FRENCH CINEMA
IN CLOSE-UP

La Vie d'un acteur pour moi

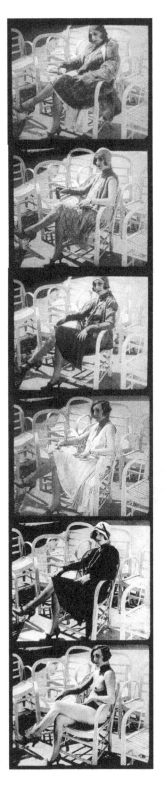

'CAN WE EXPLAIN what is magical or mysterious [about director Jean Vigo], without destroying the magic or the mystery ?' asks his daughter, Luce Vigo. †

The book's two cover stills are taken from Jean Vigo's silent documentary *À propos de Nice* (1930). This satirical portrait shows us the wealthy inhabitants of the Côte d'Azur in a new light. The elegant costumes of the uncredited model sitting on a deck chair on the Promenade des Anglais in Nice gradually strip away as the frames briskly succeed, until she is revealed completely nude.

Like an archaeologist unravelling the many bandages of a mummy to lay bare the image of the Pharaoh underneath, Vigo's camera-gaze X-rays the inner self of Nice's bourgeois society, exposing what is hidden under the apparent expensive garment in order to reveal the truth beneath the artificial. Vigo is the entomologist who shows the truest essence of the people examined in close-up under his magnifying glass.

† Michaël ABECASSIS, 'An Interview with Luce VIGO,' in *Film International*, 2012.

FRENCH CINEMA IN CLOSE-UP

La Vie d'un acteur pour moi

ILLUSTRATED MINI-DICTIONARY
OF ACTORS AND ACTRESSES
OF THE FRENCH CINEMA

edited by
Michaël ABECASSIS
with Marcelline BLOCK

caricatures by
JENNY BATLAY and IGOR BRATUSEK

PHÆTON
PUBLISHING LTD.
—— Dublin ——

French Cinema in Close-up

FIRST PUBLISHED IN IRELAND & U.K. 2015
by Phaeton Publishing Limited, Dublin

Actor and actress profile texts edited by : Michaël Abecassis (the University of Oxford) and Marcelline Block (Princeton University)

Printed and bound in U.K. and in U.S.A.

British Library Cataloguing In Publication Data: a catalogue record for this book is available from the British Library

ISBN: 978-1-908420-11-4 PAPERBACK

FOREWORD

Hi-diddle-dee-dee. An actor's life for me!
A high silk hat, and a silver cane.
A watch of gold, with a diamond chain.
Hi-diddle-dee-day. An actor's life is gay!
It's great to be a celebrity.
An actor's life for me!

—from Disney's *Pinocchio* (1940)

MANY reference works have been dedicated to the actors who have marked the history of French cinema, but most seem to take a biographical approach, focusing on their cinematographic paths and often aiming to be as objective as possible. This collection is presented alphabetically in dictionary form, and calls upon university professors alongside journalists, both francophones and Francophiles, those specialising in cinema and those who do not. Their task: to provide a brief and personal sketch of an artist, bringing out all that emerges from his or her personality, acting, and career.

A portrait is above all something that is drawn, painted, or photographed. Jenny Batlay and Igor Bratusek give free rein to their imaginations, sketching the featured artists, without having seen the written text; their sketches are the indispensable visual complement to the text. Drawing, like the text itself, provides a still image which contrasts the moving one we see on screen. How then to represent Danielle Darrieux, who has pervaded eight decades of talking pictures? For many film-lovers, she is the young starlet of 1930s cinema, but also the scatty seventy-year-old of François Ozon's *8 femmes / 8 Women* (2002). *Le Fabuleux Destin d'Amélie Poulain / Amélie* (2001) seemed to have crystallised Audrey Tautou in an image from which it will be difficult for her to escape, and yet her appearance and her influence on viewers changed in the years which followed, as she became an international star in major American productions. The drawn portrait creates an almost dreamlike image. The object is fixed in time and space in its defining features (a look, a smile, an expression often enough to represent an actor), like the petrified lovers in Marcel Carné's *Les Visiteurs du soir / The Devil's Envoys* (1942), and it is left to the viewer to uncover – between the lines, behind the phrase – all the complexity of the artist and his/her experience on screen.

Many international artists have played key parts in French cinema, and thus it is no surprise to find entries dedicated to Marie Gillain, Anna Karina, and Jean Seberg alongside portraits of French cinema icons such as Jean-Louis Barrault, Maurice Chevalier, and Jean Gabin.

This volume is far from exhaustive, but it provides an overview of the main actors who have enriched French cinema since its inception, and who today belong to the collective imaginary of those spectators whose words fill the pages which follow.

Michaël ABECASSIS, 2015

CONTENTS

FOREWORD v

Isabelle ADJANI (1955–) 1
Anouk AIMÉE (1932–) 2
   [Françoise Sorya Dreyfus]
Mathieu AMALRIC (1965–) 4
Richard ANCONINA (1953–). 6
Fanny ARDANT (1949–) 7
Pierre ARDITI (1944–) 9
Niels ARESTRUP (1949–) 11
ARLETTY (1898–1992) 13
   [Léonie Bathiat]
Antonin ARTAUD (1896–1948) 14
Ariane ASCARIDE (1954–) 16
Stéphane AUDRAN (1932–) 19
   [Colette Suzanne Dacheville]
Daniel AUTEUIL (1950–) 21
Sabine AZÉMA (1949–) 23
Charles AZNAVOUR (1924–). 24
   [Charles Aznaourian]
Jean-Pierre BACRI (1951–) 27
Edouard BAER (1966–) 29
Josiane BALASKO (1950–) 32
   [Josiane Balašković]
Jean-François BALMER (1946–) 34
Brigitte BARDOT (1934–) 37
Jean-Louis BARRAULT (1910–1994) 38
Harry BAUR (1880–1943) 40
Nathalie BAYE (1948–) 42
Emmanuelle BÉART (1963–) 44
   [Emmanuelle Béhart-Hasson]
Leïla BEKHTI (1984–). 45
Jean-Paul BELMONDO (1933–) 48
François BERLÉAND (1952–) 50
Sarah BERNHARDT (1844–1923) 52
   [Henriette-Rosine Bernard]
Jules BERRY (1883–1951) 55
   [Marie Louis Jules Paufichet]
Richard BERRY (1950–) 57
Juliette BINOCHE (1964–) 59

Michel BLANC (1952–) 61
Francis BLANCHE (1921–1974) 62
Bernard BLIER (1916–1989) 64
Richard BOHRINGER (1941–) 65
Romane BOHRINGER (1973–) 68
Sandrine BONNAIRE (1967–) 70
Dany BOON (1966–) 72
  [Daniel Hamidou]
Michel BOUJENAH (1952–) 74
Carole BOUQUET (1957–) 75
Michel BOUQUET (1925–) 78
BOURVIL (1917–1970) 80
  [André Raimbourg]
Charles BOYER (1899–1978) 82
Marcel BOZZUFFI (1928–1988) 85
Claude BRASSEUR (1936–) 87
Pierre BRASSEUR (1905–1972) 90
  [Pierre-Albert Espinasse]
Jacques BREL (1929–1978) 93
Jean-Claude BRIALY (1933–2007) 97
Guillaume CANET (1973–) 99
Julien CARETTE (1897–1966) 100
Jean CARMET (1920–1994) 102
Jean-Claude CARRIÈRE (1931–) 104
Maria CASARÈS (1922–1996) 106
  [María Victoria Casares Pérez]
Vincent CASSEL (1966–) 109
  [Vincent Crochon]
Alain CHABAT (1958–) 112
Maurice CHEVALIER (1888–1972) 115
Christian CLAVIER (1952–) 119
François CLUZET (1955–) 121
Jean COCTEAU (1889–1963) 124
COLUCHE (1944–1986) 127
  [Michel Gérard Joseph Colucci]
Clovis CORNILLAC (1967–) 130
Marion COTILLARD (1975–) 131
Darry COWL (1925–2006) 134
  [André Darricau]
Marcel DALIO (1899–1983) 136
  [Marcel Benoit Blauschild]
Béatrice DALLE (1964–) 139
  [Béatrice Cabarrou]
Gérard DARMON (1948–) 141

Danielle DARRIEUX (1917–). 144
Jean-Pierre DARROUSSIN (1953–) 145
Jamel DEBBOUZE (1975–) 147
Cécile DE FRANCE (1975–) 149
Louis DE FUNÈS (1914–1983) 151
  [Louis de Funes de Galarza]
Alain DELON (1935–) 152
Julie DELPY (1969–) 154
Catherine DENEUVE (1943–) 156
  [Catherine Dorléac]
Charles DENNER (1926–1995) 159
Gérard DEPARDIEU (1948–) 162
Julie DEPARDIEU (1973–) 167
Emmanuelle DEVOS (1964–) 170
Patrick DEWAERE (1947–1982) 171
  [Patrick Bourdeaux]
Jean-Claude DREYFUS (1946–) 174
Marie DUBAS (1884–1972) 177
Jean DUJARDIN (1972–) 181
Albert DUPONTEL (1964–) 183
Romain DURIS (1974–) 185
André DUSSOLLIER (1946–) 187
Gad ELMALEH (1971–) 189
FERNANDEL (1903–1971) 192
  [Fernand Joseph Désiré Contandin]
Edwige FEUILLÈRE (1907–1998) 194
  [Edwige Louise Caroline Cunatti]
Brigitte FOSSEY (1946–) 197
FRÉHEL (1891–1951) 199
  [Marguerite Boulc'h]
Pierre FRESNAY (1897–1975) 205
  [Pierre Jules Louis Laudenbach]
Catherine FROT (1956–) 208
Jean GABIN (1904–1976) 210
  [Jean Gabin Alexis Moncorgé]
Charlotte GAINSBOURG (1971–) 213
Michel GALABRU (1922–) 215
Nicole GARCIA (1946–) 217
Marie GILLAIN (1975–) 219
Annie GIRARDOT (1931–2011) 221
Judith GODRÈCHE (1972–) 223
  [Judith Goldreich]
Eva GREEN (1980–) 224
Sacha GUITRY (1885–1957) 227

Johnny HALLYDAY (1943–) 228
  [Jean-Philippe Smet]
Marina HANDS (1975–) 233
Isabelle HUPPERT (1953–) 235
Agnès JAOUI (1964–) 238
Louis JOUVET (1887–1951) 240
Gérard JUGNOT (1951–) 242
Élie KAKOU (1960–1999) 243
  [Alain Kakou]
Anna KARINA (1940–) 244
  [Hanne Karin Bayer]
Sandrine KIBERLAIN (1968–) 245
  [Sandrine Kiberlajn]
Bernadette LAFONT (1938–2013) 247
Christophe LAMBERT (1957–) 251
Jean-Pierre LÉAUD (1944–) 253
Madeleine LEBEAU (1923–) 256
Fernand LEDOUX (1897–1993) 257
Virginie LEDOYEN (1976–) 260
  [Virginie Fernandez]
Valérie LEMERCIER (1964–) 262
Jean LE POULAIN (1924–1988) 264
Robert LE VIGAN (1900–1972) 266
  [Robert Coquillaud]
Thierry LHERMITTE (1952–) 269
Vincent LINDON (1959–) 271
Michael LONSDALE (1931–) 273
Fabrice LUCHINI (1951–) 275
  [Robert Luchini]
Benoît MAGIMEL (1974–) 278
Jean MARAIS (1913–1998) 279
Sophie MARCEAU (1966–) 281
  [Sophie Danièle Sylvie Maupu]
Jean-Pierre MARIELLE (1932–) 283
Roxane MESQUIDA (1981–) 285
Paul MEURISSE (1912–1979) 286
Gérard MEYLAN (1952–) 289
MIOU-MIOU (1950–) 291
  [Sylvette Herry]
Eddy MITCHELL (1942–) 296
  [Claude Moine]
Yves MONTAND (1921–1991) 297
  [Ivo Livi]
Jeanne MOREAU (1928–) 299

Yolande MOREAU (1953–) 301
François MOREL (1959–) 303
Michèle MORGAN (1920–) 307
     [Simone Roussel]
Philippe NOIRET (1930–2006) 309
Vanessa PARADIS (1972–) 312
Gérard PHILIPE (1922–1959).   313
     [Gérard Philip]
Édith PIAF (1915–1963).   317
     [Édith Giovanna Gassion]
Jean PIAT (1924–)   322
Michel PICCOLI (1925–)   325
Denis PODALYDÈS (1963–).   327
Benoît POELVOORDE (1964–)   329
Jean POIRET (1926–1992)   332
     [Jean Gustave Poiré]
Albert PRÉJEAN (1894–1979).   334
RAIMU (1883–1946)   337
     [Jules Auguste César Muraire]
Serge REGGIANI (1922–2004)   340
Jean RENO (1948–)   342
     [Juan Moreno y Herrera-Jiménez]
Pierre RICHARD (1934–)   344
     [Pierre Defays]
Emmanuelle RIVA (1927–).   345
     [Paulette Riva]
Jean ROCHEFORT (1930–).   348
Viviane ROMANCE (1912–1991)   350
     [Pauline Arlette Ortmans]
Ludivine SAGNIER (1979–).   352
Édith SCOB (1937–)   354
     [Édith Helena Vladimirovna Scobeltzine]
Jean SEBERG (1938–1979)   357
Emmanuelle SEIGNER (1966–)   359
Mathilde SEIGNER (1968–).   361
Michel SERRAULT (1928–2007)   362
Delphine SEYRIG (1932–1990)   365
Simone SIGNORET (1921–1985)   367
     [Simone Henriette Charlotte Kaminker]
Michel SIMON (1895–1975) 371
Simone SIMON (1910–2005).   373
Jacques TATI (1907–1982)   375
     [Jacques Tatischeff]
Audrey TAUTOU (1976–)   377

Sylvie Testud (1971–). 379
Jean-Louis Trintignant (1930–) 382
Charles Vanel (1892–1989) 384
Lino Ventura (1919–1987) 386
Boris Vian (1920–1959) 388
Jacques Villeret (1951–2005) 394
    [Mohammed Boufroura]
Jacques Weber (1949–) 396
Lambert Wilson (1958–) 397
Elsa Zylberstein (1968–). 399

INDEX OF FILM TITLES 402

Editors and Artists 436
List of Contributors 437

[Actors' birth names (per official birth records) are
provided above (and in their profiles) for those actors
who have a stage name different to their birth names.]

Isabelle ADJANI (1955–)

*Pretty,
Pouty,
Powerfully
So*

« J E SUIS actrice pour donner de l'amour » ['I am an actress to give love'].[1] This is how Isabelle Yasmine ADJANI explains her choice of career. Love. The tormented kind: remember Camille Claudel? The tragic kind: who can forget Adèle H. ending up in an asylum because of a man who would not reciprocate her obsessive love? Adjani's mesmerizing beauty makes us feel all the sorrows of the tragic characters she portrays. She is indeed the only actress in the history of French cinema to have been awarded five Césars for Best Actress: the first in 1982 for *Possession* (Andrzej Żuławski, 1981), the second in 1984 for *L'Été meurtrier /One Deadly Summer* (Jean Becker, 1983), the third for *Camille Claudel* (Bruno Nuytten, 1988) in 1989, the fourth in 1995 for *La Reine Margot /Queen Margot* (Patrice Chéreau, 1994) – this film representing the pinnacle of her career – and the fifth in 2010 for *La Journée de la jupe /Skirt Day* (Jean-Paul Lilienfeld, 2008).

Born in a working-class neighbourhood in June 1955 on the Right Bank of the Seine, she and her younger brother Eric were raised by their Algerian father and German mother in an industrial city located to the northwest of Paris. She never forgot her roots and in 1988 went to Algeria, on the eve of the referendum, to support the birth of Algerian democracy. When very young, she was already noted for her beauty and professionalism. Her precocious successes included being the youngest player ever, at the age of 17, to be granted contract status at France's premier theatre, the Comédie-Française; and the youngest person ever nominated for a Best Leading Actress Academy Award at the age of 19 (until Keisha Castle-Hughes broke the record in 2004) for her performance in François Truffaut's 1975 *L'Histoire d'Adèle H. /The Story of Adele H.*

Indeed, Adjani's characters often include solitary, obsessive, alienated women. Despite her fragile looks, tenacity and even toughness underlie much of Adjani's best work, as illustrated by her performance as Camille Claudel. *Camille Claudel* was a very personal project, since Adjani identified with the brilliant sculptress, destroyed by her affair with the egocentric Rodin and incarcerated in an asylum for the last thirty years of her life (as was Adèle H…). Adjani, as co-producer, was nominated for an Oscar for Best Foreign Language Film. Her latest movies include *La Journée de la jupe /Skirt Day*, 2008; Jacques Weber's TV film *Figaro* (2008), and *Mamuth* (Gustave de Kervern and Benoît Delépine, 2010).

An intelligent and dedicated actress, she chooses her roles with care and works on them with single-minded application. Multilingual, she has also performed in English and German-language films. As pretty as she is pouty, treading the borderline between provocative and provoking, her performances are always full of spirited and violent emotion: she can deliver the kind of rage that comes from deep within.

However, acting has never been a priority in her life. As a matter of fact, Adjani has appeared in only 20 or so movies. A generation ago after quitting the Comédie-Française because the revered institution refused to grant her leave of absence to act in a movie, she explained that her work was not her passion. Thus, in the past decade, she has devoted most of her time to her private life, including raising her two children, Barnabé, born in 1979 and fathered by Bruno Nuytten, and Gabriel-Kane, born in 1995 and fathered by Daniel Day-Lewis. Despite being chosen by *People* magazine as one of the '50 Most Beautiful People in the World' in 1990 and selected as second-most beautiful woman (after Monica Bellucci) by the French public in 2004, she had to break off her engagement to Jean-Michel Jarre in 2002 because he cheated on her.

Adjani has never lacked courage, on the professional nor personal levels, and she was made a *Chevalier de la Légion d'honneur* in 2010. Indeed, in 2004 she openly supported 'Reporters without Borders' in the fight for the freedom of twenty-nine prisoners held in Cuba. Love. The charitable one. The selfless one. Maybe that is how we could explain her choices in her private life.

Fabienne H. BAIDER
University of Cyprus

1. 'Biographie d'Isabelle Adjani,' L'Odyssée du cinéma, accessed August 26, 2013, http://www.odysseeducinema.fr/actrice.php?id=39.

Anouk AIMÉE (1932–)
[Françoise Sorya DREYFUS]

Beloved

ANOUK AIMÉE's image is summed up in her surname, Aimée, which translates as 'beloved'. Born Françoise Sorya Dreyfus in 1932, she was renamed Anouk after the character in her debut feature *La Maison sous la mer* (Henri Calef, 1947) and Aimée after the suggestion of French poet /screenwriter Jacques Prévert. Her adopted surname was indeed a well-chosen one, firmly fixing those qualities she has come to be known for: romanticism and sensuality.

With large, soulful eyes, a soft, breathy voice, a willowy figure and graceful walk, Aimée incarnates an ethereal kind of femininity. Frequently her characters function as apparitions that haunt her male counterparts. This is the case, for instance, in *Le Farceur /The Joker* (Philippe de Broca, 1960) and *Model Shop* (Jacques Demy, 1969), where her heroines induce a spellbinding effect on the men who catch sight of them (played by Jean-Pierre Cassel and Gary Lockwood, respectively). Furthermore, Aimée's characters tend towards the tragic. Identified by an acting style that is understated and opaque, her heroines are almost invariably characterised by a sense of melancholy and *ennui*. This is most apparent in her role as Maddalena, the jaded socialite in Federico Fellini's *La dolce vita* (1960), whose suffering is silently conveyed through a black eye that she conceals under her chic sunglasses and elusive demeanour.

Alongside the mystery and fragility, however, there is a groundedness that characterises Aimée's persona, which stems from her modernity. Aimée's career takeoff coincided with the rise of European art cinema, which brought to the fore a new type of female sexuality. In fact, her career was built on three iconic films of the era: Fellini's *La dolce vita*, Jacques Demy's *Lola* (1961) and Claude Lelouch's *Un homme et une femme /A Man and a Woman* (1966). In all three, Aimée embodies an image of mature femininity; a woman who is urban, sophisticated and liberated. This is explicitly expressed in *La dolce vita*, when she unashamedly confesses to Marcello Mastroianni's character her desire to be both his wife and his whore. Similarly, in Demy's film, Aimée portrays the titular heroine, Lola – a cabaret dancer and single mother – with an unapologetic sincerity and delight that defies traditional morality and women's socially ascribed roles. So, too, in Lelouch's film (which remains her most popular and acclaimed one), does Aimée endow the character of widowed mother Anne with an emotional maturity that elegantly negotiates between the usually competing roles of mother, professional, and lover.

Since her screen debut at the age of fourteen in Calef's film, Aimée has appeared in over seventy others, working not only with French auteurs (primarily Demy and Lelouch) but also with European and American ones. Her long and prolific career notwithstanding, the majority of these films either cast her in supporting roles, or are rather unremarkable features, like George Cukor's *Justine* (1969). It appears rather odd then that the repute she enjoys till today is incommensurate with her career, resulting only from her roles in *La dolce vita*, *Lola*, and *Un homme et une femme*. Yet, this discrepancy between her reputation and limited film roles demonstrates the importance of cinéphile status in the longevity of a star's career, for it is these three films' lasting iconicity that confers upon Aimée her enduring appeal rather than her overall trajectory. This, however, does not diminish the power of the sexy melancholy she evokes in them and for which she will remain beloved.

Olga KOURELOU
King's College, London

Mathieu AMALRIC (1965–)

*It's
a Bird,
It's
a Plane,
It's …*

ONE OF THE busiest actors in cinema today, Mathieu AMALRIC has not always been famous. Not so long ago, he was a 30-year-old production assistant and house painter whose then-wife, Jeanne Balibar, was the working actor and chief breadwinner. In fact, acting was never Amalric's aspiration. Rather, he always wanted to be a director.

Born in 1965 near Paris (Neuilly-sur-Seine), Amalric spent several years of his childhood abroad, both in Washington DC and in Moscow, as his father was a foreign affairs correspondent for *Le Monde*. His mother, Nicole Zand, was that newspaper's literary critic.

Mathieu Amalric got his start as an intern ('trainee assistant director') on Louis Malle's *Au revoir les enfants* (1987), an experience which left him with a deep and lasting appreciation for the underclass of film set workers. It was not until ten years later that Amalric directed his first feature, *Mange ta soupe* (1997) – a semi-autobiographical work about a dysfunctional family – starring Jean-Yves Dubois. It was in order to raise money for his next feature

that Amalric accepted director Arnaud Desplechin's offer to star as addle-brained doctoral candidate Paul Dedalus in *Comment je me suis disputé…(ma vie sexuelle) /My Sex Life…or How I Got into an Argument* (1996), a role which garnered him a César for Most Promising Actor. This would be the first of his many collaborations with Desplechin and actress Emmanuelle Devos, and also with his then-wife Jeanne Balibar.

Amalric again won the César (for Best Actor) for Desplechin's *Rois et Reine /Kings and Queen* (2004), this time playing a neurotic musician whose complicated romantic (Emmanuelle Devos) and familial relationships both sustain and derange him. Desplechin's *Un conte de Noël /A Christmas Tale* (2008) brought the cast of *Kings and Queen* back together – Devos, Catherine Deneuve, and Jean-Paul Roussillon – but this time, the family in question and Amalric's character along with it, were even more dysfunctional.

Mathieu Amalric has directed several films, including *Le Stade de Wimbledon /Wimbledon Stage* (2001), based on Daniele Del Guidice's novel of the same name, starring Jeanne Balibar. *Tournée /On Tour* (2010), in which Amalric appears as down-on-his-luck burlesque show manager Joachim Zand, won him Cannes's award for best director. That character, Amalric has said, was partially based on his former boss, producer Paulo Branco. Amalric christened him (Zand) with his mother's maiden name as a tribute to her family, many of whom died in the Holocaust. Amalric's latest directorial effort, *The Screen Illusion* (2010), based on Corneille's play *L'Illusion comique*, was a commission from Paris's Comédie-Française. (With only 11 days to shoot, Amalric felt unprepared, and does not hide his lack of esteem for the product of his effort.)

Mathieu Amalric is perhaps best known internationally for his role as Jean-Dominique Bauby in Julien Schnabel's *Le Scaphandre et le Papillon /The Diving Bell and the Butterfly* (2007). Completely paralyzed following a massive stoke, the real-life Bauby dictated his memoirs (on which the film was based) using a system of eye blinks which his physical therapist taught him. Amalric's virtuoso performance won him a César for Best Actor.

Not restricting himself to arthouse cinema, Amalric played a Bond villain in *Quantum of Solace* (Marc Forster, 2008), and then a shifty sidekick to famed bank robber Jacques Mesrine in *L'Ennemi public n°1 /Mesrine: Public Enemy #1* and *L'Instinct de mort /Mesrine: Killer Instinct* (Jean-François Richet, 2008). In *La Question humaine / Heartbeat Detector* (Nicolas Klotz, 2007), Amalric played a corporate psychiatrist who gets caught up in a corporate power struggle involving World War II–era atrocities. Wanting to learn more about Steven Spielberg's directing technique, he joined the cast of *Munich* (2005), Spielberg's film about Israel's response to the 1972 Munich massacre.

Both polite and shrewd, and always giving of his time, Amalric is an enchanting mix of movie star and former production assistant *cum* aspiring director. He teaches at Paris's La Fémis film school. With his globe-large eyes – as curious as they are expressive – and signature loping gate, Amalric inflects the films in which he appears with a profundity beyond his unmistakable presence.

Amalric currently resides in the Belleville neighbourhood of Paris, and has been working on an adaptation of Stendhal's novel *Le Rouge et le Noir /The Red and the Black*.

Jonathan ROBBINS
Columbia University

Richard ANCONINA (1953–)

*A
Sephardic
Tough
Guy*

B ORN IN PARIS on 28 January 1953, Richard ANCONINA has had a long and relatively successful career in mainstream French cinema. His Italian sounding name is in fact derived from the typically Moroccan Jewish surname Ouaknine (from the Berber, 'son of Jacob'). Despite this name change, Anconina has frequently been cast in Sephardic Jewish roles, especially as hustler, gangster, or conman.

Anconina's breakout role came in Claude Berri's 1983 adaptation of *Tchao Pantin /So Long, Stooge*. He played a supporting role as Youssef Bensoussan, an Arab-Jewish drug dealer, opposite the illustrious comedian Coluche. Coluche's character Lambert and Bensoussan strike up an improbable friendship, which ends with Bensoussan's murder by associates from his drug ring. The film was a commercial and critical success, and Anconina won a César for Best Supporting Actor as well as the Most Promising Actor award. In 1987, he co-starred with Tunisian Jewish comedian Michel Boujenah in *Lévy et Goliath /Levy and Goliath* (dir. Gérard Oury) as an Orthodox Jew who gets mixed up in the Antwerp diamond and drugs trade. His second

César award, for Best Actor, came for his role opposite New Wave legend Jean-Paul Belmondo in Claude Lelouch's *Itinéraire d'un enfant gâté / Itinerary of a Spoiled Child* (1988). A role as the policeman tracking down a family on the run in *Le Petit Criminal /The Little Gangster* (Jacques Doillon, 1990) brought him a nomination for best actor at the Berlin Film Festival.

The first part of the 1990s was marked by a string of disappointing roles and flops. Anconina's star rose again with the smash hit *La Vérité si je mens /Would I Lie to You?* (Thomas Gilou, 1997), in which he starred as Eddie Vuibert, a down and out conman, who gets mistaken for a Jew and adopted by a wealthy Sephardic textile manufacturer in the Sentier district of Paris. Eddie works his way up the business, meeting Dov Mimran (played by Vincent Elbaz, of Moroccan Jewish origin) and Rafi Stylmode (the inimitable Elie Kakou). The film's Sephardic shtick proved to be such a success that director Thomas Gilou made *La Vérité si je mens ! 2* (2001) and *La Vérité si je mens ! 3* (2012), with Anconina reprising the role of Eddie in both sequels.

Robert WATSON
Stetson University, Florida

Fanny ARDANT (1949–)

*The
Sensational
Woman
Next Door*

FANNY ARDANT (born Fanny Marguerite Judith Ardant on March 22nd, 1949) is an internationally known and eclectic French actress whose career began on stage in the 1970s, then moved to the small screen before shifting to the big screen in the early 1980s. After interpreting Corneille, Montherlant, Racine, Claudel, Molière, and Duras in theatrical productions, she played the role of 'the woman next door' in François Truffaut's eponymous film, *La Femme d'à côté /The Woman Next Door*. For this role, Ardant received critical acclaim due to the strength of her performance. Ardant's impressive acting style is defined by her ability to move from one artistic domain to the next with ease, being driven by a passion for arts which transpires on screen and on stage through her corporeal performance. This is what distinguishes her and makes her one of the greatest French actresses.

Ardant made her screen debut in a television series directed by Nina Campaneez, *Les Dames de la côte* (1979) where she played the leading female role of Fanny Villatte. Taking place during the First World War, the series follows the passion and love of Fanny, whose striking physical characteristics and acting style made a great impact upon Truffaut as well as the French public. Describing her physique, Truffaut pertinently declared that 'her large mouth, her deep voice and its unusual intonations, her big black eyes and her triangular face... [her] penchant for secrecy, her distant, slightly unsociable side, and, above all, her vibrancy' [1] attracted him. Of course, Truffaut was seduced, but he also saw in these traits Ardant's intensity of expression and an embodiment of artistic passion. Emphasising these qualities, Truffaut was able to create for her a role that corresponded perfectly well to her state of mind in *La Femme d'à côté* (1981). The film is now seen as emblematic of Ardant's early cinematographic career, and brought her a nomination for Best Actress at the 1982 Cannes Film Festival. Ardant played the role of Mathilde Bauchard, who inadvertently moves next to her former lover, Bernard Coudray, played by Gérard Depardieu. Their body language, glances, and tone of voice betray their dormant but strong feelings for each other. Both characters are at once driven to resume their passionate but destructive love affair, which triggers in each of them a nervous breakdown. Finding it impossible to live together, but impossible to be apart, Mathilde arranges their last rendezvous in order to finally end their relationship and their lives by shooting Bernard first, before taking her own life. This symbolic death represents the intensity of the characters' passion but also stands as a purification, for in the film, death brings an end to their obsessive behaviour while at the same time glorifying their passion. While Truffaut explores the themes of love and death in a visceral way, Alain Resnais (1922–2014) handles them in a more spiritual manner in *L'Amour à mort /Love Unto Death* (1984) and *Mélo* (1986), where Ardant's roles, much briefer but no less significant in the latter film, revolve around intelligent performances. Her meditation on love and death was also brought to the stage where she interpreted Marguerite Duras's *La Maladie de la mort /The Malady of Death* in 2006.

Mind and body were reconciled for Ardant in a role once again close to her personality, that of Maria Callas, also known as the Diva or Divina. Like Ardant in cinema and on stage, Callas in opera embodied an astonishing variety of tragic heroines. In Roman Polanski's stage adaptation of *Master Class* (1996) written by Terence McNally, Callas, played by Ardant, becomes the tragic heroine. Polanski's play portrays Callas as a woman consumed by passion. After she is no longer able to sing, Callas decided to give singing lessons. In a way, the idea that the end of something (singing) can be transformed into energy is a common characteristic that Ardant shares with Callas. Although there is no physical resemblance between Callas and Ardant, Ardant was recognised as her corporeal reincarnation. As a result, in 2002 Ardant was asked to incarnate Callas once again, but this time, in a film directed by Franco Zeffirelli entitled *Callas Forever* (2002). Zeffirelli's film is a fictionalised account of the last days of Callas starring in a filmed opera of Georges Bizet's *Carmen*. Ardant excelled in simultaneously playing the roles of two most passionate and emotional women, Callas and Carmen.

Throughout her career, Ardant has received critical acclaim for her convincing performances, and was nominated five times for the Best Actress César: in 1982 for Truffaut's *La Femme d'à côté /The Woman Next Door*; in 1984 for another Truffaut film, *Vivement dimanche !/Confidentially Yours* (1983); in 1997, when she won the César for the leading female role, Eva, the owner of a gay club, in Gabriel Aghion's comedy *Pédale douce* (1996); in 2002 for her role in François Ozon's *8 femmes /8 Women*; and in 2014 for her part in Marion Vernoux's *Les Beaux Jours* (2013). It is no surprise that Ardant won the César in 1997 for Aghion's commercially popular comedy. As an excessive form of cinema, comedy is the place where Ardant can give free rein to her excessiveness, as well as tackling, at the same time, important themes, such as homosexuality. *Pédale douce* is a film about performance (gender and artistic), where the question of (female and/or male) body is paramount in its expression of an identity. In this film, bodily appearance is reconciled with its inner self, which is the main element of Ardant's representations and incarnations of female roles. In a similar way, the legendary lesbian kiss between two French stars, Catherine Deneuve and Fanny Ardant, which closes Ozon's *8 femmes*, is excessive in the sense that it serves to highlight performance and works to represent Ardant's obsessive desire for performance.

Sophie BELOT
The University of Sheffield

1. Antoine de Baecque and Serge Toubiana, *Truffaut: A Biography* (New York: Alfred A. Knopf Inc., 1999), 365.

Pierre ARDITI (1944–)

*Auteur
Cinema
&
Popular
Media
Culture*

PIERRE ARDITI began his career in the 1960s in the company of the writer and director Marcel Maréchal, interpreting his first role on stage in *L'Opéra du monde* by Jacques Audibert (1965) and *Élocoquente* by Georges Limbour (1965). He soon took on several leading parts in stagings of directors such as Jean-Pierre Bisson (*Smoking*, 1975), Pierre Mondy (*Trois lits pour huit*, 1978) and Jean-Louis Barrault (*Diderot à corps perdu*, 1979). At the same time, he made his television debut in productions by Michel Mitrani (*Reportage sur un squelette ou Masques et bergamasques*, 1970) and Serge Moati (*Le Pain noir*, 1974). In 1972 he took on the role of the protagonist of the Italian-French biopic *Blaise Pascal*, which is part of a TV series by Roberto Rossellini made in the spirit of mass education. At age 26, he had his first appearance in cinema in René Gainville's *Alyse et Chloé / Alyse and Chloe* (1970), but remained principally a theatre actor. His first important appearance in cinema is his role in the drama *L'Amour violé / Rape of Love* (Yannick Bellon, 1978), where he was cast alongside Daniel Auteuil, then a newcomer.

In 1980, he began his collabo-ration with director Alain Resnais, (1922-2014) interpreting the rather small part of Zambeaux in *Mon oncle d'Amérique /My American Uncle*, alongside Gérard Depardieu as René Ragueneau, director of a textile factory. This film was awarded the special jury prize at Cannes in 1980. Several other productions with Resnais and his favourite actors Sabine Azéma, André Dussollier, and Lambert Wilson followed: *La Vie est un roman /Life is a Bed of Roses* (1983), *L'Amour à mort /Love Unto Death* (1984), and *Mélo* (1986), the latter winning Arditi a César for Best Actor in a Supporting Role. For his starring role in Resnais's *Smoking /No Smoking* (1993), a two-part-film based on the theatre play *Intimate Exchange* by Alan Ayckbourn, Arditi won a César for Best Actor and Resnais was awarded Best Film (César and Silver Bear at the Berlin Film Festival). In this drama, Arditi portrays not only one, but four characters, and finds his counterpart in Sabine Azéma, the two of them living their lives in terms of what might have happened if they had made or failed certain choices. Arditi's last four films in collaboration with Resnais are *On connaît la chanson /Same Old Song* (1997), *Pas sur la bouche /Not on the Lips* (2003), *Cœurs /Private Fears in Public Places* (2006), and *Vous n'avez encore rien vu /You Ain't Seen Nothin' Yet* (2012).

In the 1980s and 1990s, collabo-rations with other directors followed. Arditi alternately portrays dramatic and tragicomic – often androgynous – parts, but also appears in a range of crime movies and other popular genres: Robert Enrico (*Pile ou face*

/Heads or Tails, 1980); Pierre Jolivet (*Strictement personnel*, 1985); Jacques Rouffio (*L'État de grâce /State of Grace*, 1986); Jean-Paul Rappeneau (*Le Hussard sur le toit /The Horseman on the Roof*, 1995); Claude Lelouch (*Hommes, femmes, mode d'emploi / Men, Women, A User's Manual*, 1996; *Hasards ou coïncidences /Chance or Coincidence*, 1998; *Le Courage d'aimer*, 2005); Bruno Podalydès (*Le Mystère de la chambre jaune /The Mystery of the Yellow Room*, 2003; *Le Parfum de la dame en noir /The Perfume of the Lady in Black*, 2005; *Bancs publics (Versailles rive droite) /Public Benches*, 2009; *Adieu Berthe – l'enterrement de mémé /Granny's Funeral*, 2012); Bertrand Blier (*Les Acteurs /Actors*, 2000); and Laetitia Masson (*Pourquoi (pas) le Brésil /Why (Not) Brazil?*, 2004).

Arditi also frequently appears in more commercially-oriented French TV productions, such as the four-part *Le Comte de Monte-Cristo* (Josée Dayan, 1998), starring with a wide range of prominent actors such as Gérard Depardieu (alongside his daughter Julie and son Guillaume), Ornella Muti, and Jean Rochefort, and in the crime series *Le Sang de la vigne* directed by Marc Rivière for France 3 (2011-2014), attracting more than four million viewers. Arditi maintains a consistent relationship to television, especially France 2, working particularly with Franck Apprederis and Elisabeth Rappeneau. Being known in the Francophone world as the French voice of Christopher Reeve in the first three *Superman* movies under the direction of Richard Donner and Richard Lester, he has also dubbed many other American actors

(e.g. Christopher Walken, Dustin Hoffman, Bud Spencer) and cartoons (*Kung Fu Panda*, 2008/2011). During a film career spanning 45 years, he has appeared in about 70 feature and some short films. At the same time, he has collaborated on more than 110 TV productions.

Arditi constantly insists on his loyalty to the world of Parisian theatre, having interpreted a wide range of authors including Molière, Sacha Guitry, Samuel Beckett, and Jean-Claude Gumberg. He has notably collaborated with directors such as Marcel Maréchal, Bernard Murat, and Didier Bezace in theatres such as Théâtre Montparnasse, Théâtre Edouard VII, Théâtre du Rond-Point, and the Festival of Avignon. Arditi mainly participates in theatre productions that are broadcast directly on television, thereby connecting theatre and popular entertainment.

Katharina MÜLLER
and
Daniel WINKLER
Universität Wien /University of Vienna

Niels ARESTRUP (1949–)

*Best
Supporting
Actor*

CONSISTENTLY DRAWN to bold roles where he often embodies the criminal and corrupt, Niels ARESTRUP has made a name for himself in many fields of the French entertainment scene: as a theatre, television, and film actor, writer, director, and teacher. However, despite his multifaceted career, it is in his powerhouse secondary film roles that he has found the greatest popular and critical success.

Born on February 8, 1949 in Montreuil to a Danish father and French mother, Arestrup spent a modest childhood in the Parisian banlieue. He cut his teeth at the Théâtre de la Gaîté, training under Tania Balachova, and had his theatrical breakthrough in 1969 in Calderón de la Barca's *La Vie est un songe*. Throughout his career, Arestrup would remain prominent on the French theatre scene, performing in over 30 plays as well as directing a number of them. He likewise tried his hand at playwriting, citing Chekhov, Molière, and Shakespeare as influences, and both wrote and directed *Le Temps des cerises* in 2008. Absorbed by the many aspects of his craft, Arestrup has also branched out into teaching, founding the Théâtre-École du Passage in 1987,

where he would instruct for over ten years, and heading the Théâtre de la Renaissance from 1989 to 1993.

Nonetheless, despite this theatrical success, it is in the cinema that Arestrup's work is best known. He broke onto the film scene in 1974 in Samy Pavel's *Miss O'Gynie et les hommes fleurs /Miss O'Gynie and the Flower Man*, and quickly began working with esteemed filmmakers, such as Alain Resnais on his 1974 *Stavisky...* In subsequent years, Arestrup would become known for his portrayal of figures of dubious moral character, such as in Daniel Duval's 1979 *La Dérobade /Memoirs of a French Whore* and Yves Boisset's *La Femme flic /The Woman Cop* the following year. In the 1980s, he avoided being typecast as the criminal, with principal roles in films such as Marco Ferreri's 1984 *Le Futur est femme /The Future is Woman*, in which he forms a love triangle with Ornella Muti and Hanna Schygulla, as well as in István Szabó's 1991 *Meeting Venus*, where he plays a Norwegian orchestra conductor alongside Glenn Close. Later, in 2002, he would form an unravelling married couple with Judith Godrèche in Sophie Marceau's *Parlez-moi d'amour /Speak to me of Love*, while his penchant for dark roles saw him appear in Julian Schnabel's haunting *Le Scaphandre et le Papillon /The Diving Bell and the Butterfly* (2007), Christian Carion's political espionage thriller *L'Affaire farewell /Farewell* (2009), and Gilles Paquet-Brenner's Holocaust tale *Sarah's Key* (2010). Throughout the 1980s and 1990s, he would also take on a number of television roles, in which he more regularly appeared as a principal character than in film.

Mirroring his theatrical trajectory, Arestrup was not content to remain on one side of the camera, writing and directing the 2007 political comedy, *Le Candidat /The Candidate*, in which he also plays a supporting role. The film follows hurriedly-instated politician Michel Dedieu (Yves Attal), who must replace his ill predecessor in time for a televised debate. The film received modest critical approval, and Arestrup continued to write after *Le Candidat*, including *Le Temps des cerises* (2008), and the 2009 short *L'Invitation*.

Yet while Arestrup's career is certainly multifaceted, featuring a number of starring roles, he reached the heights of his dramatic career not as a principal actor, but rather, with powerful secondary parts, particularly in Jacques Audiard's robust dramas *De battre mon cœur s'est arrêté /The Beat That My Heart Skipped* (2005) and *Un prophète /A Prophet* (2009). In both films, Arestrup epitomises the role of the domineering and corrupt father figure (which he reprises in the award-winning 2012 film *À perdre la raison /Our Children*, directed by Joachim Lafosse). In *De battre mon cœur s'est arrêté*, Tom (Romain Duris) is torn between his late mother's world of music and his father Robert's (Arestrup) realm of organised crime. Arestrup's interpretation of Robert is disconcertingly ambiguous, depicting a father at once loving, vulnerable, and baleful. Four years later, Arestrup would revisit the bad father-son dynamic in *Un prophète*. Set in a French prison divided by racial gangs, Arestrup plays the menacing Corsican mafia boss, César, who adopts the young Franco-Arab prisoner Malik (gracefully interpreted by the then-unknown Tahar Rahim) as something between a slave and a son. Audiard's thriller oozes with tension, paranoia and brutality, and Arestrup's César dominates the narrative as an omnipotent, torturous manipulator. His performance has been widely lauded as the greatest of his career.

Arestrup received a César for Best Supporting Actor for both *De battre mon cœur s'est arrêté* in 2006 and *Un prophète* in 2010. He was also nominated for the award in 2011 for his portrayal of Bartholomé in Eric Lartigeau's *L'Homme qui voulait vivre sa vie /The Big Picture* (2010), in which he again appeared alongside Duris. In 2014, Arestrup received his third Best Supporting Actor César award for his role in Bertrand Tavernier's political comedy *Quai d'Orsay /The French Minister* (2013). The cascade of awards confirmed Arestrup as a key talent on the French cinema scene.

Niels Arestrup certainly has many strings to his bow, having made his mark on the French theatre, film, and television world not only as an actor, but also in a writing, directing, and teaching capacity. His career is one of surprising diversity. Yet he remains his most arresting in films such as *De battre mon cœur s'est arrêté*, *Un prophète*, and *L'Homme qui voulait vivre sa vie*, as the supporting actor who steals the show.

After learning Corsican for *Un prophète* using the Assimil method and listening to Corsican music and radio, he played the part of the grandfather in Steven Spielberg's *Cheval de guerre /War Horse* (2011).

Gemma KING
*The University of Melbourne,
& Université Sorbonne nouvelle – Paris 3*

ARLETTY (1898–1992)
[Léonie BATHIAT]

*Paradise
Onscreen*

ARLETTY was born Léonie Bathiat to a working-class family in Courbevoie, outside of Paris. She worked in a factory before becoming a fashion model.

Her stage name comes from a Guy de Maupassant character, 'Arlette', which she changed to 'Arletty' to make it sound 'more English Fashioned', as said the writer Paul Guth.

She made her music-hall debut in 1918 at the Petit Théâtre des Capucines. Until the early 30s, she was exclusively devoted to the stage, appearing in plays and cabarets, and refused to shoot during the silent film era. Her career took off around 1936 when she appeared as the leading lady in the stage plays *Le Bonheur Mesdames*, in which she starred with Michel Simon.

The classic poetic realist Marcel Carné's films *Hôtel du Nord* (1938) and *Le Jour se lève / Daybreak* (1939) catapulted her to fame in the legendary popular Paris entertainment scene of the day. The witty lines of dialogue in these movies, notably her inimitable « *atmosphère, atmosphère* », were particularly memorable due to her voice characterized by her strong and charming Parisian accent.

Her performance, perfectly in tune with Jacques Prévert's poetry, illuminated the screen with an unusual combination of Parisian working-class humour and her romantic beauty. These qualities reached their peak with her portrayal of Garance in *Les Enfants du paradis /Children of Paradise* (1945) also directed by Marcel Carné, and considered the best role of her career.

After the Liberation, her career suffered a severe drawback owing to her liaison with a German officer during the Occupation of France. She was arrested and imprisoned. In December 1944, she was put under house arrest for another two years and condemned to three years' work suspension.

After a later period in which she reached moderate success on stage (*Huis clos /No Exit* by Sartre in 1954) and onscreen (Carné's *L'Air de Paris /Air of Paris*, 1954), an accident in 1963 left her nearly blind and forced her to retire. One of her final screen appearances was a small role in the 1962 epic *The Longest Day* (dir. Ken Annakin, Andrew Malton, and Bernhard Wicki).

Aurélie LEDOUX
École Normale Supérieure, Paris

Antonin ARTAUD (1896–1948)

*Cinema
and Its
Double*

ALTHOUGH ANTONIN ARTAUD remains better known as a literary figure, cinema represented an important part of his life. Over a relatively short period (1924–1935), Artaud wrote theoretical pieces on cinema, numerous scenarios (of which only one, *La Coquille et Le Clergyman /The Seashell and the Clergyman*, was eventually brought to the screen – controversially – by Germaine Dulac in 1928), and even planned to create a production company, while his work as an actor (with a pause in 1933) saw him appear in no fewer than 22 films. Many of the most striking portraits we have of the poet date back to his film-acting career, such as the photographic stills from *Surcouf /Adventure* (1925) or *Le Juif errant* (1926), both directed by Luitz-Morat. While it is true that most of these roles were secondary, if not altogether insignificant – considered either mere potboilers, or pretexts to travel (Italy, Germany, Algeria) – Artaud worked alongside the most important directors of the time (Claude Autant-Lara, Carl Theodor Dreyer, Abel Gance, Jean Painlevé, Georg Wilhelm Pabst), contributing to what are now considered cinematic masterpieces. Artaud's daily life was punctuated by film shoots, and the many references to his acting work found in his diaries constitute a fascinating picture of early twentieth-century cinema. When Artaud started work as a film actor, cinema was still in its infancy; and, for the first years at least, was a silent medium through which the actor was confronted with the necessary stylisation of silent roles. His background as a stage actor was paramount to his approach to cinema: actors and directors were then attempting to rid the theatre of its dusty conventions, and instead 'act true'. Although Artaud disparaged actors with tendencies for over-dramatic effects, his critics labelled his own style as one of exaggeration, overacting, and strangeness. In fact, Artaud saw his style as more akin to that of an expressionist actor seeking to express meaning or emotional experience rather than physical reality; he was influenced in this by Charles Dullin's praise of Japanese actors and their body technique, echoes of which can be found not only in his *Le Théâtre et son double /Theatre and Its Double* (1938), but also in his film acting.

Artaud's first role, in Autant-Lara's experimental *Fait-divers* (1923), is revealing: in this story of a love triangle ending in murder, Artaud plays Monsieur II with stylish and stylised efficacy: his facial and body compositions emphasise what he called 'the emotion of the images'. His body seems disjointed and radically distorted; his movements deconstructed and excessive. While some argued that Artaud appeared stilted, as though already outmoded and out of sync, it is important to note that such acting nonetheless requires enormous mental concentration on the actor's part: emotional experiences and ideas are condensed into types and transcribed through simple short-hand formulae and symbols, particularly through the actor's face and mimicry. Artaud in fact wanted to become a 'monstrous actor', playing on the ambivalence of the French word 'monstre', denoting simultaneously the act of monstration and revelation, and its monstrosity. This stance reminds us of the influence upon Artaud – and on French cinema as a whole – of German expressionism and its abstraction and stylisation, both in terms of aesthetics and acting. Artaud admired German cinema for its technical, artistic, and commercial brilliance, and revered a generation of actors who were, to him, without equals in France (Albert Bessermann, Fritz Korner, Peter Lorre, Theodor Loos, Fritz Rasp). Artaud was praised for his portrayal, most famously for a scene where hands are shot in extreme close-ups: 'One can expect much from the author of such a piece.' Marcel L'Herbier, for whom he acted twice (*L'Argent* in 1928, and *La Femme d'une nuit* in 1930), described Artaud's acting as a form of 'syntactical mistakes' expressing an inner duality symptomatic of his entire life (e.g. the light and the heavy, the physical and the spiritual). Gance used this to great effect in his *Napoléon* (1927): Artaud's portrayal of Marat, the radical journalist and defender of the Revolution, is at once effervescent and paroxystic. His eyes turn wildly, his (silent) speech is fiery and intense, and his body seems animated by some superior force. The superimposition

of his face on images of the Terror is striking, yet somehow pale in comparison with the two-minute scene that has guaranteed Artaud's surviving presence as a film actor: the death of Marat, a cinematic hybrid of Jacques-Louis David's painting and F.W. Murnau's *Nosferatu* (1922), is a showcase for Artaud's composition. His hypnotic gaze is as memorable as the wine spilling from his mouth in anticipation of the death to come; the murder itself, a model of sobriety, is in complete contrast to Artaud's acting, culminating in a final spasm which sees the actor's face looking upwards as though searching for some transcendent power.

In his second important role, as Frère Massieu in Carl Theodor Dreyer's *The Passion of Joan of Arc* (1928), his character seems again at odds: he is far-removed from the hatred lavished onto Joan by his religious brethren, entirely human and calm. Dreyer's camera, drawing ever closer to the actors' faces and making magnificent use of low-angle shots, highlights the characters' troubled psychology; Artaud, tall and upright, exudes mystic empathy and manages to communicate more through his gaze than a series of inter-titles or a dialogue perhaps ever could. His walk accompanying Joan to the stake is one of the most moving moments of cinema.

It is, of course, tempting to view Artaud's performances in light of what we know of his life: the breakdowns, the numerous sojourns in mental institutions, the drugs and physical decrepitude of later life only underlining the youthful and romantic film-star looks. His portrayals of tormented, against-the-grain characters indeed echo many of the leitmotivs of his writings – the themes of judgment, of the (in)existence of God, or of political, intellectual, and religious revolutions. To that extent, one could consider Artaud's films as a mirror reflecting, or prefiguring, the actor's life. The mirror, however, would be double-sided: watching Artaud act is not merely to witness the tensions, either psychological or metaphysical, of an individual, but also cinema's own tensions. In the 1920s and 1930s, cinema was still looking for a distinct sense of identity: Was it even an art? How specific should film acting be? It struggled with questions inherent to silent cinema: What should actors' lips do if there is no sound?, and with the transition from silent cinema to 'talkies'. Indeed, some of Artaud's films were shot twice – e.g. Léon Poirier's *Verdun, visions d'histoire* (1928 and 1931) – losing most of their beauty and value on their re-release. Artaud seems to embody these tensions and translate them to the screen; as such, watching Artaud is at once to observe the metamorphoses of a poet, and of an art and an industry in one of its first major transitional phases.

Benjamin ANDRÉO
Monash University, Melbourne

Ariane ASCARIDE (1954–)

Engagements from the South

ARIANE ASCARIDE'S cinematic activity is closely related to political *auteur* cinema and to her natal city of Marseilles. She studied sociology in Aix-en-Provence and was involved in the student union before she was trained as an actress in Paris (Conservatoire national supérieur d'art dramatique) at the end of the 1970s. At the beginning of her career, she performed in smaller productions such as *Antoine Vitez s'amuse avec Claudel et Brecht* (Maria Koleva, 1976) and *Le Barbouillé ou la mort gaie* (Koleva, 1978), both with Antoine Vitez, her teacher and founder of the Théâtre des Quartiers d'Ivry. Ascaride also performed in smaller roles in films by directors such as René Féret (*La Communion solennelle /Solemn Communion*, 1977), Christian Drillaud (*À vendre*, 1980), and René Allio (*Retour à Marseille /Return to Marseilles*, 1980), one of the most creative theatre and cinema directors of Marseilles.

Hailing from an open-minded family of a Neapolitan background, with an amateur actor father and two brothers, Pierre and Gilles – a writer and a stage designer – Ascaride also began to perform in theatre productions, often with her brother Pierre as director: *Vingt minutes avec un ange – Anecdotes provinciales* by Alexandre Vampilov (1979); *L'essuie-mains des pieds* by Gil Ben Aych (1982), and *Ma famille-revue* by Eduardo De Filippo (1985). In 1981, Ascaride began her lifelong collaboration when her husband Robert Guédiguian shot his first feature film, *Dernier été / Last Summer* (presented at Cannes). Ascaride is, together with Jean-Pierre Darroussin and Gérard Meylan, part of Guédiguian's ensemble of actors, appearing in every one of his films with the exception of *Le Promeneur du Champ de Mars /The Last Mitterrand* (2005). Guédiguian's first films have a crude and anarchic charm, referring to Marseilles' working class culture and questions of marginalization, somewhat in the tradition of Pier Paolo Pasolini. This experience is very important for Ascaride's cinematic identity; she appears in Guédiguian's movies *Ki lo sa ?* (1985), *Rouge midi* (1985), *Dieu vomit les tièdes* (1991), and *L'Argent fait le bonheur /Money Makes Happiness* (1993), all shot in Marseilles, often in the northern part of the city (L'Estaque).

Apart from the cinema of Guédiguian, Ascaride also appears in other film productions of the 1980s, while remaining faithful to her origins and convictions. She incarnates minor roles in *auteur* cinema and TV movies (*Vive la sociale !*, Gérard Mordillat, 1983 and the TV film *L'Apprentissage de la ville*, Caroline Huppert, 1982) and also in TV Series (*L'Inspecteur mène l'enquête*, 1981; *Les Amours des années folles*, 1981; *Mozart*, 1982), but she appeared in hardly more than one episode. In the first part of the 1990s, she performed in a few other movies and TV productions, mostly in smaller parts. Exceptions are a few films based on the writings of the southern French author Jean Giono (Marcel Bluwal's TV films *L'Ami Giono: Jofroi de la Maussan* and *Onorato*, 1990) and smaller parts in *Grossesse nerveuse /False Pregnancy* (made for TV), directed by Denis Rabaglia (1993), and *Calino Maneige* (Jean-Patrick Lebel, 1996).

Ascaride had to wait until Guédiguian's next two films, *À la vie, à la mort ! /Til Death Do Us Part* (1995) and *Marius et Jeannette* (1997), to become a well-known actress. While the latter film refers to Marcel Pagnol's *Marseilles Trilogy* of the 1930s, it focuses on the solidarity of several working-class couples living together on the outskirts of Marseilles. The movie was selected for the Official Competition of the Cannes Festival, and Ascaride was also awarded the César for Best Actress. She now acts in more and more films by other directors and has bigger parts in productions such as *Le Serpent a mangé la grenouille* (Alain Guesnier, 1998, with Jean Rochefort and Marisa Paredes) or *Nag la bombe* (Jean-Louis Milesi, 1999). She received leading roles in the politically engaged films of Dominique Cabrera (*Nadia et les hippopotames /Nadia and the Hippos*, 1999; the made-for-television *Retiens la nuit*, 2000) and Olivier Ducastel & Jacques Martineau (*Drôle de Félix /The Adventures of Felix*, 2000; *Ma vraie vie à Rouen /*

My Life on Ice, 2002) and has been nominated for several film prizes (European film prize, Sant Jordi, Valladolid).

Ascaride's activity in the 2000s proves her capacity to switch between diverse registers. She continues to collaborate with her husband, and appears in politically engaged films shot in Marseilles such as *À la place du cœur /Where the Heart Is* (1998), *La Ville est tranquille /The Town is Quiet* (2000), and *Marie-Jo et ses deux amours /Marie-Jo and Her Two Lovers* (2002). However, Ascaride is not only known for the films of Guédiguian, but also for her capacity to depict normal people and strong women with lots of energy and without allure. She also has become a sort of preferred actress of younger, politically engaged directors treating topics such as homosexuality, migration, and social protest. She has achieved remarkable success as Mme Mélikian in Élénore Faucher's *Brodeuses /A Common Thread* (2004) and as Nadine in Isabelle Czajka's *L'Année suivante* (2006). She has played leading roles in films of transnational and world cinema directors such as Saïd Ould Khelifa (*Le Thé d'Ania*, 2004), Mona Achache (*Le Hérisson /The Hedgehog*, 2009, the adaptation of Muriel Barbery's bestselling novel *L'Élégance du hérisson /The Elegance of the Hedgehog*), and Miel Van Hoogenbemt (*Miss Montigny*, 2005).

Her appearance in some newer movies by Guédiguian, combining political engagement with the crime genre, enable her to portray tough women, not hesitating to make use of their weapons. For two of these films she was awarded international film prizes: the Brutus film award in 2009 for *Lady Jane* (2008) and the award from the Festa Internazionale di Roma 2006 for *Le Voyage en Arménie /Armenia* (2006), for which she also collaborated as a co-screenwriter.

Ascaride also reinforces her theatrical activities in the past few years and appears mainly in plays by contemporary authors such as Véronique Olmi (*Mathilde*, 2003), Serge Valetti (*Pour Bobby*, 2004; *Ariane Ascaride lit Serge Valetti*, 2006), Dario Fo, and Franca Rame (*La Maman bohême and Médée*, 2007), in theatres in Paris as well as its suburbs. With *Algérie, je t'écris*, a reading of letters from Algerians, French, and 'Pieds-Noirs' printed in 2002 (40 years after the end of the War of Independence) in the French TV-magazine *Télérama*, she combined her theatrical activity with political engagement and was remarkably successful not only in the Parisian theatre scene, but also in the 'provinces' (2003).

In recent years, Ascaride has often performed – apart from Guédiguian's last film *Les Neiges du Kilimandjaro /The Snows of Kilimanjaro* (2011) – in leading roles in ambitious TV movies treating historic and political events, such as *George et Fanchette* and *La Femme qui pleure au chapeau rouge* (both Jean-Daniel Verhaeghe, 2010), *Les Mauvais Jours* (Pascale Bailly, 2011), and *Divorce et fiançailles /Divorce and Engagement* (Olivier Péray, 2012). But Ascaride has also come to show her comedic talent in film comedies by Emmanuel Mouret (*Changement d'adresse /Change of Address*, 2006; *L'Art d'aimer /The Art of Love*, 2011, with Frédérique Bel, François Cluzet, and Dany Brillant) and in a new cinematographic adaption of Marcel Pagnol's *Marseilles Trilogy* by Daniel Auteuil (2013), where she appears alongside Auteuil and Darroussin, both deeply connected to *auteur* cinema and the South of France. [1]

Daniel WINKLER
and
Katharina MÜLLER
Universität Wien /University of Vienna

1. Editor's Note: For further discussion of Ariane Ascaride and Robert Guédiguian, see: Annette Insdorf, '*Marius and Jeannette*,' Georgina Colvile, 'Robert Guédiguian and Ariane Ascaride: In Conversation,' and Georgina Colvile, '*Les Neiges du Kilimandjaro*,' in *World Film Locations: Marseilles*, ed. Marcelline Block (Bristol: Intellect, 2013), 72-73, 106-107, and 122-123.

Stéphane AUDRAN (1932–)
[Colette Suzanne DACHEVILLE]

A Feast for the Cinematic Senses

ELEGANT, with sharp, wondrous, glistening eyes, red hair, and refined manners, Stéphane AUDRAN became the epitome of the middle-class woman in French cinema and one of the icons of the French New Wave, as she rose to fame in the 1960s. Stern and pouty in her acting, the incarnation of the glamorous as well as the perverse adulterous, she often played characters named Hélène. Rarely taking breaks in her film and television career, she has acted in more than a hundred films. She is the multi-faceted actress of 24 movies directed by her second husband, influential filmmaker Claude Chabrol.

Born Colette Suzanne Dacheville, she was raised in Versailles, the daughter of a doctor. She made her debut in the drama school of Charles Dullin and Michel Vitol, starting her acting career in the 50s under the name Stéphane Audran in Eric Rohmer's short film *Le Signe du lion /The Sign of Leo* (1962). After a supporting role in Chabrol's *Les Cousins* (1959) next to Gérard Blain and Jean-Claude Brialy, Chabrol not only launched her career, but also helped develop her onscreen persona. Her characters combine coolness with a high degree of sophistication in Chabrol films like *Les Bonnes Femmes /The Good-Time Girls* (1960), and *Le Scandale /The Champagne Murders* (1967). With the erotic film *Les Biches /The Does* (Chabrol, 1968), for which she received the Best Actress Award at the Berlin Film Festival, she stars alongside her first husband, Jean-Louis Trintignant, as a rich lesbian that becomes involved in a love-triangle. Other notable Chabrol films include French thriller *Le Boucher /The Butcher* (1970), where she plays the part of an apparently well-balanced but neurotic schoolteacher that falls for the monstrous butcher (Jean Yanne). In *Juste avant la nuit /Just Before Nightfall* (Chabrol, 1971), for which she won the BAFTA award for Best Actress, she is the loving wife of a criminal (Michel Bouquet) who leads a double life. In *Violette Nozière* (Chabrol, 1978) for which she received a César Award for Best Supporting Actress, she is the sad and drab mother of adolescent prostitute Violette (Isabelle Huppert). In *Le Sang des autres / The Blood of Others* (1984), based on a novel by Simone de Beauvoir, she acts alongside Jodie Foster, Michael Ontkean, and Lambert Wilson.

Audran also appeared in Luis Buñuel's Oscar-winning surrealistic comedy *The Discreet Charm of the Bourgeoisie* (1972), Samuel Fuller's *The Big Red One* (1980), and as the titular character in Gabriel Axel's moving, spiritual Danish film *Le Festin de Babette /Babette's Feast* (1987), which won the Academy Award for Best Foreign Language Film (the first such honour for a Danish movie). Set in the 19th century, *Babette* made Audran an international star for her unforgettable performance as Babette, the elegant and mysterious French woman who arrives in a small town in Denmark, where she is given shelter from the violence of the Paris Commune, which has claimed her husband and son. In Denmark, Babette – who had previously been the chef of Paris's legendary Café Anglais – becomes a cook and housekeeper for two unmarried sisters, the daughters of a Protestant minister, who, along with their father's followers, lead an ascetic lifestyle in accordance with their father's teachings. After winning the French lottery, Babette spends the entire sum of her prize to prepare an elaborate, luxurious, and life-changing Parisian feast for her employers and the other townspeople invited to the meal, bringing to the town the very best French ingredients, wines, and champagne, along with silverware, crystal, and crockery. Although the villagers consider the meal sinful and initially reject it, Babette's incredible feast of French haute cuisine – sumptuously filmed – restores harmony in and even brings grace to the small community. This much- loved film is based upon a story by Isak Dinesen. In Bertrand Tavernier's masterful *Coup de torchon /Clean Slate* (1981), she is the cheating and cocky wife of Lucien Cordier (Philippe Noiret) a cop turned serial killer in a French African colony set on the eve of World War II.

In the 1990s, Audran's career

took a new turn and she completely changed registers. She can been seen in numerous comedies where she only has secondary parts, such as Claude Zidi's *Arlette* (1997), Daisy von Scherler Mayer's *Madeline* (1998), Jean-Marie Poiré's *Ma femme...s'appelle Maurice /My Wife Maurice* (2002), and Anne Fontaine's *La Fille de Monaco /The Girl from Monaco* (2008).

Stéphane Audran's persona is a paradox: popular, often burlesque, she always radiates an elegant Frenchness that makes her one of the most charismatic and seductive actresses of her generation. How can one resist a dinner of *Soupe à la tortue à la Louisianne* and *Cailles en sarcophage* served on the finest china by Babette?

Michaël ABECASSIS
The University of Oxford

Daniel AUTEUIL (1950–)

Acteur,
Auteur,
Auteuil

FEW ACTORS in the world have enjoyed such versatility and popularity as Daniel AUTEUIL. His characters range from the romantic hero Lagardère (*Le Bossu /On Guard*, Philippe de Broca, 1997) to poignant and henpecked office plankton (*Le Placard /The Closet*, Francis Veber, 2001), and he performs in psychological dramas as brilliantly as in an action-filled crime movies (Olivier Marchal's *36 Quai des Orfèvres /36 /36th Precinct*, 2004 and *MR73 /The Last Deadly Mission*, 2008). Since the beginning of his career in 1975, he has appeared in over 70 films, many of which have enjoyed both huge popular success and critical favour.

Auteuil's parents were opera and operetta singers, and he spent his childhood behind the scenes in the theatres of Avignon. At 17, he decided to pursue a career in theatre, and attended the Cours Florent in Paris. He made several attempts to enter the CNSAD (Conservatoire National Supérieur de l'Art Dramatique), attended by Isabelle Huppert and Carole Bouquet among others, but was never accepted. His theatre debut came in 1970, at the Théâtre national populaire (*Early Morning*), and he was engaged with the American musical

Godspell in 1972-3. François Périer's production *Coup de chapeau* earned him, in 1979, the Prix Gérard Philipe.

That same year, Auteuil worked with Claude Zidi in *Bête mais discipliné /Dumb but Disciplined* and *Les Sous-doués /The Under-Gifted* (released 1980), which become a major popular success and brought Auteuil instant popularity. He tried his hand at stage directing, with *Le Garçon d'appartement*, which was adapted for the screen in 1982 (*T'empêches tout le monde de dormir*, dir. Gérard Lazier).

Auteuil's early career, like that of many actors, included B-movies (*L'Arbalète /The Syringe*, 1984, dir. Sergio Gobbi), but already quite early in his film career he was working with major directors like Gérard Pirès (*L'Agression /Act of Aggression*, 1975; *Attention aux yeux ! /Let's Make a Dirty Movie*, 1976), Claude Lelouch (*À nous deux / Us Two*, 1979), and Edouard Molinaro (*Pour 100 briques t'as plus rien /For 200 Grand, You Get Nothing Now*, 1982). In his very first film, *L'Agression*, in 1975, Auteuil appeared alongside Catherine Deneuve and Jean-Louis Trintignant. Daniel Auteuil achieved recognition as a major actor with Claude Berri's 1986 *Jean de Florette* and *Manon des sources /Manon of the Spring*, where he appeared as Ugolin, alongside his then-partner Emmanuelle Béart and Yves Montand. This role brought him a Best Actor César. After this great success, Auteuil was approached increasingly by major directors, and worked with Claude Sautet (*Quelques jours avec moi /A Few Days with Me*, 1988; *Un cœur en hiver /A Heart in Winter*, 1992) and André Techiné (*Ma saison préférée /My Favorite Season*, 1993). Ugolin marks a development in Auteuil's acting style towards greater emotional depth and gravity.

The actor's other awards include a European Cinema Award (for his role in Michael Haneke's *Caché / Hidden*, 2005), another César for Patrice Leconte's *La Fille sur le pont /The Girl on the Bridge* (1999), and two 'golden stars' of the French film press, recognizing him as the Best Actor (*Après vous*, Pierre Salvadori, 2003; *Petites coupures /Small Cuts*, Pascal Bonitzer, 2003).

Auteuil's adaptable appearance and broad acting range ensure that he defies classification, and cannot be tied down to just one type of cinema. Instead, he enjoys both the recognition of critics for his more intellectual roles in independent films and a love of the wider public.

Following the success of his directorial effort *La Fille du puisatier /The Well-Digger's Daughter* (2011), a remake of the original Marcel Pagnol film, Daniel Auteuil is now preparing an adaptation of Pagnol's entire *Marius-Fanny-César* trilogy, in which he himself stars as César, showing his attachment to Pagnol's work.

Daniel Auteuil was married to Emmanuelle Béart for 11 years. He is now married to a Corsican artist and sculptor and remains very active, with 3 major films out in 2007. In 2013, Daniel Auteuil teamed up with Richard Berry for the first time on stage, triumphing in Eric Assous's play *Nos femmes* at the Théâtre de Paris.

Arina Patrikova
The University of Oxford

Sabine Azéma (1949–)

Alain Resnais's Partner & Muse

S ABINE AZÉMA was born in Paris and grew up in an upper-class milieu. After passing the Baccalauréat examination, she began her acting apprenticeship by studying at the Cours Florent in Paris, and then graduated from the CNSAD (National Conservatory of Dramatic Art) where Antoine Vitez was her teacher.

The director of the Comédie des Champs-Elysées allowed her to make her acting debut on stage by offering her the female lead in *La Valse des toréadors* (1974), a play by Jean Anouilh, featuring famous actor Louis de Funès. In 1976, Azéma appeared for the first time in a movie, *On aura tout vu /The Bottom Line* (dir. Georges Lautner), and, the year after, had a small role in Claude Goretta's *La Dentellière /The Lacemaker* (starring a young Isabelle Huppert). The turning point of Azéma's career was her encounter with and marriage to director Alain Resnais (1922–2014). She became his favourite actress and he cast her in nine movies from 1983 onward: *La Vie est un roman /Life is a Bed of Roses*, 1983; *L'Amour à mort /Love Unto Death*, 1984; *Mélo*, 1986; *Smoking /No Smoking*, 1993; *On connaît la chanson* /Same Old Song, 1997; *Pas sur la bouche /Not on the Lips*, 2003; *Cœurs /Private Fears in Public Places*, 2006; *Vous n'avez encore rien vu /You Ain't Seen Nothin' Yet*, 2012; and Resnais's final film, *Aimer, boire et chanter /Life of Riley*, 2014. Resnais's movies particularly succeeded in exploiting her special charm, composed both of elegance and humour.

In 1984, she appeared in *Un dimanche à la campagne /A Sunday in the Country* by Bertrand Tavernier, for which she won the César for Best Actress in 1985. She received another César two years later, for Best Actress in *Mélo* by Resnais.

More recently, she stood out in embodying uptight bourgeois characters in Étienne Chatiliez's satirical comedies, *Le Bonheur est dans le pré /Happiness is in the Field* (1995), *Tanguy* (2001), and *Les Derniers jours du monde /Happy End* (2009).

Aurélie LEDOUX
École Normale Supérieure, Paris

Charles AZNAVOUR (1924–)
[Charles AZNAOURIAN]

*The Saga
of Two
Portraits
(1968 &
1998)*

C HARLES AZNAVOUR, hailed as
Entertainer of the Century by
CNN (1998), was born in Paris's famous
Saint Germain des Prés area on May
22, 1924 to an immigrant Armenian
family.[1] He quit school at age nine,
favouring music over 'the three Rs.'

Not only is Aznavour recognized
as one of the greatest performers of
all time, but also he has his share of
leading parts in films as an actor, with
over 60 film credits to his name, and
has over 1000 musical compositions
he authored, performed, registered,
and sung. In this article, I shall mainly
focus on his cinematic achievements.

As a political activist Aznavour
organized a protest against Le Pen's
Front National, during which Aznavour
sang *La Marseillaise* to support his
point. He wrote the song *Ils sont tombés*
['They Fell'], which commemorates
the Armenian Genocide of 1915-1917.
Aznavour also became the Armenian
Ambassador to Switzerland. As a true
pantophile with a versatile personality,
Charles Aznavour is decorated as
Officer of the French Legion of
Honour, among many other honours.
How can one depict such a giant
phenomenon in one thousand words,
which is what I am attempting to do in

this portrait essay? Charles Aznavour
is so iconic that he overspills the limits
of my project.

Aznavour's filmic achievements are
recognised worldwide, for which he
received an honorary César Award in
1997. Aznavour was a member of the
jury of the Cannes Film Festival. He
has been featured in over 75 films and
television movies / series since he was
first cast as an extra, at age 13, in *La
Guerre des gosses* (Jacques Daroy, 1937).
François Truffaut's *Tirez sur le pianiste
/Shoot the Piano Player* (1960) shows
Aznavour in a subtle yet emotionally
moving performance as Charlie Kohler
/Edouard Saroyan, who has a hidden
past. *Tirez sur le pianiste* mingles
suspense with quiet moments of
expectation, nostalgia, and melancholia
in a film inspired by Chicago gangster
crime narratives, a film style emulated
widely by the French New Wave
cinéastes who were fascinated by it
(Jean-Luc Godard in particular, but
also Truffaut). In *Tirez sur le pianiste*,
a haunting musical score underlines
Aznavour's tired face: his deep-seated,
inquisitive eyes under the shadow of
slanted eyebrows, and his muted lips
closed on unavowable secrets visually
announce his upcoming doom.

Aznavour's film roles include
the epileptic Heurtevent in Georges
Franju's debut, *La Tête contre les murs /
Head Against the Wall* (1959), and novice
Jesuit Denis Mayeux (seeking revenge
for his sister's suicide) in the third
segment of Julien Duvivier's *Le Diable
et les dix commandements /The Devil
and the Ten Commandments* (1963). In
And Then There Were None (1974, Peter
Collinson), the second film adaptation
of Agatha Christie's eponymous
mystery novel, Aznavour plays Michael

Raven, one of ten people accused of escaping punishment for past crimes. In this movie, Aznavour performed 'The Old Fashioned Way,' an English-language version of his iconic song, *Les Plaisirs démodés*. In *The Tin Drum* (Volker Schlöndorff, 1979), based on the eponymous 1959 novel by Nobel Prize winner Günter Grass, Aznavour's supporting part as Sigismund Markus helped the film win the coveted Academy Award for Best Foreign Language Film (1980). Claude Chabrol's adaptation of Georges Simenon's novel, the 1982 thriller *Les Fantômes du chapelier /The Hatter's Ghost*, is about a serial strangler (Michel Serrault) in a small Brittany town, who is suspected by a tailor (Aznavour). Previously, Aznavour also appeared in Chabrol's *Folies bourgeoises /The Twist* (1976) in the role of Dr. Lartigue—the title *Folies bourgeoises* could be understood as an ironic play on the words *Folies bergères*, one of the most famous music-hall theatres in Paris.

Aznavour co-wrote and starred in the 1986 comedy *Yiddish Connection* (dir. Paul Boujenah); previously, Aznavour had co-written *Les Intrus / The Intruders* (dir. Sergio Gobbi), a 1972 crime drama in which he also starred. In 2002, Aznavour starred in Canadian-Armenian director Atom Egoyan's film *Ararat* as an Armenian film director, Edward Saroyan – a name purposefully referencing Aznavour's character in Truffaut's *Tirez sur le pianiste* – experiencing difficulties while making a film about the Armenian Genocide, specifically the events of the Siege of Van (April-May 1915). Oscar-winning American director Jonathan Demme's *The Truth About Charlie* (2002) – a remake of *Charade* (Stanley Donen, 1963) – pays tribute to *Tirez sur le pianiste* when Aznavour appears as himself, performing his chanson *Quand tu m'aimes*, in English and in French. Note also that the first name 'Charlie' reinforces the connection between *The Truth About Charlie* and *Tirez sur le pianiste*, in which Aznavour's character is named Charlie Kohler. In 2004, Aznavour incarnated the titular role in an adaptation of Balzac's novel *Le Père Goriot* for French television (dir. Jean-Daniel Verhaeghe) – a befitting part as Aznavour, like Père Goriot, is, in his life offscreen, a generous and thoughtful person and father, filled with empathy and kindness. In my experience, I found Aznavour humble and tolerant, and truly down to earth. Aznavour lent his voice to the 2009 animated film *Up* (dir. Pete Docter and Bob Peterson) as protagonist Carl Fredricksen when the film was dubbed into French.

CHARLES AZNAVOUR WITH ONE OF THE TWO PORTRAITS THAT JENNY BATLAY PAINTED OF HIM. [*PHOTO COURTESY JENNY BATLAY*]

I met Charles Aznavour in Beverly Hills in 1968 where he was performing in a sold-out concert, and where I was simultaneously exhibiting my oil portraits of Hollywood personalities. He kindly posed for me. I started, but did not finish, my portrait of Aznavour before he left Beverly Hills to continue on tour. He did not get to see the finished product then. Subsequently I moved to Manhattan, where I finished the canvas (from memory).

Over the next 30 years, I often exhibited my portrait of Aznavour in group and solo shows, such as at the Arthur Danziger Gallery on Spring Street in SoHo in 1993 (that gallery is no longer in existence) and in 1996 at Marylou's, which was, in its days, a celebrity hangout for directors including Abel Ferrara, Oliver Stone, and James Toback, and actors such as Robert de Niro, James Gandolfini, Chazz Palminteri, Joe Pesci, and Eric Roberts, among others, which closed in 2001. The late attorney Ken Goldstein, a fan of Aznavour, also became a fan of my portrait, which I categorically refused to sell to him, nor to anyone – but after he asked to 'borrow' it for a party at his country house, I agreed to loan it to him. When Aznavour came to perform in New York City in 1998, a time when both Aznavour and I were in the same place, Ken Goldstein was out of town and therefore unable to return my painting.

As I had made an appointment with Charles Aznavour at his midtown Manhattan hotel to show him my by then 30-year-old portrait of him, and as I still had not recovered from Ken Goldstein the original portrait I had painted in Beverly Hills, I therefore decided, the night before our meeting, to paint, from memory, another portrait of Aznavour. I arrived at the appointed time at the hotel, accompanied by a courier carrying my painting, not yet completely dried. I did not like this second version as much as the first one, and when I told Aznavour I

would finish it later, he did not bat an eye: he remembered that this was the same line I had used 30 years earlier with the previous portrait – history repeats itself. Aznavour's memory is phenomenal. He thought that mine was great, too.

Coda: In the summer of 2006, Ken Goldstein finally promised to return my original portrait of Aznavour. However, he was still uncommitted to do so as he passionately loved both Aznavour and the portrait. Unfortunately, in a tragic twist of fate, Ken, while out driving with his fiancée, hit a tree and died soon after the accident, at the age of 49. I was inconsolable at his funeral as he had been a great friend of mine over the years. But the portrait I painted of Aznavour was returned to me by Ken Goldstein's relatives.

I now have in my home the two portraits of Charles Aznavour: much drama, trauma, delays, anguish, and memory went into their creation and conservation, but for now, they hang peacefully together, side by side on the wall opposite my window. When the sun shines on them, they take on a cheerful life of their own, but when I play on my Steinway the tunes from *Tirez sur le pianiste* – a title I have re-semanticized as *Ne tirez pas sur la pianiste* – they seem to reflect a nostalgic mood.

Jenny BATLAY

PhD Columbia University

1. Charles Aznaourian are the names on his 1924 Paris birth record (with official name-change to Aznavour in July 1984). The Armenian Embassy in Switzerland gives Armenian versions of his name, spelled as follows: Shahnourh Varinag Aznavourian, and Շահնուր Վաղինակ Ազնավուրյան. —*Ed.*

Jean-Pierre BACRI (1951–)

*—and
the Art
of French
Kvetching*

J EAN-PIERRE BACRI was born
May 24, 1951, in Castiglione,
Algeria. His introduction to cinema
was relevant to the salt-of-the-
earth characters for which he would
become famous: Bacri watched films
in a movie theatre where his father
worked weekends selling tickets. In
1962, Bacri's family left Algeria during
the mass exodus of French Algerians
from the newly independent country.
Like many other *Pieds-Noirs* [1] newly
arrived in France from Algeria, the
adjustment was difficult, not least
because the entire family had to share
a small studio apartment in Cannes.

After his schooling and a rather
uninspiring stint as a bank teller, Bacri
made the leap to Paris and to acting
in 1976. From the start, writing and
acting were closely linked activities
for Bacri; he wrote his first play, *Tout
simplement*, in 1977. His breakthrough
role was as Jacky in Alexandre
Arcady's *Le Grand Pardon*, a 1982 film
about a Jewish *Pied-Noir* mafia family;
partly because of the film's success
and partly because he was thought to
have the *Pied-Noir* 'look' and accent,
he was besieged with scripts for
roles for other *Pied-Noir* thugs. Bacri
refused these roles and this particular
typecasting, especially since it was

based on his own cultural background.
In interviews, Bacri has often qualified
this type of minority identification
as clannish and separatist. He would
eventually be typecast for something
quite different, and largely of his
own making: the comically angry
grump, railing against friends, family,
hypocrisy, or snobbery.

Luc Besson's 1985 *Subway*
established Bacri as a talented
character actor; in the film, he plays
Batman, the dour cop, an *'ours mal
léché'* (literally, 'a badly licked bear,' or
in other words, an ill-bred character)
who unsuccessfully pursues suspects
in the Paris metro. The year after
Subway came another important role,
pivotal for a different reason: during
rehearsals for Harold Pinter's *The
Birthday Party*, Bacri met a young
actress named Agnès Jaoui, who was
to be his partner for over 20 years.
Jaoui and Bacri began writing plays
together, starting with *Cuisine et
Dépendances* (1991), about a dinner
party meant to reunite old friends.
Bacri wrote himself the role of a
misanthropic writer who attends
the dinner party only because he is
temporarily homeless and sleeping
on the hosts' couch. The play takes
place entirely in the wings of the
dinner party, in the kitchen, where
characters come and go, complaining
of over-salted food, social climbing,
and generally having a pretty bad
time. Typical of plays and screenplays
written by 'Ja-Bac', as the couple
is sometimes called, the emphasis
is on dialogue and the absurdity
of interpersonal relationships, with
a tone that manages to be at once
funny, biting, and tender. Bacri is
interested in observational humour

with a purpose; he once remarked in an interview that he and Jaoui did not want to make people laugh just for the sake of laughter, but that they wanted the comic moments to be linked to some human truth.

Cuisine et Dépendances was adapted into an equally successful film (Philippe Muyl, 1993), which the couple followed with another play/film adaptation, *Un air de famille /Family Resemblances* (Cédric Klapisch, 1996), chronicling family dysfunction and the plight of the neglected eldest child, played to the hilt by Bacri. But Bacri's finest role may have been a film based on another Ja-Bac screenplay, *Le Goût des autres /The Taste of Others* (2000), directed by Jaoui. A brilliant comedy of manners, the film brings together characters from different social milieux to poke fun at their cliquey prejudices, whether it be a group of theatre actors who look down their noses at an uncultured businessman (Bacri), or that very businessman who in turn snubs a more intellectual colleague because of his proper way of speaking.

In *Parlez-moi de la pluie /Let It Rain* (Agnès Jaoui, 2008), Bacri and Jamel Debbouze form an Odd Couple, with Bacri playing a tragicomically scatterbrained documentary filmmaker. *Parlez-moi de la pluie* references Algerian immigration, as does a 2009 release starring Bacri, the well-received *Adieu Gary /Goodbye Gary* (dir. Nassim Amaouche). However, given Bacri's position on what he considers sectarianism, neither film is likely to become his *Roots*. 2012's *Cherchez Hortense /Looking for Hortense* (dir. Pascal Bonitzer) touches on the question of identity in a different way,

through a female character whose apparent Frenchness means nothing in the absence of documented French citizenship. In the film, Bacri plays a put-upon father, husband, and son, and masterfully incarnates the slogan 'the personal is the political'. In *Au bout du conte /Under the Rainbow* (Agnès Jaoui, 2013), he affirmed once again that he is a true master of character acting, refining his haggard persona to a humorous and touching shorthand of gestures, grunts, and grimaces.

While Bacri's acting range goes beyond the comic, he excels in that genre, especially in ensemble films such as Jean-Marie Poiré's *Mes meilleurs copains /My Best Pals* (1989). He has appeared in over fifty films and still occasionally acts on stage, notably in a 2005 production of Bertolt Brecht's *Schweik in the Second World War*. He has won numerous awards, including four Césars, for Ja-Bac [2] screenplays.

Marina DAVIES
New York University, Paris Campus

1. '*Pied Noir* : A person of European origin who lived in Algeria during French rule' – *Oxford English Dictionary*, 6th ed., 2007
2. See also JAOUI, Agnès

Edouard BAER (1966–)

*Growing
Up
on
Screen*

EDOUARD BAER is not what you would call a high-class actor. For the general public, he is chiefly known for two things. First, his most famous role as the sickeningly cheerful scribe Otis in *Astérix et Obélix : Mission Cléopâtre /Asterix and Obelix Meet Cleopatra* (Alain Chabat, 2002). For a whole generation of French viewers, Otis is the epitome of cool. If you were in high school when the film was released, and you managed to master the intricacies of Otis's well-known declamation about loving life, you would automatically be propelled to the much-envied position of coolest kid in school. Portrayed by Edouard Baer as an inspired, oblivious, know-it-all simpleton whose only purpose in life is to build a machine that would take people to the top of buildings without much effort, Otis made such an impression on the audience that people soon started to imagine the actor as his character in real life. There can be no better proof that this role was tailor-made for Edouard Baer, as it put him in the limelight and subsequently gave him the opportunity to try his hand at more serious roles.

Secondly, Edouard Baer is famous for his boyish looks and the shabby hairstyle that gives him such a Parisian dandy look. His hair is so intrinsically connected to his acting that one could even argue that his hairstyle is a very good indicator for the quality of a film: the messier his hair, the worse the film is likely to be. The best (or the worst) example to illustrate this theory is the film *Double zéro /French Spies* (Gérard Pirès, 2004), in which Edouard Baer plays a fabulously rich megalomaniac, very logically nicknamed 'the male.' The character is absolutely ridiculous, as he cherishes the dream of being the only man left on the planet along with a large number of beautiful women at his beck and call, ready to be impregnated in order to repopulate the planet. His hairstyle and beard seem to come straight from the worst side of the eighties, and are reason enough not to see this film, the French title of which is indeed very appropriate.

But these two characteristics, which at first seem to define Edouard Baer's entire career, are unfortunately what the audience chooses to remember from his performances. The actor originally started as a comedian, and was thus pigeonholed from the start as the new hellion of French cinema: as a result, he had trouble getting away from a certain type of role. His career is indeed scattered with naïve, cynical, or disillusioned characters, who nonetheless enabled him to perfect his trademark face: a hint of bovine incomprehension mixed with charming stupidity. Edouard Baer's career is also heavily marked by secondary roles: until very recently, his contributions to film, as an actor, had been limited to unassuming, almost insignificant characters.

Edouard Baer's career obviously took off after the success of *Astérix et Obélix*, but he has only started to feature in both critically and commercially acclaimed films in the past few years. Three films in particular stand out. The first one, *Les Brigades du Tigre /The Tiger Brigades* (Jérôme Cornuau, 2006) is based on a very popular French television series from the eighties, which recounts the story of a small unit of special officers in 1912 France, trying to arrest the group of terrorists known as 'Bonnot Gang.' Edouard Baer plays Pujol, a gruff inspector dedicated to his work: the character could have been interesting without the foreseeable romantic twist. Léa, one of Pujol's prostitutes, is attacked by a member of the gang after giving tips to the officers. Predictably enough, Pujol mellows and cares for her after the attack, swearing to avenge her. But the film offered Edouard Baer the opportunity to play a dramatic role, and for the first time, to be credible in this genre.

The second film that could be considered as a landmark in Edouard Baer's career is *Un monde à nous* (Frédéric Balekdjian, 2008): the film portrays the unusual relationship between a father, Marc, and his son Noé. Running away from an invisible threat, Marc teaches Noé martial arts, and forbids him to reveal anything about their family, which isolates Noé from the real world. Edouard Baer's character is very uncommunicative, and remains mysterious about the reason that forced them to go on the run. The actor puts his body language skills (inherited from his comedian past) to good use in order to convey the father's feelings, but his acting is so cold and interiorised that he ends up appearing perfectly emotionless. The role demanded subtlety, but while Edouard Baer was not entirely convincing, he certainly showed promise and potential.

The third film, *Mon pote* (Marc Esposito, 2010) also gave Edouard Baer the opportunity to play the lead, alongside Benoît Magimel. He plays Victor, the editor of a car magazine, who agrees to give a talk about his work in a prison. During this discussion, he meets Bruno (Magimel), a former car thief, who desperately wants a chance to work for him. The film focuses on the unlikely friendship between the two men, and allows Edouard Baer to successfully play with a wide range of emotions. Even though he still overacts every now and then, the chemistry between the two actors works perfectly: Edouard Baer is good because Benoît Magimel is good, and vice versa.

Even with these significant roles, Edouard Baer made the interesting choice of continuing to play secondary roles, thus contributing to projects that interested him. In that respect, his most remarkable films include *J'ai toujours rêvé d'être un gangster /I Always Wanted to be a Gangster* (Samuel Benchetrit, 2007); *Une exécution ordinaire /An Ordinary Execution* (Marc Dugain, 2010), and *Poulet aux prunes /Chicken with Plums* (Vincent Paronnaud and Marjane Satrapi, 2011). In *J'ai toujours rêvé d'être un gangster*, Edouard Baer is both hilarious and pathetic as a wannabe gangster who tries to break into a diner and hold the waitress hostage. His wit and sense of humour is put to good use, but in a subtler way. This confirms his transformation as an actor who progressively becomes more and more respected for his choice of roles. In *Une exécution ordinaire*, Edouard Baer delivers what is, in my opinion, one of his best performances in a dramatic role. His character Vassilli is a physician madly in love with his wife who hides a terrible secret: Baer's portrayal of a man broken by torture seems chillingly powerful, and the scene when he is reunited with his wife is unsettling. Finally, in *Poulet aux prunes*, Baer's contribution is limited to the voiceover and a very small part. But his drawling voice is easily recognisable, and brings some much needed texture to the story. His role as Azraël, the Angel of Death, who bears an uncanny resemblance to what could be the evil double of the Cheshire Cat, is portentous, but brings some comic relief to the film.

But acting is not Edouard Baer's main activity: he has also tried his hand, more or less successfully, at directing. In his first film, *La Bostella* (2000), he explores the anxiety linked to writer's block. Gathered in a villa in the South of France during the summer, Edouard's company prepares a TV show based on improvisation. The film itself could not really be described as comic: instead Edouard Bear opted to show the tensions within the company, resulting in a rather melancholic film. His second film, *Akoibon* (2005), is richer, albeit a bit faltering at times. The film offers a *mise en abyme*, questioning the importance of the actors: the reflection is interesting, but the clues to uncover the nature of acting – such as the voiceover, the actors facing the camera directly, the omnipresence of theatre – are too obvious and clumsy. The film has so many layers that the reflection, supposed to be 'metacinematic', is lost in a whirlwind of references and tributes to cinema. Although the film proclaims to be absurd, this does not excuse its muddled and disorganised presentation.

Edouard Baer's tragedy was to have been marked as a comic actor at a very early stage of his career. While he certainly excels in that genre, trying to tackle more dramatic roles seems to have been incredibly difficult: one could argue that he was categorised that way for a reason, as his debuts in drama were not entirely convincing. He has certainly been bold and eccentric regarding his choice of roles: one of his latest feats was to feature in *Astérix et Obélix : Au service de sa majesté /Astérix and Obélix: God Save Britannia* (2012), but this time, as Astérix himself. While some consider this a promotion of sorts, others wonder about this risky move that can either turn out to be a success or an abysmal disaster.

But Baer is a highly proficient actor, trained in the Cours Florent, and has managed to maintain a very intense work rhythm, with an average of two or three films released almost every year. His roles are getting more and more interesting, provided he stays on the right side of French cinema. If he is not yet an A list actor, he certainly seems to be getting there.

Marion Coste
École Normale Supérieure de Lyon

Josiane BALASKO (1950–)
[Josiane BALAŠKOVIĆ]

*The
Mainstream
Anti-
conformist*

THE CAREER TRAJECTORY of Josiane BALASKO (born Josiane Balaskovic on April 15th 1950 in Paris) is inextricably linked with that of the *Splendid* comedy troupe with which she burst onto the scene in the 1970s, even if (like many of her fellow *Splendid* alumni) she has now secured a distinct place for herself in the French cultural landscape.

The *Splendid* troupe was one of the mainstays of the Paris café-théâtre scene of the 1970s, and over the next decade such names as Michel Blanc, Marie-Anne Chazel, Christian Clavier, Gérard Jugnot, and Thierry Lhermitte were to establish themselves as major players in French cinema. Their silver-screen breakthrough was *Les Bronzés /French Fried Vacation* (Patrice Leconte, 1978), based on their successful play *Amour, coquillages et crustacés.*

Les Bronzés was a huge national hit, spawning two equally successful sequels, *Les Bronzés font du ski* (Leconte, 1979) and (nearly three decades later) *Les Bronzés 3 : Amis pour la vie* (Leconte, 2006), and many of its catchphrases have been absorbed into popular culture. The

film, which also launched director Patrice Leconte into the mainstream, was an ensemble piece following the fortunes of six young French tourists on a Club-Med-style holiday in West Africa. It touched a chord in the French public through its satirical portrayal of the foibles and self-delusion of really quite unexceptional people; Balasko featured as Nathalie, a married woman attempting to live up to an ideal of sexual freedom with which she was not entirely comfortable. Following the two *Bronzés* films, Balasko continued to work with the Splendid team, co-writing and appearing in cult favourite *Le Père Noël est une ordure /Santa Claus is a Stinker* (Jean-Marie Poiré, 1982; remade in the US as 1994's *Mixed Nuts*, directed by the late Nora Ephron). Although her role in this film is relatively minor (she spends much of it stuck in a lift), her portrayal of the irritable Mme Musquin is one of its more memorable performances.

Away from the *Splendid* films, Balasko became associated with anti-sex-symbol roles, often exaggerating her 'ordinary' physique by appearing opposite more conventionally attractive actresses. A typical film from this period is *Les Hommes préfèrent les grosses /Men Prefer Fat Girls* (Poiré, 1981), based on another *Splendid* play which she had written. Balasko plays the frumpy heroine sharing her house with a model whose boyfriend (Daniel Auteuil) gradually falls for her less obvious charms. A more subversive treatment of the beautiful girl/plain girl binary comes in Bertrand Blier's

Trop belle pour toi /Too Beautiful for You (1989). This exploration of middle-aged love sees Gérard Depardieu's hero leave his beautiful wife, played by Carole Bouquet, for Balasko, his secretary. Instead of the stereotypical seductress one might expect in such a scenario, Balasko's character wins the hero through empathy, as both realise they share the same insecurities about where their lives are heading. This role was also a key moment for Balasko's career: the association with Blier gave her greater exposure in a non-comedy role than she had previously had.

Another notable performance against type was to come in the 2003 thriller *Cette femme-là / Hanging Offense* (dir. Guillaume Nicloux). The title could almost be held to refer to Balasko herself, since the director, Nicloux, wrote the central role of Michèle with her in mind. Although the film was not a huge commercial success, Balasko's portrayal of the heroine, a depressive policewoman struggling to face the anniversary of her son's death, was well received. The oneiric atmosphere which pervades the film lends intensity to a performance in stark contrast to the feisty roles for which she was better known. She has continued to alternate comic supporting roles with more sober performances like the concierge Mme Michel in Mona Achache's *Le Hérisson /The Hedgehog* (2009; a cinematic adaptation of Muriel Barbery's 2006 bestselling novel, *L'Élégance du hérisson /The Elegance of the Hedgehog*), whose lowly social standing belies an imposing but carefully hidden knowledge of intellectual culture.

Yet Balasko had already shown that she had more strings to her bow than acting. From an early age, she had exhibited a desire to try her hand at different things: she studied art and wrote science fiction before opting for the theatre. She continued writing and appearing in her own plays alongside her work with the *Splendid* through the 1970s, and it was inevitable that this pattern would repeat itself in the theatre. Thus, in 1985, she directed her first movie, *Sac de noeuds /All Mixed Up*, later claiming that this was the only way of getting her own scripts made into film. Her directorial work is characterised by a taste for social satire consonant with many of the films in which she has appeared: *Sac de noeuds* (which also stars Isabelle Huppert) is a black comedy about three misfits, and in her next film *Les Keufs /Lady Cops* (1987) she plays a police inspector investigating prostitution in a deprived area.

More recently, *Cliente* (2008) returns to the theme of prostitution but inverting the usual roles: the main character, a gigolo, finds himself having to choose between his wife and one of his customers. The difficulties in getting financing for an apparently marginal subject initially led Balasko to rewrite her screenplay as a novel; it was only following the success of the book that she found producers willing to support the film project.

Balasko's best-known work to date, especially outside France, is *Gazon maudit /French Twist* (1995) which she wrote and directed. Here, she plays the anti-sex-symbol role to the hilt, as the masculine lesbian Marijo who enters a tug of war with Alain Chabat's real-estate agent Laurent for the love of his affection-starved wife Loli (played by Victoria Abril). As in *Trop belle pour toi* and *Cliente*, the conventional love-triangle is given an almighty twist: here, the central subject over whom the suitors fight is no longer a man but a woman, and the be-suited, cigar-smoking Marijo troubles the waters of gender and sexuality. Making the still taboo subject of lesbianism a central concern of a high-profile comedy, *Gazon maudit* is a good exemplification of the two main principles of Balasko's career: the desire to entertain mainstream audiences, alongside a taste for anticonformism and challenging expectations.

Thomas HINTON
The University of Exeter

Jean-François BALMER (1946–)

Another Swiss Adopted by France

JEAN-FRANÇOIS BALMER was born on April 18, 1946, in Valangin (canton of Neuchâtel) in Switzerland. He spent most of his childhood in his native village and in Lausanne. Although many people believe that Balmer is a French actor, he actually obtained French citizenship later in life (he currently holds dual citizenship – Swiss and French). Like many other actors, he devoted more time to (more or less serious) theatrical endeavours than to school (he apparently enjoyed reading theatrical texts out loud and impersonating various imaginary characters). At age 23, he decided to pursue his dream and started studying at the Conservatoire d'art dramatique in Paris. Among his friends at the Conservatoire were other (future) actors, such as Isabelle Adjani, Francis Huster, Jacques Villeret, and others.

After his graduation, Balmer starred as Raymond Dax in Yves Boisset's war drama *R.A.S. /Nothing to Report* (1973). This was only the beginning of a long and prolific career in theatre, cinema, and television. In the 1970s, Balmer performed in a number of plays, such as Molière's *Les Fourberies de Scapin* (directed by Jacques Weber in 1973), Pierre Laville's *Les Ressources naturelles* (1974), *Petite illustration* (directed by Roger Planchon), Arthur Adamov's *A.A. théâtre* (directed by Planchon in 1976), Diderot's *Le Neveu de Rameau* (directed by Weber in 1976), and Shakespeare's *Taming of the Shrew* (also Weber in 1979). He also played in a number of relatively minor movies, such as *Le Mouton enragé /Love at the Top* by Michel Deville (1974), *Peur sur la ville /The Night Caller* by Henri Verneuil (1975), *Les Naufragés de l'île de la Tortue /The Castaways of Turtle Island* by Jacques Rozier (1976), *La Menace* (1977) by Alain Corneau, *L'Adolescente /The Adolescent* by Jeanne Moreau (1979), *Rien ne va plus /Out of Whack* by Jean-Michel Ribes (1979), and *Flic ou Voyou /Cop or Hood* by Georges Lautner (1979). It should be noted that Balmer was nominated for the César for Best Supporting Actor in 1978 for his role in *La Menace*. Alas, this is the highest recognition that he has received for his cinematographic activity so far. During this decade, Balmer could also be seen on television screens, in Jean-Roger Cadet's *Gil Blas de Santillane* (1974), Roger Vadim's *Bonheur, impair et passe* (1977), Claude Santelli's *Le Chandelier* (1977), and Peter Kassovitz's *La Vie séparée* (1979).

In the 1980s, Balmer continued his theatrical activity with roles in Beaumarchais's *Le Mariage de Figaro* (directed by Françoise Petit in 1980), Nathalie Sarraute's *Pour un oui ou pour un non* (directed by Simone Benmussa in 1986), and Molière's *Le Misanthrope* (directed by Françoise Petit at the Théâtre des Célestins in 1986 – Balmer married Françoise Petit a year later). Balmer's career as a cinema actor really took off during this period; he acted in a plethora of movies such

as *Une étrange affaire /Strange Affair* (Pierre Grenier-Deferre, 1981), *Il buon soldato* (Franco Brusati, 1982), *Le Quart d'heure américain* (Philippe Galland, 1982), *L'Africain /The African* (Philippe de Broca, 1983), *Un amour de Swann /Swann in Love* (Volker Schlöndorff, 1984), *Polar* (Jacques Bral, 1984), *Urgence* (Gilles Béhat, 1985), *Le Transfuge* (Philippe Lefebvre, 1985), and *Golden Eighties /Window Shopping* (Chantal Akerman, 1986). It is also during the 80s that Balmer began his collaboration with Claude Chabrol, which began with his role in *Le Sang des autres /The Blood of Others* (1984) and continued throughout the 1990s and 2000s. He also continued to be active as a television actor, being cast in numerous productions, such as Elie Chouraqui's *Une page d'amour* (1980), Pierre Badel's *Le Mariage de Figaro* (1981), Robert Mazoyer's *Les Poneys sauvages* (1983), Fabrice Cazeneuve's *Le Roi de la Chine* (1984), Claude Boissol's *Espionne et tais-toi* (1988), Walter Asmus's *En attendant Godot* (1989), and *La Révolution française* by Robert Enrico and Richard Heffron (in 1989, for the bicentennial of the French Revolution).

During the following decade, Jean-François Balmer continued his collaboration in the theatre with directors Françoise Petit (who directed *Une nuit de Casanova* by Franco Cuomo in 1990 and *Le Faiseur* by Balzac in 1997) and Jacques Weber (he directed *Mystification*, based on texts by Diderot, in 1992). It should be emphasised that Balmer was nominated for the Molière du comédien award for his role in *Le Faiseur*. He also worked with theatre directors Jérôme Savary, who directed

Pierre Dac's *Mon maître soixante-trois* in 1994 and Michel Pascal (*Une nuit au Moyen Age*, 1996-7). In terms of cinematographic activity, Balmer starred in two movies by Chabrol, *Madame Bovary* in 1991 (in which he played Charles Bovary) and *Rien ne va plus /The Swindle* in 1997 (as Monsieur K). He was also cast in Pierre Schoendoerffer's *Diên Biên Phu* (1992), Robert Enrico's *Vent d'est* (1993), Jacques Bral's *Mauvais garçon* (1993), Edouard Molinaro's *Beaumarchais l'insolent /Beaumarchais the Scoundrel* (1996), and *Le Temps retrouvé /Time Regained* by Raúl Ruiz (1999). For television, he starred in Philippe Lefebvre's *Antoine Rives, juge du terrorisme* (1993), Mathias Ledoux's *Le Misanthrope* (1994), Serge Moati's *Parfum de famille* (1997), and in the series *Boulevard du Palais* (1999-2014).

In 2001, Balmer was nominated again for the Molière du comédien, this time for his role in Alessandro Baricco's *Novecento*, directed by Frank Cassenti. He also performed in Jean-Marie Duprez's 2007-2008 *Débats 1974-1981*, based on the televised debates between presidential contenders Valéry Giscard d'Estaing and François Mitterrand, in *Le Talisman Balzac-Beethoven* (directed by Françoise Petit in 2007), in Daniel Colas's *Henri IV, le bien aimé* (directed by the author himself in 2010 and 2012), and in *Voyage au bout de la nuit* in 2012-13 (based on Louis-Ferdinand Céline's novel and directed, once again, by his wife, Françoise Petit). Balmer's performance in *Henri IV, le bien aimé,* earned him yet another nomination for the Molière du comédien in 2011. During the 2000s, Balmer starred in

Patricia Mazuy's *Saint-Cyr /The King's Daughters* (2000), Jean-Paul Salomé's *Belphégor – le fantôme du Louvre /Belphegor, Phantom of the Louvre* (2001), Claude Chabrol's *L'Ivresse du pouvoir /The Comedy of Power* (2006), Jacques Bral's *Un printemps à Paris /A Winter in Paris* (2006), and James Huth's *Lucky Luke* (2009). More recently, he starred in *Equinoxe* by Laurent Carcélès (2011) and *Dans la maison /In the House* by François Ozon (2012). He also made appearances in several television productions, such as Patrick Chesnais's *Bien agités !* (2004), starred as Sacha Guitry in Fabrice Cazeneuve's *L'Affaire Sacha Guitry* (2007), as Malesherbes in Pierre Aknine's *Chateaubriand* (2010), and as Georges Pompidou in Aknine's *Mort d'un président /Death of a President* (2011).

Although a relatively well-known actor, Jean-François Balmer has not earned any major distinctions for his performances (except for the nominations mentioned earlier). However, he did receive the French Legion of Honour in 2004 and was admitted to the Order of Arts and Letters with the grade of Commander in 2011.

Cristian BRATU
Baylor University, Texas

Brigitte BARDOT (1934–)

*The
Body
Artist*

BORN IN 1934 to a bourgeois family, Brigitte BARDOT studied ballet at the Conservatoire from an early age, and took René Simon's acting classes. She was only fifteen when she first appeared on the cover of *Elle* : the cover photograph identified only by the initials 'B.B.' From then on, the image of the pouting blonde belle caused anything but indifference. It was there to stay. Much to her parents' dismay, celebrity coincided with the scandal of her eroticised appearance on screen as Juliette, the 'sex kitten' in Roger Vadim's *Et Dieu...créa la femme /And God Created Woman* (1956).

She married Vadim even before her coming of age, and he created roles that suited her emancipation, constructing an emblem for the young generation's rejection of moral standards. For all its popular appeal, however, the character evolved. Only a few years later, she cast a subversive shadow on plaited Babette, exposing the social mask of candour and finding purity in its rejection in *Babette s'en va-t-en guerre /Babette Goes to War* (Christian-Jaque, 1959). She was then an unwonted epitome of the modern woman, and again controversial, in Henri-Georges Clouzot's *La Vérité / The Truth* (1960). Louis Malle followed her deification and struggle with the

pernicious side of 'bardolâtrie' in *Vie privée /A Very Private Affair* (1962). She was Jean-Luc Godard's notorious muse in *Le Mépris /Contempt* (1963), and even the titular Adorable Idiot in Edouard Molinaro's comedy *Une ravissante idiote* (1964).

Though she came close to the products of the Hollywood star machine, the French Marilyn tore apart the myth of the French *demoiselle*, thus reinventing 'a resolutely modern version of the eternal female' [1] rather than 'mythologizing the American dream' as Monroe did.[2] In her best films as in real life, she upset the canons of femininity and seduction and was a mainspring in what Simone de Beauvoir dubbed the 'Lolita syndrome'.[3] Bardot created her own myth and fascinated generations as an aesthetic object and intellectual puzzle.

At the core of everything was B.B.'s body, with its sublime inertia, as it lingered on screen always ready to be dissected in distinct frames, such as for example, Camille's feet as she lay on the bed in the opening scene of *Contempt*, slowly whispering to her husband: 'do you like my feet?' [« tu aimes mes pieds ? »]. The modulations in her voice were probably her most expressive feature, as she sang, cried, shouted, and purred. She often claimed that she did not act, and that the characters she played were 'exactly herself.' Indeed, her facial expression(s) and acting in general remained limited, and hardly suited to drama. With the exception of her world famous trance dancing at the end of *And God Created Woman*, where an upset body mimes Juliette's downfall from disturbance to dissoluteness, Bardot's acting suggested more than it actually showed. Her bare feet and wild hairstyles could repeatedly be taken as a metonymy of the character's errings and floating spirits.

Yet ultimately, Brigitte Bardot best embodied characters that were deceptively passive, and hence suited the improvisational aesthetic of New Wave cinema in an original way. She seemed to handle unscripted roles much better than constrained ones – whether they were of a comic (*Adorable Idiot*) or more tragic (*Viva Maria !*, Louise Malle, 1965) nature. When directing one of her best performances in *Contempt*, Godard even let improvisation take over at key stages of his movie, so that Bardot was unwittingly leading the plot: 'Camille only acts once or twice in the movie. And that's what triggers the three or four major twists in the movie – it's also one of its mainsprings' [« Camille n'agit que deux ou trois fois dans le film. Et c'est ce qui provoque les trois ou quatre rebondissements véritables du film, en même temps que ce qui constitue le principal élément moteur »].[4] Or was she in fact fully aware of her power? The question remains, echoing the ambivalent mixture of wantonness and even 'aggressive eroticism'[5] in a giveaway body, as if encapsulated in the initials B.B.

Caroline ROSSI
Université Stendhal – Grenoble 3

1. Vanessa R. Schwartz, *It's so French!: Hollywood, Paris, and the Making of Cosmopolitan Film Culture* (University of Chicago Press, 2007), 139.

2. Norman Mailer, *Marilyn* (Grosset and Dunlap, 1973),

3. Simone de Beauvoir, *Brigitte Bardot and the Lolita Syndrome* (Arno Press, 1976).

4. 'Le Mépris', *Ciné Club de Caen*, accessed August 26, 2013, http://www.cineclubdecaen. com/realisat/godard/mepris.htm.

5. Simone de Beauvoir, *The Second Sex*, trans. Constance Borde and Sheila Malovany-Chevallier (Vintage, 2011), 554.

Jean-Louis BARRAULT (1910–1994)

*Child
of
Paradise
on
Earth*

AT ONCE an actor, a stage director and a company manager, Jean-Louis BARRAULT is known for his profound renewal of French theatrical life, although the general public remembers him most for the few appearances he made on screen, especially as the mime Baptiste Debureau in Marcel Carné's *Les Enfants du paradis /Children of Paradise* (1945).

Jean-Louis Barrault was trained as an actor and stage director by Charles Dullin, who introduced him to the avant-garde (especially to French writer Antonin Artaud) and at the same time passed on to him his ambitions for a popular theatre. At Dullin's acting school, he met Etienne Ducroux, who taught him mime, a skill he later used in several plays and on screen. As a *pensionnaire* at the Comédie-Française between 1940 and 1946, Jean-Louis Barrault obtained his first successes as a director, especially with Claudel's *Le Soulier de satin /The Satin Slipper* in a 'reduced' five-hour version,[1] which marked the beginning of his long association with the poet.

Leaving the Comédie-Française in 1946 to gain more artistic freedom, Jean-Louis Barrault and his wife, the famous actress Madeleine Renaud, immediately created their own company, the 'Compagnie Renaud-Barrault', and settled at the Théâtre Marigny in Paris. Establishing a principle of alternation, Barrault was just as famous for his original readings of classical plays as he was for his introduction of new avant-garde plays. He often acted in his own productions, and is remembered for his performances as well as for his stagings.

In the classical repertoire, he was greatly acclaimed for his Hamlet, which he played regularly under his own direction from 1946 to 1965. He performed a particularly agile, ethereal Scapin in Molière's *Les Fourberies de Scapin*, directed by Louis Jouvet at the Théâtre du Vieux Colombier in 1948. He was also asked to stage several operas, especially Gounod's *Faust* at the Metropolitan Opera and at la Scala in 1965.

At the same time, he brought to the stage a great number of new plays: the success of Claudel's *Le Soulier de satin* in 1943 initiated a long association with the author, which continued with *Partage de Midi /The Break of Noon* in 1948, *L'Échange /The Exchange* in 1951, *Tête d'or* in 1959, and *Sous le vent des Îles Baléares* in 1972. Other authors entrusted him with the first productions of their plays, such as Jean Anouilh with *La Répétition /The Rehearsal* (1950), Eugène Ionesco with *Rhinocéros* (1960), Marguerite Duras with *Des journées entières dans les arbres* (1965), and Jean Genet with *Les Paravents /The Screens* (1966). While based in successive Parisian theatres, the company did several tours around the world in the 1950s and 1960s and were triumphantly hailed in Europe, North and South America.

Although Jean-Louis Barrault's parallel presence on screen was rarer and more discrete, it was marked by a selection of memorable films among which Marcel Carné's *Drôle de drame /Bizarre, Bizarre* (1937) introduced him to the general public in the role of a highly romantic butcher killer. He often played historical characters with whom he had some physical resemblance, such as Napoleon in *Les Perles de la couronne /Pearls of the Crown* (Christian-Jaque, 1937), composer Hector Berlioz in *La Symphonie fantastique /The Fantastic Symphony* (Christian-Jaque, 1942), King Louis XI in *Le Miracle des loups /Blood on his Sword* (André Hunebelle, 1961), and writer Restif de la Bretonne in *La Nuit de Varennes /That Night in Varennes* (Ettore Scola, 1982). But the ultimate masterpiece that made him a star is unquestionably Marcel Carné's *Les Enfants du paradis* (1945), where he was able to display his talents for mime. Jean-Louis Barrault had been fascinated by 19th century mime Baptiste Deburau for a long time, and he is the one who gave Prévert and Carné the original idea for the film. A year later, he took up some of the mime sequences of the film at the Théâtre Marigny in a pantomime show called *Baptiste*, which introduced the young mime Marcel Marceau as Arlequin.

Céline CANDIARD
Université Lumière Lyon 2

1. The unabridged version, approximately twelve hours long, was performed for the first time in the Théâtre d'Orsay in 1980.

Harry BAUR (1880–1943)

A
Neglected
Giant

THROUGHOUT THE 1930s, Harry
Baur was a force to be reckoned
with among French actors, often listed
with Raimu as the leading figure of
his generation. Baur, as his name
suggests, was of Alsatian extraction,
though born in Paris, and a more
sombre, less ebullient performer –
despite his mountainous bulk – than
the unmistakable Provençal Raimu.
He has been compared to Charles
Laughton and Emil Jannings for the
intensity of his performances, floridly
characterised in Jean-Loup Passek's
Dictionnaire du cinéma français as
follows: « Il joue en effet de toute
son âme, mais aussi de tous ses tics,
que les gros plans mettent par trop
en évidence: ses rides se creusent,
ses joues tremblent; et puis, sa voix
se fait insinuante, sifflante, hurlante
et tonitruante pour se briser dans
des sanglots selon des besoins de
l'action » [1] ['He acts, indeed, with
all of his soul, but also with all of
his features, which are emphasized
by closeups: his wrinkles deepen, his
cheeks tremble, and then, his voice is
insinuating, whistling, screaming and
booming in order for him to burst
into sobs as called for by the film's
plot'].

So heavy-duty a style, probably
carried over from a highly successful
stage career in the 1920s, suggests
one reason why Baur is nowadays
largely forgotten, for all the
ambiguous masculinity suggested
in his performances and in the
above quotation. The comparison
with Charles Laughton may seem
particularly apposite here, though
Laughton's stock is higher thanks in
part to his status as tragic gay icon,
in part to his only film as director,
the masterly *The Night of the Hunter*
(1955). Another factor is that Baur
never worked for any of the directors,
such as Jean Renoir or Marcel Carné,
whose 1930s films are most widely
available. It was for Julien Duvivier
that he produced much of his best-
known screen work, notably in *Poil
de carotte /The Red Head* (1932); *La
Tête d'un homme /A Man's Neck* (1933),
an adaptation of Georges Simenon
where Baur is one of the great cinema
Maigrets, and *Un carnet de bal /
Dance Program* (1937), as a suitor of
Christine (Marie Bell) turned priest
out of frustrated love. Yet Renoir
praised his work in an interview for
Le Travailleur du film in 1936 – the
year in which Baur was the most
successful actor at the French box
office – but also that of Renoir's *Le
Crime de Monsieur Lange /The Crime
of Monsieur Lange*, in which Florelle
has her best-known role and which
alludes to a (fictional) detective-story
magazine entitled *Javert*. This may of
course be only a coincidence, but it is
at least an appealing one.

Other major roles played by
Baur include the titular character of
Duvivier's Jewish drama *David Golder*
(1931), Jean Valjean in Raymond
Bernard's adaptation of *Les Misérables*

(1934), and for André Hugon, the titular role in the Algiers-set *Sarati, le terrible /Sarati the Terrible* (1937). One major reason for Baur's neglect is the manner of his death, one of the only partially elucidated cinematic mysteries of *les années noires*. He had been, to quote his biographer Hervé Le Boterf, 'to all intents and purposes labelled *the Jew of French cinema*,' [2] because of his roles for Duvivier in *David Golder* and Maurice Tourneur in *Volpone* (1941), in the latter of which he even sported a false nose. Le Boterf may be suspected of *parti pris* here since he was a right-wing Breton nationalist active in Nantes under the Occupation and was subsequently active in associations championing the two most prominent collaborationist French authors, Robert Brasillach and Louis-Ferdinand Céline. It seems clear that under the Occupation, Baur bent over backwards to prove himself a Gentile, declaring himself 'as much of an old Aryan as anybody,' [3] obtaining a certificate of Aryanness from the Propaganda Staffel – the German censorship authority – and attending numerous collaborationist receptions. Raymond Aron was to claim that Baur was covertly involved with the Resistance, but no concrete evidence for this appears to have been produced. He starred in Christian-Jaque's *L'Assassinat du Père Noël /Who Killed Santa Claus?* (1941), the first French film to be financed by the German-funded production company Continental, set up by Goebbels in September 1940 as a means of asserting control over the potentially subversive French industry. In 1942, Baur set off for Berlin amid much publicity to star in Hans Bertram's

Symphonie eines Lebens /Symphonie d'une vie (1943), in a further attempt at self-ingratiation that was to prove quite literally fatal. On 20 May 1942, after he had returned to Paris, he and his wife, the actress Rika Radifé, were arrested by the Gestapo. She was freed after 115 days, but Baur was to remain a prisoner until 19 September, when he was released in a dreadful state, having lost 77 pounds and allegedly been kept throughout his captivity with no change of clothing. He died in his Paris home some six months later, just short of his sixty-third birthday, and there seems to be no record of the precise circumstances of his imprisonment, though it appears all but certain that he was tortured.

Keith READER
University of London Institute in Paris

1. Jean-Loup Passek, *Dictionnaire du cinéma français* (Paris: Larousse, 1987), 31.
2. Hervé Le Boterf, *Harry Baur* (Paris: Pygmalion/Gérard Watelet, 1995), 13.
3. Olivier Barrot and Raymond Chirat, *Noir et blanc: 250 acteurs du cinema français* (Paris: Flammarion, 2000), 60.

Editor's note: Material (regarding *Les Misérables*) is excerpted from Keith Reader 'Raymond Bernard's *Les Misérables* (1934)' in *Studies in French Cinema: UK Perspectives, 1985–2000*, ed. Will Higbee and Sarah Leahy (Bristol: Intellect, 2011), 311–320.

Nathalie BAYE (1948–)

—The Discreet Charm of—

THE DAUGHTER OF PAINTERS, Nathalie BAYE was born in Normandy. Suffering from dyslexia, she did not like school very much. At the age of 14, she joined a dance school to become a ballet dancer and left for the United States at the age of 17 where she trained as a ballerina. The discipline and rigor that this entailed later helped her cinema career. While pursuing her dance class on her return to France, she joined the Cours Simon and was later admitted to the Paris Conservatoire where she obtained a second prize for comedy and drama.

After a few short appearances in films like Robert Wise's *Brève rencontre à Paris /Two People* (1973) and François Truffaut's *La Nuit américaine /Day for Night* (1973), Truffaut offered her a main part in *La Chambre verte /The Green Room* (1978), as Cécilia Mandel, the beautiful auction secretary. It was really this experience with Truffaut that made her discover and love cinema, after a career essentially oriented towards theatre. She realized at this stage in her life that she enjoyed acting more than dancing.

Alongside Miou-Miou, Isabelle Adjani, and Isabelle Huppert, Baye epitomizes the French cinema of the 1980s with her discreet natural beauty and French charm. Indeed, her big break came in the 1980s, with Jean-Luc Godard's *Sauve qui peut (la vie) /Every Man for Himself* (1980) for which she obtained her first César for best supporting actress, and then achieved consecration with Bob Swaim's *La Balance /The Nark* (1982) with a best actress César. Here, she plays Nicole, a prostitute forced to collaborate with the police, alongside Philippe Léotard, with whom Baye would have a liaison until 1981. *Une étrange affaire /Strange Affair* (Pierre Granier-Deferre, 1981) granted her a second César for best supporting actress, followed by Daniel Vigne's successful medieval romance *Le Retour de Martin Guerre /The Return of Martin Guerre* (1982) opposite Gérard Depardieu (where she keeps the spectator breathless as to whether she realizes her husband, who has just returned after years of absence, is an imposter or not). In Robin Davis's psychological drama *J'ai épousé une ombre /I Married a Dead Man* (1983), she is Hélène, a young woman abandoned by her lover for being pregnant. In 1985, she stars in Godard's cerebral comedy *Détective* with Claude Brasseur.

From 1982 to 1986, her relationship with rock singer Johnny Hallyday also made her the favourite of newspapers, which is quite an irony for such an elusive and enigmatic woman, famous for her discretion and humility. Laura Smet, their daughter, is also an actress.

In 1999, Nathalie Baye was voted Best Supporting Actress at Venice for *Une liaison pornographique /An Affair of Love* (Frédéric Fonteyne) and acted in Tonie Marshall's delightful comedy *Vénus beauté (institut) / Venus Beauty Institute*, where she plays a beautician in search of uncommitted love. Baye's energy and desire to act, as well as viewers' desire to see her act are nowhere near subsiding, as she multiplies film experiences with a host of famous directors such as Claude Chabrol (*La Fleur du mal /The Flower of Evil*, 2003) and Steven Spielberg (*Catch Me if You Can*, 2002) as well as younger directors like Xavier Bourgeois.

Not only does she excel in comedies – Diane Kury's *La Baule-les-Pins /C'est la vie*, 1990, Gabriel Aghion's *Absolument fabuleux /Absolutely Fabulous*, 2001, Léa Fazer's *Ensemble, c'est trop /Together Is Too Much*, 2010 – but also in dramatic roles: Fonteyne's *Une liaison pornographique /An Affair of Love*, 1999, Xavier Bourgeois's *Le Petit Lieutenant /The Young Lieutenant*, 2005. In the latter film, she plays Commandant Caroline Vaudieu, who, after losing her child, has to fight her alcoholic demons, a part initially written for a man but for which Nathalie Baye gained a fourth César. She stars in Xavier Dolan's Canadian drama film *Laurence Anyways* (2012) and a hit mini-series called *Les Hommes de l'ombre /The Men in the Shadows* (2012) where she played a female politician.

Nathalie Baye is a multi-talented and eclectic actress who has enjoyed a career spanning more than 80 films. She has worked with some of the most renowned directors of her generation: Bertrand Blier, Claude Chabrol, Jean-Luc Godard, Bertrand Tavernier, and François Truffaut. She is indisputably one of the greatest and most celebrated actresses of French cinema today.

Michaël ABECASSIS
The University of Oxford

Emmanuelle BÉART (1963–)
[Emmanuelle BÉHART-HASSON]

*La
Belle*

FROM THE captivating innocence of *Manon des sources /Manon of the Spring* (Claude Berri, 1986) to the troubling sensuality of *La Belle Noiseuse* (Jacques Rivette, 1991), Emmanuelle BÉART has become a cultural symbol of French cinema, embodying the feminine ideal in a variety of roles. She is probably best known for her portrayal of the young Manon in Berri's adaptation of Pagnol's eponymous novel, the role which launched her career, and one of several she played alongside her former husband Daniel Auteuil. In François Ozon's 2002 comic murder mystery, *8 femmes /8 Women*, she appeared in Ozon's representative selection of French actresses and female types as an assertive, sexually manipulative maid. Although Béart's range extends into comedy, she has tended to be cast in dramatic rather than comic roles. She has played troubled young mothers (*L'Enfer / Hell*, Claude Chabrol, 1994) and prostitutes (*J'embrasse pas /I Don't Kiss*, André Techiné, 1991) equally convincingly.

Emmanuelle Béhart-Hasson was born near St. Tropez to the singer-songwriter Guy Béhart and his wife, an ex-model of Greek descent. Her cinematic debut came in 1972, with a non-speaking child role in René Clément's *La Course de lièvre à travers les champs /And Hope to Die*. She then appeared in Jean Pourtale's science fiction film *Demain les mômes /Tomorrow's Children* (1976). She continued to star in films and television series thereafter. While in her 20s, she studied drama with Jean-Laurent Cochet, whose courses attracted many famous French actors (among them Gérard Depardieu, Isabelle Huppert, and Carole Bouquet). In 1983, Béart appeared in David Hamilton's erotic film *Premiers désirs /First Desires*, which was, arguably, the film that really got the actress noticed. Her first nomination for a César Award was in 1985, for the comedy *L'Amour en douce /Love on the Quiet* (dir. Edouard Molinaro). She met Daniel Auteuil on the set, and their collaboration continued with *Manon des sources*, culminating in the dark exploration of a *ménage à trois* in *Un cœur en hiver /A Heart in Winter* (Claude Sautet, 1992). The film, along with Sautet's last work, *Nelly et Monsieur Arnaud /Nelly and Mr Arnaud* (1995), also earned the actress a César nomination. She starred in Jacques Rivette's *La Belle noiseuse* (1991), alongside Jane Birkin and Michel Piccoli. Béart received a Best actress award at the Moscow International Film Festival in 1995 for her role in *Une femme française /A French Woman* and a César for the best supporting role in 1987 for *Manon des sources*.

Emmanuelle Béart made an excursion into Hollywood, appearing in *Mission: Impossible* with Tom Cruise (Brian De Palma, 1996). It has been suggested that this decision was motivated by her contract with Dior. Béart's career as a model and her distinctive screen presence combined to make her a beauty icon, and, like Brigitte Bardot, she has used this status for public activity, becoming a 'face' of UNICEF and protesting fiercely against legislation targeting illegal immigrants in France in 1996.

In addition to her film career, Béart acted in several major theatre productions in the late 80s and 90s. Among these are Jacques Weber's *Le Misanthrope* (1989), *On ne badine pas avec l'amour* (Jean-Pierre Vincent, 1993), *Playing with Fire* (Luc Bondy, 1995), and more recently, *Les Justes* (Stanislas Nordey, 2012).

The actress divorced Daniel Auteuil in 1998. She has two children and lives in Paris.

Arina Patrikova
The University of Oxford

Leïla Bekhti (1984–)

High-powered Actress, Style Icon, and Modern Joan of Arc

Beauty queen, celebrity, television and cinema actress Leïla Bekhti was born 1984 in Issy-les-Moulineaux, a few metro stops away from the centre of Paris. Bekhti, who as a child dreamed of becoming either a teacher or a cashier, participated in theatre productions in her lycée as a teenager. In an interview with French news magazine *L'Express*, France's shooting star who has been featured in well over twenty features and television productions, has admitted to feeling 'a bit guilty about having a job she enjoys as much as she does' [« Je me sens peut-être un peu coupable de faire un métier qui m'amuse autant »]. [1] In 2005, Bekhti landed the part of a young dancer, Yasmine, in Kim Chapiron's *Sheitan* (2006) along such well-known actors as Vincent Cassel, Olivier Barthélémy, and Monica Bellucci, a film that jump-started her career. That same year, she wrapped up several television productions, including Zakia and Ahmed Bouchaâla's *Pour l'amour de Dieu*, a teenage love story gone awry, and Alain Tasma's Harkis. Internationally, she was noticed in *Paris, je t'aime* (2006), for her role in Gurinder Chadha's segment of the film, *Quais de Seine*, as a hijab-clad Muslim teenager with whom a young Parisian (Cyril Descours) becomes smitten.

Bekhti then turned to TV, starring in Claude Scasso's series *Les Tricheurs*. In 2006, she held a supporting role in Roschdy Zem's pan-European production *Mauvaise foi /Bad Faith*, and she also performed in Pierre Aknine's TV production *Ali Baba et les quarante voleurs* (2007). In 2008, she played the role of Sarah in Rachid Hami's *Choisir d'aimer*, a love story that shuttles back and forth between Algiers and La Rochelle. That same year she starred in *Des poupées et des anges /Dolls and Angels*, a film adaption of Nora Hamdi's debut novel, alongside Sami Naceri, Karina Testa, and Samuel Le Bihan. Shot in the *banlieue*, the feature tackles an explosive cocktail of subjects such as father-daughter relationships, sexuality, violence, tradition, and female emancipation. She also had a small role in the action movie *L'Instinct de mort /Mesrine: Killer Instinct* (Jean-François Richet, 2008) again crossing paths with Vincent Cassel, Cécile de France, and Gérard Depardieu. More recently, she had a small role, Djamila, in Jacques Audiard's *Un prophète /A Prophet* (2009) about France's criminal underworld, a highly acclaimed film that received, among other awards and honours, the nomination for the Oscar for Best Foreign Language film. In 2009, she played the role of Safia in the TV series and the eponymous heroine in the television production *Le Choix de Myriam*.

In France, she finally had her breakthrough with Géraldine Nakache and Hervé Mimran's box office hit *Tout ce qui brille /All That Glitters* (2010), a comedy about two attractive young women from the Parisian suburbs, Lila (Bekhti) and Ely (Nakache), who manage to break into Parisian high society. Bekhti was awarded the prestigious César *du meilleur espoir féminin* for this film. This feature film mirrors Bekhti's own trajectory, given that the actress who is of Algerian descent and grew up in subsidized housing now owns an apartment in the posh Parisian Marais quarter. In 2010, Bekhti crossed paths again with Alain Tasma, starring in his television drama *Fracture* (2010), and she played the role of Alina in the TV miniseries *Longlasting Youth*. Turning to comedy, she starred in Anne Depitrini's comedy *Il reste du jambon ?*, a love story about a mixed race couple. In 2011, fashion-savvy Bekhti became the new ambassadress for the cosmetics company L'Oréal Paris at the Cannes Festival, following in the footsteps of celebrities such as Gwen Stefani, Jennifer Lopez, and former model Inès de la Fressange. A fashion aficionado, she has modelled for Chanel in a photo shoot with the likes of Yoko Ono, Tahar Rahim, and Sandro Kropp. The fashion shoot, organized by fashion mogul Karl Lagerfeld, was published in *La Petite Veste noire*. In 2011, she was half of an unlikely couple with Fred Testot in Jean-Luc Perreard's stilted romantic comedy *Itinéraire bis*, and she was seen in Kyan Khojandi's TV series *Bref* (2012). More recently,

Bekhti starred alongside Guillaume Canet in Cédric Kahn's feature *Une vie meilleure /A Better Life* (2011), a love story about a couple – debt-ridden chef Yann and French Lebanese waitress Nadia – who start a restaurant on a lakeside property outside of Paris to build a better life for themselves but get mired in debt. The film has received mixed reviews.

In 2011, Bekhti starred in Radu Mihaileanu's *La Source des femmes / The Source*, about a wife's revolt in an isolated Moroccan mountain village. Tired of having to fetch water from a faraway source Leïla (Bekhti) persuades other women to go on a sex strike, until the men organize for the water to be piped into the village. The Romanian-born director said he wrote the part of Leïla for Bekhti: 'I told her, you are a contemporary Joan of Arc; you set off a revolutionary movement, about love and women's place in the world.'[2] Bekhti was nominated best actress for her role in the film at the 2012 César awards. However, she was also nominated for one of the 'Gérard du cinéma' awards for that year's worst film performances – akin to the Razzie awards in the US – specifically, the 'Girard di film halal' for her role in *La Source des femmes*. She starred in the musical comedy *Toi, moi, les autres /Leila* (dir. Audrey Estrougo, 2010) alongside Benjamin Siksou and Cécile Cassel, and she played a police officer in Pierre Jolivet's 2012 action thriller *Mains armées /Armed Hands*, alongside Roschdy Zem (as her estranged father) and Marc Lavoine. In 2012, she played the role of Samia in Hervé Mimran and Géraldine Nakache's feature *Nous York*. She plans to write a film script in the near future. Bekhti is married to French actor Tahar Rahim, whom she met on the shooting of Jacques Audiard's *Un prophète /A Prophet* (2009).

Christa JONES
Utah State University, Logan

1. Géraldine Catalano, 'Leïla Bekhti: "je me sens coupable de faire un métier qui m'amuse autant," ' *L'Express*, June 17, 2011, accessed August 26, 2013, http://www.lexpress.fr/styles/vip/leila-bekhti-je-me-sens-coupable-de-faire-un-metier-qui-m-amuse-autant_1003320.html.

2. Joan Dupont, 'With *The Source*, Radu Mihaileanu Looks at the Battle of the Sexes,' *New York Times*, May 16, 2011, accessed August 26, 2013, http://www.nytimes.com/2011/05/17/arts/17iht-dupont17.html?_r=0.

Jean-Paul BELMONDO (1933–)

« Bébel »,
Born
to Act

JEAN-PAUL BELMONDO, son of the famous sculptor Paul Belmondo, was born in 1933 in Neuilly-Sur-Seine. Early on he took up boxing lessons, and his lack of discipline made his first steps into a theatrical career chaotic. He became famous after taking the lead role in the film *À bout de souffle /Breathless* (1960), shot by the still unknown director Jean-Luc Godard, which immediately became a cult film of the Nouvelle Vague. He embodied a new type of hero who was dynamic, unruly, athletic, and exuberant. He went on to make many films in France and Italy, including, among others, *Cartouche /Swords of Blood* (Philippe de Broca, 1962) and *Léon Morin, prêtre /Léon Morin, Priest* (Jean-Pierre Melville, 1961). He became a star, inviting comparisons with Humphrey Bogart and James Dean. He seemed to be regarded as the heir of Jean Gabin after their unforgettable duet in *Un singe en hiver /A Monkey in Winter* (Henri Verneuil, 1962) as dreamy and nostalgic drunkards. Despite his part in Godard's *Pierrot le fou* (1965) and Alain Resnais's *Stavisky...* (1974), he preferred acting the same kinds of roles: always characters who are

men of action, either charming louts or dispensers of justice. This type of acting became his trademark. He was later given more dramatic parts in *Itinéraire d'un enfant gâté / Itinerary of a Spoiled Child* (1988) and *Les Misérables* (1995) by Claude Lelouch, and in *L'Inconnu dans la maison /Stranger in the House* (Georges Lautner, 1992). He also acted on stage in *Kean* (1987) and in *Cyrano de Bergerac* in 1990.

As supple and agile as a big cat, Jean-Paul Belmondo is characterized by his formidable energy. He is a true chameleon, and he embodies vitality – either larger-than-life or casual in his youth, or hurt and yet ready to be reborn in his later years. As a young man, Belmondo performed his own film stunts with the help of Gil Delamare and Rémy Julienne. A great show-off, he often acts with great exaggeration that hides a deep disillusionment. In Godard's movies his restless movement is the outward sign of inner existential despair.

Belmondo's great ability can lead one to assume that he always acts naturally. This insolent fellow has a strange beauty: with his funny boxer face and his athletic figure, he is a hyperactive clown, even when he is desperate. He is often typecast as the smiling, boisterous and self-confident hero. The titles of his movies are significant in this respect: *Flic ou Voyou /Cop or Hood* (Georges Lautner, 1979), *L'As des as /Ace of Aces* (Gérard Oury, 1982), among others. In his comedies he is cunning, reckless, and impulsive. He is the French troublemaker, at ease with extreme situations in Philippe de Broca's *L'Homme de Rio /That Man from Rio* (1964) and *Les Tribulations d'un Chinois en Chine /Up to His Ears* (1965). He is a character, a type, and the film relies upon him as in *Le Guignolo* (Georges Lautner, 1980), *Le Magnifique /The Man from Acapulco* (De Broca, 1973), and *L'Incorrigible /The Incorrigible* (De Broca, 1975). The general public nicknamed him « Bébel ». He loves to mimic fools. His extravagance is audacious in itself: he has a genius for playacting; he is always on the verge of being excessive in his exclamations, his wide gestures, his insisting hushing sounds, and his dangerous stunts. As a parody, in everyday life, one refers to his dashing entrances with the cry « toc toc badaboum ! » ['knock knock, crash bang wallop!'] – and yet, in his movies, the sense of morality always remains intact. Women love his charming daredevil smile, and are almost unwillingly attracted to him. Men admire him as an irreverent lout who embodies a taste for danger and the masculine ideal of virility, as well as both casualness and class.

He has a greater sense of fancy than Alain Delon, who was supposed to be his rival. He was acclaimed as a popular actor and embodied the French spirit, with his exaggerations, his funny machismo and good-natured rudeness. Upon his return to the theatre he decided to play Cyrano.

As an older actor he was offered more serious parts. In *Itinéraire d'un enfant gâté*, his face is suddenly screwed up with pain. After a brain injury, he recently came back in *Un homme et son chien /A Man and His Dog* (Francis Huster, 2008): the now fragile Bébel found a powerful tragic density in the part of a forsaken man looking for his dog. Supporting roles of various ages such as his great fan, Jean Dujardin, and the young Hafsia Herzi made this a tribute to his talent. His acting in *Les Acteurs /Actors* by Bertrand Blier (2000) is very symbolic of his whole career. He plays his own character and is shot dead. He still jumps while he falls and confesses while laughing: 'You have always mocked me and thought I was a jester but I lived my whole life through without bothering anyone with my own troubles!'

Violaine HEYRAUD
Université Sorbonne nouvelle – Paris 3

François BERLÉAND (1952–)

*The
Invisible
Man's
Son
Exposed*

FRANÇOIS BERLÉAND likes to recall in interviews that he came to acting serendipititiously when a business school friend signed him up for a theatre class. Yet his childhood history, which he recounts in a book he published with the help of Nadine Trintignant, seems to indicate that he was a born actor. In his 2006 book *Le Fils de l'homme invisible*, the French actor explains how he took a drunken remark from his father literally, thus convincing himself that he was indeed the son of the TV character the Invisible Man (which explained why nobody seemed to notice him on buses or on the street). This deep-seeded belief eventually gave way to an equally erroneous conviction that he had Down's Syndrome and that everybody around him had been conspiring to convince him otherwise (going so far as to alter mirrors so they would distort his reflection to make it appear 'normal'). Used to living as if he were someone else, Berléand put his talent to good use, embarking upon an incredibly prolific acting career (at the age of 60 he has appeared in well over 150 films).

Between 1978 and 1994, Berléand remained almost invisible in that his screen appearances were not only few and far between (no more than three feature films per year) but also for the most part extremely short. (It takes a careful viewer to notice him in Michel Blanc's popular 1984 comedy *Marche à l'ombre*.) Nevertheless, from small part to small part, Berléand was exposed to a wide range of the French film production of his time, appearing in so called auteur films by directors such as Alain Cavalier (*Martin et Léa*, 1979; *Un étrange voyage*, 1981); Louis Malle (*Au revoir les enfants*, 1987; *Milou en mai /May Fools*, 1990) or Bruno Nuytten (*Camille Claudel*, 1988), and in more 'popular' films like Bob Swaim's crime hit *La Balance /The Nark* (1982) or Jean-Marie Poiré's comedy *Les Hommes préfèrent les grosses /Men Prefer Fat Girls* (1981). Meanwhile, his work in theatre was confined to state-sponsored productions whose appeal to audiences was as limited as the Splendid's (the troupe composed of Michel Blanc, Christian Clavier, Gérard Jugnot, and Thierry Lhermitte, among others) was massive.

Early on, Berléand's acting mentor had warned him that if he were ever to become successful, he would have to wait until the age of forty. And indeed, the actor's exposure increased in the 1990s as he was offered more regular and significant parts in films by well-respected directors such as Bertrand Tavernier (*L'Appât / Fresh Bait*, 1995; *Capitaine Conan*, 1996), Nadine Trintignant (*Fugueuses /Runaways*, 1995), Jacques Audiard (*Un héros très discret /A Self-Made Hero*, 1996), Benoît Jacquot (*Le Septième Ciel /Seventh Heaven*, 1997, *L'École de la chair /The School of Flesh*, 1998), Nicole Garcia (*Place Vendôme*, 1998), and Claude Lelouch (*Une pour toutes /One*

4 All, 1999). But it is for Pierre Jolivet that Berléand acted the most often, totaling nine feature films, including his two breakthrough roles: Barrère, the worn-out cop in *Fred* (1997) and Maxime Nassief, the sneaky insurance broker in *Ma petite enterprise /My Little Business*, a role that earned him a César as best actor in a supporting role (1999). The colossal success of the 2004 *Les Choristes /The Chorus* (dir. Christophe Barratier) – in which he plays the part of a boarding school principal with cruel disciplinary tactics – further advanced Berléand's career, and main parts started to trickle in, as was the case in Claude Chabrol's *L'Ivresse du pouvoir /The Comedy of Power* (2006) and *La Fille coupée en deux /The Girl Cut in Two* (2007).

Yet, for all the respect his talent elicits (many journalists have compared him to Michel Serrault), François Berléand certainly is not counted among those French stars whose names guarantee a film a good return on investment. The leading roles he takes on are, significantly, offered to him by first-time directors. And regardless of the quality of his performances (as an authoritarian, sleazy and impotent TV producer in Guillaume Canet's *Mon idole / Whatever You Say* (2002); as a suicidal crook in Stéphan Guérin-Tillié's *Edy* (2005); or as an emotionally detached father in Pascal Laëthier's *La Différence, c'est que c'est pas pareil*, 2009), those films' disastrous box office results consistently remind producers that Berléand's acting talent does not quite make up for a John Doe physique better suited for the supporting roles in which he has been excelling for decades.

Still, after many years spent in relative anonymity, Berléand has now become a highly visible public figure, regularly appearing on French talk shows to promote his films. His forthrightness (he openly discusses his earnings) and sense of humor, combined with his willingness to give out his personal cell phone number to journalists have indeed earned him the admiration of the press along with the so-called PAF (an acronym for *paysage audiovisuel français*, i.e. the French media). Most recently, he made public his feud with talk show host Laurent Ruquier, and, more famously, he criticized Eva Joly, the Norwegian-born judge turned presidential candidate, for her foreign accent on a national radio program in 2011. These occasional, scandalous remarks during interviews contribute to a fame that exceeds Berléand's box office worth, like so many deforming mirrors meant to convince him that he is, indeed, a big star.

François Massonnat
Villanova University, Pennsylvania

Sarah BERNHARDT (1844–1923)
[Henriette-Rosine BERNARD]

The
First
Modern
Celebrity

BOTH ON and off the stage, French actress and film star Sarah BERNHARDT could be considered a queen of theatrics, grand gestures, and dramatic excess. Possessing what Henry James described as the '*génie de la réclame*' ('the advertising genius'), she was the first modern celebrity; a woman who managed her own career, and through touring and PR, achieved fame throughout the world.[1] Her thinness was her defining feature and saw her ridiculed and caricaturized for the best part of her career. Death scenes were her speciality, as noted by the critic Jules Lemaître who commented 'she becomes herself only when she's killing or she dies.' [2]

Bernhardt is thought to have been born in Paris on 22 October 1844 although the loss of official records from the time means that one cannot be sure. The identity of her father is unknown, and similarly, the details surrounding the father of Bernhardt's own son Maurice are ambiguous. The actress offered several versions of her life story to friends, family, and the general public, the details of which were riddled with inconsistencies and contradictions. With the actress's tendency to exaggerate not limited to the stage, one could never be certain that Bernhardt was telling the truth.

It is clear, however, that the actress had a difficult childhood. She lacked the affection of her mother Youle, a high-class courtesan of Dutch-German Jewish background who left her in the care of a nurse in Brittany for the early years of her life. When the young Bernhardt's lack of education became an issue, she was shipped to a convent in Versailles and raised by nuns, this being an environment in which she would learn the manners needed to assume an upper-class Parisian life. It was during this time that Bernhardt adopted her life long motto *Quand même*, meaning 'nevertheless,' 'anyway,' or 'so what,' a mantra that captured her determination to triumph over the adverse conditions of her life. As a teenager Bernhardt wanted to become a nun herself, but her mother's frequent companion, The Duke of Morny (Napoleon III's illegitimate half brother) suggested instead that she attend the French Conservatoire de Musique et Déclamation and become an actress. It was around this time that Bernhardt first visited the theatre, an event she describes as changing her life: 'When the curtain slowly rose I thought I should have fainted. It was as though the curtain of my future life was being raised.' [3] Fortunately for Bernhardt, the Duke was able to use his position to have her admitted to the Conservatoire, and later, to find a position at the Comédie Française, France's most prestigious theatre company.

Although dedicated and enthusiastic, Bernhardt made an underwhelming stage debut in August 1862 playing the title role of Racine's *Iphigénie*. While an 1863 altercation with the Comédie Française's then most celebrated actress (Bernhardt slapped this woman who supposedly insulted her sister) brought her instant notoriety, it also meant the termination of her contract. She was offered a place at the boulevard theatre Le Gymnase soon afterwards, but it was at the Théâtre de l'Odéon that Bernhardt made her mark and established herself as an actress of note. Here, she played her most famous role, that of the male Zanetto in *Le Passant /The Passerby*, over 140 times. Following the interruption of the Franco-Prussian war, during which the actress cared for wounded soldiers, Bernhardt returned, triumphant, to the Comédie Française in 1872, cementing her star status with roles such as Joan of Arc and Camille. Tours throughout Europe in the 1870s meant that she was in demand outside of her home country and that word of her talent travelled to America.

In 1880, now incredibly famous in France, Bernhardt boldly quit the Comédie Française and established her own travelling theatre company, touring as far as Australia, as well as making several trips to America, Canada, and distant parts of Europe. The actress's international celebrity status grew not just as a result of her relentless touring and talent on stage, but due to her skills in regards to the art of generating publicity.

Ever the provocatrice, Bernhardt kept a zoo in her house, travelled with a coffin in which she was said to sleep, and wore a hat adorned with a dead bat. The actress was also said to have been involved with many of her leading men, but was unable to find long lasting romantic contentment. In a letter written to Jean Mounet-Sully in 1874 she stated, 'you must realise that I am not made for happiness. It is not my fault that I am constantly in search of new sensations, new emotions... My heart desires more excitement than anyone can give it...' [4] Whilst perhaps being a negative in terms of her emotional life, this constant search for excitement and new sensations undoubtedly drove Bernhardt to become such a prolific actress and manager of her own affairs.

In 1899, the actress established the Théâtre Sarah-Bernhardt in Paris, a venue in which she reprised the most successful roles of her career, and played the role of Hamlet in a controversial but successful 4-hour prose version of the play. It was at this point that the then 56-year-old Bernhardt become one of the first actresses to appear on film; she played the role of the youthful male Hamlet, with considerable success in the short film *Le Duel d'Hamlet* (Clément Maurice, 1900). Other films of note include *La Dame aux camélias /Camille* (André Calmettes, Louis Mercanton, and Henri Pouctal, 1912) and *Les Amours de la reine Élisabeth /Queen Elizabeth* (Henri Desfontaines and Louis Mercanton, 1912), the latter being Bernhardt's most widely distributed film and that which made her an international film star at the age of sixty-eight. *Mères françaises / Mothers of France* (René Hervil and Louis Mercanton, 1917) in which Bernhardt plays the role of a mother searching for her wounded son made a strong anti-war statement that resonated with French audiences in particular. *Daniel* (1921) saw the actress portray a morphine addict who suffers through a 5-minute death scene, from the Louis Verneuil play of the same name. By this point Bernhardt's left leg had been amputated above the knee, the result of an injury sustained whilst touring in South America in 1905; however, this did not stop her from performing, or from entertaining troops at the front during World War I. The actress was carried on a small chair, and assumed roles where she could sit or wear a prosthetic limb. Although popular, Bernhardt's film work did little to help her career as an actress. One could consider her grand gestures and florid acting style as better suited to the stage than to the newer cinematic medium.

Bernhardt worked until the very end of her life, dying in her home at the age of 78 in 1923. At this time she had been in the process of filming *La Voyante /The Clairvoyant* (Leon Abrams and Louis Mercanton, 1924), the production of which was halted and then later completed with the use of a stand-in. Upon learning that crowds had gathered outside her house, the dying star considered her large audience for the last time and commented, 'I'll keep them dangling. They've tortured me all my life, now I'll torture them.' [5] In total,

the actress appeared in nine fictional films, as well as two documentary-style biographical works. Her stage credits are numerous. Bernhardt is remembered as 'the divine Sarah,' and is arguably the most famous actress of the 19th century: an artist, mythmaker, and master of self-promotion.

Kath Dooley
Flinders University of South Australia

1. James quoted in Robert Gottlieb, *Sarah: The Life of Sarah Bernhardt* (Yale University Press, 2010), 81.
2. Ibid., 191.
3. Sarah Bernhardt, *My Double Life* (Echo Library, 2006), 45.
4. Bernhardt's letter is referenced in Gottlieb, *Sarah: The Life of Sarah Bernhardt*, 97.
5. Bernhardt quoted in ibid., 208.

Jules **BERRY** (1883–1951)
[Marie Louis Jules PAUFICHET]

*The Man
with the
Fluttering
Hands*

LOOK AT Jules BERRY's hands when you next watch *Café de Paris* (Yves Mirande and Georges Lacombe, 1938), *Carrefour/Crossroads* (Curtis Bernhardt, 1938), or *Derrière la façade* (Yves Mirande and Georges Lacombe, 1939). They are forever in motion, gesticulating, emphasising, and dissembling. The hands are an extension of his characters' busyness (less flattering reviews often referred to his 'sliminess'), and, given that Berry's career was predicated upon a stylised and declamatory performance mode, these hands are the most telling external sign of his unbridled confidence and his predatory thought-processes. Berry himself (perhaps half-jokingly) once admitted that moving his hands so exuberantly was the only way he could remember his lines, so bad was his memory. Berry was born Jules Paufichet in Poitiers in 1883, and was trained as a stage actor, performing in numerous vaudevilles and light comedies before his move into film in Marcel L'Herbier's *L'Argent* (1928). From this point on, he was remarkably prolific, appearing in nearly a hundred films between 1933 and his death in 1951.

He was the notorious 'gentleman thief' in *Arsène Lupin, Detective* (Henri Diamant-Berger, 1937) and billionaire industrialist in *Si jeunesse savait* (André Cerf, 1948), excelling in films that required a high-society sophisticate or a dubious tuxedo-clad scoundrel. Such theatrical flamboyance and dandyish gestures were frequently incorporated into roles that embodied glib elegance, linguistic dexterity, and no small degree of manipulative condescension. Paternal authority was his trademark register (often couched in highly refined use of the French subjunctive form), and he often figured as the amalgam of weak 'father' and malicious individual whose motives remained inexplicable. Berry's slicked-back black hair and waxy pallor often hinted at a malevolence that would be ultimately clinched by Marcel Carné in *Les Visiteurs du soir/The Devil's Envoys* (1942), where he cast Berry as the Devil. In this medieval allegory, made at the height of German involvement in France, Berry's versatile and elastic gestures were read by some critics as an allegorical portrayal of Hitler.

One of Berry's most memorable film performances was as the devious publisher Batala in Renoir's *Le Crime de Monsieur Lange/The Crime of Monsieur Lange* (1936). Combining a silver-tongued slipperiness and a trickster-like unscrupulousness, Berry's Batala fakes his own death, only to return in the dead of night to reclaim the co-operative that has sprung up in his absence. He is killed again, for good, by Lange, but not before he utters one of French cinema's most memorable lines: 'Who would miss you?' asks Lange. After a beat, Berry replies, his hands twisting and flicking, 'Women would...'

In Carné's *Le Jour se lève / Daybreak* (1939), he reaffirms his ghostliness, telling whoever will listen, 'I reappear like an apparition.' He plays Valentin, the original showman *raté* who manufactures cruel vaudevillian 'pleasures' by branding his dogs with hot irons. He represents the charmingly monstrous opposite of Jean Gabin's François – his character eavesdrops, drinks *fine à l'eau*, talks non-stop, and can shift from self-pity and self-loathing to steely gimlet-eyed seriousness in the space of a sentence. Such emotional legerdemain is all of a piece with Valentin's malign, implacable presence. As he says at one point, 'I am a man of imagination, a dreamer. I invent things to amuse myself.' He will even dutifully play the role of abject father if it means driving the two young lovers apart.

If Batala was a rascal, then Valentin was a villain – the harbinger of chaos and disorder, and the embodiment of the political and social forces that threaten François and the class he represents. He is well-spoken and well-dressed, and transcends class hierarchies to seduce both Clara and Françoise, whereas François's seductive allure remains class-bound. *Le Jour se lève*'s tragic overtones are reflected in Berry's performance. He is both disconcerting and beguiling, compulsively watchable. Just as he cajoles his dogs to jump through hoops in his stage act, so too does he lead us on a merry dance.

His grand theatrical gestures and excessive body language are expertly marshalled throughout the film. He spies on François and Clara while they are lying on her bed, seeking to share in the kinds of intimate sexual or emotional encounters that are always denied him. His mock-inquisitiveness on being discovered, when François opens the door, is a classic defence mechanism, masking his inadequacy in the face of the dominant heteronormative pairing of François and Clara – 'Yes, I listen at keyholes. Does that shock you?' Wherever he appears, he is an unwanted interloper. He is an actor forever acting; the malevolent flip-side to the genial Frédéric Lemaître, the self-aggrandizing ham actor in Carné's *Les Enfants du paradis /Children of Paradise* (1945). For Valentin, the purity of acting is in the end result, revealing the fundamental hypocrisy at the heart of performance. Like Batala, whose interests are dictated by unstinting greed, *Donjuanism*, and the continual manipulation of his employees' good will, Valentin exploits the full range of emotional gestures – pity, anger, sincerity – to evoke unwarranted sympathy. Clara describes him as a 'conjuror,' full of 'all that smooth talk, you'd almost think he pulled it out of his sleeve.' Her message is clear: untrustworthiness and opaqueness lie at the heart of Valentin.

Listen, as Gabin does, to Berry at the bar in *Le Jour se lève*. Listen to how he tells Gabin that he has 'tolerated' his relationship with Clara, and is 'broad-minded' enough to let it continue. Rarely are these words spoken with such faux generosity – Berry was an expert at emotional blackmail and manipulation. No wonder Gabin shoots him at the end of the film (and at the start, for good measure) – he can no longer bear to look or listen to him: 'Stop moving around like that. You remind me of a rat... Keep still, I tell you, Keep still!' At one stage, Valentin resorts to self-pity. It's a tactic signalled by a familiar Berry posture – first hands unclasped, placed contritely across his arms, followed by a contemplative stroking of the chin. It's those fluttering hands again, deflecting attention, signalling the next stage of a 'performance' that demands to be admired. Gabin was not the only one to be duped by those hands in the 1930s.

Ben McCann
University of Adelaide, South Australia

Richard BERRY (1950–)

French Cinema's Captain of Hearts

THIS DARK, HANDSOME ACTOR, with his smooth voice and smouldering looks, whom no woman can resist on the screen, is one of the major supporting performers of French cinema. Richard-Elie BERRY was born and brought up in a popular district of Paris in the 10th arrondissement, then later in Boulogne where his parents ran a ready-to-wear shop. He did not like his physique, nor his childhood in poverty, and his rubbing elbows with wealthier people nurtured Berry's *malaise* and desire to act and express himself as a way of escapism. He started acting at the age of 17 in an amateur troop which performed in town halls, with a real passion for classical theatre. In 1969, he obtained the first prize in the Conservatoire National Supérieur d'Art Dramatique (French National Academy of Dramatic Arts), and later, in 1973 joined the prestigious Comédie Française.

He has appeared in nearly a hundred films since his first cinema appearance in Claude Pinoteau's *La Gifle /The Slap*, alongside Isabelle Adjani, Nathalie Baye, Annie Girardot, and Lino Ventura in 1974, but his role in Eli Chouraqui's sentimental, moving story about a mother and a son discovering each other, *Mon premier amour* (1978), really launched his career as an actor.

In 1982, he co-starred in Bob Swaim's *La Balance /The Nark*, set in the Belleville district, with a new generation of actors: Nathalie Baye and Philippe Léotard. The film obtained César Awards for Best Film, Best Actor, and Best Actress, and Berry was nominated for Most Promising Actor. Playing the parts of seducers, he has been particularly notable in films such as Alexandre Arcady's *Le Grand Pardon* (1982) and its sequel, ten years later, *Le Grand Pardon 2* (1992), alongside Jewish godfather-like Roger Hanin as Maurice Beitoun, his son, with a group of *pied-noir* gangsters played by the likes of Jean Benguigui, Jean-Pierre Bacri, and Gérard Darmon. The following year he is one more time Roger Hanin's son in *Le Grand Carnaval* (Alexandre Arcady, 1983) facing another *monstre sacré*, Philippe Noiret. In 1986, he had a major part in Claude Lelouch's sequel *Un homme et une femme, 20 ans déjà /A Man and a Woman: 20 Years Later*, alongside Jean-Louis Trintignant and Anouk Aimée.

In 1994, he had the title part in Charles Van Damme's Franco-Belgian drama *Le Joueur de violon /The Violin Player*. He could be seen the following year in Bertrand Tavernier's *L'Appât / Fresh Bait* with Marie Gillain as the titular 'bait.'

In 1999, following a motorbike accident with French actor Patrick Timsit, he decided to direct his first film, *L'Art (délicat) de la séduction* (2001), with Timsit and Cécile de France, followed by *Moi César, 10 ans ½, 1m39 /I, Cesar* (2003), with his daughter Joséphine Berry. After these two successful comedies, he directed his first thriller with Marion Cotillard and José Garcia, *La Boîte noire /The Black Box* (2005). However, his major success came with his fourth film, starring Jean Réno, *L'Immortel /22 Bullets* (2010). [1]

In 2002, he is Jean-Pierre Darroussin's hypocritical and womanizing boss in *Ah ! Si j'étais riche /If I Were a Rich Man* (dir. Gérard Bitton and Michel Munz). He joined his longtime accomplice Patrick Timsit in 2008, for a remake of Edouard Molinaro's *L'Emmerdeur /A Pain in the Ass*, originally made with the irresistible duo of Jacques Brel (as François Pignon) and Lino Ventura. His career had never been at a halt, as he seemed to be one of the elements of major French comedies.

In 2013, he returned on stage to play the comedy *Nos femmes* with Daniel Auteuil.

Today, Richard Berry continues to be a major cinema actor. Even after the age of 60, his charm remains inalterable and he still embodies the eternal seducer with an interest for both the screen and his first love, the stage.

Michaël ABECASSIS
The University of Oxford

---

1. For further discussion of *L'Immortel /22 Bullets*, see Katherine A. Wagner, 'Interrogation in An Empty Seaport Warehouse,' in *World Film Locations: Marseilles*, ed. Marcelline Block (Bristol: Intellect, 2013), 120-121. —Ed.

Juliette BINOCHE (1964–)

« La Binoche » – What's in a Name ?

BORN IN PARIS on 9ᵗʰ March 1964, Juliette BINOCHE is an actress and dancer with an impressive filmography of over forty movies. She has become one of the leading actresses on the French scene but, also, internationally, since receiving the prestigious Academy Award for Best Supporting Actress for her part in *The English Patient* (Anthony Minghella, 1996).

She grew up in an artistic environment and started taking acting classes when she was a teenager. After performing in several stage productions, she entered the realm of auteurs with *Liberty Belle* (Pascal Kané, 1983), *Je vous salue, Marie /Hail Mary* (Jean-Luc Godard, 1985), *La Vie de famille /Family Life* (Jacques Doillon, 1985), and *Rendez-vous* (André Téchiné, 1985). It is really the latter that made her famous in France.

She made her English-language debut with a sensual part in *L'Insoutenable légèreté de l'être /The Unbearable Lightness of Being* (Philip Kaufman, 1988),[1] which launched her international career. After that, she accumulated parts in critically-acclaimed movies, such as *Les Amants du Pont-Neuf /The Lovers on the Bridge* (Leos Carax, 1991) – Carax was her partner from 1986 to 1991 – and *Fatale /*

Damage (Louis Malle, 1992) – in which she performed explicit sex scenes. Rumour has it that Steven Spielberg cast his eyes on her and wanted to offer her a part in his *Jurassic Park*, which she turned down to star in Kieslowski's trilogy: *Trois couleurs : Bleu* (Krzysztof Kieslowski, 1993), *Trois couleurs : Blanc* (Krzysztof Kieslowski, 1994), and *Trois couleurs : Rouge* (Krzysztof Kieslowski, 1994), winning the Venice Film Festival Award for Best Actress as well as a César for her starring turn in *Bleu*.[2]

After that, she starred in a number of successful films, from historical ones such as *Le Hussard sur le toit / The Horseman on the Roof* (Jean-Paul Rappeneau, 1995) to psychoanalytically-oriented ones, such as *Un divan à New-York /A Couch in New York* (Chantal Akerman, 1996), and also went back to her first love with André Téchiné's *Alice et Martin* (1998).

In 1999, she was given the opportunity to embody French writer George Sand in *Les Enfants du siècle /Children of the Century* (Diane Kurys, 1999), followed by another literary film, *La Veuve de Saint-Pierre /The Widow of Saint-Pierre* (Patrice Leconte, 2000). In 2000, she also started a collaboration with Michael Haneke, for whom she acted in *Code inconnu /Code Unknown* (Michael Haneke, 2000) and, again, in 2005, in *Caché /Hidden* (Michael Haneke, 2005), an intriguing movie about the Algerian war and the transgenerational transmission of trauma.[3]

For her part in the romantic comedy *Chocolat* (Lasse Hallström, 2000), alongside Johnny Depp, she was nominated for an Academy Award for Best Actress. After that, she starred in several romantic comedies, both in France and in the United States, alternating French and English language parts: *Décalage horaire /Jet Lag* (Danièle Thompson, 2002), *Coup de foudre à Rhode Island /Dan in Real Life* (Peter Hedges, 2007), *Paris, je t'aime* (Nobuhiro Suwa, 2006), *Quelques jours en septembre /A Few Days in September* (Santiago Amigorena, 2006), *Par effraction /Breaking and Entering* (Anthony Minghella, 2006).

Coming back to France and to drama, she acted in the powerful *Paris* (Cédric Klapisch, 2008),[4] followed by *Désengagement /Disengagement* (Amos Gitaï, 2007) and *L'Heure d'été / Summer Hours* (Olivier Assayas, 2008). 2007 was actually the beginning of an extremely busy and productive time in Binoche's life, thanks to roles in internationally acclaimed movies, from Taiwan to Palestine.

In 2009, her sister, Marion Stalens, who is a photographer and documentary director, made a television documentary about Binoche, entitled *Juliette Binoche dans les yeux /Juliette Binoche, Sketches for a Portrait* (Marion Stalens, 2009). Then, Binoche's part in *Copie conforme /Certified Copy* (Abbas Kiarostami, 2010) won her the Best Actress Award for the second time at the Cannes Film Festival, making her the first actress ever to win the European 'best actress triple crown' (at the Berlin, Venice, and Cannes film festivals).

In 2012, she starred in actress Sylvie Testud's directorial debut *La Vie d'une autre /Another Woman's Life* (Sylvie Testud, 2012) and in a romantic drama entitled *À cœur ouvert /An Open Heart* (Marion Laine, 2012), before returning to Hollywood to star in a drama science fiction film by David Cronenberg, *Cosmopolis* (David Cronenberg, 2012).

2013 was a very productive year for Binoche, with the long-awaited *Camille Claudel 1915* (Bruno Dumont, 2013) released in March, in which Binoche took up Isabelle Adjani's 1988 part as Camille Claudel in a film showing three days in the sculptor's life in a French psychiatric hospital, where she spent the last thirty years of her life, locked up against her will. Binoche also appeared in the Irish-Norwegian-produced English-language movie, *A Thousand Times Good Night* (Eric Poppe, 2013); with further roles in *Words and Pictures* (2013), *Godzilla* (2014), *Clouds of Sils Maria* (2014), *The 33 /Los 33* (2014, about the Chilean mine collapse) with Antonio Banderas and Gabriel Byrne, and co-starring again with Byrne (as the polar explorer Peary) in *Nobody Wants the Night* (2015).

Despite her extremely productive career, Binoche also found time to have two children: Raphaël (a son born on 2nd September 1993), whose father is André Halle, and a daughter, Hana (born on 16th December 1999), whose father is another famous actor, Benoît Magimel, who starred as Chopin alongside Binoche as Sand in *Les Enfants du siècle /Children of the Century* (1999).

Nathalie Ségeral
Virginia Tech.

Editor's notes: For further discussion of
1. —*The Unbearable Lightness of Being*, see Marcelline Block, ed., *World Film Locations: Prague* (Intellect, 2013), 22-23.
2. —*Trois Couleurs : Bleu*, see Marcelline Block, ed., *World Film Locations: Paris* (Intellect, 2011), 72-73.
3. —*Caché, Code Inconnu*, ibid, 94-95, 78-79.
4. —*Paris*, ibid, 116-117.

Michel **B**LANC (1952–)

*An
Atypical
Actor*

MICHEL **B**LANC (born in April 1952 in Courbevoie, France) is undoubtedly one of the best known French actors. He has played hypochondriacs and losers in most of his films.

Michel Blanc was first known through the Splendid theatre group, which he co-founded with Josiane Balasko, Christian Clavier, Gérard Jugnot, and Thierry Lhermitte. Blanc started to become extremely popular when he took roles where he was a moaner, such as in *Circulez y'a rien à voir! /Move Along, There is Nothing to See* (Patrice Leconte, 1983).

In 1983, Jean-Marie Poiré directed *Papy fait de la résistance /Gramps is in the Resistance*, in which Blanc acted for the last time with the Splendid troupe. After they separated, each member of the Splendid went on to have a successful career in French cinema. In 1984, Blanc directed his first film, called *Marche à l'ombre*, which was a phenomenal success with the French audience. One of his most interesting and intriguing roles was when he and Gérard Depardieu portrayed a gay couple in *Tenue de soirée /Ménage* (1986), which was directed by Bertrand Blier. In addition, Blanc collaborated with

Blier in *Merci la vie* (1991), where he played Raymond Pelleveau.

In 1989, Blanc took on a new and intriguing role far from his previous burlesque roles in *Monsieur Hire* (Patrice Leconte), based on Georges Simenon's novel, for which Blanc was nominated for the César for Best Actor. Blanc challenged himself even more when he played the role of a communist in *Uranus* (1990). *Uranus* was directed by Claude Berri and adapted from the novel of the same name, written by Marcel Aymé (1948).

In the 1990s, Blanc focused more on being a director and released comedies of manners such as *Grosse fatigue /Dead Tired* (1994) and *Embrassez qui vous voudrez / Summer Things* (2002). Nonetheless, the most intriguing film released by Blanc in the 1990s was *Mauvaise Passe /The Escort* (1999). *Mauvaise Passe* narrates the story of a French literature teacher named Pierre (Daniel Auteuil) who is in his forties. Pierre has writer's block and decides to go to London in order to find inspiration for his new novel. Being far from his family, Pierre meets a gigolo called Tom and follows him into prostitution.

In 2005, the French media acclaimed Blanc in Isabelle Mergault's comedy *Je vous trouve très beau /You Are So Beautiful*. Blanc played the role of Aymé Pigrenet, a grumpy farmer living in La Drôme. Aymé has just lost his wife following a domestic accident. We learn that Aymé did not truly love his dead wife but that she was useful in the sense that she could properly look after his house and farm. Aymé consequently resolves to find a new wife as soon as possible because he cannot manage all these chores on his own.

In that same year, Blanc joined the Splendid troupe in the third Les Bronzés film, *Les Bronzés 3 : Amis pour la vie* (Patrice Leconte, 2006), due to audience demand for a third instalment of this famous series. The film was an immense success at the box office; however, film critics were not impressed and the troupe was accused of '*médiocrité artistique.*' Furthermore, some members of the public were also disappointed by the mediocrity of the film.

Stéphane NARCIS
Bath Spa University

Francis BLANCHE (1921–1974)

The Joker

FRANCIS BLANCHE was born in Paris to a family of theatre actors and artists, which is why he would always say, 'I am an artist by heredity.' At age 14, he became the youngest *bachelier* in France. He made his film debut in Jean Boyer's *Frédérica* (1942) and started his theatre career in 1948 with the comedy troupe Les Branquignols. With comedian Pierre Dac, he formed one of the funniest radio duos of the 1950s, with over 1,000 episodes of their *Signé Furax* airing on Europe 1. The radio drama of this pair of humorists attracted a very wide audience. Dac and Blanche were a perfect blend of innovative humour that made people roar with laughter. He was also famous in the 1960s for his phone pranks, which were also broadcast on radio. Francis Blanche wrote songs, notably the famous *Débit de l'eau, débit de lait* and *Le Complexe de la truite*, both interpreted by Charles Trénet. The sketches he wrote with Pierre Dac, including *Le Fakir*, the *Sar Rabindranath*, and *Le Parti pris*, have become all-time classics. In 1956, he won the Grand Prix de l'humour.

One of his most famous film roles is that of the Nazi commandant

Obersturmführer Schulz in *Babette s'en va-t-en guerre /Babette Goes to War* (Christian-Jaque, 1959) alongside Brigitte Bardot. He appears in Claude Autant-Lara's *La Jument verte /The Green Mare* (1959), with other performances in Jean-Pierre Mocky's *Un couple /A Couple* (1960), *Snobs !* (1962), *Les Vierges /The Virgins* (1963), *Un drôle de Paroissien /Heaven Sent* (1963), *Les Compagnons de la Marguerite /Order of the Daisy* (1967), *La Grande Lessive /The Big Wash* (1968) and *L'Étalon / The Stud* (1970). Inspector Cucherat in *Un drôle de Paroissien* was initially to be played by Louis de Funès, but for financial reasons the part was eventually given to Blanche. He also became one of Georges Lautner's favourite actors with memorable film roles such as Maître Folasse in *Les Tontons flingueurs /Monsieur Gangster* (1963); eccentric uncle Absalon, an anthropologist who works in the coffin industry in *Des pissenlits par la racine /Salad by the Roots* (1964), and Boris Vassilief in *Les Barbouzes /The Great Spy Chase* (1964) with Lino Ventura and Bernard Blier. With Darry Cowl, he acted in a series of minor roles in *Les Livreurs* (Jean Girault, 1961), *Les Bricoleurs / Who Stole the Body?* (Jean Girault, 1963), and *Les Veinards /People in Luck* (Jean Girault, 1963). In 1968, he performed in Luis Buñuel's *Belle de jour* with Catherine Deneuve. He directed *Tartarin de Tarascon* (1962) with Bourvil and Jacqueline Maillan, but the film was quite unsuccessful. As a scriptwriter, he wrote the screenplay of the controversial film *La Grande Bouffe* for Marco Ferreri (1973).

With his rotund physique and laughing eyes, Francis Blanche was a talented and creative actor whose madcap films were burlesque and his roles were both poetic and almost surrealist. He would revisit films or would create his own texts and make them truculent with his physicality and scatty interpretations. In his career of thirty years, he appeared in over a hundred films.

Francis Blanche died in his fifties from a heart attack, apparently caused by improperly treated diabetes. Pierre Dac would follow him a few months later. Blanche is buried in the small medieval city of Èze near Nice, where he bought a house and spent his holidays since 1947. His daughter Barbara Blanche, in the wake of her great grandmother and great uncle who were, respectively, a ceramist and a painter, still runs an art gallery in Èze that specializes in china dolls and puppets.

Michaël ABECASSIS
The University of Oxford

Bernard BLIER (1916–1989)

*The
Eternal
Sidekick*

Though he mainly found success as a supporting character, Bernard BLIER managed to have one of the biggest careers amongst the French actors of his generation. Quite short and endowed with a stout stocky figure topped by a thick neck and a quickly balding head, a round face stricken with slightly droopy features, Blier's performances could not rely on a conventional physique – but all those things made him easily recognizable to the French public for over fifty years. Indeed, he proved able to develop a stunning versatility in a plentiful filmography of over 180 performances.

Like many others of his time, he started as a stage actor at the Conservatoire, where he met his classmate François Périer, who became a life-long friend. In drama school, he studied under the great Louis Jouvet, a leading actor, stage director, and mentor with influential theories about his craft; the master soon hired the pupil and gave him his first parts in his renowned company. Unsurprisingly, Blier's screen debuts concur with Louis Jouvet's main appearances; together, under the direction of Marc Allégret or Marcel Carné, they gave substance to a body

of work that would soon be known as 'poetic realism,' with such titles as the iconic *Hôtel du Nord* or the lesser known but no less successful *Entrée des artistes /The Curtain Rises*, both released in 1938.

Posing as a man of the people, mainly playing working-class characters in heartfelt social melodramas (although he really came from an intellectual family), in those years, Blier developed a rich on-screen collaboration with the super-star of the time, Jean Gabin, which soon evolved into an enduring friendship. With his honest, joyful and sometimes naive presence, Blier subtly contributed to give some balance to the more dramatic leading characters played by Gabin, such as in Carné's *Le Jour se lève /Daybreak* in 1939.

After being detained in a wartime camp in 1940 for a year, he managed to be sent back to Paris, where he resumed his flourishing acting career, but with a new slimmer figure, which enabled him to endorse a more diverse range of characters as a ladies' man. He then began a long series of minor parts for major filmmakers, including Claude Autant-Lara, Christian-Jaque, Jean-Paul Le Chanois, Henri-Georges Clouzot, and Sacha Guitry. He soon became a reliable, almost unavoidable regular value of what was then called 'French quality' cinema. By the end of the fifties, he followed many of his fellow French actors who found work in Italian cinema, where he played parts that were sometimes more interesting than those he had previously been given.

For Blier, the sixties became the most successful decade of his career, thanks to director Georges Lautner and screenwriter Michel Audiard. In a body of modern films noirs often verging on parody, when not openly made as comedies or spy-film spoofs, Bernard Blier created the new stock character of the comic villain. Sturdy as ever, subject to violent outbursts of anger, his characters often appeared as the main point of interest to the public eye; to a deeper extent, Bernard Blier achieved iconic status making a series of films that have since then entered the French collective memory through many television airings (Lautner's *Les Tontons flingueurs / Crooks in Clover* or *Monsieur Gangster*, 1963 and *Les Barbouzes /The Great Spy Chase*, 1964; Yves Robert's *Le Grand Blond avec une chaussure noire /The Tall Blond Man with One Black Shoe*, 1972). From then on, Bernard Blier never stopped working, but he met one of his last and most memorable parts in *Buffet froid /Cold Cuts* (1979) under the direction of his son, Bertrand Blier, a renowned filmmaker who achieved fame in the seventies. The fact that in this film, the elder Blier shared the screen with the then rising star Gérard Depardieu, commonly seen as a new Jean Gabin, appeared like the perfect passing of the torch and the crowning of a very full career. In the end, Blier is remembered for his sarcastically grumpy presence, a trait that made him the epitome of a certain *franchouillardise*, or Frenchness.

Jean-Christophe Blum
Lycée Blaise Pascal, Clermont-Ferrand

Richard Bohringer (1941–)

The Tender -hearted Rebel

'Anger keeps one alive. One is screwed when one is not angry anymore.' This quotation is an excerpt from Richard Bohringer's autobiography entitled *C'est beau une ville la nuit* (Editions Denoël, 1988) and it sums up perfectly the philosophy of a man whose screen roles for over four decades mirror his strong personality and troubled life. His image as the gently charismatic loudmouth of French cinema is inseparable from the deep-voiced rebel whose career was marked by great highs, but also the lows of alcohol and drug addiction. Bohringer, who claims to have 'broken into' cinema by accident, became one of the most popular French actors of the 1980s and 1990s. A man of multiple talents, he has also been a successful writer, singer, and director.

Richard Bohringer was born on January 16th 1942 in Moulins, from a German father and a French mother. World War II greatly impacted his life as his mother fled France to join her lover in Germany, leaving him in the care of his grandmother. For young Richard, who was raised in Paris, the first years were difficult. At age six he contracted a disease that left him blind for nearly two years; he then suffered from a severe case of scoliosis that trapped him in a body cast for two years. Upon recovery, he lived a tumultuous childhood on the streets of Saint-Germain and probably sharpened his *gouaille*, the cheeky and brash Parisian attitude that would later be his on-screen trademark. He became a fixture of the jazz clubs where he met his idols: John Coltrane, The Doors' Jim Morrison, Claude Nougaro, Charlie Parker, and Vince Taylor. It was Taylor who encouraged him to step onto the musical stage under the moniker 'Richard Blues.'

The struggling writer made his first breakthrough in 1967, when his play *Les Girafes* was picked up by famed producer Claude Lelouch and presented at the Théâtre de la Gaîté Montparnasse. The play already featured key elements of Bohringer's life: alcohol, a passion for Africa, and a troubled yet endearing protagonist. He also had a number of small roles in films and plays. His first major role was in 1972 in Charles Matton's *L'Italien des roses /The Italian of the Roses*. In this film, he is Raymond, a suicidal man who is sitting on the edge of his apartment, reflecting upon the events that led to his suicide attempt. This role was the first of a long line of tortured characters that defined his career as an actor.

In 1973, his daughter Romane was born. He raised her alone, and they share an extremely close relationship. Bohringer, who fathered three other children (Mathieu, Richard, and Lou), describes fatherhood as 'the best role of his life.'

Throughout the 1980s, Richard Bohringer acted in more than fifty films and plays. He earned a spot in the pantheon of French actors thanks to his roles in popular films such as Claude Zidi's *Les Sous-doués* (1980) and Claude Pinoteau's *La Boum / The Party* (1980). In 1981, he earned critical and popular acclaim as Serge Gorodish, the suave manipulator of Jean-Jacques Beineix's *Diva* (1981). The actor whose screen presence increasingly mirrored a troubled life performed the role of often angry or tortured men who are still lovable despite the ravages of multiple addictions. In 1987, he played opposite actress Anémone in Jean-Loup Hubert's *Le Grand Chemin / The Grand Highway*. His character, Pello, is a bitter man who has been unable to overcome the death of his child and who is entrenched in constant bickering with his grief-stricken wife. The arrival of a nine-year-old child allows the couple to bury their painful ghosts and move on with their lives. Pello's mixture of hardness and fragility won the favour of the public and earned Bohringer the César for Best Actor in 1988. This award was the second César for Bohringer who previously won the prize for his supporting role as Lorca, the vengeful and sadistic warden of Denis Amar's *L'Addition* (1984).

In 1988, he publicly revealed his battle with addiction in his autobiography *C'est beau une ville*. The bestseller chronicles his struggles with alcohol, drugs, violence, and the financial setbacks that resulted from his addictions.

His more than forty performances

throughout the 1990s bear the mark of his deep voice and strong personality. In 1990, the actor, who never strayed away from the musical scene, released *Errances*, an intimate album whose jazzy tunes such as *Au fond des bars* and *Alcools* tell the tale of his addiction and his insecurities. Bohringer, who was then famous for his charisma, stubbornness, and violent outbursts, established his reputation throughout roles where he brought life to characters that were virile and cheeky. Toubib, the homeless man that he played in Gérard Jugnot's *Une époque formidable... /Wonderful Times* (1991) illustrates these roles of outspoken and endearing outcasts. Toubib encounters Michel Bertier (Gérard Jugnot), a former executive who finds himself homeless after losing his job and his wife, and takes him under his wing. Bohringer's charisma defined the film and won him, once again, the favour of the public. In 1997, he played the no-nonsense Victor Benzakhem in Thomas Gilou's popular movie *La Vérité si je mens /Would I Lie to You?*. Benzakehm is a boss in the Sentier, the famous Jewish quarter of Paris, whose uncompromising character strangely resembles Bohringer's real-life personality.

At the beginning of the new millennium, the actor turned away from the silver screen and established himself in popular television roles. In 2002, he affirmed his love for Africa and became a citizen of Senegal. In 2006, he directed and played himself in the adaptation of his autobiography *C'est beau une ville la nuit /A City is Beautiful at Night*, with his daughter playing herself.

The actor has remained faithful to his image as an idealistic dreamer determined to correct society's flaws. He eventually returned to his first love, literature, and has authored several books including *Traîne pas trop sous la pluie* (Flammarion, 2009) and *Les Nouveaux contes de la cité perdue* (Flammarion, 2011), an ode to his disenchantment with capitalism.

Mame-Fatou NIANG
Carnegie Mellon University, Pittsburgh

Romane BOHRINGER (1973–)

*More Than
Just
Daddy's
Little Girl*

ROMANE BOHRINGER was born on August 14th 1973 in Pont-Sainte-Maxence in the northern département of Oise. She is known for her angelic face and youthful looks. Growing up in the shadow of her father, actor Richard Bohringer, Romane managed to make a name for herself as an actress.

Named after Roman Polanski, Romane was born from the union of two free spirits. In the early 1970s, her father Richard was living a penniless bohemian life in Parisian artistic circles. Her mother, Marguerite Bourry, was a Franco-Vietnamese refugee who was born in Saigon and had been adopted in France. Marguerite left the little family when Romane was only nine months old. Just like her father had been abandoned by his mother three decades earlier, Romane was abandoned by hers. The child grew up in her paternal great-grandmother's house, surrounded by Richard's unconditional affection. The strong bond between the two was certainly born during these first years. Romane and her father were inseparable, and she grew up on movie sets watching her father develop his career. The little girl, who was dazzled by this world, dreamed of working behind a camera,

and never contemplated becoming an actress.

In 1986, Romane made her debut as an actress alongside her father in Didier Grousset's *Kamikaze*, written by Luc Besson. In 1991, her role as Miranda in Shakespeare's *The Tempest*, directed by Peter Brook, persuaded her to abandon her studies and pursue a career in acting. When she was eighteen, she starred alongside her father in Claude Miller's *L'Accompagnatrice / The Accompanist* (1992). The movie is set in 1942 German-occupied France and features Romane as Sophie Vasseur, a talented but shy pianist who lives vicariously through famed singer Irene Brice (Yelena Safonova). Sophie becomes Irene's maid and travels with her to London where she witnesses Irene's infidelities. The film presents the entwined lives of three characters: Sophie, Irene, and her husband Charles Brice (played by Richard Bohringer). Romane's expressive acting compensated for Sophie's silences and withdrawn personality. She transformed Sophie into a key character of the movie. The bond between Romane and Richard was evident in the scenes that they shared. Her performance in the film earned her critical and popular acclaim but it was really her role that same year in Cyril Collard's *Les Nuits fauves /Savage Nights* that brought her recognition on both sides of the Atlantic. Romane played Laura, a beautiful young woman who dove into the throes of a passionate relationship with Jean (Cyril Collard) who is bisexual and HIV positive. The film was a stunner and triggered an unprecedented discussion about

AIDS in French society. Bohringer's performance garnered wide acclaim and she was soon considered one of the rising stars of French cinema. In December 1993, Bohringer was awarded the coveted César Award for Most Promising Actress for her role in Collard's movie. She received her award from the hands of famed sculptor César himself. She delivered an emotional tribute to the man of her life, her father Richard, and to her co-star Cyril, who had passed away a few days before the ceremony.

These two movies foreshadowed the roles that Romane Bohringer would play in the cinema of the 1990s. She became famous portraying troubled characters who are often at odds with love. This is the case when Romane incarnates Mina, the introverted young artist afraid to approach men in Martine Dugowson's *Mina Tannenbaum* (1994); Alice, the unbalanced and manipulative woman of Gilles Mimouni's *L'Appartement /The Apartment* (1996); Zoe, the unfaithful wife of Bigas Luna's *La Femme de chambre du Titanic /The Chambermaid on the Titanic* (1997); Marguerite, one half of a dysfunctional couple in Bertrand Bonello's *Quelque chose d'organique /Something Organic* (1998), or Lydu Lozinska, in Julien Temple's biopic *Vigo, histoire d'une passion* (1998) where she plays the role of the late cinéaste Jean Vigo's passionate wife and muse.

Romane opens up to other genres and takes on new projects and directions. In 1995, she starred with Leonardo DiCaprio in Polish director Agnieszka Holland's *Total Eclipse*, about the troubled relationship between 19th century French poets Arthur Rimbaud (DiCaprio) and Paul Verlaine (David Thewlis). In 2001, she was costume designer for Bertrand Bonello's *Le Pornographe / The Pornographer*. She also directed Carole Fréchette's play *Les Sept jours de Simon* and acted in Olivier Dahan's film adaptation of *Le Petit Poucet /Tom Thumb*, Charles Perrault's fairytale. After a two-year hiatus, she resumed her cinematic career in Benoît Cohen's *Nos enfants chéris / Our Precious Children*. In 2005, she narrated Luc Jacquet's successful wildlife documentary *La Marche de l'Empereur /The March of the Penguins* (2005). The following year, she yet again collaborated with her father, when she played herself in his adaptation of his autobiography *C'est beau une ville la nuit /A City is Beautiful at Night* (2006). Romane has moved away from movie sets and shines on theatrical stages where she plays both contemporary and classic texts. Passionate and curious, she has managed to shake the image of a celebrity offspring and made a name for herself in roles that resemble her: passionate yet tender, troubled yet endearing.

Mame-Fatou NIANG
Carnegie Mellon University, Pittsburgh

Sandrine BONNAIRE (1967–)

*Poignant
Movies,
Serious
Acting*

BORN IN AUVERGNE to a poor family in May 1967 (she is a Gemini), with ten brothers and sisters, Sandrine BONNAIRE never imagined becoming an actress. Her ambition was to become a hairdresser but, growing up in the Parisian suburbs (Grigny), she was given the opportunity to try her luck in film. By chance she discovered acting through her father's friend, who was in casting for movies. He offered her a role as an extra in *La Boum 2* (1982), the sequel of the very popular *La Boum /The Party* (1980), directed by Claude Pinoteau. Later on, she discovered that this kind of very light comedy was not really her style, or her calling, but for now she accepted other contracts for the same type of movie, working with Claude Zidi in *Les Sous-doués en vacances* (1982), among others.

Again by chance, she found what she really wanted to do. One of her sisters answered an advertisement, in the daily newspaper *France-Soir*, looking for would-be actresses. Sandrine went along to the interview with her sister. There she met the famous director Maurice Pialat with whom she would work for many years. Their first collaboration, *À nos amours /To our Loves* (1983) won the César

for best movie. The critics appreciated Sandrine Bonnaire as much as the movie itself and she was awarded 'Most Promising Young Actress' (Prix du jeune Espoir Féminin) César. Bonnaire's natural acting style contrasted sharply with the slightly overdone style of the actresses in the 80s.

In fact, Sandrine Bonnaire has acted in many different styles of movies: in thrillers such as *Tir à vue /Fire on Sight* (Marc Angelo, 1984), *Police* (Maurice Pialat, 1985) and *Monsieur Hire* (Patrice Leconte, 1989); in romantic comedies such as *Le Meilleur de la vie /A Better Life* (Renaud Victor, 1985) and *Quelques jours avec moi /A Few Days with Me* (Claude Sautet, 1988); in dramas such as *Sous le soleil de Satan /Under the Sun of Satan* (Pialat, 1987) which received the Palme d'Or in Cannes; in *Sans toit ni loi /Vagabond* by Agnès Varda (1985) for which she received the César for Best Actress; and in *Jeanne la Pucelle* by Jacques Rivette (1994). More recently she has appeared in *Le Cou de la girafe /The Giraffe's Neck* by Safy Nebbou (2004) and in *Un cœur simple /A Simple Heart* by Marion Laine (2008), the cinematographic version of the famous Gustave Flaubert novel. The invitation to be a member of the jury of the 58th Berlin Film Festival (2008), presided over by Costa-Gavras, testifies to her international reputation.

Her roles have also been diverse. In turn she has been a young and dynamic woman (*Le Meilleur de la vie*), a likeable youthful offender (*Tir à vue*), a disturbed young woman obsessed with the idea of evil who will finally commit suicide (*Sous le soleil de Satan*), a woman enlightened by faith (*Jeanne la Pucelle*), a vagrant without any family (*Sans toit ni loi*), and a bubbly maid (*Quelques jours avec moi*). She can also portray disturbing characters such as a murderess (Claude Chabrol's *La Cérémonie*, 1995; *Secret défense /Secret Defense*, Jacques Rivette, 1998) or a murder accomplice in *Monsieur Hire*. Well-known for her professionalism, Bonnaire always tries to, literally, 'incarnate' her characters. To portray as truthfully as possible the vagrant Mona Bergeron in *Sans toit ni loi*, Bonnaire did not wash her hair during the whole period of the film's shooting.

In 2007, she became a director herself, producing a powerful movie about her sister Sabine who is autistic. Her aims were to make the French public aware of the problems encountered by disabled people and to raise awareness about the poor services in France for them. This extremely touching and impressive movie, *Elle s'appelle Sabine /Her Name Is Sabine*, released in 2009, encapsulates Bonnaire's career as much as her personal life, her twenty years of filming and her spiritual evolution. She was herself the victim of a violent assault in 2000, while she was in Paris making the movie *C'est la vie* (directed by Jean-Pierre Améris). She directed the 2012 *J'enrage de son absence /Maddened by his Absence*, which screened at Cannes. Starring William Hurt, this film is again a personal and poignant journey. *J'enrage de son absence* had its US premiere in October 2013 at the French Institute/ Alliance Française in New York City – with Bonnaire presenting it in person – as part of a retrospective devoted to Bonnaire's films.

This good-looking brunette, with her distinctive high forehead and lively features, does not lack a sense of humour, or a sense of modesty either. When receiving her award for Best Actress, she commented that any award can collect dust. Neither does she lack a sense of dignity for that matter, asking to have manure poured in front of the popular magazine *Voilà* in protest against the publication of stolen photos of her autistic sister Sandrine.

She has two daughters: Jeanne, whose father is Bonnaire's ex-partner William Hurt and Adèle, whose father is Guillaume Laurant, actor and screenwriter, Bonnaire's husband since 2003. An avowed socialist, she openly supported Jospin and then Martine Aubry (2012). However she never liked Dominique Strauss-Khan, who according to the actress, is « *complètement malade sexuellement* » ['unbalanced sexually'].[1]

Fabienne H. BAIDER
University of Cyprus

1. Joséphine Simon-Michel, 'Bonnaire: « J'ai toujours été contre DSK »,' *Le Figaro TV*, November 10, 2011, accessed August 27, 2013, http://tvmag.lefigaro.fr/programme-tv/ article/telefilm/65609/bonnaire-j-ai-toujours-ete-contre-dsk.html.

Dany Boon (1966–)
[Daniel HAMIDOU]

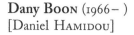

—*The Planet's Best-known Ch'ti?*

BORN DANIEL HAMIDOU in Armetières (in the Nord-Pas-de-Calais region) in 1966, his stage name was inspired by the American television series *Daniel Boone* (1964-1970). Boon has acted in some twenty feature films, a list that while heavy on popular comedy (Francis Veber's *La Doublure /The Valet*, 2006) runs the gamut from heritage film (*Joyeux Noël /Merry Christmas*, Christian Carion, 2005) to auteur cinema (Jean-Pierre Jeunet's 2009 *Micmacs à tire-larigot /Micmacs*). Since being cast in his first major role in the uneven *Le Déménagement* (Olivier Doran, 1997), Boon has appeared in numerous comedies, including *Mon meilleur ami /My Best Friend* (Patrice Leconte, 2006), *De l'autre côté du lit /Changing Sides* (Pascale Pouzadoux, 2008), *Le Code a changé /Change of Plans* (Danièle Thompson, 2009), and *Astérix et Obélix : Au service de sa majesté /Astérix and Obélix: God Save Britannia* (Laurent Tirard, 2012). Boon has also played voice-over roles in the animated features *Mia et le Migou /Mia and the Magoo* (Jacques Rémy-Girerd, 2005) and *Pollux : Le Manège enchanté /Sprung! The Magic Roundabout* (Dave Borthwick,

Jean Duval, Frank Passingham, 2005).

Despite his long list of acting appearances, Boon is best-known as the director and writer of *Bienvenue chez les Ch'tis /Welcome to the Sticks* (2008), in which he also starred.[1] While he also directed *Rien à déclarer /Nothing to Declare* (2010) and *La Maison du bonheur* (2006), *Welcome to the Sticks* is by far his greatest popular success. The film draws on regional customs, cuisine, and dialect, the latter being a variation of Picard, generating many laughs in particular by reinforcing or debunking common stereotypes about the north of France. A veritable sensation at the box office, the film attracted over 20 million spectators in France alone, inspired an Italian remake (*Benvenuti al sud /Welcome to the South*, Luca Miniero, 2010) and earned Boon a reported twenty-six million Euros. American actor and producer Will Smith purchased the option for an American remake of *Welcome to the Sticks* but was ultimately unable to find a script that appealed to Boon and the project was shelved in late 2012. The enormous success enjoyed by the film in France helped transform Boon into regional folk hero – he was labelled the 'planet's best-known Ch'ti'[1] by the magazine *Marianne* – but also led to a great deal of critical derision. Boon boycotted the 2009 César awards ceremony to protest *Welcome* being snubbed in every nomination category with the exception of best screenplay. Writing in *Le Monde*, Thomas Sotinel opined that Boon's film owed its success to its nostalgic depiction of an idealized, largely homogenous French past.

Sotinel also complained that Boon presented social issues in a reductive fashion. *Marianne*'s critic wondered if the film – and Boon himself – were too *beauf* (best translated as yokel or bumpkin) to be true. Indeed it is true that *Welcome to the Sticks* has on display a seemingly anachronistic world in which everyone has typical Gallic names such as Philippe, Antoine, or Annabelle, as Sotinel charges. Scratching the surface of these characters reveals considerably more complexity, however. Boon (who played Antoine in *Welcome*) is the son of an immigrant from the Kabylia region of Algeria and himself converted to Judaism at the time of his marriage in 2003 to Yael Harris, while his co-star Kad Merad (as Philippe) was born to a Muslim family in Algeria. Moreover, the actor-director has often commented on the diversity of origins found in his native *Nord*, an industrial region that was once a major site of immigration from Europe and North Africa.

Boon has mined his simpleton-from-the-North persona since the very start of his career. Indeed *L'Express* was asking if Boon was not a bit too *beauf* as early as 2003, when he was well-known for his comedy routines and one-man shows in Paris but had yet to become a major film star. After studying theatre across the border in Tournai, Belgium, Boon moved to Paris to work as an actor and would become a fixture at theatres such as the Lucernaire, Café de la gare, and l'Olympia. He began his career performing sketches inspired by Northern stereotypes and regional customs. One of his *spectacles* revolved around life in a typical Northern 'fry shack' – a tradition with a central place in *Welcome to the Sticks* – called 'Moulekerque.' His successful 2003 show, bearing the *chti* title *À s' baraque /At One's House*, comprised a series of sketches in the Northern dialect that has become inextricably linked to Boon in French popular imagination. Beyond the thematic continuities between his stage and screen work, Boon's background in theatre has had a significant impact on his work in cinema. His early theatre performances incorporated elements of sketch comedy, singing, dancing, and even miming, traces of which can be found in his subsequent films.

Michael GOTT
University of Cincinnati

1. *Ch'ti, ch'timi*: Northern French (person or dialect). —Ed.

Michel Boujenah (1952–)

*Rocking
the
Cradle*

WITH HIS characteristic *pied noir* accent, Michel Boujenah has become a major figure of French theatre and cinema, very popular among all generations. Unlike *pied noir* 'godfather' Roger Hanin and his disciples Jean-Pierre Bacri, Jean Benguigi, and Gérard Darmon, among many other entertainers who hailed from Algeria, Michel Boujenah is a French humorist of Jewish origins who was born in Tunisia. He is the brother of film director Paul Boujenah, and the uncle of actor Matthieu Boujenah. In 1963, at the age of 11, Michel left the capital Tunis with his parents to settle in the suburbs of Paris. This rupture with his roots and his nostalgia for Tunisia, his homeland, would become one of the main themes of his one-man shows.

After failing to enter the prestigious École Supérieure d'Art dramatique in Strasbourg because of his accent, he created his own theatrical group named La Grande Cuillère ('The Big Spoon'), and wrote and staged his own one-man shows. His shows *Albert* (1980), *Les Magnifiques*, (1984), *Les Nouveaux Magnifiques* (2004), and *Enfin libre* (2008) – depicting the lives of Franco-Tunisians who have immigrated to France – were particularly successful.

Michel Boujenah appeared in around 30 films and television series. He starred in Jan Saint-Hamont's rather mediocre 1980 comedy *Mais qu'est-ce que j'ai fait au bon Dieu pour avoir une femme qui boit dans les cafés avec les hommes ? /What Did I Ever Do to the Good Lord to Deserve a Wife Who Drinks in Cafes with Men?* (a film which is famous for having the longest title in the history of French cinema). The characters he subsequently played are distinguished by their kindness and naïveté. His main film success that granted him a César in the best supporting role was Coline Serreau's *Trois hommes et un couffin /Three Men and a Cradle* (1985). Here, he plays Michel, one of the three titular hedonistic bachelors who finds a baby girl on his doorstep and is compelled to move from woman chasing to baby caring and nappy changing, which leads to a range of hilarious farcical misunderstandings. The film's enormously successful American remake, *Three Men and a Baby*, released in 1987, was directed by veteran *Star Trek* actor Leonard Nimoy (although Serreau was initially engaged by Touchstone Studios to direct the remake, but she withdrew from the project). After the box office smash of *Three Men and a Baby* – the number one film of 1987 – its American sequel, *Three Men and a Little Lady* (dir. Emile Ardolino, 1990) followed, while the French sequel, *18 ans après /18 Years Later*, directed by Serreau, was released in 2003, in which the now fifty-something daddies are still as endearing, though the comedy lacks the freshness of the original 1985 film. In Gérard Oury's unmistakably

Jewish comedy *Lévy et Goliath* (1987), Albert (Michel Boujenah) who has negated his faith and married a non-Jew, faces his orthodox brother Moses (Richard Anconina) who works as a diamond cutter in Antwerp. In Ariel Zeitoun's *Le Nombril du monde* (1993) Boujenah pursues his Jewish saga, but is completely transformed. With his extra fifteen kilos, his fake belly and dental prosthesis, he is unrecognizable. In 1998, he played Sganarelle in Jacques Weber's directorial debut *Don Juan* (1998), a part that he had already played at the theatre in Jacques Rosner's adaptation (1990).

In 2003, Michel Boujenah directed Philippe Noiret and Charles Berling in his first film, *Père et fils /Father and Sons*, about the difficult relationship of a father to his three sons. *Père et fils* was nominated for a César Award for Best Debut. Its sensibility combined with the wonderful acting of its cast makes this comedy worth seeing. Boujenah's second feature-length directorial effort, *3 amis* (2007), is a pleasant comedy about the ups and downs of friendship, starring Mathilde Seigner and Kad Merad, but very much inferior to his first film. In *3 amis*, Philippe Noiret only has a cameo appearance as a garage owner, but this short scene is very touching, as it is his last role.

Moving, funny, and charismatic, Michel Boujenah knows how to make the viewer laugh or cry, and he impregnates each part he plays with a dose of melancholy and tenderness.

Michaël ABECASSIS
The University of Oxford

Carole BOUQUET (1957–)

From Buñuel to Bond Girl to the Bouquet of Her Sangue d'Oro Wine

CAROLE BOUQUET, born in the chic suburb of Neuilly-sur-Seine on August 18, 1957, was mainly brought up by her father after her parents separated during her childhood (she is not related to veteran French actor Michel Bouquet). She left her philosophy studies at the Sorbonne for theatre classes at the Paris Conservatoire d'art dramatique. After being discovered by chance, she landed her first film role, in Luis Buñuel's last film, *Cet obscur objet du désir /That Obscure Object of Desire* (1977), starring as the young Conchita, a role she shared with Spanish actress Angela Molina: Bouquet's Conchita is more aloof whereas Molina's is fiery. Fernando Rey is Mathieu, an older gentleman pursuing Conchita as she deflects his sexual advances, thus driving him to madness and violence. This film explores a twisted/obsessive relationship and introduces audiences to Bouquet's luminous, regal beauty, for which she is famous. Her flawless physical appearance was put to good use by Chanel, for which she modeled, and is showcased onscreen in John Glen's *For Your Eyes Only* (1981), where she is Bond Girl Melina Havelock opposite Roger Moore as the fictional British Secret Service agent.

Bouquet is much more than a pretty face and near perfect physique, as attested to by the accolades she has received throughout her career – such as the Best Actress César for Bertrand Blier's *Trop belle pour toi /Too Beautiful for You* (1989) – and the high calibre of her theatrical work in performances of classical French theatre: Racine's *Phèdre* (at the Théâtre national de Nice and Paris's Théâtre Déjazet, 2002, dir. Jacques Weber) and later on, his *Bérénice*, at the Théâtre des Bouffes du Nord, in a 2008 production directed by Lambert Wilson. Her offscreen activities include being spokesperson for the French children's charity *La Voix de l'enfant* (see below). Bouquet is a respected winemaker, whose Sangue d'Oro Passito di Pantelleria wine is made on the volcanic island of Pantelleria in Southern Italy (between Sicily and Tunisia), where she owns property and vineyards. Her wine is well regarded, and she is often invited to speak about it at conferences, such as being interviewed by gastronomic historian John Mariani, among others. Bouquet speaks Italian fluently.

Since *Cet obscur objet*, Bouquet has had roles in over 40 films, in *œuvres* by major French filmmakers: Patrice Leconte (*Tango*, 1993); Claude Berri, for whom she incarnates the titular figure in the biopic *Lucie Aubrac* (1997), which is based upon the memoirs of the heroic Resistance fighter Aubrac (1912-2007); and André Téchiné, in 2011's *Impardonnables /Unforgivable*, as the younger, real-estate agent wife of a novelist (André Dussolier), living on an island estate near Venice. Bouquet also appears in the Francis Ford Coppola short film *Life Without Zoe* (1989; co-written by Francis and

Sofia Coppola), one of the three films of the omnibus *New York Stories*. In this film, Bouquet plays Soroya, a Middle Eastern princess, to whom precocious preadolescent protagonist Zoe (Heather McComb) helps return her diamond earring, known as 'a tear of Sharez.'

Bouquet is noted for her collaborations with Bertrand Blier, as in her César-winning performance in *Trop belle pour toi* in which she is Florence, the beautiful, elegant, upper-class wife of a BMW salesman, played by Gérard Depardieu, who falls for his ordinary-looking – even homely – secretary (Josiane Balasko), with whom he has a passionate affair. Along with Bouquet's award, this film won several Césars, among others, Best Film and Best Director, as well as the Grand Prize of the Jury at Cannes. Ten years earlier, Bouquet appeared in Blier's cult black comedy *Buffet froid* (1979), a satire of violence and anomie.

Some of Bouquet's other memorable roles include Nada, a French journalist in New York City, in Ulli Lommel's cult film *Blank Generation* (1980), an homage to the punk rock scene – the film bears the same name as the 1977 album by Richard Hell and the Voidoids – the centre of which is the now-defunct legendary nightclub CBGB on Manhattan's Bowery, featured in the film. In *Blank Generation*, Andy Warhol appears (as himself), while Richard Hell co-stars as Nada's love interest, punk rocker Billy. For Philippe Labro's drama *Rive droite, rive gauche* (1984), Bouquet received her first César nomination (Best Supporting Actress), for playing Babée, the wife of a lawyer (Gérard Depardieu) who falls for another woman (Nathalie Baye). In 2004, Bouquet appeared in 'An American Girl in Paris, Part *Deux*,' the series finale of the hit American television show *Sex and the City*, as fashion executive Juliet, ex-wife of Russian artist Aleksandr Petrovsky (Mikhail Baryshnikov). Meeting with Petrovsky's new girlfriend, *Sex and the City*'s protagonist Carrie Bradshaw (Sarah Jessica Parker), over lunch at the sleek Kong restaurant in Paris, Bouquet, wearing a red silk jacket, cuts a striking figure as she sips a glass of wine while speaking fluent English with a charming French accent. Juliette emblematizes the sophisticated and elegant *Parisienne* whose warmth toward her ex-husband's new love interest surprises Carrie, a New Yorker recently transplanted to the City of Light. Commiserating over a post-lunch cigarette with Carrie, Juliette candidly discusses her own experience of living with the difficult Petrovsky, who has attained fame and success in the art world to the detriment of his personal relationships with women, including his marriage to Juliette, since he always prioritizes his art over his love life. When Carrie states that Petrovsky is supportive of her writing, Juliette expresses surprise, foreshadowing how he will eventually sabotage Carrie's book party.

Apropos of private lives, Bouquet's love life is a topic of interest in France, as she has been romantically involved with public figures such as the deceased, controversial French-Lebanese film producer Jean-Pierre Rassam, the father of her son Dmitri, born in 1982. With photographer Francis Giacobetti, she had son Louis in 1988. Bouquet was in a relationship with Gérard Depardieu starting in the late 1990s; they were engaged from 2003-2005, ultimately parting ways without getting married. Bouquet has acted opposite Depardieu on numerous occasions, such as in the previously mentioned films *Buffet froid*; *Rive droite, rive gauche*; and *Trop belle pour toi*; as well as in 1999's *Un pont entre deux rives /The Bridge* – which Depardieu co-directed with Frédéric Auburtin – and Jacques Weber's adaptation of Victor Hugo's *Ruy Blas* for French television (2002).

Offscreen, Bouquet is the spokesperson for the French children's charity *La Voix de l'enfant* /'The Child's Voice,' which, since 1981, has promoted 'awareness and protection of children in distress in France and all over the world.' 'The Child's Voice,' whose Honorary Chairman was former French Resistance member, political activist, and bestselling author Stéphane Hessel (until his death in February 2013), has twice been decorated with the French Republic's Human Rights Award, in 1987 and 1992. In 2011, for her contributions to French gastronomic culture, Carole Bouquet was named Commander of the Order of Arts and Letters.

Marcelline BLOCK
Princeton University and SAG-AFTRA

Michel Bouquet (1925–)

*A Bouquet
of Talent
for Over
Six Decades
of Film
and Theatre*

Michel Bouquet's lengthy stage and screen career, spanning more than sixty years, has brought him international acclaim and renown. He is the recipient of France's highest honours and awards for film and theatre, as well as holds the title of Commander of the Legion of Honour. Bouquet received the Best Actor César after being nominated for this award for the very first time (and as a septuagenarian, no less) for his performance in Anne Fontaine's psychological drama *Comment j'ai tué mon père /How I Killed my Father* (2001) as Maurice, a father alienated from his adult son. Bouquet also received a Lumière Award for Best Actor for this role. Bouquet was again honoured with the César for Best Actor for the biopic *Le Promeneur du Champ de Mars /The Last Mitterrand* (Robert Guédiguian, 2005), his second César nomination (at age 80), in which he starred as François Mitterrand (1916-1996), the President of France who had the longest tenure in French history, as he was in office for fourteen years (1981-1995). Bouquet's work in theatre has been twice awarded the Molière prize for Best Actor:

first for Bertrand Blier's 1998 *Les Côtelettes*, a role Bouquet reprised, again starring opposite Philippe Noiret, in Blier's 2003 cinematic adaptation of his own play, and next in 2005 for his starring performance as King Berenger I in Eugène Ionesco's *Le Roi se meurt /Exit the King* (dir. Georges Werler), in which he also starred in the 2006 made-for-television version (dir. Roberto Maria Grassi). In both these stage and film versions of *Le Roi se meurt*, Bouquet's wife, the actress Juliette Carré, played King Berenger's first wife, Queen Marguerite (Carré and Bouquet often perform together).

Bouquet was born to a family of rather modest means in Paris on November 6, 1925, and was inspired by viewing Parisian theatrical productions to go into acting, eventually meeting, in 1943, the distinguished Comédie-Française actor Maurice Escande who became Bouquet's mentor and professor. Bouquet was admitted to the prestigious Paris Conservatoire (CNSAD) where he studied theatre and made his stage debut in 1944 in Paul Géraldy's *Première Étape* (dir. Jean-Jacques Daubin) at the Studio des Champs-Elysées. Bouquet performed with his fellow Conservatoire student, Gérard Philipe, in Paul Oettly's 1945 production of Albert Camus's *Caligula*, with Philipe as the mad emperor and Bouquet as Scipio, at the Théâtre Hébertot in Paris. In the late 1990s, Bouquet returned to the Conservatoire as a professor.

With over 100 film and television roles from the 1940s onward – his first credited onscreen appearances date from 1947, as the killer in Gilbert Gil's *Brigade criminelle / Criminal Brigade* and as a tubercular in Maurice Cloche's Vincent de Paul biopic, *Monsieur Vincent* (written by Jean Anouilh), a film that won an honorary Academy Award for best foreign language film – Bouquet has worked with leading figures in French culture, literature, arts, and entertainment, and was instrumental in bringing Harold Pinter's works to France.

Between 1946-47, Bouquet appeared in three Anouilh plays, all directed by André Barsacq at the Théâtre de L'Atelier: *Roméo et Jeannette, Le Rendez-vous de Senlis,* and *L'Invitation au château.* He also originated the role of Bitos/Robespierre in Anouilh's *Pauvre Bitos ou le dîner de têtes* at the Théâtre Montparnasse – Gaston Baty in 1956 and appears in Anouilh's last film, his cinematic adaptation of his own play, 1951's *Deux sous de violettes /Two Pennies Worth of Violets.* Bouquet also worked with Henri-Georges Clouzot, in *Manon,* 1949; with Abel Gance, as King Louis X in the period film *La Tour de Nesle /The Tower of Lust,* 1955 (based on the 14th century Tower of Nesle Affair); with Alain Resnais, for whom Bouquet narrated the important early Holocaust documentary *Nuit et Brouillard / Night and Fog,* 1955; with François Truffaut in *La Mariée était en noir / The Bride Wore Black,* 1968 (Bouquet depicts Coral, one of the men on whom Jeanne Moreau exacts her revenge) and in *Mississippi Mermaid,* 1969 (as inspector Comolli, opposite Jean-Paul Belmondo and Catherine Deneuve); and with Francis Veber,

in *Le Jouet /The Toy,* 1976, among others.

Bouquet productively collaborated with Claude Chabrol, appearing in numerous Chabrol films such as *Le Tigre se parfume à la dynamite /Our Agent Tiger,* 1965; *La Route de Corinth /Who's Got the Black Box,* 1967, starring Jean Seberg; *La Femme infidèle /The Unfaithful Wife,* 1969, in the role of cuckold Charles Desvallées who murders his wife's lover (for which Bouquet won Best Actor from the National Society of Film Critics – sharing the award with Robert Redford for *Butch Cassidy and the Sundance Kid*); *La Rupture /The Breach,* 1970; *Juste avant la nuit /Just Before Nightfall,* 1971; and 1985's *Poulet au vinaigre /Chicken with Vinegar.* Bouquet narrated Chabrol's powerful and disturbing documentary *L'Oeil de Vichy /The Eye of Vichy* (1993), which exposes the actual propaganda newsreels used by the Vichy regime to further its collaborationist agenda.

Bouquet appeared in Belgian films such as Jaco van Dormael's critically acclaimed 1991 *Toto le Héros /Toto the Hero* as protagonist Thomas in his elder years, a performance for which Bouquet won the European Film Award for Best Actor as well as the Joseph Plateau Award for Best Belgian Actor, and Harry Kümel's cult horror film *Malpertuis /Legend of Doom House* (1971) with a cast whose members include Orson Welles, Jean-Pierre Cassel, and Sylvie Vartan.

Bouquet has memorably and successfully taken on a range of classic and iconic characters in film and theatre, whether portraying

Javert – opposite Lino Ventura as Valjean and Jean Carmet as Thénardier – in Robert Hossein's 1982 version of *Les Misérables*, Argan in Molière's *Le Malade imaginaire*, or Prince Hal in Shakespeare's *Henry IV*, among others. Primarily retired from theatre (but not film), Bouquet, in his late 80s, is one of France's living icons; he was commemorated in Jean-Pierre Larcher's 2011 documentary *Le Temps des vertiges*, broadcast on France 2 television.

Michel Bouquet recently incarnated another legendary figure of French culture, that of artist Pierre-August Renoir, in Gilles Bourdos's *Renoir* (2012), France's submission to the Academy Awards for consideration for nomination in the Best Foreign Language film category.

Marcelline BLOCK
Princeton University and SAG-AFTRA

BOURVIL (1917–1970)
[André RAIMBOURG]

The Embodiment of Kindness and Innocence

BORN IN a village of Normandy in 1917, André Raimbourg's first stage name 'Andrel' was directly inspired from Fernandel, showing his attachment to this actor. Like him, he was an actor who also sang in shows or cabarets, but they only acted together once in his career (*La Cuisine au beurre*, Gilles Grangier, 1963). Actually he is still associated nowadays with Louis de Funès, although they only worked together in a few movies (Gérard Oury's *Le Corniaud /The Sucker* and *La Grande Vadrouille /Don't Look Now... We're Being Shot At!*, in the 1960s). These were such blockbusters that this partnership remains a classic of French Cinema.

He eventually used the name of the village of his childhood 'Bourville' as the definitive stage name 'BOURVIL,' in order to avoid any confusion with his cousin Lucien Raimbourg, who was already an actor.

Singing and acting came together. At the end of World War II, he played in *La Ferme du pendu /Hangman's Farm* (Jean Dréville, 1945) in which he sang his song *Les Crayons*, the starting point of his successful career. In the fifties, he was offered more and more main roles: in *Le Passe-muraille /Mister Peek a Boo* (Jean Boyer, 1951), Claude Autant-Lara's *La Jument verte /The Green Mare* (1959), and *La Traversée de Paris /Four Bags Full* (1956) for which he won an award. Even though in *La Traversée de Paris* (1956) he played a scene with Louis de Funès, the mythical 'couple' was to be set some ten years later. However, in this movie, he inaugurates acting with a partner: indeed, the story is about two 'Sunday smugglers' during World War II who have to carry meat throughout occupied Paris. Bourvil plays a rather cowardly and clumsy smuggler in contrast with Jean Gabin who is his partner, provocative, and teasing him with his fears. Even though the story is rather pessimistic about the human condition, the duo manages to give a funny touch to the movie. Comic roles are what would characterize Bourvil's acting. In a movie with Bourvil, humour is guaranteed. Indeed, throughout the fifties and the sixties, most of his movies were comedies. Bourvil's comic effect lies in his way of acting as honest, naive, kind, and non-scheming characters. Thus in *Le Corniaud* or in *La Grande Vadrouille*, the comic effects are created by the opposition of two different characters, and also by the fact that the intrigues of the sophisticated and nervy Louis de Funès are constantly being thwarted by Bourvil's clumsiness and innocence. The latter represented a lower middle class painter with little education and a modest living standard, whereas de Funès embodied an arrogant conductor at the Opéra de Paris, with sophisticated taste but rude behaviour: two contrasting characters bound to help each other in occupied France during World War II. Both of them had to help English parachutists pass across the border of the unoccupied part of France. This movie – *La Grande Vadrouille* – produced in 1966, remained number 1 at the French box-office for more than 30 years (only overtaken by Cameron's *Titanic*, in 1998).

Bourvil seemed so sincere in his acting that these kinds of roles made him very likeable. He became so typecast in these characters, that it is often forgotten that he also played roles of bad guys or in sad and dramatic stories (*L'Arbre de Nöel /The Christmas Tree*, Terence Young, 1969; *Le Miroir à deux faces*, André Cayatte, 1958, and *Les Misérables*, Jean-Paul le Chanois, 1958 in which he embodies Thénardier). Even though his acting could adapt to such characters, the audience did not expect him in these types of roles, so that these movies are barely associated to him. Therefore he was the ideal actor to play the servants or sword-bearer (*Les Trois Mousquetaires /The Three Musketeers*, André Hunebelle, 1953; *Le Bossu*, Hunebelle, 1959; etc). In *Le Cerveau /The Brain* (Gérard Oury, 1969) he played the friend of Jean-Paul Belmondo whose character claimed to be superior to the 'Brain' (David Niven) of a train attack: in the end nobody knows really which one is brainy. Even though Bourvil here is the accomplice of a hold-up, he is still naive enough to be a simple follower, not as ambitious and brave as his friend.

Although he was very popular in France, Bourvil did not really have an international career. However he had a role in the D-Day epic *The Longest Day* (Ken Annakin, Andrew Marton, and Bernhard Wicki, 1962) as the Mayor of Colleville-sur-Mer.

He died at the height of his glory, in 1970, probably from Kahler's disease, at the age of 53.

He embodied so much kindness and generosity in the roles he played, that for the majority it is hard to dissociate his characters from his own personality in real life.

Igor BRATUSEK
Université Paris–Sorbonne

Charles BOYER (1899–1978)

A Franco-American Love Affair

THROUGHOUT A CAREER lasting five decades, Charles BOYER (1899-1978) embodied the beauty, ironies, and ravages of love. Not a tame love, close to friendship, marriage, or devotion. Not the malodorous and slobbery goo of Pepé Le Pew – an inexcusably nasty caricature – said to be based on Boyer's reprisal of *Pépé le Moko* in *Algiers* (John Cromwell, 1938). Instead, it is an absolute love, at odds with society, above the law, even beyond life itself. Such love ends at times in death (in tragedy), at times in laughter (in comedy), but it grants nobility and a better self – it seems worth the sacrifices it requires.

Boyer's characters always have something transgressive to them. In his first film, Marcel L'Herbier's *L'Homme du large /Man of the Sea* (1920), Boyer appears with devilish black eyeliner around his famously dark eyes and lets his hair flow long as he leads an adolescent away from a loving family and into booze and sexual dissipation. He would return to this diabolical key later, as with the enchanting killer of *Algiers* and, especially, with his iconic villainy opposite Ingrid Bergman in *Gaslight* (George Cukor, 1944). Playing a psychopath who marries a beautiful young woman in order to drive her insane, Boyer is a virtuoso of smarmy, insincere evil.

In most of his work, however, Boyer expresses a noble, but no less dangerous love. In *Garden of Allah* (Richard Boleslawski, 1936) he plays a Trappist monk in the Sahara who has betrayed his vows and falls for Marlene Dietrich who is exploring the desert on the advice of her spiritual guide. The lovers are clearly close to God: his return to the monastery is made only with her complicity, and temporarily, until death reunites their souls. His most iconic portrayal of tragic love comes in the film that made him an international star: *Mayerling* (Anatole Litvak, 1936). Boyer plays Prince Rudolf, who suffers keenly from the awareness that everyone – friends, family, wife – wants something from him, and that he is loved by none. He falls torridly in love with a girl, Marie, played by a radiant Danielle Darrieux. Later, with just a silent and tortured gaze, he will tell Darrieux that he will kill her and then himself. The famous close-ups of their faces detach them from a world that has no space for them.

In many roles Boyer plays a nobleman, either of soul or by birth, who, in love, drags into death or murder. In *Arch of Triumph* (Lewis Milestone, 1948) Boyer is a self-assured Austrian doctor and resistance fighter living in Paris at the outbreak of war. He falls hopelessly for Joan Madou (Ingrid Bergman), a beauty marked with a death wish (he saves her from killing herself at the beginning of the film, and she is killed by another admirer at the end).

The stark noir lighting casts him into shadows, recreating their turbulent love story in an appropriately sombre despair (at her death he gives himself up to the Gestapo). Then, eighteen years after winning Darrieux's eternal love in *Mayerling*, he loses her to dashing Vittorio de Sica in *Madame de... /The Earrings of Madame de...* (Max Ophüls, 1953); Boyer plays the stiff military husband, wearing his epaulettes with dignity and indulging his wife's flirtations with young men. Even so, it is apparent that he kills de Sica out of a deep jealousy of their real love. As the Duc de Praslin, in *All This, And Heaven Too* (Anatole Litvak, 1940), he falls in love with a kind governess, Bette Davis, while married to a neurotic, manipulative wife. After Davis is chased from the home, he kills his wife in rage and protects Davis until killing himself. It even makes sense for his Comte Muffat to go against Zola and end Nana (Christian-Jaque, 1955) by strangling the *cocotte* himself.

In his American career, the late 1930's and 1940's, aging into his own forties, Boyer turned more frequently to comedy. Notably, in a series including *Love Affair* (Leo McCarey, 1939), *When Tomorrow Comes* (John M. Stahl, 1939), and *Together Again* (Charles Vidor, 1944), Boyer formed a superb comic team with Irene Dunne. During the same period he also notably worked with Joan Fontaine (*The Constant Nymph*, Edmund Goulding, 1943) and Jennifer Jones (*Cluny Brown*, 1946, directed by Ernst Lubitsch and in which Boyer is a resistance fighter, a role he would play in several films). Of the many great comic roles of this productive period, *Love Affair* is emblematic: Boyer plays a slightly aging athlete, Michel, who meets Dunne while crossing the Atlantic from France to America, where he plans to marry for money. They fall in love and arrange a date at the top of the Empire State Building for New Year's Eve – if they still love each other, and if Boyer is able to support himself, they will wed. But while crossing the street, Dunne is hit by a car: she hides her battered body and they do not meet until a year later. But Boyer's love is constant, and though she may never walk again, he remains with her.

One scene from *Love Affair* illustrates Boyer's marvellous technique. He plays the sophisticated Frenchman, the handsome playboy, immune to the endless attention he inspires in women. But his unflappability is gradually flapped. When the ocean liner stops over in Madeira, he and Dunne visit his grandmother, widowed, who had lived on the island with her husband. This scene has him speaking English and French – the stiffness and conscious control of his English contrasting with the fluent bonhomie of his French. His grandmother's devotion, a song by Dunne, and a visit to the private chapel give the scene a tranquil depth. When Dunne crosses herself and leaves, he begins the same gesture, one that this womanizer probably has not made since childhood. He quickly stops himself and adjusts his tie. It is a touching moment in which his superficiality is undermined by a sincerity driven by love.

Such is Boyer's marvellous range and subtlety: sometimes his whole body speaks, sometimes he modulates the inflections and origins of his accent (the map of his characters' origins spreads from Russia to Canada), at other times he expresses ideas and emotions through a raised eyebrow, a faraway glance, or a mere change of focus in his eyes. In comedy he is befuddled, confused, understanding, patronizing, seduced as much as seductive. Even where his physique had shortcomings, he effectively employed prosthetics to make up for them: a toupee that he wore only for acting, extensions in his heels, even a box he had to stand on to kiss Ingrid Bergman.

In his offscreen life, Boyer was anything but a playboy. He married the starlet Pat Patterson three weeks after meeting her: they remained together for 44 years. Two days after her death, Boyer took an overdose of barbiturates and joined her again.

Joseph MAI
Clemson University, South Carolina

Marcel Bozzuffi (1928–1988)

'The Quintessential Marseilles Bad Guy'

Several of the most memorable scenes of William Friedkin's Oscar-winning film, *The French Connection* (1971), feature Marcel Bozzuffi as coldblooded thug Pierre Nicoli. Nicoli is the righthand henchman and assassin working for dapper Marseilles drug lord Alain Charnier (Spanish actor Fernando Rey), whose plan to smuggle heroin via automobile to New York City – based on true criminal events – is eventually uncovered by Detective 'Popeye' Doyle (Gene Hackman, who received the Best Actor Academy Award for his performance). Yet Bozzuffi, as Nicoli, frequently steals the show, such as in the film's opening scene, with his assassination of a plainclothes detective who has been investigating Charnier. Stealthily following his target through the winding streets of Marseilles' Panier district, the city's most ancient neighbourhood, Nicoli effortlessly shoots the man point blank in the entryway of his apartment building. What makes this introductory scene so unforgettable, however, is how, after he has killed his victim, Nicoli casually breaks off a piece of the baguette the dead man still clutches under his arm. Nicoli's brazen violence, in daylight, emblematizes Marseilles' reputation as a locus of brutality and crime. Moreover, Nicoli's misgivings about drug mule Henri Deveraux (Frédéric de Pasquale) – a television anchor and media personality Charnier has selected because of his public profile which allows him to travel freely (based on the real-life television host Jacques Angelvin of *Télé-Paris*[1] and *Paris-Club*, whom director William Friedkin, in the film's DVD commentary calls 'The French Johnny Carson') – are accurate, foreshadowing the operation's failure. However, Nicoli proves to be no match for New York City when the drug ring travels there to deliver their product. In *The French Connection*'s most famous sequence, which is one of the most memorable chases in cinema history, Popeye pursues Nicoli through Brooklyn, first by foot and then by car. The prelude to the chase is Nicoli's failed attempt to assassinate Popeye from the rooftop of a building in Popeye's own apartment complex; Nicoli, fleeing Popeye, commandeers an elevated subway train, taking its conductor and riders hostage on a terrifying joyride. The cool, collected demeanour Nicoli exhibited in Marseilles as he carried out his bloody mission is lost in New York City, as he becomes unhinged, shooting two transit officers while the train hurtles along the tracks without stopping. Popeye catches up, chasing the train by car underneath the elevated subway, during which 'Hackman accents the tenseness of the scene perfectly, pounding on the horn and yelling at pedestrians as he speeds through the streets of Brooklyn, often against oncoming traffic. Friedkin makes terrific use of tracking shots, sometimes showing Hackman zooming underneath the elevated train in a single frame.' [2] After the train crashes, Doyle confronts Nicoli on the subway steps, shooting Nicoli as he attempts to flee; Nicoli collapses, his face twisted in a lurid grimace, arms flailing in desperation, in total contrast to the stone cold confidence he demonstrated at the start of the film which took place on his home turf, the Phocaean City. This final, iconic image of the stricken Nicoli, pitching forward on the subway steps – with Popeye closely behind, gun in hand – has been immortalized on the film's poster. Bozzuffi did his own stunt work when, after being shot, he tumbles down the stairs and lands at Hackman's feet.

It is said of Bozzuffi, 'Never forget the great, prodigious actor of Italian heritage, Marcel Bozzuffi. Whether in Melville, Parrish, or Friedkin, he is *the* quintessential Marseilles bad guy.' [3] Along with *The French Connection*, Bozzuffi appeared in several classic Marseilles-set crime films, such as Costa-Gavras's 1965 *Compartiment tueurs /The Sleeping Car Murders* (Bozzuffi later collaborated with Costa-Gavras on *Z*, 1969, appearing as another bad guy, Vago, who is tasked with assassinating The Deputy, played by Yves Montand); Jean-Pierre Melville's *Le Deuxième Souffle /Second Breath* (1966), as mobster Jo Ricci; as Inspector Blot

in José Giovanni's *Le Gitan /The Gypsy* (1975), and in Robert Parrish's *Marseille contrat /The Destructors* (1974). [4] In Lucio Fulci's 1980 *Luca il contrabbandiere /Luca le contrebandier /Contraband*, the name of the French criminal boss Bozzuffi plays is 'Il Marsigliese' (aka 'the Marseillais'). Bozzuffi directed his *Z* co-star, Jean-Louis Trintignant, in *L'Américain / The American* (1969). Along with writing and directing *L'Américain*, Bozzuffi directed the made-for-television films *Les Grands Ducs* (1982, co-written and co-directed with Patrick Jamain), in which he starred, and *Bon anniversaire Juliette* (1983), with his wife, actress Françoise Fabian, in a leading role. In a career whose highlights include roles in films by directors such as Yves Allégret (*La Meilleure Part / The Best Part*, 1955); Robert Altman (*Images*, 1972); Michelangelo Antonioni (*Identificazione di una donna /Identification d'une femme / Identification of a Woman*, 1982); Marcel Carné (*Le Pays d'où je viens /The Country I Come From*, 1956); Réné Clément (*Le Jour et l'Heure / The Day and the Hour*, 1963); Claude Lelouch (*Un homme qui me plaît / Love is a Funny Thing* and *La Vie, l'amour, la mort /Life Love Death*, both 1969), and Edouard Molinaro (*La Cage aux folles II*, 1980), Bozzuffi is also remembered as the voice of American actors Charles Bronson, Paul Newman, and Robert Duvall, among others, when their films were dubbed into French. Despite often being typecast as the archetypal Marseillais tough guy, Bozzuffi – also an author, whose collection of stories, entitled *Forfana*, was published after his death of a brain haemorrhage – was actually born in Rennes.

Marcelline BLOCK
Princeton University and SAG-AFTRA

1. In 1953 (ten years before Angelvin's conviction in New York), the very young artist Jenny Batlay was interviewed on *Télé-Paris* by hosts Jacques Angelvin and Jacques Chabannes about her recent painting exhibit, in particular, her portrait of Maurice Chevalier. She has fond memories of that interview and was impressed by the tall, redheaded Angelvin, but was very saddened to hear later that Angelvin was convicted of drug possession and imprisoned in the United States in 1963 (he was released four years later, and returned to France where he died in 1978).

2. 'The Five Best Car Chase Scenes in Movie History,' *MovieFanFare*, March 23, 2011, accessed October 6, 2013, http://www.moviefanfare.com/the-five-best-car-chase-scenes-in-movie-history/.

3. Olivier Bohler, 'The Underworld is in His Lands: Marseilles Gangster Films,' in *World Film Locations: Marseilles*, ed. Marcelline Block (Bristol: Intellect, 2013), 49.

4. For further discussion of *The French Connection*, *Le Deuxième Souffle*, *Le Gitan*, and *Marseille contrat*, see Block, *World Film Locations: Marseilles*, 38-39, 46-47, 54-55, 58-59.

Claude BRASSEUR (1936–)

A Deceptive Elephant

SON OF Pierre Brasseur and Odette Joyeux, Claude BRASSEUR grew up under the benevolent gaze of such notables as Simone Signoret, Jean-Paul Sartre, and Ernest Hemingway (his godfather). In addition to a vocation for acting, Claude inherited a mish-mash of talents and physical features from his parents: a great natural fluidity, a diminutive but athletic body (he was part of the French national bobsled team and won the 1983 Paris-Dakar Rally as a co-pilot), an unconventional face (round, a receding hairline, and a large mole just next to the nose), and an immediately recognizable raspy voice. This physiognomy reflects an ambiguity at play in almost all of his roles: he is at once strong and mediocre, aggressive but vulnerable, attractive while somewhat ordinary.

Befitting such a prestigious lineage, Brasseur's career has been diverse in scope (covering stage, television, and cinema), prodigious in number (his filmography includes over a hundred titles), and has spanned at least five decades. He has collaborated with big-name cineastes (Marcel Carné, Georges Franju, Jean Renoir), worked the New Wave (Jean-Luc Godard twice,

François Truffaut), and scored at the box office (with Yves Robert). He has specialized in historical costume pieces (playing Maupassant, Georges Dandin, Fouché opposite Talleyrand in Edouard Molinaro's 1992 *Le Souper /The Supper*, and, famously, François Vidocq on television). He is entirely at home in contemporary melodrama and in daft comedy. Brasseur's career peaked from the mid-1970's to about the mid 1980's, when he starred in hit after hit, and earned several César nominations: for best actor (won for Robin Davis' *La Guerre des polices /The Police War*, 1979) and best supporting actor (twice nominated in 1976, won for Yves Robert's *Un éléphant ça trompe énormément /Pardon Mon Affaire*). During this time, his natural talents were fused with cultural evolution to make him something of an index of a changing masculinity, as can be illustrated with a couple of his exemplary roles.

With his combination of vulnerability and *bon enfant* assertiveness, Brasseur became a perfect foil for the rise of newly empowered women (Godard had already foreseen this in the beautiful scene in the métro in *Bande à part /Band of Outsiders*, 1964, where Brasseur plays a vexed petty criminal eclipsed by the 'stupid' girl he tries to exploit and seduce). One of the landmark victories of the feminist movement was, of course, the granting of abortion rights to women in 1974. In 1978, Claude Sautet concocted the last of his Romy Schneider vehicles, *Une histoire simple /A Simple Story*, in which Schneider decides to dump her lover, abort his baby, and return to her ex-husband (whom she will also leave after becoming pregnant again). Brasseur plays the lover: a balding failure that drinks heavily and generally comes unhinged. In contrast to Schneider, radiant and sturdy centre of the film, Brasseur sweats anxiously throughout and even beats her out of frustration. When Schneider reveals the abortion, he bitterly assents to the ascendency of all women: « c'est toi la femme ».

Brasseur is threatened or over-whelmed by women in many roles of the period. In *Les Seins de glace /Someone is Bleeding* (Georges Lautner, 1974, here the title says it all), he is almost murdered by a psychopathic Mireille Darc (the more handsome and heartless manly man Alain Delon gets to kill her at the end). In *La Guerre des polices*, his copper bravado is a reaction to his wife's departure with their child. A younger female cop admires him and sleeps with him, but she also uses him to obtain information for a rival. The film surrounds him with porn images, suggesting that in the absence of the traditional family, male/female relationships have been reduced to mere sex. Even in the epoch-defining comedy *La Boum / The Party* (Claude Pinoteau, 1980) he plays the curious adolescent Sophie Marceau's genial but overwhelmed father, only to become her drunkard and paunchy husband a few years later in *Descente aux enfers /Descent into Hell* (Francis Girod, 1986).

But the 'war of the sexes' is just one dimension of the crisis in masculinity. Brasseur has, since his bromantic pairing with Jean-Pierre Cassel in Renoir's POW film *Le Caporal épinglé /The Elusive Corporal* (1962), been drawn to parts played in an all-male universe. But if Cassel and Brasseur managed to escape and reassert themselves in 1962 (looking back to the Resistance), by the 1970's it is another story. Brasseur dies of his bravado in *La Guerre des polices*, and his vigilantism is futile against a soulless group of murderers in *Légitime violence* (Serge Leroy, 1982) (perhaps a reference to the 'emasculating' abolition of the death penalty in 1981). *Un éléphant ça trompe énormément* (1976) captures male anxiety in a comic net. The film follows a gang of *copains* reaching middle age and losing their former bearing: one friend has an affair, another loses his wife, and the third is incapable of overcoming his stereotypically overbearing mother. Brasseur's character, outwardly the most macho, turns out to be gay. Brasseur won a César for this discrete and funny performance (two years before Edouard Molinaro's *La Cage aux folles*, 1978). This does not, however, prevent his homosexuality from fitting tightly into an atmosphere of masculine angst and impotence.

Though he has represented these anxieties, Brasseur's work is rarely sombre, and whether a victim or a tyrant, he comes off as likeable. He is perfectly built for all kinds of gags, such as when he revives a real-life routine of his in *Un éléphant*: disguised as a blind man, he walks into a posh restaurant and proceeds to destroy glasses and porcelain with his cane while the polite waiters and bourgeois diners stare in disbelief. Brasseur rescues *Les Seins de glace* from complete humourlessness – no mean feat opposite a Mireille Darc who serves a plate of psychosis with a side of serious malnourishment and a frigid Alain Delon: even while being beaten by thugs he manages to fall eye-first on a corner of a coffee table in a pratfall as much comic as it is violent. But do not write Brasseur off entirely: in later films the adaptable actor has flipped the equation, his raspy voice now emerging from an old body to indicate a stony interior, as witnessed by his cold and vulgar Fouché in *Le Souper* (1992).

Joseph MAI
Clemson University, South Carolina

Pierre BRASSEUR (1905–1972)
[Pierre-Albert ESPINASSE]

A Second Role of First Choice

Pierre Brasseur was born Pierre-Albert Espinasse on December 22, 1905 in Paris, and was raised by his mother whose maiden name he chose as his stage name. He spent his childhood in a boarding school in Montlhéry. In his autobiography, *Ma vie en vrac* (Calmann-Lévy, 1972), he gives comical details of these experiences, with mentors, women, figures of authority, and theatre. Indeed, above all, Brasseur was a man of theatre: 'by age twenty Brasseur had become a star of light stage comedy. From the 1920s through the 1940s he wrote successful comedies as well as acted in them.' [1] Brasseur wrote several plays: *L'Ancre noire* (1927), *Sainte Cécile* (1944), *Un ange passe* (1943), and *L'Enfant de Poméranie* (1945). His most notable interpretations are in *Le Sexe faible* by Edouard Bourdet, and in plays by Jean-Paul Sartre, such as *Les Mains sales*, *Le Diable et le Bon Dieu* and his adaptation of Alexandre Dumas's play, *Kean*. Brasseur worked closely with *monstres sacrés* such as Louis Jouvet, Henry de Montherlant, Sartre, and Boris Vian.

Brasseur's artistic surroundings were enlivened by encounters with talent and genius. In *Ma vie en vrac*, he mentions his friendship with the great Marcel Dalio (who starred in Renoir's *La Grande Illusion* /*Grand Illusion* (1937), Yves Allégret's *Dédée d'Anvers* /*Dédée* /*Woman of Antwerp* (1948), and Renoir's *La Règle du jeu* / *The Rules of the Game*, 1939), [2] and his experiences during the amazing 1920s in Montparnasse, such as sharing red wine with Modigliani [3] or stories with Hemingway. [4] He met Jean Cocteau in 1923 and showed great admiration for the prince of poets who dreamed of being an actor. [5] Through Louis Aragon, Brasseur was introduced to the world of Parisian Surrealists. He met with all the leaders of the intellectual scene, such as Paul Eluard, whom he admired, and André Breton, who frightened him, as well as Antonin Artaud, Robert Desnos, and Max Jacob. Brasseur also travelled abroad, for example, to Berlin in the 1920s where he met the devil in person, Hitler. [6] He also travelled to London, where he did some research on Kean, the Shakespearian actor he interpreted in the eponymous play by Sartre. In 1934, he reached New York and its Cotton Club where the first dances of Josephine Baker were born. [7]

His screen debut was in Jean Renoir's 1924 *La Fille de l'eau*. He initially portrayed characters who were gigolos, but that would change with his encounter with the poet who would change the course of his career for the better: 'of his nearly eighty films, many of Brasseur's best were scripted by Prévert.' [8]

On a personal level, he married Odette Joyeux in 1935 and they had a son, the actor Claude Brasseur (b. 1936). They divorced in 1945 and he remarried Lisa Magrini in 1947, before living with singer Catherine Sauvage. He died on August 14, 1972 in Brunico (Italy) of a heart attack during the shooting of *La Plus Belle Soirée de ma vie /The Most Wonderful Evening of My Life* by Ettore Scola. He is buried in the Père Lachaise Cemetery (division 59).

The most famous roles of Brasseur's career are:

1938 – *Le Quai des brumes /Port of Shadows* (Marcel Carné).

Brasseur and one of the greatest names of Poetic Realism, Carné, collaborated on three films from 1938 to 1946. Brasseur portrays 'characters with oversized ego in three of Carné's films, *Le Quai des brumes*, *Les Enfants du paradis* and *Les Portes de la nuit*.' [9] In what is probably the 'masterpiece' [10] of Poetic Realism, Brasseur interprets Lucien, the gangster who stands between the beautiful blue-eyed and lost-souls couple of Jean (Jean Gabin) and Nelly (Michèle Morgan). His character does not appear in Mac Orlan's novel, but here it helps to reinforce the contrast between Jean's masculinity and humanity. Weak and pitiful, Lucien is never able to talk back or to fight against Jean. Jealous, he will eventually shoot him in the back, to prevent his departure for Venezuela and end his dream of a sunny paradise, far from the titular port of shadows.

1942 – *Lumière d'été* (Jean Grémillon).

Cricri (Madeleine Renaud) is a former opera dancer who now owns an inn in Provence and is courted by Patrice (Paul Bernard). Michèle (Madeleine Robinson) arrives at the inn to wait for her lover, the painter Roland Maillard (Brasseur). Patrice falls in love with Michèle, fanning Cricri's jealousy. About Grémillon, Brasseur writes: 'He loved actors, from the tiniest to the greatest. He never got angry...he knew what he wanted and he respected authors and interpreted way more than producers... Charming, authoritarian, you were respectable and now you are the regrettable, dear, very dear Grémillon. *Lumière d'été* is a film that resembles you.' [11]

1945 – *Les Enfants du paradis /Children of Paradise* (Marcel Carné).

This other masterpiece of Poetic Surrealism (screenwriter: Jacques Prévert) portrays the tumultuous artistic, romantic scene of 19th-century Paris, bringing together theatre, literature, mimes, music, and love around the eternal figure of Garance (Arletty), loved by four different men: the mime Baptiste (Jean-Louis Barrault), the count of Montray (Louis Salou), the comedian Frédérick Lemaître (Pierre Brasseur), and the intimidating Lacenaire (Marcel Herrand). Lemaître becomes a famous comedian, and his *Othello* is very successful. He is accused by Montray, Garance's husband, of having an affair with his wife, when she is actually seeing the mime Baptiste ...

1958 – *Les Grandes Familles /The Possessors* (Denys de La Patellière).

After the novel by Maurice Druon and a script by Audiard, this film offers a fantastic encounter between a powerful Noël Shoudler (Jean Gabin) and a rejected Lucien Maublanc (Brasseur). In *Ma Vie en vrac*, Brasseur thanks Druon: 'Thank you for *Les Grandes Familles*, astonishing film, superbly interpreted by Gabin, and a bit by me, but nothing more. I love Audiard, he never betrayed the works he adapts (one should say "he adopts"). As for Denys de La Patellière, he has the amiable sharpness and the gravity.' [12]

1960 – *Les Yeux sans visage /Eyes Without a Face* (Georges Franju).

Brasseur and Franju collaborated on three features, *La Tête contre les murs /Head Against the Wall* (1959), *Pleins feux sur l'assassin /Spotlight on a Murderer* (1961), and *Les Yeux sans visage* (1960), in which Brasseur interprets Docteur Génessier, a specialist in surgical reconstruction. With his nurse Louise (Alida Valli), they kidnap, kill, and remove the faces of young women in order to give back his daughter (Edith Scob) the face she lost in a car accident. Spanish Director Pedro Almodóvar explained at the 2011 American Film Institute Festival that Dr Génessier is one of the great sources of inspiration for the character of Dr Ledgard (Antonio Banderas), in his *La piel que habito / The Skin I Live In* (2011). Mentioning the lyricism and the elegance of the film, he also described it as 'an exquisite gem of horror cinema.' [13]

It is worth stating that Brasseur's other great collaborations include Christian-Jaque's *Souvenirs perdus / Lost Souvenirs* (1950), *Barbe-Bleue* (1951), *Les Bonnes Causes /Don't Tempt the Devil* (1963), Claude Autant-Lara's *Vive Henri IV…vive l'amour ! / Long Live Henri IV…Long Live Love* (1960), *Le Magot de Josefa /Josefa's Loot*

(1963), *Humour noir /Black Humour* (1965), and Jean-Paul Rappeneau's *La Vie de château /A Matter of Resistance* (1965) and *Les Mariés de l'an deux /The Scoundrel* (1971).

Candice NICOLAS
Loyola Marymount University, Los Angeles

1. Edward Baron Turk, *Child of Paradise: Marcel Carné and the Golden Age of French Cinema* (Cambridge: Harvard University Press, 1989), 261.
2. Pierre Brasseur, *Ma Vie en vrac* (Paris: Calmann-Lévy, 1972), 117-23.
3. Ibid., 133.
4. Ibid., 134.
5. Ibid., 140.
6. Ibid., 219.
7. Ibid., 251.
8. Turk, *Child of Paradise*, 261.
9. Ibid., 12.
10. François Truffaut, 'Une certaine tendance du cinéma français,' *Cahiers du cinéma* 31 (January 1954): 16.
11. Brasseur, 309.
12. Ibid., 308.
13. Pedro Almodovar, personal communication at the American Film Institute Festival.

Jacques BREL (1929–1978)

« Le Plus Grand Belge »

BELGIAN *chanson* star Jacques BREL, one of the most important and influential singer-songwriters of the 20ᵗʰ century, was born on April 8, 1929, in the Brussels municipality of Schaarbeek. Brel's often dark, cynical, and melancholic songs explore mortality, faith, love, and loss, such as *Le Moribond*, in which he tells a buddy that he is going to die, but since the friend was his wife's lover, he trusts that he will take good care of her. His songs also deal with social and political issues, such as poverty, addiction, and war. For Julian Barnes, 'it was Brel's mixture of satire, wisdom, and heart that did it for me: alongside the snarl and the lush contempt was a bursting emotionalism, a celebration of love as *la tendre guerre*, an aching sympathy for the weak, the lost, the *amputés de cœur*, … bundling you up in that rich gargly tonsilly voice and whirling you round in his thrilling taunts and joyous dreams.' ¹ Brel influenced Anglophone *chansonniers* including Leonard Cohen – whose style differs widely from that of Brel – and David Bowie. Among Brel's iconic songs are *Amsterdam*, an emotional rendering of the sailors on leave in this Dutch port; *Marieke*; *Mathilde*; *Madeleine*; and his classic *Ne me quitte pas* /'Don't

Leave Me,' in which the singer pleads with a lover not to abandon him. This song is one of Brel's best known, and has been performed by many artists, including American singer Mary J. Blige at the February 2014 White House State dinner held by US President Barack Obama in honour of French President François Hollande. In 2013, at age 86, Juliette Gréco, co-writer with Brel of his *Ne me quitte pas* (among other works), released the album *Gréco Chante Brel*, in which she interprets 12 of his most iconic songs, such as *Amsterdam* and *Bruxelles*. In a two-day concert in May 2014, Gréco performed songs from this recording at the Olympia in Paris.

As a singer, Brel toured the world tirelessly for years, and because of the extraordinary intensity of his performances (his profuse sweating was legendary), he was physically exhausted – 'down there, on that familiar equine face, the sweat famously poured: Brel was said to lose 800 gm during a recital.' ² Yet, despite his immense success and influence – including sold-out concerts at prestigious venues such as Bobino and the Olympia in Paris, as well as Carnegie Hall, numerous awards, and tours around the world – Brel decided, in the summer of 1966, to forego singing live (finishing any outstanding contracts until 1967 and continuing to record albums, four in total) in order to pursue other interests, in particular, acting in film.

Brel organized a goodbye tour that led him around the world, with farewell concerts from 1966-1967 at the Paris Olympia, the Palais des Beaux-Arts in Brussels, London's Royal Albert Hall, and Carnegie Hall in New York City; his last concert was held on May 16, 1967, in Roubaix, France.

Immediately after quitting performing *chanson*, Brel embarked on a career in film acting and directing (he had previously appeared in the 1956 short film *La Grande Peur de Monsieur Clément*, shot in Brussels, which he co-wrote with director Paul Diebens; and he played himself, alongside Jean-Luc Godard, Anna Karina, and Edouard Molinaro in the short 1960 musical film *Petit jour*, directed by Jackie Pierre). As an actor, he took on a variety of roles, including historical fiction, comedy, and drama, and worked with some major names in the French film industry, including directors Marcel Carné, Claude Lelouch, and Edouard Molinaro, as well as actors such as Bernard Blier, Annie Girardot, Isabelle Huppert, Claude Jade, Emanuelle Riva, and Lino Ventura. As a director, he was nominated for the Palme d'Or at Cannes. Moreover, Brel was commemorated with the 1968 off-Broadway tribute, *Jacques Brel is Alive and Well and Living in Paris* (Eric Blau and Mort Shuman), in which 25 of his songs were translated into English (the show's fifth anniversary gala performance at Carnegie Hall in 1972 was attended by Brel himself). Denis Héroux adapted the musical to screen in 1975. This show has been revived numerous times throughout the 1990s and the 2000s, most recently in Los Angeles in 2010.

Brel's first role in a feature film was in 1967's *Les Risques du métier /Risky Business* (directed by André Cayatte). Here, Brel performed opposite famous French actress Emmanuelle Riva. His character, Jean Doucet, is a schoolteacher, falsely accused of sexual abuse by a female student, after which several other students follow suit. Not only was Brel's acting acclaimed in the film, but also, he was the author of the film's soundtrack, along with his longtime collaborator and friend François Rauber. Next, in 1968, Brel had an important part in *La Bande à Bonnot /Bonnot's Gang* (dir. Philippe Fourastié), in which he played opposite another major French star, Annie Girardot. Again he composed the soundtrack with his friend Rauber. This period piece, taking place in 1911 in Paris, is about the historical Bonnot Gang, a group of anarchists who terrorized France and Belgium between 1911-1912 and who are credited with being the first criminals to escape in a car after committing a crime (after they robbed the Société Génerale Bank in Paris on December 21, 1911). In the film, Brel incarnates the Bonnot Gang member Raymond Callemin, aka 'Raymond la Science' (who, along with several other gang members, was guillotined on April 21, 1913, after refusing to ask for a pardon). Incidentally, Callemin, like Brel, was born in Belgium. A year later, in 1969, Brel played the part of Benjamin in *Mon oncle Benjamin /My Uncle Benjamin* (directed by Edouard Molinaro), set in pre-revolutionary France of the 1750s. Among his co-stars are Bernard Blier (father of director Bertrand Blier) and Claude Jade, star of several of François Truffaut's Antoine Doinel films, including *Baisers volés /Stolen Kisses* (1968), *Domicile conjugal /Bed and Board* (1970), and *L'Amour en fuite / Love on the Run* (1979). Brel, along with François Rauber, composed the soundtrack of *Mon oncle Benjamin*. Brel starred as disgraced cavalry officer Georges Dormond in Jean Valère's 1970 film *Mont-Dragon*, a story of love, seduction, and betrayal. In Marcel Carné's 1971 *Les Assassins de l'ordre /Law Breakers* – one of Carné's later films – Brel had the leading role as Judge Bernard Level, a magistrate investigating police corruption. In the 1972 *L'Aventure, c'est l'aventure /Money, Money, Money*, directed by Claude Lelouch, Brel starred alongside Lino Ventura in this narrative about a group of bank robbers who decide to kidnap high profile victims such as Johnny Hallyday (playing himself) and ambassadors. Also in 1972 Brel had the leading role in the World War I era drama *Le Bar de la fourche /The Bar at the Crossing* (directed by Alain Levent), alongside a young Isabelle Huppert in her first major film role. This film was nominated for the Golden Berlin Bear at the Berlin Film Festival. With Rauber and Gérard Jouannest, Brel composed the film's soundtrack.

In his final film role, Brel would again play opposite Ventura in another work directed by Molinaro, the comedy *L'Emmerdeur /A Pain in the Ass* (1973), for which Brel and Rauber also contributed the soundtrack. Brel stars as François Pignon, the film's titular 'pain,' a man whose wife recently left him and whose subsequent emotional breakdown impacts the life and work of contract killer Milan (Ventura), who is staying in an adjacent hotel room where he is on a contract. This film was adapted from Francis Veber's 1971 play *Le Contrat*, with Veber writing the screenplay for the film adaptation. *L'Emmerdeur* represents a major moment in the history of French cinema, namely, the first time that the character of the endearing loser François Pignon appears onscreen. It was Brel who originated this character, one of the most recognizable in recent French cinema. After *L'Emmerdeur*, different iterations of the hapless François Pignon would recur frequently throughout Francis Veber's *œuvre* (indeed, Pignon is synonymous with Veber's filmography), played by a variety of actors. Some of the most famous examples of the actors who interpret François Pignon in subsequent Veber films include Pierre Richard in *Les Compères* (1983), Jacques Villeret in *Le Dîner de cons /The Dinner Game* (1998; remade in the United States as Jay Roach's 2010 *Dinner for Schmucks*), Daniel Auteuil in *Le Placard /The Closet* (2001), and Gad Elmaleh in *La Doublure /The Valet* (2006). In 2008, Veber remade *L'Emmerdeur*, starring Patrick Timsit as Pignon and Richard Berry as Milan.

Not only was Brel an onscreen presence as an actor, but he also stepped behind the camera to direct films such as the tragic drama *Franz* (1972), which he co-wrote and in which he starred as the recovering wounded Belgian mercenary Léon, opposite French singer Barbara as his love interest Léonie. *Franz* was a commercial disappointment although it received positive criticism. However, Brel's second directorial effort, the comedy *Le Far-West /Far West* (1973) – which, like *Franz*, he also co-wrote with Paul Andréota – was better received, as it was nominated for the Palme d'Or at the Festival de Cannes in 1973. In this film, Brel was influenced by Claude Lelouch (who has an uncredited role as a psychiatrist) and Luis Buñuel. Brel composed the soundtracks for both the films he directed.

A heavy smoker, by 1973, Brel's health was declining, and he would soon be diagnosed with terminal lung cancer, undergoing several operations for it. Brel was aware of the gravity of his condition, and was able, toward the end of his life, to attend his older daughter Chantal's wedding, even though he had abandoned his wife Miche and their three daughters, Chantal, France, and Isabelle for his career – yet he left his entire estate to Miche, whom he never divorced. He spent much of the last years of his life on his yacht *Askoy II*, hoping to sail around the world in three years, travelling to the Azores, the Canary Islands, and the West Indies, periodically returning to Brussels and France where he received medical treatment. He was particularly enamoured with Hiva-Oa, one of the French Polynesian Marquesas Islands, where Paul Gauguin had painted; Brel's final album, *Les Marquises*, is named for the islands. The climate of the islands, due to their humidity, was not recommended for his ailing lungs, yet he continued to live there, with his girlfriend, dancer/actress Maddly Bamy. Brel died in a hospital near Paris on October 9, 1978, at age 49: like so many legendary entertainers, he left this world far too soon. Shortly after his death, his body was returned to Hiva-Oa and interred there in its Calvary Cemetery, which is also the final resting place of Gauguin.

Jacques Brel made major impact in the world of entertainment, as the third bestselling Belgian recording artist in history (following Salvatore Adamo and Frédéric François). Although Brel's legacy is mostly for performing, singing, and songwriting, he also influenced the world of film, not only by being featured on many movie soundtracks, but also in his own filmography as an actor and Palme d'Or nominated director, as well as the first François Pignon, introducing this memorable character to French film spectators. In 2005, on the Belgian television program *Les Plus Grandes Belges /The Greatest Belgians*, Jacques Brel was voted by the francophone public as *Le Plus Grand Belge* : 'The Greatest Belgian.'

Marcelline BLOCK
Princeton University and SAG-AFTRA

1. Julian Barnes, *Something to Declare: Essays on France and French Culture* (Vintage, 2003), 22.
2. Ibid., 25.

Jean-Claude BRIALY (1933–2007)

*Commandeur
of the
Nouvelle
Vague*

JEAN-CLAUDE BRIALY was born in 1933 in Aumale, Algeria. As his father was an officer in the French army, the young Brialy and his family often moved from town to town. Settled in Strasbourg, he obtained his Baccalauréate and successfully took drama studies at the Conservatoire. During his military service, he worked at the Cinematographic Centre of the Armies, thus discovering cinema from within.

Leaving for Paris in 1955, Brialy made his debuts as an actor in 1956, in *Elena et les hommes /Elena and Her Men* (Jean Renoir) and two short movies, *Le Coup du Berger* by Jacques Rivette and *La Sonate à Kreutzer* by Eric Rohmer. He quickly found his place in the early *Nouvelle Vague*, including one of the leading roles in what is often termed the 'first' New Wave film, Claude Chabrol's *Le Beau Serge* (1958), alongside Gérard Blain as the titular character (a year later, Blain and Brialy again performed opposite each other in Chabrol's *Les Cousins*). New Wave actors and film directors appreciated his manners, wit, lightness, and charm. He performed in Louis Malle's first two movies (*Ascenseur pour l'échafaud /Elevator to the Gallows*, 1958, and *Les Amants /The Lovers*, 1958) and appeared in *Les Quatre Cents Coups /The 400 Blows* (François Truffaut, 1959)

and *Paris nous appartient /Paris Belongs to Us* (Jacques Rivette, 1958). Collaboration with film directors issued from the *Nouvelle Vague* continued until the 1970s.

Throughout his entire career, Brialy met and made friends with the most important French and international actors and film directors of the time. He was often caricatured for his boasting of it. More deeply, however, Brialy felt early on a duty to recall great figures from the past to the present. He admired older actors such as Arletty and Jean Gabin, with whom he was delighted to act in relative flops (respectively *Et ta soeur*, Maurice Delbez, 1958, and *L'Année sainte /Holy Year*, Jean Girault, 1976). He also reconnected with the late Jules Berry, one of his models, by assuming the role of the charming 'gentleman thief' Arsène Lupin (*Arsène Lupin contre Arsène Lupin /Arsène Lupin vs. Arsène Lupin*, Edouard Molinaro, 1962; and a 1980 TV mini-series, *Arsène Lupin joue et perd*). He wrote anthologies and memoirs, endlessly fighting against oblivion.

Brialy's first major role was in *L'Ami de la famille /A Friend of the Family* (Claude Pinoteau, 1957). But *Le Beau Serge* (Claude Chabrol, 1958) was his public revelation: returning to his home village, his character tries to help, heal, and redeem his formerly charismatic friend Serge (Gérard Blain), now a shameful and pathetic alcoholic. The pair of actors then appeared together in *Les Cousins /The Cousins* (Chabrol, 1958) where Brialy, as a festive law student, is a Luciferian mix of brightness and sarcasm against his pure, innocent, and laborious cousin who came from the farm to study at La Sorbonne. In 1961, he symbolizes, in a light manner, the ambivalent position of an individualistic young man confronted with the desire of his girlfriend Angela (Anna Karina) to bear a child, be it with him or another man (Jean-Paul Belmondo) in Jean-Luc Godard's *Une femme est une femme /A Woman is a Woman*. In 1961, he is the model of a very useless and charming Parisian *beau-parleur* (*Les Lions sont lâchés /The Lions are Loose*, Henri Verneuil) seducing the gorgeous Claudia Cardinale but revealing himself a poor lover.

Brialy appreciated beautiful women. In *Le Genou de Claire /Claire's Knee* (Eric Rohmer, 1970), he played a settled man, about to be married, suddenly troubled by the deep sensuality of young women. Brialy, though, never hid his homosexuality. He remained very active in promoting the fight against AIDS. He also often played ambiguous or clearly homosexual characters. In 1970, he was the poet Paul Verlaine, with Terence Stamp as Rimbaud (*Una stagione all'inferno /A Season in Hell*, Nelo Risi). In 1976, his performance as a dandy, melancholic prosecutor (*Le Juge et l'Assassin /The Judge and the Assassin*, Bertrand Tavernier) won him a César for best supporting actor. In a scene of *La Nuit de Varennes /That Night in Varennes* (Ettore Scola, 1982), he makes the disastrous passing of time most palpable, as a young effeminate hairdresser who gets to speak to the old and puffy Casanova (Marcello Mastroianni). In *Les Innocents /The Innocents* (André Téchiné, 1987), he is an alcoholic, gay music conductor – a role which won him another César for best supporting actor.

Brialy was also good in comedic roles, because of his firefly-like acting. He was very popular in *Le Roi de cœur /King of Hearts* and *Julie pot de colle /Julie Gluepot* (Philippe de Broca,

1966 and 1977). By contrast, he, who hated vulgarity, found himself most successfully cast against type in *S'en fout la mort /No Fear, No Die* (Claire Denis, 1990), where he is a filthy nightclub owner organizing dangerous cock-fights. In the baroque and controversial *La Reine Margot /Queen Margot* (Patrice Chéreau, 1994), he appears as the brutal Amiral de Coligny, though only in a supporting role.

Brialy was a sensible and talented film director, paying homage to his own childhood and family (*Églantine*, 1972, won a Silver Concha in San Sebastian), to moments of history (*Les Volets clos /Closed Shutters*, 1973, describes life in brothels in the 1930s) or to past writers (*L'Oiseau rare /A Rare Bird*, 1973, is inspired by Sacha Guitry, while *Les Malheurs de Sophie*, shot for television in 1981, and the popular movie *Un bon petit diable* in 1983, adapt novels by the Countess of Ségur). He also directed TV films until 2006, and, as an actor, mostly appeared on television from 1990 onwards.

Jean-Claude Brialy loved life in all its positive forms: elegance, wit, seduction, sensuality, joy. A man of theatre, he organized the festivals of Anjou and Ramatuelle. He had been the director of the Théâtre Hébertôt and the Bouffes Parisiens. His dramatic sense for the frailty of life made him play many roles treating what bites and bitters men: alcohol, burning passion (*Le Gigolo /The Gigolo*, Jacques Deray, 1960), melancholia, old age. For reasons of discretion, he decided to keep his cancer a secret to his friends and family until his death on 30th May 2007.

Nicolas RIGAUD
The University of Oxford

Guillaume CANET (1973–)

*Riding
the Horse
of Fame
and Success*

GUILLAUME CANET's passion for horses comes from his family background. As the son of horse breeders, he was brought up mostly in the countryside near Paris and hoped to be a professional equestrian, but a bad fall ended that dream. After a successful stage career and enrolling in the famous Cours Florent, he made his cinema debut in Philippe Landoulsi's short *Fils unique* (1995). In 2001, he appeared alongside Gérard Depardieu in the fantasy film *Vidocq* (Pitof, 2001). He rose to fame in Danny Boyle's *The Beach* (2000) co-starring Leonardo Di Caprio and Virginie Ledoyen. Canet later earned positive reviews for his performances in *Jeux d'enfants /Love Me If You Dare* (Yann Samuell, 2003) with Marion Cotillard, his real-life partner since 2007, with whom he has a child (son Marcel, born May 19, 2011); in the World War I drama *Joyeux Noël /Merry Christmas* (Christian Carion, 2005), and in the French comedy *Ensemble, c'est tout /Hunting and Gathering* (Claude Berri, 2007) with Audrey Tautou.

Along with being an acclaimed actor, this natural heart-throb is also very successful as a film director – with films like *Mon idole /Whatever You Say* (2002), his first feature as a director (which he also co-wrote),

starring his first wife, German actress Diane Kruger; *Ne le dis à personne / Tell No One* (2006), starring François Cluzet and Kristin Scott Thomas, for which he won the César for Best Director; the friendship movie drama *Les Petits Mouchoirs /Little White Lies* (2010); and the family drama *Blood Ties* (2013). With Marina Hands and Daniel Auteuil, he returned as a horse rider in Christian Duguay's equestrian drama *Jappeloup* (2013). More recently, he starred opposite Catherine Deneuve in André Téchiné's latest film, the 2014 drama *L'Homme qu'on aimait trop /In the Name of My Daughter*, which was screened out of competition at that year's Cannes Film Festival.

In *Icon*, the upcoming Lance Armstrong biopic, directed by Irish director Stephen Frears, Canet plays Italian physician and cycling coach Michele Ferrari, who worked with Armstrong and other cyclists. Dr Ferrari was found guilty of doping by Italian and US authorities, ultimately receiving a lifetime ban from sports. This film, in post-production in 2014, stars Ben Foster as Armstrong, Jesse Plemons as Floyd Landis, and Chris O'Dowd as sports journalist David Walsh.

With his chiselled features, Guillaume Canet is more than just a *belle gueule du cinéma*. He is a multitasking, talented artist, an accomplished actor and director, as well as a natural equestrian.

Michaël ABECASSIS
*The University of Oxford
and*
Marcelline BLOCK
Princeton University and SAG-AFTRA

Julien CARETTE (1897–1966)

*Too Short
to Play
the
Leading
Man*

H E WAS SHORT, Julien CARETTE (born Julien Henri Carette [1] in 1897), too short to serve in the military, too short to play the role of the leading man. Jean Renoir once jokingly remarked that Carette was as tall as a marionette, a slight exaggeration as he was nevertheless five feet three inches tall. For some of his directors (Roger LeBon, Reinhold Schünzel, Richard Pottier) his stature as well as his gestures made him the best choice for roles that required cross-dressing. During the thirties, Carette successfully pushed the boundaries of gender. In the early thirties, while working in the film studios in Berlin, he was chosen for the musical comedy *Georges et Georgette* (Roger Le Bon and Reinhold Schünzel, 1934), playing an impoverished ham cross-dressing on stage. The original German version *Viktor und Viktoria* (Reinhold Schünzel, 1933) was also lucratively adapted for the British market as *First a Girl* (Victor Saville, 1935). Carette was so effective in this role that Pottier asked him to play in *Fanfare d'amour /Fanfare of Love* (1935), as one of two hapless musicians who dress up as women to garner jobs in an all-female orchestra; of course, Billy Wilder remade it as *Some Like it*

Hot (1959), starring Marilyn Monroe. It is, however, in Renoir's *La Grande Illusion* (1937), in which Carette plays an actor putting on a musical show in a German WWI prisoners' camp that normative gender notions are brought into question. Carette plays Cartier, a comical male singer, surrounded by tall British male prisoners dressed as women, who let go of their female alter ego once they hear of a French victory, and together with Carette and all the other male prisoners begin singing *La Marseillaise*. By centering the beginning of the rebellion on cross-dressers and a mawkish male, Renoir invites the viewer to question 1930s perceptions of gender roles and the values that accompany them. As Carette states in one of his later films (*Archimède, le clochard /The Magnificent Tramp*, Gilles Grangier, 1959), playing the role of the clever clochard Félix: 'You shouldn't trust the physical appearance of people.'

Julien Carette was born in Paris, December 23, 1897. He initially dreamt of pursuing a career as a painter and for a while attended the *École des arts décoratifs* where he developed a friendship with Claude Autant-Lara. However, he soon realized that he was not cut out for this profession. Instead, he attempted theatre. Carette auditioned, unsuccessfully, for the Conservatoire, and eventually got a job as an extra at the Théâtre de l'Odéon, where they accepted him despite his height as all male extras had been drafted because of the war. Initially, he had to dabble in many professions and take on various 'roles,' before being able to begin a real acting career. But all this prepared him well for the many character roles his directors would ask him to play. Eventually, his persistence paid off; he received acting roles on stage and in silent movies, but it was really with the talkies that his career took off. His musical and comedic talent as well as his plebeian accent worked wonders. While today's viewers might be more ambivalent about the slapstick quality of his early films such as *L'Affaire est dans le sac /It's in the Bag* (Pierre Prévert, 1932), the humorous quality of his later films appears more timeless: *Sylvie et le fantôme /Sylvia and the Ghost*, Autant-Lara, 1946; *L'Auberge rouge /The Red Inn*, Autant-Lara, 1951; *Archimède, le clochard*, Gilles Grangier, 1959. In these films he would essentially play a funny male oddball, a major supporting role. In *L'Auberge rouge* the lead is played by Fernandel and in *Archimède* the lead is played by Jean Gabin, who according to Bernard Tavernier would be well remunerated. Carette was hence quite an expensive actor, but also someone whose popularity would significantly contribute to the financial success of any film.

It was most likely Renoir who enabled Carette to broaden his repertoire as an actor, casting him in less comical roles, which would allow him to play characters such as the volunteer, the loyal comrade or the poacher /servant (*La Marseillaise*, 1938; *La Bête humaine*, 1938; *La Règle du jeu /The Rules of the Game*, 1939).

During the Occupation years, Carette rekindled his friendship with Autant-Lara. The two would begin a close working relationship that would last throughout the rest of Carette's cinema career. Famous Autant-Lara films such as *Sylvie et le fantôme* (1946), *Occupe-toi d'Amélie..! /Keep an Eye on Amelia* (1949), *L'Auberge rouge* (1951), and *La Jument verte /The Green Mare* (1959) all showcased Carette.

Carette was truly one of the few actors who transitioned seamlessly from the 1930s to the German Occupation to the post war years. He acted in over a hundred films and worked with a large number of French film directors including the Prévert brothers, Marc Allégret, Yves Allégret, Henri Decoin, Pierre Caron, Jean Grémillon, and Julien Duvivier. Carette, well aware of the fact that spectators are too easily taken in by appearances, ended his filming career when he was diagnosed with a severe form of arthritis. In a last ironic twist, Carette who had his break-through in cinema dressing up in women's clothes, died tragically trapped in a wheelchair, wearing a nylon shirt that had caught fire.

Elisabeth-Christine MUELSCH
*Angelo State University,
San Angelo, Texas*

1. *Editor's note:* Many sources have incorrectly indicated that 'Julien Carette' was an adopted stage name (with the actor's birth name variously given as Victor Jullien, Victor Julien, and Julien Victor). However, his birth records in Paris show that he was born (on 23 December 1897) Julien Henri Carette, son of Félix Marius Carette and Valentine Véronique [née] Oursel.

Jean CARMET (1920–1994)

*A
Life(time)
in the
Service
of Acting*

JEAN CARMET was born on April 25, 1920, in Bourgueil, near Tours. Realizing that acting was his true vocation, he interrupted his studies at a fairly young age and left for Paris to begin his acting career. Like many other actors, he started at the bottom of the acting ladder, as an extra for the Théâtre du Châtelet and then the Opéra.

After working as a stage manager intern for a while at the Théâtre des Mathurins, he realized that he could put his acting talent to good use in film. He started, once again, as an extra or playing minor parts in several movies in the 1940s: *Le Pavillon brûle* (1941) and *Les Mystères de Paris /The Mysteries of Paris* (1943) by Jacques de Baroncelli; *Les Visiteurs du soir /The Devil's Envoys* (1942) and *Les Enfants du paradis / Children of Paradise* (1945) by Marcel Carné; *François Villon* (1945) by André Zwobada; *Les Démons de l'aube /Dawn Devils* (1946) by Yves Allégret; *Copie conforme /Confessions of a Rogue* (1947) by Jean Dréville; *Monsieur Vincent* (1947) by Maurice Cloche; and *Bonheur en location* (1949) by Jean Wall, among others.

Towards the end of the 1940s, Jean Carmet joined the Branquignols, a group of comedians founded by Robert Dhéry and Colette Brosset, which included Louis de Funès, Michel

Serrault, Jean Lefebvre, Micheline Dax, Annette Poivre, Jacqueline Maillan, and Jacques Legras. Carmet starred in the theatre play *Les Branquignols* (1948) at the Théâtre La Bruyère, and in the movies *Branquignol /Crazy Show* (1949) and *La Patronne /The Patron* (1949), both directed by Robert Dhéry.

In the 1950s, French audiences become accustomed to Carmet's voice in his role as Gaston Duvet in the radio show series *La Famille Duraton* – an extremely popular show which focused on the daily lives of characters resembling ordinary French people, first broadcast on Radio Cité in 1937, and discontinued in 1966, when Radio Andorre stopped broadcasting it. During the 1950s, Carmet also acted in movies such as *Dieu a besoin des hommes /God Needs Men* (1950) by Jean Delannoy; *Knock* (1951), *Elle et moi /She and Me* (1952), and *Bonjour la chance* (1957) by Guy Lefranc; *Le Vicomte de Bragelonne /The Last Musketeer* (1954) by Fernando Cerchio; *La Madelon* (1955), *Mademoiselle et son gang* (1957) by Jean Boyer, and *La Bigorne, caporal de France* (1958) by Robert Darène, to name only a few.

The following decade, Carmet continued his collaboration with Robert Dhéry in *La Belle Américaine* (1961) and *Allez France* (1964), and with Guy Lefranc in *L'Auvergnat et l'autobus* (1969). He starred in several movies directed by Jean Renoir: in *Le Caporal épinglé* (1962) and *Le Petit Théâtre de Jean Renoir* (1970); also in *Les Trois Mousquetaires : Première époque – les ferrets de la reine* (1961) by Bernard Borderie; *Nous irons à Deauville* (1962) by Francis Rigaud; *Mélodie en sous-sol /Any Number Can Win* (1963) by Henri Verneuil; *La Bourse et la Vie* (1965) by Jean-Pierre Mocky; *Un idiot à Paris* (1967) by Serge Korber; *Alexandre le bienheureux*

(1968) by Yves Robert; and *Une veuve en or* by Michel Audiard (1969).

By the 1970s, Jean Carmet had become an established actor, and the many roles that he incarnated during this decade (and beyond) are proof of his growing fame. He starred in several movies by Claude Chabrol, such as *La Rupture /The Breach* (1970), *Juste avant la nuit /Just Before Nightfall* (1971), *Alice ou la dernière fugue /Alice or the Last Escapade* (1977), and *Violette Nozière* (1978). He became a constant presence in Michel Audiard's movies, starring in *Elle boit pas, elle fume pas, elle drague pas, mais... elle cause ! /She Does Not Drink, Smoke, or Flirt, But... She Talks* (1970), *Le Cri du cormoran le soir au-dessus des jonques /Cry of the Cormoran* (1971), *Le Drapeau noir flotte sur la marmite /The Black Flag Waves Over the Scow* (1971), *Elle cause plus... elle flingue /She No Longer Talks, She Shoots* (1972), *Comment réussir quand on est con et pleurnichard /How to Make Good When One Is a Jerk and a Crybaby* (1974), and others. In 1972, he starred as Maurice Lefebvre in Yves Robert's (commercially) successful movie *Le Grand Blond avec une chaussure noire /The Tall Blond Man with One Black Shoe* and in the sequel *Le Retour du grand blond /The Return of the Tall Blond Man with One Black Shoe* (1974). In 1976, Carmet was cast as Antoine Robineau in Jean-Jacques Annaud's *La Victoire en chantant (noirs et blancs en couleurs) /Black and White in Color*. Two years later, he played the part of Adrien Courtois in Jacques Rouffio's *Le Sucre* – a role which earned him a nomination for Best Actor and Best Supporting Actor at the Césars in 1979.

French audiences were used to seeing Jean Carmet play the role of an average Frenchman finding himself in silly or absurd situations. However, over time, Jean Carmet diversified his acting to include comedic as well as dramatic roles. In the 1980s and 1990s, critical recognition came for Carmet in the form of several prestigious cinema awards and nominations. In 1983, he won the César for Best Supporting Actor for his role as Thénardier in Robert Hossein's 1982 *Les Misérables*. In 1987, he was nominated for Best Supporting Actor for his role as Martin in Francis Veber's 1986 *Les Fugitifs /Fugitives*; the following year, he was nominated again for a César, this time for Best Actor for his starring role in Mehdi Charef's *Miss Mona* in 1987. In 1991, he earned the Sept d'Or (a French television award similar to the Emmy) for Best Actor in the two-part series *Bouvard et Pécuchet* (Jean-Daniel Verhaeghe), based on Flaubert's novel, in which he starred as Pécuchet. The following year, he received the César for Best Supporting Actor for his role as an old father in Bertrand Blier's *Merci la vie* (1991). He also received an Honorary César in 1994, as well as a post-mortem Sept d'Or for Best Actor for his role as Félix Grandet in the televised film *Eugénie Grandet* (Jean-Daniel Verhaeghe, 1994), adapted from Balzac.

Carmet died on April 20, 1994, and many actors and directors came to pay their last homage at the Montparnasse cemetery. In 1999, the editor Plon published *Je suis le badaud de moi-même*, a book written by Carmet before his death. Ten years after Carmet's death, his son Jean-François Carmet published a book entitled *Carmet intime* (a play on words, since '*carnet intime*' means personal or intimate diary), dedicated to the memory of the great French actor.

Cristian BRATU
Baylor University, Texas

Jean-Claude Carrière (1931–)

*From
Burlesque
to
Buñuel*

Jean-Claude Carrière (born Jean-Claude François Carrière, 19th September 1931 in Colombières-sur-Orb, Hérault, France) is a screenwriter, novelist, playwright, and actor. The screenwriter is a typically invisible species, absent from publications on the cinematic medium; instead, academic consideration and critical reviews are preoccupied with the influences of the director, the auteur, and the star. In the case of Carrière, the screenwriter works in a process of collaboration with the director: the two formulate ideas and create a coherent vision. It is Carrière's role as a screenwriter to transfer these collaborative ideas on paper.

Carrière made the transition from a literary background to the film industry, after having been selected to write a story based on Jacques Tati's *Les Vacances de M. Hulot /Monsieur Hulot's Holiday* (1953), a film that had been released eight years previously. It was this nascent relationship with Tati that introduced Carrière to the filmmaking medium. Tati's influence formed the early career and screenwriting techniques of Carrière, emphasizing the art of observation and contemplation as a method for creating and developing scenes. Tati's films are developed in his psyche from life that takes place around him and from what he could witness, and, as a consequence, mime is heavily engaged with in his corpus of films. The ossification of Tati's influence is evident in Carrière's first two short films, which were directed by another member of Tati's constellation of film talent, Pierre Étaix (born 1928). Étaix had previously worked as Tati's first assistant. These two short films, *Rupture* (1961) and *Heureux anniversaire /Happy Anniversary* (1962), garnered a positive reputation for Carrière as screenwriter, launching his film career on both a national and international scale: the latter film won the Oscar for best short in 1962. These short films consequently cultivated an emerging wave of burlesque and slapstick comedies à la française.

Both *Rupture* and *Heureux anniversaire* provide a French accent to the Buster Keaton-esque silent era slapstick comedies. The shorts are formulated by a string of slapstick events borne out of everyday situations. For example, *Heureux anniversaire* charts the events of a man as he attempts to buy a gift for his wife on his way home, and *Rupture* outlines the problems in writing a letter in reply to his lover. Comedy is derived from a subversion of expectations and a comedic interpretation of the French poetic realist cinematic tradition of pessimism and fatalism, which encapsulated the mood that pervaded France in the 1930s. For instance, towards the conclusion of *Rupture*, the spectator is lured into expecting the male protagonist's suicide: a gun is drawn and cocked, epitomizing the doomed protagonist embracing his inevitable fate (that he will never complete his letter). The gun is, however, revealed to be a cigarette dispenser, and the main character dies moments later, after slipping on the spilt ink and falling to his death out of his window. Carrière and Étaix's translation of the American burlesque movement pertains to the next dimension of Carrière's film career, since the surrealist movement had a level of imbrication, and a degree of kinship, with the slapstick and burlesque genre.

The Buñuelian period of Carrière's corpus of works began in May 1963 at the Cannes Film Festival, after the completion of Carrière's first feature length production, *Le Soupirant /The Suitor* (Pierre Étaix, 1962). At the time, Buñuel was searching for a French writer to adapt Octave Mirbeau's 1900 book *Le Journal d'une femme de chambre /Diary of a Chambermaid* into a feature film production. Both Buñuel and Carrière originated from a Mediterranean heritage, in addition to having similar Catholic educational experiences. This background led to his inclusion, beyond the writing stage, to the screen in Buñuel's filmic opuses, since he played the role of a priest in Buñuel's 1964 film *Diary of a Chambermaid* and the role of a heretic bishop in *La Voie lactée /The Milky Way* (1969). These roles necessitated the articulation of Latin, which Carrière was able to master.

The French corpus of Buñuel's work, in particular in collaboration with Carrière, critiqued the ideal of Spanish morality and Spanish bourgeois values. The French language, actors, and film location facilitated a prism through which Buñuel was

able to explore his exilic journeying and banishment from Spain under the Franco regime. The film *Diary of a Chambermaid* concentrates upon the French bourgeoisie, and could be interchangeable with the perception of the Spanish bourgeoisie, from which Buñuel derives. They are perceived as static and immobile, trapped inside their bourgeois microcosm, alienated from external influences. This critiques the bourgeoisie, postulating that they have no hope and suffer from tedium by means of repetition. *The Milky Way* is set against the Spanish pilgrimage to Santiago, a tradition conceived in order to purge one's sins and receive divine blessing. During this odyssey, the film draws upon the politics of heretics and a theology of the Church's suppression of these heresies.

This quest is dictated by the heresies and the dogmas of Catholicism, deconstructing the contemporary and traditional views of the religion as the film progresses. The film is set in France and its language is French, despite its narrative setting in Spain, which thus necessitates the inclusion of Carrière in the writing and development stages of the project. The religious and Catholic subject matter is a point of imbrication between the auteur, Buñuel, and the screenwriter, Carrière, due to their shared educational experiences. The film is additionally infused with French influences and points of comparison, since it is a multi-strand opus that experiments with narrative forms. This inspiration is derived from its contemporary films by Alain Resnais, *Hiroshima mon amour* (1959) and *L'Année dernière à Marienbad /Last Year at Marienbad*

(1961), in addition to Jean-Luc Godard's *Made in U.S.A.* (1966) and *Week-end / Weekend* (1967). The Buñuel-Carrière film projects thus exist as a convergence of not only French and Spanish dialectics, but also represent the meeting of two components of a film industry with shared histories, heritages and cultures. This was salient for the auteur, Buñuel, since Carrière provided much of the writing for this corpus of works, and therefore needed to share a degree of mental kinship.

The Buñuel-Carrière collaborations focus upon the absurdities of two key tropes: bourgeois life and Surrealism. The notion of absurdity has pervaded Carrière's corpus of works, in particular from the burlesque to the Buñuel period. His engagement in burlesque *à la française* enabled his most prolific and successful collaboration with Luis Buñuel, which comprised nine manuscripts and six completed feature format movies. His collaborations with the notable filmmakers Jacques Tati and Luis Buñuel influenced his writing style in polarized ways. Tati championed reality and observation as the source of his filmic creations, whereas Buñuel believed that imagination is a muscle that needs to be trained. Creativity and inventiveness were at the centre of his opuses. This combination of influences created a prolific screenwriter with a prominent place in the French film industry.

Jamie STEELE
University of Exeter

Maria CASARÈS (1922–1996)
[María Victoria CASARES PÉREZ]

Enchantress's Charms

ALTHOUGH MARIA CASARÈS may not be as much of a household name as, for instance, Jean Gabin or Jean Marais, her image is nonetheless instantly etched in the memory of whoever has seen her act or perform: an upright, statuesque, intense, and beautiful woman (green eyes, piercing in black and white photography, mesmerising in colour), with classical inflections in her voice. These all served to translate onto the screen the most direct and most real – but also the darkest – emotions, passions and sufferings of the human heart.

It is, however, difficult to account for Maria CASARÈS's cinematic career and the place she holds amongst twentieth-century actors, so complex was her relationship with cinema. The effects she had on it are, although subtle, undeniable. Casarès herself remained somewhat detached from cinema: she wrote, in *Résidente privilégiée* (the memoirs she published in 1980), that 'cinema is not [her] adventure.' Indeed, her name and her entire life remain linked to the theatre (to the extent that, in her personal mythology, she claimed to have been born in November 1942 on the stage of the Théâtre des Mathurins). As much for the variety as for the quality of her interpretations, Casarès is regarded as one of the most talented tragédiennes of the second half of the twentieth century: she not only performed the great classical authors (Shakespeare, Marivaux), but also took part in numerous creations of contemporary theatre (Strindberg, Genet, Copi, Koltès); in so doing, Casarès took on some of the most famous roles (Lady Macbeth, Mother Courage, Phaedra, Medea) and won, in 1989, the Molière prize for 'best actress' for her role in *Hecuba* by Euripides. Maria Casarès really stands in the tradition of other theatrical greats such as Sarah Bernhardt or Ludmilla Pitoëff. However, we also remember Maria Casarès's name through cinema – and, beyond the name, a voice and a face so striking that they resonate long after the curtains have fallen over the screen. Throughout her career, she graced and served (in the truest sense of the word) several French cinematic masterpieces.

María Victoria Casares Pérez was born in A Coruña (Spain) on 21 November 1922. Her father was an important Republican politician and her family left Spain when Franco came to power. In Paris, Maria Casarès learnt French and discovered theatre. At the Conservatoire National d'Art Dramatique, she followed Béatrix Dussane's classes – incidentally, whilst she failed her first entrance examination on the grounds of 'approximate grasp of the French language' and 'dreadful delivery,' we now remember her for her mastery of the French language and its rhythm, as well as for her distinctive diction. In 1944, Casarès met Albert Camus. Until his accidental death she remained his mistress as well as the favoured actress for his plays (*Le*

Malentendu ['The Misunderstanding'], 1943; *L'État de siège* ['State of Siege'], 1948; *Les Justes* ['The Just Assassins'], 1949). Casarès's acting career, and the long list of her roles (both on stage and on screen), also bears witness to two important shifts in post-war French theatre and cinema. On the one hand, it points to the development of quality short films: for example, Casarès will lend her voice to the commentary on *Guernica* (Alain Resnais and Robert Hessens, 1949), *Varsovie, quand même...* (Yannick Bellon, 1954) and *Le Théâtre national populaire* (Georges Franju, 1956); on the other, she took part in both the adventure of the Théâtre National Populaire of Jean Vilar and the Avignon Theatre Festival. Amongst the group of friends who established the latter as one of the major theatre festivals in the world, many will effect the transition between stage and screen (to name but a few: Gérard Philipe, Philippe Noiret, Jeanne Moreau, Georges Wilson). All will contribute to the reinvention of cinema which François Truffaut praised in his famous polemical essay « Une certaine tendance du cinéma français » ['A Certain Tendency in French Cinema'] (January 1954). The same Truffaut, in several film reviews, will refer to 'the' Casarès, hinting both at the exceptional dimension and the exemplary nature of this great lady of cinema. For if her film roles are, all things considered, few and far between, the vast majority of these are remarkable. Indeed, Maria Casarès is an admirable actress not only because of the excellence of her interpretations but also because the roles she chose were always that of exceptional, unconventional, or marginal characters. Her first feature film is widely considered a mythical film of French poetic realism. In *Les Enfants du paradis /Children of Paradise* (Marcel Carné with dialogues by Jacques Prévert, 1945), Casarès plays Nathalie, the daughter of a theatre director; she is married to Baptiste (Jean-Louis Barrault) who has an affair with Garance (Arletty). Casarès, in this film, embodies the betrayed woman and mother, self-effaced but proud, whose courage, verging on the sacrificial, culminates in the confrontation scene when Nathalie catches Baptiste and Garance in an embrace. She wants to 'know everything' and does not shy away from suffering ('everyone suffers'); she makes sense of these emotions for us that no one can truly understand. The martyr's trajectory ('And me, Baptiste? And me?') is, however, somewhat inverted in her second film, *Les Dames du Bois de Boulogne /Ladies of the Park* (Robert Bresson, with dialogues by Jean Cocteau, 1945), based on the story of Madame de la Pommeraye in Denis Diderot's anti-novel *Jacques le fataliste et son maître* (1796). Casarès plays Hélène in what must be her most famous cinematographic role. The heroine, devastated by passion, frustrated and shocked at the idea that her lover, Jean (Paul Bernard), no longer desires her, decides to vilely and cruelly manipulate the one she loves until he weds an ex-cabaret dancer and she shames him to the world. Her face expresses at once vengeance, pleasure, and suffering, all encompassed in one Machiavellian smile which also manages to be full of doubt and tenderness. The close-ups truly convey on film the 'enchantress's charm,' as well as her charms. Casarès moves through the film as a fine

tragedienne, combining two opposite poles that tear her apart; she paints the fury of a murdering semi-goddess who toys with her subjects, mere human beings reduced to the state of objects by an all-destructing Eros.[1]

Classical tragedy is also Casarès's trademark in *La Chartreuse de Parme / The Charterhouse of Parma* (Christian-Jaque, 1948), adapted from Stendhal's novel, in which she plays a delightful and lovely Sanseverina, a role for which she won 'Best Female Interpretation' at the Locarno International Festival. However, it is Jean Cocteau, under whom she had worked for *Les Dames*, who offered Casarès one of her most memorable roles in 1950, and again in 1960. In both *Orphée /Orpheus* and *Le Testament d'Orphée /The Testament of Orpheus*, Casarès is the Princess (Death): both temptress and cruel seductress who leads Orpheus (Jean Marais) to the underworld. Jealousy is, here again, the great motivator as the Princess kills Eurydice; she does, however, sacrifice her own feelings and allows the Poet to remain on Earth. Casarès revisited the role for the *Testament*, still bringing her hoarse and bewildering voice as well as her hands (a manipulator's hands, which Cocteau filmed in close-ups, revealing the tension that is also seen on her face), to a character who is now in the position to judge Orphée/ Cocteau himself. After this film, her screen appearances were rare indeed. For instance, she appeared in Jean-Luc Godard's *Histoire(s) du cinéma* (1988-1998) and, of course, in *La Lectrice /The Reader* (Michel Deville, 1988) in which her superb General's widow, passionate about Marx and Tolstoy, will bring her the César for

Best Supporting Actress. Her final screen appearance was in *Someone Else's America* (Goran Paskaljevic, 1995) where she played the endearing, offbeat mother of the film's hero, with her characteristic spirit. Apart from these notable exceptions, she remained, from the 1960s onwards, mainly a voice on film, lending her deep and passionate delivery to yet more documentaries and short-length films such as *Hieronymus Bosch* (François Weyergans, 1963), *Les Rencontres de Mérimée* (Jacques de Casembroot, 1971) and *Les Deux mémoires* (Jorge Semprún, 1974). But whoever hears this voice (for instance reading Antonin Artaud's texts) will hear a voice that has suffered, travelled, and come back (the Orphic voice *par excellence*). Watching or listening to Maria Casarès today reminds us that cinema, and life, are never far removed from classical tragedy. Casarès not only brought grace, elegance, nobility of heart, generosity of spirit, and some enchantress's charm(s) to cinema, but also revitalized its cathartic function. She died on 22nd November 1996; her house (La Vergne, in Alloue) has been converted to the *Maison du Comédien Maria Casarès*, a place where screen and stage actors come to experiment, exchange, and revive their art. A fitting testimony if ever there was one.

Benjamin ANDRÉO
Monash University, Melbourne

1. See also Marcelline Block, 'Vendetta and Veritas in Diderot's *Madame de la Pommeraye* and Bresson's *Les Dames du Bois de Boulogne*' in Giovanna Summerfield, ed., *Vendetta: Essays on Honor and Revenge* (Newcastle: Cambridge Scholars Publishing, 2011), 93-126. —Ed.

Vincent CASSEL (1966–)
[Vincent CROCHON]

Hothead
For
Hire

BORN VINCENT CROCHON in Paris on 23rd November 1966, CASSEL followed his father Jean-Pierre Cassel (1932-2007) into acting, and most of his films have achieved notoriety both in France and internationally. Though his first appearance in cinema was 1991's *Les Clés du paradis /The Keys to Paradise* (Philippe de Broca), his breakthrough came in Mathieu Kassovitz's *La Haine /Hate* (1995). This powerful film follows a day in the lives of three friends growing up in the deprived Parisian suburbs. Cassel's character, Vinz, is the most volatile of the three, intent on avenging a friend's severe beating at the hands of the police. In an early scene, he re-enacts the mirror scene from Scorsese's *Taxi Driver*, wielding an imaginary gun; this image of apparent adolescent impotence takes on more serious overtones when Vinz later gets his hands on a real gun. *La Haine* was an important film for both Kassovitz and Cassel, garnering success and acclaim both in France and abroad despite being shot in black and white on a low budget (the then prime minister Alain Juppé even organised a compulsory viewing for his cabinet). By the time the two friends next worked together, on *Les*

Rivières pourpres /The Crimson Rivers (2000), their careers had moved into the mainstream. The monochrome of *La Haine* was replaced by the brooding dark reds and blues of a big-budget crime thriller which, despite a fairly involved plot, was another hit at home and abroad. Here Cassel plays Inspector Max Kerkerian, the young gun working with Jean Reno's seen-it-all superintendent to investigate a mysterious murder in the French Alps. Despite the great differences of tone and subject matter between *La Haine* and *Les Rivières pourpres*, Vinz and Max both share a maverick intelligence, short temper, and lack of self-control.

Cassel has also been a secondary character in a number of high-profile productions. He plays the effete villain of *Le Pacte des loups /Brotherhood of the Wolf* (Christophe Gans, 2001), another international box-office success, and has more minor parts in the period-dramas *Elizabeth* (Shekhar Kapur, 1998) and Luc Besson's *The Messenger: the Story of Joan of Arc* (1999). Alongside his penchant for portraying suave aristocrats, Cassel has popped up with increasing frequency in English language films playing European characters. In *Birthday Girl* (Jez Butterworth, 2001), he and Kassovitz are the sinister associates of Nicole Kidman's Russian mail-order bride; in David Cronenberg's *Eastern Promises* (2007), his character is again Russian, this time the spoilt and unstable son of a mafia boss in London. The connection between these two characters is their volatile natures, a trait shared by Vinz, Max, and other Cassel roles. More recently, Cassel appeared in Darren Aronofsky's

Black Swan (2010) as Thomas Leroy, a prestigious French director who casts fragile ballerina Nina (Natalie Portman) in a performance of *Swan Lake*. While the focus of the film is on Nina's mental disintegration, Leroy's position on the cusp between single-minded professionalism and sadistic manipulation suggest a more controlled direction in which Cassel may take his portrayals of moral ambiguity. A notable exception to this evolution comes in Cassel's most commercial minor role to date, as the jewel thief Night Fox in Steven Soderbergh's *Ocean's Twelve* (2004). This performance played less on Cassel's own cinematic reputation and more on general stereotypes of Frenchness, with the sophisticated yet overly confident Night Fox coming off second best to George Clooney's dream team of con artists.

Moonlighting in Hollywood movies has not distracted Cassel from pursuing his own career as a leading man, and his choice of films has generally seen him portraying anti-heroes, characters on the edge of moral respectability. After the success of *La Haine*, his next major role was in *L'Appartement /The Apartment* (Gilles Mimouni, 1996). His character, Max, is caught between a respectable future with his fiancée and a sense of unfinished business with a previous lover, played by Monica Belucci. It is this morally dubious yet sympathetic character's intrusion into the titular flat which sets in motion the subsequent developments of the narrative. This is also the first of several collaborations between Cassel and Belucci, who married in 1999 (the couple separated in 2013). Jacques Audiard's *Sur mes lèvres /Read My Lips*

(2001), a romantic thriller, sees Cassel playing another anti-hero, a small-time criminal on parole whose romantic involvement with a deaf, socially ostracised office worker develops into a high-risk robbery scam. The parallel developments of the tender relationship and the increasingly dangerous criminal activity make it hard to decide whether the lovers represent a positive or negative influence on each other. Without being a classic, *Sur mes lèvres* represents one of Cassel's most satisfying performances to date, his initially charmless criminal believably developing in sensitivity as his involvement with Emmanuelle Devos's office worker deepens. In a different register, the eponymous hero of Jan Kounen's cartoonish *Dobermann* (1997) is an outlaw hero. His nemesis, a sadistic policeman, is clearly the villain of the piece, but *Dobermann's* own ethics are muddy to say the least, and the outlandish violence perpetrated by all sides never really engages moral issues. Cassel's ramped-up performance – all jutting jaw and mirrored shades – matches the tone of the film, favouring style over depth. One memorable moment, in which he kisses his girlfriend while at the wheel of a high-speed vehicle, is parodied in a scene involving Night Fox in *Ocean's Twelve*, yet *Dobermann* as a film comes across as its own parody.

Cassel's most significant role in French-language cinema to date saw him take on a role perhaps tailor-made for him, as the criminal Jacques Mesrine who earned notoriety for a series of robberies and kidnappings in the 1960s and 1970s. Told over two films (*Mesrine : l'instinct de mort / Mesrine: Killer Instinct* and *L'Ennemi public n°1 /Mesrine: Public Enemy #1*, both 2008) by Jean-François Richet, the life story of Mesrine is one of heists, prison escapes, and false identities, and earned Cassel the 2009 César for Best Actor (he had previously been nominated for his performance as Vinz in *La Haine* in 1996). The accumulation of spectacular and improbable events allows Cassel, who is in virtually every scene of the two films, to keep the audience in thrall to his charisma while evincing ruthless and repulsive brutality. As usual, his performance eschews any easy identification of a moral compass for the character, except perhaps for a committed anti-authoritarianism.

Perhaps Cassel's most controversial performance is in Gaspar Noé's *Irréversible* (2002), as a man out for revenge after his girlfriend (played by Belucci) is brutally sexually assaulted. While the revenge quest allows Cassel to display a similar anti-hero persona to that of Vinz or Mesrine, Noé's shock tactics ensure that the acting is not what stays in the audience's mind. The film's approach to chronology, consisting of a series of single takes viewed in reverse order, and a nine-minute rape scene, were thus the main focus of critical comment. Nevertheless, Cassel's involvement says much about the duality of his cinematic interests, mixing mainstream work with continuing forays into the more confrontational or experimental material with which he first made his name.

Thomas HINTON
University of Exeter

Alain CHABAT (1958–)

A LAIN CHABAT never aspired to a successful career in cinema: as a child, he wanted to be a cartoonist. After a few unsuccessful attempts, he decided to focus on radio, which turned out to be a more auspicious enterprise. The turning point appeared to be his contribution as a presenter to Canal+, a dynamic private TV channel. In this context, Chabat formed a group of comedians called *Les Nuls*, with Chantal Lauby, Dominique Farrugia, and Bruno Carette (who died in 1989). The group became so popular that they decided to turn to cinema, which resulted in four films of uneven quality. Subsequently, Alain Chabat's cinematic career seems to have evolved around two main axes: collaborations with *Les Nuls*, and more personal projects.

Alain Chabat has always been the driving force behind the films made by *Les Nuls*: he usually acts as scriptwriter, and sometimes director. It is indeed very interesting to examine the type of comedy Alain Chabat has used in those films, and more generally, its evolution throughout his career. The first film the group made was *La Cité de la peur /Fear City: A Family-Style Comedy* (1994), directed by Alain Berbérian, but partly written

by Chabat. The film recounts the story of a series of murders that replicate the murders staged in a low-budget film, 'Red is Dead.' Alain Chabat plays a bodyguard whose mission is to protect the main actor of the aforementioned film. The character is lame, stupid, and inefficient, but the role offers some memorable scenes, such as the mythical dance scene in which Chabat and Gérard Darmon dance *La Carioca*. The humour of the film is based on simple mechanisms: one of the most recurrent is quoting idiomatic French expressions and applying them to the letter. For instance, when Odile Deray asks the driver to drop her off, she is literally ejected from the car. This literal sense of humour may not be subtle or sophisticated, but it definitely works. It usually borders on scatology, but is mildly amusing: one of the main characters vomits whenever he feels happy, and the joke never gets old.

The second film written and directed by Alain Chabat, *Didier* (1997), and in which *Les Nuls* star, moves away from this kind of humour: it is more of a slapstick comedy. The film itself is unforgettable, puzzling, grotesque, and insane (and sometimes very uncomfortable to watch). Some spectators will see the director as a comic genius, others as a deranged lunatic. The film tells the story of a dog, Didier, who is magically transformed overnight into a human being, played by Alain Chabat. His feat was not that he played a dog: the achievement was that he actually *was* a dog. The facial expressions are pitch-perfect, as Chabat faithfully portrays the behaviour of a brave but stupid Labrador and many funny situations arise from the character's predicament: a dog, trapped in a human body, battling his canine instincts, is bound to be hilarious. Didier sniffs ladies' bottoms, swallows flies, tears clothes, and breaks into side-splitting dance moves. Alain Chabat's performance is so striking that he was nominated for the second time in the best actor category at the Césars in 1998, and won a César in the best first work category, thus giving him the opportunity to steer his career whichever way he wanted.

But *Astérix et Obélix : Mission Cléopâtre /Asterix and Obelix Meet Cleopatra* (2002), which Alain Chabat wrote, directed, and produced, is the real treasure among all the other films. This film can easily be classified as one of the best French comedies of all time: it simply encompasses all the best aspects of French cinema. It is subtle, clever, and layered with so many references about French culture that even ten years after its original release and countless viewings, you can still discover jokes that had eluded you. It became an instant success, as it managed to capture the essence of the original comic book but made it its own (referring to Claude François in a film about Astérix is a very bold move). It is also a tribute to the French language which, incidentally, makes it very difficult to translate into other languages. Many puns border on poetry and it is not often that you see a film whose aim was to cram thirty jokes into one minute actually live up to that expectation: every scene is an instant classic.

The fourth film, *RRRrrr !!!* (2004) was directed by Alain Chabat, but he only contributed to the script,

as it was mainly written by another group of comedians, *Les Robins des Bois*. Thus Chabat comes back to a more literal sense of humour ('What's your type of girl?' 'Alive'), but some of the recurrent jokes offer some great catchphrases. After seeing this film, whenever you hear the sentence 'It's gonna get dark soon,' you will invariably reply with a laconic and cynical 'Shut up!' Alain Chabat plays a sort of shaman who invents the first crime of History in order to avenge the death of his beloved 'Yorkmoth,' a subtle prehistoric mix between a Yorkshire Terrier and a mammoth. Overall, the film is quite insignificant, and seems to mark Chabat's gradual detachment from *Les Nuls*.

Alongside his work with *Les Nuls*, Chabat pursued a more personal career, collaborating with some of the great names of French cinema, such as Claude Berri, Alain Corneau, Agnès Jaoui, and Michel Gondry. As an actor, Alain Chabat favours comedies, but has made a few forays into more dramatic films, with a greater or lesser degree of success. Four films in particular stand out. First, *Gazon maudit /French Twist* (Josiane Balasko, 1995), for which Alain Chabat was nominated for the first time in the best actor category at the Césars in 1996. The film portrays a couple living in the South of France: the husband, played by Alain Chabat, is a misogynous womanizer who repeatedly cheats on his wife, played by Victoria Abril. The latter finds comfort in the arms of a lesbian (played by the film's director and co-writer, Josiane Balasko) she has just met, and who decides to stay at her house. The story itself is well written and appealing, but the film drifts too much towards a farce to be truly satirical.

The second film is *Trésor* (2009), Claude Berri's very last film, starring Chabat and Mathilde Seigner. Unfortunately for Berri, the film is at best atrocious. It tells the story of an upper-middle class Parisian couple who have to deal with a puppy the husband gave his wife for their anniversary. The acting is beyond appalling (the award for the worst acting goes to Mathilde Seigner), and the dog's performance, which elicits the only positive reactions the spectator will experience throughout the film, outshines those of the main actors. The film is supposed to be a social satire, which would aim at criticising a certain upper-middle class sentimentality: the dog is treated in every respect like a new-born smothered by his mother, and the couple ends up seeing a behavioural specialist for pets. It could have been a lot better had the script not been so ludicrous and simplistic.

If these two films can be defined as comedies, the other two are slightly more (or completely) dramatic. The first one is a detective film which explores the relationship between a policeman and his informer: *Le Cousin* was directed by Alain Corneau in 1997, and offers Alain Chabat his very first dramatic role. His performance as the policeman haunted by the suicide of his colleague is gripping, and his duo with Patrick Timsit is excellent: the traditional duality between a brave and upright policeman and a slightly less honest informer is twisted in order to portray their partnership and its consequences. Alain Chabat has not acted in many dramatic films. This is a pity since he is quite convincing in such roles, but his appearances were too brief to be of importance.

This is why one could argue that *Papa*, directed by Maurice Barthélémy in 2005, represents Alain Chabat at his best, showing his impressive range of emotions. The film tells the story of a young boy and his father, driving towards the South of France. In the first part of the film, Chabat keeps cracking jokes to entertain his son, and they seem to have a close relationship. Some scenes are extremely funny, such as the improvised dance to a song called 'Jesus was born in Provence' and the scene where the son has to wear a shopping bag to protect himself from the rain. But the second part of the film gradually reveals that if the father wants to make his son laugh at any cost, it is because they recently had to deal with a tragedy. Thus the film becomes subtler, more intimate, and infinitely more dramatic. Comedy is used here as a means to deflect the unbearable burden that this tragedy represents, and gives the expression 'comic relief' its full meaning.

Alain Chabat has certainly earned respect as an actor, director, and scriptwriter, especially in the field of comedy. But his roles in more dramatic films suggest that there is still a whole side of his acting abilities to be discovered.

Marion Coste
École Normale Supérieure de Lyon

Maurice CHEVALIER (1888–1972)

*From
Belleville
to
Hollywood*

ALTHOUGH his renown as a singer of popular *chanson* – especially 'Thank Heaven for Little Girls,' 'Louise,' 'Valentine,' and *Ma Pomme* – eclipses his prolific acting career, Maurice CHEVALIER (September 12, 1888 – January 1, 1972) played many important roles in films made in France and the United States. In the U.S., Maurice Chevalier's French accent (which he purposefully exaggerated onstage and onscreen), his protruding lower lip (the famous *lèvre en lippe*), and his grumpy mood offset by a *bon vivant* attitude – in other words, his idiosyncratic Gallic persona and mannerisms – endeared him to the American public. His spoken English was in fact rather good offstage.

Chevalier was born and raised in picturesque Belleville, the lower middle class *faubourg* in Northern Paris that had cradled celebrities such as singer/actress Édith Piaf and actor Jean Gabin, who, like Chevalier, came from impoverished families. Philanthropist and friend of the arts, Marcel Bleustein-Blanchet – creator of the Publicis Drugstore on the Champs-Elysées in Paris (and who also posed for me for an oil portrait in 1968) – writes in his memoirs, entitled *La Traversée du siècle* (1994, ed. Robert Laffont) that he grew up in the destitute yet legendary Belleville, where Parisians refused to capitulate to the invading Prussian army in 1871, stocking cannons in order to defend their country during the Franco-Prussian War (1870-1871).

Son of a housepainter and a mother of Belgian origin nicknamed 'La Louque', Maurice Chevalier left school early to sing and dance onstage, and as a teenager he held several *petits boulots*. It is ironic that although Maurice never completed his education, several schools throughout France are now named after him, along with streets, avenues, and boulevards such as Avenue Maurice Chevalier in Cannes and Avenue Maurice Chevalier in Marnes-la-Coquette. Marnes-la-Coquette, near Paris, is one of the smallest but wealthiest villages in France, and it is where, in 1952, Chevalier acquired a fine property he named 'La Louque,' where he is buried. Marnes-la-Coquette is famous because Eugénie de Montijo – who became Empress Eugénie after her marriage to Napoléon III – had consecrated this area where a church is named after her. Coincidently, Chevalier thought that my name, 'Jenny,' was short for 'Eugénie' and he always called me 'Eugénie' (as did some of my teachers in Montpellier, where I was born and spent my earliest years, and where the first name 'Jenny' was not well known at the time).

After being injured in combat, captured, and held prisoner in Germany during World War I, Chevalier was released early from the POW camp thanks to Alfonso XIII,

King of Spain (the only king at the time with both German and British lineage) and he returned to Paris. In 1917, Chevalier became a success at the Casino de Paris and a household name in France. After signing a contract with Paramount Pictures in 1928, he starred in numerous musical films, including *Playboy of Paris* (Ludwig Berger, 1930), *The Smiling Lieutenant* (Ernst Lubitsch, 1931), *One Hour with You* (Ernst Lubitsch, 1931), *Love Me Tonight* (Rouben Mamoulian, 1932), and *The Merry Widow* (Ernst Lubitsch, 1934). For his artistic and cinematic accomplishments, Chevalier received an honorary Academy Award in 1958 after appearing, that same year, in Vicente Minnelli's enormously successful Hollywood musical comedy film *Gigi*, set in Belle Epoque Paris (based on Colette's eponymous 1944 novella). In *Gigi*, Chevalier plays Honoré Lachaille, whose playboy nephew Gaston (Louis Jourdan, 1921-2015) unexpectedly falls in love with Gilberte/Gigi (Leslie Caron), a young girl being trained for a life as a high-class mistress/courtesan for wealthy men such as Gaston himself. In this film, Chevalier sings his iconic song 'Thank Heaven for Little Girls' (a title that Leslie Caron recuperated for her 2009 autobiography, *Thank Heaven: A Memoir*). After an unsuccessful Broadway adaptation in 1973 by Alan Jay Lerner and Frederick Loewe, *Gigi* – directed by Eric Schaeffer with a new adaptation by playwright Heidi Thomas, and produced by Jenna Segal – is revived on Broadway in 2015. (The original novel had first been adapted for Broadway in 1951 in a play by Anita Loos, in which Audrey Hepburn made her Broadway debut in the titular role.) Previously, Chevalier was nominated for the Oscar for Best Actor (for *The Love Parade*, dir. Ernst Lubitsch, 1929, and *The Big Pond*, dir. Hobart Henley, 1930).

In the US, Chevalier relished the adulation of starlets and female fans, but remained uncomfortable with the more sophisticated Charles Boyer, who epitomized the French bourgeois spirit. Boyer, revered as a true romantic hero, had more appeal, whereas Chevalier's adventures, peppered by the comic, did not tug at the heart. Maurice, his cocked *canotier* (straw hat), and eternal bowtie, provided lighter entertainment. Boyer and Chevalier starred in Joshua Logan's 1961 film adaptation of the 1954 Broadway musical *Fanny* produced by David Merrick, with music/lyrics by Harold Rome, and book by Logan and S.N. Behrman – itself an adaptation/resemantization and condensation of Marcel Pagnol's famous *Marseilles Trilogy* films from the early 1930s.[1] In *Fanny*, Chevalier, as in *Gigi*, is a gentleman of means, Panisse, who obliges by marrying the young Fanny, pregnant by Marius. Boyer incarnates César, father of Marius, who abandoned his lover Fanny to yield to the call of the sea. In *Fanny*, as in *Gigi*, Leslie Caron starred in the titular role.

In a 1958 American variety show, *The Lucy-Desi Comedy Hour*, Chevalier appears with Ricky Ricardo (Desi Arnaz), singing *Valentine* in French. Arnaz follows in turn, singing *Valentina*, in Spanish, followed by 'Little Ricky', son of Arnaz and Lucille Ball, who sings

'Valentine' in English. The song's teasing tune (written in 1925) has survived over the years into the new millennium, as part of Chevalier's musical legacy. Valentine – with her *petit menton* /'small chin,' *petit petons* /'small feet,' and *petit tétons* /'small breasts' – prefigures Georges Brassens's 1955 song, *Une jolie fleur* /'A Pretty Flower,' written in ironic praise of a woman with a small brain: « *Ell' n'avait pas de tête, ell' n'avait pas /L'Esprit beaucoup plus grand qu'un dé à coudre* » /'She did not have much sense, she did not have /A mind much bigger than a thimble.' [2]

When I was fourteen years old, I was commissioned to paint Maurice Chevalier's portrait and when the portrait was finished, we were invited to his estate at Marnes-la-Coquette to present him with the painting. Chevalier had also invited the press – including a reporter from *Le Midi-Libre*, the local newspaper from Montpellier, France, my hometown – for a photo shoot with the portrait. I had painted Maurice with his cocked *canotier*, bowtie, and *lèvre en lippe*,

MAURICE CHEVALIER PHOTOGRAPHED IN THE GARDEN OF 'LA LOUQUE' AT MARNES-LA-COQUETTE WITH 14-YEAR-OLD JENNY BATLAY AND THE PORTRAIT SHE PAINTED OF HIM.

smiling widely. Maurice Chevalier confided to me that he also loved to paint, but he did not think that he had much talent for painting, and with a sweeping gesture of his left hand toward my portrait of him, he said, 'I certainly could never paint like that.'

That year, when I had my first solo painting exhibition at the Galérie Marcel Bernheim, 26 rue la Boétie, Paris 8ᵉ (rue la Boétie was then thought of as 'the French Florence… the thoroughfare wherein the most important American, Swiss, and German collections were born' and was, according to Ambroise Vollard, the 'incontestable centre of the art market' at the time [3]), Maurice Chevalier came to my exhibit, mingling with *le tout Paris*. The only photograph of the painting that I have is the one that appeared in the newspaper from Montpellier, *Le Midi-Libre* (opposite); my extensive file of my portrait of Maurice Chevalier has since disappeared.

Maurice Chevalier was rumoured to have collaborated with the Nazi regime during World War II, a rumour probably brought about because he had sung to French prisoners at a German POW camp where he himself had been held captive during World War I – Chevalier received the Croix de Guerre for his military service in the First World War. He was also decorated with the French Legion of Honour. Archival footage of Chevalier denying the rumours of his collaboration is the penultimate scene of the two-part television documentary *Le Chagrin et la Pitié /The Sorrow and the Pity* (Marcel Ophüls, 1969). *The Sorrow and the*

Pity furthermore features several of Chevalier's songs, in particular, his diegetic performance of *Ça fait d'excellents français* during the film's opening credits and 'Sweepin' the Clouds Away' – one of his most popular songs – playing over the film's final scene and closing credits. Both of these upbeat songs are used ironically, given the rumours about Chevalier's possible collaboration. Moreover, they are juxtaposed with the solemn and tragic mood of this documentary, an exposé casting a critical eye upon France's collaborationist activities during the Occupation.

Although Chevalier's name was cleared of such charges, his worldwide reputation remained somewhat tainted. During the McCarthy Era, he was denied entry to perform in the US. This decision was, however, reversed, and he was allowed to go into the US in 1954. After two decades away from Hollywood, he starred with Audrey Hepburn and Gary Cooper in *Love in the Afternoon* (Billy Wilder, 1957); with Leslie Caron in the aforementioned *Gigi* (1958), and with Shirley MacLaine and Frank Sinatra in *Can-Can* (Walter Lang, 1960).

Along with his honorary Oscar for contributions to film, Chevalier received the George Eastman Award (1957). Furthermore, he has a star on the Hollywood Walk of Fame and his handprints are visible in cement in front of the TCL Chinese Theatre. He was given the Cecil B. DeMille Award (honorary Golden Globe) in 1959. Chevalier's complex journey from Belleville to worldwide reputation is a remarkable

rags-to-riches story in itself, on the background of two World Wars, two continents, two languages, and two careers: acting and singing.

Jenny BATLAY
PhD Columbia University

1. For further discussion of Pagnol's *Marseilles Trilogy* and Logan's *Fanny*, see Marcelline Block, ed., *World Film Locations: Marseilles* (Intellect, 2013). —Ed.

2. *Une Jolie Fleur* at 'The Songs of Georges Brassens with English Translation,' http://brassenswithenglish.blogspot.com/2008/02/une-jolie-fleur-by-georges-brassens.html. Accessed Jan. 1, 2013.

3. Hector Feliciano, *The Lost Museum: The Nazi Conspiracy to Steal the World's Greatest Works of Art* (Basic Books, 1997), 59-60.

Christian CLAVIER (1952–)

*Un
acteur
hors du
commun*

THE CAREER trajectory of Christian CLAVIER (born 1952 in Paris) is inextricably linked with that of the *Splendid* comedy troupe, which was created by a group of authors and actors in the 1970s. Michel Blanc, Christian Clavier, Gérard Jugnot, and Thierry Lhermite were four childhood friends who attended Le Lycée Pasteur in Neuilly-sur-Seine. Christian Clavier is now one of the most known actors within the French cultural landscape. As a result of the popularity of the *Splendid*, famous actors and actresses such as Josiane Balasko and Marie-Anne Chazel (who married Clavier) joined the troupe. The troupe's performers also included Anémone, Dominique Lavanant, and Martin Lamotte, who joined the troupe on stage and behind the camera although they did not belong to it. This famous theatre was located in 10 rue des Lombards in the fourth arrondissement in Paris, before moving to Rue du Faubourg-Saint-Martin.

One of the most famous films released by the *Splendid* troupe was *Les Bronzés /French Fried Vacation*, a 1978 French comedy film directed by Patrice Leconte, in which Clavier played Jérôme Tarayre. The film parodies life at holiday resorts such as Club Med. *Les Bronzés* obtained cult status in France but also sold 2.2 million tickets throughout its preliminary theatrical announcement. *Les Bronzés* was then followed by two sequels, also directed by Patrice Leconte: *Les Bronzés font du ski* (1979) and *Les Bronzés 3 : Amis pour la vie /Friends Forever* (2006).

Clavier made his debut in *L'An 01 /The Year 01*, a French film released in 1973, written by Gébé, the editor of *Charlie Hebdo*, and directed by Jacques Doillon, Alain Resnais, and Jean Rouch. The film was an adaptation of Gébé's comic strip of the same title.

Clavier had a strong work collaboration with Jean-Marie Poiré (as an actor and director) in which he contributed to the following films: *Papy fait de la résistance / Gramps is in the Resistance* (1983), *Twist again à Moscou /Twist Again in Moscow* (1986), *Mes meilleurs copains /My Best Pals* (1989), and *L'Opération corned-beef /Operation Corned-beef* (1991), which revealed a strong acting collaboration and friendship between Clavier and Jean Reno.

Clavier's biggest hit to date was *Les Visiteurs /The Visitors* (Poiré, 1993), a cult French film released in 1993 in which he played Jacquouille la Fripouille. This symbolic character repeatedly uses the word "Okkkayyy !!" which became a prevalent exclamation after the film's achievement. *Les Visiteurs* was a commercial success, with 13,782,846 tickets sold. In order to make the film more attractive to French audiences, the director Poiré used the eye-catching tagline « *Ils ne sont pas nés d'hier* » ['They weren't born yesterday']. For his outstanding role in *Les Visiteurs*, Clavier received a César nomination for Best Actor and Best Screenplay. Clavier and Reno reprised their roles in a sequel entitled *Les Visiteurs 2 : Les Couloirs du temps* (Poiré), which was released in 1998 and sold 8,035,299 tickets. Due to its phenomenal success there was an American remake entitled *Just Visiting* (Poiré, 2000, starring Reno, Clavier, and American actress Christina Applegate), but it did not match the success of the French original. According to French news, Poiré and Clavier are preparing to add a third chapter to this incredible success story for release in 2015, entitled *Les Visiteurs 3 : La Terreur.*

Clavier then took on the role of Astérix, based on the comic book series of the same name by French comic book artists Albert Uderzo and René Goscinny. Interestingly, Gérard Depardieu kept the role of Obélix for the entire film series whereas Clavier appeared in the first two films and was replaced by Clovis Cornillac for the third instalment, and by Edouard Baer in the fourth.

In conclusion, Clavier has been known for his comical performances, where he has been compared to Louis de Funès. Clavier was made *Chevalier* (Knight) of the *Ordre national du Mérite* on 13 June 1998 and *Officier* in 2005. In addition, Clavier was made *Chevalier* of the *Légion d'honneur* in 2001.

Even though Clavier has encountered success throughout his cinematic career, one of his last works *On ne choisit pas sa famille /* *You Don't Choose Your Family* (2011), which he directed, was a total disaster at the French box office. The French media blamed this disaster on his friendship with former French president Nicolas Sarkozy. Clavier also recently left France for England because of François Hollande's 'unfair' tax policy in which 75% of income exceeding one million euro is to be given back to the French State. Clavier's departure from France reflected his colleague Gérard Depardieu's recent actions: Depardieu was granted Russian citizenship on 3rd January 2013 by Russian President Vladimir Putin and exiled himself to Belgium. In 2014, Clavier starred alongside Chantal Lauby in *Qu'est-ce qu'on a fait au Bon Dieu ?* (dir, Philippe de Chauveron) and returned to box-office success with more than 10 million cinema admissions.

Stéphane NARCIS
Bath Spa University

François CLUZET (1955–)

*Changing
With
the
Times*

FRANÇOIS CLUZET started his career in 1980 in Diane Kurys's *Cocktail Molotov*: ever since, he has been surprisingly productive. With only a couple of breaks here and there, Cluzet managed to sustain the impressive work rhythm of two or three films a year. He worked with some of the greatest French directors, such as Bertrand Tavernier (*Autour de minuit* /*'Round Midnight*, 1986), Tony Gatlif (*Rue du départ* / *The Way Out*, 1986), Pierre Jolivet (*Force majeure* /*Uncontrollable Circumstances*, 1989), Bertrand Blier (*Trop belle pour toi* /*Too Beautiful for You*, 1989), and Jean-Paul Rappeneau (*Le Hussard sur le toit* /*The Horseman on the Roof*, 1995). François Cluzet also tried to broaden the scope of his career by landing a few roles in American productions, such as *Prêt-à-porter* in 1994, directed by Robert Altman, and *French Kiss*, directed by Lawrence Kasdan in 1995.

In spite of this diversity, he maintained a close relationship with Claude Chabrol, with whom he collaborated on five different films over the course of twenty years. The last two films they made were particularly striking. *L'Enfer* / *Hell*, directed by Chabrol in 1994 is gripping. The film tells the story of Paul Prieur (François Cluzet), who marries a beautiful woman, Nelly (Emmanuelle Béart): slowly, Paul begins to suspect his wife is cheating on him. Cluzet's performance is chilling as he painstakingly portrays his character gradually becoming paranoid and violent. The open ending of the film also adds to the frightful deterioration in the couple's relationship. In the second film, *Rien ne va plus* /*The Swindle* (1997), Cluzet plays the paymaster general of a big nameless company who is fooled by a duo of swindlers. His death is the most surprising scene of the film, and a feat for the actor: it is not every day that you get to play someone who has been murdered by a knitting needle thrust in their eye (evoking the 'Moe Greene Special' of Francis Ford Coppola's 1972 *The Godfather*).

During his career, François Cluzet's talent was acknowledged many times. His first nomination at the César Awards for Most Promising Actor was in 1984 for *Vive la sociale !* (Gérard Mordillat, 1983), but he was also nominated the same year for Best Supporting Actor for Jean Becker's *L'Été meurtrier* /*One Deadly Summer*, in which he played the main character's brother. After that, Cluzet was nominated three more times in the Best Supporting Actor category: in 1990 for the above-mentioned *Force majeure*, directed by Pierre Jolivet, in 2003 for *L'Adversaire* /*The Adversary* (2002), directed by Nicole Garcia, and finally in 2007 for Christian Vincent's *Quatre étoiles* (2006). But Cluzet was also nominated five times in the Best Actor category: four of those nominations occurred after the start of his collaboration with Guillaume Canet.

One could argue that Cluzet's career is defined by two characteristics. The first one is the fact that the actor often vacillates between thrillers (or more generally dramatic films) and romantic comedies. Although Cluzet can be a brilliant actor, good thrillers or romantic comedies are hard to come by, which is why most of the films he has made are merely average.

For instance, *Blanc comme neige /White Snow*, directed in 2010 by Christophe Blanc, is certainly not the most amazing thriller of the year. The film focuses on a car salesman caught up with thugs who killed his partner because he could not pay them. The story feels unoriginal and unsubstantial, and the film as a whole lacks rhythm and energy. Cluzet's performance is not entirely convincing, and his dreadful English is the only thing worth noticing. The same goes for romantic comedies: François Cluzet is usually on automatic pilot, resorting to the same expressions, gestures, modulations, and looking either perpetually annoyed or arrogant. *La Vérité ou presque /True Enough* directed by Sam Karmann in 2007, is, for instance, appalling. The characters have no substance whatsoever, and the plot is uninteresting.

But there are some real treasures in his filmography, which have been rightfully rewarded with a nomination in the Best Supporting Actor or Best Actor categories. For example, Cluzet's portrayal of

Antoine in *Les Apprentis*, directed by Pierre Salvadori in 1995, is both funny and deeply moving. Antoine shares a flat with Fred, but both men are completely different: the situation gives rise to delectable dialogues, and some hilarious scenes, such as the burglary and the visit paid to their flatmate's grandmother.

Another example (although it did not lead to a nomination at the Césars) is *Enfants de salaud / Bastard Brood* (1996), directed by Tonie Marshall. The film recounts the story of a man tried for murder: his daughter, whom he abandoned when she was a child, comes to the trial in order to discover more about her dad. There, she discovers that she has in fact two stepsisters and a stepbrother (played by Cluzet), who were all abandoned by their father. The film is remarkable: the newly reunited family is extremely dysfunctional, and the children have to come to terms with the fact that they are the offspring of a murderer, which leads them to question their respective lives. The upper class sister starts to mix with riffraff and asks her stripper sister to have sex with her husband, while the third sister hooks up with their brother. The film is hilarious, albeit quite cringe-inducing at times. Cluzet is perfect in the role of Sandro, the misogynist and cynical stepbrother, and his scenes with Nathalie Baye are simply superb.

The second characteristic of François Cluzet's career is his cinematic revival in 2006, thanks to actor-director Guillaume Canet, which leads to a pre-/post- Canet divide in his filmography. This turning point allowed François Cluzet to have access to more diverse roles, but also to more commercial films (which can either be a good or a bad thing). It can be described as a revival in the sense that younger generations were able to discover him in successful films, even though his long filmography had already ensured him a faithful audience.

In 2006, François Cluzet starred in Guillaume Canet's first significant film, *Ne le dis à personne /Tell No One*. It recounts the story of a doctor, played by Cluzet, who tries to uncover the truth about his wife's death. The rhythm of the film is steady and intense, and Cluzet's performance is the keystone: he looks like an animal being hunted down, looking for a way out at any cost. The film earned him his first César for Best Actor in 2007, and his collaboration with Canet thrived, as he is now known as being part of the director's group of favourite actors. They worked together again on the set of *Les Liens du sang / Rivals*, directed by Jacques Maillot in 2008, in which the two actors played brothers, and in *Les Petits Mouchoirs /Little White Lies* (2010), a big commercial success directed by Canet.

Cluzet's latest success was *Intouchables /The Intouchables* (Olivier Nakache and Eric Toledano, 2011), which tells the true story of Philippe, a rich tetraplegic man who hires Driss (Omar Sy), a young man from the suburbs of Paris, to look after him. Although Cluzet's performance is outshone by Omar Sy's, his portrayal of a man trapped in his own body is powerful. The film

actually drew Harvey Weinstein's attention: he seized the film in order to commercialize it in the United States, hoping to give it the same fabulous success as *The Artist* (Michel Hazanavicius, 2011), which he also distributed. Incidentally, this could re-launch Cluzet's career in the United States.

His filmography so far is interesting as it seems to symbolise the meeting of two periods in the history of French cinema: Cluzet could be seen as the cornerstone between the era of the aging (or dead) great French directors (Becker, Blier, Chabrol, Tavernier) and the new generation of French directors, such as Guillaume Canet. In that sense, François Cluzet truly succeeded as an actor, as he has been able to navigate effortlessly between trends, styles and techniques, thus symbolising the permanence of French cinema, and its capacity to reinvent itself.

Marion Coste
École Normale Supérieure de Lyon

Jean COCTEAU (1889–1963)

*A Life in
One Act,
or
Cinema
and Its
Double*

A LTHOUGH the inclusion of Jean Cocteau in this collection might not seem the most obvious editorial choice, I would argue that it may in fact be one of the most relevant. It is indeed difficult to 'define' or summarise Cocteau: an artistic jack of all trades, he has methodically and constantly shifted the boundaries within and between genres, always preferring to pursue a 'quest for Poetry.' Such an enterprise is of course reflected in his artistic nomenclature: he always referred to his works, for instance, as novelistic poetry (*poésie de roman*), critical poetry (*poésie critique*), graphic poetry (*poésie graphique*), or cinematographic poetry (*poésie de cinéma*). Cinema was, in fact, at the heart of Cocteau's life and career long before his first feature film, *Le Sang d'un poète /The Blood of a Poet* (1932). For Cocteau, the virtue of this 'tenth muse' was as another writing medium, which explains his insistence upon calling it 'the cinematograph' (as opposed to 'cinéma'). Of course, his cinematic reputation is now established, albeit mainly based on just a few films. Cocteau directed some of the most memorable and, arguably, influential films of the twentieth century, most of which managed to achieve both popular and critical success: *La Belle et la Bête /Beauty and the Beast* (1946), *Orphée /Orpheus* (1950), and *Le Testament d'Orphée / The Testament of Orpheus* (1960). He collaborated, as a dialogue- or scriptwriter, on such 'cult' films as *Les Dames du Bois de Boulogne /Ladies of the Park* (Robert Bresson, 1945). And, indeed, he filmed many of French cinema's greats: Paul Bernard, Roger Blin, Maria Casarès, Jean-Pierre Mocky, and, of course, Jean Marais. It was his relationship with Jean Marais, however, that would often take centre stage, making him a household name in France and abroad. This supremacy of his private over his artistic life in turn became one of the core themes of a body of work that incessantly plays with and on self-referentiality (to the extent that many people criticised him for having developed a 'showy' cinema, shot for the sole benefit and pleasure of his friends, lovers, and fashionable relationships). Nonetheless, beyond the famous and celebrated films – beyond the socialite life even – one often overlooks the fact that Cocteau was also an actor. Indeed, a quick look at Cocteau's filmography reveals no fewer than twelve or thirteen films whose credits attribute him an acting role. Each of these goes a long way to shedding some light on the conception(s) of cinema, life, and poetry of a prolific artist, for whom 'disrupting the order of things' constituted a veritable ethos.

Jean Cocteau was born to a wealthy bourgeois family in Maisons-Laffitte near Paris on 5th July 1889 (which led him to declare famously that he and the Eiffel Tower were the same age). Very young, Cocteau grew tired of studying and made the decision to dedicate his life to poetry. He would be forever untiring in his effort to do so. The list of his friends and relations reads like a *Who's Who* of the political, literary, and artistic worlds of the period running from the 1920s to the mid-1960s: Charles Aznavour, Maurice Barrès, Yul Brynner, Coco Chanel, Queen Elizabeth of Belgium, André Gide, Edith Piaf, Pablo Picasso, Marcel Proust, Erik Satie, and the Groupe des Six (Georges Auric, Louis Durey, Arthur Honegger, Darius Milhaud, Francis Poulenc, Germaine Taillefer). On the one hand, his relationship to the avant-gardes was often tumultuous (a consequence, amongst other things, of his 'worldliness'): the Surrealists (André Breton in any case) abhorred him, all the more so since Cocteau's work (his films, most often) were at times described as 'surrealist' (ironically, the group owes its name, in part, to Cocteau since the term 'surrealist' was coined by Guillaume Apollinaire following the performance of *Parade*, a ballet written as a collaboration between Cocteau, Satie, and Léonide Massine). His role and place in occupied France was also put into question (e.g. his artistic collaboration with Arno Breker, Hitler's favourite sculptor). On the other hand, his literary success and influence were recognized with an election to the Académie française in 1955, along with an array of awards, prizes, and commendations (including a Doctorate *honoris causa* from the University of Oxford, which was the occasion for the famous Oxford speech, as well as a mischievous reference in *The Testament*). As far

as cinema is concerned, the French New Wave authors acknowledged him as both one of their forefathers and one of their equals, saluting his experimentations, his intertextuality, his humour, his improvised techniques, and his unwillingness to quit. François Truffaut even financed Cocteau's last film with the profits from his own *Les Quatre Cents Coups /The 400 Blows* (1959).

Cocteau-the-actor remains nonetheless mysterious and much less known. His screen (dis-)appearances are rather badly recorded, so much so that, besides his obvious 'presence' in the *Testament*, the list of films he acted in is blurred and, one suspects, still incomplete. These range, however, from feature films such as *Le Baron fantôme /The Phantom Baron* (Serge de Poligny, 1943), *La Malibran* (Sacha Guitry, 1944), the superb *8 × 8, A Chess Sonata in 8 Movements* (Hans Richter, 1957), to shorts such as *Désordre* (Jacques Baratier, 1949) and documentaries such as *De Jeanne d'Arc à Philippe Pétain* (Sacha Guitry, 1944). One thing is certain: Cocteau regarded his contribution to these works, documentaries included, as that of an actor and not merely an extra. Paradoxically, the same list reveals that the majority of Cocteau's roles as an actor consisted in playing... Jean Cocteau (albeit sometimes only as a voice). When this is not the case, Cocteau played Alfred de Musset, a fallen poet (*La Malibran*) or Baron Julius Carol, the ghost baron of the eponymous film. Cocteau's game, and his aim as an actor and an author, was to testify to this presence-absence dynamic. His interpretations all point towards the duality of life, the theme of the double and the distance between the self and the subject/object. Nowhere is this more striking than in *The Testament*, culminating in the missed encounter between the Poet and his double. Such an occurrence is amusing (Cocteau's face feigning surprise and then indignation) but ultimately disconcerting: it very much fits the framework of a 'realistic document of unreal happenings,' but Cocteau's interpretation also unsettles and disturbs, placing the spectator in the uncomfortable position of the dawning realisation that our own paths follow the same trajectory of non-encounters with our own self. Cocteau-the-director always looked to achieve a 'sublimation of the documentary style.' This led him, in the valedictory instalment of the Orphic trilogy, to shatter the boundaries between cinema and life, between acting and living. This is first visible in the distribution for the film: Cocteau plays himself and/as the poet; Edouard Dermithe plays himself and Cégeste, who utters the famous lines: 'This time, it is no longer a film. This is life'; the characters of the Princess of Death (Maria Casarès) and her aide (François Périer) both acknowledge that they are taking part in a sequel but concurrently fail to recognise characters from the previous film. But Cocteau's directing and, above all, his acting, also transpose to the screen the desired irruption of poetry in reality. In a 'realist' and 'material,' almost 'mechanical,' setting, Cocteau's acting seems, at times, to jar: his body is tensed, angular, and performs Cocteau's own version of the distancing effect (*Verfremdungseffekt*), thereby 'preventing the audience from losing itself passively and completely in the character created by the actor.' This in turn leads the audience to realise that all is not as it seems with the surrounding reality, and to become a consciously critical observer (the out-of-focus shot of Cocteau finally walking out of his film only reinforces such an impression). As such, Cocteau's cinematography and oneiric form of acting – whilst the film 'is not a dream,' it 'adopts its logic' – both function as a form of virus that disrupts our expectation of what an actor, and of what a film, ultimately is. *The Testament* makes for a touching series of appearances and disappearances (both literal and metaphorical) which tell of Cocteau's vision of the actor as yet another channel for poetry. In fact, each of his films – and each of his screen appearances – follow this basic principle: they are a series of disruptive 'stripteases.' Indeed, Cocteau-the-actor plays with the (un-)veiling of the truth: what constitutes a lie, if all the world is a stage? Cocteau invents a form of cinema, contradictory and demanding, in search of truth and mystery. For him, cinema's function is first and foremost to show – through slow motion, reverse chronology, '(un) special effects' – forms that, until then, were only imagined. But his cinema also sets out to prove these things: they are true because I show them (what Cocteau called cinema's *vérisme*). Art coincides with artifice and the art of the actor is part of this process. *The Testament*, again, is a worthy example (and certainly the most poignant and beautiful): Cocteau walks through his life as though he were floating over it, his voice (the opening voiceover) bearing witness to the fact that he is already the ghost of his own work. His hands, trembling, do things and then undo them, push, touch, and ultimately know that they will soon die (death and disappearance remain two leitmotifs of the author-actor). In fact Cocteau-the-actor is yet another face of Cocteau-the-poet. For Cocteau, the poet is defined as 'A man who puts his foot in it. My method has always been to put my foot in it.' This methodical disruption of the consensual, this sublimation of reality (visible directly both through the sublimation of the documentary style but also through Cocteau's own understated, self-depreciative, humorous, and subtle interpretations of his own character) emphasises the theatrical dimension of one's existence. Cocteau's life, it is true, was an endless game whose rule was to relentlessly and irreverently lead us astray. Such is reflected in his 'work' as an actor. But what more serious, and liberating, game could it have been than that of looking for poetry in every corner of life, leaving us a legacy that, just like the phoenix, will rise from its ashes?

Benjamin Andréo
Monash University, Melbourne

COLUCHE (1944–1986)
[Michel Gérard Joseph Colucci]

*Comedian,
Presidential
Candidate,
Philanthropist,
Motorcyclist*

TOGETHER with Fernandel, Louis de Funès, Pierre Desproges and a few others, COLUCHE is one of the larger-than-life figures of French comedy. Comedy did make Coluche famous but it is really his flamboyant personality and socio-political *engagement* that have transformed him into the quasi-legendary figure that he is in the French collective imagination.

Michel Gérard Joseph Colucci was born in Paris on October 28, 1944, to a French mother, Simone (Monette) Bouyer and an Italian immigrant from Lazio, Honorio Colucci. His father died at age 31 from polio and, as a result, his mother had to bring up her two children on her own. Despite financial problems and her own health issues, Monette constantly tried to dress and educate her children in a bourgeois-like manner. The young Michel, however, was not fond of living in denial. Instead, he preferred to spend time with his friends in the less-than-bourgeois Parisian suburb of Montrouge. With his friends, Michel regularly committed petty larcenies and other minor offences, which caused him to have frequent encounters with the police. Since his childhood, his life never was very structured. Later, he took on several small jobs working as a telegrapher, ceramicist, waiter, apprentice photographer, delivery boy, shop assistant, and florist; he did not keep any of these jobs for extended periods of time. In 1964, he joined the infantry in Lons-le-Saunier but was soon imprisoned for insubordination. It is quite possible his behaviour as a young man, together with the future comedian's later activism, both stemmed from his rejection of his mother's bourgeois ideals (and, psychoanalysts might add, the absence of a father figure in his life).

In the 1960s, Michel Colucci wanted to become a singer and tried his luck performing consecrated songs in Parisian cafés around Saint-Michel and the very happening rue Mouffetard. Although he was not too successful as a singer, he had the opportunity to meet many fellow entertainers and even founded a short-lived band, 'Les Craignos Boboys' ('The Scary Yuppies' would be an approximate translation). He also performed in a certain number of cabarets, such as Chez Bernadette, where he met the singer-songwriter Georges Moustaki.

His career as a comedian began in the 60s when, together with Romain Bouteille and other comedians such as Patrick Dewaere, Miou-Miou, and Martin Lamotte, he performed various skits at the Café de la Gare (a café-théâtre or 'dinner theatre'). The late 60s and 70s marked his television debut on shows such as *Madame êtes-vous libre ?* and *La Cloche tibétaine*. He also appeared in several commercial advertisements. In 1971, he created a comedic group called the *Le Vrai Chic Parisien* ['The True Parisian Chic'], which he later left because of his behavioural disorders and alcohol addiction. He started performing solo skits such as *C'est l'histoire d'un mec* (the French equivalent of 'So, this guy walks into a bar'), in which he derides failed attempts to tell a funny story. Little by little, Michel Colucci becomes Coluche, the comedian figure loved by so many French people. In his skits, Coluche impersonates a poor urban character who is jovial yet foul-mouthed ('though never vulgar,' as he liked to point out), racist without even realizing it, and who lives in a world whose main (sub) cultural references are commercial advertisements and radio games. In a sense, Coluche impersonated the typical proletarian Frenchman, which was the absolute opposite of the bourgeois ideal that his mother had tried to inculcate in him.

In the following years, he toured France as a comedian with both older skits and new ones ('Le Schmilblick,' in which he poked fun at radio games). In 1977, he directs the movie *Vous n'aurez pas l'Alsace et la Lorraine /You Won't Have Alsace-Lorraine*, in which he also plays the role of the protagonist, the king Gros Pif ['Big Nose']. In the late 70s and early 80s, he features in several radio shows but is repeatedly laid off for using licentious language. For a while, he is even banned from radio and television shows.

In 1980, he officially announced his bid for the French presidency. Although most people thought it a joke, the left-wing comedian was supported by major intellectual figures such as Gilles Deleuze, Félix Guattari, and Pierre Bourdieu, and was credited in a survey with approximately sixteen per cent of the vote. Several politicians, including some on the left, tried to dissuade him. Ultimately, it seems that only the assassination of his friend and studio manager René Gorlin convinced him to abandon the bid. The assassination of Gorlin was apparently unrelated to politics, which Coluche did not know at the time. At any rate, his dropping out cleared the path for the Socialist candidate François Mitterrand to the Elysée.

The following years were not very auspicious for Coluche. He lived for a while in Guadeloupe and invited Elsa, the wife of his friend Patrick Dewaere, to join him in the Caribbean. Elsa left her husband for Coluche, and in 1982 Dewaere committed suicide with a rifle that had been given to him by Coluche himself. As a result, Coluche fell into a deep depression and his various addictions worsened.

In 1983, he starred in Claude Berri's *Tchao Pantin /So Long, Stooge* (1983) for which he was awarded the César for Best Actor in 1984. Over the years, Coluche played (mostly) comedic roles in numerous movies – Claude Berri's *Le Pistonné /The Man with Connections* (1970) and *Le Maître d'école* (1981); Claude Faraldo's *Themroc* (1973); Claude Zidi's *L'Aile ou la Cuisse /The Wing or the Thigh*[1] (1976), *Inspecteur la Bavure /Inspector Blunder* (1980), and *Banzaï* (1983), to name just a few. After performing in several other movies and slowly emerging from his depression, he got more involved in the social and political life of the city by creating (with Harlem Désir) the influential organization *SOS Racisme*. In 1985, he created a charity named *Restos du cœur* ['Restaurants of the Heart'] with the purpose of feeding the poor.

Coluche was also a big fan of motorcycles. He participated in the Paris-Dakar on one occasion and even broke a world speed record for a 750 cc motorcycle in 1985. Unfortunately, in 1986, he died at age 41 in a motorcycle accident near Cannes.

Cristian BRATU
Baylor University, Texas

1. *L'Aile ou la Cuisse* sometimes titled in other ways in English: *The Wing or Thigh?* etc. —Ed.

Clovis CORNILLAC (1967–)

*The Best
Act You're
Not
Watching:
The
Versatile—*

DESPITE his encyclopedic résumé, Clovis CORNILLAC has not become an international household name – which is surely the household's oversight. The actor, born in 1967 in Lyons, has performed alongside Depardieu, Devos, and Tautou; been directed by Barratier, Davis, and Jeunet; featured in police dramas, fantastic thrillers, and surfer comedies; played roles from a disenfranchised 1980s teenager to a rough-tempered police captain, from David against a pharmaceutical-industry's Goliath to the minute Gaulois warrior, Astérix. He has received César nominations – *meilleur espoir masculin* (most promising male actor) for *Karnaval* (Thomas Vincent, 1999), and best supporting actor for *À la petite semaine /Nickel and Dime* (Sam Karmann, 2003) – and was crowned with the Best Supporting Actor César for *Mensonges et trahisons et plus si affinités /The Story of My Life* (Laurent Tirard, 2004).

Son of actors Myriam Boyer and Roger Cornillac, Cornillac married the classically trained Caroline Proust in 1994 (best known for Éric Besnard's *Ca$h* in 2008; and, more recently, four seasons of *Engrenages / Spiral* on Canal+). The couple had twin daughters in 2001 and divorced in 2010. In 2013, he married actress Lilou Fogli (the couple has a son, Nino, born May 28, 2013).

After a childhood believing he would become a boxer (and indeed, his physique still reflects this early ambition), Cornillac left home at age fourteen to try his luck in theatre. He began with street theatre and subsidized plays before getting picked up for Robin Davis's 1985 *Hors-la-loi /Outlaws*. From there his career has been a starburst of performances in every genre, including some of the most iconic roles of contemporary French cinema. His filmography lists fifty-plus blockbusters and art films alike from the 1980s to today; and that is to say nothing of his appearances in short films, plays, and television series. His feature films include titles like *Carnages /Carnage* (Delphine Gleize, 2002), *Maléfique* (Eric Valette, 2002), *Un long dimanche de fiançailles /A Very Long Engagement* (Jean-Pierre Jeunet, 2004), *Brice de Nice /The Brice Man* (James Huth, 2005), *Le Nouveau Protocole /The New Protocol* (Thomas Vincent, 2008), *Astérix et Obélix aux jeux olympiques /Asterix at the Olympic Games* (Frédéric Forestier and Thomas Langmann, 2008), and *Requiem pour une tueuse /Requiem for a Killer* (Jérôme Le Gris, 2011), to name just a handful.

His dark glare makes him perfect for haunting performances in thrillers and mysteries, though he also plays a great straight man in comedies (and adaptations of René Goscinny's beloved comic-book series). But aficionados of the *polar* genre will know Cornillac for his role as the brutish Capitaine 'Viking' Techouet in Matthieu Fabiani's *Central Nuit / Night Squad* (2001-2009), about a nighttime Parisian police brigade whose members solved crimes from shoplifting to serial murder with wit and solidarity. For three seasons, he played the rough-exteriored Viking, whose proverbial teddy-bear interior made him a faithful team member and friend, even following his dismissal from the squad.

We might also recognize Cornillac for his voice, which has made appearances in the French-dubbed releases of *Happy Feet* 1 and 2 (2006; 2011); and in Christophe Barratier's nostalgic musical, and music-hall-themed, comedy *Faubourg 36 /Paris 36* (2008), for which he took voice and dance lessons. Cornillac played Milou, the local Jewish communist who is also the love-interest of music-hall star Douce (Nora Arnezeder).

2012 showed Cornillac in two important roles: he played Maxime in *Mes héros* (Eric Besnard), and added his charisma as Arnold in Romain Lévy's *Radiostars*. With the thirtieth anniversary of his film debut, and a universe of roles behind him already, *cinéphiles* should expect to see Cornillac keep flexing his muscles and exploring new artistic paths on screens of all sizes.

Rosemary A. PETERS
Louisiana State University, Baton Rouge

Marion COTILLARD (1975–)

*She
Stoops
to
Conquer?*

WELL ON HER WAY to becoming as famous internationally as she is at home, Marion COTILLARD is undoubtedly one of the biggest French stars of the twenty-first century. Notable performances in films by some of the most influential directors in contemporary Hollywood have solidified Cotillard's fame outside France, which initially stemmed from her Academy Award winning performance as Édith Piaf in Olivier Dahan's *La Môme /La Vie en Rose* (2007).

Recalling Charlize Theron's Oscar winning turn as Aileen Wuornos in *Monster* (Patty Jenkins, 2003), Cotillard is utterly unrecognisable in her embodiment of the older Piaf in *La Môme*. After the manner of another Academy Award winner, Robert de Niro as Jake La Motta in *Raging Bull* (Martin Scorsese, 1980), Cotillard undergoes an extraordinary physical transformation over the course of Dahan's film, from the young and vibrant *môme* of the 1930s to the prematurely aged and strikingly frail Piaf in the period leading up to her untimely death in 1963. With Cotillard picking up best actress prizes at the Golden Globes, BAFTA, and the Césars as well as the Oscar, her role in *La Môme* was clearly predisposed to appeal to juries, but this should not blind us to the skill and power of her performance. To embody persuasively such an extensive physical transformation is notable in itself but Cotillard's real achievement is in how she uses the restrictions imposed by Piaf's physical decline, employing very subtle movements of the head, eyes, lips, and hands to convey the star's emotional turmoil. Though it is Piaf's own singing voice that is heard through the greater part of the film's soundtrack, Cotillard's vocal performance also deserves recognition, her natural huskiness becoming increasingly prominent as her character ages, suggesting a physical brittleness that conceals a spiritual force, most powerfully communicated by Piaf's seemingly unquenchable desire to perform.

Beyond the particularities of the performance itself, Marion Cotillard's 2008 Academy Award represented a very significant achievement. The first time that a French actress had won the top acting prize since Simone Signoret in 1960 for *Room at the Top* (Jack Clayton, 1959), Cotillard's win was also the first for a lead actress in a non-English speaking part since Sophia Loren picked up the 1962 award for her role in Vittorio De Sica's *La ciociara /Two Women* (1960). Beating such celebrated figures as Cate Blanchett, Julie Christie, and Laura Linney, recognition of the range and the affecting nature of Cotillard's performance in *La Môme* signalled the advances that she had made from her first film roles in which she was employed as little

more than eye candy. In her brief, scantily-clad appearance in Arnaud Desplechin's 1996 *Comment je me suis disputé...(ma vie sexuelle) /My Sex Life...or How I Got into an Argument*, Cotillard's Juliette has a marked effect on the seminary bound Ivan (Fabrice Desplechin) who describes the sight of her dancing in her underwear as 'the most perfect image of the Holy Spirit.' Rather less philosophically elevated (though arguably as sensible) discussion accompanies Cotillard's appearance as Lilly Bertineau in the first instalment of the hugely successful *Taxi* series (Gérard Pirès, 1998) – a role which she reprised in the next two *Taxi* sequels (2000 and 2003), directed by Gérard Krawczyk, for which she received her first César nomination (*Meilleur jeune espoir feminin* /Most Promising Actress). In a relative state of undress for the greater part of her screen time in *Taxi*, an introductory lingering pan over Cotillard's figure signals Pirès's priorities in his employment of the actress.

Born in 1975 and raised in Orléans by thespian parents, Marion Cotillard was not content to rest on the laurels of the burgeoning fame which came with her reprisal of the Lilly role in the Gérard-Krawczyk-directed *Taxi 2* (2000) and *Taxi 3* (2003) – but not in the fourth and final film in the series, *T4xi* (2007). Seeking to broaden her experience and to hone her acting skills, she appeared in a number of films by first time French directors including *Du bleu jusqu'en Amérique /Blue Away to America* (Sarah Lévy, 1999), *Les Jolies choses / Pretty Things* (Gilles Paquet-Brenner, 2001, garnering her a second César nomination for *Meilleur jeune espoir féminin* /Most Promising Actress), and *Ma vie en l'air /Love Is in the Air* (Rémi Bezançon, 2005). Appearing in French auteur Jean-Pierre Jeunet's 2004 *Un long dimanche de fiançailles /A Very Long Engagment*, she won the César for Best Supporting Actress for her portrayal of prostitute Tina Lombardi, bent on avenging the murder of her beloved pimp – even if she destroys herself in the process. The actress's fluent English was clearly a major asset in her early attempts to gain a foothold in Hollywood, and she successfully landed roles alongside Ewan McGregor in Tim Burton's *Big Fish* (2003) and Russell Crowe in Ridley Scott's *A Good Year* (2006).

Really taking off with her 2008 Oscar win, Cotillard's Hollywood career risked being immediately grounded with the unearthing of some ill-advised comments concerning the 9/11 terrorist attacks which the actress had made on French television in 2007. Swift apologies saw the controversy passing and media interest in the star's off-screen persona has more recently tended to focus on her relationship with actor/director Guillaume Canet with whom she has a son, Marcel (born in 2011). After appearing together in *Jeux d'enfants /Love Me If You Dare* (Yann Samuell, 2003), Cotillard and Canet became an item after his divorce from Diane Kruger in 2006. Since then, the couple has appeared together in Karim Dridi's *Le Dernier Vol /The Last Flight* (2009) while Canet has directed Cotillard in two films, the risible *Les Petits Mouchoirs /Little White Lies* (2010)

and the English language production *Blood Ties* (2013). Ginette Vincendeau notes the importance of cosmetic advertising for French film stars' international recognisability and Marion Cotillard is one of the current faces of Dior. Though film stars regularly communicate contradictory messages, it remains to be seen whether Cotillard's commitment to Dior can remain compatible with her frequently proclaimed support for Greenpeace for whom she made a 2010 film about the disastrous environmental impact of logging in the Congo.

Since her Oscar win, except roles in French films by partner Canet and Jacques Audiard (*De rouille et d'os / Rust and Bone*, 2012, for which she received a César nomination for Best Actress), Cotillard's primary focus seems to have been on advancing her career in Hollywood and she has forged productive relationships with such recognised *auteurs* as Michael Mann (*Public Enemies*, 2009), Steven Soderbergh (*Contagion*, 2011), Woody Allen (*Midnight in Paris*, 2011), Christopher Nolan (*Inception*, 2010; *The Dark Knight Rises*, 2012), as well as James Gray (*The Immigrant*, 2013). In 2015 she received a Best Actress Oscar nomination for her role in the Dardenne brothers' film, *Deux jours, une nuit /Two Days, One Night* (2014). To date, she has seemed content to occupy supporting roles, attempting to elevate apparently one-dimensional characters (e.g. *Midnight in Paris*'s sexy French muse Adriana or *Inception*'s woman as/of mystery Mal) into something more complex through the subtleties of performance. Yet she is now taking on meatier roles, starring as Lady Macbeth, opposite Michael Fassbender, in Justin Kurzel's highly anticipated *Macbeth* adaptation, currently in production and set for a 2015 release. In summer 2015, she will appear onstage in the titular role of Arthur Honegger's *Joan of Arc at the Stake* – its US premiere – which is to be performed at Avery Fisher Hall in New York City's Lincoln Center.

Will Cotillard be able to end her career singing *Je ne regrette rien* ? Will her strategy see her landing the leading Hollywood roles that her talents unquestionably deserve? Only time will tell.

Jim Morrissey
Newcastle University

Darry Cowl (1925–2006)
[André Darricau]

Sweet Madness

DARRY COWL, born André Darricau on August 27th, 1925, in Vittel (in the eastern part of France), was not only a famous postwar actor, but also a talented musician originating from the Conservatoire and was employed as such. Starting his career in the music-hall and piano-bars in the 1950s, he began to create a stammering blundering fool while accompanying actors like Bourvil; with this character gaining popularity he was eventually noticed by the famous playwright Sacha Guitry, who advised him to consider playing in films and who gave him a role in 1956 in *Assassins et Voleurs /Lovers and Thieves*. From the start of his film career in 1955 he was often asked to play clumsy, vacant, and stammering characters, such as in one of his first movies, *Le Triporteur /The Tricyclist* (Jacques Pinoteau, 1957), where he is the lead actor. The simple story about a joyful and absent-minded tricycle rider fond of soccer made the movie – and consequently the actor – very popular. But he stuck so much to such a character that he was mainly asked to keep acting this way. Even though such characters brought him popularity and a sympathetic image, with time his clumsiness and unintelligible stuttering eventually wearied his audience and even himself. However, this weariness did not affect his popularity and he kept acting up to his death: if he had not died of lung cancer in 2006, he would have been playing Jean Barbier's *Hold Up* on stage with Jacques Balutin.

The more recent characters he had to play were no longer clumsy but rather naïve or embodying kindness and simplicity – his age bringing him also a wiser touch. In *Ah ! Si j'étais riche /If I Were a Rich Man* (Gérard Bitton and Michel Munz, 2002) he plays an old manufacturer basically overwhelmed by industrial production, and who barely understands how a lottery billionaire managed to give a second birth to his quality products in selling them at a good price, which gives a sweet comical touch to this sour comedy: the character embodied by Darry Cowl is far from being an 'aware' manager and he does not even try to understand the sudden success of his business.

Conscious that many of his films were third-rate, Cowl acknowledged that his best role happened to be in Marco Ferreri's *Touche pas à la femme blanche /Don't Touch the White Woman!* (1974) and the critics congratulated him in 1999 for his supporting role in *Augustin roi du kung-fu /Augustin, King of Kung-Fu* (dir. Anne Fontaine). However, in 2001 he received a César award for his long career, with a second one in 2004 for his role in *Pas sur la bouche /Not on the Lips* (Alain Renais, 2003). He even admitted to being tired of the image sticking to him and to the characters he played. Paradoxically the audience

started to get bored of this recurrent character in movies, but could not have understood nor accepted another kind of role which would have been more serious or dramatic. People would have expected some funny issue, or would not have believed in the sincerity of his dramatic or his sad acting. His popularity as a clumsy, stupefied, lisping, and stuttering actor/ character (the one sticking so much to the other) started with *Le Triporteur* in 1957, at a time when comic situations coming from involuntary blunders (as in Jacques Tati's films) suited a post-war audience in providing simple comic effects to forget the trauma of WWII. However, the evolution of cinema and the passing of time (with trauma becoming a far-away memory, and new post-war generations growing up), and also the recurrent style of his acting, eroded his popularity in the late 1960s, after an impressive score of 60 films. In 1964, he experienced his first big failure not only as an actor but also as a director – for the first and last time – with *Jaloux comme un tigre*.

L'Increvable /The Indestructible (Jean Boyer, 1959) is not a famous film but is worth watching for the way his clumsiness is used: Cowl, as the main character – the owner of a café – has signed a juicy life-insurance policy. Because of his stupid, naïve behaviour, his wife thinks she can easily get rid of him. Therefore she plans to use three greedy and gullible clients to kill her husband. Somehow his faults save him and the criminals end up, one after the other, as the victims. Darry Cowl's genuine astonishment and compassion as he reads in the newspaper of the 'accidental' death of three of his clients provides one of the funniest moments of the film. This film was an interesting mixture of cruelty and innocence: the cruelty of killing but also the compassion of the victim for his murderers.

Jean-Pierre Mocky, a director well-known for his subversive style, asked Darry Cowl to act in *Les Saisons du plaisir* (1988). Even though he had never stopped acting, working in Mocky's film was seen as a comeback for Darry Cowl, maybe because one has to watch this director's films with second-degree interpretation.

Many people in France are unaware that Darry Cowl composed the music of a few films between 1967 and 1977, including that of *Ces messieurs de la gâchette* (Raoul André, 1970), *Le Concierge* (Jean Girault, 1973), and *Arrête ton char...bidasse !* (Michel Gérard, 1977), because what remains of Darry Cowl in people's minds is an image of a simple, sincere and honest person; and this image of the actor – of the person – finds its sources in the characters he played and stuck to him perfectly.

Igor BRATUSEK
Université Paris–Sorbonne

Marcel DALIO (1899–1983)
[Marcel Benoit BLAUSCHILD]

Dalliance with 'L'immortel' Dalio

'MARCEL DE BLANCHEVILLE or Marc de Beauchili? I was fifteen years old, and on the eve of leaving for the first time on tour with a company of actors I had to choose a name for myself. Something properly French, also a bit grandiloquent, and naturally aristocratic. Because there was no question of appearing on the poster under my real name: Israël Mosche Blauschild![1] It was enough to make the brave Swiss for whom we were to perform flee!

'Blancheville or Beauchili? My decision was made: neither one nor the other...I had my idea. I was still dazzled by the memory of the handsome prince Danilo in *The Merry Widow* and a name formed itself in my head: Dalino...Dalo... DALIO !!! I was baptized.'[2]

It is not, perhaps, too much of an exaggeration to say that the destiny of Marcel DALIO, and that of twentieth century Europe, intersected with one another to the extent that the former could almost be considered to be the personification of the latter. As the above anecdote reveals, even Dalio's stage name resonated with broader historical significance; by his own explanation, the soubriquet was simultaneously a nod to a certain variety of gilded Old World charm, and a kind of portent or premonition of the ultimate demise of that world in the concentration camps of Europe. David Thomson interprets Dalio's final speech in what was unquestionably his finest role, as the world-weary Marquis de la Chesnaye in Jean Renoir's 1939 film *La Règle du jeu /The Rules of the Game*, as a thinly veiled metaphor for the threat posed by the worsening political situation in Germany. As he stands in the darkness on the steps leading to his château, the Marquis calls for his guests to come in from the evening chill after one of their number, mistaken for someone else, has been shot by his gamekeeper. In a perfect *mise en abime*, as Thomson declares, '[f]or both the character – a French aristocrat of Jewish descent – and the Jewish actor, Marcel Dalio, that speech was to prove a farewell to France.' [3]

'From the ghetto to Fouquet's,' [4] as Dalio puts it in his lively autobiography, and, from there, on to Hollywood, his was, in many ways, the archetypical European émigré story: larger-than-life, propelled by its protagonist's personal resourcefulness and capacity for self-reinvention, finding both its happy ending and a new beginning in America. Born into a family of Eastern-European Jews in Paris in 1900, Dalio studied at the *Conservatoire d'art dramatique*, from which he graduated to performing in the theatre and the music hall. When he turned to cinema, his appearance – short and dark with

expressive face and pronouncedly 'exotic' features – precluded his casting as the *jeune premier* in romantic leading roles, yet Thomson's assessment that he 'would never be a star' [5] underestimates the impact of a number of brilliant supporting performances which helped to establish him, alongside personalities like Carette and Modot, as a *vraie gueule* of French cinema.

Dalio's perceived 'otherness' was often central to his characterizations. In fact his cultural affiliations would become such an integral aspect of his onscreen persona that, as Elizabeth Ezra and Valerie Orpen point out, the Nazis later employed his photograph to identify the features of 'The Typical Jew' [6] in anti-Semitic propaganda. In the European phase of his career, his Jewishness would manifest itself both in the negative and villainous stereotypes of films like *Pépé le Moko* (Julien Duvivier, 1937) and *La Maison du Maltais /Sirocco* (Pierre Chenal, 1938), in which he played the 'typical Oriental bastard' required by xenophobic imagery,[7] and as the enviable cosmopolitanism and inherent nobility of the banker's son Rosenthal in Renoir's *La Grande Illusion* (1937). Even after Dalio fled occupied Europe for Hollywood, he continued to play the role of a cultural outsider, perhaps most notably as one of the many European refugees employed in Rick's Café Américain in *Casablanca* (Michael Curtiz, 1942, in which Dalio's wife, Madeleine Lebeau, plays Yvonne). Yet somewhat ironically, as Ezra and Orpen put it, '[h]is American roles traded greatly on his Frenchness, rather than his Jewishness.' [7] Indeed one of the characters Dalio played, 'Gerard' in Howard Hawks' Hemingway adaptation *To Have and Have Not* (1944), was called, simply, 'Frenchy.' However, nearly three decades later in the 1973 French farce *Les Aventures de Rabbi Jacob /The Mad Adventures of Rabbi Jacob* (dir. Gérard Oury), a comedy of mistaken identity and a send–up of French conventions of class, religious, and social identity, Dalio incarnates the titular figure: a respected rabbi who returns to Paris after 30 years in New York City. The comical misadventures begin the moment Rabbi Jacob's plane touches down in France when he crosses paths, in the airport, with the casually racist, xenophobic, and anti-Semitic bourgeois French snob Victor Pivert (Louis de Funès), who forcefully takes on Rabbi Jacob's identity in order to flee both the French police and a group of Arab government agents pursuing him (as Pivert unwittingly prevented them from executing a rebel leader attempting a coup d'état). High jinks ensue as Pivert poses as Rabbi Jacob, ultimately rejecting his prejudices in favour of tolerance.

Though he would never be given the opportunity to surpass his achievement in *La Règle du jeu*, Dalio's later career produced some memorable cameos in classic films like *Gentlemen Prefer Blondes* (Howard Hawks, 1953), *Sabrina* (Billy Wilder, 1954), *Pillow Talk* (Michael Gordon, 1959), *Donovan's Reef /La Taverne de l'Irlandais* (John Ford, 1963), and *Catch-22* (Mike

Nichols, 1970), in which he appears briefly as a pragmatic 107 year-old Italian who councils Art Garfunkel's Captain Nately that 'it's better to live on your feet than to die on your knees.' It was, perhaps, his most fitting epitaph.

Celia NICHOLLS
University of Alberta, Edmonton

1. Dalio's full birth-name [as entered (without circumflex) on his Paris 5e birth record of November 1899] was 'Marcel Benoit Blauschild' (son of Isidore Blauschild, *maroquinier*, and Sarah Cerf); 'Israël' and 'Mosche' were names used more personally by him and his family. —Ed.

2. Marcel Dalio, with Jean-Pierre de Lucovich, *Mes années folles* (Paris: Éditions J.C. Lattès, 1986 [original pub. 1976]), 13. [Translated: Ed.]

3. David Thomson, *The New Biographical Dictionary of Film* (London: Little Brown, 2010), 227.

4. Dalio, *Mes années folles*, 11.

5. Thomson, *The New Biographical Dictionary of Film*, 227.

6. Elizabeth Ezra and Valerie Orpen, 'Marcel Dalio,' in *Journeys of Desire: European Actors in Hollywood, A Critical Companion*, ed. Alastair Phillips and Ginette Vincendeau (London: BFI, 2006), 224.

7. Jean-Loup Passek, ed., *Dictionnaire du cinéma français* (Paris: Larousse, 1987), 99; quoted in Keith Reader, *La Règle du jeu* [French Film Guide] (London: I.B. Tauris, 2010), 16.

8. Ezra and Orpen, *Journeys of Desire*, 224.

Béatrice DALLE (1964–)
[Béatrice CABARROU]

« *La Grande Bouche* »

Béatrice DALLE (born Béatrice Cabarrou in 1964) is popularly known in France by the epithet « La grande bouche ». Stemming from her physically prominent mouth and gapped teeth, this characterisation sums up figuratively, albeit rather harshly, the defining characteristics of Dalle's star image: carnality (her embodiment of a voracious sexuality) and volubility (her projection of a confrontational, sharp-tongued personality).

This image was established as early as her first film appearance in Jean-Jacques Beineix's cult classic, *37°2 le matin /Betty Blue* (1986). A box-office hit nationally and internationally, the film propelled the newcomer Dalle, who had until then been working as a model, to high stardom. Yet, *37°2 le matin*'s success, which was partly the result of its explicit sexual content, proved to be both a blessing and a curse for Dalle. For although her debut role as the free-spirited and brazen Betty turned her into an iconic sex symbol, it also significantly reduced the variety of parts she has been offered to play. Since *37°2 le matin*, Dalle has become inextricably associated with an image of disturbed

sexuality that echoes the film's story of *amour fou*. Betty exhibits a raw, unapologetic, all-consuming passion, which while acting as a catalyst for the realisation of her lover Zorg's creative potential (Zorg, played by Jean-Hugues Anglade, moonlights as a writer), at the same time it becomes an agent of destruction, as it not only wreaks havoc on those around her, but also precipitates her descent into depression, self-harm, and ultimately madness.

This linking of passion with disturbance has taken a rather extreme turn in recent years that have seen Dalle's erstwhile sexual abandon and mental fragility transmute into full-blown carnal violence and disorder. The development of her career in this direction coincides with the rise of the so-called *cinéma du corps* in the early noughties. Characterised by its focus on extreme sexuality and viscerality, this new tendency in French cinema is the province of art cinema and female stardom. However, unlike those of her contemporaries who specialise in similarly extreme parts, such as Émmanuelle Béart, Sandrine Bonnaire, and Isabelle Huppert, Dalle is never endowed with subjectivity and psychological depth. Rather, she is cast stereotypically, physiognomically even, with her mouth metonymically standing for a transgressive and abject sexuality. Emblematic of this is her role as Coré in Claire Denis's *Trouble Every Day* (2001). Here Dalle plays the wife of a scientist whose experiments into the human libido have left her suffering from a clinical disorder that induces her to cannibalistic sexual acts. The film presents Dalle as feral, a wild beast on the prowl for carnal satisfaction. Given no dialogue, she is treated as an object of fascination, with close-ups either fetishising her voracious mouth as it devours the flesh of her lovers, or scrutinising her as a clinical case, a curiosity best kept locked up.

This stereotyping has affected both her leading and supporting roles. As a lead, Dalle is now confined to monstrous feminine parts in horror flicks, such as *À l'intérieur / Inside* (Alexandre Bustillo and Julien Maury, 2007), in which she plays an unnamed character, credited as 'The Woman,' who obsessively tries to take the unborn baby of a young widow. In general, however, Dalle has tended to appear in supporting roles that can be divided into two major types. On the one hand, Dalle is cast as a kind of truth-teller, who confronts other characters by voicing those ideas and fears they refuse to acknowledge. This is her function, for instance, in Jim Jarmusch's *Night on Earth* (1991) and Michael Haneke's *Le Temps du loup /Time of the Wolf* (2003). On the other hand, Dalle is typically used as a female archetype. This is the case in *Clubbed to Death (Lola)* (Yolande Zauberman, 1996), where her function is relegated to that of a sex goddess, and in *L'Intrus /The Intruder* (Claire Denis, 2004), where her striking iconography (an animal-skin clad Dalle surrounded by huskies) graphically conjures up her archetypal role as the 'Queen of the Northern Hemisphere.'

Dalle's wild image on screen is matched by her notoriety off screen. Her personal life has been marked by a series of high-profile scandals. First are her various law offences, ranging from assault, shoplifting, and possession of class-A drugs. Furthermore, her infamy is bolstered by her rather controversial choices of partners, most notably her marriage to Guénaël Meziani in 2005. Meziani was an inmate serving a sentence for raping his ex-girlfriend, whom Dalle met while shooting *Tête d'or* (Gilles Blanchard, 2006) in Ploemeur prison in Brittany. When rumours of his alleged assault against Dalle reached the press soon after their marriage, the self-destructive streak of Dalle's volatile persona was confirmed once more. It remains to be seen what other extremes are left for the impulsive and provocative Béatrice Dalle to cross.

Olga KOURELOU
King's College, London

Gérard DARMON (1948–)

« Sais-tu danser la Carioca ? »

WITH A CAREER spanning over four decades, including more than 90 film and television roles to his credit, performing onstage in plays and as a singer, Gérard DARMON (born in Paris) is a very familiar face in French cinema, as he worked, over the years, with some well-known names in the French and European film industries, including directors Jean-Jacques Beineix, Luc Besson, Bertrand Blier, Alain Chabat, Neil Jordan, Tony Gatlif, Claude Lelouch, Bigas Luna, Gérard Oury, and an array of stars, too numerous to cite individually here.

As a child, Darmon idolized Fernandel and Jerry Lewis, known for their comic roles. Darmon never obtained his Baccalaureate nor did he make it through the audition process for the Conservatoire national supérieur d'art dramatique (CNSAD) in 1972. Yet in 1972, he made his onscreen debut in not one, but two feature films: as a valet in the Jacques Brel vehicle *Le Bar de la fourche /The Bar at the Crossing* (dir. Alain Levent) – a World War I era drama in which Isabelle Huppert garnered her first major role – and with a small part in *L'Humeur vagabonde /Vagabond Humour* (directed by Edouard Luntz), starring Michel Bouquet, Jeanne Moreau, and Madeleine Renaud. With Jean-Pierre Bacri, Darmon spent about ten years in *café-théâtres*, honing his craft.

With the help of actor/director Roger Hanin – who cast Darmon as Blumenfeld in his 1975 *Le Faux-cul / The Phoney* – Darmon received more work in film, including a small role in Claude Lelouch's *Nous deux /Us Two* (1979), starring Catherine Deneuve and Gérard Depardieu. Darmon would work again with Lelouch as the moody policeman in *Il y a des jours… et des lunes /There Were Days…and Moons* (1990) and in *La Belle Histoire /The Beautiful Story* (1992) as well as *Tout ça…pour ça ! /All That…for This?!* (1993). By 1982, Darmon was co-starring with Hanin in the drama *La Baraka* (Jean Valère, 1982), as Julien, who, living in the wild outside the bounds of civilization, rescues Hanin, a Marseilles chef, after a fishing accident. Darmon then had a substantial role in another film set in the south of France, Juliet Berto and Jean-Henri Roger's *Cap Canaille* (1983), which was nominated for the Golden Bear at the Berlin Film Festival. Darmon starred as Nara in Tony Gatlif's acclaimed and award-winning drama *Les Princes* (1983), the first instalment of Gatlif's 'Gypsy' trilogy, about the plight of a Roma family living in government housing on the outskirts of Paris, with Darmon portraying the obstinate and temperamental leading character, the father. *Les Princes* received the Golden Charybdis at the Taormina Film Festival, and in 1997 Gatlif received the Grand Prix Spécial des Amériques from the Montréal World Film Festival for his entire 'Gypsy' trilogy. Darmon collaborated again with Gatlif in the crime drama *Rue du départ /The Way Out* (1986), as the inspector, and as the titular Gaspard in *Gaspard et Robinson /Gaspard and Robinson* (1990). In 1983, Darmon received the Prix Jean-Gabin given annually to the most promising actor (which, as of 2008, was renamed the Prix Patrick-Dewaere).

Darmon's early collaboration with Beineix was particularly fruitful. Darmon appeared in Beineix's first feature film, *Diva* (1981), as the killer thug 'L'Antillais' ('The Antillean') and a few years later in Beineix's third directorial effort, which is considered his chef d'oeuvre, *37°2 le matin /Betty Blue*, a hugely successful contemporary drama. Darmon's character in Betty Blue is that of the supportive Eddy, a charismatic pizzeria owner, who is a friend of Betty (Béatrice Dalle) and Zorg (Jean-Hugues Anglade). In this film, as Eddy, Darmon received top billing following the two stars, Dalle and Anglade (Darmon worked with Dalle again in Lelouch's 1992 *La Belle Histoire*). Eddy is Betty's friend Lisa's (Consuelo de Haviland) boyfriend, who tries to help Betty and Zorg, first by hiring the couple at his restaurant, a move that proves disastrous due to Betty's emotional instability which prevents her from being able to handle customers against whom she can turn violent. Eddy then allows Betty and Zorg to live in his late mother's home in the South of France, but Betty's emotional decline leads to her inability to go on. *Betty Blue* was something of a breakthrough for Darmon: for his memorable performance as Eddy, he was nominated for his first César, for Best Supporting Actor. (He was again nominated for the Best Supporting

Actor César in 2003 for his role as Amonbofis in Alain Chabat's 2002 *Astérix et Obélix : Mission Cléopâtre / Asterix and Obelix Meet Cleopatra*.) *Betty Blue* was nominated for major awards the world over, including the Oscar, Golden Globe, César, BAFTA, and more, receiving prizes such as the Best Foreign Language Film award from the Boston Society of Film Critics, Grand Prix des Amériques from the Montréal World Film Festival, and the César for Best Poster.

Darmon is of Algerian Jewish descent (although in July 2012 he was naturalized as a citizen of Morocco by King Muhammed VI). Some of his roles, in numerous films that explore Jewish themes and/or have Jewish characters, relate to his cultural background as a Jew from Algeria. One of Darmon's earliest films was Oury's 1973 comedy *Les Aventures de Rabbi Jacob /The Mad Adventures of Rabbi Jacob*, although here he incarnated one of the non-Jewish characters, a henchman of Colonel Farès (Renzo Montagnani), attempting to prevent opposition leader Mohamed Larbi Slimane (Claude Giraud) from overthrowing the current government in place in their country. Darmon took on the role of Roland, the nephew of the North African Jewish Beitoun crime family, in Alexandre Arcady's 1982 *Le Grand Pardon* and its 1992 sequel, *Le Grand Pardon 2*. In another Arcady film, *Pour Sacha / For Sasha* (1991), a tale of friendship, love, and loss set on an Israeli kibbutz in 1967 against the backdrop of the Six-Day War, Darmon plays attorney David Malka. David is the brother of Myriam (Shlomit Cohen), a young woman, who, before she committed suicide, had been in love with Sacha (Richard Berry), writing him the film's titular letter ('For Sasha') prior to her death. Renowned French actors Sophie Marceau and Emmanuelle Riva are also members of the film's cast. In Arcady's 2004 comedy *Mariage mixte*, Darmon incarnates Max Zagury, a wealthy Jewish casino proprietor who is displeased with his daughter marrying a man who is of a different religious faith. In Idit Cebula's Jewish family film *Deux vies...plus une / Two Lives Plus One* (2007), Darmon plays Sylvain Weiss, whose wife, schoolteacher Eliane (Emmanuelle Devos), decides to pursue a writing career.

A versatile performer, Darmon demonstrated his gift for comedy as well as singing and dancing in the first film by the comedy group *Les Nuls*, the cult farce *La Cité de la peur /Fear City: A Family-Style Comedy* (Alain Berbérian, 1994), written by members of 'Les Nuls' (Alain Chabat, Dominique Farrugia, Chantal Lauby). Darmon, in the role of Detective Patrick Bialès, together with Chabat, perform a song and dance routine. They croon *La Carioca* in French and dance together onstage in what has become one of the film's iconic scenes. In 1994, Darmon met Mathilda May on the set of Spanish auteur Bigas Luna's *La Lune et le téton /La teta y la luna*. May and Darmon married, and had two children: Sarah (born on August 17, 1994) and Jules (born on March 4, 1997), before divorcing in 1999. (Darmon also has a daughter, Virginie, born in 1968, from his first marriage to Nicole Recoules.) May and Darmon also co-starred in Paul Boujenah's *Le Voleur et la Menteuse*

(1994).

Darmon has recorded three albums, sang seven times as part of *Les Enfoirés* for *Les Restaurants du cœur*, and covered the classic *Mambo Italiano*. He has also performed his songs at the prestigious Olympia in Paris, where he also celebrated the 50th anniversary of Enrico Macias' singing career onstage with Macias. Darmon is politically engaged, having campaigned for François Hollande and criticized French deputy Gilbert Collard, who is part of a coalition that supports Marine Le Pen of the Front National.

Among Darmon's recent films is Valérie Lemercier's *100% cachemire / The Ultimate Accessory* (2013). Judging from his long and successful career, one can expect to see and hear much more of Gérard Darmon's singing and acting on French stages, screens, and airwaves.

Marcelline BLOCK
Princeton University and SAG-AFTRA

Danielle DARRIEUX (1917–)

Nine
Decades
of
Stardom

DANIELLE DARRIEUX's remarkable and lengthy career spans almost the entire history of sound cinema, from the early 1930s up to the present day. She began by playing children in such films as *Le Bal* (Wilhelm Thiele, 1931) and *Coquecigrole* (André Berthomieu, 1931), before progressing to leading roles in comedies with Albert Préjean. From the mid-1930s onwards her fame developed further, with her starring in *Quelle drôle de gosse !* (Léo Joannon, 1935) and a number of films produced and directed by her manager Henri Decoin (whom she also married in 1935). For the remainder of the 1930s, she was the main star of the films she appeared in, a rarity for a French female star at this time. Decoin also influenced her career by encouraging her to appear in dramas as well as comedies, and by taking her to Hollywood in 1938, where she made *The Rage of Paris* (dir. Henry Koster), before returning to France.

While many stars of the 1930s were taken from the stage, as they were actors with the vocal skills required to meet the demands of the new sound medium, Darrieux entered the cinema directly, making her, along with a number of other stars of the period, such as Annabella, Simone Simon,

and Michèle Morgan, an example of the period's 'cinematic' stardom, a French response to the glamorous stars found in Hollywood at the time. She was indeed exceptionally beautiful, with a youthful appearance, wide eyes, long lashes, and pouty lips. These elements were channelled into two main aspects of her persona. On the one hand, she was a young, delicate and innocent ingénue, particularly in historical melodramas like *Mayerling* (Anatole Litvak, 1936), co-starring Charles Boyer, and *Katia* (Maurice Tourneur, 1938). At the same time, she was a prominent French example of the internationally ubiquitous 'modern woman.' This was especially the case in *Club de femmes* (Jacques Deval, 1936) – a surprisingly modern film, containing Art Deco sets, a cast composed almost entirely of women, a lesbian narrative, and hints of transvestism – in which Darrieux wore up-to-date fashions and demonstrated the energy and spontaneity associated with this form of femininity. Her tall, thin body and long neck (one magazine article dubbed her *la giraffe*), meant that she also possessed the physique typical of this female type. She also played women who had 'modern' jobs – she was a stenographer in *Quelle drôle de gosse !* and a lawyer in *Un mauvais garçon* (Jean Boyer, 1936), as well as in *Abus de confiance /Abused Confidence* (Henri Decoin, 1937). Her modernity was particularly important to her comedies in which her roles combined comedy and romance, making her a French equivalent of the screwball heroines found in Hollywood at this time, such as Claudette Colbert and Katherine Hepburn.

During the Occupation years,

Darrieux continued to be a big star, though her decision to work for the German-run Continental Films was controversial. After the war, with her identity shifting from the precocious young woman to a personification of French sophistication, she made a few more Hollywood films, including *5 Fingers* (Joseph L. Mankiewicz, 1952), co-starring James Mason, and became one of the big stars of the French 'tradition of quality,' particularly through three films directed by Max Ophüls – *La Ronde* (1950), *Le Plaisir* (1952), *Madame de... /The Earrings of Madame de...* (1953) – and *Le Rouge et le Noir* (Claude Autant-Lara, 1954), in which she co-starred with Gérard Philipe. Into the 1960s her career slowed down, but she continued to appear in some high profile films, including *Les Demoiselles de Rochefort / The Young Ladies of Rochefort* (Jacques Demy, 1967), the second of five films in which she played Catherine Deneuve's mother, the others being *L'Homme à femmes /Ladies Man* (Jacques-Gérard Cornu, 1960), *Le Lieu du crime / Scene of the Crime* (André Téchiné, 1986), *8 femmes /8 Women* (François Ozon, 2002), and *Persepolis* (Vincent Paronnaud and Marjane Satrapi, 2007). Darrieux also commenced a successful stage career, mostly in Paris, but she also appeared on Broadway in 1970 replacing Katherine Hepburn in *Coco*. With a career spanning from 1931, when she was just 14 years old, to the present day (she turned 97 in 2014), she has had one of the longest careers in the history of cinema.

Jonathan DRISKELL
Monash University Malaysia

Jean-Pierre DARROUSSIN (1953–)

*A Tender
and
Iconic
Actor*

JEAN-PIERRE DARROUSSIN was born in Courbevoie, near Paris. Darroussin's career began with theatre: between 1974 and 1979, he studied in Paris at the Cours Florent, the Rue Blanche drama school, and the Dramatic Art Conservatoire, making friends with Ariane Ascaride, Catherine Frot, and Sam Karmann. Since 1976, he has continuously acted on stage, in parallel to his career in the cinema.

Jean-Pierre Darroussin first appeared in a movie as an extra in Jean-Jacques Annaud's second film *Coup de tête /Hothead* (1979). In 1981, he played the supporting role of a paranoiac in the comedy *Psy* (Philippe de Broca) with Catherine Frot and starring Patrick Dewaere. He then obtained one of the leading roles, an invigorating embalmer, in the situational comedy *Celles qu'on n'a pas eues* (Pascal Thomas, 1981) with Michel Aumont, Michel Galabru, and Bernard Menez. Until 1988, though, Darroussin's career was mostly oriented towards theatre. He appeared as a supporting role in very different movies such as *Est-ce bien raisonnable ?* (Georges Lautner, 1981), *Notre histoire /Our Story* (Bertrand Blier, 1984), *On ne meurt que deux fois /He Died with His Eyes Open* (Jacques

Deray, 1985), and *Ki lo sa ?* (Robert Guédiguian, 1985).

A turning point in Darroussin's career is *Mes meilleurs copains /My Best Pals* (Jean-Marie Poiré, 1989), which brings him public notoriety. Meeting up with his 'best friends' (Gérard Lanvin, Christian Clavier, Jean-Pierre Bacri, and others), Darroussin's character was a revelation as a post-traumatic, slow, and sluggish musician refusing all conflicts and playing the electric guitar like a god. From then, popular roles followed in successful movies, mainly from three different universes: Paris and its prickly irony with screenwriters Agnès Jaoui and Jean-Pierre Bacri; hearty or petty humble people caught in social conflicts in/near Marseilles with film director Robert Guédiguian; and bitterweet comedies of manners with film director Jeanne Labrune.

Cuisine et Dépendances /Kitchen with Apartment (Philippe Muyl, 1993) is the adaptation of a famous and award-winning play written by Agnès Jaoui and Jean-Pierre Bacri. It was performed by Jaoui, Sam Karmann, and Darroussin on stage between 1990 and 1992. In the movie, the same actors, adding Jean-Pierre Bacri, evolve from the dining room to the kitchen in an electric atmosphere as a former friend, now a famous man, is invited for dinner. Darroussin's character, a sensible and lucid gambler, makes an amusing counterpoint to a stiff-necked atmosphere. It won him a César nomination as Best Supporting Actor. In 1996, he is a clumsy bartender in *Un air de famille /Family Resemblances* (Cédric Klapisch) written by Jaoui and Bacri, a performance which won him a César for Best Supporting

Actor. His first collaboration with Cédric Klapisch (*Riens du tout /Little Nothings*, 1992) showed him as a comical music teacher whom the new manager of a declining department store (Fabrice Luchini) asks to build up team spirit. He also appeared in *On connaît la chanson /Same Old Song* (Alain Resnais, 1997), also written by Jaoui and Bacri. In 1999, the successful comedy *La Bûche /Season's Beatings* (dir. Danièle Thomson), with Sabine Azéma and Emmanuelle Béart, recalls *Un air de famille.*

With his hangdog look, Darroussin has performed in eleven movies by the film director Robert Guédiguian and with actress Ariane Ascaride. All refer to a communist past, solidarity in hard times, and social injustice. They take place in the Estaque neighbourhood in Marseilles, a popular place near the beach with its small harbour and atmosphere of sunny loneliness. *Marius et Jeannette* (1997) is undoubtedly Guédiguian's best success and won Darroussin a nomination for the Best Supporting Actor César.[1]

Finally, film director Jeanne Labrune is a great fan of Jean-Pierre Darroussin. His monotonous voice, tender and ironic looks, and extinct eyes fit perfectly with the hypercritical characters he plays in her witty comedies, such as *Ça ira mieux demain /Tomorrow's Another Day* (2000), *C'est le bouquet ! /Special Delivery* (2002), and *Cause toujours !* (2004).

Full of artistic curiosity, Darroussin has accepted original leading roles. In *Le Poulpe /The Octopus* (Guillaume Nicloux, 1998), he was a Rock & Roll style Parisian detective investiga-ting small-town rubes with actress

Clotilde Courau. The role won him a nomination for best actor. The dark comedy *Qui plume la lune ?* (Christine Carrière, 1999) let him fully express sadness, rage, and tenderness, for which he received Best Actor Awards at the Namur International Festival of French-speaking films and the Thessaloniki Film Festival. The nerve-racking *Feux rouges /Red Lights* (Cédric Kahn, 2004) made him a drunk husband confronted with murder and rape. Darroussin directed his first full-length movie in 2006, *Le Pressentiment*, which won the Prix Louis Delluc for Best First Film, among other awards.

Darroussin has become one of the key performers in French cinema. He plays alongside André Wilms in Aki Kaurismäki's *Le Havre* (2011), and is once more one of the major ingredients of Guédigian's films: he shines again in *Les Neiges du Kilimandjaro /The Snows of Kilimanjaro* (2011), and as usual almost a label for Darroussin's part, with finesse and emotion.

Nicolas RIGAUD
The University of Oxford

1. For further discussion of *Marius et Jeannette*, see Annette Insdorf, scene review, in *World Film Locations: Marseilles*, ed. Marcelline Block (Bristol: Intellect, 2013), 72-73. —Ed.

Jamel DEBBOUZE (1975–)

Jack of All Trades

JAMEL DEBBOUZE was born in Paris and spent the first four years of his life in Morocco before his parents came back to France. From then on he grew up in a humble background in the heart of a workers' housing estate in Trappes, near Paris. Indeed, nothing suggested that he would one day become one of the most important actors of his generation, the odds being rather against him, and yet he proved able to make use of imbalances to become what he is today.

He started on stage with improvisation theatre, before working for radio and then for television, on Canal+, where his programme *Le Cinéma de Jamel* brought him success. And he soon evolved from presenting the latest releases to becoming a film actor himself.

On screen, he first embodied a new type of French humour, claiming to take his inspiration from *Saturday Night Live*, Eddie Murphy, Jerry Seinfeld, and Albert Dupontel. But he soon turned to more dramatic roles. In ten years of success on screen, he alternated between comic roles in *Le Ciel, les oiseaux...et ta mère ! / Boys on the Beach* (Djamel Bensalah, 1999) and *Astérix et Obélix : Mission Cléopâtre /Asterix and Obelix Meet*

Cleopatra (Alain Chabat, 2001), to more serious ones such as *Zonzon* (Laurent Bouhnik, 1998) and *Indigènes /Days of Glory* (Rachid Bouchareb, 2006). In parallel, he pursued his career as a stand-up comedian, became a producer (*She Hate Me*, dir. Spike Lee, 2004, and *Indigènes*), had a go at rap music with Joeystarr (of the band NTM), and confirmed his role as a TV clown in various shows on Canal+. This variety of roles and functions reflects the personality he created for himself. Mixing up genres and being on a precarious balance have become his trademarks.

From the point of view of language, Jamel's acting is built on broken diction, approximations, in between dyslexia and neologism, a language not devoid of swear words and colloquial phrases, giving birth to a world of nonsense and imagination close to the naïve language of a young child. He is a permanent creator and every text that passes through his hands comes out modified, 'jamelified', so that even in his non-comic roles, some of the language gimmicks that made him famous reappear. This new language that he helped create is used nowadays by many members of the younger generation. A new grammar and syntax appeared, flouting the rules learnt in school or in society.

On this account, it must be acknowledged that Jamel Debbouze is of major importance in French creation nowadays. As all great artists, he is able to draw from the legacy of previous generations, to modify and transgress the rules in order to produce something new that the young generations can make theirs.

As for body language, here again, Jamel makes use of approximation and imbalance. He is of a puny, child-like, fragile appearance, with something of Pee-Wee Herman and Charlie Chaplin. Bending his body in all directions, he often seems on the verge of breaking into pieces, but he always rebounds. He bends but never breaks, just like in the accident which befell him when he was a teenager: while he was playing on a railway with a friend, he was hit by a train which killed his friend and left his left arm atrophied and unusable. Yet Jamel managed to turn this disability into an asset: always thrust deep into his jeans pocket, forcing his body to lean towards one side, little by little, this ghost-hand became part of the character he had built. It materializes an unavoidable asymmetry and modifies the actor's centre of gravity, forcing him to run after an inaccessible position of balance. Animated with inexhaustible energy and movement, he ends up having to occupy the whole space in each scene, at the risk of falling.

Some might reproach him for spreading himself too thin, on screen, on stage, and in life, but they would be wrong, because dabbling in everything is part and parcel of his personality.

Caroline Rossi
Université Stendhal – Grenoble 3

Cécile DE FRANCE (1975–)

*High
Tension
and
Charming
Diversity*

SOME NAMES may deceive as much as appearances: born in Namur (Belgium), it is only after turning seventeen that actress Cécile DE FRANCE moves to Paris where, after studying drama with Jean-Paul Denizon, she gains acceptance to the École Nationale Supérieure des Arts et Techniques du Théâtre (ENSATT). Related to her namesake, Cécile de France, discovered by the French actor and agent Dominique Besnehard, started a successful career by acting in French hit films such as Richard Berry's *L'Art (délicat) de la séduction* (2001) and Ivan Calbérac's *Irène* (2002). Within Europe she is best known for her César-award-winning roles in Cédric Klapisch's romantic comedy *L'Auberge espagnole /The Spanish Apartment* (2002) and its sequels *Les Poupées russes /Russian Dolls* (2005) and *Casse-tête chinois /Chinese Puzzle* (2013), as well as for her girl-next-door performance in *Quand j'étais chanteur* (Xavier Giannoli, 2006). The North-American audiences have known harder versions of cinematic sexiness starring de France: it is, to say the least, by wielding the chainsaw and fighting for her life alongside actress Maïwenn in Alexandre Aja's horror slasher *Haute tension /High Tension* (2003), that this charming short-haired beauty – whose image was once compared remarkably by *Screen* magazine with that of Jean Seberg – provides a completely different body language.

Steady preparatory training with classes in fencing, dancing, and singing, in the context of her former theatre training provided her with a wide repertoire that is manifestly displayed in the above-mentioned films. Her performance as the character Isabelle, the lesbian confidante and romantic tutor of French actor Romain Duris in Cédric Klapisch's *L'Auberge espagnole /The Spanish Apartment* (2002), a Barcelona-set tale of a group of European exchange students learning intensively about life by flat-sharing, was a huge success with the public as well as a milestone in French lesbian cinema history.

De France's popularity spread further when in 2004 she gave her English-language debut in Frank Coraci's remake of Jules Vernes' *Around the World in 80 Days*, interpreting the French avant-garde painter Monique alongside Steve Coogan as Phileas Fogg and action-film icon Jackie Chan as Passepartout. Already awarded the 'most promising actress' César and Prix Louis Lumière, it is notably after *Les Poupées russes* (for which she received the César for Best Supporting Actress) that film roles continue following aplenty: besides starring in Xavier Giannoli's Golden Palm-nominated musical romantic drama *Quand j'étais chanteur* (where, as a young estate agent, she seduces Gérard Depardieu as a down-on-his-luck ballroom singer), she appeared in two other films shot in 2005: Danièle

Thompson's delightful theatre feature *Fauteuils d'orchestre /Avenue Montaigne* (2006) [1] and Roschdy Zem's intercultural Arab-Jewish comedy *Mauvaise foi /Bad Faith* (2006).

De France's visibility on the stage of international film is reinforced by Gilles Jacob inviting her to host the Cannes Film Festival in 2005. This incontestable honour is followed by numerous feature-film appearances: an abandoned wife in Alain Berliner's *J'aurais voulu être un danseur /Gone for a Dance* (2007); a lieutenant assigned the investigation of a murder tracing back to Algeria's struggle for independence in Laurent Herbiet's *Mon colonel /The Colonel* (2006), and a mother alongside Patrick Bruel in Claude Millers's *Un secret /A Secret* (2007), an Occupation-period-related drama raising questions about collective memory. She finally embodies a successful diver awaking from a coma, coached by an obsessive father (interpreted by German star actor Ulrich Tukur) in Guillaume and Stéphane Malandrin's psychological drama *Où est la main de l'homme sans tête /Hand of the Headless Man* (2007).

Embodying exceptionally diverse forms of human passion, de France's acting reaches even 'compassionate' levels: after appearing alongside Vincent Cassel in Jean-François Richet's crime thriller *Mesrine : l'instinct de mort /Mesrine: Killer Instinct* (2008), she impresses by starring as an outstanding Dominican nun Jeannine Deckers in Stijn Coninx's 2009 Franco-Belgian biopic *Sœur Sourire /Sister Smile*, and as police officer Julie going undercover to the world of drugs in Nicolas Boukhrief's *Les Gardiens de l'ordre /Off Limits* (2010).

Having graced the cover of countless French magazines such as *Elle* or *L'Express Style*, she continues to appear in diverse movies by a wide range of international directors. She not only continues her American career but also an art of acting in its most existential value: by starring alongside Matt Damon in Clint Eastwood's Oscar-nominated drama *Hereafter* (2010), she once again appears as a woman facing a near-death experience. In 2011, de France appears in the Golden Palm nominated and almost universally acclaimed feature by Jean-Pierre and Luc Dardenne, *Le Gamin au vélo / The Kid with a Bike*. Her recent film appearances include Xavier Giannoli's *Superstar*, co-starring Kad Merad, as well as reprising her role as Isabelle in the third instalment of Klapisch's *Auberge espagnole* trilogy, *Chinese Puzzle* (2013), set in New York City.

Daniel WINKLER
and
Katharina MÜLLER
Universität Wien /University of Vienna

1. For further discussion of this film, see Douglas King, review of *Fauteuils d'orchestre* in *World Film Locations: Paris*, ed. Marcelline Block (Bristol: Intellect, 2011), 102-103. —Ed.

Louis DE FUNÈS (1914–1983)
[Louis DE FUNES DE GALARZA]

Fun
Fun
Fun...
Funès

INDISPUTABLY the most successful French comedian of all time, although almost unknown in the English-speaking world, Louis DE FUNÈS is famous for the hyperactive, quick-tempered characters he played in Gérard Oury's blockbusters such as *Le Corniaud /The Sucker* (1965), *La Grande Vadrouille /Don't Look Now...We're Being Shot At!* (1966), and *Les Aventures de Rabbi Jacob / The Mad Adventures of Rabbi Jacob* (1973). In addition to his huge popular success, he also received tributes from intellectuals and artists such as dramatist Valère Novarina (*Pour Louis de Funès*, 1986).

The son of Spanish immigrants, Louis de Funès had to do all sorts of odd jobs before becoming a full-time actor. He acted on stage as well as on screen, in countless small parts and extras (he is credited in 128 films), before being noticed in a secondary role in *La Traversée de Paris /Four Bags Full* by Claude Autant-Lara (1956). He eventually met with late popular success in the beginning of the 1960s, with the unexpected hit *Pouic-Pouic* by Jean Girault (1963).

The next two decades established Louis de Funès as France's favourite comedian, with major successes like the *Gendarme de Saint-Tropez* series (6 films by Jean Girault, between 1964 and 1982); the *Fantômas* trilogy (by André Hunebelle, between 1964 and 1966); *Le Corniaud* (1965) and most of all, *La Grande Vadrouille* (1966), which attracted 17 million spectators – a record unbeaten in France until James Cameron's *Titanic* in 1997. Continuing his association with Gérard Oury, he was much acclaimed in 1971 for *La Folie des grandeurs /Delusions of Grandeur*, a comic remake of Victor Hugo's drama *Ruy Blas*, and in 1973 for *Les Aventures de Rabbi Jacob*, in the role of a snappy fake rabbi.

In 1975, a serious heart attack forced him to abandon the stage permanently and to slow down his film acting career. His comeback on screen with Claude Zidi's *L'Aile ou la Cuisse /The Wing or the Thigh* in 1976, co-starring with French comedian Coluche, proved a tremendous success. In 1979 he fulfilled an old dream by co-directing with Jean Girault an adaptation of Molière's *L'Avare / The Miser* (1980) where he played Harpagon, but the film was not as warmly received as expected. Louis de Funès starred in another two movies, *La Soupe aux choux* (1981) by Jean Girault, which introduced Jacques Villeret, and *Le Gendarme et les Gendarmettes /The Troops & Troop-ettes* (1982), the last opus of the *Gendarme de Saint-Tropez* series, before dying from a final heart attack in January 1983.

Louis de Funès's success is all the more remarkable since his characters are extremely similar; in this respect, he could be compared to ancient Roman *senes* or *commedia dell'arte*

Pantaloons, which could be found in many different plays. With his very ordinary physique (he was short, skinny, and bald) and his bad temper, he was often identified with the average Frenchman. A keen admirer of Charles Chaplin and Buster Keaton, he was a very rigorous, systematic worker, basing a great part of his comic effects upon facial expressions and twitches, as well as very energetic physical reactions, but unlike Bourvil he always refused to strike the emotional chord. He invented most of his gags out of everyday observation, and was particularly inspired by all kinds of power struggles: his characters are often bossy, tyrannical little men who become obsequious in front of powerful people. His high sense of dance and music (he was a jazz pianist for several years) was used in several films, especially *Le Corniaud*, *Le Grand Restaurant /What's Cooking in Paris* (Jacques Besnard, 1966), *L'Homme-orchestre /The Band* (Serge Korber, 1970), and *Les Aventures de Rabbi Jacob*.

His physical stature made him ideal for work in contrasting duos: most of his successful movies are based on this principle, which proved particularly successful with tall, quiet, good-tempered Bourvil in *Le Corniaud* and *La Grande Vadrouille* (cf. Bourvil). Other effective contrasts were made with Yves Montand in *La Folie des grandeurs*, with Michel Galabru in the *Gendarme* series, with Coluche in *L'Aile ou la Cuisse*, and with Jacques Villeret in *La Soupe aux choux*.

Céline CANDIARD
Université Lumière Lyon 2

Alain DELON (1935–)

The Bad and the Beautiful

FOR MANY, Alain DELON embodies the epitome of beauty and grace on screen. Though not a character actor, his sheer presence contributed to making his name almost synonymous with French acting in such countries as Japan or Italy. After a difficult and rebellious childhood, and some time spent in the French army during the Indochina War, his flamboyant movie debut helped him build an international career in acting that has only been diminished by a more pathetic development as an aging man, leading him to slowly retire and remain in a self-proclaimed and often proud position as the last survivor of a great generation of actors.

Born in 1935, Delon was not at first meant to be an actor, since he was about to embrace unenthusiastically the family career of pork butcher, before being rescued from this dreary fate, as he said, by discovering acting. Driven and ambitious, Alain Delon however did not break through on the stage, but on the silver screen, where his charisma and mesmerizing beauty worked wonders, especially in combination with those of a young and still relatively unknown Austrian actress, Romy Schneider, to whom he was briefly engaged, after they starred together in one of his earliest films, *Christine* (Pierre Gaspard-Huit, 1958).

Delon quickly gained fame, especially through playing on screen and on stage under the direction of Luchino Visconti, in a series of performances that were to build his mythical aura, first in *Rocco e i suoi fratelli /Rocco and His Brothers* (1960), and then as the aristocratic heir Tancredi in the dying world of *Il gattopardo /The Leopard* (1963). He also worked at that time for another acclaimed Italian director, the more modernist Michelangelo Antonioni, in *L'Éclipse /The Eclipse* (1962). First praised as some kind of new James Dean, Delon's acting however is placed on a more subdued level of underplaying. Not being a character actor, he relies on the mere presence and intensity that allow him to remain almost low-key. Nevertheless, Delon's intense magnetism relies on a somewhat tainted quality, making it all the more memorable: his ambiguous looks work marvels in René Clément's 1960 *Plein soleil / Purple Noon* (adapted from Patricia Highsmith's *The Talented Mr. Ripley*), displaying a profound duality which is not only moral but also social and sexual and which would fascinate audiences and become his most praised trademark.

Contrary to the sunnier Jean-Paul Belmondo, his joyful friend and rival leading man at the time, Alain Delon tended to choose less flamboyant, at times almost silent parts, with few words harshly uttered

at a machine gun pace. However, his behaviour and posture remained most of the time smoothly elegant and attractive, all things seeming to revolve around him once he enters a scene. Those assets have been his strongest trumps as he played a series of dark *film noir* heroes in movies directed by Henri Verneuil (*Mélodie en sous-sol /Any Number Can Win*, 1963; *Le Clan des siciliens / The Sicilian Clan*, 1969); Jean-Pierre Melville (*Le Samouraï*, 1967 and *Le Cercle rouge /The Red Circle*, 1970), and Jacques Deray (*Borsalino*, 1970, and its sequel *Borsalino and Co. / Blood on the Streets*, 1974).

Seeking to become a popular icon, the second part of Delon's career has been less overwhelming, with the exception of what remains one of his greater parts to date, Mr. Klein in Joseph Losey's eponymous 1976 film. Once again, he turned to a dual character, in search of an identity as cloudy as his blue eyes are clear. Gradually retiring or turning to production, Alain Delon became a national symbol of French cinema, mostly interested in strengthening his stardom. It is indeed as such that directors would use his presence from now on: at the beginning of the nineties, Jean-Luc Godard's 1990 *Nouvelle vague /New Wave* sets a good example of this new twist (alongside Edouard Niermans' 1992 *Le Retour de Casanova /Casanova's Return*), offering the aging actor, now almost a spectre of what he used to stand for, another dual part, and one of his last truly great performances. Due to the lack of great parts, the end of Delon's career saw him regularly (re)turn to the stage from the end of the nineties, though he would claim to be one of the only 'pure' film actors (insisting on the gap between *acteur* on screen and *comédien* on stage). He also tried to remain popular by playing the parts of recurrent detective heroes on television, such as Fabio Montale in the 2002 televised version of Jean-Claude Izzo's neo-noir *Marseilles trilogy*, with limited success.

Emilie FRENKIEL
Université Paris 8

Julie DELPY (1969–)

The Adaptable Nomad

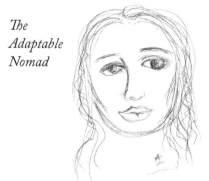

JULIE DELPY's life was divided between France and the USA, both because of the choices she made as an artist and her personal life. She was born in Paris. Her parents were both actors, and, influenced by the rich and eclectic cultural environment in which she was raised, she decided to become an actress at an early age. She began her career working with some of the great French auteurs. Discovered by Jean-Luc Godard at 14, she appeared in his feature-length film *Détective* (1985) and then worked with other leading French directors, notably Leos Carax in *Mauvais sang /The Night Is Young* (1986).

Nominated for a César for Most Promising Actress, she was not afraid to take on challenging parts despite her young age, such as that of a woman who makes a pact with the devil in Bertrand Tavernier's *La Passion Béatrice /Beatrice* (1987). Using her talent for foreign languages, she then began to appear in films made outside France. She worked first with the Spanish filmmaker Carlos Saura in *La noche oscura* (1989). This was followed by her breakthrough role, in German, as a young Nazi, for the Polish director Agniezska

Holland in *Europa Europa* (1990), which made her a well-known figure on the international scene. She then starred, speaking English, alongside Sam Shepard in the French-German-Greek production of *The Voyager* (1991). With an ethereal and pure face, cold and distant but also passionate, she played romantic leads in several independent films, for instance as Dominique in Krzysztof Kieslowski's *Trois couleurs : Blanc /Three Colours: White* (1994). She did not, however, turn her back on more commercial cinema, even if she did not take on major roles (for example she starred in Stephen Herek's 1993 Hollywood production, *The Three Musketeers*). Flexible and willing to appear in a variety of productions, she has often played French characters in English-speaking Anglo-French productions. She appeared as a prostitute in Roger Avary's debut feature film *Killing Zoe* (1993), a cult 'bank caper' film, and a werewolf in Anthony Wallers' *An American Werewolf in Paris* (1997).

But she has always been much more than just a pretty face. Julie Delpy has throughout her career been very much her own woman, one of the generation born following May 1968, who wanted to gain experience in all aspects of film production from screenwriting, scriptwriting, directing to editing. After her initial success as an actress, she left France to study filmmaking in New York. Whilst searching for backing for her own films, she collaborated with Richard Linklater and the actor Ethan Hawke on the screenplay for *Before Sunrise* (1995) and then the subsequent *Before Sunset* (2004) and *Before Midnight* (2013), starring in all three

films alongside Ethan Hawke. The originality and the success of these films was due in large part to the dialogue in scenes featuring extended conversations, which both actors received the credit for, though not without some controversy. Following her short film *Blah Blah Blah* (1995), her final project for film-school, she directed, with the help of friends, *Looking for Jimmy* (2002) which described the life of a French artist in the USA. The semi-autobiographical feel of this film was characteristic of her subsequent feature films. It was with *2 Days in Paris* (2007) that she at last had the financial backing to enable her to produce a film that was a box-office success and was also acclaimed by the critics. This was followed by her *2 Days in New York* (2012).

As a director she blurs the boundaries between fantasy and reality, mixing comedy with politics, and casting family members such as her parents alongside stars such as Chris Rock, Adam Goldberg, and Vincent Gallo. Her films deal with modern relationships, cultural differences, and the status of women in both contemporary society and in the past, such as in *La Comtesse / The Countess* (2009), portraying the Countess Elizabeth Báthory de Ecsed, a 17th century Hungarian serial killer. Through her creativity, both in front of and behind the camera, Delpy could exploit her position as an artist able to work in both Europe and the US. Although she became a US citizen in 2001, she has never lost touch with her roots and made *Le Skylab / Skylab* in 2011 with the French actors Bernadette Lafont, Emmanuelle Riva, and Noémie Lvosky, which, set in 1979, portrayed the French society of her youth. To conclude, Julie Delpy's background and her innate talents have given her a chameleon-like adaptability, enabling her to shift between languages and genres, and to master all the skills essential to any great filmmaker.

Karine CHEVALIER
University of Roehampton, London

Catherine DENEUVE (1943–)
[Catherine DORLÉAC]

*Icon
of
Icons*

WITH AN acting career spanning more than five decades and roles in over 100 films as well as two Césars for best actress, Catherine DENEUVE is arguably France's most internationally recognized contemporary female film star and *the* face of French cinema. She has enjoyed fruitful collaborations with the world's leading *auteurs* and cinéastes, including Luis Buñuel, Leos Carax, Jacques Demy, Claude Lelouch, Jean-Pierre Melville, Manoel de Oliveira, François Ozon, Roman Polański, Raúl Ruiz, Tony Scott, André Téchiné, Lars von Trier, François Truffaut, and Roger Vadim, to whom she bore a son in 1963, actor Christian Vadim.

Deneuve is a true icon whose name and image are synonymous not only with French cinema, but also with the country itself: from 1985–1989, she was elected to incarnate France, whose national symbol is 'Marianne,' a semi-nude female figure donning a Phrygian cap. An official bust of Marianne, sculpted in Deneuve's likeness, was displayed in town halls throughout the nation for the duration of her elected term. Upon hearing this news, Deneuve was surprised and delighted, stating: 'I never thought that one day I would embody the Republic...I imagine that what people see in me is the image of a classical woman... straightforward and sophisticated,'[1] which is certainly true of many of the characters she portrays on screen as well as her offscreen persona exuding a quality of 'Frenchness' associated with classic glamour and luxury items, discussed below.

Born Catherine Dorléac during the Occupation of France on October 22 1943 to parents who were themselves actors, Renée Deneuve and Maurice Dorléac, Deneuve followed in their footsteps, and began acting at a very young age, debuting in the 1957 film *Les Collégiennes* (dir. André Hunebelle). She was thrust into the spotlight upon the death of her older sister, also an actress, Françoise Dorléac (1942–1967), who was barely 22 at the time of the car crash in the south of France that took her life. For Deneuve, the pain of losing her sister at such a young age, and so unexpectedly, never fully dissipated and haunts her to this very day. Deneuve took her mother's maiden name professionally in order to distinguish herself from Dorléac at the time when both sisters were up-and-coming actresses: it was Dorléac who was poised for imminent stardom, and Deneuve who was in her shadow.

About one year apart, Deneuve and Dorléac worked together, playing the 25-year-old lovelorn twins Solange and Delphine Garnier in Jacques Demy's 1967 feel-good musical romantic comedy *Les Demoiselles de Rochefort / The Young Ladies of Rochefort*. This film was to be Dorléac's penultimate onscreen role before her death, and it was Deneuve's second time working with Demy after her breakthrough performance as the pregnant out-of-wedlock protagonist Geneviève in the enormously successful bittersweet musical film *Les Parapluies de Cherbourg / The Umbrellas of Cherbourg* (1964), one of Deneuve's best-remembered roles, remaining her favourite of all. Deneuve enjoys singing: in 1997, in a live performance with singer/actor Alain Souchon, she sang the heartfelt melody *Allô maman bobo* at the annual charity concert supporting the French organization *Restaurants du cœur* (founded by the actor Coluche), which distributes hot meals to the hungry. Along with the Demy musicals, Deneuve sang in numerous films, among others, Lars Von Trier's melodrama *Dancer in the Dark* (2000), in which she plays factory worker Kathy alongside Icelandic singer Björk, and in Christophe Honoré's *Les Bien-aimés / Beloved* (2011), in which she is cast as the mother of the character played by Chiara Mastroianni (b. 1972), who, is, in real-life, her own daughter, fathered by Marcello Mastroianni. Deneuve and Chiara Mastroianni have acted together in other films, including Raúl Ruiz's critically acclaimed *Le Temps retrouvé / Time Regained* (1999), an adaptation of Marcel Proust, and Arnaud Desplechin's 2008 *Un conte de Noël / A Christmas Tale*, Deneuve's 100th film.

With her mane of blonde hair and pale skin, Deneuve emanates a cool elegance and glamour, for which she has garnered monikers such as 'Ice Maiden,' 'Ice Princess,' and 'Ice Queen' – a female counterpart to French actor Alain Delon, known as the 'Ice Cold Angel,' and with whom she has shared screen time, such as in Jean-Pierre Melville's *Un flic / A Cop* (1972) and Robin Davis's *Le Choc / Contract in Blood* (1982). Deneuve's signature aesthetic intersects with the personae of the often cold, lofty characters she portrays onscreen. These qualities are perhaps best exemplified in her role as a psychotic murderess in Roman Polański's disturbing psychological horror film *Repulsion* (1965); in Luis Buñuel's controversial erotic film *Belle de jour* (1967), adapted from Joseph Kessel's eponymous novel, in which she plays a frigid, respectable doctor's wife who becomes a prostitute at a brothel during the day – not for money, but for thrill – while her husband is at work and does not have the slightest clue about her double life, and as the con artist seducing, robbing, and ultimately falling in love with Jean-Paul Belmondo in Truffaut's *La Sirène du Mississippi / Mississippi Mermaid* (1969). Deneuve would have been an archetypal Hitchcock blonde, ('something subtle and mysterious always remain[s] beneath their immaculately groomed surfaces'[2]) and indeed, around 1970, she was supposed to be cast in Hitchcock's *The Short Night*, a film that never materialized. Her pallor, coupled with a regal demeanour, made her the perfect choice for the ageless, centuries-old vampire Miriam in *Les Prédateurs / The Hunger*, the 1983 cult film by Tony Scott, co-starring David Bowie and Susan Sarandon.

In *Indochine* (Régis Wargnier, 1992), for which she received her only Academy Award nomination and her second best-actress César – her first was for Truffaut's Nazi-occupation drama *Le Dernier Métro / The Last Metro* (1980), for portraying a gentile woman hiding her Jewish theatre director husband – Deneuve portrays Eliane Devries, a wealthy French plantation owner in colonial Indochina in the 1930s. This powerful narrative received the Oscar and Golden Globe awards for Best Foreign Film. The year after *Indochine*, she starred alongside Daniel Auteuil in Téchiné's family drama *Ma saison préférée / My Favorite Season* (1993), a sensitive portrayal of a complex relationship between a brother and a sister as they confront the demise and eventual death of their elderly mother and its impact upon their entire family. *Ma saison préférée* was named Best Foreign Film by the Boston Society of Film Critics. Another memorable Deneuve role is that of the fallen woman Madame Malivert, the alcoholic wife of a wealthy jeweller in Nicole Garcia's thriller/drama *Place Vendôme* (1998), in which she awakens from the demons of her past in order to rescue an ambitious young woman who reminds her of herself as she attempts to enter the dangerous and thrilling world of the high-end jewelry market. Deneuve was awarded the Volpi Cup at the Venice International Film Festival for her portrayal of Madame Malivert.

In the transatlantic romantic comedy *Au plus près du paradis / Nearest to Heaven* (Tonie Marshall, 2002), she plays a woman who tries to recapture a past love, but in the process, while in New York City, ends up falling for a handsome American, played by William Hurt. In Téchiné's *La Fille du RER / The Girl on the Train* (2009), Deneuve is Louise, a working-class single mother living in a pedestrian Parisian suburb, who is baffled by her young adult daughter's public deception which brought her fifteen minutes of fame (or rather, infamy) and jail time for falsely claiming she was the victim of a hate crime. This film was based on the true 2004 case of Marie-Léonie Leblanc. In François Ozon's retro comedy, *Potiche /Trophy Wife* (2010), Deneuve's character, Suzanne – the film's titular 'trophy wife' – is swept into the heady days of the second wave feminist movement of the 1970s, becoming a strong female leader, yet without losing her sense of style, for which Deneuve is consecrated beyond the screen.

Indeed, Deneuve emblematizes French luxury goods and products such as designer clothes, accessories, and perfume: she has her own perfume line, 'Deneuve.' Furthermore, she was the spokesperson for Chanel No. 5 perfume and L'Oréal (as well as the American brand MAC) cosmetics; a friend and muse of Yves Saint-Laurent, and model for Louis Vuitton luggage.

Catherine Deneuve, an enduring cultural icon and living legend who continues her reign as the *grande dame* of French cinema, was celebrated at a gala tribute held in her honour in New York City's Alice Tully Hall in April 2012, where she was presented with the prestigious Chaplin Award from the Film Society of Lincoln Center.

Marcelline BLOCK
Princeton University and SAG-AFTRA

1. 'Brigitte Bardot Loses Out to Catherine Deneuve in France's Clash of Symbols,' *People* Magazine, vol. 24, no. 20, November 11, 1985, http://www.people.com/people/archive/article/0,,20092137,00.html.

2. Ian Scott Todd, 'Hitchcock's Good Looking Blondes : First Glimpses and Second Glances,' in *Situating the Feminist Gaze and Spectatorship in Postwar Cinema*, ed. Marcelline Block, (Newcastle, UK : Cambridge Scholars Publishing, 2010), 52.

Charles DENNER (1926–1995)

The Man Who Loved Women

A GEM of the French big screen whose films have yet been overlooked today, Charles DENNER embodied the artist who graciously and successfully combined theatre with cinema. Throughout his career, the actor performed on the stage of the Théâtre National Populaire in Paris and filmed with famous directors such as Claude Chabrol, Costa-Gavras, Jean-Luc Godard, Claude Lelouch, Louis Malle, and François Truffaut.

Charles Denner was born in 1926 in Poland to a Jewish family and moved to France when he was four. At an early age, he received the *Croix de guerre* distinction for his activity in the French resistance during World War II. Beginning his acting career on stage, Denner remained active in theatre throughout his entire life, even after he became a cinema actor. He worked for a long time with the Théâtre National Populaire team directed by Jean Vilar and with famous actors such as Michel Galabru, Jeanne Moreau, and Gérard Philipe. He appeared in various famous plays such as Fiodor Dostoïevski's *L'Idiot /The Idiot*, Bertolt Brecht's *La Résistible ascension d'Arturo Ui /The Resistible*

Rise of Arturo Ui, Alfred de Musset's *Lorenzaccio*, and Molière's *Les Fourberies de Scapin*.

One of his first complex performances in cinema was in Claude Chabrol's *Landru /Bluebeard* (1963), a highly theatrical black comedy that allowed Denner to perform at his highest potential. With a script written by Françoise Sagan, *Landru* stars Denner as a leading actor who plays a serial killer during World War I. The film is based on a real story of a twentieth century Bluebeard, a married man who seduced single, rich women before murdering them, in order to support his bourgeois family. Part of an exceptional cast that includes Michèle Morgan as Célestine and Danielle Darrieux as Berthe, two of Landru's victims, Denner did not impose himself through his physical stature, but rather through his ability to convey a wide spectrum of emotions. Dark and seductive, grotesque and poetic, an expressive figure with a deep voice and thick eyebrows, Denner succeeded in making spectators believe in a certain hidden sensitivity behind his monstrous acts. Denner's interpretation comes to reinforce what is already known as the director's critique of bourgeois hypocrisy.

Soon after interpreting Landru, in 1964, Denner performed in an equally dark and amusing, much-celebrated film, *La Vie à l'envers / Life Upside Down*, directed by Alain Jessua. Here, Denner's character, Jacques Valin, tells spectators « J'ai le secret ». His secret to happiness consists of a nonconformist celebration of solitude. He plays a Paris Real Estate developer who decides to withdraw from social life, being convinced that happiness can be attained in seclusion, in a dreamlike state. In the film, a series of theatrical monologues in black and white, to which Denner brings value by his convincing, spiritual presence, express a simultaneously humorous, tragic, and philosophical take on life. Positively welcomed by audiences and critics alike, *La Vie à l'envers* has been a source of inspiration for a series of filmmakers and actors.

During the 1960s and 1970s, Denner gave other admirable performances in films by classic directors, notably those of Claude Lelouch and Costa-Gavras. In Lelouch's best comedy and gangster film parody, *L'Aventure, c'est l'aventure /Money, Money, Money* (1972), Denner interprets Simon Duroc, one of five gangsters, next to Lino Ventura playing Lino Massaro, and Jacques Brel in the role of Jacques. The five steal artwork and cars, rob banks, hijack airplanes, and kidnap celebrities starting with Johnny Hallyday (playing himself). Denner's character, Simon, is the 'brain' behind the adventures, the one who finds solutions with a calm diplomacy. Pleading for the *carpe diem* credo « profitez de la vie, il est plus tard que vous ne le pensez » ['profit from life, it's later than you think'], the film combines fine humour with a subtle critique of the materialism of the consumerist society developing in 1970s France. Loyal to the New Wave theory of the *caméra-stylo*, Lelouch wrote the script, creating numerous dialogues which seem improvised. With his comic-serious tone, Denner contributes to these memorable dialogues that make *L'Aventure, c'est l'aventure* an intelligent, humorous, and well-received comedy.

Denner's most memorable role was in François Truffaut's tragicomedy, *L'Homme qui aimait les femmes /The Man Who Loved Women* (1977). Before this film, Truffaut had cast Denner in a series of secondary roles in *La Mariée était en noir /The Bride Wore Black* in 1968 and *Une belle fille comme moi /Such a Gorgeous Kid Like Me* in 1972. *L'Homme qui aimait les femmes* brings to the screen the story of a man permanently in love, an *éternel amoureux errant*, Bertrand Morane. He is driven in life by his two passions: women and writing. Bertrand is sincerely in love with several women at the same time, admiring each of them for their specific beauty. He follows, observes, and writes about them. The same deep voice, which inspires fear in *Landru*, acquires musicality in *L'Homme qui aimait les femmes* where it expresses passion, sensuality, and desire. Bertrand passionately lives and poetically writes an entire philosophy of desire while observing, fragmenting, and rendering abstract women's bodies.

Conceived by Truffaut as an homage to women and specifically created with Denner in view, this film is augmented by Raoul Coutard's brilliant cinematography. Truffaut's film has remained one of the most important collaborations between the New Wave director and Denner, providing the actor with the opportunity to perform in a role that placed him in the pantheon of talented French actors. Truffaut declared: « Nous avons écrit, Suzanne Schiffman, Michel Fermaud, et moi, le scénario de *L'Homme qui aimait les femmes*, à l'intention de Charles Denner et par admiration pour lui » ['Suzanne Schiffman, Michel Fermaud, and I wrote the screenplay of *The Man Who Loved Women* with Charles Denner in mind and out of admiration for him'].[1] We will undoubtedly remember Denner as 'the man who loved women.'

Adela LECHINTAN-SIEFER
The Ohio State University, Columbus

1. *'L'Homme qui aimait les femmes,'* *Classiques du Cinema,* May 16, 2012, accessed September 17, 2013, http://www.classiquesducinema.com/article-l-homme-qui-aimait-les-femmes-truffaut-1977-77093467.html.

Gérard DEPARDIEU (1948–)

*France's
Most Famous
Actor Is
Alive
and Well
and Living
in Belgium*

GÉRARD DEPARDIEU, who appears in nearly 200 films, is acclaimed throughout the world as France's greatest contemporary film star and the most globally recognizable French actor living today. Those with even only cursory knowledge of and/or experience with French cinema are aware of his ubiquitous presence on the French and international film scenes.

Born into a modest family in Châteauroux, a town south of Paris, Depardieu went from dropping out of school at the cusp of adolescence to dabbling in juvenile delinquency before studying the dramatic arts and acting with the Parisian Café de la Gare troupe alongside, among others, Miou-Miou and Patrick Dewaere, his co-stars in his breakthrough film, Bertrand Blier's ode to *épater le bourgeois*, 1974's *Les Valseuses /Going Places*. Depardieu debuted onscreen in the 1967 short film *Le Beatnik et le Minet* (dir. Roger Leenhardt) as the titular Beatnik (the film also featured Jacques Doniol-Valcroze).

Throughout his career, Depardieu has worked with a range of legendary directors, a who's who of leading names in the European and American film industries, including fruitful collaborations with Blier (the above-mentioned *Les Valseuses* as well as *Préparez vos mouchoirs /Get Out Your Handkerchiefs*, 1978, which won the Oscar for Best Foreign Language Film; *Buffet froid /Cold Cuts*, 1979; *Tenue de soirée /Ménage*, 1986; *Trop belle pour toi /Too Beautiful for You*, 1989; *Merci la vie /Thank You, Life*, 1991; *Combien tu m'aimes ? /How Much do You Love Me?*, 2005); and with Francis Veber (*La Chèvre /The Goat*, 1981; *Les Compères /ComDads*, 1983; *Les Fugitifs /Fugitives*, 1986; *Le Placard / The Closet*, 2001; *Tais-toi /Ruby and Quentin*, 2003).

He has also appeared in films by: Jean-Jacques Beineix (*La Lune dans le caniveau /The Moon in the Gutter*, 1983); Claude Berri (*Je vous aime /I Love You All*, 1980; *Jean de Florette*, 1986; *Uranus*, 1990; *Germinal*, 1993); Bernardo Bertolucci (*1900*, 1976); Kenneth Branagh (*Hamlet*, 1996, as Reynaldo); Claude Chabrol (Depardieu acted in only one Chabrol film, in the titular role of the *policier Bellamy*, 2009, which would be the director's last movie); Marguerite Duras (*Nathalie Granger*, 1972; *Baxter, Vera Baxter*, 1977; *Le Camion /The Lorry*, 1977); Marco Ferreri (*La Dernière Femme /The Last Woman*, 1976; *Rêve de singe /Bye Bye Monkey*, 1978); Jean-Luc Godard (*Hélas pour moi /Oh, Woe is Me*, 1993); Mathieu Kassovitz (*Babylon A.D.*, 2008); Ang Lee (*Life of Pi*, 2012); François Ozon (*Potiche /Trophy Wife*, 2010); Maurice Pialat (*Loulou*, 1980; *Police*, 1985; *Sous le soleil de Satan / Under the Sun of Satan*, 1987; *Le Garçu*, 1995); Alain Resnais (*Stavisky...*, 1974; *Mon oncle d'Amérique /My American Uncle*, 1980; *I Want to Go Home*, 1989); Claude Sautet (*Vincent, François, Paul* et les autres... /Vincent, François, Paul and the Others, 1974); André Téchiné (Barocco, 1976; Les Temps qui changent /Changing Times, 2004); François Truffaut (Le Dernier Métro /The Last Metro, 1980; La Femme d'à côté /The Woman Next Door, 1981); and Agnès Varda (Les Cent et une nuits de Simon Cinéma /One Hundred and One Nights, 1995). He stepped behind the camera to direct the 1984 cinematic adaptation of Molière's Le Tartuffe, in which he incarnated the titular role of the religious hypocrite par excellence, an iconic character of the French canon. A television documentary devoted to his life and career, entitled Depardieu, vivre aux éclats (dir. Jean-Claude Guidicelli), was released in 2000.

For his contributions to French cinema, Depardieu is the recipient of countless awards and honours, including being named Chevalier de la Légion d'honneur and Chevalier de l'Ordre National du Mérite, as well as receiving two Best Actor Césars. His first César was for François Truffaut's 1980 Occupation-era drama Le Dernier Métro /The Last Metro, in which Depardieu plays a theater actor who participates in French Resistance activity. He received the César a second time for starring as the tragic figure and eponymous protagonist of Jean-Paul Rappeneau's 1990 adaptation of Cyrano de Bergerac, a career-defining role for which Depardieu also received the Best Actor award at Cannes and a nomination for the Best Actor Oscar. The film itself won ten Césars including Best Film; the Golden Globe for Best Foreign Film; the Academy Award for Best Costume Design, and in 1995 was awarded the 'César des Césars' prize. Some of

Depardieu's other accolades include 16 Best Actor César nominations (more than any other French actor); a Golden Globe award for Best Actor for Peter Weir's Green Card (1990); a Career Golden Lion from the Venice Film Festival, as well as awards from the British Film Institute, the German Golden Camera, the London Film Critics Circle, the Lumière Awards, the Montréal World Film Festival, the Moscow Film Festival, the San Francisco International Film Festival, and the United States' National Society of Film Critics, among others.

Depardieu's career has brought him not only fame in his native France but also international glory, including roles in Hollywood, earning him the previously mentioned Oscar nomination for starring as the titular figure of Rappeneau's iconic adaptation of Cyrano, which is particularly noteworthy as it was a nomination for a non-English-language role. Another recent example of a French actor receiving Academy Award recognition is Marion Cotillard who won the Best Actress Oscar for her turn as Édith Piaf in Olivier Dahan's 2007 biopic La Môme /La Vie en Rose, in which Depardieu appears. Yet Depardieu has also taken on numerous English-speaking roles, notably in Weir's 1990 romantic comedy Green Card, written specifically with Depardieu in mind, for which he earned the Golden Globe award for Best Actor (in a musical or comedy) as a Frenchman illegally living in the United States whose sham 'green card' marriage to an American woman actually leads to love between the two of them – albeit, too late for him to avoid being deported. In Roland Joffé's English-language *Vatel* (2000), based on the true story of François Vatel (1631-1671), the 17th century master chef to the French aristocracy, Depardieu incarnates the eponymous protagonist who ultimately takes his own life due to his frustrations with the rigid class hierarchy in pre-Revolutionary France as well as his doomed love for an aristocrat (Uma Thurman).

Depardieu's great variety of roles as a leading man cut a wide swath across genre. His breakthrough came in the 1974 cult film *Les Valseuses / Going Places* (dir. Blier) as Jean-Claude, one of two antiheroes – the other played by Patrick Dewaere – whose picaresque journey leads to crime sprees and erotic escapades in this unconventional, raunchy narrative which confronts bourgeois values and sensibility, skewering conventional morality. *Les Valseuses*, adapted from Blier's novel, features Miou-Miou and Jeanne Moreau as well as a young Isabelle Huppert in an early performance as a bored 16-year-old girl, seeking the thrills and sexual pleasures offered by the trio of Depardieu, Dewaere, and Miou-Miou.

He has appeared in blockbusters such as the four live-action *Astérix* films (1999-2012) based on the adventures of the beloved cartoon character, in which he co-stars as Astérix's trusty sidekick, the hefty stonemason Obélix (in fact, Depardieu is the only member of the original film's cast who appears in all four films). Depardieu's manifold roles in literary adaptations include playing the titular victimized hunchback in Claude Berri's adaptation of Marcel Pagnol's *Jean de Florette* (1986); the priest Donissan who encounters

Satan in Maurice Pialat's Palme d'Or winning *Sous le soleil de Satan /Under the Sun of Satan* (1987), taken from the eponymous George Bernanos novel; an outsize performance as Léopold, a bar owner and aspiring poet falsely accused of harboring a former collaborator in Berri's bleak *Uranus* (1990), based on Marcel Aymé's controversial novel about a small French town struggling to rebuild after World War II; Maheu in Berri's adaptation of Emile Zola's *Germinal* (1993), and Ursus in *L'Homme qui rit /The Man Who Laughs* (Jean-Pierre Améris, 2012) from the Victor Hugo novel of the same name, which had previously been adapted for the screen, including several silent film versions as well as a television film.

Many of the characters Depardieu has played over the years exude a masculinity that is endorsed by his strong, muscular physique, which has become considerably bulkier over the years. In the comedy *Les Compères / ComDads* (Veber) – in which he is reunited with Pierre Richard, his co-star from Veber's earlier *La Chèvre / The Goat* – Depardieu is Jean Lucas, the macho foil to sensitive François Pignon (Richard), when both are called by a former girlfriend to search for her missing son after she tells each man that he is the teenage boy's biological father. (*Les Compères* was remade as the 1997 US film *Father's Day* by Ivan Reitman, starring Billy Crystal and Robin Williams.) In Maurice Pialat's *Loulou* (1980), Depardieu plays the titular figure, an unemployed ex-convict having an affair with the bourgeois, married Nelly (Isabelle Huppert). As Loulou, Depardieu's 'heavier, more powerful physique became a foil for the dark, lanky balding figure of Guy Marchand'[1] who played Nelly's husband. In a later Pialat film, *Police* (1985) – Pialat's only *polar*[2] – Depardieu is a detective who relies upon brutal interrogation techniques. For his performance in *Police*, Depardieu received the Best Actor Award at the Venice Film Festival and was also nominated for the Best Actor César. In Veber's *Le Placard /The Closet* (2001), he is cast as Félix Santini, a homophobic rugby enthusiast and bully who gets his comeuppance. Yet Depardieu's often macho, tough appearance as well as screen presence belies an underlying gentleness and tenderness, as reflected in his 'marvellously modulated voice...that can boom like a fog horn and then sink into an insinuating whisper.'[3] This contrast at the core of Depardieu's onscreen persona has been described as 'his intuitive playing of his formidable but undeniable plebeian physique against the poetry of his voice.'[4] In other words, Depardieu 'combines brutishness, intelligence and profound emotion with a subtlety that has no equal.'[5]

He memorably played philandering husbands on numerous occasions, including in François Truffaut's 1981 *La Femme d'à côté /The Woman Next Door*, in which a cruel twist of fate reunites his character, Bernard, with former lover Mathilde (Fanny Ardant), leading to tragic consequences evoking the ending of Truffaut's earlier New Wave classic *Jules et Jim* (1962). Bertrand Blier's *Trop belle pour toi /Too Beautiful for You* inverts the cliché of the cheating husband: in this film, Depardieu again plays a man named Bernard, who, despite being married to a conventionally beautiful woman (Carole Bouquet), falls for his much less attractive secretary (Josiane Balasko). This film won a Special Jury Prize at Cannes and the Best Film César. In *Nathalie...* (Anne Fontaine, 2003) he once more is cast in the role of married man named Bernard whose wife Catherine (Fanny Ardant) discovers his infidelity after which she hires a sex worker – the titular Nathalie (Emmanuelle Béart) – to confirm her suspicions about her husband. The film however foregrounds the unlikely friendship that develops between the two women – the older, financially secure and professionally established gynecologist Catherine and Nathalie, whose sordid experiences in the harsh world of prostitution is at the antipodes of Catherine's bourgeois existence. *Nathalie...* was remade in the US by Atom Egoyan as the 2009 psychosexual thriller *Chloe*, a far cry from the more subtle original French film.

Depardieu has often incarnated historical figures, such as Christopher Columbus in Ridley Scott's *1492: Conquest of Paradise* (1992), and some of his most iconic roles were based on real people: he played the imposter Arnaud du Tilh in Daniel Vigne's *Le Retour de Martin Guerre / The Return of Martin Guerre*, 1982, (based on a notorious 16th century incident of identity fraud researched by Natalie Zemon Davis, a cultural historian who assisted with the film's production and wrote the eponymous book), a film which was subsequently remade in the United States as Jon Amiel's 1993 *Sommersby* (set in the Civil War era, starring Jodie Foster and Richard Gere); he played

Georges Danton in Polish auteur Andrzej Wajda's critically acclaimed treatment of the French Revolution in the Franco-Polish co-production *Danton* (1983), which won, among other accolades, the BAFTA Award for Best Foreign Language Film; and he played sculptor Auguste Rodin opposite Isabelle Adjani as Rodin's former student/lover whom he abused and whose career and life he ruins in Bruno Nuytten's 1988 *Camille Claudel*, for which Adjani won the Best Actress César as well as received an Oscar nomination. One of his best-known performances is his starring turn in *Cyrano de Bergerac* as the aging, ailing, older man (ashamed of his prominent nose), forever doomed to unrequited love for the beautiful Roxane. In *La Môme*, the 2007 Édith Piaf biopic, which landed Marion Cotillard the Academy Award, he played a small but pivotal part as nightclub owner Louis Leplée (1883-1936) who hired Piaf to sing in his Parisian club Le Gerny in 1935. Leplée is credited with giving Piaf (born Édith Gassion) her stage name *La Môme Piaf* ['The Kid Sparrow'], renaming her for posterity. Piaf was identified as a person of interest by the police investigating Leplée's murder, which occurred barely a year after he discovered her. She was cleared of all charges yet suffered substantial damage to her reputation.

Despite his humungous career success, Depardieu has not been spared tragedies such as the death of his estranged son Guillaume (1971-2008) at age 37 due to viral pneumonia. Although his short life was marked by struggles with drugs, serving several prison sentences, and getting badly injured in a motorcycle accident, which required the amputation of a leg, Guillaume was a gifted actor who received the César for Most Promising Actor for Pierre Salvadori's 1995 *Les Apprentis / The Apprentices*. Guillaume appeared with his father in several films, including Alain Corneau's 1991 *Tous les matins du monde /All the Mornings of the World*, in which Depardieu plays Marin Marais (1656-1728), a composer and master viol player, with Guillaume cast in the role of the younger Marais. Depardieu's daughter Julie (born 1973 - *see following*) is a steadily working, two-time César-winning actress with over 70 roles to her name, including a part in Yves Angelo's *Le Colonel Chabert /Colonel Chabert* (1994), in which her father starred.

Beyond the screen, Depardieu, a gourmand and oenophile dedicated to sharing his passion for food and wine, wrote *My Cookbook* (2005), a book featuring his preferred recipes. He is the owner of La Fontaine Gaillon, a restaurant situated near the Opéra in Paris's second arrondissement. He is also the proprietor of vineyards around the world, from the Loire valley and Bordeaux regions in France to countries as far as Argentina and Morocco. His love of wine is reflected in his occasionally driving under the influence, for which he has been penalized.

His decision to give up his French citizenship in 2012 was controversial, as was his relocation to the Belgian town of Néchin, close to the French border, where he was welcomed with open arms by the local residents who fondly refer to him by his nickname 'Gégé.' As was the case of many top-earning French citizens, Depardieu also left

France supposedly in reaction to the 2012-2014 French policy of raising taxes to 75% for income exceeding 1 million euros. On January 3rd 2013, Vladimir Putin, President of Russia, gave Depardieu Russian citizenship and the actor was also offered the position of culture minister of the city of Saransk, capital of the Russian Republic of Mordovia, where he now also has a residence. Depardieu was photographed, beaming, wearing the embroidered shirt given to him by residents of Saransk upon his arrival in the city.

A towering figure of French cinema, the now self-avowed 'Franco-Russian' Depardieu incarnates a character based on fallen political personality Dominique Strauss-Kahn in Abel Ferrera's *Welcome to New York* (2014). In 2014, Depardieu released his autobiography *Ça c'est fait comme ça*.

Marcelline BLOCK
Princeton University and SAG-AFTRA

1. Marja Warehime, *Maurice Pialat* (Manchester University Press, 2006), 95.

2. *Polar* : slang for detective novel/film.

3. Anwar Huda, *The Art and Science of Cinema* (Atlantic Publishers and Dist., 2004), 111.

4. Ibid.

5. Janet Maslin, 'Film Festival: Maurice Pialat's *Police* with Gérard Depardieu,' *New York Times*, September 20, 1986, accessed March 30, 2014, http://www.nytimes.com/movie/review?res=9A0DE1D8103DF933A157 5AC0A960948260.

Julie DEPARDIEU (1973–)

A Julie in the Depardieu Tree

JULIE MARION DEPARDIEU, born in 1973 to the illustrious family of actors – Gérard Depardieu (b. 1948) and his first wife Elisabeth Guignot (born 1941) – is the sister of late actor Guillaume Depardieu (1971-2008). Yet Julie thrives in her own right and her own light in a successful acting career. Since age 23, she has steadily acted in films (with the exception of the years 2009 and 2010); in 2005, she even appeared in seven films, and in 2006, in six.

I never met Julie Depardieu personally, but did meet her father Gérard in New York City during the filming of *Green Card* (Peter Weir, 1990) when he starred opposite Andie MacDowell. Note that Gérard Depardieu was apparently so unknown in Manhattan at the time that he could walk anywhere freely without being recognized: he told me, on the set of *Green Card*, that this is why he loved working in Manhattan. Even on the very set of *Green Card*, some members of the film's American crew did not realize that Depardieu was such a celebrity in France. When I told a Production Assistant during *Green Card*'s filming that Depardieu was indeed one of the best known French actors, so famous that he could not walk around Paris without being recognized, this PA was surprised: 'Oh really?' he said, 'that guy over there is so famous in France?' – which made Gérard Depardieu, who had overheard the conversation, grin from ear to ear. Gérard truly enjoyed this moment of non-celebrity in Manhattan. It was quite a treat for him to be able to roam Manhattan's labyrinthine subways and walk in the downtown urban canyons, or anywhere else in the city, without being accosted even once. He savoured his incognito to the fullest then and could even stare at passers-by without anyone requesting an autograph.[1]

By 2013, 23 years post-*Green Card*, this welcome incognito status was quickly vanishing, as Gérard Depardieu, back in Manhattan, acted the part of disgraced Dominique Strauss-Kahn (with Jacqueline Bisset in the role of his now ex-wife, Anne Sinclair) in the 2014 film *Welcome to New York* (dir. Abel Ferrara). With an even larger grin on his portly face, Gérard Depardieu was photographed in front of the very same multimillion-dollar TriBeCa townhouse that DSK had occupied under house arrest in 2011, accused of sexually assaulting a housekeeper at the luxury Manhattan hotel in which he had been staying. In an interview on Swiss television in 2012, Depardieu stated that he was happy to portray DSK, whom he described as 'very French: arrogant and smug.'[2]

Although much saddened by the early demise of their son Guillaume, Julie's older brother, the Depardieu family continues to be a true French cinematic dynasty with household name recognition.

Julie Depardieu, although she projects a more discreet profile about her personal life than her father, is well-liked in filmic circles, among the establishment or aficionados: she obtained the Best Supporting Actress César along with the César for Most Promising Actress for *La Petite Lili /Little Lili* (Claude Miller, 2003) – a French adaptation of Anton Chekov's 1896 play *The Seagull* – in which she incarnates Jeanne-Marie. She won her second César award for Best Supporting Actress in 2008 for her performance as Louise in *Un secret /A Secret* (Claude Miller, 2007), which explores the tragic experience of a French-Jewish family during the Nazi Occupation of France. The titular 'secret' from those days was kept hidden for many years until Louise confides it to the family's son, who was born after World War II and was unaware of his parents' past.

Besides acting, in 2008, Julie directed an *opérette*, *Les Contes d'Hoffmann /Tales of Hoffmann*, in the majestic setting of the Château de Vaux le Vicomte. This château is not alien to tragedy: Louis XIV, the Roi Soleil [Sun King], upon visiting it, became so envious of its owner Fouquet, that he had Fouquet incarcerated, and he gathered Fouquet's cultured entourage (that included playwrights now considered the best French authors), and installed them in his own castle at Versailles, where they entertained him and his court. In the film *Les Témoins /The Witnesses* (André Téchiné, 2007), Julie Depardieu was once again associated with opera, playing an aspiring opera singer named Julie, whose brother dies of AIDS in the 1980s, the early days of the terrifying epidemic.

Julie Depardieu's filmography includes, among other titles, the 1998 *Count of Monte Cristo*, a French TV mini-series in which she incarnated Valentine de Villefort. In Jean-Pierre Jeunet's *Un long dimanche de fiançailles /A Very Long Engagement* (2004), Julie Depardieu is Véronique Passavant; in the 2005 French TV mini-series *Les Rois maudits*, based on *académicien* Maurice Druon's historical novels about the French kings, Julie incarnates Jeanne de Poitiers. She plays the role of yet another Jeanne, this time Jeanne Faussier – a prostitute who becomes a Resistance operative during World War II – in *Les Femmes de l'ombre /Female Agents* (Jean-Paul Salomé, 2008).

Not yet as famous as her father, Julie Depardieu, on her way to reaching the highest rungs of stardom, holds her own.

Jenny BATLAY
PhD Columbia University

1. Subsequent to his fictitious role in *Green Card* (1990), Gérard Depardieu, Julie's father, moved to Russia in 2012, after throwing away his French passport: does one need a green card to move to Russia? Or perhaps, rather, a *red* card? From a coveted role in *Green Card*, to throwing away his French passport in exchange for a new Slavic ID in 2012, to playing the controversial figure of DSK – DSK, the man who might have been elected President of France – Gérard Depardieu is never far from public scrutiny. He now juggles international borders and crosses over country boundaries as one would cross the avenue des Champs-Elysées.

2. Andy Soltis, 'Hey, it's "DSK"!' *New York Post*, April 27, 2013, 3.

Emmanuelle Devos (1964–)

The Awkward Beauty

EMMANUELLE DEVOS is an actress to be reckoned with, as anybody who has seen some French movies in the last few years would have surely come across her earthy physique and heard her unforgettable, piping voice. Born to a family of stage actors, Emmanuelle Devos left school at 16 to enrol in a theatre school. Starting her cinematic career in the early 90s, she quickly became famous as the muse of the film director Arnaud Desplechin. Fresh from the prestigious FEMIS, the French School of Cinema, and part of what the press called the *New Nouvelle Vague*, she was consequently labeled as a cerebral actress, which never fails to make her smirk, noting that she never even obtained the most basic academic degree. In the following two decades, she went on to play in the five most acclaimed Arnaud Desplechin films. Among the powerful parts she played for him are Esther in *Comment je me suis disputé...(ma vie sexuelle) /My Sex Life...or How I Got into an Argument* (1996), an anxious young woman who is mourning her unexplainable absence of menstruation, and Nora, the single mother of *Rois et Reine / Kings and Queen* (2004) who cannot express her love to the men in her life (i.e. the Kings) and has to care for her terminally ill father. But it is for Jacques Audiard's *Sur mes lèvres / Read My Lips* in 2001 that she wins professional recognition with the César for best actress. In the film, she plays Clara, a shy and prejudiced hearing-impaired young woman who falls for a mediocre thug who happens to be on parole – managing to have the audience believe that she could pass for an ugly duckling.

In past interviews, Emmanuelle Devos has spoken extensively about her decision to become an actress, explaining that, as a child, she was not the sort to entertain a crowd but realised at a young age that acting would help her discover who she was and heal still open wounds (she lost a sister to cancer). She is a hard worker and goes from one shooting to the other, appearing in lead roles as well as supporting roles, in her belief that no one should dismiss a good part, however minor it may be. She says that her life has been filled with lucky encounters, including Desplechin and Audiard.

In recent years, she has played varied roles: a town mayor in *À l'origine /In the Beginning* (Xavier Giannoli, 2009), a police inspector in *Complices /Accomplices* (Frédéric Mermoud, 2009) and a passionate Israeli mother whose son was exchanged at birth with a Palestinian family in Lorraine Lévy's 2012 *Le Fils de l'autre /The Other Son*, never handicapped by a voice that she hates and calls girlish while admitting that it does not prevent her from being heard when necessary (she has been a supporter of the French Socialist Party). She co-stars with Irish actor Gabriel Byrne in *Le Temps de l'aventure /Just a Sigh* (Jérôme Bonnel, 2013).

One may find her characters awkward at times as they are always out of step with others around them. Emmanuelle Devos confessed that she herself feels out of place most of the time, especially in places where glitter and bling are required: a modern Annie Hall.

Gaëlle PLANCHENAULT
Simon Fraser University,
British Columbia

Patrick DEWAERE (1947–1982)
[Patrick BOURDEAUX]

The
Free
Mind

PATRICK DEWAERE, born Patrick Bourdeaux on January 26th, 1947, committed suicide on July 16th, 1982. Like his five brothers and sisters, he made early debuts in dramatic arts, performing on stage, television, and cinema. He first appeared in a movie at the age of four (*Monsieur Fabre*, Henri Diamant-Berger, 1951). Among other movies, he was an extra in *The Happy Road* (Gene Kelly, 1957) and *Les Espions /The Spies* (Henri-Georges Clouzot, 1957). As a child, Patrick sometimes assumed the family name of his mother, the comedian Mado Maurin. At 17 years old, he learned that he was the natural son of Michel Tétard, a conductor who had died four years earlier. This piece of news, a climate of competition among his brothers and sisters, and an argument with his mother about inheritance issues lead him astray from the family. He then chose the pseudonym Dewaere from his great-grandmother's name Devaere. This independent adventure started with a role in *Paris brûle-t-il ? /Is Paris Burning?* (René Clément, 1966).

In 1967-1968, Dewaere was not a University student protesting in the streets. He hated school and had failed the Baccalaureate thrice. Nor was he a believer in political ideology. He participated in the creation of the Café de la Gare in Montparnasse, with a group of jolly 'anticonformist' artists, among whom were the actor Romain Bouteille, the comic Coluche (who became a close friend of his), and the actress Miou-Miou who inspired him with deep passion. Many other actors and artists gradually came and found a home in this very democratic, libertarian, and communal place, including Anémone, Josiane Balasko, Gérard Depardieu, Gérard Jugnot, Diane Kurys, Martin Lamotte, Gérard Lanvin, Thierry Lhermitte, Coline Serreau, and others. The theatre opened in July 1969. Dewaere performed there for ten years, in parallel with his career in cinema. He also earned some money in US/French dubbing: he is Dustin Hoffman's French voice in *The Graduate* (Mike Nichols, 1967).

In 1970, on Coluche's advice, Jean-Paul Rappeneau came to the Café and chose Dewaere for the role of a soldier in the film *Les Mariés de l'an deux /The Scoundrel* (1971). The film director Claude Faraldo then recruited the whole Café de la Gare troupe to play in *Themroc* (1973), an anarchist and barbaric satire of society. The movie had almost no impact in France, but it stunned a part of the British public and became a cult movie there.

Les Valseuses /Going Places (Bertrand Blier, 1974) revealed Dewaere as a major actor. He played with precision and truth an uncompromising, bored, and crude outcast. The lost and wandering trio he formed in the movie with Gérard Depardieu and Miou-Miou was a great public success. Dewaere would remain faithful to Blier's cinema: in 1978's *Préparez vos mouchoirs /Get Out Your Handkerchiefs*, he performed another duet with Gérard Depardieu, trying to heal a woman (Carole Laure) from her baffling frigidity; in *Beau Père* (1981), he played a weak man tempted by the love and sexual desire of his stepdaughter following her mother's death.

Anxious to preserve his freedom, the actor adopted personal choices in his career, combining some art and underground movies (*Au Long de la rivière Fango*, 1975, produced by the Café de la Gare and written/directed by his wife Sotha) and popular films such as *Pas de problème ! /No Problem!* (Georges Lautner, 1975) and *Adieu, poulet /The French Detective* (Pierre-Granier Deferre, 1975). He remained adventurous enough to discover and help new creators, accepting the leading role in Maurice Dugowson's first movie (*Lily, aime-moi*, 1975) and forming a perverse duet with Patrick Bouchitey in Claude Miller's first film (*La Meilleure Façon de marcher / The Best Way to Walk*, 1976).

Dewaere was most at ease with anti-heroic characters drifting from society or refusing its common rules of power and corruption. With a popular Parisian accent, he easily mixed softness and vulgarity. In *F comme Fairbanks* (Maurice Dugowson, 1976), he is the tragic figure of a man who believed his life would be as easy as Douglas Fairbanks's, but suffers from economic crisis and unemployment.

The dark *Le Juge Fayard, dit le Shérif /Judge Fayard Called the Sheriff* (Yves Boisset, 1977) is inspired by the recent murder of the examining magistrate François Renaud, and depicts the character's rough fight against a gangster organisation and its political allies. In the sarcastic comedy *Coup de tête /Hothead* (Jean-Jacques Annaud, 1979), Dewaere's character, a common worker, is confronted with the political and industrial powers that lie within local soccer competition; distant lucidity fits well with the actor's apparent tranquillity. Later, *Mille milliards de dollars /A Thousand Billion Dollars* (Henri Verneuil, 1982) shows him as an idealistic journalist aiming to reveal a political and industrial affair. Used to playing outcasts, Dewaere, in *Série noire* (Alain Corneau, 1979) is an unimpressive worker who, squashed by financial problems and with the help of Mona (Marie Trintignant), becomes a thief and a murderer.

In 1980, Dewaere punched a journalist who had revealed private information about his prospective wedding. The French media decided to boycott the actor, refusing to interview him or to review his movies. Financial settlement only happened in 1982. Until then, producers did not see the actor as a seller anymore. Great roles continued, though. In *Un mauvais fils /A Bad Son* (Claude Sautet, 1980), he played the angry and frustrated son of a factory-worker (Yves Robert), trying to find his place after some time in prison. The romantic *Hôtel des Amériques /Hotel America* (André Téchiné, 1981) makes him the wounded and passionate lover of a woman from higher society (Catherine Deneuve).

In July 1982, shortly after the release of *Paradis pour tous* (Alain Jessua, 1982) with Fanny Cottençon, Patrick Dewaere shot himself with a rifle, a gift from his friend Coluche, with whom his girlfriend Elsa had eloped to Guadeloupe. It is said that a phone call from Elsa in the morning announced he would never see her or his daughter Lola again. He was preparing a movie with the film director Claude Lelouch and had other projects with Blier, Boisset, and others.

Nicolas RIGAUD
The University of Oxford

Jean-Claude Dreyfus (1946–)

*The
Pig's
the
Thing*

ALTHOUGH he is recognizable for his robust physique, as a child, César-nominated stage and film actor Jean-Claude DREYFUS (born in Paris), suffered from the early symptoms of tuberculosis. Between the ages of 7 and 10, he was sent to a preventorium to treat his condition. This is where he first began performing onstage, in comedies and farces. Not only was this Dreyfus's first exposure to acting, but also to playing female characters (as there were not enough girl patients available to perform the female roles), prefiguring how, as an adult, he would be part of the élite transvestite theatre troupe, *La Grande Eugène*, during the 1970s. With *La Grande Eugène* – located on the rue de Marignan in the 8th arrondissement of Paris – Dreyfus incarnated a variety of female figures and characters, including Sarah Bernhardt, Lilli Marleen, Mistinguett, Pola Neri, and Barbra Streisand, among others.

Prior to performing in drag in *La Grande Eugène*, however, Dreyfus, as a teenager, started out as a magician and an illusionist in his father's medical theatrical revue, called *Art et Sana*, which travelled throughout France, performing in sanatoria, retirement homes, prisons (and even Parisian cabarets). Although Dreyfus spent about ten years with *Art et Sana*, as he continued with it, he realized more and more that his interest and talent lay in the theatre rather than in performing prestidigitation. He therefore joined another travelling troupe, the theatre group *Les Classiques de France*, performing the works of Molière throughout the south of France. After seeing a performance of *La Grande Eugène* in Paris, however, Dreyfus found his true calling and immediately decided to join the group, staying with it for 8 years; he is its only remaining member. In 1974, while still with *La Grande Eugène*, he obtained his first role in a major film, Michel Audiard's *Comment réussir quand on est con et pleurnichard /How to Make Good When One Is a Jerk and a Crybaby*, in which he appears in a few scenes – as a Baudelaire-reading transvestite – opposite Jane Birkin and Jean-Pierre Marielle. He continued working in theatre, playing Thomas Pollock Nageoire in the 1976 revival of Paul Claudel's *L'Échange* at the Theatre de la Ville. More small roles in film and television (often in drag) followed, and he began working with major names in the film industry, such as when he played a parody of Sarah Bernhardt (uncredited) in Werner Herzog's *Fitzcarraldo* (1982), and a neighbour in Bertrand Blier's *Notre histoire /Our Story* (1984).

Dreyfus's breakthrough arrived in the mid-1980s, when he became the spokesperson of the 'Marie' brand of frozen and prepared foods, a role he would keep for over 15 years. As 'Monsieur Marie,' Dreyfus was a familiar face on French television, in commercials that were directed, early on, by Patrice Leconte (Leconte would cast Dreyfus in his 1987 film *Tandem*). Dreyfus's next major breakthrough was in the post-apocalyptic black comedy *Delicatessen* (1991), set in a bleak futuristic society in which food is scarce. In this film, Dreyfus incarnates Clapet, the cannibalistic butcher who owns the apartment building in which his delicatessen is located and who preys upon the handymen he hires, turning them into his (and his building's occupants') next meal – somewhat recalling *Sweeney Todd*. *Delicatessen*, Jean-Pierre Jeunet and Marc Caro's award-winning debut feature, introduced their signature aesthetic, mise-en-scène, and visuals. Dreyfus's over the top performance as the evil butcher who prepares meals from human flesh brought him instant recognition and a César nomination. He worked with Jeunet and Caro on their next film, the dark, surreal *La Cité des enfants perdus /The City of Lost Children* (1995) about a mad scientist, who, unable to dream, kidnaps children in order to steal theirs. Here, Dreyfus plays the flea-tamer, Marcello, who aids protagonist One (Ron Perlman) to find his brother, one of the kidnapped children. Jeunet and Dreyfus collaborated again on Jeunet's 2004 film adaptation of Sébastian Japrisot's *Un long dimanche de fiançailles /A Very Long Engagement*, a World War I drama and love story, in which Dreyfus has a role as the nefarious Commandant

Lavrouye who could have pardoned the five French soldiers condemned to death for self-mutilation (a role that Dreyfus did not initially want to accept). This epic film features an all-star cast, including Audrey Tautou as protagonist Mathilde, a young woman determined to prove that her fiancé Manech (Gaspard Ulliel) is still alive, and Marion Cotillard in her César-winning supporting performance as a vengeance-seeking prostitute. The cast also features Jean-Pierre Darroussin, André Dussollier, Jodie Foster, and Dominique Pinon. In 2001, Dreyfus had the leading role of Philippe, Duc d'Orléans, in Eric Rohmer's *L'Anglaise et le Duc /The Lady and the Duke*, a historical drama based on real events that occurred during the French Revolution (adapted from Grace Elliott's memoir *Ma vie sous la revolution*). This film noted for its use of innovative digital effects to create its period setting, and was nominated for a César for Best Production Design. Dreyfus starred as Renaud Duraquet opposite Noémie Merlant in Jacques Richard's 2012 *L'Orpheline avec en plus un bras en moins*, based on a story by Roland Topor, about a young woman, Eléonore (Merlant), who is missing an arm due to a childhood accident that claimed her parents. This bizarre and surreal thriller – shot entirely digitally – explores Eléonore's encounters with the men in her life: the Judge (Pasquale d'Inca) who adopts her and takes her to live in his castle, observing her every move; Robinson the magician (Melvil Poupaud), the man she loves; the Inspector

(Dominique Pinon), examining a series of crimes against women, and Duraquet, an unsavory character, the proprietor of a fetishist cabaret. Dreyfus greatly enjoyed playing this role.

A prolific actor, with approximately 150 film (feature and short) and television credits to his name, Dreyfus incarnates a wide range of characters onscreen and onstage, often provocatively crossing and blurring boundaries of gender. Throughout his career, Dreyfus has worked with some of the top names in French theatre and film; along with his César nomination for *Delicatessen*, he was awarded the Cognac-Tonic Award in 1995 from the Cognac Festival du Film Policier. For his one-man drag show, *Le Mardi à Monoprix*, he was nominated for the prestigious Molière Award for Best Actor in 2010 and 2011 (for which he had previously been nominated in 1991 for *La Nonna* and in 1998 for *Hygiène de l'Assassin*).

This versatile performer and somewhat eccentric personality – one of his hobbies is collecting pigs, for which he has a well-known fondness, passion, and fascination, with a collection containing over 5,000 pieces of porcine art, which has been exhibited in Paris and at the Musée du Jambon in Bayonne – is also a writer. His publications include his book celebrating the pig and his admiration for this species, entitled *Du cochon considéré comme l'un des beaux-arts* (Editions du Cherche-Midi, 2005) while the title of his 2012 autobiography, *Ma bio dégradable* (Editions le Cherche-Midi, prefaced by Patrice Leconte) demonstrates his wit. The character Théodem Falls, titular figure of Anthony-Luc Douzet's 2012 fantasy crime thriller novel *Les 13 Crimes de Théodem Falls*, is based on Dreyfus (Douzet and Dreyfus collaborated on this project, with Dreyfus contributing the book's preface). In this book, Falls, the proprietor of the 'Les Divines Pagailles' merry-go-round in Paris's place Saint Sulpice – with pigs as carousel animals – is bored with his life; after he finds an old telephone book in a trash bin, mysterious crimes occur. A film adaptation is already in place, to be directed by Julien Seri.

Marcelline BLOCK
Princeton University and SAG-AFTRA

Marie Dubas (1884–1972)

*Not La
du Barry
but La
Dubas
Marie*

Trained as a stage actress, Marie Dubas (1884-1972) aspired to be a classical actress like Sarah Bernhardt or Rachel; like them, Dubas had dark hair, a vivacious stage presence, and immense talent. Dubas debuted at the Théâtre de Grenelle at age 14, before achieving stardom as a *chanteuse* and *diseuse*. She had initially sung for many years in the Montmartre cabarets and music halls before performing on the most coveted Parisian stages, including L'ABC, Bobino, the Casino de Paris, and L'Olympia. She incorporated comedy routines into her singing performances and invented a new genre, a kind of dramatic monologue where she is alone on stage, in the manner of the Belle Epoque cabaret star Yvette Guilbert (1865-1944). Dubas's signature dress, a white silk *mousseline* gown – which floated around her – brings to mind Isadora Duncan. She was endowed with an incredible energy – truly a *force de la nature*, the incarnation of *joie de vivre*. She well deserved her soubriquet « La Maréchale de la joie » ['the Marshal of joy'].

Marie Dubas sang without a microphone all of her life as she disliked any electronic devices, including being recorded in a studio, which is one of the reasons why she might be less remembered today. She inspired many followers, in particular, Édith Piaf, who admitted having decided to perform like Dubas after watching her and after attending all of her performances in Paris. Dubas was considered one of the most intelligent performers of her time; her lucidity impressed many. Colette, herself passionate about music halls, was a fan of Marie Dubas, so much so that in her 1933 novel *La Chatte*, Colette modelled her heroine Camille after Marie Dubas.[1] Colette described Dubas as « une femme belle comme un tison qui compose une chanson avec une lucidité de peintre ardent et patient » [2] ['a woman as beautiful as fire, who writes a song with the lucidity of a painter, ardent and patient'].

In a textbook entitled *Histoire contemporaine : classe de philo*, we read that 'music hall demands exceptional talents of mime and diction. Examples: Maurice Chevalier and Marie Dubas.' [3] The names Chevalier and Dubas are often cited together. Dubas was also admired by Simone de Beauvoir, Roland Barthes, and Charles Oulmont, among other important literary and theatrical critics. Dubas elevated her songs to the level of theatre, as in her act *Pedro*; she was mostly an actress. Indeed, her performance style was highly cinematic: according to French film scholar Ginette Vincendeau, Marie Dubas's recitals were an 'ascetic spectacle, with expressionist lighting, pared-down decor and costume, all drawing the audience's attention to the face of the singer on which the emotions were concentrated, as in a film close-up.'[4] Moreover, 'the descriptions of Marie Dubas, "alone in front of the audience, without any decor, without any *mise en scène*, without a garish costume"... is a *mise-en-scène* which owes its techniques to the small-scale cabaret, but also to the cinema.'[5]

As an actress, Dubas greatly admired Katharine Hepburn and Charlie Chaplin. Dubas's film credits include singing the theme song, *La Java d'un sou*, in Louis Valray's *Escale /Thirteen Days of Love* (1935), and roles in Pierre Gautherin's *Au fil des ondes* (1951) as well as Jean-Claude Roy's *Une nuit au Moulin Rouge* (1957). Some of Dubas's most memorable theatrical performances include that of the *deuxième* servant (soprano) in the original cast of Sacha Guitry and André Messager's musical comedy *L'Amour masqué* at the Théâtre Edouard VII in Paris in February 1923, as well as roles in the 1926 *opérette Le Temps d'aimer*, with music by Reynaldo Hahn (whose name is forever linked to that of Marcel Proust, his lover and friend) at the Théâtre de la Michodière; René Sarvil's *La Main de ma soeur* (1947) at the Théâtre de l'Ambigu; the 1949 production of Tristan Bernard's *Le Petit Café*, and the 1950 musical review *Drôle de monde* at the Théâtre de la Porte Saint Martin. Dubas was a household name in Paris and at the height of her career, her performances were sold out.

During World War II, Marie Dubas was not allowed to perform in Occupied France. Instead, performed in South America, Africa, and Canada. In Canada, she acted in the film *Utrillo*, made for television, in which she plays the part of the painter Suzanne Valadon, mother of artist Maurice Utrillo. Unfortunately, this film was not shown in France. Valadon's part was well suited to Marie Dubas, a lover of art who owned an Utrillo painting, which she used to carry around on her tours all over the world, along with a painting by André Derain. These paintings decorated the walls of her successive dressing rooms. Toward the end of her life, Dubas unfortunately had to part with her Utrillo as money had become scarce. She was painted by Edouard Georges MacAvoy (1905-1991), whose Parisian studio was located at 102, rue du Cherche-Midi. MacAvoy painted the portraits of many celebrities at the time (including writers, entertainers, and politicians). Toward the end of her career, in 1958, I also painted Marie Dubas's portrait after meeting her, upon her request.

During World War II, when Marie Dubas was not allowed to perform in France because of her Jewish heritage, Édith Piaf, who was determined not only to emulate Dubas, but to surpass her, was doing well, thanks to Raymond Asso, whom Marie Dubas had hired as a part-time secretary to rescue him when he was in dire straits. Raymond Asso wrote the song *Mon Légionnaire* for Marie Dubas. It was one of the signature songs in her repertoire, although it was one of the few songs that made the public cry rather than laugh. Dubas wanted, above all, to bring joy to her audience; her style had a definite Chaplinesque quality. While Dubas was performing *Mon Légionnaire* for the first time in a Marseilles music hall, Édith Piaf was entangled in the tragic murder of her first manager/promoter, Louis Leplée. Dubas received a moving letter from a woman whose son, a legionnaire, had died. This letter contained a 50 franc note. Marie Dubas bought a striped scarf with that money, and she wore it during all her performances of *Mon Légionnaire* in his memory. In the days when a singer had the ownership of his/her repertoire, Dubas kindly allowed Édith Piaf to borrow and sing that song, written for Dubas. *Mon Légionnaire* also made Édith Piaf famous.

Édith Piaf put *Mon Légionnaire* in her own repertoire, while acknowledging her debt to Marie Dubas (and today, *Mon Légionnaire* is more closely associated with Piaf). Although much was written about the rivalry between these two among the greatest of French singers, Marie Dubas's son François Bellair-Dubas, in his excellent co-written biography of his mother, *Marie Dubas : comédienne de la chanson* (2003) – with a preface by Jacques Tati – explains that in fact these two women singers were friends and were willing to help each other. There was a great mutual admiration, but if today Marie Dubas is less remembered than Piaf, it is because of Dubas's dislike of recording her songs or singing on the radio, akin to how, in Jean-Jacques Beineix's 1981 film *Diva*, the fictitious American opera singer Cynthia Hawkins (played in the film by real-life American soprano Wilhelmina Fernandez), refuses to be recorded. This refusal is the driving force of *Diva*'s plot, as an admirer clandestinely records her voice during a public performance.

Marie Dubas's dislike of the reproduction of her voice on radio or disc can be acknowledged as proof of her genuine, authentic talent: nothing artificial, no subterfuge, only her own voice. In his essay entitled 'The Work of Art in the Age of Mechanical Reproducibility,' German philosopher Walter Benjamin is of similar mind about his distrust of mechanical or technological reproduction. These two great minds suffered tremendously during the Occupation of France for being of the Jewish faith: Walter Benjamin lost his life when he was stranded at the border between France and Spain while attempting to escape occupied France. Marie Dubas lost her two beloved sisters, Rachel and Stephanie, as well as her nephew who disappeared in a concentration camp.

Most importantly, Dubas's singing voice is only one part of her performance. Equally important was the way she moved on stage, dancing; she spoke, narrating stories, such as 'Pedro,' which she acted out – to the fascination of crowds. Her facial expressions form a major part of the spectacle. Marie Dubas is the one who truly invented the 'recital', a formula which Maurice Chevalier, after the war, also selected, as it allows the singer to express him or herself totally.

Since 2003, Edwige Bourdy's one-woman cabaret *Stupéfiante : Marie Dubas de haut en bas* (dir. Vincent Vittoz), commemorating Dubas, has played at numerous theatres and venues throughout France, including the Avignon Theatre Festival. In *Stupéfiante*, Bourdy, a classically trained soprano, interprets 22 of Dubas's signature songs, such as *Mon Légionnaire* and *Le Tango stupéfiant*, among others, which might signal that a possible revival of Dubas is underway.

It seems surprising that Dubas, with such a phenomenal talent and a great variety of expressions, has not yet been commemorated in a filmed biography. There is no counterpart to the acclaimed Piaf biopic, *La Môme /La Vie en Rose* (Olivier Dahan, 2007), for Dubas; whoever would tackle a biopic of Marie Dubas should find an actress capable of reproducing such a versatile, multitalented personality.

Dubas, who, in her youth, had studied at the Conservatoire d'art dramatique, sang and danced at Bobino, the Moulin Rouge, and the Casino de Paris, and also around the world, and was, during her lifetime, a household name in music, theatre, dance, song, and film – decorated with the Legion of Honour for her excellent propaganda for France during World War II – died quietly in 1972, the same year as Maurice Chevalier. Dubas now reposes at the Père Lachaise Cemetery, along with the likes of Colette, Jim Morrison, Marcel Proust, among other luminaries. Marie Dubas should be rightfully commemorated among the greatest entertainers and performers of all time.

Jenny BATLAY
PhD Columbia University

1. Robert de Laroche and François Bellair-Dubas, preface by Jacques Tati, *Marie Dubas : comédienne de la chanson* (Paris: Christian Pirot, 2003), 207.
2. Catherine Galitzine, 'Critique : "Stupéfiante ! Marie Dubas de haut en bas" au Vingtième Théâtre,' July 12, 2011, http://www.musicalavenue.fr/Critiques/Spectacle/Critique-Stupefiante-Marie-Dubas-de-haut-en-bas-au-Vingtieme-Theatre.
3. De Laroche and Bellair-Dubas, *Marie Dubas*, 317.
4. Ginette Vincendeau, 'The *Mise-en-scène* of Suffering: French *chanteuses réalistes*,' *New Formations 3* (Winter 1987): 124.
5. Ibid.

Jean DUJARDIN (1972–)

*From the
Outskirts
of French
Cinema
to the
Oscar*

JEAN DUJARDIN recently achieved sudden international notoriety thanks to the Academy Award for Best Actor that was awarded to him in the spring of 2012 for his splendid performance in Michel Hazanavicius's silent movie *The Artist*. Quite remarkably, he is the first Frenchman to have earned an Academy Award for Best Actor. However, it should be pointed out that very few people would have predicted this outcome a few years ago. Especially in Dujardin's native France, the general public tended to associate him with his slapstick comedic roles in the TV series *Un gars, une fille* (1999-2003), *Brice de Nice /The Brice Man* (James Huth, 2005), and the two *OSS 117* movies (Michel Hazanavicius, 2006; 2009). His talent earned him a certain degree of fame within the Hexagon but could surely not suffice for an Oscar – or so most people thought. At any rate, given Dujardin's somewhat peripheral status within the French star system, very few people would have believed that the first Oscar for a French actor would go to Dujardin and not to the likes of Gérard Depardieu. Thus, we are dealing with a very interesting case. Was Dujardin a fast learner in terms of acting? Was he grossly underrated in France or is he simply overrated internationally? Such questions might never receive a proper or unbiased answer but in order to attempt to answer them, one is compelled to take a closer look at Dujardin's career.

Jean Edmond Dujardin was born on June 19, 1972, in Rueil-Malmaison, a western suburb of Paris. He spent his childhood in Plaisir, just west of Versailles, and he earned a baccalaureate in philosophy and arts. After a short spell as a locksmith in his father's company, he formed the « *Bande du Carré Blanc* » ['The Band of the Carré Blanc' or 'White Square'] which was a small Parisian theatre, together with several friends: Luc Antoni, Eric Collado, Eric Massot, Bruno Salomone, and Philippe Urbain. After the singing-cum-comedic band changed its name to « *Nous C Nous* » ['We Are Us'], they featured regularly in the show *Fiesta* on the television channel France 2 and even won the M6 show *Graines de star* on three occasions. Later, Dujardin performed several comedic skits with Bruno Salomone for the show *Farce attaque* on France 2. His first major role was the character Jean (or Loulou) on France 2's television series *Un gars, une fille*. It is thanks to this part that Dujardin became a celebrity in France. But no sooner did Dujardin become a recognizable face on television screens than he jumped ship to the big screen.

From 2002 to 2004, he starred in several short films (*À l'abri des regards indiscrets*, Ruben Alves and Hugo Gélin, 2002; *Rien de grave*, Renaud Philipps, 2004) and comedies

(*Ah ! Si j'étais riche /If I Were a Rich Man*, Gérard Bitton and Michel Munz, 2002; *Toutes les filles sont folles /All Girls are Crazy*, Pascale Pouzadoux, 2003; *Les Clefs de bagnole /The Car Keys*, Laurent Baffie, 2003), which helped him hone his acting skills. In *Le Convoyeur /Cash Truck* (Nicolas Boukhrief, 2004), Dujardin tackled his first major non-comedic role. Soon after, he was noticed for his acting in Valérie Guignabodet's *Mariages !* (2004). But it is really in roles such as the protagonist of *Brice de Nice* (2005), an amusing yet clueless character whose first and foremost desire is to catch the perfect wave in a waveless bay of the Mediterranean, that Dujardin seems to fecel the most comfortable. In fact, in *Brice de Nice*, Dujardin was both an actor and a co-writer. In 2006, Dujardin was cast by the French director and screenwriter Michel Hazanavicius in *OSS 117 : Le Caire, nid d'espions / OSS 117: Cairo, Nest of Spies*, which was a spoof of the Eurospy genre. In this movie, Dujardin impersonates Hubert Bonisseur de La Bath, a French secret agent whose code number (OSS 117) is an ironic (if not self-deprecating) hint to the more famous agent 007. Like Brice de Nice, Hubert Bonisseur de La Bath – a self-important, ludicrous, erratic, racist, sexist, inefficient, yet remarkably lucky and arguably handsome secret agent – seems to be the perfect role for Dujardin. It is thanks to this role that Dujardin earned an Étoile d'Or for the Best Actor (awarded by the Academy of French Cinema Journalists) and was nominated for the César Award for Best Actor. One could argue

that the Étoile d'Or and the César nomination convinced Dujardin that he was on the right path and that his conversion to cinematography was successful.

After starring in a few minor movies (*Hellphone*, James Huth, 2007; *Contre-enquête /Counter Investigation*, Franck Mancuso, 2007), Dujardin was awarded the Raimu Comedy Award for his role as Octave Parango in the 2007 film *99 francs* (dir. Jan Kounen), which was an adaptation of Frédéric Beigbeder's novel of the same title. Two years later, Hazanavicius directed a sequel to his previous *OSS 117* movie, this time with the title *OSS 117 : Rio ne répond plus /OSS 117: Lost in Rio*. A year later, Dujardin starred in the role of the real estate agent Marc Palestro in Nicole Garcia's *Un balcon sur la mer /A View of Love*, for which he received the Golden Swann award at the Cabourg Film Festival.

But Jean Dujardin's real consecration came, as suggested earlier, with his performance as George Valentin in Hazanavicius's *The Artist* (2011). In this movie, Dujardin manages to blend his characteristic comedic style with a dramatic performance and a gravitas which he had not fully shown in his previous roles. His performance earned him a remarkable number of awards. Aside from the highly prestigious Academy Award and the BAFTA, the Golden Globe, and the Screen Actors Guild awards for Best Actor, he also received awards for best actor from the London Film Critics' Circle, the Australian Academy, the Santa Barbara International Film Festival, the Las Vegas Film Critics Society, and the Phoenix Critics

Society. The year 2012 was nothing short of magical for Dujardin, for it consecrated him far beyond what the young actor from *Un gars, une fille* would have probably ever imagined.

More recently, Dujardin wrote the screenplay, directed, produced, and starred in *Les Infidèles /The Players* (2012), a comedy on the topic of male infidelity. Also, he is featured in the cast of *The Wolf of Wall Street*, a 2013 crime drama by Martin Scorsese, starring Leonardo DiCaprio. One can only assume that Dujardin's future performances will be eagerly awaited by the general public and closely scrutinized by film critics.

Cristian BRATU
Baylor University, Texas

Albert DUPONTEL (1964–)

*Reinventing
Black
Humour*

ALBERT DUPONTEL is undoubtedly a special case in French cinema. What he likes above all in cinema are crazy stories with little commercial appeal. This actor, film director and scriptwriter was not intended to be a member of the world of motion pictures. He was meant to be a doctor just like his father, and he actually studied medicine for several years. But he was not interested in the medical art and wanted to write and perform comedies.

He began to follow Yves Pignot and Antoine Vitrez's classes in the Théâtre de Chaillot for two years, during which he was hired for small roles in *Encore /Once More* (Paul Vecchiali, 1988) and in *La Bande des quatre /The Gang of Four* (Jacques Rivette, 1989). Thanks to the TV creative channel Canal+, he wrote and directed, in 1990, *Sales Histoires* – brief and cruel social satires. This kind of black comedy is qualified by the expression *au vitriol* in French because there is no concession to political correctness: that will be the genre Dupontel will never leave.

He quickly attracted the attention of humorist Patrick Sebastien, who first believed in his cruel and acidic humour, and became the producer of a successful one-man show: *Le Sale Spectacle*. The funniest sketch, entitled 'Rambo,' became very famous. He was popular when he came back onto the screen in 1995 and was immediately congratulated by the critics for playing Dionnet in Jacques Audiard's film, *Un héros très discret /A Self-Made Hero* (1996). Thanks to the money he had earned with his one-man show, he directed his first movie, the successful *Bernie* (1996), which is an amazing and crazy film about a thirty-year old orphan who decides, in a fantastic delirium, to find and protect his parents from a Mafia plot.

Insane and peculiar characters in black humour movies remained after this first one his favourites, whether in *Serial Lover* (James Huth, 1998) with Michèle Laroque or, of course, in his second masterpiece, *Le Créateur /The Creator* (1999), a wonderfully absurd piece of thinking about what an artist is.

From *La Maladie de Sachs /Sachs' Disease* (Michel Deville, 1999), there was nevertheless something like a turning point: he got new roles, less comic, more eclectic and sometimes classic, but always anti-heroes, extreme and provocative – which shows how much his singularity is now absolutely accepted and recognised by film directors – such as Alexandre Demarre in *Le Convoyeur* (Nicolas Boukhrief, 2004), Célestin Poux in *Un long dimanche de fiançailles /A Very Long Engagement* (Jean-Pierre Jeunet, 2004), the pianist Jean-François Lefort in *Fauteuils d'orchestre / Avenue Montaigne* (Danièle Thompson, 2006), the president in *Président* (Lionel Delplanque, 2006), and Balthazar Balsan in *Odette Toulemonde* (Eric-Emmanuel Schmitt, 2006).

With his profound and worrying looks, Dupontel is not only a gifted actor, but also an anti-star who definitively refuses French cinema conformism and consensus. 'The most important thing is to be able to find how to do your own cinema,' he says. He ironically called his production company « Contre Production ». The only time he accepted to go to the Cannes Festival was in order to support Gaspard Noé's ultra-violent and scandalous movie with Monica Bellucci and Vincent Cassel, *Irréversible* (2002). In 2009, he went back to directing with the release of *Le Vilain /The Villain* starring Catherine Frot, which was a commercial success.

Many members of the cinema world, such as Terry Gilliam and Terry Jones, have regard for his provocative and burlesque creativity, his art for aggressive and pungent humour, his dark and involved treatment of social distress, and his will to do what he wants in cinema even if that can hardly reach consensus. His fourth feature as a director, *Enfermés dehors /Locked Out* (2006), shows that he has now reached, after 40 years, complete maturity, managing to combine extreme gravity (the issue is social precariousness) and acid humour. For his most recent writing and directing effort, *9 mois ferme /Nine Month Stretch* (2013) – in which he also starred – he received numerous César nominations, including Best

Film, Director, and Actor, ultimately winning the award for Best Original Screenplay.

As are a lot of his characters, Dupontel is without a doubt a drop-out of French cinema, but he loves living on the fringes: 'I am indebted to nobody. I live like Gandhi, I need nothing. Nobody can fool me. The real luxury in my job is this – you are free to say yes or no. You just have to know what you want.'

Christophe MIQUEU
Université Montesquieu – Bordeaux IV

Romain DURIS (1974–)

The New Kid on the Block

ROMAIN DURIS is undoubtedly one of the most, if not *the* most, exciting newcomer of contemporary French cinema, which is always in search of fresh faces. His freshness, energy, and humour have already made him a crowd-pleaser as well as an actor relished by the *auteurs*.

Unlike a good number of his predecessors from the thirties to the sixties (in spite of some famous exceptions such as Alain Delon or Brigitte Bardot), he did not attend the Conservatoire, nor did he have any previous experience on stage when he first hit the screen. He is pure movie material, and a natural-born actor, which easily makes up for his lack of proper training in the craft of theatre. Discovered almost by chance in the streets (thus fulfilling the perfect dream of the wannabe he never was), he began his career with the successful director Cédric Klapisch. *Le Péril jeune /Good Old Daze* (1994) started for both of them a very special creative relationship, crowned with no less than seven pictures in nineteen years. This is almost a unique case in the history of French cinema, perhaps only surpassed by the legendary collaboration that united Jean-Pierre Léaud with François Truffaut.

This first feature film introduced Romain Duris's main character to the French viewers, helping to make him a familiar silhouette: surprisingly unathletic, he kept an adolescent body, often gracefully moving, not unlike a dancer; but most of all, he won the masses thanks to a devastatingly witty and juvenile smile. *Le Péril jeune* was meant to be a bitter-sweet group portrayal, but it was Duris who really stood out. His incandescent impersonation of the charismatic but lost Tomasi led a whole generation of youngsters to adopt him as their own, making him the symbol of a disenchanted post-seventies era. Romain Duris thus found his niche portraying a series of cocky young men, relying strongly on the stereotype of the *titi parisien* (which shows in his distinctive accent), and the Romani/Algerian filmmaker Tony Gatlif made perfect use of it in *Gadjo Dilo /The Crazy Stranger* (1997), for which he received his first César nomination (Meilleur jeune espoir masculin /Most Promising Actor) and *Exiles* (2004).

However, Duris proved to be much more versatile: if he could easily embody the young leading male typical of comedies, as in Klapisch's 2002 blockbuster *L'Auberge espagnole / The Spanish Apartment*, its 2005 sequel *Les Poupées russes /Russian Dolls*, and the concluding film of the *Spanish Apartment* trilogy, 2013's *Casse-tête chinois /Chinese Puzzle* – filmed in New York City – his performance always reveals a more tortured or unsettled side to his characters, and most of the time, he avoids picturing them as nice guys. Going even further, Duris truly hit the spot with both critics and the public playing a genuine gangster

partially redeemed by the grace of music in Jacques Audiard's most acclaimed *De battre mon cœur s'est arrêté /The Beat That My Heart Skipped* (2005), for which he was nominated for the Best Actor César, though he never went as far as making his character one-sided in one way or the other. He is as equally gifted for goofy science-fiction (Klapisch's 1999 *Peut-être*, garnering him a second Most Promising Actor César nomination); period movies (Laurent Tirard's 2007 *Molière* and Régis Roinsard's 2012 comedy *Populaire*, which is set in 1958); romantic dramas and contemporary auteur cinema (like in *17 fois Cécile Cassard /17 Times Cécile Cassard*, Christophe Honoré, 2002). He was utterly stunning in Christophe Honoré's *Dans Paris /In Paris* (2006). [1] This last film was conceived as a sort of homage to the French New Wave, the two main characters standing for the two opposite faces of the movement: the young and reckless side is shown by the virtuoso Louis Garrel, whereas a thick-bearded skinny Romain Duris displayed a more melancholic component, holding the challenging part of a brilliant but edgy photographer completely sunk into depression.

In *Paris*, [2] his 2008 collaboration with his mentor Cédric Klapisch, he takes on the role of a dancer whose career is just taking off while he discovers he has cancer. Gifted for life, but promised to death, since his first embodiment of Tomasi, Romain Duris has in a word been embodying the modern hero, despite an attempt to reach a broader audience as a rom-com leading man in the witty hit *L'Arnacœur /Heartbreaker* (Pascal

Chaumeil, 2010), for which he was nominated for the César for Best Actor, or in Michel Gondry's rendering of Boris Vian's reportedly inadaptable *L'Écume des jours /Mood Indigo* (2013). A recent film appearance is in François Ozon's *Une nouvelle amie /The New Girlfriend*, 2014.

Jean-Christophe BLUM
Lycée Blaise Pascal, Clermont-Ferrand

1. For further discussion of *Dans Paris /In Paris* (2006), see Adam Bingham, 'To help his brother cope with heartache, a student runs through Paris,' in *World Film Locations: Paris*, ed. Marcelline Block (Bristol: Intellect, 2011), 100-101. —Ed.

2. For further discussion of *Paris* (2008), see Adrienne Angelo, 'Pierre's Parisian Peregrination' in *World Film Locations: Paris*, ed. Marcelline Block (Bristol: Intellect, 2011), 116-117. —Ed.

André DUSSOLLIER (1946–)

*Not
the Same
Old Song*

ONE OF France's best-loved actors, André DUSSOLLIER has appeared in more than 100 films, and worked with an amazing array of directors. The theatre, however, was his first love. After receiving an arts degree, Dussollier, aged 23, studied to become an actor, and immediately received excellent results, including the prestigious Premier prix du Conservatoire, thus becoming Pensionnaire de la Comédie-Française in 1972. That same year, François Truffaut noticed him in a Büchner play, *Léonce et Léna*, and offered him his first big role on screen in *Une belle fille comme moi /Such a Gorgeous Kid Like Me*. This was the beginning of Dussollier's regular appearance in New Wave films, working with Claude Chabrol (*Alice ou la dernière fugue /Alice or the Last Escapade*, 1977), Éric Rohmer (*Perceval le Gallois /Perceval*, 1978, and *Le Beau Mariage /A Good Marriage*, 1982), Jacques Rivette (*L'Amour par terre /Love on the Ground*, 1984), and especially with Alain Resnais (*La Vie est un roman / Life is a Bed of Roses*, 1983; *L'Amour à mort /Love Unto Death*, 1984; *Pas sur la bouche /Not on the Lips*, 2003; *Cœurs /Private Fears in Public Places*, 2006, and *Les Herbes folles /Wild Grass*, 2009, among others).

Dussollier seems to excel at everything he undertakes, be it comedy, tragedy, detective or fantasy/horror genres, working with art-house as well as mainstream directors – such as Marguerite Duras (*Les Enfants / The Children*, 1985), Costa-Gavras (*La Petite Apocalypse /The Little Apocalypse*, 1993), Ettore Scola (*Le Roman d'un jeune homme pauvre*, 1995), Valérie Lemercier (*Quadrille*, 1997), Bertrand Blier (*Les Acteurs /Actors*, 2000), Étienne Chatiliez (*Tanguy*, 2001), Guillaume Canet (*Ne le dis à personne /Tell No One*, 2006), the Taviani brothers (*Le Mas des alouettes /The Lark Farm*, 2007), Anne Fontaine (*Mon pire cauchemar /My Worst Nightmare*, 2011), or André Téchiné (*Impardonnables / Unforgivable*, also 2011).

Dussollier has enjoyed long-lasting partnerships with some directors: along with Alain Resnais, he has worked several times with Yves Angelo, Jean Becker, and Jean-Pierre Jeunet (besides roles in *Un long dimanche de fiançailles /A Very Long Engagement* in 2004, and *Micmacs à tire-larigot / Micmacs* in 2009, for instance, his is the narrating voice in *Le Fabuleux Destin d'Amélie Poulain /Amélie*, 2001). He has also recently worked with Pascal Thomas on three adaptations of two Miss Marple novels and a collection of short stories by Agatha Christie, which became respectively, in 2005, *Mon petit doigt m'a dit...* (from *By the Pricking of My Thumbs*), in 2008, *Le Crime est notre affaire* (from *4.50 from Paddington*) and, in 2012, *Associés contre le crime* (from *Partners in Crime*), in which he plays the main protagonist, Bélisaire Beresford, a retired colonel quite overwhelmed by the endeavours of an intrepid wife (played by Catherine Frot) to solve crimes which he feels at first are figments of her imagination, only to find himself completely involved in them in his efforts to rescue his beloved yet ironically named wife, Prudence...

Light comedy, however, was not always Dussollier's trademark. He was originally perceived as a *comédien intellectual*, which is why he welcomed the opportunity to completely change his image in 1985, with Coline Serreau's comedy *Trois hommes et un couffin /Three Men and a Cradle*, which unexpectedly proved to be a huge box-office success. In it, Dussollier's comic genius comes to the fore in the scene where, very drunk, his character places a pillow under his sweat-shirt and, thus looking very pregnant, walks to a public park and declares to the world men's frustration at their inability to give birth – a scene removed from the film's enormously successful Hollywood remake, *Three Men and a Baby* (Leonard Nimoy, 1987).

Despite being highly appreciated and constantly receiving critical acclaim from film professionals and from the public, Dussollier had to wait until Resnais's *Mélo* in 1986 to receive a nomination for Best Actor at the Césars. He finally received this prize for his role in Resnais's *On connaît la chanson /Same Old Song* in 1997. This represented a consecration as, in the meantime, with Claude Sautet's *Un cœur en hiver /A Heart in Winter* in 1993, he had already received the César for Best Supporting Actor (he received another in 2002 for his role in *La Chambre des officiers /The Officers' Ward* by François Dupeyron).

In a recent interview Catherine Frot declared loving her experience of working with André Dussollier for his very personal approach to comedy, in particular his sense of rhythm and natural capacity to bring subtle humorous touches wherever needed. But compliments seem to put him ill at ease; Dussollier is a very modest star. Yet, lately, he was thrilled to open the new library which now bears his name, in Cruseilles, the small town in Haute-Savoie, where he grew up, especially because, as he says, the collective experience of reading in a library is similar to that of watching films in a cinema-house, a shared pleasure which can never end – probably because, as Alain Resnais once said, these are encounters, meetings of minds, forms of friendship – and André Dussollier's career in French cinema is indeed a good illustration of his generous nature.

Brigitte LE JUEZ
Dublin City University

Gad ELMALEH (1971–)

Humorist, Performance Artist, Actor, and Comedian

MOROCCAN-BORN GAD ELMALEH is a charismatic, versatile, and popular artist in the francophone world, and he is increasingly making an impact internationally as well. A naturalized French citizen, Elmaleh is an actor, singer, stand-up comedian, director, and performance artist; polls consistently rank him among the fifty most popular figures in France, such as in 2007, when he was elected the funniest person in France, and in 2009, when he was elected most popular public figure, along with former tennis-star-turned-singer Yannick Noah and film director Dany Boon. Elmaleh is a member of the *Ordre des Chevaliers des Arts et des lettres* and was awarded a medal by the French government in March 2007. In his award speech, French politician Renaud Donnedieu de Vabres applauded him as '... one of the most moving artists, an irresistible comedian, and a highly gifted actor.'

Elmaleh was born on April 19, 1971 in Casablanca where he attended the Georges Bizet School and the prestigious Lycée Lyauteau. The son of a mime-turned-businessman whose first name means 'joy' in Hebrew and whose last name means 'salty' in Arabic, Elmaleh grew up speaking colloquial Moroccan Arabic French and is 'very proud' of his Jewish Moroccan origins. In 1988, Elmaleh moved to Montréal, Canada, to study Political Science, while working as a stand-up comedian. At the age of 22, he moved to Paris to study drama.

In 1996, he became part of the *Morning d'Arthur* team on Europe 2 where he interpreted fictive callers such as a young Moroccan called Momo Zemio who gained French citizenship through a fake marriage. His first one-man show, *Décalages*, was performed at the Palais des Glaces in 1995. This autobiographical show explored themes linked to identity, travel, and cultural differences through the travels of David from Casablanca to Montréal, on to Paris and through the people he encounters, like a grandfather at McDonald's and his friend Abderrazak. *Décalages* was followed by the highly successful one-man show, *La Vie normale* in 2000 – directed by Isabelle Nanty – and *L'Autre c'est moi* in 2005, a stand up comedy show that relied on interaction with the audience. In 2000, Elmaleh's son Noé was born from his two-year relationship with French actress Anne Brochet. He has dated ballet dancer Aurélie Dupont and Monaco's royal princess Charlotte Casiraghi, with whom he has a son.

Elmaleh has a most impressive filmography: he has starred in numerous comedies, including his first breakthrough part in Algerian filmmaker Merzak Allouache's comedy *Salut cousin ! /Hey Cousin!*

(1996), followed by *Chouchou* (2003) which he co-wrote with Allouache and in which he played a romantic transvestite alongside Alain Chabat, and in *La Vérité si je mens ! 2 /Would I Lie to You? 2* (Thomas Gilou, 2001), where he played a charmer named Dov. He has also played roles in dramas, such as *L'Homme est une femme comme les autres /Man Is a Woman* (Jean-Jacques Zilbermann, 1998) and *Train de vie /Train of Life* (Radu Mihăileanu, 1998). In 1997, he played a role in *XXL* (dir. Ariel Ziétoun) alongside French actor Gérard Depardieu. In the 2005 comedy *Olé* (dir. Florence Quentin), he again starred with Depardieu (in the role of a chauffeur named Ramon), before joining Francis Veber's comedy *La Doublure /The Valet* (2006) where he played a parking valet named François Pignon who lets himself be persuaded by a businessman (Daniel Auteuil) to act as the lover of his mistress, a supermodel (Virginie Ledoyen).

In Pierre Salvadori's 2006 romantic comedy *Hors de prix / Priceless*, Elmaleh starred alongside French actress Audrey Tautou. Elmaleh plays Jean, a shy young bartender who becomes a gigolo at a luxury hotel in an attempt to win over the affection of a beautiful girl named Irene who drops him after finding out that he is not a millionaire. Tautou and Elmaleh were awarded the NRJ Ciné Award for Best Kiss for their performance in *Hors de prix*.

In 2009, he directed his first feature, *Coco*, inspired by *La Vie normale* and which received a Gérard du cinéma award, which, since 2006 have been annually given to the year's worst French acting performances and films, as a parody of the César Awards (similar to the Razzies in the US). *Coco* was awarded the 2009 « Gérard de la feignasse tellement décontractée du gland qu'elle recycle un de ses vieux sketches en film d'une heure et demie ».[1] In *Coco*, Elmaleh played a wealthy head of a family, ready to ruin himself to organize his son's bar mitzvah. Around the same time, he played his 2010 show *Papa est en haut du Palais des sports* (a reference to the French lullaby *Fais dodo, Colas mon p'tit frère*).

Outside France, Elmaleh is probably best known for his film *Chouchou* (2002) where he plays an illegal immigrant transvestite – starring with Alain Chabat, Claude Brasseur, Roschdy Zem, and Catherine Frot – in a role that was based on the character of Chouchou in *La Vie normale*. More recently, he played a Jewish head of a family in Rose Boche's *La Rafle /The Round Up* (2010), alongside Jean Reno and Mélanie Laurent, a film about the round-up of French Jews in the Vel d'Hiv as well as their deportation to concentration camps during World War II. More recently, he has done voice-overs for animation films, such as the character Gru in *Moche et Méchant /Despicable Me* (Chris Renaud and Pierre Coffin, 2010) and Omar Ben Salaad in Steven Spielberg's *Les Aventures de Tintin : Le Secret de la Licorne /The Adventures of Tintin: The Secret of the Unicorn* (2011). He has also had a role in Woody Allen's feature *Midnight in Paris* (2011). In one of his latest project, a romantic comedy called *Un bonheur n'arrive jamais seul /Happiness Never Comes Alone* (James Huth, 2012), Gad stars alongside Sophie Marceau.

After his highly popular one man-show *Papa est en haut*, Elmaleh toured France with another one-man show, *Gad Elmaleh : One Man /Woman Show*, in 2012. In 2011 and 2012, he proved that he is anything but lazy, starring in a number of features, including Dennis Dugan's Adam Sandler vehicle, *Jack and Jill* (2011), and *Les Seigneurs* (dir. Olivier Dahan, 2012).

In 2012, he was seen in Costa-Gavras's *Le Capital* with Gabriel Byrne, and in 2013, in Michel Gondry's *L'Écume des jours /Mood Indigo*, based on Boris Vian's novel.

Christa JONES
Utah State University, Logan

1. 'Lazybones Gérard for having such loose glands as to recycle one of one's old sketches into a 90-minute feature.'

FERNANDEL (1903–1971)
[Fernand Joseph Désiré CONTANDIN]

*More
Than
Just a
Funny
Face*

FERNANDEL was much more than an actor, he was « une gueule » – a face; he was pretty much visual, very expressive, not only in movies, but also in shows or simply when singing. This characteristic was a combination of a heritage of his *comique-troupier* period (at the Alcazar in Marseilles) – a certain tradition of visual acting in silent films, even though he started in talking ones – and probably a very strong and typical characteristic of his home town.

He was born in 1903 in Marseilles, a place where people are known to be natural-born actors (in the way they talk, in trying to convince you, and also in exaggerating…).[1] Fernand Joseph Désiré Contandin – nicknamed at the age of 8 « Fernand d'elle » ['Fernand of hers'] by his mother since he was always playing around with a girl who was later to become his wife – seemed to carry genes of drama added to this local particularity: his father was already in the Music-Hall and his ancestors were immigrants from the country of the *Comedia dell arte.*

Before starting to play in movies, Fernandel had already acted on stage in his home town at the Alcazar. At that time cinema, even though quite popular, was not really an institution, and being an actor was not as glamorous as today. Thus, actors rarely started a career directly in cinema, and film budgets were tighter than nowadays: actors were mostly sought in cabarets or theatres where they had proven to be already professionally trained. Shows and music-halls on the one hand and cinema on the other were close in the 1930s, so that Fernandel naturally came to act quickly in films. When his film career started in earnest with *Le Rosier de Madame Husson /He* (dir. Dominique Bernard-Deschamps) in 1932, he had already shot 15 movies. His career was uninterrupted for 40 years and he acted in 148 films. However, among them quite a number were popular if not third-rate films (i.e. *Les Gueux au paradis /Hoboes in Paradise*, René le Hénaff, 1946); for such movies, his main interest was to make 'easy money,' to ensure a certain level of well-being for him and his family. At the same time he maintained his popularity and fame, and could not be easily forgotten.

Fortunately for French cinema he was also approached by great authors (Jean Giono, *Crésus /Croesus*, 1960) and could develop his dramatic acting talent more fully: one of them was his fellow Marseilles native Marcel Pagnol. Sharing the same French southern culture, their collaboration was successful and proved to be a real fusion (*Angèle*, 1934; *Le Schpountz*, 1938; *La Fille du puisatier*, 1940; *Naïs*, 1945; *Topaze*, 1951). In 1947, he accepted to shoot the first film of Henri Verneuil (the short *Escale au soleil*), thus offering him his fame to promote the director's work as well as future notoriety. They shot many films together, and the most famous one was also Fernandel's greatest success in the French box-office: *La Vache et le Prisonnier /The Cow and I* (1959): in this movie he really considered the cow as an actress, which gave his acting a very convincing touch and complicity.

In 1951, he acted as a priest, not one known all around the world, but a priest confronted by a strong dilemma: betraying a confession in order to save the lives of people staying in an inn owned by deadly thieves (*L'Auberge rouge /The Red Inn*, 1951, Claude Autant-Lara). In this movie Fernandel had to combine dramatic and comic effects; his character had to lie to the threatened clients in order to save them without betraying his promise not to reveal the confession of one of the two owners. This film is considered to be a kind of pre-Don Camillo, the world famous priest. Shot the same year with a French director, Julien Duvivier, and with an Italian team in Italy, *Don Camillo /The Little World of Don Camillo* (1952) was to be a real success, giving birth to four sequels and an unfinished one which could have been his last (he died in 1971).

This character stuck to him so much that he even had requests from fans to bless their children. He was the perfect incarnation of Don Camillo. He showed in this film a great sense of humanity behind a curtain of political rivalry.

Furthermore behind the character's responsibilities given to him by the cassock, he showed he could have as many faults as any other ordinary man. In *Don Camillo*, as in most of his films, Fernandel showed a sense of comic talent, and the audience expected him to play this way. When he played more tragic roles the film did not really work (*L'Armoire volante /The Cupboard was Bare*, 1948, Carlo Rim; *Le Voyage du père /Father's Trip*, 1966, Denis de la Patellière), except for *Heureux qui comme Ulysse... /Happy He Who Like Ulysses* (1970, Henri Colpi), in which he combined tragic and comic acting.

But even though acting in comic films brought him the reputation of a third-rate actor, due to his ability to change a large smile into a very expressive astonished attitude with ample gestures, his style was also convincing in movies nowadays considered classics (*François premier /Francis the First*, 1937, Christian-Jaque; *La Cuisine au beurre /My Wife's Husband*, 1963, Gilles Grangier). Because of his unique face, he was often compared to a horse (mainly because of his big teeth), but he seemed to play a lot with his physical aspect in his acting, in order to be as expressive as possible, as if he were acting in a silent movie: *Les Rois du sport* (1937, Pierre Colombier) being a good example, since this film was based on almost exclusively gestural acting with very few dialogues. Incidentally, Philippe Halsman's photographic interview (*The Frenchman*, 1948) is a very good and convincing example and collection of Fernandel's attitudes and grimaces; the photographer asked the actor to answer his questions with facial expressions alone.

Fernandel brought thus to the cinema a touch of humanity and often portrayed characters with minor vices, faults, and a lot of insincerity. The comic effects which made this popular even brought people attracted by his fame to watch a film only because he was in it.

Igor BRATUSEK
Université Paris–Sorbonne

1. For further discussion of Marseillais culture and cinema, see Marcelline Block, ed., *World Film Locations: Marseilles* (Bristol: Intellect, 2013). —Ed.

Edwige FEUILLÈRE (1907–1998)
[Edwige Louise Caroline CUNATTI]

Grande Dame of Cinema and Theatre

EDWIGE FEUILLÈRE was born Edwige Louise Caroline Cunatti on October 29, 1907 in Vesoul, France, and spent her early childhood in France and in Italy. She knew at a very young age that she wanted to act. As a young girl, when her father or a teacher would ask her what she wanted to do in life, she would respond: « Je ferai du théâtre ! » [1]

She attended the Conservatoire d'art dramatique in Dijon, and in 1928, she won a Premier prix de comédie for her role in Molière's *Le Malade imaginaire*. Soon after, she left for Paris to apply to the Conservatoire, where she studied both declamation and singing. Using the stage name Cora Lynn, an anagram of her middle name, Caroline, she launched her theatrical career in Paris in 1930 and played several secondary roles. She joined the Comédie-Française and made her official debut in Paris on November 2nd, 1931 as Suzanne in *Le Mariage de Figaro*. On screen, her career would start with the 1931 short film, *La Fine Combine* (dir. André Chotin), for which she used the stage name, Cora Lynn.

She began to use the name Edwige Feuillère after her marriage to Pierre Feuillère, whom she had met at the Conservatoire that same year.

Feuillère was beloved for her work both on screen and on the stage, and her career encompassed periods where she focused more on one medium than on the other. In the 1930s and 1940s, she concentrated more on her film career than on her theatre work. Her early roles included Suzy Courtois in *Topaze* (Louis J. Gasnier, 1933), Diane in *Les Aventures du roi Pausole /The Adventures of King Pausole* (Alexis Granowsky, 1933), Claudia Procula in *Golgotha /Behold the Man* (Julien Duvivier, 1935), and Giacinta in *Barcarolle* (Gerhard Lamprecht and Roger Le Bon, 1935). Later, Feuillère's image as a *femme fatale* began to take shape with roles such as her Véra in *J'étais une aventurière /I was an Adventuress* (Raymond Bernard, 1938), Marthe in *Marthe Richard, au service de la France /Marthe Richard* (Raymond Bernard, 1937), Edwige Elno in *Feu !* (Jacques de Baroncelli, 1937), Catherine in *L'Honorable Catherine* (Marcel L'Herbier, 1943), and the duchess in *La Duchesse de Langeais /Wicked Duchess* (Jacques de Baroncelli, 1942).

Critical and audience reception of Feuillère's performances in the films that she made before and during the war were, for the most part, very positive. Audiences loved Feuillère's sophisticated demeanour, and she was extremely well-known for her elegant image. Newspaper headlines would laud her manner of dress. For example, one headline read « Une nouvelle reine pour la ville de Paris : Edwige ». Another read « Edwige Feuillère est l'actrice la plus élégante du monde ».[2] For Feuillère, elegance was not a question of dress or of couture; rather, it was a state of mind. She had modelled her stature on that of her paternal grandmother, who was a peasant with nine children. When her grandmother would come back to her village carrying wet laundry on her head, Feuillère would watch her and tell herself that she had to stand and hold herself as straight as her grandmother did.[3] Feuillère's demeanour and elegance were integral components of her cinematic image.

By the end of the 1940s, Feuillère had established herself as a distinguished and well-respected film actress, to the point that she had secured the reputation of being the *Grande Dame du cinéma français*.[4] Yet in the 1950s, she began to work more regularly in the theatre. In the 50s and 60s, she worked very frequently with Paul Claudel and Jean Giraudoux, and she spent relatively little time working on film projects. The theatre was especially dear to Feuillère, who suffered from bouts of depression, anger, and self-doubt throughout her career and was often plagued by migraines. Acting was her way of escaping her maladies, and the admirations of her public never failed to bring her out of whatever was ailing her. Though she loved acting in film, her preference for the theatre was noticeable. Feuillère had remarkable success in the theatre, both in France and in England. She made regular performances in

Parisian theatres like the Théâtre de Paris, the Théâtre Marigny, and the Théâtre Sarah Bernhardt. She also made several trips to London to act in a variety of plays between 1951 and 1968. Her first performance in London was in Claudel's *Partage de Midi*. Her performance so captivated audience members that they were 'mesmerized by a beautiful woman who had the power to communicate the most complex words and thoughts to a foreign audience.' [5] Such was Feuillère's impression on English audiences that Harold Hobson, a well-known critic for the British *Sunday Times*, was compelled to call her 'the greatest actress in the world.' [6] Yet in spite of this immense success in the theatre, Feuillère still felt a need to make films as well. Even though she preferred the energy of the theatre, she noted in her interview with *Monsieur Cinéma* that she greatly appreciated the sense of team spirit in filmmaking and the numerous congenial people she met while working. She clearly wanted to return to making films.

Despite the amicable working relationships she fostered in the cinema, Feuillère's productivity on the screen would never again attain the level that it did before the War. Between 1951 and 1961, Feuillère made only eight films, as opposed to her thirty-one films made between 1931 and 1941 or her fourteen made between 1941 and 1951. In a 1961 television interview, Feuillère noted that it was extremely difficult to work on film and in the theatre at the same time. At that time, she was preparing for her role in two sketch films for Paul Gordeaux, which

she told the interviewer was to be her « retour au cinéma ». Feuillère, however, would make only seven more films after 1961. Her theatre career continued to flourish until 1992, and she worked in television for several years. She made appearances in several sketches, television shows and made-for-TV movies between 1967 and 1995. Her last television appearance was only three years before she died on November 13, 1998.

Julie PARSON
The Ohio State University, Columbus

1. « Je ferai du théâtre ! » ['I will work in theatre!']: Françoise Giroud, 'Edwige Feuillère,' in *Françoise Giroud Vous Présente Le Tout-Paris* (Paris: Gallimard, 1952), 85.

2. TF1, *Edwige Feuillère : la rêveuse éveillée*, February 15, 1981.

3. Ibid.

4. 'Edwige Feuillère,' Cinémathèque française, accessed September 17, 2013, http://cinema.encyclopedie.personnalites.bifi.fr/index.php?pk=31653.

5. John Stokes, *The French Actress and Her English Audience* (Cambridge: Cambridge University Press, 2005), 162.

6. Ibid, 159.

Brigitte Fossey (1946–)

Bienvenue chez la ch'ti !

Who could have forgotten little Paulette, as blonde as she was fragile, heroine of the movie *Jeux interdits /Forbidden Games* (René Clément, 1952)? The film surely left its mark at the Venice Film Festival where it was presented while the soundtrack was also a hit in France at the time. Born in Northern France in June 1947, Brigitte Fossey, or 'Paulette', then only 6 years old, became instantly world famous. At 10 years old she was Jane Duval in Gene Kelly's *The Happy Road /La Route joyeuse* (1957), a young schoolgirl escaping secondary school.

Forgotten 10 years after her early successes: it had been her parents' decision that, as a teenager, she leave aside her new movie career to enjoy a normal upbringing and continue her studies in translation and philosophy. Only later, at the age of 20, did she accept director Jean-Gabriel Albicocco's offer to play the beautiful and romantic Yvonne de Gallais in his screen adaptation of Alain-Fournier's well-known French novel *Le Grand Meaulnes /The Wanderer* (1967). Her performance in *Raphaël ou le débauché /Raphaël or the Debauched One* (dir. Michel Deville) in 1971 made her a second-time-around star. Her return to the cinema gave her the opportunity to work with the most well-known directors, for example, François Truffaut in *L'Homme qui aimait les femmes /The Man Who Loved Women* (1977); *Chanel solitaire* (George Kaczender, 1981), and Giuseppe Tornatore's Academy Award winning *Nuovo Cinema Paradiso / Cinema Paradiso* (1988). Her best years were the 70s when she acted in Jean-François Adam's 1973 *M comme Mathieu* with Sami Frey; in Bertrand Blier's 1974 *Les Valseuses / Going Places* with Gérard Depardieu, Patrick Dewaere, Miou-Miou, and Jeanne Moreau; in René Gilson's *La Brigade /The Brigade* (1975); in *Les Fleurs du miel /The Honey Flowers* (Claude Faraldo, 1976); in Claude Lelouch's *Les Bons et les Méchants / The Good Guys and the Bad* (1976) and in *Les Enfants du placard / Closet Children* (Benoît Jacquot, 1977). Despite the fact that she may not be a well-known French actress outside France or French-speaking countries (too sensitive, too blonde for a French actress?), she has won Oscar nominations for the two last-mentioned movies, and was also a member of the jury for the Berlin Film Festival in 1982, proving a European reputation. In the late 80s and 90s she was still one of France's favourite actresses although she was not acting as much. Her later films include *La Boum /The Party* and its sequel, *La Boum 2* (Claude Pinoteau, 1980, 1982) with Sophie Marceau, and *Un mauvais fils /A Bad Son* (Claude Sautet, 1980), with Patrick Dewaere. She has often acted in TV movies (téléfilms) or series, such as *Les Gens de Mogador* (Robert Marzoyer, 1972), *Le Château des Oliviers* (Nicolas Gessner, 1993), and more recently in *La Mort dans l'île* (Philippe Setbon, 2008).

Very early in her life, she realised she should nurture her talents. Taking courses in drama and dance, she was trained by some of the biggest names such as Jean Vilar, Roger Blin, and Laurent Terzieff. Her theatrical career includes *L'Eté* (Jean-François Adam, 1967), *La Surprise de l'amour* (Marivaux), *Macbeth* (Shakespeare), *La Mouette* [*The Seagull*] (Tchekhov), *Le Jeu de l'amour et du hasard* (Marivaux), *L'Homme en question* (Marceau, 2002), *Grosse chaleur* (Laurent Ruquier, 2005), and more recently *La Nuit de l'audience* (Patrice Kerbrat, 2009) directed by Jean des Cars and Jean-Claude Idée. In 2006, she was on stage in Northern France with her daughter Marie Adam (from her ex-husband, the movie director Jean-François Adam, with whom she had a brief five-year marriage). Mother and daughter both acted in *Cocteau l'invisible vivant*. Fossey has also participated in operas such as *Jeanne d'Arc au bûcher* (Arthur Honegger). The organ player, Loïc Mallié, admires her voice which 'espouses the musical form.'

Brigitte Fossey's personal tastes are as classic as her looks. While admiring the artists Rembrandt, Matisse, and Carpacccio, her true love is literature. Since she was not allowed by her parents to watch television at home, she would find the greatest pleasure in reading the classics such as Stendhal and Dostoyevski. Her favourite composers are Mozart and Handel and also Duke Ellington.

Fossey is also involved in social activism, particularly in good causes involving children: with the actress Danièle Delorme she wrote a report on the artistic awakenings of children and has taken part in international conventions regarding children.

Her biggest regret is not having been a singer … in order to be able to put on weight!

Fabienne H. BAIDER
University of Cyprus

FRÉHEL (1891–1951)
[Marguerite BOULC'H]

Ubi
Sunt?

F RÉHEL and 'The Future of Nostalgia'.[1]

 Ce sont amis que vent emporte.

—Rutebeuf, *La Complainte Rutebeuf*
(1262) [2]

 Les sanglots longs
 Des violons
 De l'automne
 Blessent mon cœur
 D'une langueur
 Monotone.

 [The long sobs
 Of the autumn violins
 Wound my heart
 With a monotonous
 Languishing.]

 ...

 Quand sonne l'heure
 Je me souviens
 Des jours anciens
 Et je pleure.

 [When the clock strikes
 I recall
 The olden days
 And I cry.]

—Paul Verlaine, *Chanson d'automne* (1867)

 Qu'as-tu fait, ô toi que voilà
 Pleurant sans cesse,
 Dis, qu'as-tu fait, toi que voilà
 De ta jeunesse ?

 [What have you done, oh you
  over there
 Crying non-stop,
 Tell me, what have you done,
  you over there,
 With your youth?]

—Paul Verlaine, *D'une prison* (1894)

With an expression of sadness and nearly tearful despair on her moonlike face – as if carrying all the tragedy of the world – Fréhel sings *Où est-il donc ?* (1926) in Julien Duvivier's celebrated poetic realist 1937 film *Pépé le Moko*, starring Jean Gabin. In *Pépé*, Fréhel plays Tania. Singing *Où est-il donc ?* with her melancholic expression and gripping voice, with an accent that belies the faubourg (as well as raw emotion and self-taught singing), evoking the Paris that Pépé *le Moko* (or Pépé, 'the Toulon Man,' a dangerous gangster), is pining for, summarizes the plot as well as announces the film's denouement: Pépé, exiled in the Algiers Casbah in order to escape the French police, longs to return to Paris. Not the commodified, touristy Paris, but the proletarian Paris with its clichés which have been romanticized, then commercialized through books, brochures, and postcards: *café-crème*, *frites*, a bottle of wine, and the smell of the metro, artefacts that the 'people' hold on to, and retell each other to commemorate their existence, and to consecrate and validate their *raison d'être*. These objects symbolize the *classe ouvrière* [working class] from which hail Gabin/Pépé and Fréhel, emblematic of the Paris mythology. Fréhel, at the helm of the 1930s and 1940s, with a slight *parigot* accent, becomes the muse of that era with her nostalgic songs such as *La Chanson des fortifs* ['The Song of the Fortifications' – which fortifications were already gone by the time she sang about them]. Fréhel 'the sublime',[3] *la grande Fréhel* – *grande* meaning 'tall' and 'great', as she was both – grew up in Montmartre, Belleville, and later Pigalle, where she died in 1951 at age 50, in a shabby hotel, forgotten, having lost her youth and beauty.

Fréhel has been hailed as one of the best performers of *la chanson réaliste* (also called *chanson vécue*). What makes her believable is that she sang truly from the heart, each song a *cri du cœur* revealing a personal experience, *du vécu*. For example, not without irony, after her relationship with Maurice Chevalier fell apart – he left her for the older and more established Mistinguett – she sang, in *Tout change dans la vie* ['Everything Changes in Life'] (1936):

J'ai mis au-dessus de ma cheminée
La photo d'Maurice Chevalier.

[I hung Maurice Chevalier's photo
Above my fireplace.]

After their breakup, Fréhel attempted suicide: she was not even 19 years old.

In *Pépé le Moko*, after listening to Fréhel sing *Où est-il donc ?*, Pépé decides to leave the Casbah and return to the France he misses so much, risking his life and liberty in the process. It is as if Pépé, emoting

from Fréhel's song, can no longer bear his Casbah confinement. He must see Paris again (as in Luis Mariano's *Revoir Paris ... /C'est magnifique* [To see Paris again ... /is wonderful], which is how Pépé feels).

There is a manifest reason for Pépé's decision to go back to France: a new love interest – *cherchez la femme !* Yet underlying, in *filigrane*, there is the latent aching desire for Paris, a desire re-activated by Fréhel's nostalgic voice, whose lyrics act as a catalyst:

Y'en a qui vous parle de
    l'Amérique
Ils ont des visions de cinéma...
[There are those who tell you
    about America
They saw it at the cinema...]

Où est-il mon moulin de la place
    Blanche ?
Mon tabac et mon bistrot du coin ?
Tous les jours pour moi c'était
    dimanche !
Où sont-ils les amis les copains ?
...Où sont-ils donc ?

[Where is my windmill on Place
    Blanche?
My coffee shop and my corner
    bistro?
Everyday was Sunday for me![4]
Where are all my friends, my
    buddies?
So, where are they?]

The *chanteuse réaliste mise en abyme* in Duvivier's film romanticizes the *bas-fonds* of Paris (or Marseilles for that matter), sometimes raising crime to an aesthetic level, anticipating *film noir*.

Fréhel was born Marguerite Boulc'h, on July 14, 1891, Bastille Day. As a child, she might have thought that fireworks and music were for her birthday, a form of compensation for a childhood lived in poverty. Born poor, she also died poor. In between, she lived a bohemian life, travelled East, exiled herself for 10 years, and made a glorious comeback before dying.

If the essence of poetry, of tragedy, is the coming to terms with the passage of time, Fréhel inscribes herself within this lineage of poets. The flight of time is lamented in François Villon's *Ballade des dames du temps jadis* ['Ballad of the Ladies of Yesteryear'] in his *Grand Testament*, 1461–1462, in which he pleads « Mais où sont les neiges d'antan ! » ['But where are the snows of yesteryear!'], a metaphor for the ladies who are no longer in this world:

La royne Blanche comme lis,
Qui chantoit à voix de seraine;
Berte au grant pié, Bietris, Allis;
Haremburgis qui tint le Maine,
Et Jehanne, la bonne Lorraine,
Qu'Englois brûlèrent à Rouan;
Où sont-ils, où Vierge souvraine ?
Mais où sont les neiges d'antan !

[Queen Blanche de Castile, as white as a lily / With the voice of a Siren, / Bertha–Broadfoot, Beatrice, Adelaide of Paris; / Ermengarde, Countess of Maine, / And Jeanne d'Arc, the good child of Lorraine, / Who was burned at the stake in Rouen by the English; / Where, oh where, are they, Virgin sovereign? / But where are the snows of yesteryear!]

And in Ronsard's 1578 *Sonnets pour Hélène* (II, 24):

Quand vous serez bien vieille, au soir, à la chandelle
Assise auprès du feu, dévidant et filant,
Direz, chantant mes vers, en vous émerveillant :
« Ronsard me célébrait du temps que j'étais belle ».

[When you'll be very old, at night, by candlelight,
Sitting by the fireplace, spinning and sewing wool,
You will say, as you sing my verses, in wonder:
'Ronsard did praise me when I was beautiful.']

Other examples include Lamartine's poem *Le Lac* ['The Lake'] (1820) in which the poet pleads for Time to stop its flight: « Ô temps ! Suspends ton vol, et vous, heures propices ! Suspendez votre cours : Laissez-nous savourer les rapides délices. Des plus beaux de nos jours ! » ['Oh Time! Stop your flight and you, opportune hours! Suspend your course: let us savour the rapid delights. Of our most beautiful days!']

Or Hugo's *Tristesse d'Olympio* ['Olympio's Sadness'] (1837), in which the poet complains that time has robbed him of his lover; or Verlaine's verses, cited above in the epigraph: « Quand sonne l'heure /je me souviens /des jours anciens /et je pleure »… – coincidentally, there is a poster of Fréhel that states « Fréhel pleure » ['Fréhel cries'].

Twentieth-century French poet Apollinaire states, in *Le pont Mirabeau*

['The Mirabeau Bridge over the Seine River'] (1912), « Le temps s'en va...je demeure ». ['Time goes by, but I remain.'] Songwriters such as Charles Aznavour advise young people to seize the day before it is too late: « mais les jours passés ne reviennent pas...ils passent » ['but days that have gone by never come back']. In *Marquise* (1961), singer Georges Brassens set Corneille's *Stances à Marquise* (1658) to music (adding a final verse from Tristan Bernard):

Marquise, si mon visage
A quelques traits un peu vieux
Souvenez-vous qu'à mon âge
Vous ne vaudrez guère mieux

Le temps aux plus belles choses
Se plaît à faire un affront
Et saura faner vos roses
Comme il a ridé mon front

[Marquise, if my face
Has a few slightly old features
Remember that at my age
You won't do any better

Time injures
    the most beautiful things
It will fade your roses
As it has wrinkled my face]

Fréhel, who cries over her past beauty now lost forever, also cries because her lovers have gone away, along with her good looks: the title and eponymous refrain of her song *Où sont tous mes amants* (1935) rhymes with Villon's refrain *Mais où sont les neiges d'antan !* The topos *ubi sunt ?*, already in vogue in medieval times, is an eternal one: yesterday everything

seemed so much better than today, as sung by the Beatles:

Yesterday, all my troubles seemed
    so far away,
Now it looks as though they're
    here to stay.
Oh, I believe in yesterday.
Yesterday, love was such an easy
    game to play,
Now I need a place to hide away.
Oh, I believe in yesterday.

And where is Fréhel today? I found her, rosy-cheeked and filled with energy, in Joann Sfar's biopic *Gainsbourg (vie héroïque) /Gainsbourg: A Heroic Life* (2010), in which Fréhel (played by César-winning actress Yolande Moreau) makes an entrance in a restaurant where Gainsbourg, then a young boy, exclaims excitedly: « Madame Fréhel !». He rushes to tell her that he knows one of her songs by heart, not *La Java bleue*, which is mild enough to be sung by children, but rather, a song about prohibited drugs, *La Coco*, whose lyrics proclaim: « j'ai tué mon gigolo ». During this episode in the film, Fréhel sways along with her song, a bit of bravado in her stance. Filled with humour and brio, Fréhel laughs when singing the line about killing her gigolo with a knife while she was under the influence! Serge Gainsbourg, whom François Mitterrand, then President of France, compared to Baudelaire and Apollinaire, seems to have particular affinities with Fréhel, who was herself, in a way, a kind of *poétesse maudite* in the tradition of Nerval, Rimbaud, Verlaine, and Marceline Desbordes-Valmore (the only *poétesse maudite*). Serge Gainsbourg as a little boy as represented in Sfar's film is a mischevious smart-aleck, a would-be counterpart for Raymond Queneau's character Zazie in his 1959 novel *Zazie dans le métro*, made by Louis Malle into the eponymous film (1960). In Olivier Dahan's 2007 biopic of Édith Piaf, *La Môme /La Vie en Rose*, Édith as a little girl is a more pathetic character, neglected by her mother, unkempt, with a runny nose, travelling with her father's circus. In *La Vie en Rose*, Cosette of Hugo's *Les Misérables* is recalled when Édith's father brings her a doll, hidden under his overcoat: does he become a Jean Valjean figure at this juncture? Édith can also be compared to Fellini's Gelsomina in *La strada* (1954), travelling with a strong man and performing circus tricks. Édith, raised in her grandmother's brothel, recalls Louis Malle's *Pretty Baby* (1978), in which a little girl named Violet, played by child star Brooke Shields, is auctioned into prostitution in a New Orleans brothel (where she, too, was abandoned by her mother). Like *La Vie en rose*, named after Piaf's iconic song, the title *Pretty Baby* is that of a well-known old song preceding the film (the Tony Jackson ragtime melody from the early 1900s). Other literary reminiscences in *La Vie en Rose* occur: Louis Leplée, *La Môme Piaf*'s first manager, brings to mind Henri Danglard, played by Jean Gabin in Jean Renoir's *French Cancan* (1954), the cabaret director who discovers a young washerwoman and makes her a famous Cancan dancer. Raymond Asso became Piaf's manager after Leplée's murder: in *La Vie en Rose*, a scene reminiscent of *My Fair Lady* (adapted from Shaw's *Pygmalion*) occurs when Asso teaches Piaf how to

hold her body, how to sing with her hands extended, and with 'emotion' – she thrived under his training. But Fréhel did not need to be taught how to emote: she was emotion made woman; her tears were real, her sighs true, her performance a window open entirely into her heart and soul.

Fréhel's name is mentioned at the beginning of Dahan's *La Vie en Rose* : when Piaf's mother abandons her daughter Édith, she gives the excuse that she aspires to be like 'the great Fréhel' who toured the world as a singer. Piaf's mother recognizes her desire to emulate Fréhel, and later, according to François Bellair-Dubas in his biography of his mother, Marie Dubas,[5] Piaf acknowledged that she wanted to emulate Marie Dubas and subsequently had hired Dubas's manager, Asso. The rest is history.

Tempus fugit. This theme was the obsession of philosophers: for the Greeks, time was the enemy; for Nietzsche, time's circularity allows one to erase existential angst, because everything that is and that has been will occur again – the theory of *l'éternel retour*. Marcel Proust was able, through writing, to regain lost time.

But Fréhel, the uncommodified, and therefore, more authentic preacher of nostalgia, with her pout, corners of her lips turned down, mask of sorrow, loneliness, and lovelessness, a pitiful mask above her aging body – yet when she was young, she had the face of a porcelain doll with small features, a smooth complexion, and a sweeping updo, as represented in a photograph which appears in *Pépé le Moko* when she sings to Jean Gabin, and she states that when she looks at that picture, it is like looking in the mirror – represents the brokenhearted female who could never recapture her past, her lost beauty, and lost lovers. In her youth, with flowers in her hair, she was so lovely. She is the true *chanteuse réaliste.*

Édith Piaf's commodification allowed her to transcend her station in life and although born in poverty – « je ne suis qu'une fille du port, une ombre de la rue » ['I am only a girl from the harbour, a shadow in the street'] [6] – Piaf died in glory, having won New Yorkers' hearts as well as those of all France and the rest of the world, truly a showstopper, her funeral procession halting Parisian traffic. Piaf's *chanson réaliste* is somewhat in dissonance with her later, more glamorous lifestyle (yet after her death, there was little left to her heir except for debt – not unlike many other performers). However Fréhel lived and died in approximately the same economic hardship and never became a currency; she remained the uncommodified voice of the proletariat. She was known as a singer and an actress: along with *Pépé le Moko*, she appeared in 17 films between 1932 and 1950, among them Anatole Litvak's *Cœur de lilas /Lilac* (1932) and Sacha Guitry's *Le Roman d'un tricheur /The Story of a Cheat* (1936), and her songs feature on the soundtracks of a wide array of films, both during her lifetime – including *Frou-frou*, the opening song of Jean Renoir's *La Grande Illusion* (1937) – and after her death, as in Jean Eustache's *La Maman et la Putain / The Mother and the Whore* (1973), Jean-Pierre Jeunet's *Le Fabuleux Destin d'Amélie Poulain /Amélie* (2001), and her famous *La Java bleue* in Gillian

Armstrong's French Resistance drama *Charlotte Gray* (2001), all of which commemorate Fréhel's 'sublime' countenance and tremendous voice for posterity.

Marcelline BLOCK
Princeton University and SAG-AFTRA

1. Svetlana Boym, *The Future of Nostalgia* (Basic Books, 2001).

2. 'Friends are what the wind carries away.' —Translation mine.

3. Ginette Vincendeau, 'The *Mise-en-scène* of Suffering: French *Chanteuses Réalistes*,' *New Formations 3* (winter 1987): 107.

4. Sunday, for Fréhel, is a day of joy – as opposed to Charles Trenet's song *Les Enfants s'ennuient le dimanche* ['Children are Bored on Sundays']:
    « Les enfants s'ennuient le dimanche,
    Le dimanche, les enfants s'ennuient.
    En knickerbockers ou en robes blanches,
    Le dimanche, les enfants s'ennuient.
    …
    Gamins et gamines
    Sont plus tristes que maman ne croit
    …
    Les parents s'ennuient le dimanche,
    Le dimanche, les parents s'ennuient.
    Avec leurs lorgnons et leurs barbes blanches,
    Le dimanche, les parents s'ennuient. »

5. François Bellair-Dubas and Robert de Laroche, *Marie Dubas : Comédienne de la chanson* (Editions Christian Pirot, 2003).

6. *Milord* (1959), sung by Édith Piaf, lyrics by Georges Moustaki, music by Marguerite Monnot.

Pierre FRESNAY (1897–1975)
[Pierre Jules Louis LAUDENBACH]

*From
Barman to
Boëldieu
…and
Everything
In Between*

IN ONE OF the many wonderful moments of casual lucidity speckled throughout Marcel Pagnol's *Marius* (1931, Alexander Korda), the titular protagonist remarks that 'Monsieur Brun needs collars just for the purpose of bleaching them.' Those who, by some great misfortune, have never seen *La Grande Illusion / Grand Illusion* (1937, Jean Renoir) will grin at Marius' keen provincially-pronounced observation. Those who have, however, may read the phrase as a supreme statement of the extraordinary range of Pierre FRESNAY, who, within these two films alone, demonstrated that no role could ever define him. Anyone who has seen both films knows all too well that *le Capitaine* Edmond de Boëldieu would staunchly defend the importance of his own impeccably clean gloves (and Monsieur Brun's collars) and that he would certainly not have lowered his taste to the point of granting young Marius the well-deserved chuckle elicited from the audience. Herein lies the conundrum: by the end of his career, Fresnay had left us with a multitude of impeccably portrayed characters, of which three appear in undisputed classics of French cinema: *Marius, La*

Grande Illusion, and *Le Corbeau / The Raven* (Henri-Georges Clouzot, 1943). However, if you ask the average film-goer or even the classic film fan about his/her favourite stars of the cinema, Jean Gabin's name generally dominates the responses whilst Fresnay's name is unlikely to be mentioned. At best, one can jolt the film-goer's memory by mentioning *La Grande Illusion* but the average viewer will still choose to tout Gabin's performance.

This negligence arguably stems from the exemplary malleability that makes Fresnay's work so rich, varied and endlessly rewarding. Fresnay was acting at the same time as some of the great *monstres sacrés* of French cinema such as Gabin, Michel Simon, and Jules Berry. Unlike many of his contemporaries, however, Fresnay never confined himself to a set type, and his own personality never intruded on his characterization. When articles were published in fan magazines, they generally praised his chameleon-like malleability, and even included photographs of him in a number of roles that demonstrated his versatility.[1] That Alec Guinness cited Fresnay as his favourite actor is a sign of the extent to which the latter is an actor's actor rather than a star destined for the teenage girl's bedroom wall or even the thinking man's office.[2]

In his youth, he was reportedly moved by Henri Étiévant in *Les Deux Orphélines* and by Édouard de Max and Jean Coquelin in *Notre-Dame de Paris*.[3] While still a student, he entered the stage with his uncle at the Réjane Theatre. Following the completion of his baccalauréat at the Lycée Henri-IV, he enrolled in classes at the Conservatoire de Paris, where he was taught by playwright Georges Berr. During the same period, he entered the Comédie-Française. Here he found himself surrounded by a number of France's great faces including Blanche Pierson, Edouard de Max, Jeanne Julia Bartet, and Eugène Sylvane, who all incarnated a style of acting which was dying on the cusp of worldwide political change. Fresnay valued it immensely, seeing it as a defence against the insufficiencies inherent in the qualities of the modern school.[4] Indeed, one sees especially in Fresnay both Berr's masterly nuance and the qualities he learned to appreciate in Bartet: elegance, discretion and an absolute absence of artifice.[5] Fresnay adamantly believed that his own generation would never be able to attain the artistic acme achieved by those who had dominated the stage before the war. However, he also placed great emphasis on the importance of modernity and of being linked to one's era.[6]

Thus Fresnay brought his classical expertise to Pagnol's revolutionary stage production of *Marius*. His immediate success led him to star in the 1930 film adaptation.[7] As one might expect, Fresnay was initially sceptical of talking films.[8] He placed great emphasis on the preparation and development of his characters and disliked the lack of rehearsal time for filming.[9] It is tempting to view Fresnay as a French Laurence Olivier, fresh from the stage, but their individual approaches to acting are immediately evident: with Fresnay, there is no contempt for the camera, whereas we can imagine Olivier striding around the set, daring the machine to capture both of his best sides.

Fresnay achieved further international acclaim following the success of the film adaptation of *Marius* and its sequel, *Fanny* (Marc Allégret, 1932). He later starred opposite Sacha Guitry's former wife, Yvonne Printemps, in an adaptation of Dumas fils's *La Dame aux camélias* (Abel Gance and Fernand Rivers, 1934). The two became inseparable and would remain together for the remainder of his life. He next had the opportunity to test his English – three years before *La Grande Illusion* – in the minor but significant role of Louis Bernhardt in Alfred Hitchcock's first version of *The Man Who Knew Too Much* (1934). Other roles followed, including the final instalment of Pagnol's Marseilles Trilogy, *César* (Marcel Pagnol, 1936), also *La Bataille silencieuse* (Pierre Billon, 1937) opposite Michel Simon, and *Les Trois Valses / Three Waltzes* (Ludwig Berger, 1938) in which he starred once more opposite Printemps.

He met one of his most notoriously fruitful associates, Henri-Georges Clouzot, in 1939.[10] Clouzot wrote the script for Fresnay's sole directorial effort, *Le Duel* (1941), and another two plays in which Fresnay starred: *On prend les mêmes* (performed in December 1940), and *Comédie en trois actes* (performed in March 1942).[11] Employment in the film industry during the Occupation depended on German approval [12] and Fresnay signed a contract with the Franco-German company, Continental Films.[13] Fresnay's contract provided him with the steady, varied work merited by his talent: he provided a voice-over for *Les Inconnus dans la maison / Strangers in the House* (Henri

Decoin, 1942), played a struggling artist in the Faustian *La Main du diable* / *Carnival of Sinners* (Maurice Tourneur, 1943) and a World War I amnesiac in Jean Anouilh's adaptation of his own play, *Le Voyageur sans bagages* (1944). It was during this time that he headlined two of Clouzot's own films, *L'Assassin habite...au 21* / *The Murderer Lives at Number 21* (1942), and, most notoriously, *Le Corbeau* / *The Raven* (1943). In the latter, his doctor bears all the rigid composure of Boëldieu, but without the strict adherence to principles. Viewing these films side by side reveals the nuances that differentiate each of Fresnay's performances and characterise the sheer precision of his craft. Perceived as a scathing vilification of the French people, Fresnay's participation in Continental Film was duly punished: he was arrested in September 1944 and spent six weeks in prison, although no charges were ever brought against him.[14] Quarrels eventually erupted between Clouzot and Printemps, after which Fresnay's relations with Clouzot were irreparably broken.[15]

Despite any dents to his reputation resulting from his success during France's dark years, Fresnay continued to perform and further expand his range, most notably as Vincent de Paul in *Monsieur Vincent* (Maurice Cloche, 1947), for which he won the Volpi Cup for Best Actor at the Venice Film Festival. Thereafter, less prominent roles followed, and from the 1960s Fresnay worked chiefly in the theatre.

Today, Fresnay's work is scarcely revived except to study Pagnol, Renoir, and Clouzot. The fault arguably lies with Fresnay, whose accuracy as an actor in the best work of some of these directors encourages us to believe that he and his characters are one and the same, and makes us forget that there is ultimately one man behind the many masks. The tragedy is ours.

Barry NEVIN
National University of Ireland, Galway

1. Colin Crisp, *The Classic French Cinema, 1930-1960* (Bloomington: Indiana UP, 1993), 361.
2. Alec Guinness, *My Name Escapes Me: The Diary of a Retiring Actor* (New York: Penguin, 1998), 65.
3. Pierre Fresnay, *Je suis comédien* (Paris : Éditions du Conquistador, 1954), 37.
4. Ibid., 46-7.
5. Ibid., 49.
6. Ibid., 4.
7. For further discussion of Pagnol's Marseilles Trilogy (*Marius, Fanny, César*) see Marcelline Block, ed., *World Film Locations: Marseilles* (Intellect, 2013).
8. Jean-Pierre Jeancolas, *Le Cinéma des français : 15 ans d'années trente, 1929–1944* (Paris: Nouveau monde, 2005), 54.
9. Fresnay, 100-1.
10. Christopher Lloyd, *Henri-Georges Clouzot* (Manchester UP, 2007), 6.
11. Ibid.
12. Ibid., 33.
13. Evelyn Ehrlich, *Cinema of Paradox: French Filmmaking Under the German Occupation* (New York: Columbia UP, 1985), 46.
14. Lloyd, 173.
15. Ibid., 6.

Catherine FROT (1956–)

France's Reigning Sweetheart, Beloved by 'Toulemonde

Born in Paris, distinguished stage and film actress Catherine FROT is one of France's most beloved contemporary entertainers. She has received extensive recognition in her homeland, including induction into L'Ordre National du Mérite (2008). Frot received the César Award for Best Supporting Actress for her performance as Yolande in Cédric Klapisch's cinematic adaptation of Agnès Jaoui and Jean-Pierre Bacri's play *Un air de famille /Family Resemblances* (1996) – a role Frot had originated onstage, for which she was honoured with the Molière Award for Best Supporting Actress in 1995 (Jaoui and Bacri, also known as 'Jabac,' collaborated with Klapisch on the screenplay for the film adaptation).

Since her onscreen debut in 1980 in Alain Resnais's *Mon oncle d'Amérique /My American Uncle*, Frot has worked nonstop in French cinema and television with more than 90 credits to her name, often with major directors such as Lucas Belvaux (in his 2002 Prix-Louis-Delluc-winning trilogy, consisting of the films *Cavale /On the Run*, *Un couple épatant /An Amazing Couple*, and *Après la vie / After Life*); with Catherine Corsini (*La Nouvelle Eve /The New Eve*, 1999),

and Claire Denis (*J'ai pas sommeil /I Can't Sleep*, 1994), among others. Along with her Best Supporting Actress César award for *Un air de famille*, Frot has been nominated for this award on numerous occasions – for her performances in *Escalier C* (Jean-Charles Tacchella, 1985), and *Le Dîner de cons /The Dinner Game* (Francis Veber, 1998), as well as for Best Actress in *La Dilettante* (Pascal Thomas, 1999), *Chaos* (Coline Serreau, 2001), *La Tourneuse de pages /The Page Turner* (Denis Dercourt, 2006), *Odette Toulemonde* (Eric-Emmanuel Schmitt, 2006), *Le Crime est notre affaire /Crime Is Our Business* (Pascal Thomas, 2008, based on an Agatha Christie story), and *Les Saveurs du Palais /Haute Cuisine* (Christian Vincent, 2012). Among her other accolades are the Best Actress Award for *La Dilettante* from the Moscow Film Festival.

By the time Frot made her film debut in Alain Resnais's *Mon oncle d'Amérique* (1980) as the young Arlette (played as an adult by Nelly Borgeaud), she already had several roles in television movies and series, as she had previously studied theatre, starting at the Versailles Conservatory when she was only fourteen and continuing at L'École nationale supérieure des arts et techniques du théâtre (ENSATT) in Paris (then known as the 'Rue Blanche' conservatory in reference to its address before it moved to its current location in Lyon in 1997). In the late 1970s, Frot, along with fellow actors Yann Collette, Alain Gautré, and Thierry Gimenez, was one of the founding members of the Compagnie du Chapeau Rouge theatrical troupe in Avignon, directed by Pierre Pradinas. Frot appeared in many Chapeau

Rouge theatrical productions at the annual Avignon Theatre Festival and was directed by Sir Peter Brook in a 1982 production of Anton Chekov's *The Cherry Orchard*.

Frot is primarily hailed for her performances as Prudence Beresford who, with her husband Colonel Bélisaire Beresford (André Dussollier), forms a detective duo in *Mon petit doigt m'a dit... /By the Pricking of My Thumbs* (2005), *Le Crime est notre affaire /Crime Is Our Business* (2008), and *Associés contre le crime /Partners in Crime* (2012) – Pascal Thomas's French adaptations of Agatha Christie's *Tommy and Tuppence* series; as Odette Toulemonde in the film of the same name; in her César-winning turn in Klapisch's *Un air de famille* (as bourgeois wife and mother Yolande, whose 35th birthday dinner becomes the site of her husband's family drama while also revealing her own disappointments in her birthday presents, husband, marriage, and children); and in her supporting role as Marlène, mistress of cruel publisher Pierre Brochant (Thierry Lhermitte), in Veber's internationally acclaimed *Le Diner de cons* (remade in the US as 2010's *Dinner for Schmucks*, directed by Jay Roach).

In *Boudu*, Gérard Jugnot's 2005 remake of Jean Renoir's iconic *Boudu sauvé des eaux /Boudu Saved from Drowning* (1932), Frot plays Yseult, the bourgeois recovering alcoholic wife of Aix-en-Provence art gallery owner Christian (Jugnot). *Boudu* transposes Renoir's film's Parisian setting to the South of France. Yseult's debilitating neuroses, manifesting themselves in her malapropisms and insomnia, are healed by her erotic encounter with the lustful and vulgar yet energizing and inspiring vagrant Boudu, played by Gérard Depardieu, a role unforgettably and inimitably originated onscreen by Michel Simon in the original *Boudu sauvé des eaux*.

In *Odette Toulemonde* – bestselling author Eric-Emmanuel Schmitt's directorial debut – Frot incarnates the titular character, a fortysomething widow and department store saleswoman in the industrial Belgian city of Charleroi, who raises her two children (now on the cusp of adulthood) on her own. Toulemonde leads a rather simple and basic life as the 'everywoman' – as reflected by her last name – finding joy in the bestselling novels of her favourite author, Balthazar Balsan (Albert Dupontel), and in the music of Josephine Baker. As Odette, Frot won hearts with her portrayal of this 'everywoman' who lives a life free of irony and intellectual pretension, despite her 'Proustian name,' as Balsan tells her when he autographs his book for her – a reference that she does not understand. But it is Odette who inspires the worldly, successful, and yet melancholy Parisian author Balsan to change his attitude and perspective, prompting him to spend time with her in her hometown after he reads the touching and genuine letter she writes to him about how much his books mean to her. Through her sensitive and three-dimensional portrayal, Frot immerses herself completely in the character, imbuing Odette with sincere optimism.

By often playing against type and taking on darker, dramatic roles, such as that of troubled police captain Fabienne in the *polar* [1] or neo-noir

Coup d'éclat /Fabienne (José Alcala, 2011) or the disturbing, abusive mother nicknamed 'Folcoche' ('Crazypig') by her sons in *Vipère au poing /Viper in the Fist* (Philippe de Broca, 2004, based on Hervé Bazin's novel), Frot demonstrates her range and versatility.

Catherine Frot continues her reign as one of France's most popular leading contemporary actresses. She was recently nominated – for the sixth time – for the Best Actress César for *Les Saveurs du Palais / Haute Cuisine* (2012), in which she memorably incarnates brilliant and stubborn Périgordian chef Hortense Laborie, who breaks the glass ceiling by becoming the first female chef at the Elysée Palace, a character based upon Danièle Delpeuch, President François Mitterrand's personal chef from 1988 to 1990.

Marcelline BLOCK
Princeton University and SAG-AFTRA

1. *Polar* : Slang for detective novel/film.

Jean GABIN (1904–1976)
[Jean Gabin Alexis MONCORGÉ]

Marianne's Fiancé

BORN Jean Gabin Alexis Moncorgé, Jean GABIN is a complex figure and one of the most popular actors of twentieth century France. Indeed, he was one of the very few superstars of the French film industry, and his popular impact could only be rivalled by Maurice Chevalier's, with whom Gabin shared a similar background: if Gabin would mainly work as an actor, he began his career as a music hall entertainer, was perfectly skilled in the techniques of singing and dancing, and the two artists, of similar complexion, embodied the very figure of the casual Parisian guy, that is to say, a man of the people with much charm, street smarts, and a typical class accent (a certain popular cockiness the French usually name *la gouaille*). However, Chevalier starred in Hollywood musicals and mainly remained a singer, while Gabin bloomed in a full-fledged dramatic career with the French studios.

Jean Gabin actually first stepped into his father's shoes as a stage entertainer: after a few cameos at the famous cabaret Les Folies Bergères, he worked as a regular stand-in at the Bouffes parisiennes starting in 1926 and joined the Moulin Rouge as a singer in 1928 thanks to Mistinguett, the then cabaret star, who had spotted and tutored him. It was only a matter of time before he was recruited for the screen in the 1930's musical *Chacun sa chance /Everyman for Himself* (René Pujol and Hans Steinhoff, 1930). Unlike Maurice Chevalier, Gabin really was pure film material: his natural ways made him less artificial than the musical star and more versatile as an actor, suitable not only for romantic but also realistic and dramatic productions. Gabin also owned his success to a stout and flawless physique, whose most famous assets were a pair of piercing blue eyes and seductive blond hair, making him a natural choice for playing the part of young candid lovers, as attested to by the titles of his early films (*Gloria*, Hans Behrendt, 1931; *Tout ça ne vaut pas l'amour*, Jacques Tourneur, 1931; *Paris-béguin /The Darling of Paris*, Augusto Genina, 1931; *La Belle Marinière*, Harry Lachman, 1932). Later, the title of Jean Grémillon's 1937 film, *Gueule d'amour /Lady Killer* definitely sums up this characteristic of the actor. One often associates a distinctive voice with those mesmerizing beautiful looks: besides the charming popular accent, Gabin knew how best to use his voice when going from a plain and friendly conversational tone to a tender whisper, loaded with controlled emotion, making a sensitive gentleness emerge from a tough guy appearance, and in many respects, by his great physical presence and soft voice, Gérard Depardieu carried on Jean Gabin's heritage in the seventies and eighties.

Like Marlon Brando in America after World War II, whose modern acting he anticipates by a little less than two decades, Gabin personifies a myth of the pre-war years, a quality directors like Julien Duvivier deeply took advantage of for the better. His characters are rebellious, but true to their word, and he makes good portrayals of romantic mobsters (Julien Duvivier's *La Bandera /Escape from Yesterday*, and *Pépé le Moko*, 1935 and 1937), or melancholic working-class heroes. With Julien Duvivier's *La Belle Équipe /They Were Five* (1936) and above all Jean Renoir's *Les Bas-fonds /The Lower Depths* (1936) and *La Grande Illusion* (1937), Gabin becomes the symbol of the *Front populaire* /Popular Front generation (after the name of the united government of the coalition of leftist parties that came to power in 1936) and embodies its often shattered political dreams. Gabin represents the common man with good common sense, unwilling to compromise his freedom but still defiant towards any kind of ideology. An incarnation of the average republican citizen of France, at ease with the elite as well as with the people, he is, as some scholars have put it, a perfect 'fiancé of Marianne,' and the first of a long series in French film. Even in dramas like Jean Renoir's 1938 screen adaptation of Zola's *La Bête humaine*, Gabin's performances maintain a strong social component. The thirties end for him with a string of realistic melodramas by Marcel Carné (*Quai des brumes /Port of Shadows*, 1938, and *Le Jour se lève /Daybreak*, 1939) and Jean Grémillon (*Remorques /Stormy Waters*, 1941), shot in the poetic visual style that is considered the climax of

French classic cinema, forever sealing Gabin's mythical status.

The war interrupted this legendary film series for Gabin, who took a shot at a Hollywood career, among others with Duvivier; but besides his glamorous long encounter with Marlène Dietrich, the enterprise was not a success at all. Returning to France after the war ended, things also changed for Jean Gabin. When he left, he embodied more or less the cute romantic hero, but he went back as a different man. Heavier and older, his presence was intact, but his good looks had faded, and in his maturity he started to resemble a French Spencer Tracy and could not be cast anymore in his former roles. A new career thus began, after a few struggling years, truly taking off in 1952 with Max Ophüls's *Le Plaisir*. Always aware of his superstar status, Jean Gabin was one of those actors with power on and off the set, whose sole name was enough to trigger a project. In return, he always felt an obligation towards 'his' audience: since people went to see a movie if he was in it, he thought his presence should warrant a program of quality. That is why from then on, he preferred to take on the roles of bourgeois family men or old gangsters with morals, and pretty much stuck to genre film, whether history pieces (Jean Renoir's *French Cancan*, 1954, or Sacha Guitry's *Napoléon*, 1955) or gangster movies for the most part, directed by reliable but often uninspired filmmakers (Claude Autant-Lara, Jacques Becker, Jean Delannoy, Gilles Grangier, Pierre Granier-Deferre, Jean-Paul Le Chanois, and Henri Verneuil), defining what was known as the French 'Tradition of Quality' cinema. The most successful among those films, *Touchez pas au grisbi / Grisbi* (Becker, 1954), *Razzia sur la chnouf /Razzia* (Henri Decoin, 1955), *Le Pacha /Pasha* (Georges Lautner, 1968), and *Le Clan des siciliens /The Sicilian Clan* (Henri Verneuil, 1969), do a more than decent job, but he always stays in the same range of expression. It is significant that the New Wave directors never felt the need to conjure up Jean Gabin, since he had become the potent representative of *le cinéma du papa* ['Daddy's cinema']. Despite a few gems, his career ends on a successful but rather mediocre tone, unworthy of his talent, restraining the elderly star to the status of a grumpy, once legendary, patriarch of French cinema.

Jean-Christophe BLUM
Lycée Blaise Pascal, Clermont-Ferrand

Charlotte GAINSBOURG (1971–)

*From Shy
Teenager
to Lars
von Trier's
Muse*

BORN ON 21 July 1971 in London to French singer Serge Gainsbourg and British singer, actress, and model Jane Birkin, Charlotte was immersed in an artistic lifestyle from an early age. In 1984, when she was only 13, she suddenly became the focus of public attention when her controversial father had her sing and star in his video clip *Lemon Incest*, which sparked public outrage over the intended double entendre of the lyrics and the suggestive poses.

Shortly afterwards, Charlotte acquired her own letters of fame thanks to Claude Miller's *L'Effrontée /An Impudent Girl* (1985), for which she was awarded the 'César du meilleur espoir féminin' in 1986. In the movie, she plays Charlotte, a rebellious thirteen-year-old teenager who hates her boring life in a small French provincial town. Because of her awkwardness, she is bullied by her classmates, and her only friend is her six-year-old neighbour, a little girl suffering from a severe illness. When Charlotte meets a young gifted pianist, Clara, who is the same age as her, she starts dreaming of leaving everything behind so as to start a new life as the pianist's 'demoiselle de compagnie.' The movie

has been widely critically acclaimed as providing a powerfully accurate depiction of teenage angst; however, there have been controversies as to the origin of its script, which bears striking similarities with Carson McCullers's novel *The Member of the Wedding* (1946), but which has not been acknowledged by Miller.

Gainsbourg's following movie, *Jane B. par Agnès V. /Jane B. for Agnès V.* (Agnès Varda, 1988), echoes Marguerite Duras's novel *Le Ravissement de Lol V. Stein* (1964). She was then again cast as a rebellious teenager in another big hit, *La Petite Voleuse /The Little Thief* (Claude Miller, 1988). The stereotype of the eternal teenager, or the young woman who has trouble 'fitting in,' characterized many of her following roles: *Merci la vie* (Bertrand Blier, 1991), *Grosse fatigue /Dead Tired* (Michel Blanc, 1994), *Jane Eyre* (Franco Zeffirelli, 1996), *Passionnément* (Bruno Nuytten, 2000), and *La Bûche* (Danièle Thompson, 1999), for which she received the 'César de la meilleure actrice dans un second rôle.'

Her performance as Fantine in the TV mini-series *Les Misérables* (Josée Dayan, 2002) was a turning point in her career. From then on, she became an aficionada of more dramatic roles, such as *L'Un reste, l'autre part /One Stays, the Other Leaves* (Claude Berri, 2005), along with two films directed by her husband Yvan Attal: *Ma femme est une actrice /My Wife is an Actress* (Yvan Attal, 2001) and *Ils se marièrent et eurent beaucoup d'enfants /...And They Lived Happily Ever After* (Yvan Attal, 2004). These films revolve around themes that come across as central to French cinema to a foreign audience, such as love triangles (the husband, the wife, and the lover) and couple issues.

Then, in 2009, another turning point in Gainsbourg's career occurred, when she accepted to star in Danish director Lars von Trier's *Antichrist*, in which she plays a young woman whose two-year-old son died by falling out of a window while she and her husband (Willem Dafoe) were having intercourse. Her devastating grief later on gives way to a descent into madness when her husband insists that she stop taking psychiatric medication and that she follow him to their cabin in the woods. Like most of von Trier's movies, *Antichrist* is open to many interpretations and can be seen either as a horror movie or as a depiction of madness. When the film was screened at the 2009 Cannes Film Festival, the scene of female genital auto-mutilation in which it culminates elicited such strong reactions from the audience that many spectators left the room or booed. Gainsbourg nevertheless received the 'Prix d'interprétation féminine' for her role, of which she said that her late father, who particularly enjoyed shocking people, would be proud. *Antichrist* was only released in its entirety in Europe and Latin America, but remains partly censored in the United States and Asia.

Two years later, Gainsbourg renewed her partnership with Lars von Trier and starred in his film *Melancholia* (2011), as Kirsten Dunst's sister, in a plot that combines von Trier's fascination for mental illness and the imminent end of the world due to a planet approaching the Earth's orbit.

Gainsbourg seems to have taken to following in her father's provocative footsteps insofar as she incarnated a fifty-year-old nymphomaniac reflecting upon her past sexual adventures in von Trier's *Nymphomaniac*, the third von-Trier-Gainsbourg collaboration. The first volume of this film premiered in February 2014 at the Berlin International Film Festival, and the second in September 2014 at the Toronto International Film Festival. *Nymphomaniac* stirred heated controversy among critics and was threatened with censorship due to its explicit sexual content.

Since 1991, Gainsbourg has been Yvan Attal's partner. He is also an actor and a director. They are parents to three children (Ben, Alice Jane, and Joe). Gainsbourg also has a parallel career as a singer and her songs are famous both in America and Europe. In 2008, she suffered a stroke, which led her to record, the following year, an album entitled *IRM* ['MRI']. Despite being now over forty, Gainsbourg still embodies the figure of the eternal teenager in the French collective imagery.

Nathalie Ségéral
*Virginia Polytechnic Institute
and State University*

Michel GALABRU (1922–)

*A Living
and
Acting
Legend*

SEVERAL generations of Frenchmen have grown up seeing Michel GALABRU perform on stage, as well as on the big and small screens. Indeed, Galabru has performed in hundreds of theatre plays and starred in over 250 movies and televised series. Equally responsible for this are the actor's undeniable talent and remarkable longevity. Michel Galabru was born in 1922 in Safi (nowadays in Morocco), where his father, Paul Galabru, helped build the city's harbour. Michel spent his childhood in Morocco and in his family home in the Hérault region in the south of France. He has always been a supporter of the local soccer club, Montpellier HSC, and for a while he was even tempted to become a professional player.

His results as a student seem to have been mediocre. Galabru claims that he was expelled from seven different schools, almost like one of his idols, Sacha Guitry, who was expelled a dozen times. He studied at the Saint François-Régis high school in Montpellier, then at a Jesuit high school, Saint-Louis de Gonzague, in Paris, and completed a year of college studying law, apparently only in order to please his father. During the war, Galabru was sent to a forced

labour camp in Klagenfurt, Austria, by the *Service du Travail Obligatoire* (the institution in charge of finding and sending French workers to Nazi forced labour camps). He was also sent to Yugoslavia to work as a blacksmith and, according to Galabru, was liberated by Tito's partisans.

After his return to France, he went to Paris to study at the Conservatoire with Denis d'Inès, under whose direction he studied for three years. He was awarded the first prize of the Conservatoire d'art dramatique and shortly thereafter, he was hired at the Comédie-Française in September 1950. Thus, like many other cinema actors, Galabru started off as a theatre actor. He made his debut as a stage actor with *George Dandin ou le mari confondu* and then continued with roles in various classical plays by Shakespeare, Molière, Marivaux, and others. He made his cinema debut in 1952 in Jean Devaivre's *Ma femme, ma vache et moi*. After this movie, Galabru returned to his theatrical endeavours for almost a decade, playing only minor roles for cinema and television.

In 1962, he starred in Yves Robert's *La Guerre des boutons /War of the Buttons*; but it was really his role as sergeant major Jérôme Gerber in the comedic series *Le Gendarme de Saint-Tropez /The Troops of St. Tropez*, directed by Jean Girault, that made him famous and endeared him to French audiences. The first movie of the series was *Le Gendarme de Saint-Tropez* (1964), in which the gendarme Ludovic Cruchot (Louis de Funès) was reassigned from a small village to the coastal (and much glitzier) city of Saint-Tropez. Gerber, played by Galabru, is Cruchot's hierarchical superior and one of the eight gendarmes in Saint-Tropez (the others being Beaupied, Perlin, Tricard, Berlicot, Fougasse, and Merlot, incarnated respectively by Maurice Risch, Patrick Préjean, Guy Grosso, Michel Modo, Jean Lefebvre, and Christian Marin). In 1965, Jean Girault directed *Le Gendarme à New York /The Troops in New York*, followed by *Le Gendarme se marie /The Troops Get Married* in 1968, *Le Gendarme en balade /The Troops on Vacation* in 1970, *Le Gendarme et les Extra-terrestres /The Troops & Aliens* in 1979, and finally *Le Gendarme et les Gendarmettes /The Troops & Troop-ettes* in 1982. Jean Girault died during the shooting of *Le Gendarme et les Gendarmettes*, which thus became the last episode of the series. Michel Galabru played in all six episodes; of all the 'Gendarmes', Galabru and Patrick Préjean are the only ones still alive.

It should be noted that Galabru also played in a number of movies directed by Girault which were not part of the *Gendarme* series such as *Les Gorilles* (1964), *Monsieur le président-directeur général* (1966), *Un drôle de colonel /A Strange Kind of Colonel* (1968), *Jo /The Gazebo* (1971), *Le Concierge* (1973), *Deux grandes filles dans un pyjama* (1974), *L'Intrépide* (1975), and *Le Mille-pattes fait des claquettes* (1977), *L'Horoscope* (1978), and *L'Avare /The Miser* (1980). During his career, Galabru collaborated with cinema directors such as Richard Balducci (*La Honte de la famille* in 1969, *Par ici la monnaie* in 1973, *On l'appelle catastrophe* in 1983), Michel Gérard (*Les Joyeux Lurons* in 1972, *Les Vacanciers* in 1974, *Soldat Duroc, ça va être ta fête ! /The Dangerous*

Mission in 1975, and *On s'en fout... nous on s'aime* in 1982), and others (Gilles Béhat, Philippe Lefebvre, Jean Pignol, etc.). However, considering the number of movies Galabru shot with Jean Girault, it is quite obvious that the two had forged a very special professional relationship.

Although Galabru specialized primarily in comedies, critical consecration in the form of a César for best actor came in 1977 for his performance in Bertrand Tavernier's drama *Le Juge et l'Assassin /The Judge and the Assassin*, (1976). In this movie, Galabru incarnates the role of Joseph Bouvier, a former infantry sergeant who attempted to kill his fiancée and then commit suicide. Because of both the failed suicide and murder attempts, Bouvier became a wandering assassin who murdered shepherds and raped shepherdesses in the region of Ardèche (this happened at the end of the nineteenth century). Eventually, Bouvier was captured through the efforts of a provincial judge who also had him sentenced to death.

In the 1980s, Michel Galabru became a benefactor for various theatres and acting-related activities. Thus, in 1984, he bought a theatre founded in 1850 by Renée Maubel known as the Conservatoire Maubel. By the 1980s, the building was in terrible condition but after Galabru purchased it for his daughter Emma, the new management renovated the building and transformed it into what is now known as the Théâtre Montmartre-Galabru. A year later, Galabru bought the Théâtre de Dix Heures in the eighteenth arrondissement of Paris. Galabru intended this theatre to promote young actors, but unfortunately, he was able to use and maintain it for only four years. Around the same time, the French actor created a theatre festival in the Vaucluse (south of France) entitled 'Les Estivales de Malaucène.' Though successful for a while and attracting crowds of tens of thousands of people, the festival was only organized for eight years.

More recently, in 2007, Galabru was awarded the Prix Plaisir du théâtre. The following year, he received the Molière award for best comedian. In 2011, the Association de la Régie Théâtrale (ART) awarded him the *Prix du brigadier* for his entire acting career. Over the years, Galabru performed in major plays by Anouilh, Goldoni, Ionesco, Molière, Pagnol, and Shakespeare; under directors such as Jean Anouilh, Jean Vilar, Georges Vitaly, Alain Sachs, and Jérôme Savary. As of this writing, Galabru continues to perform for the Comédie-Française.

Cristian BRATU
Baylor University, Texas

Nicole GARCIA (1946–)

An Ambiguous Object of Desire

NICOLE GARCIA ranks among French actresses such as Josiane Balasko, Agnès Jaoui, or more recently, Julie Delpy, who made a name for themselves for the quality of the performances they gave in front of the camera as well as for the critical acclaim they received for the films they have directed.

Born in Oran, French Algeria on April 22, 1946, Nicole Garcia left the African continent to study law in France. She then enrolled in the famous Conservatoire de théâtre de Paris where she was awarded the first prize for modern comedy when she was barely twenty years of age. In the first ten years of her career she distinguished herself by the choice of films she played in: films that opposed the mainstream status quo by their themes (the Algerian war in *La Question*, Laurent Heynemann, 1977; psychoanalysis in *Les Mots pour le dire*, José Pinheiro, 1983) or that were daring with regards to their aesthetics (such as Alain Resnais's jigsaw-film *Mon oncle d'Amérique / My American Uncle*, 1980).

In the seventies and eighties, she collaborated with the most acclaimed French directors of the time: the aforementioned Alain Resnais, as well as Bertrand Blier, Jacques Deray, Michel Deville, Claude Lelouch, Jacques Rivette, Claude Sautet, and Bertrand Tavernier, to name but a few. She shared the stage with legends of the French screen: Jean-Paul Belmondo, Yves Montand, Philippe Noiret, and Lino Ventura – giants with regard to their physical presence as well as the size of their talent. If the flawless and uncompromising trajectory of her career provokes respect, she received little professional recognition. She obtained her first and only César in 1980 (Best Supporting Actress) for a comedy, *Le Cavaleur* (dir. Philippe de Broca). From then on, she was nominated 9 times for Césars (4 times as an actress, 4 times as a director, and once for screenplay) and received 3 nominations at Cannes (in 1986 for her short film *15 août* ; in 2002 for *L'Adversaire / The Adversary*, and in 2006 for *Selon Charlie /Charlie Says*), but remained a blatant omission among the final awardees.

Nicole Garcia was still a young woman when she decided to get behind the camera and was also quickly hailed by the critiques as an auteur. For the lead roles of her films, she chose among the best actresses (Nathalie Baye, Catherine Deneuve) but, in contrast with actors-directors such as Josiane Balasko or Julie Delpy, preferred not to act in her own films (in her words, she explained that by this choice she made a radical move from the desire to be looked at to the desire to look for herself). However, she never abandoned her career as an actress and recently

gave unforgettable performances, such as the dysfunctional mothers she portrayed for Claude Miller in *Betty Fisher* in 2001 and *La Petite Lili /Little Lili* in 2003.

What will one remember of Nicole Garcia: the woman is elegant, seductive (with the cold beauty of Hitchcock's blonde muses – not surprising that Kim Novak is one of Garcia's models), sharp, and intense. There is a constant duality (masculine-feminine, director-actor, French and Algerian-born) that she affirms. Her rasping voice is both seductive and unnerving. Talking of her profession as an actress, she describes it as a precarious position: sometimes comparing the actress with an object of desire, forced to constantly attract male attention or perish (see Rigoulet and Odicino, *Télérama*, 2010),[1] sometimes as a low-ranking officer, always on the front (see her interview in *Studio Magazine*, 1998).[2] She said: « Je n'aime pas le langage des mots, je préfère celui des corps » ['I don't like the language of words, I prefer the one of bodies.'] [3] It is true that she was never afraid to expose her body on the screen, as everyone will remember Michel Deville's 1985 *Péril en la demeure*'s very sensuous poster that was displayed on the front of many French cinemas.

Today in her late sixties, she is a vibrant woman, her gaze still inquisitive. Throughout her career, it seems that she constantly explored the same theme, ceaselessly looking for a place that she describes as « celle qu'on tient, celle que l'on prend ou que l'on usurpe, celle qu'on voudrait avoir et celle qui, dans l'ombre, nous hante » ['the one we have, the one we take or the one that we usurp, the one we would like to occupy and the one, in the shadows, that haunts us.'] [4]

Gaëlle PLANCHENAULT
*Simon Fraser University,
British Columbia*

1. Laurent Rigoulet and Guillemette Odicino, 'Nicole Garcia en compagnie des ombres,' *Télérama*, December 13th, 2010.

2. Nicole Garcia, 'Entretiens avec Nicole Garcia,' *Studio Magazine*, October 1998.

3. Ibid.

4. Rigoulet and Odicino, 'Nicole Garcia en compagnie des ombres.'

Marie GILLAIN (1975–)

*The
Becoming
of a
Classic
Star*

MARIE GILLAIN (born in Liège, Belgium) arrived on the panorama of French cinema in 1991 like a breath of fresh air. At 16 she gave Gérard Depardieu a run for his money in Gérard Lauzier's movie *Mon père ce héros /My Father the Hero* (1991). Her acting performance was so well reviewed and appreciated by the public that she was nominated for a César award. In a sense, Marie Gillain's début in this film could be compared to Sophie Marceau's first appearance in the now classic movie *La Boum /The Party* (Claude Pinoteau, 1980). This incredible success could be due to the fact that Marie Gillain did not attend any formal acting courses and therefore was not moulded as a 'Parisian actress.'

Marie Gillain was immediately recognised by directors and other actors as a very promising young actress, and that allowed her to avoid the pitfall of playing the same kind of roles as in *Mon père ce héros*. She seized the opportunity to work with the Belgian director and screenwriter Marian Handwerker in a movie entitled *Marie* (1993). This drama in which Marie Gillain plays the role of a troubled pregnant teenager was not an enormous success at the box office but nevertheless showed the extent of her talent not only as a comedian but also as a dramatic actress. Critics were ecstatic about her and from then on her career took off and she never looked back.

Indeed, after her experience with Handwerker, it was Bertrand Tarvernier who offered her next role in *L'Appât / Fresh Bait* (1995). Marie Gillain went on to explain that this role was her first real role as a professional actress. It was, as she said, 'a real role with real responsibilities.' This intense drama tells the story of a young woman dreaming of a better life in America playing the bait in nightclubs. She pretends to seduce or to be seduced by men. As soon as she gets back to the men's room she lets her accomplices in and they rob the poor middle-aged men. For this role, Bertrand Tavernier asked her to develop the character of Nathalie herself, and she did so with gusto. Marie Gillain gave her character a personality mixed with insouciance and determination. Once again critics recognised the work and the talent, and Marie Gillain was again nominated for a César but more importantly, she received the Romy Schneider Award.

At that time, Marie Gillain's talent was so appreciated that even Quentin Tarantino was contemplating her for the role of Fabienne in his *Pulp Fiction* (1994), which ultimately went to Maria de Medeiros. Unfortunately the connection between the two artists did not happen and Marie Gillain did not perceive the experience as a success. However, it gave her the wonderful opportunity to play Anne Frank on stage. With this performance, Marie Gillain gained enormous maturity as an actress and once again was

recognised for it. She was nominated for a Molière Award.

What is fascinating about Marie Gillain's career is that she did not let herself be cornered into accepting the same kind of role twice. She managed to work with many great French and Italian directors such as Bertrand Tavernier, Paulo and Vittorio Taviani in *Les Affinités électives /Elective Affinities* (1996), Philippe De Broca in *Le Bossu /On Guard* (1997), Ettore Scola in *Le Dîner* (1998), Emmanuel Mouret in *Laissons Lucie faire !* (2000), Bruno Chiche in *Barnie et ses petites contrariétés* (2001), Cédric Klapisch in *Ni pour ni contre (bien au contraire) / Not For, or Against (Quite the Contrary)* (2003), Jean-Paul Salomé in *Les Femmes de l'ombre /Female Agents* (2008), and more recently, Philippe Lioret in *Toutes nos envies /All Our Desires* (2011). Marie Gillain acted also with most of the great contemporary French actors: Daniel Auteuil, Emmanuelle Béart, Guillaume Canet, Jacques Gamblin, Fabrice Lucini, Denis Podalydès, Jean Rochefort, Karin Viart, and many others.

One cannot put aside the magnificent roles played by Marie Gillain in recent movies such as *L'Enfer /Hell* (Danis Tanovic, 2005), *Les Femmes de l'ombre, Coco avant Chanel /Coco Before Chanel* (Anne Fontaine, 2009), and *Toutes nos envies*. Such diversity and quality of interpretation are taking Marie Gillain to the path of classic stardom, a very select pantheon in which she is about to take her place next to actresses such as Fanny Ardant, Catherine Deneuve, and Romy Schneider.

Jean-Fréderic HENNUY
National University of Ireland, Maynooth

Annie GIRARDOT (1931–2011)

Votre cousine,
votre tantine,
votre maman,
votre fiancée

DESPITE THE ALLURE of Brigitte Bardot, Annie GIRARDOT (1931–2011) was the highest earning French actress of 1969, proving the popular appeal of the classically trained actress. Girardot acted in 158 European films – the majority in her native language, yet she is also a celebrated actress of Italian cinema and starred in several Yugoslavian features. Her presence and subtlety allowed audiences to imagine her in a variety of roles and genres, a few of the most important: a maid in the comedy *Elle boit pas, elle fume pas, elle drague pas, mais… elle cause ! /She Does Not Drink, Smoke or Flirt, But… She Talks* (Michel Audiard, 1970), a prostitute in the melodrama *Rocco et ses frères /Rocco and His Brothers* (Luchino Visconti, 1960), and a teacher taken to court for an affair with a student *Mourir d'aimer /To Die of Love* (André Cayatte, 1971). It was precisely this talent and range that made Annie Girardot an icon of mainstream French cinema, most notably during the 60s and 70s.

Raised solely by her mother, a nurse, Girardot's humble beginnings gave her access to the everyday woman on screen. However, the Conservatoire de la rue Blanche recognized Girardot's talent, where she won first prize in Classical and Modern Comedy before graduating in 1954. This paved the way for a brief theatrical residence at the Comédie-Française where Girardot demonstrated her mastery of classical theatre. There, Jean Cocteau spotted the young actress and proved her breadth by casting her in a new production of his 1941 play, *Une machine à écrire*. Although Cocteau's critique of provincial life was his least successful play (financially and artistically), his accolades of Girardot enhanced her growing reputation.

While Girardot had already played in a film with Jean Gabin (Gilles Grangier's 1957 *Le Rouge est mis /Speaking of Murder*), it was her theatrical training that led her to Luchino Visconti, who directed her on stage before casting her alongside Alain Delon in *Rocco et ses frères*, a film loosely based on Dostoyevsky's *The Brothers Karamazov*. Girardot finally won the renown of the cinema public as a fragile but fierce prostitute whose allegiance glides between two competitive brothers. The melodrama demonstrates neo-realism's influence on Visconti; though the role of Nadia lacks glamour, her part exudes a natural sensuality. In many respects Nadia is the key role, as her intensity sparks the brothers' rivalry at the centre of the narrative. The role also began Girardot's career as an international actress; after marrying her *Rocco* co-star, Renato Salvatore, she continued to act in Italian productions.

Yet only a year after their marriage Girardot began her cinematic and romantic relationship with the director Claude Lelouch, a relationship that continued through five films. The two had met when Lelouch was the assistant director for her 1956 film

L'Homme aux clefs d'or /The Man with the Golden Keys (dir. Léo Joannon), but it was after the enormous success of Lelouch's film *Un homme et une femme /A Man and a Woman* (1966), that he cast Girardot opposite Yves Montand in *Vivre pour vivre /Live for Life* (1967). In this film Girardot plays the housewife of a playboy journalist (Montand). However, after the journalist's romance with an American model (Candice Bergen) goes sour, his once docile wife begins her own infidelities. Girardot was central to the film's success, as her character shows how confidence transforms the girl next door. Girardot continued to act in popular films throughout the 70s, and won the César for best actress in 1976 for playing an adulterous doctor, who realizes the importance of family when struck with cancer (Jean-Louis Bertuccelli's *Docteur Françoise Gailland*).

Lelouch cast the actress four times after *Vivre pour vivre* including their last collaboration in 1995, a retelling of Victor Hugo's *Les Misérables* set in World War II. The popularity of Lelouch's *Les Misérables* was uplifting for Girardot as the 1980s and early 1990s were largely a string of unsuccessful features and television work for the aging actress. She tearfully accepted her César for her secondary role in the film, telling the audience that she had profoundly missed French cinema, and that the award signified that « peut-être je ne suis pas encore tout à fait morte ».

Michael Haneke selected Girardot at 69 to play the mother at the root of a masochist piano teacher's (Isabelle Huppert) personality disorder in *La Pianiste /The Piano Teacher* (2001) – Girardot and Huppert were also paired as mother and daughter in *Docteur Françoise Gailland*. Along with the starring actors Huppert and Benoît Magimel, Girardot received a César for her refined performance, which portrayed a controlling woman brought to rage and fear. Four years later Haneke chose Girardot for a smaller role as the mother of a literary TV host in his post-colonial thriller *Caché /Hidden* (2005). Here Girardot's character fails to remember a debacle concerning an Arab orphan that occurred forty years prior. Girardot played another woman struggling with memory loss in *Je préfère qu'on reste amis* (Olivier Nakache and Eric Toledano, 2005). Although Girardot's friends and family had not yet revealed Girardot's malady to the public, the actress's lack of memory mirrored her characters', as she suffered from Alzheimer's disease.

Although celluloid makes Girardot's contribution to cinema undeniable, she continued to act on stage throughout her career. In fact the school teacher, Mme Marguerite, in the play of the same title, became her signature role. Jean-Loup Dabadie adapted the first person Brazilian novel, and though Mme Marguerite is the sole actress on stage, Girardot claimed that *Mme Marguerite* was not a monologue, but rather, a dialogue with the students. Girardot reprised the role for the last time in 2003, aided by an earpiece as her memory began to fail her. Annie Girardot is remembered for her ability to play and connect with many types of average people, and was aptly called *Madame tout le monde* by the popular press.

Nicole Beth WALLENBROCK
The City University of New York

Judith GODRÈCHE (1972–)
[Judith Goldreich]

*From
Japanese
Chocolate
Commercials
to
Hollywood
Fame*

JUDITH GODRÈCHE, whose real last name is Goldreich, was born on 23 March 1972 in Paris to psychologist parents. After starting out as a model for teen magazines and in a commercial for a Japanese chocolate maker, she received her first screen role as Claudia Cardinale's daughter in *L'Été prochain /Next Summer* (Nadine Trintignant, 1985).

In the wake of that first movie, she went on to play several teenage parts: Catherine in *Les Mendiants / The Beggars* (Benoît Jacquot, 1988), Ophélie in *Les Saisons du plaisir* (Jean-Pierre Mocky, 1988), Laurence in *Un été d'orages /Stormy Summer* (Charlotte Brandström, 1989), and Juliette in *La Fille de 15 ans /The 15 Year Old Girl* (Jacques Doillon, 1989), until her nomination for the César du Meilleur Espoir Féminin for her part in *La Désenchantée /The Disenchanted* (Benoît Jacquot, 1990).

The second part of her career, which can be seen as her coming-of-age, marks a shift from teenage roles to young, bourgeois, uptight women, much like a younger Catherine Deneuve, from *Paris s'éveille /Paris Awakens* (Olivier Assayas, 1991) to *Tango* (Patrice Leconte, 1993), *Une nouvelle vie /A New Life* (Olivier Assayas, 1993), *Beaumarchais l'insolent /Beaumarchais the Scoundrel* (Edouard Molinaro, 1996). She was nominated for the César du Meilleur Second Rôle féminin (Best Supporting Actress) two years in a row, for the now cult movie *L'Auberge espagnole /The Spanish Apartment* (Cédric Klapisch, 2002) and for *France boutique* (Tonie Marshall, 2003). Her part as Anne-Sophie in *L'Auberge espagnole* epitomizes her cinematic image of the 'ingénue' bourgeoise which characterizes so many of her parts, including her role as Mathilde de la Mole in the made for TV adaptation of the canonical Stendhal novel *Le Rouge et le Noir /The Red and the Black* (Jean-Daniel Verhaege, 1997). It was on the set of *Bimboland* (Ariel Zeitoun, 1998), in which she stars as a shy doctoral student who falls in love with her adviser (Gérard Depardieu), that she met French actor and humorist Dany Boon, with whom she had a son, Noé, in 1999.

In 1996, her career also took on an international turn when the film *Ridicule* (Patrice Leconte, 1996) contributed to making her known to the American audience. From then on, she starred in a few Hollywood productions, such as *The Man in the Iron Mask* (Randall Wallace, 1998) with Leonard DiCaprio, Gabriel Byrne, Jeremy Irons, John Malkovich, and Gérard Depardieu. More recently, still in keeping with her bourgeois persona, she starred in François Ozon's *Potiche /Trophy Wife* (François Ozon, 2010) and in *L'Art d'aimer /The Art of Love* (Emmanuel Mouret, 2011). In 2010, she directed a film entitled *Toutes les filles pleurent*, in which she also played the main part and for which she wrote the script. Unfortunately, the film did not receive good critique.

Although not as discrete in real life as she is in her movie roles, she has imposed herself as one of the most productive actresses in contemporary French cinema, with an impressive filmography for a woman who is in her early 40s. Her career was first initiated through her relationship with director Benoît Jacquot, with whom she moved in when she was only sixteen years old. Since 2004, she has been living with Maurice Barthélemy, an actor and director, with whom she had a daughter, Tess, in 2005.

Nathalie SÉGERAL
*Virginia Polytechnic Institute
and State University*

Eva GREEN (1980–)

*Indecent
Beauty*

BERNARDO BERTOLUCCI said of Eva GREEN that 'she is so beautiful, it's indecent.' [1] The Italian director had recently cast Green to play Isabelle in *The Dreamers*, known in France as *Innocents* (2003). Her role as Isabelle, who has a quasi-incestuous, three-way relationship with her twin brother Théo (Louis Garrel) and visiting American student Matthew (Michael Pitt), set the tone for much of what has followed in Green's career – namely a propensity to act predominantly in English and to play characters notable for their sensuality and psychological instability.

The Dreamers achieved some notoriety, with Green at its centre, because of prolonged scenes featuring sex and nudity. The open, but eventually jealous, *ménage à trois* that Isabelle, Théo, and Matthew have in the film is set against the backdrop of the events leading up to the protests in Paris in May 1968. Three avowed cinephiles (who first meet at the Cinémathèque française, no less), they retreat into an enclosed world, alienating themselves from the crumbling society that surrounds them. The film seems to suggest, therefore, that the utopian aspects of their relationship (and those of the

May '68 movement more generally) can only be sustained in a bubble, and even then only temporarily.

After *The Dreamers*, Green had what to date is her only role uniquely in French, playing Countess Clarisse de Dreux-Soubise in Jean-Paul Salomé's film version of *Arsène Lupin* (2004), the latest adaptation of Maurice Leblanc's early twentieth century 'gentleman thief' stories. It is ironic that Green should here play the innocent love interest for the titular hero (Romain Duris), since she has as her rival for Lupin's hand Joséphine, the Countess of Cagliostro (Kristin Scott-Thomas). It is ironic because while the witch-like character of Joséphine is played by British actress Scott-Thomas, it is French actress Green who in her English-language films will play characters more akin to Joséphine. In other words, where Englishness seems to make of Scott-Thomas an evil temptress in this French-language film, it is her Frenchness that will make of Green a temptress in her English-language films.

This is the case in Ridley Scott's Crusades-era epic *Kingdom of Heaven* (2005), in which Green plays Sibylla of Jerusalem. Although the relationship that Sibylla has with Balian (Orlando Bloom) is affirmed at the film's end (Balian and Sibylla leave the crusades behind, having renounced all power), Sibylla is depicted as a corrupt and unfaithful woman whose sanity is only questionable. Most often Sibylla is shrouded in semi-darkness, lending to her a sense of mystery, intensified by the henna tattoos that feature prominently on her body. In the director's cut of the film we see Sibylla

killing her own son because he is born with leprosy, further suggesting her psychological instability.

Vesper Lynd, the character that Green plays in *Casino Royale* (Martin Campbell, 2006), is also a woman with psychological scars that manifest themselves in a fatale way: although James Bond (Daniel Craig) falls in love with Vesper, she nonetheless steals from him (and by extension from the British government) the winnings from Bond's high stakes poker game against the evil banker Le Chiffre (Mads Mikkelsen) in order to liberate her real boyfriend, who has been taken hostage by a terrorist organisation. Vesper prefers to die at the film's climax rather than be rescued by Bond.

After unstable temptress /fatale characters, Green played a heroine in her next film, *The Golden Compass* (2007), which was Chris Weitz's adaptation of Philip Pullman's *Northern Lights*. While Serafina Pekkala advises and then helps the film's child protagonists in their battle against the evil Tartars, she is nonetheless a witch, who is characterised as barefoot and in thin, translucent clothing – suggesting not only sensuality, but also mystery and magic.

Thereafter, Green starred in a series of relatively small budget, British, independent films. In *Franklyn* (Gerald McMorrow, 2008), Green has two parts: Sally, the imaginary childhood friend of Milo (Sam Riley), who has recently been jilted, and Emilia, an art student who was abused by her father and whose work now consists of recorded suicide attempts and documentaries about stalking strangers. In *Cracks* (2009), made by Ridley Scott's daughter, Jordan, Green plays Miss G, a teacher at an isolated girls' school who is responsible for leading her students astray while falling in love with an aristocratic Spanish pupil (María Valverde), whom she ultimately kills. In *Womb* (Benedek Fliegauf, 2010), Green plays a woman who gives birth to the clone of her dead boyfriend, only eventually to have a relationship with her own clone-son. And in *Perfect Sense* (David Mackenzie, 2011), Green plays an epidemiologist, Susan, who struggles – along with the rest of humanity – with losing her senses one by one. Although not as identifiably unstable as her other characters, the latter film offers a strong emphasis on sensuality, reinforcing the link between Green and the sensual and psychological instability.

This string of independent films might suggest the 'curse' of James Bond – in that Bond girls struggle to have high profile acting careers after going to bed with 007. However, in 2012 Green appeared in Tim Burton's major Hollywood production of *Dark Shadows*, starring, perhaps predictably, as a witch who fails to keep the heart of Barnabas Collins (Johnny Depp).

If Green seems often to play sensual, unstable *fatale* types, she spreads this type across genres, including action films, dramas, fantasy, and comedy. This versatility was already manifest in her earliest stage performances in Esther Vilar's drama *Jalousie en trois fax* in 2001, for which she was nominated for a Molière, and Alain-René Lesage's comedy *Turcaret* in 2002.

In conclusion, Green is one of France's best-known actresses despite only having played in one film that could be fully classified as French. Perhaps it is by way of distinguishing herself from her mother, the actress Marlène Jobert, that she has chosen to shy away from France – which in turn has led to her being cast more often than not as a sensual, often unstable, *femme fatale* or witch-type character, including as Vanessa Ives in the American cable television series *Penny Dreadful* (Showtime, from 2014), set in Victorian England.

William BROWN
University of Roehampton, London

1. Geoffrey Macnab, 'Julia Roberts – Has Cinema Queen Lost Her Crown?' *The Independent*, March 13 2009, accessed September 20, 2013, http://www.independent.co.uk/arts-entertainment/films/features/julia-roberts--has-cinemas-queen-lost-her-crown-1643714.html.

Sacha **GUITRY** (1885–1957)

*Me,
Myself,
and
Sacha*

ALEXANDRE-PIERRE 'SACHA' GUITRY'S figure stands alone and shines bright in the landscape of cinema. Both an actor and a playwright, and then a director, his incomparable wit makes him the equivalent of a French Oscar Wilde, or even more acutely, in the words of François Truffaut, a 'French sibling of Ernst Lubitsch.'

Sacha Guitry's life reads like a thrilling play, a comedy of manners full of twists, contradictions, and famous punch lines. To begin with, Sacha grew up in the constant admiration of his father Lucien Guitry (1860-1925), who was undoubtedly the most famous actor of his time. This blessing turned into a curse, since the son spent nearly his whole career emulating and eventually surpassing his flamboyant father. Sacha owes to his successful father his Russian birth, his Russian nickname (in homage to Alexander III, in whose theatre houses Lucien was a regular guest-star) as well as his precocious theatrical debuts in Saint Petersburg and Paris. The pair competed in everything, sharing their passion for the stage and sometimes even for the same women. As it could easily be foreseen, Lucien and Sacha completely split apart in 1905 – for almost thirteen years: Lucien never forgave his son for arriving late and without his wig at a performance he was supervising, and most of all, for stealing his latest lover, the young Charlotte Lysès.

If Lucien had a quick temper, Sacha was more of the ironic kind, and this ability became the core of his acting and writing style. The young star kept on working copiously as a playwright, for Charlotte Lysès, whom he married, and then for his second wife, the actress Yvonne Printemps, even becoming some sort of an official playwright of the Third Republic. First reluctant to engage in an art he saw as an impoverished version of the stage, Sacha Guitry eventually embraced a creative filmmaker's career under the influence of his third wife, actress and modern art connoisseur Jacqueline Delubac. In the mid-1930s, once the technical transition from silent to sound pictures had been secured, Guitry finally found a medium worthy of his tremendous verbal virtuosity. Adapting to the screen his most successful stage plays, Sacha Guitry managed to transcend the boundaries of traditional filmmaking, with no less than three masterpieces during 1936, namely, *Le Roman d'un tricheur /The Story of a Cheat*, *Mon père avait raison /My Father Was Right*, and *Faisons un rêve /Let's Make a Dream*. As a perfect ironist, and quite a narcissist, 'Mr Me' is constantly on display in front of the camera, while commenting upon his own actions on voice-over, and using the camera with the openly casual manners of a god-like narrator. Like that of his American counterparts Frank Capra or Ernst Lubitsch, the Guitry touch can seem theatrical, always elegant, sometimes insignificant, but this cheerful filmmaking fuels a visual and narrative boldness that inspired Orson Welles and the whole French New Wave. For many, it embodies creative freedom in its purest childlike form.

The events of World War II, however, cast a shadow on Guitry's reputation. The man's luxurious taste for honours, a fondness for collecting art, and the deep passion for his craft led him to some dubious commitments. During the Occupation of France, he befriended Otto Abetz, the very Francophile Reich ambassador in Paris, and became a regular on the programmes of the pro-German radio station; he also worked until very late in the course of war on adapting to the screen his own art book, perhaps dictated by the circumstances: *From Joan of Arc to Philippe Pétain* (1944).

The Liberation of France brought trouble for the actor and director since the French Résistance unsuccessfully attempted to try him for collaboration with the enemy. Though his critical and political aura ended up tarnished, Guitry achieved fame again in the fifties, through a series of ambitious patrimonial pieces (such as *Si Versailles m'était conté /Royal Affairs in Versailles*, 1954; *Napoléon*, 1955 or *Si Paris nous était conté /If Paris Were Told To Us*, 1956), maybe a little out-dated, but forever gay and quick-witted.

Jean-Christophe BLUM
Lycée Blaise Pascal, Clermont-Ferrand

Johnny HALLYDAY (1943–)
[Jean-Philippe SMET]

From the 'French Elvis' to Man on the Train

IN JULY 2011, the French town of Epinal was the setting for a violent showdown between a Serge Gainsbourg lookalike /impersonator, Denis Colnot, and his rival, Michel Pacchiana, a Johnny Hallyday impersonator, who, over the years, had had frequent run-ins with each other as they competed in the same lookalike contests. After a particularly heated confrontation during which Pacciana insulted Colnot by calling him a 'social misfit,' Colnot, 48, stabbed the 50-year-old would-be Johnny Hallyday in the throat, barely missing his carotid artery (Colnot previously filed harassment complaints against Pacchiana). Pacchiana survived the attack, although it could have been fatal. In June 2013, Colnot, found guilty, was sentenced to two years in prison (he could have received 30 for his crime); although he admitted to stabbing Pacchiana, Colnot maintained that he never intended to kill him. Pacchiana, for his part, insists that he is the more talented of the two celebrity impersonators: 'I won the last two competitions that we took part in, and he was livid... When I sing as Johnny, I become a total animal on stage. Whereas Denis Colnot stays completely motionless when he impersonates Serge Gainsbourg.'[1] Does life imitate art, or is it the other way around (as one headline screamed: « Gainsbourg a poignardé Johnny… et ce n'est pas du cinéma »[2])? In the recent biopic *Gainsbourg (vie héroïque) /Gainsbourg: A Heroic Life* (Joann Sfar, 2010), Gainsbourg (Eric Elmosnino) states that he would rather die ('plutôt crever') than ever have to write lyrics for Johnny Hallyday.

These two incidents reflect how Johnny Hallyday is at once an idol and also an object of scorn/ridicule. Hailed as the true French rock star, who many consider comparable to the American Elvis Presley – whom Hallyday claims as an influence – others find him unpalatable, not deserving of his popularity, fame, and reputation. Born on June 15, 1943 in Paris as Jean-Philippe Smet to a French mother and Belgian father, recalling other successful French entertainers of Belgian heritage such as Maurice Chevalier and Jacques Brel, although unlike Hallyday, Chevalier had a Belgian mother (named 'La Louque') and Brel was actually born in Belgium. Johnny Hallyday has become an icon of French popular culture, performing his French rock n'roll music at sold out concerts in prestigious venues including the Paris Olympia and the Stade de France. Smet reached the heights of fame and success, including being named Chevalier of the Légion d'Honneur in 1997, under the pseudonym Johnny Hallyday, a name borrowed from his aunt's American husband Lee, an entertainer at the Café de Paris who called himself 'Lee Hallyday' (Johnny Hallyday was raised by his aunt and

uncle and started out at the Café de Paris with Lee as his agent).

Since his 1961 version of Chubby Checker's song 'Let's Twist Again' went gold, Hallyday has had many hit singles and albums as well as sold out concerts, receiving, among his many accolades, the Male Artist of the Year award from the Victoires de la Musique in 1987 and the Victoire d'Honneur in 2009, comprising 8 Victoire awards over the course of his career. Despite his many gold (40) and platinum (22) records as well as selling over 100 million albums, Hallyday's immense popularity and household name status has not transcended beyond the French speaking public: Hallyday never broke into the Anglophone music world/ market, despite appearing on *The Ed Sullivan Show* with Connie Francis and performing with Jimi Hendrix (The Jimi Hendrix Experience's first concert was as the opening act for Hallyday in France in 1966) and Bono of U2 writing Hallyday a song in English ('I am the Blues') which appeared on his 2007 bestselling album *Le Cœur d'un homme*. Peter Frampton accompanied Hallyday on the guitar on the original recording of Hallyday's 1985 song *Quelque chose de Tennessee*, a tribute to the American playwright Tennessee Williams (1911-1983) which has become a staple of Hallyday's touring repertoire and one of his most beloved songs. On March 20, 1988, Hallyday performed *Tennessee* at the grand meeting of the Rassemblement pour la République (RPR) party held at the Hippodrome de Vincennes in Paris. In front of a crowd of more than 80,000, Hallyday shook Prime Minister Jacques

Chirac's hand onstage and dedicated the song to Chirac – who was then running for president as the RPR candidate, against François Mitterrand – by announcing « nous avons tous en nous quelque chose de Jacques Chirac » ['we all have something in us of Jacques Chirac'], a modification of the song's final line, « y'a quelque chose en nous de Tennessee » ['there is something in us of Tennessee']. In December 2008, the musical special *Johnny Hallyday : ça ne finira jamais !* aired on France 2 television, with Hallyday and Carla Bruni-Sarkozy together singing *Quelque chose de Tennessee* (Hallyday concluded their performance with « y a quelque chose en nous de…Carla »). After singing this duet, Sarkozy-Bruni appears totally charmed by Johnny and says it is an honour for her to sing with him; Hallyday likewise expresses his gratitude to her – Hallyday was a supporter of Nicolas Sarkozy during his campaigns, although he attended a dinner with François Hollande in 2012. In 2011, Hallyday commemorated Williams again – during the centenary of the playwright's birth – this time, by making his stage acting début at the Théâtre Édouard VII in Paris as Chicken in Williams's 'Paradise on Earth,' performed for the first time in France (as *Le Paradis sur terre*).

Johnny also has a cinematic career. Starting in 1955 with an uncredited part in Henri-Georges Clouzot's iconic noir thriller, *Les Diaboliques / Diabolique*, Hallyday has worked as an actor, with over 32 film and television credits to his name (occasionally playing himself or thinly fictionalized versions of his rock star persona). Along with Clouzot, Hallyday has worked with several of the biggest names in French cinema, including Claude Lelouch in 1972's *L'Aventure, c'est l'aventure /Money, Money, Money*, in which he plays himself, taken hostage by a gang of criminals who kidnap high profile victims (Hallyday's latest collaboration with Lelouch, *Salaud on t'aime /We Love You, You Bastard* was released in 2014); in another uncredited role as a sailor who kisses Sylvie Vartan (Hallyday's then wife) in Belgian director Harry Kümel's cult horror/fantasy film *Malpertuis / Legend of Doom House* (1971),[3] whose cast includes Michel Bouquet, Jean-Pierre Cassel, and Orson Welles; with Jean-Luc Godard in *Détective* (1985), as the boxing manager Jim Fox Warner, and in Costa-Gavras's *Conseil de famille /Family Council* (1986), as a thief and head of household known as 'Le Père' ['The Father'], who initiates his son into his profession, co-starring with Fanny Ardant as 'La Mère' ['The Mother']

Hallyday has also had roles in big budget action/adventure films such as *Les Rivières pourpres 2 – Les Anges de l'apocalypse /Crimson Rivers 2: Angels of the Apocalypse* (Olivier Dahan, 2004) as well as in the comedy *The Pink Panther 2* (Harald Zwart, 2009). In the 2009 revenge action drama *Vengeance*, directed by prolific Hong Kong auteur Johnnie To, Hallyday starred as Francis Costello, a former hitman now suffering from memory loss and seeking to avenge himself against a gang that attacked his daughter and her family. Hallyday's character's name pays homage to Jeff Costello (played by Alain Delon), the protagonist of Jean-Pierre Melville's 1967 *Le Samouraï /The Samurai*, while his use of Polaroid pictures as a memory device recalls Christopher Nolan's *Memento* (2000).

With his starring role in French auteur Patrice Leconte's critically acclaimed and award winning drama, *L'Homme du train /Man on the Train* (2002), Hallyday achieved serious recognition as an actor. In this film, he plays the aging bank robber Milan, who arrives in a small town where his partners assigned him to hold up a bank. Milan's chance encounter with lonely retired poetry professor Manesquier (Jean Rochefort), who invites Milan to stay in his home as Milan has nowhere else to go, develops into a friendship that leads each man to introspection, reflecting upon and examining his path in life – choices, regrets, unfulfilled desires – each being envious of the other and wishing that they could switch places. For his highly praised performance as Milan, Johnny Hallyday was awarded the 2003 Prix Jean-Gabin (which since 2008 has been known as the Prix Patrick-Dewaere), for most promising male actor of the year and he was also nominated for the Audience Award for Best Actor from the European Film Awards that year. The film itself was honoured by numerous film festivals and organizations, including the Venice Film Festival (Audience Award for Best Film), as well as the Los Angeles Film Critics Association Awards (Best Foreign Film), among others. The less successful 2011 US remake, *Man on the Train*, stars Donald Sutherland and Larry Mullen Jr, and is directed by Mary McGuckian.

As mentioned above, Hallyday was married to singer-actress Sylvie Vartan (aunt of French-American actor Michael Vartan) from 1965 until their divorce in 1980; their 1973 duet, *J'ai un problème*, reached the top position on the French charts. Their son, David Hallyday (born in 1966), is a singer, performer, songwriter, and racecar driver, who has written songs for his father. Laura Smet (born in 1983), Hallyday's daughter from his relationship with actress Nathalie Baye, made her powerful screen debut in Xavier Giannoli's *Les Corps impatients /Eager Bodies* (2003), as a young woman suffering from a terminal illness who is withering away while her boyfriend and best female friend – who have developed romantic feelings for each other – attempt to care for her and cope with the gravity of their situation, an exploration of the triangulation of desire. For this role, Smet – appearing emaciated and with a shaved head, as the disease ravaged her youth and beauty – was nominated for a César and received the Étoile d'Or for Best Female Newcomer as well as the Prix Romy Schneider for most promising actress of the year. Hallyday – married briefly several times after his split from Vartan – married his current wife, Laeticia (née Boudu), a former model, in 1996, when she was 21 years old. They adopted two daughters from Vietnam, Jade (born in 2004) and Joy (born in 2008) (Hallyday dedicated his 2005 hit song *Mon plus beau Noël* /'My Happiest Christmas' to Jade, who is featured throughout the video with Hallyday). Hallyday is also a grandfather, as his son David has three children.

When Hallyday attempted to flee France for a fiscal haven in Belgium in 2005, he was rejected by the Belgian government because he had not spent enough time there, and therefore, he turned to Gstaad, the luxurious Swiss ski resort, where he spent part of the year, and became a citizen in 2006. He spends the other part of the year in California, where he loves riding his Harley-Davidson in the California desert and can go relatively incognito, which he greatly enjoys. Recently, his health has given him worries, after colon cancer and back surgery, for which he received treatment in France and in Los Angeles, and at one point he was placed in a medically induced coma. He is not the picture of health and it is rumoured that he wants to sue one of his surgeons for malpractice. Despite these health issues and setbacks (which primarily occurred in 2009), Hallyday continues performing and touring: he played in the UK for the first time in October 2012 at the age of 69 at the Royal Albert Hall, and held his first public concert in New York City at the Beacon Theater in November 2012, returning to play the Beacon in May 2014. During one of the concerts of his 'Born Rocker' tour in 2013, he fêted his 70th birthday – June 15, 2013 – on stage to a full house of over 20,000 spectators at the Palais Omnisports de Paris-Bercy. Accompanying Hallyday was a veritable entourage of French music icons, including Hallyday's great friend Eddy Mitchell – with whom he sang *La Musique que j'aime* – and Charles Aznavour. Together, Aznavour and Hallyday sang Aznavour's 1955 song *Sur ma vie*, his first chart-topper in France, which opens with the famous declaration « sur ma vie je t'ai juré un jour /de t'aimer jusqu'au dernier jour de mes jours », forming

a poignant and emotional moment during Hallyday's birthday concert, especially given that Hallyday refers to Aznavour as his 'père.' Hallyday has openly expressed his admiration for Aznavour and declares that Aznavour is one of his main inspirations as a singer, and that he, too, hopes to be on stage at the age of 90, like his idol Aznavour (who turned 90 in May 2014).

Marcelline BLOCK
Princeton University and SAG-AFTRA

1. Henry Samuel, 'Serge Gainsbourg Impersonator Sentenced for Stabbing Johnny Hallyday Rival,' *The Telegraph*, June 18, 2013, accessed July 1, 2013, http://www.telegraph.co.uk/news/worldnews/europe/france/10127782/Serge-Gainsbourg-impersonator-sentenced-for-stabbing-Johnny-Hallyday-rival.html.

2. Yann Soudé, « Sosie: Gainsbourg a poignardé Johnny ». *LePoint.fr*, June 6, 2013, accessed July 1, 2013, http://www.lepoint.fr/insolite/gainsbourg-juge-pour-avoir-poignarde-johnny-14-06-2013-1680877_48.php

3. For further discussion of this film, see Michael Cramer, '*Malpertuis /Legend of Doom House*,' in *Directory of World Cinema: Belgium*, edited by Marcelline Block and Jeremi Szaniawski (Intellect, 2013), 132-33. —Ed.

Marina HANDS (1975–)

French
Actress
Anglaise

T HE DAUGHTER OF actress Ludmilla Mikaël and British theatre director Terry Hands, Marina HANDS (b. January 10, 1975) grew up in England and France. Being bilingual, she is often cast as a non-French character, often speaking English and/or playing characters from or living in Canada. Indeed, Hands describes herself on Twitter as a 'French actress *anglaise,*' lending to her a liminal identity that feeds into the outsider status of many of her characters, who are notable for their open sexuality, troubled domestic lives, and associations with nature.

All of these qualities are prominent in what is perhaps Hands' best-known role, as Constance Chatterley in Pascale Ferran's *Lady Chatterley* (2006). In one scene, Constance dances naked in a field in the rain, only to be joined by groundsman Parkin (Jean-Louis Coullo'ch), with whom she is having an affair, unbeknown to her husband, Sir Clifford (Hippolyte Girardot). Nature here is combined with a sense of sexual liberation, which stands in stark contrast to the repressive character of Constance's home life.

Hands won the Best Actress César for *Lady Chatterley*; her persona's open sexuality is identifiable even in earlier films. Hands plays Julia in Andrzej Żuławski's anarchic *La Fidélité / Fidelity* (2000), the unstable daughter of a media tycoon who declares her undying, quasi-lesbian friendship for lead character Clélia (Sophie Marceau) during their first meeting – on the deathbed of her would-be father-in-law. In the Canadian production *Les Invasions barbares /The Barbarian Invasions* (Denys Arcand, 2003), Hands' Gaëlle meanwhile upbraids dying academic Rémy (Rémy Girard) for his libido-driven lifestyle. However, Gaëlle is not simply a dutiful wife to Rémy's estranged son, Sébastien (Stéphane Rousseau). Rather, she understands Rémy's sexual drives all too well because, she explains, her upbringing was characterised by her parents' arguments and separations. In other words, Gaëlle is also from a broken family, something that leads Rémy to believe that her fidelity to Sébastien cannot last. And in *Les Âmes grises /Grey Souls* (2005), her second collaboration with Yves Angelo after 2002's *Sur le bout des doigts /At My Fingertips*, Hands plays Lysia Verhareine, who in 1917 travels to a small town near the Western front, where her boyfriend is fighting. All men seem to fall in love with Lysia, including town prosecutor Pierre-Ange Destinat (Jean-Pierre Marielle), on whose land she lives. Lysia discovers via a letter delivered by Destinat that her boyfriend has died at the front, which prompts her to kill herself, though there is a brief (unsubstantiated but also unproven) suggestion that Destinat might have murdered her. In other words, Hands here represents a natural, innocent love that the corrupt world of the Great

War seems incapable of tolerating.

Open sexuality features in *Ne le dis à personne /Tell No One* (2006), directed by her Fidelity co-star Guillaume Canet, with whom Hands also made a short film in 1996 called *Sans regrets*. Hands plays Anne Beck, the lesbian sister of pediatrician Alexandre (François Cluzet), who finds himself caught up in a murder mystery revolving around his believed-dead wife, Margot (Marie-Josée Croze). Meanwhile, in *Le Scaphandre et le Papillon /The Diving Bell and the Butterfly* (Julian Schnabel, 2007), Hands plays Joséphine, the ex-girlfriend of Jean-Dominique Bauby (Mathieu Amalric), who develops locked-in syndrome. Memorable shots of Joséphine's hair flying in the wind, together with a sequence in which she takes Bauby to Lourdes only for him to refuse to make love to her because of the presence of a glowing statue of the Madonna, further enhances the sexual openness of Hands's characters.

In *L'Histoire de Jen /Story of Jen* (François Rotger, 2008), Hands plays young mother Sarah. Set amid the beautiful forests of Ontario, Sarah drinks and sleeps with random local men in an attempt to get over her dead husband, who has recently committed suicide – again reaffirming the relationship between nature, overt sexuality, and a dysfunctional family that Hands seems to embody.

Open sexuality and a dysfunctional family life also characterise her roles as Juliette in Danièle Thompson's *Le Code a changé /Change of Plans* (2009) and as Audrey in Julie Lopes-Curval's *Mères et Filles /Hidden Diary* (2009). In the former, Juliette is a globe-trotting actress who blames her absent father (Pierre Arditi) for the death of her mother, while having an eventually abortive relationship with aging actor and obvious replacement father-figure, Erwann (Patrick Chesnais). In the latter, a recently pregnant Audrey falls out with her mother, Martine (Catherine Deneuve), while also discovering from a previously lost diary that her absent grandmother Louise (Marie-José Croze again) did not necessarily abandon Martine, but might have been the victim of a much more sinister, misogynistic crime at the hands of her husband.

In *Une exécution ordinaire /An Ordinary Execution* (Marc Dugain, 2010), Hands's Anna is a doctor with healing hands who in early 1950s Moscow is forced to leave her husband, Vassilli (Edouard Baer), in order to treat a dying Stalin (André Dussollier). Evidently, Anna's powers to heal people make of her a force of nature that cannot fit Stalin's would-be rational worldview, resulting not only in the imprisonment and torture of Vassilli, but also that of her whole family.

Hands is pictured in nature – walking through fields and on horseback – in knockabout comedy *Ensemble nous allons vivre une très, très grande histoire d'amour* (Pascal Thomas, 2010), in which her character significantly is called Dorothée Duchamp ('Dorothy of the Field'). Hands plays Lise in Claude Miller's *See How They Dance* (2011), a videographer crossing rural Canada in search of her missing husband – again reinforcing the link between her, nature, and broken families.

Finally, Hands's link with horses in reaffirmed in both Patricia Mazuy's

Sport de filles (2011) and Christian Duguay's *Jappeloup* (2013). In the former, she plays horse rider Gracieuse, who turns her hand from riding to show jumping, while in the latter she plays the love interest of Olympic show Pierre Durand (again Guillaume Canet). Both films reinforce Hands's link with the natural world and also reflect her own biography, in that before becoming an actress Hands wanted to be a professional dressage rider.

Hands has also appeared in many TV movies and stage productions, for which she has won three Molière awards, including for plays directed by Patrice Chéreau and Jacques Weber. However, as mentioned, *Lady Chatterley* remains her best-known work – a film in which her association with nature, with open sexuality, and with a troubled domestic life is made most clear.

William BROWN
University of Roehampton, London

Isabelle HUPPERT (1953–)

*The
Charms
of Icy
Perversion*

ISABELLE HUPPERT was born in Paris on 16 March, 1953. Her father was the owner of a safe company and her mother a piano player. She, her three sisters, and one brother were initiated early on to the charms and excesses of French intellectual bourgeoisie, including culture, discipline, and secrets. As a child, she had no deep interest for cinema, though she remembers seeing movies such as *Le Triporteur / The Tricyclist* (Jacques Pinoteau, 1957), with Darry Cowl. She sang and dreamt of being an ice skater. Her mother pushed her into theatre when she grew to be a teenager. In parallel with her first successes, however, she pursued Russian studies at university, until she obtained a BA.

Isabelle Huppert started playing short and secondary roles in *Faustine et le bel été* (Nina Companeez, 1972), with Jacques Brel in *Le Bar de la fourche /The Bar at the Crossing* (Alain Levent, 1972), or as Romy Schneider's little sister in *César et Rosalie /César and Rosalie* (Claude Sautet, 1972). Quite soon, the cheeky young red-haired girl stunned the public in two movies from the new generation of French film directors: *Les Valseuses / Going Places* (Bertrand Blier, 1974) and *Le Juge et l'Assassin /The Judge and the Assassin* (Bertrand Tavernier, 1976). She had a strange look, both icy and arrogant, provocative and indolent. In *La Dentellière /The Lacemaker* (Claude Goretta, 1976) she was Pomme [Apple], a discreet hairdresser silently living her first amorous disappointment as an existential turn. The role was her first great international success and won the movie a BAFTA and an Italian Donatello award. Two years later, Claude Chabrol cast her in *Violette Nozière* (Claude Chabrol, 1978), which won her a Best Actress award at the Cannes Film Festival for her interpretation of a true story, that of a mad woman poisoning her parents in 1933 and being accused by her surviving mother. The movie shows the poverty, mediocrity, and triviality Violette had to suffer with her parents, and her walking in the street to charm men and smoke it all away.

Chabrol and Huppert's reciprocal *estime* led to their very prolific collaboration, starting ten years later with *Une affaire de femmes / Story of Women* (1988), the true story of a woman sentenced to death for practising abortion under Maréchal Pétain's political regime. With many closeups on Huppert's imperturbable face, Chabrol focuses on her gradual decision to help women, respectful of their individual decisions, despite the legal dominance and hypocrisy of a man-made political regime. The movie won a Golden Globe and Huppert a Best Actress award at Venice. Since then, the iconic film director has been playing the role of a Pygmalion for Isabelle - a relationship very

palpable in *L'Ivresse du pouvoir /The Comedy of Power* (2006). In *Madame Bovary* (1991), the actress seems to melt with Flaubert's iconic character, while Chabrol's camera shows how boundless desire, frigidity, and frustration are given the intellectual appearance of romanticism. With *La Cérémonie* (1994), Huppert is an unstable mail-woman, forming a frightening murderous duo with an illiterate maid (Sandrine Bonnaire) humiliated by the French small-town bourgeoisie. The role won her a Best Actress award at Cannes and great success in Venice and the USA. Other successes under Chabrol's direction include *Rien ne va plus / The Swindle* (1997), an ambiguous comedy where Huppert and Michel Serrault play with lies, false stories, and manipulation, and her dark, poisoning, perverse, and mellow acting in *Merci pour le chocolat* (2000) with Jacques Dutronc.

Since *Violette Nozière*, Isabelle Huppert has given body and flesh to women's solitudes and acceptances and to the complex relations of power and desire they share with men, often perverse and beyond plain morality. In *Retour à la bien-aimée /Return to the Beloved* (Claire Denis, 1979), she ends up making love with her ex-husband (Jacques Dutronc) who, she has discovered, is responsible for the murder of a man and the mistaken arrest of her second husband (Bruno Ganz). *La Vengeance d'une femme /A Woman's Revenge* (Jacques Doillon, 1990) displays a sadistic Huppert, exacting psychological revenge on the mistress (Beatrice Dalle) of her recently dead husband. The shiveringly cynical hypocrisy of Parisian bourgeoisie can be felt in *Pas de scandale /Keep it Quiet* (Benoit Jacquot, 1999), where Isabelle Huppert plays the very castrating wife of a formerly convicted CEO (Fabrice Luchini). In *Saint-Cyr / The King's Daughters* (Patricia Mazuy, 2000), sadism and power will intertwine with religious fanaticism, as Huppert plays the role of Madame de Maintenon, King Louis XIV's secret second wife and the founder of a school for poor noble girls. As the girls grow adolescent, she excels in showing how a feminist ideal of rational independence can gradually cause brutal repression, mortification, and religious terror. Huppert has also recently played ambiguous and disturbing roles. She obtained a César award for the rigid and borderline character of *La Pianiste / The Piano Teacher* (Michael Haneke, 2001), a piano professor reacting to one of her pupils' advances (Benôit Magimel) by self-mutilation, violent sex, and sadomasochism. *Ma mère / My Mother* (Christophe Honoré, 2004), inspired by Georges Bataille's novel, presents incest with extreme morbidity, as a son (Louis Garrel) is seduced by his perverse and shameless mother following his father's death. *Histoire de Piera* (Marco Ferreri, 1983), by contrast, only showed sexual incest between a mother and her daughter as a metaphor for pre-birth communion.

Huppert is certainly an exception among French actresses. With pure presence, clarity, and precision, she has worked with the most influential French film directors, including Assayas, Blier, Chéreau, Godard, Jacquot, Kurys, Ozon, Tavernier, and Téchiné. She is of the few French actresses who have accessed a truly international career, working under the direction of Otto Preminger (*Rosebud*, 1975), Michael Cimino (*Heaven's Gate*, 1980), Hal Hartley (*Amateur*, 1994), Joseph Losey (*La Truite /The Trout*, 1982), Andrzej Wajda (*Les Possédés /The Possessed*, 1988), and Paolo and Vittorio Taviani (*Le affinità elettive /Les Affinités électives /Elective Affinities*, 1996). Huppert has also attained many successes on stage. She has, at times, given public lectures, with a sharp, calm, and mysterious voice, for instance on Maurice Blanchot in 2006 at the French Cinémathèque in Paris.

Isabelle Huppert was the President of the Jury at the Cannes Festival in 2009. In 2012 she played the part of Eva in Haneke's successful *Amour* alongside Jean-Louis Trintignant and Emmanuelle Riva, with further roles (among other film appearances) in Marc Fitussi's comedy *La Ritournelle /Paris Follies* (2014), and in New York with Gabriel Byrne in Joachim Trier's *Louder than Bombs* (2015).

Nicolas RIGAUD
The University of Oxford

Agnès Jaoui (1964–)

*Neither
Cinderella
nor Her
Stepsister*

Agnès Jaoui was born October 19, 1964 in the Parisian suburbs to parents of Tunisian Jewish descent; her father was a business executive and her mother a psychotherapist. Jaoui has remarked that, as a daughter of a psychotherapist, she was encouraged to analyse human motivation from a very early age. Earlier magazine articles on Jaoui often asserted that she attended the prestigious preparatory school Henri IV, but she later stated that this was in fact untrue. She began studying acting with Patrice Chéreau at the Théâtre des Amandiers in Nanterre in 1984, a formative experience which led her to believe that there existed only two possible roles for actresses: the pretty girl and the wicked stepmother. Although strikingly attractive, Jaoui felt that she was pigeonholed in the second category and therefore had a difficult time establishing herself as an actress.

In 1986, she met Jean-Pierre Bacri, 13 years her senior and much better known. Partly as a way of resolving her typecasting dilemma, Jaoui began writings plays with Bacri that included more interesting and multi-dimensional roles for herself. Their works owe their appeal in large part to their humorous observations on interpersonal relationships. The spiritual heir to popular theatre playwrights like Georges Feydeau, Jaoui grounds her plays in witty dialogue, playing with language in a way that is often lighthearted and thought provoking at the same time. Jaoui and Bacri's plays *Cuisine et dépendances* (1991) and *Un air de famille* (1995) were very well received (to this day, *Cuisine et Dépendances* is often reprised in France) and subsequently adapted by the couple into successful films: *Cuisine et Dépendances /Kitchen with Apartment* (Philippe Muyl, 1993) and *Un air de famille /Family Resemblances* (Cédric Klapisch, 1996).

In the 1990s, Jaoui collaborated on several projects with the director Alain Resnais. She and Bacri adapted playwright Alan Ayckbourn's *Intimate Exchanges* into the diptych *Smoking / No Smoking* (released in 1993 as two separate films), which presents twelve different denouements in a narrative that begins with a frustrated housewife who chooses to smoke a cigarette (*Smoking*) or not (*No Smoking*). Two actors, Sabine Azéma and Pierre Arditi, play all the characters in this small-town soap opera, and Jaoui and Bacri's talent for well-honed and nuanced dialogue is consequently put to excellent use. Not unlike *Cuisine et Dépendances*, the decor is deliberately artificial and spare, concentrating the spectator's attention on the sometimes microscopic changes in language and in the characters' rapport. Bacri and Jaoui wrote the screenplay and starred in Resnais's 1997 *On connaît la chanson /Same Old Song*, also about intersecting lives. Jaoui won the César for Best Supporting Actress for her performance as an eternal doctoral student who finally completes her dissertation at the very moment that her life is falling apart (or coming together). A spin on the musical genre, the film is punctuated by short excerpts from popular songs, lip-synced by the character whose life mirrors the sentiment expressed by the song.

Jaoui, Bacri, and three colleagues founded the production company Films A4, whose first success was also Jaoui's directorial debut, *Le Goût des autres /The Taste of Others* (2000). Widely hailed as a funny and touching tour de force, *Le Goût des autres* won the César for Best Film and catapulted Jaoui to a new level of stardom. Although now out of Bacri's shadow, Jaoui still valorised collaboration; like Bacri, she almost always used 'we' rather than 'I' when discussing their work and artistic vision.

Jaoui directed and starred in 2004's *Comme une image /Look At Me*, whose title in French evokes the idiom *sage comme une image* ('very obedient'). In this film, she played Sylvia, a voice coach whose husband is a struggling writer and whose student Lolita is, auspiciously, the insecure daughter of a famous writer who knows many publishing VIPs. Sylvia tries to capitalise on these contacts for her husband while still giving Lolita a voice and maintaining her own integrity. The film's critical reception was mixed, as is often the case for a director's second film. Its release was soon followed by Richard Dembo's 2005 *La Maison de Nina*, with Jaoui as the determined and loving director of a French orphanage for Jewish children during and after World War II. As in *Comme une image*, Jaoui played a decidedly maternal role, something she seemed previously reluctant to try.

Of late, Jaoui has also concentrated her energies on singing; she is not a complete novice, having studied voice on and off from a young age. In 2006, she released the CD *Canta*, which included songs in Spanish and Portuguese. In 2008, she directed and performed in *Parlez-moi de la pluie / Let It Rain* (2008); the same year, on the personal front, she adopted two children from Brazil. In 2012, Jaoui appeared in *Du vent dans mes mollets / The Dandelions* (Carine Tardieu, 2012), and though the film is perhaps most striking as an example of the recent nostalgic trend toward a 1980's, pre-Ikea decor, Jaoui also stood out in her thoughtful and sensitive turn as a clucky Jewish mother. She reunited with Bacri [1] on screen in 2013's *Au bout du conte /Under the Rainbow*, which they co-wrote and she directed; in this fine ensemble effort, she fittingly played the role of a fairy godmother, having left the Cinderella /stepsister dilemma and its pat ending behind in favour of more interesting and complicated questions.

Marina Davies
New York University, Paris Campus

1. See: Bacri, Jean-Pierre.

Louis Jouvet (1887–1951)

'The
Boss'

Born in 1887, Jules Eugène Louis Jouvet became, under the name Louis Jouvet, one of the most revered French stage and screen actors of the twentieth century. Though he may not be the best known star of the time, even though he made relatively few pictures compared to his fame on stage, Jouvet remains the most frequently quoted artist by his fellow workers and among the following generations of actors (noticeably by Michel Bouquet, Denis Podalydès, or Fabrice Luchini).

Early in his life, between 1907 and 1913, Louis Jouvet developed a talent for acting and enhancing his features with many theatrical props. After fighting in the trenches of World War I, he avoided taking up the pharmaceutical family business to begin his career on stage in Paris, in association with modern theatre pioneer Jacques Copeau. The theatre is truly the place where his skills matured and to which Jouvet will remain associated throughout his life. Indeed, he took on every existing job, from prop manager to supporting actor, stage director to troupe leader, both as a leading man on stage and as a theatre director (first at the Théâtre du Vieux-Colombier,

then at the Comédie des Champs-Élysées, and for the longest time at the Théâtre de l'Athénée, which truly was his thing). Later in his life, he achieved everlasting fame through his teaching experience for the Conservatoire's master classes, a job which he strongly loathed but for which his solid craftsmanship and biting wit worked wonders. Often comparing actors to mere whores (not supposed to enjoy themselves when doing their work properly) or often offering unforgiving advice to young debutantes playing alongside him, Jouvet's snippets of wisdom and punchlines remain famous to this day, even leading the way to new plays based on his numerous classes (such as *Elvire Jouvet 40*, about the rehearsals of *Dom Juan*'s main female part). Since his authority was unchallenged by his partners and employees, with the notable exception of his temperamental wife Madeleine Ozeray, he was always referred to as 'the boss' (or in French, *le patron*).

On stage, Jouvet embodied long-remembered characters from the repertoire through his mesmerizing performances as Tartuffe or Don Juan. However, he owed his reputation above all to his tremendously successful collaboration with celebrated authors Marcel Achard, Jean Giraudoux, and Jules Romains. The latter gave him his most famous part in *Knock*, as a mastermind physician who convinces a whole town that even the healthiest man is virtually prone to sickness. Jouvet's tall skinny figure, piercing gaze, and severe face were so convincing – and the success of the play so powerful (almost 1,300 performances!) – that he took this part with him to the screen twice: *Knock, ou le triomphe de la médecine* (Roger Goupillières and Louis Jouvet, 1933) and *Knock* (Guy Lefranc, 1951). But what was perhaps his most fruitful collaboration occurred with Giraudoux, whose new plays Jouvet systematically directed and acted as they opened in Paris theatres.

Due to his intense dramatic activity on stage, in Paris as well as on tour (for instance, he toured in South America for more than three years during World War II), Jouvet's presence in movies does not seem as dense as it could or should have been in respect to his fame and talent. It began in the mid-thirties, and of course, such an actor was not overlooked by the main French directors of the time, such as Marcel Carné, Henri-Georges Clouzot, Henri Decoin, Julien Duvivier, and Jean Renoir. Carné later gave Jouvet a memorable role as a libertine bishop in *Drôle de drame /Bizarre, Bizarre* (1937), opposite Michel Simon. The illustrious and absurd line « Bizarre, vous avez dit bizarre ? » made his glory, and imposed Jouvet's self-conscious and staccato voice. Even with a distinctively nasal but precise diction, he shared with Sacha Guitry or, in the following generation, Gérard Philipe, a great sense of theatricality in his performances in contradiction with the psychologically naturalist principles that ruled the American and Russian dramatic traditions. Jouvet's altogether funny, touching, and cruel portrayal of a pimp in Carné's *Hôtel du Nord* (1938) opposite Arletty proved him to be equally skilled in comedy and drama: although

in the beginning the director Carné and the screenwriter Jeanson fought harshly about Jouvet participating in the original project, the final choice resulted in a star-making part and ensured the success of the film. Clouzot's *Quai des Orfèvres* (1947), where he plays a detective, shows that his intense presence similarly suited *film noir* atmospheres. An actors' actor, memorable both on stage and on screen, Jouvet, the man and his career, could be summed up with the most famous quote from Allégret's 1938 *Entrée des artistes /The Curtain Rises* (picturing the every-day life of a drama school), when his experienced character gives a tip to a newbie actress: 'Baby, one ought to put a little art in his life and a little life in his art.' Indeed, Jouvet deeply cherished this motto, striving to make it truly his.

Jean-Christophe BLUM
Lycée Blaise Pascal, Clermont-Ferrand

Gérard JUGNOT (1951–)

*France's
Extraordinarily
Average
Man*

GÉRARD JUGNOT is a French actor, director, screenwriter, and producer. Born in 1951 in Paris, Jugnot first launched his career with the comedy troupe *Le Splendid*, made up of four high school friends who would go on to success. Around the same time, Jugnot made his movie debut in *Les Valseuses /Going Places* (1974) and Bertrand Tavernier's *Le Juge et l'Assassin /The Judge and the Assassin* (1976). With *Le Splendid*, Jugnot made three smash hit film comedies: *Les Bronzés /French Fried Vacation* (Patrice Leconte, 1978), its sequel *Les Bronzés font du ski* (Patrice Leconte, 1979), and *Le Père Noël est une ordure /Santa Claus is a Stinker* (Jean-Marie Poiré, 1982). Made familiar to the French public by his diminutive stature, blooming moustache, and bald head, Jugnot came to embody the image of the comically average Frenchman.

Jugnot began his directing career with *Pinot simple flic* (1984), in which he played the eponymous Parisian policeman whose soft heart and bumbling ways lead him astray. Although often humorous and entertaining, Jugnot's films, in particular those he directed, often engaged with the pathos of the human condition, and the force of choice in the face of moral quandaries. *Monsieur Batignole* (2002), for example, deals with one Frenchman's response to the treatment of Jews during World War II. *Casque bleu /Blue Helmet* (1994) put the spotlight on the war in the former Yugoslavia through the prism of comedy. He has directed eleven films in all, some of which he has co-written.

Perhaps Jugnot's most famous role is that of Clément Mathieu in Christophe Barratier's drama *Les Choristes /The Chorus* (2004), in which he played an unemployed music teacher who is hired as a supervisor at a reform school for unruly boys. The film was nominated for eight French Césars, two BAFTAS, and two Oscars.

Jugnot appeared in Franziska Buch's *Upgrade* (2012), Éric Besnard's *Mes héros* (2012), and alongside Gérard Depardieu and Catherine Deneuve in Laurent Tirard's *Astérix et Obélix : Au service de sa majesté /Astérix and Obélix: God Save Britannia* (2012).

Made Chevalier of the Légion d'Honneur in 2004, Jugnot has garnered seven César nominations. He is a member of the charitable group *Les Enfoirés*, which combats hunger, as well as a spokesman for gay and minority rights.

Jugnot lives with his companion, actress Saïda Jawad; with costume designer Cécile Magnan, he had a son, Arthur (b. 1980) – also an actor – with whom he has made several public appearances. Gérard Jugnot is now a grandfather, as Arthur Jugnot and actress Cécilia Clara welcomed a son, Célestin, in March 2013.

Jonathan ROBBINS
Columbia University

Élie KAKOU (1960–1999)
[Alain KAKOU]

A
Comedian
of the
Maghrebi
Jewish
Diaspora

E LIE KAKOU was born Alain Kakou
to a Sephardic Jewish family
in Nabeul, a costal town in the Cap
Bon region of Tunisia in 1960. The
country had gained its independence
from France only four years before,
and the European and Jewish
populations were leaving in large
numbers due to the rising tide of
anti-colonial Arab nationalism.
Kakou's family left soon after
his birth, arriving in Marseilles
where they made their home
with thousands of other migrants
from North Africa. Growing up
in a French-Arabic house with
a constant stream of Tunisian
relatives arriving from *le pays*, Kakou
gathered plenty of material for his
burgeoning stand up comedy act.
After stints in Israel (where he
served with the IDF and lived on a
kibbutz), and at various Club Med
locations in Turkey and Morocco,
Kakou began doing standup at
small clubs around Marseilles. His
most successful comic creation was
Madame Sarfati, a cantankerous
Tunisian Jewish grandmother who
constantly bemoaned her 34-year-
old daughter Fortunée's inability to
find a husband.

With some hesitation, Kakou
began a career in film in the middle
of the 1990s. His first role was as
high-strung couturier Rafi Styl'mode
alongside fellow Sephardic actors
Richard Anconina, Vincent Elbaz,
and Gilbert Melki in Thomas Gilou's
blockbuster *La Vérité si je mens /Would
I Lie to You?* (1997). Kakou played
supporting roles in two mediocre
comedies, first as a crime boss in
Graham Guit's *Les Kidnappeurs*
(1998), then as the sympathetic
police commissioner confronting
an overcrowded penitentiary system
in *Prison à domicile /House Arrest*
(Christophe Jacrot, 1999). Finally
with Olivier Schatzky's *Monsieur
Naphtali* (1999), Kakou earned a title
role. His Monsieur Napthali was an
outsider who refused to grow up and
holds on to his unique child-like
view of the world. When he arrives
in Paris, he changes all those around
him. While Kakou's performance
was applauded, the film faced
negative reactions from critics, such
as *Le Monde*'s Jacques Mandelbaum
who called the film a failed comic
remake of Pasolini's *Teorema /
Theorem* (1968). Not long after the
film's release, Kakou's career was cut
short by his tragic death resulting
from lung cancer.

Robert WATSON
Stetson University, Florida

Anna KARINA (1940–)
[Hanne Karin BAYER]

From
Denmark
with Love
—Her
Fabulous
Life and
Times

Anna Karina, born Hanne Karin Bayer on September 22, 1940 in Solbjerg, Denmark, began her career as a model, singer, and actress in commercials and short films. Her unstable childhood and rocky relationship with her mother led her to leave Denmark for Paris at the age of 17, where none other than Coco Chanel helped her change her name to Anna Karina.

Jean-Luc Godard spotted her in a Palmolive soap commercial, and offered her a role in *À bout de souffle /Breathless* (1960) which she turned down because it required nudity. None of this, however, stopped her from marrying Godard that same year.

The marriage would represent only one aspect of her fruitful collaboration with Godard. In 1961, Karina won the award for best actress at the Berlin Film Festival for her portrayal of Angela in Godard's *Une femme est une femme /A Woman is a Woman*. She would go on to feature prominently in Godard's work for several years, in such films as *Vivre sa vie /My Life to Live* (1962), *Le Petit Soldat /The Little Soldier* (1963), *Bande à part /Band of Outsiders* (1964), *Pierrot le fou* (1965), *Alphaville* (1965), and *Made in U.S.A.* (1966).

Karina's onscreen accomplishments as an actress were not limited to Godard's films, though. She appeared in Agnès Varda's groundbreaking *Cléo de 5 à 7 /Cleo from 5 to 7* (1962), Chris Marker's *Le Joli Mai* (1963), and Roger Vadim's *La Ronde /Circle of Love* (1964). She starred in Jacques Rivette's *La Religieuse /The Nun* (1966) and alongside Marcello Mastroianni in Visconti's *The Stranger* (1967), a film based on Camus's celebrated novel. Karina also acted under the direction of George Cukor, Rainer Werner Fassbinder, Raúl Ruiz, and Volker Schlöndorff. She co-starred with Anthony Quinn and Michael Caine in Guy Green's *The Magus* (1968). Karina herself directed and wrote *Vivre ensemble* (1973).

True to her roots as a cabaret singer, Karina appeared in a made-for-TV movie musical whose soundtrack was written by none other than Serge Gainsbourg, entitled *Anna* (1967), directed by Pierre Koralnik. Her renditions of *Sous le soleil exactement* and *Roller Girl* turned both songs into hits. Her musical career also includes a 1999 album recorded with Philippe Katerine, entitled *Une histoire d'amour*. She also sang in Jonathan Demme's film *The Truth About Charlie* (2002), a star-studded remake of Stanley Donen's *Charade* (1963).

Karina acted for the stage in such productions as *La Religieuse /The Nun*, by Denis Diderot, directed by Jacques Rivette (1966) and *After the Rehearsal* by Ingmar Bergman (1997). Karina has written four novels. Most recently, Karina appeared in Jacques Rivette's film *Up, Down, Fragile* (1995), and in *Victoria* (2008), which she wrote and directed.

Jonathan ROBBINS
Columbia University

Sandrine KIBERLAIN (1968–)
[Sandrine KIBERLAJN]

A (Gold)
Star
on the
Horizon

B ORN IN Boulogne-Billancourt,
Sandrine KIBERLAIN (birth-name
Kiberlajn – her four grandparents
were Polish Jews who relocated to
France in 1933 [1]) has appeared in
some fifty-six films since her acting
debut (an uncredited appearance in
Pierre Granier-Deferre's 1986 *Cours
privé*).

Her impressive career has earned
her seven César nominations (in
1995, 1996, 1997, 1998, 1999, 2010 and
2013); she was awarded the Most
Promising Actress (*Meilleur jeune
espoir féminin*) César for Laetitia
Masson's 1995 *En avoir (ou pas) /To
Have (or Not)* and in 2014 the Best
Actress César for Albert Dupontel's
9 mois ferme /Nine Month Stretch
(2013). In addition, Kiberlain has won
the Prix Romy Schneider (1995), the
Étoile d'argent in the Brussels Film
Festival (1995), two Molières (1997),
two Étoiles d'or (1999, 2001), and
prizes at the Montreal and Chicago
film festivals (both in 2001).

After receiving the baccalauréat,
Kiberlain entered the Cours
Florent from 1987 to 1989, then the
Conservatoire national supérieur
d'art dramatique from 1989 to 1992.

Her breakthrough came in 1990
when she played Sister Colette
in Jean-Paul Rappeneau's *Cyrano
de Bergerac*, though the next four
years saw her in mostly minor roles.
It was not until 1994 and Éric
Rochant's *Les Patriotes /The Patriots*
that her talent was truly recognized:
her performance as a call girl earned
her a nomination for the César for
Most Promising Actress, which she
won the following year for Masson's
first feature-length film *En avoir
(ou pas)*. The freckled blonde with
gauche appeal perfectly incarnated
the lovelorn Alice, searching for her
place in the world.

Since then, Kiberlain has
performed in such recognizable
roles as the eponymous Betty in
Claude Miller's *Betty Fisher et
autres histoires /Alias Betty* (2001);
Blanche Grimaldi, the patient ex-
girlfriend in Pierre Salvadori's
culinary comedy *Après vous* (2003);
the teacher in Laurent Tirard's *Le
Petit Nicolas* (2009); and the jealous
wife Suzanne Joubert in Philippe le
Guay's *Les Femmes du 6e étage /The
Women on the 6th Floor* (2010).

She has gained visibility on a
national scale with roles in theatrical
adaptations (Guitry's *Quadrille*,
Marivaux's *La Fausse Suivante*),
psychoanalytical character studies
(most notably the kleptomaniac
Mathilde in Benoît Jacquot's *Le
Septième Ciel /Seventh Heaven*,
1997). Her subtle charm and
sensitivity come through most
clearly perhaps in the title role of
Stéphane Brizé's quiet 2009 drama
Mademoiselle Chambon, about the
unlikely – and illicit – romance
between a schoolteacher and a shy

building contractor.

Kiberlain has more than one string in her instrument, however, as she is also a singer whose two albums have been well-received in France. Her first album, *Manquait plus qu'ça*, released in 2005, met with wide acclaim; her second, *Coupés bien net et bien carré*, was released in 2007. Her voice is clear and dry, a simple sound that may not win her a place in the musical halls of fame, but that works well with the instrumentation and production of her EMI team.

Her work in films has followed a distinct trajectory, one involving two prominent figures: director Laetitia Masson, and actor Vincent Lindon. Masson and a young Kiberlain developed a close friendship during the production of *En avoir (ou pas)*, and the director worked closely with her discovery for two more prominent roles, women on a certain identity quest (in *À vendre /For Sale*, 1998, then *Love Me*, 2000). As for Lindon, he featured alongside Kiberlain in *L'Irrésolu /The Indecisive Guy* (Jean-Pierre Ronssin, 1994), *Le Septième Ciel* (1997), *Filles uniques / Only Girls* (2003) and *Mademoiselle Chambon* (2007) – not to mention his starring role as Kiberlain's lover, husband (the couple married in 1998), and the father of her daughter, Suzanne. The couple divorced in October 2006.

Kiberlain does not practice the faith of her ancestors, but does not deny its importance in her identity and her upbringing. « Je sais d'où je viens. Je viens du froid, d'un endroit dont on nous a exclus » ['I know where I come from. I come from the cold, from a place where we were excluded'], she told an interviewer in 2007.[2] Still, when a talk-show host cites her 'Polish' origins, Kiberlain is quick to correct him: 'Jewish-Polish.' Like her characters, who tend toward the sharply self-deprecatory, Kiberlain carries her self-knowledge with her, both on and off the set.

Rosemary A. PETERS
Louisiana State University

1. In a 2009 *Paris Match* interview, the actress noted that her grandfather had 'Frenchified' the family name during the last war; however Kiberlajn is listed in her birth record at Boulogne-Billancourt. —Ed.

2. Luc Le Vaillant, 'La Passante du sans chichi,' *Libération*, April 27, 2013, accessed October 12, 2013, http://www.liberation.fr/portrait/2007/04/27/la-passante-du-sans-chichi_91562. —With author's translation.

Bernadette LAFONT (1938–2013)

*La
Fiancée
de la
Nouvelle
Vague*

SINCE MAKING her screen debut at age 19 in François Truffaut's short film *Les Mistons /The Mischief Makers* (1957) – opposite her then-husband Gérard Blain, as her lover – filmed in her hometown of Nîmes in southern France, Bernadette LAFONT had roles in over 120 films. She is associated with the auteurs and cinematic production of the French New Wave.[1] Lafont's impertinent spirit was noted by many directors, including Truffaut: 'The New Wave style was an impulsive one, of youthful insolence tinged with self-conscious theatricality, and Lafont had a natural gift for both, as seen in the treasure trove of movies that she sparked in the sixties and seventies.'[2] Michel Marie lists Lafont first in his discussion of New Wave actresses, stating that with her 'natural sensuality, her stunning smile, and her liveliness,' Lafont was 'the closest to a Renoir-inspired actress that the New Wave could generate' and 'the first real model of a New Wave woman.'[3] According to Ginette Vincendeau, Lafont 'occupied a specific niche in the New Wave female galaxy, against Jeanne Moreau and Emmanuelle Riva's cerebral heroines on the one hand and Jean Seberg and Anna Karina's Godardian gamines on the other.'[4]

Lafont was cast in a leading role in what is often considered the first New Wave film, Claude Chabrol's directorial debut, *Le Beau Serge /Handsome Serge* (1958). Here, Lafont incarnates Marie, bent on seducing François (Jean-Claude Brialy), who has just returned to his home village and is devastated by his best friend Serge's (Blain) downward spiral into alcoholism. In Chabrol's 1960 *Les Bonnes Femmes /The Good-Time Girls*, Lafont is Jane, a Parisian shopgirl who enjoys singlehood: staying out all night with male strangers, yet seeing another man during the day. In this brutal single-girl-in-the-city narrative, Lafont embodies the 'good time girl' as alluded to by the film's title in its English translation, whereas her co-worker, the soulful Jacqueline (Clotilde Joano) succumbs to her bad luck at the hands of a motorcyclist drifter who preys upon gullible women. Along with *Le Beau Serge* and *Les Bonnes Femmes*, Lafont collaborated with Chabrol on several films, including his first thriller, *À double tour /Leda* (1959), as a maid named Julie who flaunts her half-naked body in front of an open window in the initial scene (in Jacques Doniol-Valcroze's 1960 *L'Eau à la bouche /A Game for Six Lovers*, Lafont was again cast as a maid); in the 1961 revenge tale *Les Godelureaux / Wise Guys*, she is Ambroisine who is sent by Roger (Brialy) to seduce a man who had publicly humiliated him; in *Violette Nozière* (1978), she is the prison cellmate of Violette (Isabelle Huppert in her César-nominated turn), and she is two-time widow Hélène Mons in *L'Inspecteur Lavardin* (1986), the second Chabrol film to feature Jean Poiret as the titular investigator, one year after his first appearance in *Poulet au vinaigre / Chicken with Vinegar* (1985).

More than ten years after *Les Mistons*,

Truffaut cast Lafont as Camille, the manipulative and seductive murderess in the black comedy *Une belle fille comme moi /Such a Gorgeous Kid Like Me* (1972). Camille fancies becoming a musical comedy *chanteuse*: she introduces herself as such, stating « je suis chanteuse ». ['I am a singer.'] In this film, 'Lafont's exuberant embodiment of gleeful feminine ferocity cuts cleverly against Truffaut's grim vision of a world that both represses and craves it.'[5]

In Jean Eustache's controversial and critically acclaimed *La Maman et la Putain /The Mother and the Whore* (1973), a *ménage-à-trois* exploring sexual freedom, Lafont portrays Marie, the film's titular *maman*, a boutique owner who supports her younger live-in boyfriend Alexandre (Jean-Pierre Léaud), who simultaneously pursues Veronika (Françoise Lebrun). Rather than incarnating 'the sassy working-class woman' in *La Maman et la Putain*, Lafont 'winds up an exploited and victimized older woman…a climactic shot focuses on a bereft Marie as she listens to a lovely Édith Piaf song, *Les Amants de Paris*.'[6] Previously, Lafont shared screentime with Léaud in *Out 1, noli me tangere* (1971), Jacques Rivette's 'nearly thirteen-hour, quasi-improvised Balzacian extravaganza,'[7] inspired by *La Comédie humaine* (especially the stories in *Histoire des Treize /The History of the Thirteen*) as well as the shortened (225-minute) version, *Out 1 : Spectre*, released in 1974.

Lafont's knowing coquettishness and irreverence – expressed through her tousled dark mane, unmistakable wide grin, and loud, high pitched laughter – lasted from her days as an ingénue to her later years. In Chabrol's 1987 *Masques*, she forms part of the entourage of game show host Christian Legagneur (Philippe Noiret), who hides his nefariousness under a mask of congeniality toward elderly contestants on his 'love connection' type programme as well as toward his ailing goddaughter. Lafont, as Patricia, a masseuse who claims to be a fortune teller, is as flirtatious as ever – giggling like a young girl, even though she is a married, middle-aged woman – especially toward handsome young Roland Wolf (Robin Renucci), hired to write Legagneur's biography. But Roland hides an ulterior motive, which is uncovering Legagneur's misdeeds and then exposing them.

Divorced from Blain in 1959, Lafont married Hungarian artist/film director Diourka Medveczky. They had a son, David, and two daughters, Elisabeth and Pauline, both actresses. In 1988, Pauline, at age 25, died during a hiking accident. Lafont, understandably devastated, found comfort in her work.

Highlights of Lafont's recent filmography include the romantic comedy *Prête-moi ta main /I Do: How to Get Married and Stay Single* (Eric Lartigau, 2006), winner of the NRJ Ciné Award for Best Comedy, in which Lafont is Geneviève Costa, a widowed matriarch heading a large family almost entirely made up of women. With her pet pug in tow, surrounded by her married daughters, Geneviève is so determined to marry off her only son, bachelor Luis (Alain Chabat) to Emma (Charlotte Gainsbourg), that when the wedding plans collapse, she ends up in the hospital. Lafont was nominated for a Best Supporting Actress César for this role. She lent her voice to Jean-Loup Felicioli and Alain Gagnol's Oscar-nominated animated film *Une vie de chat /A Cat in Paris* (2010), as the duplicitous

Claudine. Claudine poses as a nanny, but in fact is a dangerous con artist/member of a criminal gang who has infiltrated the home of her intended victim. In 2012, Lafont starred as a marijuana-selling grandmother, the titular figure of the box office hit *Paulette* (dir. Jérôme Enrico).

Lafont was awarded the César for Best Supporting Actress in 1986, for her performance opposite Charlotte Gainsbourg – who herself won the César for Most Promising Actress – in *L'Effrontée /An Impudent Girl*, Claude Miller's 1985 coming of age tale. *Waiting for the Moon* (Jill Godmilow, 1987), a historical fiction about Gertrude Stein and Alice B. Toklas, in which Lafont is Picasso's lover/model Fernande Olivier, won the Sundance Film Festival Grand Jury Prize. Along with her Best Supporting Actress César, for her contributions to French cinematic culture, Lafont received a lifetime achievement César in 2003. In 2009, she became an *Officier* of the French *Légion d'honneur*. André Labarthe commemorated the 50th anniversary of Lafont's film career with his 2007 cinematic 'portrait' of her, the documentary *Bernadette Lafont, exactement*, which was broadcast on France 3 television.

Lafont's passing on July 25, 2013 at age 74 was commemorated by an outpouring of media tributes emphasizing how she was an iconic figure of the French New Wave, as well as commemorated her lengthy career in which she worked with major actors and directors in French and international cinema, including roles in films by, among others, Costa-Gavras (*Compartiment tueurs /The Sleeping Car Murders*, 1965); Louis Malle (*Le Voleur / The Thief of Paris*, 1967); as one of three characters, the mother of the child, in Philippe Garrel's silent, black and white

Le Révélateur (1968); as 'the spitefully avenging heroine' [8] of Nelly Kaplan's 1969 debut film, *La Fiancée du pirate /A Very Curious Girl*, 'a comic critique of masculinity in which Lafont's Marie uses her sexuality as a weapon to take revenge on the men who humiliated her mother,' a role which 'marked Lafont deeply to the point that she entitled her 1978 autobiography *La Fiancée du cinéma*'.[9] Also with Jacques Rivette (*Noroît*, 1978); Raul Rúiz (*Généalogies d'un crime / Genealogies of a Crime*, 1997), and Julie Delpy (*Le Skylab*, 2011). Despite her long and versatile acting career lasting more than five decades, Lafont's funeral, held in a village in the Gard near her hometown of Nîmes, was not an elaborate media event, nor was she buried in Père Lachaise Cemetery in Paris as are so many of her fellow celebrities, but rather, she was interred close to the place of her birth. Indeed, rather than portraying cold and sophisticated *parisiennes*, Lafont was a southern woman at heart, exuding 'a sunny screen presence, inimitable voice, and warm personality' [10] and 'during the 1950s, Lafont...offered a more modern image of the young southern French woman who is comfortable with her full figure, as well as natural, spontaneous, and populist.' [11]

One of the only members of the film community present at her funeral was cinéaste Jean-Pierre Mocky, who directed Lafont on several occasions. Mocky denounced the lack of cinema colleagues in attendance: « Si peu de monde pour son enterrement, c'est dégueulasse. Même si Bernadette était quelqu'un de solitaire et indépendant, le cinéma devait être là. Or, même pas l'équipe de son dernier succès *Paulette* n'est venue. Quand on pense aux foules qu'il y a eu pour l'enterrement de Brialy, sans parler de celui de Raimu. » ['So few people at her funeral, it's disgusting. Even if Bernadette was a solitary and independent person, the film industry should have been there. Not even the team from her last success, *Paulette*, showed up. When we think of the crowds that were there for the funeral of Brialy, not to mention that of Raimu.'] [12] Yet Mocky suggests that perhaps this low turnout at the funeral is due to the fact that Lafont had the misfortune to die at the end of July, during the French *grandes vacances* period when most people are unavailable as they are away on vacation. This is a rather flimsy excuse, however, as one cannot imagine anything, no matter what the season – *neither snow nor rain nor heat nor gloom of night*, as the saying goes – preventing crowds of film colleagues and hordes of loyal fans from gathering to pay tribute at a funeral for a household name celebrity such as Brigitte Bardot, Catherine Deneuve, or Jeanne Moreau. Lafont has not become an international celebrity at their level, despite Carnegie Hall presenting 'A Tribute to Bernadette Lafont' over two days in November 1977.

Bardot, Deneuve, and Moreau are arguably more solidly ensconced than Lafont within the French cinematic/ cultural landscape and collective unconscious, each occupying a recognizable and stable onscreen persona: Bardot, *la femme enfant* and eternal sex symbol; Deneuve, whose career followed a stable trajectory, growing into and remaining in her icy blonde beauty persona starting with *Les Parapluies de Cherbourg /The Umbrellas of Cherbourg* (Jacques Demy, 1964), and Moreau, the *femme fatale* of Truffaut's *Jules et Jim* (1962) and *La Mariée était en noir /The Bride Wore Black* (1968). Lafont perhaps suffered from overexposure, and might even be taken somewhat for granted, due to having worked in so many films and taken on so many types of roles – an intersection of the highbrow and the low: secondary characters, works of popular cinema, made-for-television movies as well as TV series alongside groundbreaking experimental and New Wave auteur films (all told, she has nearly 200 film and television credits to her name, not counting theatrical performances). Compared with some of her contemporary French female film stars such as Bardot, Deneuve, and Moreau, discussed above, Lafont does not have as fixed nor immediately recognizable an onscreen identity or persona; rather, she tends to elude codification/classification, and for that reason, she is somewhat neglected and perhaps less remembered, as evidenced by the lack of fanfare surrounding her funeral, although upon her passing, she was commemorated by major news outlets the world over, including an obituary in the *New York Times*. The Nîmes Theatre will be named after her in homage, a most fitting tribute, as Nîmes is where Lafont began her life, onscreen and off: the place of her birth and the start of her cinematic career with Truffaut's *Les Mistons* filmed on location there.

Lafont was set to play Nicolas' grandmother in Laurent Tirard's 2014 *Les Vacances du petit Nicolas*, but after her death, she was replaced by Dominique Lavanant. Lafont's final role is as one of the mute protagonist's (Guillaume Gouix) elderly aunts in *Attila Marcel*, Sylvain Chomet's first live action film. Released after Lafont's death, *Attila Marcel*'s world premiere was at a special presentation screening at the Toronto International Film Festival in September 2013.

Marcelline BLOCK
Princeton University and SAG-AFTRA

1. The phrase « *La Fiancée de la nouvelle vague* » is from André Labarthe's 2007 documentary film, *Bernadette Lafont, exactement* (shown on France 3 television), http://www.vodeo.tv/documentaire/bernadette-lafont-exactement.

2. Richard Brody, *The Mother and the Whore* Revisited, the *New Yorker*, July 30, 2013, accessed October 5, 2013, http://www.newyorker.com/online/blogs/movies/2013/07/the-mother-and-the-whore-revisited.html.

3. Michel Marie, *The French New Wave: An Artistic School*, trans. Richard Neuport (Malden, MA: Blackwell Publishing, 2003), 121.

4. Ginette Vincendeau, 'Bernadette Lafont, 1938-2013,' *Sight and Sound*, July 30, 2013, accessed October 3, 2013, http://www.bfi.org.uk/news-opinion/sight-sound-magazine/comment/obituaries/bernadette-lafont-1938-2013.

5. Richard Brody, 'DVR Alert: *Such a Gorgeous Kid Like Me*,' the *New Yorker*, July 12, 2013, accessed October 2, 2013, http://www.newyorker.com/online/blogs/movies/2013/07/dvr-alert-such-a-gorgeous-kid-like-me.html.

6. Jonathan Rosenbaum, '*The Way We Are (THE MOTHER AND THE WHORE)*,' January 22, 1999, accessed October 3, 2013, http://www.jonathanrosenbaum.com/?p=6507.

7. Brody, '*The Mother and the Whore* Revisited.'

8. Rosenbaum, '*The Way We Are.*'

9. Vincendeau, 'Bernadette Lafont.' Bernadette Lafont with Alain Lacombe, *La Fiancée du cinéma* (Paris: O. Oroban, 1978).

10. Vincendeau, 'Bernadette Lafont.'

11. Marie, *The French New Wave*, 121.

12. 'Jean-Pierre Mocky à propos des obsèques de Bernadette Lafont : 'C'est dégueulasse !', *Première*, July 31, 2013, accessed October 4, 2013, http://people.premiere.fr/News-People/Jean-Pierre-Mocky-a-propos-des-obseques-de-Bernadette-Lafont-C-est-degueulasse-3810908. [Translation mine.]

Christophe LAMBERT (1957–)

From Tarzan to Tartan

CHRISTOPHE LAMBERT was born on Long Island, New York in 1957, but grew up in Geneva, where his family moved in 1959. Having headed to Paris at sixteen to pursue a career in film, he was persuaded by his parents into brief sojourns in the French military and the London Stock Exchange, but soon returned to acting.

Lambert played roles in a handful of French productions in the late 1970s and early 1980s (his debut was in Sergio Gobbi's *Ciao, les mecs /Ciao, You Guys* (1979), playing an unnamed hooligan), but he has his 'introductory' credit on a British film: Hugh Hudson's reverent *Greystoke: The Legend of Tarzan, Lord of the Apes* (1984). Cast as Tarzan – although the character is never named as such outside of film's title – Lambert's accent is explained, in a detail consistent with Edgar Rice Burroughs' 1912 novel, as due to having learned English from a French naval officer. The film was nominated for several writing and technical awards, with Lambert's highly physical performance as a lithe and sinuous ape-man, in stark contrast to the musclemen of previous incarnations, also drawing positive critical attention. Ironically, the 'intense gaze' so admired by casting director Patsy Pollock was attributable to the actor's acute myopia. His subsequent career as an action star often saw him, forced for safety reasons to work without contact lenses, fighting practically blind.

Initially turning down further English-speaking parts, Lambert returned to France, appearing in Élie Chouraqui's *Paroles et musique / Love Songs* (1984) alongside Catherine Deneuve, and in Luc Besson's *Subway* (1985), with Isabelle Adjani. The latter, in which Lambert plays the shock-headed Fred, dodging cops and gangsters in the Paris Métro, formed part of the vanguard of the so-called *Cinéma du look*, achieving the third-highest box office gross in France during its year of release, and securing Lambert a César award for best actor (as well as an iconic and enduring poster image, in which he brandishes a neon light).[1]

Lambert's next film and his return to non-francophone cinema, was *Highlander* (Russell Mulcahy, 1986). Connor McLeod, part of a race of sword-fighting immortals, battling over centuries for the final 'prize' of ultimate knowledge, would prove to be Lambert's signature role, despite his eccentric casting as a Scotsman (his Scottish co-star Sean Connery, meanwhile, plays an Egyptian recently relocated from Spain). The film's director, Russell Mulcahy, recalls choosing Lambert solely on the basis of a photograph in a magazine (that intense Tarzan stare again), and only discovered the language barrier once the contracts had been signed. Against these apparent odds however, Lambert proved to be essential to the film's success. Re-cut and then buried by studio Fox in the US, with a patchy release and non-existent marketing, Lambert's presence in the film, post-*Subway*, ensured that it was nevertheless an enormous hit in France and the rest of Europe, leading to a long-running franchise.

Comedies, dramas, and romances in the US, France, and Italy followed over the next five years, including Michael Cimino's *The Sicilian* (1987). But it was *Highlander* that sealed Lambert's screen presence as predominantly an action star for the next two decades. *Highlander II: The Quickening* (Mulcahy, 1991) was an expensive disaster, filmed in Argentina as the country's currency collapsed, and 'ret-conning' the immortals as having come from space (subsequent alternate cuts of the film have been re-edited and re-dubbed to pretend this never happened). *Highlander III* (Andrew Morahan, 1994; variously subtitled *The Final Dimension*, *The Final Conflict*, and *The Sorcerer*) ignored its predecessor completely, and *Highlander: Endgame* (Douglas Aarniokoski, 2000) merged the films' dubious continuity with that of the spin-off TV series. Lambert returned as McLeod for all three films, finally passing the franchise torch to Adrian Paul in *Endgame* (he had also appeared alongside Paul in the TV series' pilot episode in 1992).

In between *Highlander* films, Lambert starred in the sci-fi prison thrillers *Fortress* (Stuart Gordon, 1992) and *Fortress 2* (Geoff Murphy, 2000); Deran Serafian's action films *Gunmen* (1993, with subsequent *Highlander III* co-star Mario Van Peebles) and *Roadflower* (1994); Paul Anderson's videogame adaptation *Mortal Kombat* (1995, as the white-robed thunder god Lord Rayden); Albert Pyun's *Adrenalin: Fear the Rush* (1996) and *Mean Guns* (1997, with Ice-T); Graham Baker's odd futuristic version of *Beowulf* (1999); the critically-mauled historical epic *Vercingétorix /The Gaul* (Jacques Dorfmann, 2001); and frequent James Bond director John Glen's *The*

Point Men (2001), among many similar, often direct-to-video projects. He has also often served as a producer, beginning with *Génial, mes parents divorcent !* (Patrick Braoudé, 1991), and has a story credit on *Resurrection* (Mulcahy, 1999).

Lambert at one point seemed resigned to his action-centric casting niche – he suggested it was appropriate to his, in his own words, 'limited' acting ability – but recent years have seen him moving towards more taxing roles in independent and arthouse films, a gradual process he attributes both to aging and to financial independence from his business interests. *Donnie Darko* director Richard Kelly cast him as an anarchist arms dealer in his garbled *Southland Tales* (2006), and Lambert led the introspective *Le Lièvre de Vatanen / Vatanen's Hare* (Marc Rivière, 2006), based on a novel by Arto Paasilinna. But it was Claire Denis' *White Material* (2009) that brought Lambert some of the best notices of his career to date, for his sensitive portrayal of the fragile André, husband to Isabelle Huppert's Maria, struggling on an African coffee plantation in the shadow of imminent civil war.

Most recently though, Lambert was wielding a sword once again for the Marvel property *Ghost Rider: Spirit of Vengeance* (Mark Neveldine and Brian Taylor, 2011), and was seen in the drama *Ma Bonne Étoile /My Lucky Star* (Anne Fassio, 2012). The arthouse may beckon, but it seems that the cult end of mainstream will remain a comfortable retreat.

Owen WILLIAMS
Journalist, Southampton

1. For further discussion of *Subway*, see Marcelline Block, ed., *World Film Locations: Paris* (Bristol: Intellect, 2011), 62-63. —Ed.

Jean-Pierre LÉAUD (1944–)

L'Enfant terrible, and Darling of the French New Wave

SON OF actress Jacqueline Pierreux and scriptwriter and assistant director Pierre LÉAUD, Jean-Pierre Léaud (born 5th May 1944, Paris) remains one of film history's most enduring icons. Scenes of a triumphant François Truffaut alongside a 15-year-old Léaud being carried aloft at the 1959 Cannes Film Festival on the success of *Les Quatre Cents Coups /The 400 Blows* (1959), were to encapsulate his eternal 'adolescent' figure – the child of modern French cinema was born.

Most well-known as Truffaut's *acteur fétiche* and the semi-autobiographical role of Antoine Doinel, Léaud's body of work equally extends to collaborations with other acclaimed directors as diverse as Bernardo Bertolucci, Jean Eustache, Philippe Garrel, Jean-Luc Godard, Aki Kaurismäki, Serge Le Péron, Pier Paolo Pasolini, Jacques Rivette, Jerzy Skolimowski, and Tsai Ming-liang.

Léaud's unique performance style incorporates a rich visual vocabulary – his glazed look, uncompromising stare, flick of the hair, frenzied gestures, spontaneous outbursts of laughter, and manic protestations over love and life. There is something inherently anachronistic about Léaud – the symbol of a generation, representative of youth in 1960s France amid a changing socio-political climate. Thus his star image came to embody the French New Wave myth, portraying somewhat marginal characters that were troubled and vulnerable, clumsy with women, and tinged with a sense of melancholy.

Having already had a taste of the cinema at a very young age, appearing briefly in Marcello Pagliero's *Un homme marche dans la ville /A Man Walks in the City* (1950), Léaud's first major screen role was as Pierrot in Georges Lampin's *La Tour, prends garde ! /King on Horseback* (1958), alongside Jean Marais. And then came *Les Quatre Cents Coups* which, along with the Doinel character, would leave its indelible mark on cinema. With the birth of Doinel, Léaud found himself growing up on screen in tandem with Doinel, whilst becoming a kind of alter-ego of Truffaut himself, born into a cinematic lineage at the heart of the construction of the French New Wave. Truffaut became a father figure for Léaud, just as André Bazin had been for Truffaut. Indeed Léaud has often referred to Truffaut as his 'father' and Jean-Luc Godard as his 'uncle.'

Les Quatre Cents Coups follows the plight of its young protagonist, Antoine Doinel – neglected at home and rebelling against authority, Antoine seeks solace in his love of literature, his close friendship with René, and in the city of Paris itself. Truffaut's subsequent Doinel films saw Léaud in a short segment in *L'Amour à vingt ans /Love at 20* (1962) in which Antoine becomes infatuated with the beautiful, yet indifferent, Colette (Marie-France Pisier); *Baisers volés /Stolen Kisses* (1968) as Antoine enters married life; *Domicile conjugal /Bed and Board* (1970) with the birth of his child and his continued confusions over love and women, and *L'Amour en fuite /Love on the Run* (1979) with the now divorced Doinel in a new relationship, and a published author. Léaud also starred in Truffaut's *La Nuit américaine / Day for Night* (1973) – an ode to the seventh art – and the literary adaptation *Les Deux Anglaises et le continent /Two English Girls* (1971).

Whilst Léaud may be most well known for his role as Doinel, his eternal *soixante-huitard* image was equally formed through other films of the 1960s and early 1970s. Jean-Luc Godard's *Masculin féminin* (1966), *La Chinoise* (1967), and *Le Gai Savoir / Joy of Learning* (1969) saw Léaud perpetuate an image of vulnerable male and adorer of women, politically motivated, and passionate about literature. Parallels with literature are none more pronounced than in Marcel Cravenne's adaptation of Flaubert's *L'Education sentimentale* (1973) as a TV mini-series, with Léaud as the lovelorn Frédéric Moreau, the quintessential literary (anti)hero.

Léaud began his collaboration with Jean Eustache as Daniel in *Le Père Noël a les yeux bleus /Santa Claus has Blue Eyes* (1962) before what would arguably become the pivotal role of his career: a Doinel-like character and extension of Daniel who had matured during the politically charged years of the 1960s, incarnated by an increasingly politically motivated Léaud. Alexandre in *La Maman et la Putain /The Mother and the Whore* (Jean Eustache, 1973) embodied Godard's so-called 'generation of Marx and Coca-Cola' that had come of age post-May 1968. The French New Wave icon, eternal *soixante-huitard*, and voyeur and adorer of women were all captured at once within this very role. Alexandre seemingly does nothing other than while away time with his friend, creating anecdotes out of everyday moments replete with cinematic references, cursory observations, and wild declarations of love – an ultimate *flâneur*.

Melancholic undertones run through many of Léaud's characters, and he too was himself touched personally by tragedy. In 1981, Jean Eustache committed suicide, and in 1984, François Truffaut suffered an untimely death, leaving Léaud an orphan from his cinematic family. Léaud's career subsequently took a downturn with few roles of note other than Godard's *Détective* (1985).

Léaud's career saw a revival in the mid 1990s, with several roles recalling his *soixante-huitard* image, notably in Bernardo Bertolucci's *The Dreamers* (2002) in which he played himself intercut with archive footage of himself from 1968, and as François Marcorelle in Serge le Péron's *L'Affaire Marcorelle /The Marcorelle Affair* (2000). Léaud was awarded the César d'honneur in 2000, whilst over the last decade he has continued to work with such directors as Aki Kaurismäki, Serge Le Péron, and Tsai Ming-liang.

Perhaps what is most striking about Léaud is the way in which his star image is intrinsically linked to cinema itself – playing the role of a film director or actor (*La Nuit américaine* ; *Last Tango in Paris*, Bernardo Bertolucci, 1972; *Irma Vep*, Olivier Assayas, 1996; *Le Pornographe /The Pornographer*, Bertrand Bonello, 2001), or simply himself (*Et là-bas quelle heure est-il ? /What Time is it Over There?*, Tsai Ming-liang, 2000; *The Dreamers*). In *Les Quatre Cents Coups*, the cinema was represented as a place of refuge and a symbol of rebellion, somewhat pre-empting Léaud's life in the cinema. The freeze-frame at the end of *Les Quatre Cents Coups*, an image at once bleak and full of hope, is inscribed in the memory of almost every cinephile. As Tsai Ming-liang himself once said of Léaud, his face is almost more than a cinematic experience in itself.

Sonali JOSHI
Film Curator, London

Madeleine LEBEAU (1923–)

*La Belle
Lebeau*

MARIE-MADELEINE BERTHE LEBEAU was barely sixteen when she wed divorced actor Marcel Dalio – more than twice her age – in 1939. They fled together to the US from France in 1940, and both appeared in Michael Curtiz's 1942 film *Casablanca*, which was made in Hollywood. During the filming, however, Dalio (who plays Emil the croupier) filed for divorce, which was granted in California in June 1943.

Lebeau, born on June 10, 1923, in the commune of Antony [1] (south of Paris), acted in stage productions in Paris and was featured in over thirty films in Hollywood and Europe. Yet she is best remembered for her performance as Yvonne in the iconic *Casablanca*, ranked at the top of the American Film Institute's list of the '100 Greatest American Films of All Time': #2 in 1998, and #3 in 2007. Not only does the Academy-award-winning *Casablanca* contain and represent much of the pathos of the World War II era, but it also held personal significance for Dalio and Lebeau, whose exile from France resembles that of many of the film's characters. Since Dalio was Jewish, he and Lebeau had to flee their homeland in 1940. The couple followed a circuitous path similar to that taken

by countless refugees 'en route from Paris to Marseilles and from Marseilles across the Mediterranean, to the shores of North Africa' [2] as described in *Casablanca*'s opening voiceover. Dalio and Lebeau's desperate journey took them from France to Hollywood via Portugal, Mexico (where their Chilean visas we found to be forgeries), and Canada. *Casablanca*'s production notes from Warner Bros Studio state that Lebeau's participation in the film 'graphically parallels her own harrowing flight to America.' [3] In Lebeau's own words, 'we were somewhat like those poor unfortunate refugees in *Casablanca*. We tried in every way we knew to get to America.' [4]

In *Casablanca*, Lebeau's character Yvonne is left brokenhearted by Rick Blaine (Humphrey Bogart), and later consoles herself with a German soldier. Lebeau is featured in one of the film's most memorable scenes: at Rick's Café Américain, while the Nazi patrons sing the anthem *Lieb' Vaterland...*, Czech resistance leader Victor Laszlo (Paul Henreid) disrupts them by having the café's musicians play the French national anthem. *La Marseillaise* ('a sound cue for an absent map of France,' according to Tom Conley [5]) generates so much excitement among the café's clients that their voices drown out the Nazis' singing, ultimately silencing them.

Yvonne sings *La Marseillaise* with raw emotion, shedding tears, and concluding passionately with cries of « Vive la France ! » and « Vive la démocratie ! ». Lebeau's performance reflects her own exile, since, together with her husband, she was stranded far away from friends and family suffering during France's Occupation (including her younger brother who went missing after attempting to join the Free French). Thus there is a convergence of the actress Lebeau with her character Yvonne: both lament their native country, their defeated *patrie*. Lebeau's unforgettable turn in this scene has left a powerful impression upon generations of film spectators, and continues to resonate with the viewing public: at *Casablanca*'s 60th anniversary screening held at Lincoln Center in New York City in 2003, 'the audience erupted into applause' for Lebeau.[6]

In 1988, Lebeau married Italian screenwriter Tullio Pinelli, whose credits include Federico Fellini's *8 ½* (1963), in which Lebeau plays a French actress, also named Madeleine. Pinelli and Lebeau remained together until his death in 2009. When Madeleine Lebeau celebrated her 91st birthday in 2014, she had outlived all other credited cast members of *Casablanca*.[7]

Marcelline BLOCK
Princeton University and SAG-AFTRA

1. Lebeau's sister, Marie-Thérèse Ernestine Lebeau (1921-1981), was born in Bourg-La-Reine in the southern suburbs of Paris in February 1921; as both sisters were actresses, they are occasionally mistaken for one another.
2. Tom Conley, 'A Writer and His Movie,' afterword to Marc Augé, *Casablanca*, trans. (University of Minnesota Press, 2009), 91.
3. *Casablanca*, Special Edition DVD (Warner Home Video), released August 5, 2003, disc 2, 'Production Research' feature.
4. *Biography of Madeleine Le Beau [sic]*, Harry Bond, Director of Publicity, 20th Century Fox Studios, Hollywood, p. 3 (archived at the Academy of Motion Picture Arts and Sciences' Margaret Herrick Library, Los Angeles).
5. Tom Conley, *Cartographic Cinema* (University of Minnesota Press, 2007), 95.
6. Liz Smith, *New York Post*, August 27, 2003.
7. Her name is written as 'LEBEAU' in the film's credits.

Fernand LEDOUX (1897–1993)

Not
So
Sweet?

B ELGIAN-BORN, FERNAND LEDOUX was a recognisable stalwart of French cinema for four decades, an actor of great sensitivity and range who was a comfortably reassuring presence across an assortment of genres and styles, film fads, and fashions. Alongside his career in film (which began in 1918, in the short *La Faute d'orthographe* directed by his compatriot Jacques Feyder, followed by Feyder's 1921 feature *L'Atlantide /Missing Husbands* or *Lost Atlantis*), Ledoux was contracted at the Comédie-Française, working prolifically there from the early 1920s through to the 1950s. Ledoux was part of a troupe of actors who worked on stage and screen (Pierre Blanchar, Edwige Feuillère, Pierre Fresnay, and Pierre Renoir). Stentorian is often the word associated with him; extremely loud, often declamatory, rarely 'the sweet one' (*le doux*). 'Theatrical,' perhaps, but not in a retrograde, *cinéma de papa* way. Rather, theatrical in the sense that he brought truthfulness, stillness, and often sudden bursts of anger or rage from within a seemingly calm, collected exterior. While the Big Stars of this period, like Jean Gabin, Louis Jouvet, or Raimu often took the plaudits,

Ledoux was frequently their co-star, generously providing these actors with their necessary performance space and freedom. *Remorques /Stormy Waters* (Jean Grémillon, 1941) would be a poorer film without Ledoux's amiable quartermaster, no matter the humming masculinity of Gabin, while *Untel père et fils /The Heart of a Nation* (Julien Duvivier, 1943), for all of its star cast, relies on Ledoux's quieter, less showy turn as the mayor. He is the very definition of a 'character actor' – solid, reliable, a team player.

Ledoux's most memorable role was that of the stationmaster Roubaud in Jean Renoir's 1938 adaptation of Emile Zola's *La Bête humaine*. When Roubaud discovers that his wife Séverine (Simone Simon) has been seduced by her godfather Grandmorin, the jealous Roubaud murders Grandmorin on a train. The murder scene is grim and macabre, but you cannot take your eyes off Ledoux: rage, fury, but also, ultimately, impotence. Rarely has jealousy resulted in such a tragic sense of unfulfilment and moral emptiness, and Ledoux's slumped, slouching frame captures this perfectly. Ledoux's patrician nature was put to good use in the role of Baron Hugues in Marcel Carné's *Les Visiteurs du soir /The Devil's Envoys* (1942). That lingering sense of impotence in *La Bête humaine*, that sense that unseen class structures were determining the fates and fortunes of ordinary working Le Havre men, resonates in Carné's film. *Les Visiteurs du soir* is set in medieval France, and Ledoux's Hugues is forever piously devoted to the picture of his dead wife Berthe. He lives in the past, and is easily manipulated by Jules Berry's

Devil to kill his future son-in-law in a joust. Once again, forces beyond his control seem to dictate Ledoux's behaviour. Did directors like Carné and Renoir see in Ledoux's external vigour a vulnerability that could be easily corrupted or weakened? Later on, he is easily seduced by Arletty, and eventually gives into her totally, abdicating all power and responsibility: 'My life belongs to you now. Wherever you go, I will go.'

Ledoux worked steadily throughout the Occupation, and was a familiar face in many a melodrama, costume drama, and *film noir*. Not many actors can boast collaborations with such formidable directors as Jacques Becker, Christian-Jaque, and Julien Duvivier. Each turned to Ledoux during the early 1940s, and he was often the default choice whenever a role required physical heft and authority. Big roles in smaller films also followed, like his jealous jailor in the prison film *Le Lit à colonnes* (Roland Tual, 1942), or his Prince Charming *manqué* in Henri Decoin's *Premier rendez-vous /Her First Affair* (1941), seeking to 'seduce' the young Danielle Darrieux through a series of anonymous letters. Indeed, as has often been noted, Ledoux stepped up from supporting roles in the 1930s to a position of pre-eminence during the Occupation. He starred in nearly a dozen films in this period, playing paternal roles (whether actual fathers, father figures, or substitute fathers).

His professionalism, adaptability, and reliability allowed him to continue to work constantly with some of France's emerging and established directors in the post-war era: for Jules Dassin in *Celui qui doit mourir*

/He Who Must Die (1957), for Henri-Georges Clouzot in La Vérité /The Truth (1960), and for Claude Chabrol, as the old doctor in Alice ou la dernière fugue /Alice or the Last Escapade (1977). There were lighter roles too, to offset the darker strains of his earlier work. A particular gem was Roger Richebé's Monseigneur /Monsignor (1949), in which Ledoux's historian passes off Bertrand Blier as a descendant of Louis XVI to a rich duchess. It is a wonder Hollywood has not remade this delightful romantic comedy, with its lightness of touch and bright, breezy mise en scène. Add to this a number of telefilms and documentary voiceovers, and Ledoux was rarely out of work. He even starred in two versions of Les Misérables: first as Monseigneur Myriel for Jean-Paul Le Chanois in 1958, and then as Gillenormand in the 1982 Robert Hossein version. 1962 was an important year in Ledoux's filmography: he played the court clerk in Orson Welles' version of The Trial, a minor role in The Longest Day, and plays neurologist Jean-Martin Charcot alongside Montgomery Clift's Freud in John Huston's Freud, The Secret Passion. The scene in which Ledoux uses hypnosis to transfer the symptoms of one patient to another was particularly shocking for audiences only gradually becoming acquainted with psychoanalysis.

No one would have expected to see Ledoux as the Red King in Jacques Demy's fairytale musical romance Peau d'âne /Donkey Skin (1970), but there he was, alongside Catherine Deneuve and Delphine Seyrig, a regal presence in a land of fairies, queens, and princesses. At over 2 million spectators, the film was one of Ledoux's most successful.

He eventually slowed down, returning more and more to the stage, and directing Molière, Shakespeare, and Pirandello. The great left-wing film critic, Georges Sadoul, describes Ledoux in La Bête humaine as follows: 'he reveals himself to be one of the screen's greatest tragedians…bitter, tortured, vindictive, and pitiful.' That word 'tragedian' once again conjures up the theatre, death-bed scenes, and characters with fatal flaws. Ledoux's film performances often traded in this doomed register, but occasionally, in films like Goupi mains rouges /It Happened at the Inn (Jacques Becker, 1943), glint of subversiveness and black humour, or distraught lyricism of Pattes blanches /White Paws (Jean Grémillon, 1949) would emerge, and show Ledoux in the sweetest of lights.

Ben McCann
The University of Adelaide, Australia

Virginie LEDOYEN (1976–)
[Virginie FERNANDEZ]

*The
Daring
Ingénue*

WHEN thirteen-year-old Virginie Ledoyen (born on 15th September 1976, in Paris) was cast in *Mima* (Philomène Esposito, 1990), she was already an experienced performer, having appeared in several publicity spots since the age of two. A young Ledoyen plays Mima, an immigrant girl living in Sète, who, after having witnessed the murder of her Italian grandfather by the Mafia, needs to reconcile the family traditions with her new French identity. Ledoyen's moving performance, illustrating the struggles of immigrants to integrate their heritage into the French culture, launched her career.

Immediately after her successful debut, Ledoyen was cast, alongside Marcello Mastroianni and Michel Piccoli in *Le Voleur d'enfants /The Children Thief* by Christian de Chalonge (1991), acquiring very early the reputation of an art-house actress. For three consecutive years, Ledoyen was nominated for the César Award for Most Promising Actress for *Les Marmottes /The Groundhogs* (Elie Chouraqui, 1993), *L'Eau froide /Cold Water* (Olivier Assayas, 1994), and *La Fille seule /A Single Girl* (Benoît Jacquot, 1995).

L'Eau froide was Olivier Assayas's contribution to the highly popular television-film series *Tous les garçons et les filles de leur âge* in which Ledoyen plays a rebellious adolescent in the 1970s, delivering a powerful and mature performance. Ledoyen's collaboration with famous directors – such as Marcel Carné in *Mouche*, adapted from Guy de Maupassant (1992, unfinished), Claude Chabrol in *La Cérémonie* (1995), Assayas again in *Fin août, début septembre /Late August, Early September* (1998), and James Ivory in *La Fille d'un soldat ne pleure jamais /A Soldier's Daughter Never Cries* (1998) – have established her as a daring young actress, unafraid to take on demanding, dramatic roles, remarkable not only for her sensitive presence, but also for her rigorous interpretation.

Throughout the 1990s, Ledoyen continued to solidify her reputation as being highly selective of her roles in auteur films. For instance, encouraged by Assayas, she chose to act in *Mahjong* (1995), a film directed by the Taiwanese filmmaker Edward Yang. Despite the fact that the film was never released in France, Ledoyen considers it as one of her best. In 1998, the actress starred in her tenth film, the musical drama *Jeanne et le garçon formidable /Jeanne and the Perfect Guy*, directed by Olivier Ducastel and Jacques Martineau. In this revival of the French musical, she plays a girl who passionately looks for love and finds it in a boy who has AIDS, the haunting illness of the contemporary era. Through a luminous performance, Ledoyen displays her acting and singing skills in the difficult genre of a hybrid musical, which mixes both comedy and tragedy.

In 1999, Virginie Ledoyen took the first steps to establish herself as a more popular star, becoming one of the official ambassadors for the French cosmetic corporation L'Oréal. Chosen for her charismatic beauty as well as her artistic work, Ledoyen will become a regular presence at the Cannes French film festival since L'Oréal is its official sponsor. The same year, Ledoyen also starred in her first major international production, the thriller *The Beach* (2000), directed by Danny Boyle. Despite its all-star cast, including Leonardo DiCaprio, the film failed to achieve a full-scale success. Even though Ledoyen was typecast in the role of a highly seductive and sultry French girl, her performance attracted positive reviews both in France and abroad.

After this brief Hollywood experience, Ledoyen returned to France and received a leading role in François Ozon's *8 femmes /8 Women* (2002) alongside some of the biggest female stars in French cinema, including Fanny Ardant, Danielle Darrieux, Catherine Deneuve, and Isabelle Huppert. Ledoyen plays Suzon, the ingénue daughter of a bourgeois family who is attending college in England and comes home for the winter holidays. Ozon uses her image of a luminous and innocent ingénue, but also adds a dark and erotic undertone to her character, as Suzon hides an awful truth under the tidy image inspired by Audrey Hepburn in *Sabrina* (Billy Wilder, 1954). Not only is she pregnant by her own adoptive father, but she is also revealed to be deceitful, manipulative, and cruel. While dark innuendos trouble the clear and luminous image of the ingénue played by Ledoyen, the actress incarnates both traits in the challenging register of a musical comedy, earning well-deserved praise for her performance.

In 2003, Ledoyen plays a more traditional type of an ingénue in *Bon voyage* by Jean-Paul Rappeneau, which represents the period of the Occupation in a nostalgic and comedic mode. Ledoyen's character, Camille, actively participates in the French Resistance and is also a very young science genius, working at the Collège de France. In this role, her innocent yet intelligent aura is exploited by Rappeneau and allows Camille to become the unlikely love interest of the main protagonist, Frédéric Auger (Grégori Derangère), who had completely succumbed to the charms of a superficial actress, Viviane Denvers (Isabelle Adjani), in the first part of the film. After these two important roles, Ledoyen continued to star in more popular but less successful comedies, such as *La Doublure /The Valet* (Francis Veber, 2006), *Mes amis, mes amours /London mon amour* (Lorraine Lévy, 2008), and *L'Emmerdeur /A Pain in the Ass* (Francis Veber, 2008).

In 2011 Ledoyen returned to a more dramatic role, collaborating again with Benoît Jacquot in *Les Adieux à la reine /Farewell, My Queen* (2012). The actress convincingly plays the aristocrat Gabrielle de Pollignac, Marie-Antoinette's love obsession, and her presence on screen, although secondary, is unforgettable. Combining experience with intuition and restraint with emotion, Ledoyen's performance, both detached and natural, constructs a memorable character. Several times in her career, the actress has been compared to Jeanne Moreau and Isabelle Huppert, due to the detailed attention and instinctive emotion put into the creation of the film characters. The daring ingénue, Virginie Ledoyen, proves in *Les Adieux à la Reine* that she can follow in Moreau and Huppert's footsteps, in particular through her defining capacity of expressing emotional lucidity and intelligent sensuality on screen.

Nicoleta Bazgan
University of Maryland, Baltimore County

Valérie LEMERCIER (1964–)

Crude,
Chic,
and
Sharp

WHEN SHE CLAIMS to Sydney Pollack in *Fauteuils d'orchestre /* *Avenue Montaigne* [1] (Danièle Thompson, 2006) that she would not only play but that she 'would *be* Simone de Beauvoir' for his next film, Valérie LEMERCIER speaks the truth: a real chameleon, she is as convincing when impersonating the disturbed four-year-old daughter of a psychoanalyst or a rustic drunkard ('Me, a fag? I'd rather get f...'). But this scene also reflects her typical modus operandi: beyond mocking, through this begging TV actress, the French submission to American cinema, she also pokes fun at Hollywood megalomania. Inspired by Michel Simon and following the footsteps of Josiane Balasko, Valérie Lemercier has become an icon – well beyond the stuck-up bourgeoise she often caricatures – as well as the best-paid actress. As a versatile comedian, actress, writer, TV/film director, producer, singer, dancer, model, and illustrator, she has imposed a distinctive signature onto the groove of France's comic landscape with three Molière (theatre) awards and two César (cinema) awards.

Born in 1964, Valérie Lemercier grew up on a farm in Normandy (Gonzeville, Seine-Maritime), in a well-to-do family with three sisters. Very early on, she became aware of her comic potential and her call for the stage. An acute observer and impersonator, she enrolled at the Conservatoire de Rouen and later on went to Paris where she took theatre courses while working at odd jobs such as a salesperson which will inspire several of her stage characters. She performed Bourvil songs at the Piano Zinc cabaret in Paris and made her TV debut in 1987 in *M'as-tu vu ?* written and staged by Jean-Michel Ribes. In 1988, Ribes gave her the highly popular role of Lady Palace in the six-part mini-series *Palace /* *Ça, c'est palace*, which established her notoriety but also somewhat encaged her in this uptight *grande bourgeoise* role. However, she soon had the opportunity to portray a wide variety of personalities for her own one-woman shows (Palais Royal in 1989, Théâtre de Paris in 1995-96, Folies Bergères in 2000, Palace in 2008). Free to give voice to her wild characters, she also refuses to record these successful shows.

Louis Malle gave her her first movie role in *Milou en mai /May Fools* (1990). She played in three comedies with both actors Jean Reno and Christian Clavier: *L'Opération corned-beef* (Jean-Marie Poiré, 1991); *Sexes faibles ! /The Weaker Sexes!* (Serge Meynard, 1992); and the hit that will establish her as a leading comedian and actress, *Les Visiteurs /* *The Visitors* (Jean-Marie Poiré, 1993), with a total of 14 million tickets sold. In this comedy, Valérie Lemercier portrays both a medieval damsel and her descendant, the contemporary aristocratic wife of a dentist. Her highly praised performance won her a César award for best supporting actress. Now recognized as one of the funniest comedians in France, she plays with the most prominent French humorists, Les Nuls, in *La Cité de la peur /Fear City: A Family-Style Comedy*, and Gérard Jugnot, in *Casque bleu / Blue Helmet*, in 1994. A year later, she appeared in Sydney Pollack's remake of *Sabrina* (1995) with Harrison Ford. She also recorded successful kitsch/ pop music songs, collaborating with musician-producer Bertrand Burgalat.

After her *coup d'essai*, adapting Sacha Guitry's play *Quadrille* to the screen in 1997, she goes on to direct, co-write, and star in *Le Derrière / From Behind* (1999), a comedy about homosexuality and the excess of political correctness. Eager to expand her repertoire, she lends a French voice to Jane in Disney's *Tarzan* (Chris Buck and Kevin Lima, 1999) and Ginger in *Chicken Run* (Peter Lord and Nick Park, 2000) when these animated films were dubbed into French; adds a decisive presence to Claire Denis's lyrical and sensual *Vendredi soir /Friday Night* (2002), as well as her unfailing humor to Alain Chabat's *RRRrrr !!!* (2004) and *Narco /The Secret Adventures of Gustave Klopp* (Tristan Aurouet and Gilles Lellouche, 2004). No longer dedicating most of her time to her own stage shows, she is increasingly focusing on cinema, both as a director (*Palais royal !*, 2005, and the recent *100% cachemire /The Ultimate Accessory*, 2014), and as an actor – from *Fauteuils d'orchestre* (2005) for which she received a César for best supporting actress, to her latest films: Frédéric Beigbeder's *L'Amour dure trois ans /Love Lasts Three Years*

(2011), *Adieu Berthe – l'enterrement de mémé /Granny's Funeral* (Bruno Podalydès, 2012), *Astérix et Obélix : Au service de sa majesté /Astérix and Obélix: God Save Britannia* (Laurent Tirard, 2012), and *Main dans la main /Hand in Hand* (Valérie Donzelli, 2012). Even if comedies such as *Agathe Cléry* (Étienne Chatillez, 2008) and *Bienvenue à bord* (Eric Lavain, 2011) received a cool reception, Valérie Lemercier is widely and consistently praised for her acting performance.

Always a protagonist in her own shows and films, Valérie Lemercier offers both an incisive and intimate description of society, in her polite and self-restrained demeanour. Crude but never vulgar, she prefers to work on the least obvious traits to mock the characters she interprets. For instance, her description of the family estate 'La Renardière' is encapsulated in the very pronunciation of this name, with softened 'r' and deep-throat 'a' sounds. In the same skit, in order to better represent the sexual frustration of this high society, she mimics the lexical 'riffraffing' of the French upper-class, with downright obscene words for explicit and unexpected taboo realities. A painter more than a novelist, she also excels at portraying characters of all ages and genders.

Thanks to an expendable palette and thorough preparation – she says she cannot improvise – Valérie Lemercier easily switches from lowbrow comedies to cutting-edge production, from a fashion show ('Anti-jeunisme' for Jean-Paul Gaultier), to designing the posters of her shows. She also contributed illustrations to the *Larousse* dictionary. Whether commenting on contemporary monarchy or a certain Parisian gay elite, her statements are never tepid and reflect an intransigent perspective that consistently questions gender, race, or society at large. Both private in her emotions and raw in her words, Valérie Lemercier is uncompromising in denouncing bourgeois behaviours, racism, charity, and more generally politically correct hypocrisy when, for instance, she asks the Césars audience not to forget the 'homeless of *Loft Story*,' a French *Big Brother* reality show.

Both restrained and blunt, Valérie Lemercier aims at confronting her audience with her own and their fears and insecurities. With mixed results as a director, she probably is at her best as a comedian and an actress, when she can give the full measure of her talent. But what probably strikes us most is her ability to make her public feel, beyond her creative and unbridled energy, a fundamental blend of tenderness, grief, and life.

Noëlle ROUXEL-CUBBERLY
Bennington College, Vermont

1. For further discussion of *Fauteuils d'orchestre /Avenue Montaigne*, see Marcelline Block, ed., *World Film Locations: Paris* (Bristol: Intellect, 2011), 102-103. —Ed.

Jean LE POULAIN (1924–1988)

—Le Fabuleux Destin de—

SCREENWRITER Jean-Claude Carrière once stated in an interview with the *Guardian* that, 'if you want fame, don't be a screenwriter.'[1] The same could be said of stage actors whose fame and wealth are at times nothing when compared with film actors. During each and every performance, the stage actor must fight his demons, memory lapses, and stage fright, while in film acting, the scene can be reshot as many times as needed. Jean LE POULAIN is an actor who marked the mid-1960s and the 1970s with the popularization of theatre on television in programmes such as Pierre Sabbagh's *Au théâtre ce soir*. He also had his own TV show, *Le Poulain au galop* (literally translated as 'the galloping foal'), punning on his name. *Au théâtre ce soir* was a rare occasion for the average viewer to see successful plays that were performed in Paris before they toured the country. Television thus made important works of theatre accessible to a wider, popular audience. However, who remembers Jean Le Poulain today, apart from this generation of spectators that had the chance to see him in some of his most notable parts: *Le Minotaure* (1969), *Le Noir te va si bien* (1972) with Maria Pacôme, *De doux dingues* (1972), and

Le Don d'Adèle (1972), among many others? In his career, he performed more than 100 roles onstage.

Jean Le Poulain was born in Marseilles, but spent most of his youth in Phnom Penh in Cambodia, as his father was a colonial administrator. He returned to France at the age of 19, and his destiny was to act. With his round physique, laughing eyes, and deadpan air, he was very distinctive and would strut around the stage with bonhomie and mischief for more than three decades. His scatty imagination as an actor would make every single performance unique. He would compose his own universe with its own rules. When Le Poulain arrived onstage, there was no limit. He would improvise, make puns, and even create unforeseeable gags, flirting with excess and absurdity. Peals of laughter were guaranteed among spectators. More of a stage actor than a cinema actor like the wonderful Michel Duchaussoy, Jacques Fabbri, Jean-Jacques, Robert Hirsch, Jean Piat, Laurent Terzieff, and Jacques Weber, he was a true stage actor in the pure tradition, taught by his master René Simon alongside comedienne Jacqueline Maillan. What remains of stage actors is not only a presence, but also, an inimitable laughter and voice. In his rare TV interviews, his round face would light up with a cigar in his mouth.

After receiving a first prize for comedy at the National Conservatory of Theatre Arts in Paris in 1949, Le Poulain later joined eminent stage actor Jean Vilar's Théâtre National Populaire (TNP) alongside Michel Bouquet, Maria Casarès, Gérard Philipe, and Georges Wilson.

Behind the hilarious faces of this Falstaff-like actor that entered the venerable *Comédie française* in 1978 and who a few years later became its general administrator (from 1986-1988) could hide some fierce, even violent personae, as well. In 1958, he played the fearful Baron Massacre in Jacques Audiberti's *La Hobereaute*. In Pinter's *Un pour la route* (1987), he was the enigmatic judge or executioner Nicolas. This very talented actor could play everything: classical texts from Shakespeare to Corneille as well as contemporary theatre and *théâtre de boulevard*, comedy as well as tragedy: from punchbag Victor Emmanuel Chandebise and his uncanny double, the hotel porter Poche in Feydeau's *La Puce à l'oreille* (1954) – whose humour is essentially based on the resemblance between the two characters – to Turelure in Claudel's *Père humilié* (1962) and Arnolphe in Molière's *École des femmes* (1983), both funny and sinister. Jean Anouilh's adaptation of Shakespeare's *La Nuit des Rois* with Suzanne Flon was performed more than 400 times at the Théâtre du Vieux-Colombier.

Throughout his career, Le Poulain appeared in a good score of films, but mainly as secondary parts or cameo appearances that sadly did not take advantage of his full potential. His first film was Marcel Aboulker's *Les Aventures des pieds-nickelés* (1948) drawn from the eponymous comic strips. In André Hunebelle's classic version of Féval's swashbuckling novel *Le Bossu* (1959), he plays the trustworthy Peyrolles, alongside Jean Marais and Bourvil. In the 1960s, he has parts in run-of-the mill *franchouillard* comedies with humourists Darry Cowl and Fernand

Raynaud. Dominique Delouche's musical *Divine* (1975), which is both a hymn to theatre and to cinema, put him for the first time in the foreground, as Danielle Darrieux's theatrical impresario. In Jean-Pierre Mocky's *L'Ibis rouge /The Red Ibis* (1975), he does not pass unnoticed either as Margos, starring with Michel Simon and Michel Serrault. His last film is Jean Yanne's *Signé Furax* (1981) adapted from *Le Boudin sacré* by Francis Blanche and Pierre Dac.

The title of Le Poulain's autobiography *Je rirai le dernier* (1977) seems to imply that he would have the last laugh on his spectators. However, let's hope that generations of spectators will rediscover this exceptional, indefatigable comedian. His nieces Corinne and Vannick Le Poulain are also stage actresses. They have perpetuated the brand name Le Poulain and at the same time the memory of a *monstre sacré* of the French stage.

Michaël ABECASSIS
The University of Oxford

1. Ryan Gilbey, 'Jean-Claude Carrière: If You Want Fame, Don't Be a Screenwriter,' *Guardian*, June 28, 2012, accessed September 10, 2013, http://www.theguardian.com/film/2012/jun/28/jean-claude-carriere-fame-screenwriter.

Robert LE VIGAN (1900–1972)
[Robert COQUILLAUD]

A French Eccentric

ROBERT LE VIGAN is seen by many as a one-of-a-kind actor, unmatched in the history of French cinema; for others he was a tormented soul haunted by the dark, crackbrained, aggressive characters he played.

He was born on January 7, 1900 as Robert Coquillaud, the son of a veterinarian. In 1972, shortly before his death in Argentina, Le Vigan wrote to André Bernard about his early childhood years, 'I was born in Barbès, in the 18th district, rue de la Charbonnière, street of the bordellos!' This slightly roguish self-portrayal was quite typical of him.

Le Vigan, cultivated and well educated (in Argentina he would teach French and Greek) was an actor who always liked to put on a show, not only on stage where he immersed himself completely in the characters he played, but also in real life. For Renoir, he was the actor *par excellence* who lived for the stage and who was unable to cope with the demands of the real world. Film director Pierre Chenal with whom Le Vigan had worked in the thirties and whom he would meet again in Argentina attributed his intense acting style to the fact that Le Vigan had a hard time memorizing texts; he would thus fill the void with crazy laughs and aggressive outbursts.

Le Vigan was a precocious and bright adolescent. In 1918, encouraged by a philosophy teacher with a knack for theatre, he auditioned at the Conservatoire. His brilliant performance guaranteed him a spot, but he abandoned the institution soon thereafter and began playing in various *variété* theatres. It was in this environment that he formed his first long lasting professional friendships with actors such as Jean Brochard, Marcel Dalio, and Guy Derlan. Living in Montmartre, the handsome Le Vigan devoted himself fully to a bohemian life-style and by chance, succeeded in receiving a role at the Théâtre des Arts (today Théâtre Hébertot). He alternated between the world of the music hall and the world of classical theatre, sometimes playing two different roles on the same night. According to his biographers Claude Beylie and André Bernard, playing two different genres almost simultaneously and assuming a dual personality was the foundation of his art, an art he demonstrated even more successfully on screen.

In 1930, while giving a stellar performance in Jules Romain's play *Donogoo*, he was noticed by Julien Duvivier, who offered him a role alongside Harry Baur and René Lefèvre in the stylistically creative film *Les Cinq Gentlemen maudits / Moon Over Morocco* (1931), filmed on location in Morocco. Duvivier cast him as a duplicitous character, which became – much to the actor's chagrin – the Le Vigan trademark. Le

Vigan preferred to explore different characters and viewed Duvivier as the director who had limited his choices. This perception might not be all that accurate as Duvivier chose him, despite bewildered reactions from commentators in the film industry, for the role of Jesus in the film *Golgotha /Behold the Man* (1935) and gave Le Vigan the opportunity to play Lucas, the sly police agent in *La Bandera* (1935) who is following Gilieth (Jean Gabin), only to become his comrade; indeed, in this film he almost eclipses Gabin. On the other hand, Le Vigan did not seem to mind playing the evil merchant Monsieur Lheureux in Jean Renoir's *Madame Bovary* (1934) or an alcoholic actor driven to suicide in another Renoir film, *Les Bas-fonds /The Lower Depths* (1936) as he stated that filming with Renoir was his most enjoyable acting experience. He dedicated an entire article to Jean Renoir, giving homage to this director whom he admired for his leadership style, his intelligence, and kindness – certainly a noteworthy fact as Le Vigan mistrusted the written word and refused to write his own memoirs, believing that writing facilitates misrepresentation.

It was also during those years that Le Vigan developed a close friendship with Louis-Ferdinand Céline, who has been seen by many as the driving force behind Le Vigan's anti-Semitism. During the Occupation years, Le Vigan would work with the German forces, appearing in Christian-Jaque's film *L'Assassinat du Père Noël /Who Killed Santa Claus?* (1941), a film produced by La Continental, and more importantly, participate in a radio programme *Les*

Juifs contre la France /The Jews against France, which was aired by Radio-Paris. However, Le Vigan's most successful film during those years was Jacques Becker's *Goupi mains rouges /It Happened at the Inn* (1943), a film produced by Minerva just like *L'Homme qui vendit son âme* (Jean-Paul Paulin, 1943). Noteworthy also is his appearance as one of the actors in Carné's *Les Enfants du paradis / Children of Paradise* (1945). Here he played, how could it be otherwise, the rather dislikable *clochard* Jericho. When the Allies landed in France and the German defeat was predictable, Le Vigan, who was a member of the pro-fascist PPF, fled to southern Germany, following Céline.

While trying to escape to Austria, Le Vigan was arrested by the Swiss Military Police and was handed over to the French authorities. On November 16, 1946, Le Vigan was tried by the Courts of Justice for collaboration. Many French actors and film directors came to his defence, but despite their intervention he received – compared to other actors who had worked for La Continental or Radio-Paris – a rather harsh sentence: ten years of hard labour and imprisonment, confiscation of his property and 'national unworthiness' for life. In 1948, he obtained a conditional discharge, but unable to rebuild his life in France, he escaped with Jacques Becker's help to Spain. Duvivier, who knew Franco, requested a work permit on Le Vigan's behalf, enabling the actor to play in two films, *Ley del mar* (Miguel Iglesias, 1952) and *Correo del rey* (Ricardo Gascón, 1951). However, according to Le Vigan, the French

undermined his career in Spain, forcing him to finally turn his back on Europe for good. Although he played in two Argentinian films as well, he ultimately abandoned his acting career, living in poverty in Tandil, where he taught languages and drove a cab.

Whilst he considered Céline his friend, Le Vigan also believed that in his novels (*D'un château l'autre /Castle to Castle*, *Nord /North*, *Rigodon /Rigadoon*) the writer had immortalized him as a Nazi. Céline's character 'La Vigue' had turned him into an immutable person, something that was fundamentally contrary to Le Vigan's self-understanding as an actor. In the eyes of Le Vigan, acting was 'a permanent metamorphosis leading to the renewal of the self, physically, morally and emotionally.' [1]

Elisabeth-Christine MUELSCH
Angelo State University, Texas

1. *Paris-Soir*, November 7, 1934.

Thierry LHERMITTE (1952–)

A Playboy
for
French
Comedy

THIERRY LHERMITTE (born 1952 in Paris) is a prominent film and theatre actor who is closely associated with café-théâtre and popular cinema. He made a name for himself with the Parisian troupe *Le Splendid* in the 1970s, performing in successful plays with Josiane Balasko, Michel Blanc, Marie-Anne Chazel, Christian Clavier, and Gérard Jugnot. In this period, he was also close to the *Café de la gare* group, especially Coluche and Patrick Dewaere. In his career, Lhermitte has appeared in over 100 films and contributed to a few screenplays. Unlike some of his *Splendid* friends, he is less interested in directing (he tried once), but he was involved in film production in the 1990s and worked with a media production company in the 2000s. He returned to theatre in the mid-2000s and has recently featured in a Television series for TF1, *Doc Martin*.

A founder member of the *Splendid* in 1975 with Blanc and Jugnot whom he met at school, Lhermitte collaborated in the writing and mise-en-scène of most of the *Splendid* shows *Je vais craquer* (1975), *Pot de terre contre pot de vin* (1976), *Amour, coquillages et crustacés* (1977). He interpreted some of their most iconic characters, first on stage,

then in cult comedy film adaptations. The French public still identify him with Popeye, the irresistible play-boy of *Les Bronzés /French Fried Vacation* and its sequel *Les Bronzés font du ski* (Patrice Leconte, 1978 and 1979) the film adaptation of *Amour, coquillages et crustacés*, and with Pierre Mortez, the stuck-up middle-class volunteer of the SOS-Amitié association in the stage version of *Le Père Noël est une ordure /Santa Claus is a Stinker* (1982) and the film adaptation which became a huge success in 1982, directed by Jean-Marie Poiré.

Lhermitte had appeared in small roles in a number of films in the 1970s, but following the success of *Le Splendid*'s films, he was one of the first of the group to break away into mainstream cinema and continue a solo career as actor in a diverse range of films, alongside Austrian-born actress Romy Schneider in *La Banquière /The Lady Banker* (Francis Girod, 1980), and co-starring with Isabelle Adjani as a *bande dessinée* [1] author in *L'Année prochaine si tout va bien /Next Year if it All Goes Well* (Jean-Loup Hubert, 1981), and as a teacher, Bertrand, in *Clara et les chics types* (Jacques Monnet, 1981). Some of the films in which he appeared that decade were comedies directed and written by his former companions, such as *Papy fait de la résistance /Gramps is in the Resistance* (Jean-Marie Poiré, 1983) in which he plays an SS colonel, and *Nuit d'ivresse* with Balasko (Bernard Nauer, 1986). He was also called upon over that period by established directors, such as Bertrand Blier's *La Femme de mon pote /My Best Friend's Girl* (1983).

In the 1980s and 1990s, Lhermitte featured as lead actor in comedies and police dramas. He worked repeatedly with Claude Zidi, for instance for the successful *Ripoux* trilogy (Zidi, 1984, 1990, and 2003). The first film, *Les Ripoux /My New Partner*, sees him as policeman François Lesbuche who teams up with corrupt cop René Boisrond played by Philippe Noiret. The sequels *Ripoux contre ripoux / My New Partner II* and *Ripoux 3* are variations on the same theme of police corruption. Other major roles include François Voisin, the undercover secret agent of *La Totale !* (Zidi, 1991) another box-office comedy (later remade as *True Lies*, with Arnold Schwarzenegger in Lhermitte's role). In *Un indien dans la ville /Little Indian, Big City* (Hervé Palud, 1994), a hit comedy that he co-wrote and co-produced, he interprets a trader absorbed by his professional life who finds out one day that he has a 13 year-old son in South America, brings him back to Paris and is confronted with the difficulties of family life.

Outside France, Lhermitte's best-known roles to date are the comedies *Le Dîner de cons /The Dinner Game* (1998) and *Le Placard /The Closet* (2001) both written and directed by Francis Veber. As Pierre, the cruel editor of *Le Dîner de cons*, he convincingly teams up with Jacques Villeret to create one of the most hilarious duos of French comedy. In this film, he changes his acting style though, as he is not really the funny one, but rather the catalyst of the jokes imagined by Veber. In *Le Placard*, where he holds a secondary role, he again plays a cruel and irresponsible manipulator who is prepared to do anything for a bit of fun at the expense of his colleagues.

Lhermitte's star image is associated with the figure of middle-class playboy, helped by his blue eyes and young premier looks that he fully exploits for many of his roles, including his performance as incompetent government minister Alexandre Taillard de Vorms in Bertrand Tavernier's most recent film, the political satire *Quai d'Orsay /The French Minister* (2013), which premiered at the Toronto International Film Festival in a special screening presentation. For his performance in *Quai d'Orsay*, Lhermitte was nominated for the Lumière Award for Best Actor. His laid-back attitude and engaging personality make it easy for audiences to engage with most of his characters, whether they are surreal in the Splendid period, or more realistic in dramas, police films, and romantic comedies. He is also known for his sarcastic humour (sometimes cruel, often witty). However, he has also regularly changed roles and played with his star image over the years. In the 2000s, he took up roles in two noir *polars* directed by Guillaume Nicloux the stern detective François Manéri in *Une affaire privée /A Private Affair* (2002) and *La Clef / The Key* (2007), showing that he could also excel at serious noir compositions after being a labelled as a comic for so long. He also played in two American films: *Until September* in 1984, which was shot in France and in which he is Karen Allen's French lover, and in James Ivory's *Le Divorce* in 2003, in which he plays a Frenchman.

Lhermitte is a typical example of a French actor with a clear national identity and a popular star image within Francophone countries. He has remained associated with Le

Splendid and comedy: however, the mitigated reception of their reunion for *Les Bronzés 3 : Amis pour la vie* (dir. Patrice Leconte) in 2006 seems to indicate that if the troupe was a fantastic stepping stone for a whole generation of French actors, the likes of Balasko, Blanc, Clavier, and Jugnot have now all found their own ways to stardom, and *Le Splendid* is a thing of the past. Lhermitte is possibly the one in the group who most retained the spirit of the comedy acting that made him famous, even if unlike some other members of the group, this also means that he abandoned writing and directing to concentrate his energy on acting, and for a while producing films.

Isabelle VANDERSCHELDEN
Manchester Metropolitan University

1. *Bande dessinée* : French-language comic strip. —Ed.

Vincent LINDON (1959–)

Passionate Man and Perfectionist Actor

VINCENT ALFRED FERNAND LINDON is a prominent French actor whose filmography exceeds 50 films and who also made a few films as screenwriter and one as director. He was nominated for four Césars over the years, but is still to receive one. He comes from a high bourgeois family that counts industrialists and intellectual figures – his grandfather Raymond took part in the founding of the state of Israel, and his uncle Mathieu Lindon founded the prestigious Editions de Minuit.

After working as assistant costume designer and tour manager, he joined the Cours Florent in Paris in 1982, and started with small film parts in the 1980s, for example in *37°2 le matin /Betty Blue* (dir. Jean-Jacques Beineix) in 1986. His first leading role was alongside Sophie Marceau in *L'Étudiante* (dir. Claude Pinoteau) in 1988, for which he received the Prix Jean Gabin. He became a prominent lead star in France in the 1990s, often making several films with the same director, thus becoming a sort of screen messenger through whom they could express themselves. For example, he worked with Benoît Jacquot (*L'École de la chair /The School of Flesh*, 1998; *Pas de scandale /Keep it*

Quiet, 1999); with Pierre Jolivet (Fred, 1997; Ma petite enterprise /My Little Business, 1999), with Coline Serreau in successful social comedies (La Crise, 1992; La Belle verte, 1996; Chaos, 2001), and with Claude Lelouch (La Belle Histoire, 1992; Tout ça...pour ça ! /All That...for This?!, 1993).

In La Crise (1992), his first real comedy hit, he plays a selfish husband who discovers one morning that his wife has left him, he has lost his job, and his mother is leaving his father. He meets by chance a homeless man played by Patrick Timsit, who will help him realise what is important in life. For this role, he received a César nomination, and became an important figure in popular French cinema, sometimes appearing in two or three films per year, many of which were commercial successes, such as Paparazzi (Alain Berbérian, 1998), for which he was also one of the screenwriters.

Lindon's characters come from different social and professional backgrounds (ranging from surgeon, teacher, or paparazzo to woodworker, bricklayer, crane driver, restaurant owner, or swimming instructor), but they tend to represent ordinary middle class or working class men. Welcome (Philippe Lioret, 2009) is a typical example: Simon, a swimming instructor whose wife is leaving and who, partly to impress her in the first instance, gets involved with an illegal immigrant who wants to swim across the Channel to England. In Chaos (2001) Paul and his wife, by chance, meet a prostitute (Rachida Brakni) in danger and, at first, he refuses to help her. Lindon's roles often include more intimate personal facets, such as problematic relationships and complex love stories.

Lindon has been cast in different film genres, including social or romantic comedies, intimate dramas and thrillers. His star image tends to remain linked more to popular French cinema, with him often featuring as ordinary types in realist dramas, some with a societal or psychological edge, such as Fred, Ma petite enterprise, and Welcome, for which he was nominated for a César. He has also worked with less commercial auteur-directors, as illustrated for example by Emmanuel Carrère's La Moustache (2005); L'Avion (2005), directed by Cédric Kahn, which blends realism and fantasy; Vendredi soir /Friday Night (2002) by Claire Denis, or more recently the experimental film Pater by Alain Cavalier (2011) which was presented at Cannes.

Since becoming known as an actor, Lindon has also become a public figure in France. He does not hesitate to engage in political debates (for example, he was linked to the politician François Bayrou for the 2007 presidential election). He has also attracted attention in the celebrity press, his private life often becoming the subject of media speculation. His friendships or relationships with Caroline de Monaco, Claude Chirac, and more recently, Chiara Mastroiani and Rachida Dati earned him an image of jet-set seducer, which adds to his star persona. He was married to the actress Sandrine Kiberlain between 1998 and 2006, and they have appeared together in Le Septième Ciel / Seventh Heaven (Benoît Jacquot, 1997) and more recently in Mademoiselle Chambon (Stéphane Brizé, 2009).

Lindon evokes a unique masculinity,

mixing personal charm and an element of ruggedness. He admires Jean Gabin and Lino Ventura, two stars to whom he is sometimes compared, the former because he often plays working-class characters, the latter because his performance style, like Lindon's, does not necessarily rely on dialogue, but more on physical expression and movement. He is also characterised by excess and contradictions. One minute he can appear introverted (and is notorious for his twitches), angry and *grande gueule* the next. Like many of his characters, he has a rebellious streak and is known for his frankness – he does not hesitate to speak his mind and takes a stand, such as his strong position against Sarkozy's illegal immigration policy, as illustrated upon the release of the film *Welcome*, which addresses the trials and tribulations of illegal immigrants in France.

Described in 2010 in *Le Figaro* as 'forever nostalgic', Lindon is also hypersensitive, anxious, and full of energy. There is a compulsive perfectionist side to his performance style, a method-like approach to his acting, and an obsessive quest for realism through every little detail of the construction of his characters. Lindon sees himself as an actor with a physical performance style: 'I let my body guide me … the right movement is what matters most,' he explains in a *Télérama* interview in 2009. He also invests a great deal of research in his characters' state of mind and their social background.

Isabelle VANDERSCHELDEN
Manchester Metropolitan University

Michael LONSDALE (1931–)

Calm and Content: The Life and Career of an English Enthusiast in Paris

THE BENEVOLENT spirits watching over MICHAEL LONSDALE when he came into the world on 24th May 1931 were, without doubt, a tad eccentric. But they were generous nonetheless. He effectively grew up without a father – he was born to an English naval officer whose itinerant existence took a radical change of direction into the fertiliser trade just before World War II, only to return him to frontline military service shortly thereafter – and was correspondingly overprotected by the gentle but omnipresent figure of his mother, an English teacher and pianist whose various talents were much sought after. Small wonder that the young Lonsdale ended up living a rather nomadic life. His early years saw him wander far and wide, often in apparently chaotic fashion, from France to Guernsey, then briefly to London, then via Casablanca to his final destination of Paris at the age of nineteen. Here he was nurtured by an aunt and uncle who combined geniality and genius: Marcel Arland, who eventually became a member of the French Academy (chair 26) and director of the *NRF*,[1] and Janine Arland, a painter and art connoisseur who was at heart a committed pioneer.

His compulsory schooling irked him, and so in 1950 he started his literary, philosophical, and artistic education all over again in the best possible environment, in highly literary circles. A precociously gifted painter who also settled into acting at a young age, and endowed with a great love and appetite for film, Lonsdale was soon drawn to the distinctive richness of Georges Rouault's work (like Alfred Hitchcock before him) and, in the Vieux-Colombier theatre, Tania Balachova's acting prowess (in particular her work with Delphine Seyrig and Jean-Louis Trintignant).[2] 'You will never make a young lead,' was Tania Balachova's verdict, no doubt because of Lonsdale's distinctive and somewhat unconventional physique. Indeed, his physical makeup was an unusual combination of contrasts: heaviness and authority, grace and gentleness, the net effect of which was far removed from any of the physical stereotypes in cinema's firmament. With similar foresight she added, 'You will achieve nothing of note before you turn thirty-five.'[3] Lonsdale's distinctly English acting style – often minimalist, generally contained but capable of sudden and unexpected flights of fancy, and touched with a discreet and mischievous humour – came to full fruition in his maturity, as did his peculiar and unmistakable delivery. Again, it was with age that his voice, by turns syrupy and shrill, acquired infinite modulations and subtle inflexions, accentuating or even lingering over the final syllables of words, an effect unique to Lonsdale.

He became a solid and eventually indispensable pillar of French cinema, playing more than 120 supporting roles, an astonishing range which included many significant and some major roles in both art-house and popular cinema, especially in the years following his much admired performance as Charles Duffaut in Jean-Pierre Mocky's *Snobs !* (1962) and as Georges Tabard in François Truffaut's *Baisers volés /Stolen Kisses* (1968). On several occasions he has played the brilliant villain in American or international films – the slippery, ambiguous, devious abbot in Jean-Jacques Annaud's cinematic adaptation of Umberto Eco's novel *The Name of the Rose* (1986); the spy of multiple allegiances in Steven Spielberg's *Munich* (2005); and the expression of pure evil, the would-be destroyer of the human race Hugo Drax in Lewis Gilbert's *Moonraker* (1979), whom he played as an almost affable, cultivated aesthete. By contrast, he took on the role of the indefatigable detective as Lebel, the model of upright honesty in Fred Zinnemann's *The Day of the Jackal* (1973), in which he ended up stealing the show.

Seemingly able to turn his hand to pretty much anything, over a period of more than fifty years, Lonsdale invaded the theatre, cinema, radio, audio book – where he introduced a vast audience to the joys of Rudyard Kipling and Pauline Réage – television, opera, musical theatre, painting, and the written word.[4] Not so much a nomad as an eclectic genius, impossible to pin down. It was natural that a man of his talent would reach the pinnacle of his profession: it was slow in coming, admittedly, but his magnificent performance as Brother Luc, the monk and medic in Xavier Beauvois's *Des hommes et des dieux /Of*

Gods and Men (2010) – a role made to measure for a man like Lonsdale, apparently touched by divine grace and a model of selflessness – earned him the highest honours at Cannes.[5]

Of the many associations and collaborations he enjoyed on the stage and the film set – with figures including Samuel Beckett, Luis Buñuel, Joseph Losey, Alain Resnais, Jacques Rivette, and Orson Welles – the most remarkable is without doubt the relationship of great friendship and deep trust he shared with Marguerite Duras, in whose work his intense presence was a discreet but powerful agent.

Pierre LETHIER
University of Buckingham (BUCSIS)

1. *La Nouvelle Revue Française* – Editions Gallimard.

2. Jean Cléder and Michael Lonsdale, *Michael Lonsdale : entretiens avec Jean Cléder* (Paris: François Bourin Editeur, 2012), 46

3. Ibid., 50.

4. Lonsdale is the author of five books: *Oraisons* (Paris: Actes Sud, 2000), *Visites* (Paris: Pauvert, 2003), *Un cri dans les images* (Paris: Editions de Champtin, 2003), *L'Amour Peut Tout* (Mesnil-Saint-Loup: Le Livre Ouvert, 2010) and *L'Amour sauvera le monde: mes plus belles pages chrétiennes* (Paris: Philippe Rey, 2011).

5. Laurie Goodman, 'A Gentle Screen Giant Subtly Shines,' *Wall Street Journal*, 3 December 2010.

Fabrice LUCHINI (1951–)
[Robert LUCHINI]

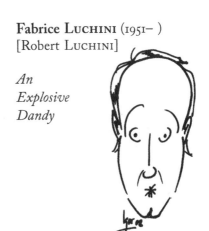

An Explosive Dandy

FOR THE French public, Fabrice LUCHINI is first of all a performer. He first learned the tricks of stage performance with a popular audience. Fabrice, born in Paris as Robert Luchini in 1951, the son of Italian immigrants, was selling fruits and vegetables in the working-class neighbourhood of La Goutte d'Or with his parents. He became a hairdresser's apprentice at age 13 in a chic salon where he renamed himself 'Fabrice' (the same name as the son of the proprietor), but was nevertheless a self-educated literary man who could not put down Balzac, Flaubert, or Proust. Nor did he receive formal theatrical training. Above all, he was also a great appreciator of soul music. Although he later praised Johnny Hallyday in the film *Jean-Philippe* (Laurent Tuel, 2006), his first true idol was James Brown.

It may be because of soul music that he became interested in acting in the cinema. In 1969, he was spotted by Philippe Labro in a discothèque where he used to go. Labro gave him his first role with Catherine Allégret, Jean-Claude Bouillon, Jean-Claude Brialy, and Catherine Deneuve in

Tout peut arriver /Don't Be Blue (1969). Eric Rohmer truly revealed his talent with *Le Genou de Claire /Claire's Knee* (1970) and *Perceval le Gallois /Perceval* (1978). During these years, he also discovered theatre, which was the true revelation of his life and changed everything: an authentic love story. He followed the famous Jean-Laurent Cochet's classes and from that moment, he understood he was meant to be an actor on the stage.

This did not exclude screen performances. Fabrice is known for his various roles as a dandy. In *Beaumarchais l'insolent /Beaumarchais the Scoundrel* (Edouard Molinaro, 1996) he maintains a provocative style in the duel scenes – the best incarnation of one kind of dandy: a very precious and eccentric one. But before and after Edouard Molinaro's masterpiece, Fabrice was also used to playing impertinent, refined, but most of the time unsuccessful men, who do not succeed in matching Beaumarchais's style. His first popular success was *P.R.O.F.S.* (Patrick Schulmann, 1985) with Patrick Bruel. But he very quickly focused on the pleasure of the spoken word, such as in 1990 in Claude Berri's *Uranus*. In *La Discrète* (Christian Vincent, 1990), he was Antoine, an emotional and complicated writer who tried to be immoral in love. Cédric Klapisch, for his first film, offered him, in *Riens du tout* (1992) the chance to play Director General of the Grandes Galeries who has revolutionary – but not realistic – methods of management. With *Rien sur Robert* (Pascal Bonitzer, 1999), he is still

the *anti-héros* who reviews a film he never saw and gets lost in the ups and downs of his love life. *Barnie et ses petites contrariétés* (Bruno Chiche, 2001) is a vaudeville set between London and Calais, where he had to commute back and forth and never managed to choose between his wife Lucie and his two lovers, Margot and Mark. He also received the César for best actor for his performance as a character also named Fabrice in the Lelouch film, *Tout ça...pour ça ! /All That...for This?!* (1993), his third of seven César nominations: he was nominated for Best Supporting Actor for his roles in Eric Rohmer's *Les Nuits de la pleine lune /Full Moon in Paris* (1984), *Le Retour de Casanova* (Edouard Niermans, 1992), *Le Colonel Chabert /Colonel Chabert* (Yves Angelo, 1994), and Laurent Tirard's *Molière*, 2007 (for which he won the Silver St. George Award for Best Actor at the Moscow Film Festival); and he was nominated for Best Actor for *La Discrète /The Discreet* (Christian Vincent, 1990), Edouard Molinaro's *Beaumarchais l'insolent /Beaumarchais the Scoundrel* (1996), *Dans la maison /In the House* (François Ozon, 2012), and *Alceste à bicyclette /Bicycling with Molière* (Philippe Le Guay, 2013). In 1991, Luchini received the Prix Jean Gabin, which since the 1980s was awarded to the most promising actor each year (in 2008, the prize was renamed in honour of the late actor Patrick Dewaere).

On stage, Luchini is better known for his solo explosive performance and literary verve – a real 'stage animal.' He is now absolutely successful in declaiming

Céline, La Fontaine, and Nietzsche, because of his flight of oratory. In the way he brings the verses to life, one can find the passion of this lover of texts, who was not born among books but who always delighted in literature – for what great texts have to say about our human condition. Indeed, not only is Luchini an avid and passionate reader, but he is also a published author: he was one of the contributors to the recent edition of the *Cahiers d'histoire de la philosophie* devoted to the late writer Philippe Muray (1945-2006), edited by Jacques de Guillebon and Maxence Caron and published by Les Editions du Cerf in November 2011. Luchini has also contributed prefaces to Jean-Laurent Cochet's *À la rencontre de Sacha Guitry* (Editions Oxus, 2010), and Laurent Terzieff's posthumous *Seul avec tous* (Presses de la Renaissance, co-written with Marie-Noëlle Tranchant and published in September 2010, shortly after Terzieff's death in July of that same year). Luchini's TV performances are famous for the same kind of pleasure he gives to theatre spectators: when he is invited onto various French talk shows, he always bursts out unexpectedly quoting classical French authors, which has made him very well known and liked – or hated – by a very large public today. Fabrice is a 'frequent guest' on TV shows. Barthes, Chrétien de Troyes, Molière, and Valéry have been favourites of his in the recent performances of his long-running one-man show *Le Point sur Robert* at various theatres including the Théâtre de la Gaîté–Montparnasse

('Robert' being his original given name).

Resisting any set categorization, yet ranking among the top ten best French actors today, he is a man who likes words, and who seduces people by this genuine love of words. And although he agreed to answer Jean-Dominique Brierre's questions on his life in *Le Mystère Luchini* (Plon, 2007), he remains a mind of great depth, who always, as Nietzsche said, 'needs a mask.'

Christophe MIQUEU
Université Montesquieu – Bordeaux IV

Benoît MAGIMEL (1974–)

*Good
Bad
Boy*

A VERSATILE and prolific actor, MAGIMEL began his career at the early age of 12, landing the leading role in *La Vie est un long fleuve tranquille /Life is a Long Quiet River* (Étienne Chatiliez, 1988) by responding to a newspaper ad. He left school at 16 to become a full-time actor, and appeared with Virginie Ledoyen in *La Fille seule /A Single Girl* (Benoît Jacquot, 1995) and in Matthieu Kassovitz's *La Haine /Hate* (1995).

After André Techiné casts him with Catherine Deneuve and Daniel Auteuil in *Les Voleurs /Thieves* (1996), Magimel comes into demand as a serious actor. He turns to independent cinema and challenging roles, working with Olivier Dahan and Florent-Emilio Siri. Some of Magimel's particularly memorable roles show him as the younger lover of an older woman. Thus, he plays Alfred de Musset in *Les Enfants du siècle / Children of the Century* (Diane Kurys, 1999), alongside Juliette Binoche – his partner at the time – in the role of George Sand. In *Selon Matthieu /To Matthieu* (Xavier Beauvois, 2000), he played a young lover of Nathalie Baye. In 2001, he appears beside Isabelle Huppert in Michael Haneke's *La*

Pianiste /The Piano Teacher, for which he received 'best actor' at Cannes. The role of a handsome and able music student drawn into a strange and traumatising relationship with his troubled teacher, who ends up bringing out his violent and perverse side, was particularly difficult, and definitively proved the maturity of Magimel's talent.

Magimel became a favourite with Siri (*Nid de guêpes /The Nest*, 2002; *L'Ennemi intime /Intimate Enemies*, 2007) and with Claude Chabrol (*La Fleur du mal /The Flower of Evil*, 2003; *La Demoiselle d'honneur /The Bridesmaid*, 2004; *La Fille coupée en deux /The Girl Cut in Two*, 2007). His roles tend to engage his physical appeal, but this is often presented with troubled, ambiguous undertones. One of Magimel's most interesting appearances was in Gérard Corbiau's lavish period drama *Le Roi danse / The King is Dancing* (2000), where he plays Louis XIV rising to maturity and power through dance performances.

Although the actor seemingly prefers working with young directors, and selects challenging roles in independent cinema, he has also participated in making blockbusters, such as *Les Rivières pourpres 2 – Les Anges de l'apocalypse /Crimson Rivers 2: Angels of the Apocalypse* (Olivier Dahan, 2004) and *Les Chevaliers du ciel /Sky Fighters* (Gérard Pirès, 2005). He also appeared, with Jacques Villeret, in the moving dramatic comedy *Effroyables jardins /Strange Gardens* (Jean Becker, 2003).

Magimel remains much sought-after. He appeared in the 2008 film *La Possibilité d'une île /Possibility of an Island*, which was directed by the novelist Michel Houellebecq, who adapted his own book for the screen, and in the recent Diane Kurys film, *Pour une femme /For a Woman* (2013). Magimel has a number of film and television projects in the works – unlike many famous French actors, Magimel has worked purely with film and television, and is not credited in a single theatre production.

Arina PATRIKOVA
The University of Oxford

Jean MARAIS (1913–1998)

An Ephebe in Tights and Cloaks

'TO PAINT illustrious heroes, to rid them of all fantastic mythology, to throw them into the world of the night without depriving them of their greatness – this is no easy work.' [1] These words depicting the creation of *L'Éternel retour /Love Eternal* (Jean Delannoy, 1943) could have been referring to Jean MARAIS – the main actor in the film – both to his life and his career.

After several years of playing the extra on stage and screen, it was this wartime version of *Tristan and Isolde* that brought Marais fame and recognition, as he and his co-star Madeleine Sologne became symbols for French youth during the Occupation. It was also the first cinematographic offspring of his collaboration and close friendship with Jean Cocteau. Many would follow, like *La Belle et la Bête /Beauty and the Beast* (1946), *Les Parents terribles /The Storm Within* (1948), *Orphée /Orpheus* (1950), or *Le Testament d'Orphée /The Testament of Orpheus* (1960). He was a versatile actor, with a repertoire ranging from cloak-and-dagger stories (Robert Vernay's 1954 *Le Comte de Monte-Cristo /The Count of Monte-Cristo*; Pierre Gaspard-Huit's 1961 *Le Capitaine Fracasse /Captain Fracasse*;

Henri Decoin's 1962 *Le Masque de fer /The Iron Mask*) and costume dramas (Jean Delannoy's 1961 *La Princesse de Clèves /Princess of Cleves*; André Hunebelle's 1962 *Les Mystères de Paris*) to popular novel adaptations (André Hunebelle's *Fantômas* trilogy, 1964-7), to more serious roles with movie icons of the period: *Elena et les hommes / Elena and Her Men* (Jean Renoir, 1956) with Ingrid Bergman; *White Nights* (Luchino Visconti, 1957) with Maria Schell, and *Stealing Beauty* (Bernardo Bertolucci, 1996) with Liv Tyler.

What would first strike men and women alike about Jean Marais was his classical beauty and charisma. He was a tall and charming man, whose muscular elegance made him a natural for stunts and sword battles. There was something about him of a 19th century James Bond in tights and a cloak. No wonder policemen's wives kept portraits of his Orpheus on their nightstands, when his shoulders were so much broader than Death's that it seemed he would get Eurydice back and belie the legend.

His regal physique endowed characters with eloquent theatrical gestures, which had lost the awkwardness of his debut. One wave of Fandor's hand had the energy of fifteen of Juve's somersaults.

His wavy hair and raised eyebrows gave him the tragic aura of the myths he was impersonating. His Orpheus's piercing glances were often looking away into nothingness, as if perpetually trying to decipher the car radio's oracles – 'silence goes faster backwards…mirrors are the doors through which death comes and goes…'

There was also something deceitful about the perfection of his looks, his muscular cheeks, and square jaw, symmetrically beautiful. He managed to turn beasts into Byronic outcasts with ancient powers and gentle natures, and to make us forget, if not forgive, the incestuous desires of a princess's father.[3]

But he also proved that beauty could be polymorphous, and became a master of the masks. He was the face behind Cocteau's dreamy drawings; he was the young man, the beast, and the prince in the black-and-white interpretation of the tale. When his face was nothing but glued beastly hair, after 5-hour make-up sessions, it seemed that his hallucinated eyes alone brought life to his pantheist universe of speaking mirrors and moving chandeliers. When Fandor the hero was wearing the sleek mask of the evil Fantômas, as well as that of his victim Professor Lefebvre, we got to the essence of Marais's power – one actor could be all characters thanks to his metamorphoses.[4] The only mask missing from his collection was certainly that of old age. But then again, 'it is the privilege of a legend to be ageless.' [5]

Emilie L'Hôte
Université Paris Diderot – Paris 7

1. Article by Jean Cocteau in *Présent*, September 27, 1943.

2. Louis de Funès in the *Fantômas* trilogy.

3. *Peau d'âne /Donkey Skin* (Jacques Demy, 1970).

4. Philippe Azoury and Jean-Marc Lalanne, Fantômas, *Style Moderne* (Paris: Centre Pompidou /Crisnée, Belgium: Editions Yellow Now, 2002).

5. *Orpheus*, Jean Cocteau.

Sophie MARCEAU (1966–)
[Sophie Danièle Sylvie MAUPU]

Growing Up After La Boum

DISCOVERED BY filmmaker Claude Pinoteau, Sophie MARCEAU (born in Paris in 1966) made her silver-screen debut in the cult comedy in Pinoteau's *La Boum / The Party* (1980) at the young age of thirteen. Her unforgettable role as the teenager Vic Beretton in *La Boum* had a lasting impact on her future career and stardom. Resonating with an entire generation of adolescents, the film tells the story of a girl next door who has problems with her parents and friends, goes to school, parties, and discos, and finds support in her grandmother. The innocent and fresh appearance of Sophie Marceau compensates for what the comedy lacks in narrative depth and style. The young actress instantly became an iconic model for the contemporary young generation and illustrated the potential appeal of French popular cinema to international audiences. Two years after the great success of *La Boum*, the film producers released a sequel, *La Boum 2* (Pinoteau, 1982), starring a fifteen-year-old Marceau and depicting the problems her character now faces in her burgeoning love life. Again, France fell in love with

Vic, and Marceau received the César Award for Most Promising Actress in 1983.

After these two enormous successes, the biggest challenge that Marceau faced was to start anew. The 'Vic' image was now not only a key part of her persona, but it would also impact the choice and appraisal of her future roles. In a predictable manner, several parts played by Marceau throughout her career have been, more or less, variations on *La Boum*. Pinoteau's *L'Étudiante* (1988), for example, follows Vic as she grows up and tells the story of a student who is preparing her *agrégation*. Even in the more recent *LOL (Laughing Out Loud)* (Lisa Azuelos, 2008), Marceau plays the mother of a teenager, inviting an inevitable comparison to her role as Vic. In addition, Marceau's popular appeal made her a preferred candidate for more serious roles in France's heritage cinema. For instance, she appeared in the costume drama *Fort Saganne* (Alain Corneau, 1984), alongside well-known actors such as Catherine Deneuve and Gérard Depardieu, and held the main role in the swashbuckling production *La Fille de d'Artagnan /Revenge of the Musketeers* (Bernard Tavernier, 1994).

Marceau also began a search for authenticity on her own terms, choosing more challenging roles, and directly undermining her image of an innocent adolescent. On this path, the encounter with the film director Andrzej Żuławski was decisive in Marceau's transition from an innocent *gamine* to a young actress, in particular through excessive sexualization. In their first film, *L'Amour braque* (1985), inspired by Dostoievskis's novel *The Idiot*, Marceau's role as a prostitute completely shattered her image as *la fiancée des français*. In Maurice Pialat's *Police* (1985), she accepted once more a role that went against her well-established star image, playing a young woman living with criminals. In *Joyeuses Pâques* (Georges Lautner, 1984), Marceau, the teenager next door, becomes the lover of the fifty-year-old Jean-Paul Belmondo, and in 1986, she shocked her adoring fans, yet again, with *Descente aux enfers* (Francis Girod, 1986) in which she plays a young woman who attempts to overcome a traumatic rape, and begins a self-destructive relationship with a married, alcoholic writer. The scandal was only intensified by the fact that Marceau's lover in the film is played by Claude Brasseur, who starred as her father in *La Boum*.

In the other three collaborations with Żuławski – *Mes nuits sont plus belles que vos jours /My Nights are More Beautiful than Your Days* (1989); *La Note bleue* (1991), a biopic about Georges Sand and Chopin, and *La Fidélité /Fidelity* (2000), a modern adaptation of *La Princesse de Clèves* – Marceau was cast in similar roles, in a poetic and erotic style. The opinions of the critics were divided: they either praised Marceau as a mature artist or harshly criticized her. Regardless of the ambiguous reception, it is clear that through these demanding roles, Marceau attempted to carve out an alternative path for her film career, challenging her star image defined exclusively through *La Boum*. In

the mid-1990s, the '*Marquise* affair' reinforced Marceau's reputation as a difficult actress. Filmmaker Véra Belmont accused the star – who had the leading role in Belmont's film *Marquise* (1997) – of publicly criticizing the film and thus not fulfilling her obligations to promote it. At the same time, Marceau became more visible in international productions as her key appearances in Mel Gibson's *Braveheart* (1995), Michelangelo Antonioni's *Par-delà les nuages /Beyond the Clouds* (1995), and Bernard Rose's *Anna Karenina* (1997) attest. Her most important international role was, arguably, that of a James Bond girl in *The World is not Enough* (Michael Apted, 1999). The Gallic actress convincingly and delightfully plays a seductive villain, remaining a memorable and refreshing character in the dull gallery of passive Bond girls.

The end of the professional and private relationship with Żuławski prompted Marceau to start a filmmaking career as well. *Parlez-moi d'amour /Speak to me of Love* (2002), her first film, is an introspective look into a love relationship, inspired by her personal past with Żuławski. Exploring a different direction in her second film, *La Disparue de Deauville /Trivial* (2007), she found inspiration in the tradition of the psychological thriller. Even in the first decade of the twenty-first century, Marceau relentlessly pursued her career in popular films through collaborations with Jean-Paul Salomé in *Belphégor – le fantôme du Louvre /Belphegor, Phantom of the Louvre* (2001) and in the historical drama *Les Femmes de l'ombre /Female*

Agents (2008), through her lead role in the sentimental thriller *Anthony Zimmer* (Jerôme Salle, 2005), and, finally, through her part in a recent romantic comedy alongside a younger French star, Gad Elmaleh, *Un bonheur n'arrive jamais seul / Happiness Never Comes Alone* (James Huth, 2012). Despite the ups and downs of her career, Marceau has maintained a constant presence on the silver screen. Since her debut in 1980, she has made roughly one film per year, establishing herself as a solid and popular female star in the landscape of French contemporary cinema.

Nicoleta BAZGAN
University of Maryland,
Baltimore County

Jean-Pierre MARIELLE (1932–)

The Disillusioned Seducer

Like Philippe Noiret and Jean Rochefort, Jean-Pierre MARIELLE belongs to a tradition of French actors renowned and loved for their inimitable and instantly recognizable voices. Born on April 12, 1932 in Dijon, Marielle first discovered acting while in high school. He was accepted to the Conservatoire in the same cohort as Jean-Paul Belmondo and Jean Rochefort, forging a close and enduring friendship with them both. Like Belmondo, Noiret, Rochefort, and also Jean-Claude Brialy, Jean Carmet, and Annie Girardot, Marielle counts among the leading figures of the French cinema of the 1970s.

Profiting from his classic training at the Conservatoire, Marielle first turned to the theatre, where he performed works by Jean Anouilh, Paul Claudel, Sacha Guitry, Harold Pinter, and Luigi Pirandello, among others. He then tried his hand at cabaret, alongside Guy Bedos, prior to becoming more consistently involved in cinema from the late 1960s onwards. Of particular note is his role as playboy Jean-Jacques Leroy-Martin in Philippe de Broca's *Le Diable par la queue /The Devil by the Tail* (1969), which signalled the beginning of a series of colourful figures of disillusioned and aging romantic losers that contributed greatly to Marielle's fame and his endearing popularity with audiences.

His reputation as a solid comic actor exploded in the 1970s with films like *Sex-shop /Le Sex Shop* (Claude Berri, 1972); *La Valise /Man in the Trunk* (Georges Lautner, 1973), *Calmos /Femmes Fatales* (Bertrand Blier, 1976), and, to a lesser extent, *Que la fête commence... /Let Joy Reign Supreme* (1975), his first collaboration with Bertrand Tavernier. Despite his participation in a number of successful movies directed by a wide array of French directors – Chantal Akerman, Claude Berri, Bertrand Blier (who directed him four times), Alain Corneau, Georges Lautner, Patrice Leconte, Claude Miller, Yves Robert, and Henri Verneuil – Marielle remained, for the most part, a supporting actor. It is only in 1991, with the character of Monsieur de Sainte-Colombe in the film adaptation of *Tous les matins du monde /All the Mornings of the World* (Alain Corneau), that the French public discovered Marielle's pathos and gravitas in a lead role and his ability for dramatic performances.

Given his looks – stature, voice, premature baldness – Marielle could have been employed to play intimidating figures, but it is his ability to incarnate the typical French 'beauf' – a slightly idiotic, misogynistic and loud-mouthed skirt-chaser – that brought him fame. He excels in portrayals of womanisers and in social satires, such as Claude Berri's *Sex-shop*, where he plays the character of Lucien, a man of two passions: refurbishing old houses and

group sex! His talent lies in his ability to avoid vulgarity and his capacity to introduce an ounce of *gravitas* into these satirical parts.

Marielle's main screen persona can also be encapsulated as that of the 'friend', a man surrounded by other males for whom friendship and the ability to fool around with his mates – as with Philippe Noiret and Jean Rochefort in *Les Grands Ducs* (Patrice Leconte, 1996) – is of primary importance. The public's love for him is no doubt born of his ability to impersonate this typical 'déconneur,' with a deadpan sense of humour, delivered with impeccable comic sense through his deep baritone voice and imperturbable facial expression.

Widely celebrated as an actor, Jean-Pierre Marielle did not, however, receive many awards for his cinematographic and his theatrical career, with the exception of one Molière, the highest French award for theatre acting in 1994. Both *Les Grands Ducs* (1996) and *Les Acteurs / Actors* (Bertrand Blier, 2000) failed to meet with success and some of his choices surprised the profession, such as the very strange *Atomik circus, le retour de James Bataille /The Return of James Batalle* (Didier Poiraud and Thierry Poiraud, 2004). Two years later, however, he appeared in the highly anticipated Ron Howard-directed adaptation of Dan Brown's *The Da Vinci Code*, where he played Le Louvre's curator Jacques Saunière. A year later, in 2007, Marielle lent his voice to the character of head chef Gusteau in the Pixar animated film *Ratatouille* (dir. Brad Bird and Jan Pinkava).

Combining cinema, theatre, and

television, and with over 100 movies under his belt, Marielle's career shows no sign of slowing down. Not only is he willing to try his hands at many genres, this is also an actor in tune with a younger generation of comedians like Omar Sy, José Garcia, and Gad Elmaleh who all appear with him in Olivier Dahan's *Les Seigneurs* (2012).

In *Le grand n'importe quoi*, the autobiography he published in 2010 (Calmann-Lévy), Jean-Pierre Marielle describes his fondness for the average, seeing himself as an average actor, with an average career, having played in a number of average films. But it is precisely this ability to embody normality that contributes to the public's ongoing love for this disillusioned seducer.

France GRENAUDIER-KLIJN
Massey University, New Zealand

Roxane MESQUIDA (1981–)

*Not
Cyrano's
Roxanne*

BEST KNOWN for her role in Catherine Breillat's *À ma soeur !* /*Fat Girl* (2001), a controversial film by a controversial director, Roxane MESQUIDA appeared mostly in films focusing on sexuality and on the problems of adolescence. She was discovered by Manuel Pradal while he was shooting *Marie baie des anges* /*Marie from the Bay of Angels* (1997), and played one of the several lost, hedonistic teenagers engaged in a misguided quest for self-discovery through sex and violence on the French Riviera. She then acted in Benoît Jacquot's *L'École de la chair* / *The School of Flesh* (1998), based on a novel by Yukio Mishima, alongside Isabelle Huppert, and in Olivier Panchot's *Les Paradis de Laura* (2002), a TV film exploring the mundane troubles and budding sexuality of a schoolgirl.

Fat Girl engages the actress's youthful sex appeal and romantic looks to show the darker side of sex, with outright brutality characteristic of Breillat's work. In this film, her most important so far, Mesquida plays a 15-year-old teenage beauty, whose loss of innocence is watched and analysed by her unprepossessing younger sister (Anaïs Reboux). The film was famously banned by the Ontario Film Board for its depiction of sexual intercourse between characters under 18, and received mixed reviews, as some critics found it too heavy-handed and failing in its message, but it was recognised as important. For the young actress, it was the beginning of apprenticeship and friendship with Breillat. She appeared in Breillat's *Sex is Comedy* (2002), a cinematic reflection of the director's difficulties in making *Fat Girl*, and in *Une vieille maîtresse / The Last Mistress* (2007), based on the 1851 novel by Barbey d'Aurevilly. Mesquida also played in *Sheitan* (Kim Chapiron, 2006), alongside Vincent Cassel, and then moved to the United States, where she was cast in several TV series, while also continuing her modelling career over the years.

Like Emmanuelle Béart, Roxane Mesquida said that she was influenced by Romy Schneider in her decision to become an actress. Indeed, her roles depend overwhelmingly on representations of idealised female beauty, but the actress has eschewed the stereotypes of popular cinema. For instance, she starred in *Sexes très opposés /Very Opposite Sexes* (Eric Assous, 2002), a 'mockumentary' about love as it happens in Paris according to statistical evidence aimed to overturn the conventional depictions of love as 'happily ever after' in romantic comedy, just as Breillat's films aim to break away from the sexual stereotypes in cinema.

Arina PATRIKOVA
The University of Oxford

Paul MEURISSE (1912–1979)

The Elegant Art of Sarcasm

BORN IN Dunkirk, the son of a local bank branch manager, Paul Gustave MEURISSE was brought up in Corsica, then Burgundy, and finally Provence. As a student he was a tenacious plodder, and wound up as an apprentice clerk to a *notaire* in Aix, but he found ample distraction outside this humdrum working life. Every inch the young dandy, with a remarkable head of hair the colour of Indian ink, Meurisse was idolised by women; away from his apprenticeship he spent what remained of the day working in the stables, while by night he was to be found in the *cafés-concerts* and clubs. He soon caught the acting bug, and in 1933 came to the realisation that this was to be his path in life.[1] It was his triple education in matters sentimental (or sensual), equestrian and sybaritic, rather than his formal studies, which laid the foundations of the distinctive style which Jean Anouilh came to admire: self-assurance in the face of any challenge, the discreet vanity of the successful lothario, and the affected stiffness of the accomplished dressage rider, all cloaked in a veil of irony which ranged from gentle mockery to sardonic wit to occasional cynicism.

Although   Meurisse   was   of

Flemish origin, from a young age he effectively belonged to the Midi, while his impassive, slanting features were more redolent of the Far East; his already impeccable diction and the timbre of his voice – by turns dry and soothing – set him on his course, with performances in song recital gaining him access to the theatre stage and eventually the film set.[2] He spent three years singing himself hoarse in Corsica and on the Riviera, adopting a contrary style in which he interpreted burlesque ditties in a mournful tone, until eventually he won a singing contest on the radio.[3] This success attracted considerable attention, and in 1936 it earned him his first appearance in the clubs of Pigalle.

Meurisse was encouraged, indeed pushed forward, by a series of female benefactors, famous names who were used to playing to packed audiences – Marie-Louise Damia, Huguette Duflos, Marie Dubas and, above all, Édith Piaf, for whom Meurisse was much more than just another passing fancy.[4] The new boy, a sort of French Buster Keaton – at once droll and coolly impassive – flourished on stage among the feathers of the Bluebell Girls, and soon made inroads into the theatre, where Jean Cocteau wrote *Le Bel indifférent* (1939) for him and Piaf.

Meurisse became a pillar of the very best comedy theatre of the boulevards, often performing alongside Danielle Darrieux,[5] with whom he also appeared onscreen on five occasions – Léonide Moguy's *Bethsabée* (1947), Henri Decoin's *L'Affaire des poisons / The Case of Poisons* (1955), Raymond Bernard's *Le Septième Ciel /Seventh Heaven* (1958), Julien Duvivier's *Marie-Octobre* (1959), and André Hunebelle's *Méfiez-vous, mesdames !* (1963). On July 10, 1954, however, Meurisse the former variety artist was confirmed as an accomplished tragic actor when he played to an audience of 10,000 at the Roman amphitheatre in Arles, in Jean Renoir's grandiose staging of Shakespeare's *Julius Caesar*. His performance as Brutus, in which he portrayed the character as a paragon of moral rectitude, earned him his stripes as a *sociétaire* of the Comédie-Française, where he bore the insignia of the mighty Roman general Coriolanus.[6]

In 1941 his first foray into film began, as did his stage career, in the shadow of Édith Piaf (*Montmartre-sur-Seine*, directed by Georges Lacombe), but he soon emerged from her influence and protection, blossoming into a pivotal, often central actor in genre cinema. Whether playing a gangster, an elegant crook, or a policeman, whether sardonic, good-natured, or displaying the cold humour of the archetypal phlegmatic gentleman,[7] Meurisse brought to his performances two great components of the prolific police/crime genre – insouciant comedy and film noir.

Meurisse displayed his particular brand of oblique humour as Inspector Sergil in a sequence of three eponymous films by Jacques Daroy produced between the years 1947 and 1952, all of them filmed in the Midi,[8] before going against the grain of the espionage genre of the day in Georges Lautner's *Monocle* series between 1961 and 1964, films with strong Gaullist overtones which veered between comedy and detective cinema.[9] While the eccentric and grandiose figure of Commander Théobald Dromard of the SDECE and his curious way of carrying a revolver remain unforgettable, Meurisse's fame as a film actor rests more on the Série Noire films – characterised by their atmosphere of terror and their exploration of criminal psychology – and in particular the roles he played in the great works of Henri-Georges Clouzot and Jean-Pierre Melville. Meurisse had featured in the rebirth of the film noir in the immediate post-war years – in Jacques Feyder and Marcel Blistère's *Macadam* (1946) – but it was in the genre's transformation during the mid-1950s that he played a crucial role.

His status as an actor was conspicuously enhanced by Clouzot's *Les Diaboliques /Diabolique* (1955), in which he renewed the fruitful partnership he had established with Simone Signoret.[10] The important on-screen association between Signoret and Meurisse began with *Macadam*, and was followed by *Impasse des deux anges /Dilemma of Two Angels* (Maurice Tourneur, 1948), *Les Diaboliques*, and then *L'Armée des ombres /Army of Shadows* (Jean- Pierre Melville, 1969). He reached his apogee in Melville's *Le Deuxième Souffle /Second Breath* in 1966 – which today is still regarded as one of a handful of unsurpassed French police dramas.[11] Literally inhabiting the character of the elegant, indomitable Inspector Blot, Paul Meurisse offers a master class in the art of sarcasm, and is the focus of one of the genre's greatest and most unforgettable sequences [12] – a breathtaking long take of around five minutes containing a remarkable monologue, a true *tour de force* which

was universally acclaimed at the time, and is still celebrated today. [13]

Paul Meurisse was not destined to live to an old age; he died at age 66 in Neuilly in January 1979.

Pierre LETHIER
University of Buckingham (BUCSIS)

1. Paul Meurisse, *Les Éperons de la liberté* (Paris: Robert Laffont, 1979), 64.
2. Olivier Barrot and Raymond Chirat, *Noir et blanc: 250 acteurs du cinéma français 1930–1950* (Paris: Flammarion, 2000), 376.
3. Meurisse, *Les Éperons*, 80.
4. Barrot and Chirat *Noir et blanc*, 376; Meurisse, *Les Éperons*, 107.
5. Yanick Dehée and Christian-Marc Bossino, *Dictionnaire du cinéma populaire français* (Paris: Nouveau Monde Éditions, 2009), 593.
6. Yvan Foucart, *Dictionnaire des comédiens disparus* (Mariembourg: Éditions Grand Angle, 2001), 581.
7. Dehée and Bossino, *Dictionnaire du cinéma populaire français*, 593.
8. Georges Guarracino, *L'Écran provençal: histoire et géographie du cinéma en Provence et Côte d'Azur* (Saint-Rémy-de-Provence: Éditions Equinoxe, 2006), 219.
9. François Guérif, *Le Cinéma policier français* (Paris: Henri Veyrier, 1981), 128.
10. Simone Signoret, *Nostalgia Isn't What It Used to Be* (London: Crafton Books, 1979), 92, 95, 140.
11. Barrot and Chirat, *Noir et blanc*, 378.
12. Jacques Zimmer and Chantal de Béchade, *Jean-Pierre Melville* (Paris: Edilig, 1983), 87.
13. Ginette Vincendeau, *Jean-Pierre Melville, an American in Paris* (London: BFI Publishing, 2003), 159.

Gérard Meylan (1952–)

*L'Estaque
Embodied*

G ÉRARD MEYLAN has a job, and
it is not acting. After finishing
studies in his hometown, the
disenfranchised Marseilles suburb of
L'Estaque, Meylan became a nurse in
1972, eventually settling into a night
shift in a pulmonary ward. This career
choice was guided by a social idealism
(he was a co-leader of the communist
youth group of L'Estaque): he wanted
to make himself 'useful' to his
community. Meylan would not act in
his first film for another seven years,
and continues to do so today on days
off or during sick and occasionally
more extended leave.

It was a propitious friendship that
brought Meylan to the cinema. The
other co-leader of the communist
youth of l'Estaque happened to be a
young man named Robert Guédiguian,
whom Meylan had met in school.
The two had grown close listening to
Meylan's relatives talk about politics,
and developed a love for both political
organizing and cinema. When Gérard
took his diploma in nursing, Robert
left to study sociology and met Ariane
Ascaride and Jean-Pierre Darroussin.
Of this famous Guédiguian family,
Meylan is the eldest, the only real
Estaquéen, and the only one to retain
a literal place in the economic and

social forces of Marseilles.[1]

Guédiguian did not forget his
friend when he returned to l'Estaque
to make his first film. *Dernier été / Last
Summer* (1981) contains in vitro the
sum of the Meylan persona that will
mature over the decades. Handsome
but mysterious, Meylan's character
anchors a group of friends and family
facing the economic changes in
L'Estaque during the late 1970s. He
is gregarious, intercedes in friends'
disputes, and falls in love. He refuses
to work, preferring the anarchist's life
of petty crime, and prefers to move
between others to create a social bond
and sense of solidarity. This social-
anarchist radicalism remains a steady
undercurrent throughout his work
with Guédiguian (in just one example,
Marius et Jeannette (1997), Meylan
feigns a disability to win a watchman's
job and helps the neighbourhood kids
with their homework).[2] Meylan is the
actor Guédiguian aligns most closely
with the community of L'Estaque.

This identification is forged
in Meylan's body: tall, svelte, and
handsome. A memorable image from
Dernier été has Meylan silhouetted
against the Mediterranean sunset,
wearing only his speedo, on what
looks like the ruin of a dock crane
set on a cliff overlooking the bay,
his long hair blowing in the wind
as he executes a beautiful dive into
the ocean far below. Only someone
born in L'Estaque, the destination
for Cézanne and other painters
seeking the shapes and colours of the
Mediterranean port city, could mirror
the town's unique light. Guédiguian
loves to film nude bodies and frank
sexuality, and Meylan (with the
possible exception of Ascaride) is the

actor he films most naked. Even when Meylan grew into middle age, in films like *Marius et Jeannette* and *Marie-Jo et ses deux amours /Marie-Jo and Her Two Lovers* (2002), Guédiguian's lighting and framing emphasize most the smoothness and tan colour of Meylan's skin. This is one of the unique techniques in Guédiguian's so-called 'fairy tale' style, and Meylan's roughed up handsomeness obliges.

But Meylan also reflects the city's eclipse. In one scene of *Dernier été* he sits in front of a café at night, while a voiceover conveys his inner thoughts in his Marseillais drawl: « ce quartier est mort et moi avec » ['this neighbourhood is dead and me with it']. Meylan's handsome face is also scarred from acne, his hair dark and unwieldy, his clothes dirty, and his stare worried. In more recent films, like the wintry *Lady Jane* (Guédiguian, 2008), Meylan has lost much of his tan, grown thick around the middle, and his face has fallen. Meylan's /l'Estaque's beauty becomes pockmarked, punished, and past.

This sinister side can burst into sudden violence. Nastiness erupts from a bitter nostalgia, as the pent up anger of L'Estaque bubbles to the surface like the pockmarks on Meylan's face: in films like Guédiguian's *Ki lo sa ?* (1985) and *Dieu vomit les tièdes* (1991), Meylan plays skulking marginals who refuse to work and who spew disdain on childhood friends who have betrayed their ideals during the Mitterrand years and the rise of the Front National. In *Dieu...*, Meylan's character has an obsessive focus on the past, leading him – despite his friends' opposition – to commit a rash of politically motivated murders. In

Guédiguian's *La Ville est tranquille /The Town is Quiet* (2000) he is a vicious political hit man.[3] With Meylan, one cannot always be sure whether one is dealing with utopia or dystopia.

Meylan's textured body seems to contain layers of history, good and bad, an effect deepening as the years pass. And it has indeed been moulded by a life of work that has given it character, strong lines, and despite its scars, a mature beauty. In a *Libération* interview from 1997 he compares nursing and acting: 'A woman at the hospital once wrote to me: "Thank you for helping me live." Our history is like that. Our proposition in terms of society is not to accept fatality... Robert has gone from a relatively pessimistic nostalgia to a flight of hope.' More than any other actor, Meylan has helped Guédiguian give l'Estaque a face and a body that express the pessimism of bleak times, but also the flights of hope.

Joseph MAI
Clemson University, South Carolina

1. Robert Guédiduian and Ariane Ascaride: see Georgiana M. M. Colvile, 'Robert Guédiguian and Ariane Ascaride: In Conversation,' in *World Film Locations: Marseilles*, ed. Marcelline Block (Bristol: Intellect, 2013), 106-107. —Ed.

2. *Marius and Jeannette*: see Annette Insdorf, 'Making the Aioli,' in *World Film Locations: Marseilles*, ed. Marcelline Block (Bristol: Intellect, 2013), 72-73. —Ed.

3. *La Ville est tranquille* : see Jean-Luc Lioult, 'The Old Port and The Canebière,' in *World Film Locations: Marseilles*, ed. Marcelline Block (Bristol: Intellect, 2013), 28-29. —Ed.

Miou-Miou (1950–)
[Sylvette Herry]

*Small
Turbulence
in French
Cinema*

The French audience became aware of her uncommon name and her presence through the scandalous *Les Valseuses /Going Places* (Bertrand Blier, 1974). It was not her debut film, though. She started earlier in 1971. Some early films were *Les Aventures de Rabbi Jacob / The Mad Adventures of Rabbi Jacob* (Gérard Oury, 1973), a Louis de Funès comedy, and *Elle court, elle court la banlieue /The Suburbs Are Everywhere* (Gérard Pirès, 1973). Over the past forty years, Miou-Miou, whose real name is Sylvette Herry, has managed to become France's most popular actress, cherished by all, and yet she is somewhat atypical when it comes to the French film landscape and its actresses. She stands out, and stands apart from other glamorous French actresses, whose names and fame are celebrated abroad, and at home, as spokespersons for fashion products in commercials. She is not as *médiatique* as Isabelle Adjani, Brigitte Bardot, Juliette Binoche, Carole Bouquet, Catherine Deneuve, Isabelle Huppert, or Jeanne Moreau.

Her uncharacteristic trajectory is worthy of attention since she struggled for many years to find her voice and always questioned her place as an actress. She was at first timid: « J'ai mis beaucoup de temps, beaucoup, à m'avouer que j'aimais jouer, que c'était un métier…Pendant assez longtemps, j'ai joué en m'excusant. C'est pour cela que j'avais cette voix ténue. » ['It took me a long long time to recognize that I loved to act, that it was a profession…For a long time, I acted while excusing myself.'] [1]

Born in 1950, Miou-Miou came of age in the late 1960s, and embodies the winds of rebellion that shook France then with the May 68 revolution and French women's emancipation. Several unique roles anchored her in the 60s, shaping the image of a liberated woman. Navigating through different genres, styles, and periods, she never stays firmly put in a specific one: she circulates between mainstream cinema, auteur, and avant-garde cinema as well as heritage cinema. She moves from comedies to dramas, crime stories, and *mélos* (melodramas). She started as a comedian with café-theatre roles. Her early parts were controversial, and as she has aged, the roles have mellowed. Many Miou-Miou characters are memorable. She has dabbled with theatre, but not extensively, although her acting in Marguerite Duras's plays is remarkable.

Les Valseuses may well represent a provocative acting 'debut' – a catalyst for several subsequent rebellious roles, where she plays against trends. Many associate her with the rebellious spirit of May 68: *Milou en mai /May Fools* (Louis Malle, 1990) casts May 68, as the *toile de fond* [backdrop] of the film.[2] Malle proposed a vision of rural France and of a French family during the May '68 events, displacing the centre for the periphery. The director chose her for a rather unsympathetic role, thinking she would bring a certain sincerity to the film.[3]

Her persona evolved. For a long time, although an adult, she performed the *gamine*. She appears as Marie, the supermarket cashier who befriends members of a Marxist commune near Geneva, in Alain Tanner's hymn to 68: *Jonah qui aura 25 ans en l'an 2000 /Jonah Who Will Be 25 in the Year 2000* (1976). The endearing character shows a compassionate side in her friendship with different generations, as she brings groceries to Charles La Vapeur (Raymond Bussières), a retiree who connects the film to Popular Front ideology. Together with Charles, they 'reenact memories in song, dance, and sketch.'[4]

Of the same generation as Josiane Balasko (born in 1950), and Isabelle Huppert (born in 1953), by a few years, Miou-Miou maintains a rather low profile, selecting roles that are demanding and charismatic. She has acted for the following French directors: Jacques Becker, Claude Berri, Yves Boisset, Michel Deville, Michel Gondry, Diane Kurys, Louis Malle, and Alain Tanner, and played opposite famous actors and actresses such as Maria Casarès, Gérard Depardieu, Patrick Dewaere, Sami Frey at the theatre, Yves Montand, Michel Piccoli, Isabelle Huppert, Rufus, Michel Bouquet, Charles Berling, and Niels Arestrup, among others. On the heels of her success with *Les Valseuses*, she was recruited by foreign directors Marco Bellochio, Luigi Comencini, and Joseph Losey.

Many times, she appears as the 'woman next-door,' a working-class girl, the best friend, the (nice) girl or *gamine*, the homemaker, the mother, and more recently a 'young' grandmother. Her performances are strongly gender-inflected, and at the edge of shifting perspectives on women's positions in French society in World War II and after. Diane Kurys's *Coup de foudre /Entre Nous /At First Sight* cast her as a young French woman who befriends a Jewish Belgian woman (Isabelle Huppert). The latter survived the war, and resettled in France in the immediate aftermath of World War II. Incidentally, this is the first role when Miou-Miou is given children. Both women fall in love with each other, to the point of leaving their respective husbands, and moving in together despite 1950s conventions. The focus originates from Kurys's biography, revealing her mother's lesbian friendship. It leans toward the character of Léna, yet Madeleine stands out, strong, vulnerable, artsy, and 'chic' in the middle of a Bohemian relationship with her husband (Jean-Pierre Bacri), her feminized son, and her partner's macho and future ex-husband (Guy Marchand) until the end, when she breaks down and is hospitalized before being rescued by Léna. Madeleine is an artist, who somehow abandoned painting after her first husband was killed by the Militia in Lyons at the end of the war. She still engages with sculpting. She is not afraid to express her feelings for Léna and is sensual, sensitive, and natural in her behaviour. She is more cosmopolitan and cultivated than her friend and decides to take the lead and open a fashion shop for them. One recalls that at that time, women in France did not have the right to open their own bank accounts and had to ask permission from their husband in order to do so, as well as to learn how to drive. Madeleine represents France during *les trente glorieuses*. Miou-Miou's acting 'is remarkable in these half-tone sequences where her burgeoning desire brushes against a shyly, trembling, sensual Isabelle Huppert.'[5]

Miou-Miou's style is classical and…natural. She enters the profession through the café-theatre door and rather stumbles into acting without passing through an acting school. She was in her late teens when she started. Some refer to this moment as fairy-tale-like; in her own words: « C'est l'histoire d'une petite fille pauvre qui soudain s'est transformée en princesse. Ça a l'air d'un petit conte de fées, les gens aiment bien » ['It is the story of a poor little girl who is suddenly transformed into a princess. It looks like a fairy tale and people like that'].[6]

She comes from a working-class background, as her mother worked at Les Halles market and her father was a policeman; she was apprenticing for another profession, that of a tapestry maker. Coluche, her boyfriend, baptized her Miou-Miou, referring to her small voice and demeanour. The name close to a catcall stuck. It has become a household name.

She demonstrates early on that she is not afraid to take on rather difficult roles, some of them sexually explicit. Yet, in many of these she is mistreated. Her acting debut coincides with the 1970's wave of liberalization in cinema, and the influx of mainstream erotic/ pornographic films on screens. She became popular during the 1980s, a moment that witnesses the discomfiture of males, the crisis of masculinity, the rapid rise of women on the job market, yet the strong belief that they should be at home raising children according to polls.[7]

In *Les Valseuses* (Blier, 1974), Marie-Ange, a hairdresser, is kidnapped by two male punks (Patrick Dewaere and Gérard Depardieu) who alternately try to molest her then please her, and coerce her into a marginal life on the road, rendered powerless by her frigidity. Jill Forbes describes her as 'in appearance, an uninhibited girl, complete with mini-skirt and contraceptives.'[8] Later on, she meets up once more with Depardieu and Blier in the 1980s, in the role of a rather castrating wife in the parodic *Tenue de soirée /Ménage* (Blier, 1986), caught in a *ménage à trois* situation between her husband Antoine (Michel Blanc) befriended by a small time criminal Bob (Gérard Depardieu). Miou-Miou's roles from *Les Valseuses* to *Tenue de soirée* show a deepening of the male crisis.[9] The threesome situation is reenacted in the more recent and sombre crime film *Nettoyage à sec /Dry Cleaning* (Anne Fontaine, 1997) in which a couple – with a now middle-aged Miou-Miou – falls for an androgynous young character who seduces them both.

Many directors project her into the past of World War II, as in *Folle embellie* (Dominique Cabrera, 2004), *Coup de foudre* (Diane Kurys), and, in *Les Routes du sud /Roads to the South* (Joseph Losey, 1978, written by Jorge Semprún), the aftermath of the Spanish Civil War. *Blanche et Marie / Blanche and Marie* (Jacques Renard, 1985) takes a look at women's resistance during the war. Her persona adapts well to historical reconstructions and wartime scenarios, maybe because of her classical features.

Miou-Miou does not consider herself a star. On the other hand, she draws the line between her position and 'stars' like Deneuve, by her claims that 'to me a star is inaccessible, mysterious, an impossible dream – and should stay that way. Adjani's a star, Deneuve's a star…not me.'[10] She became a star despite herself, according to the film critic Isabelle Regnier. Yet in 1976, she was considered the number one French star by *Paris Match*, her picture displayed on the front cover, with Julien Clerc: « Miou-Miou : Amour, Gloire et Beauté. »[11] The same issue traces her move to the countryside, and her decision to raise her two daughters there with Clerc, privileging her maternal side with the ensuing image that the audience keeps of her. She is low-key and far from glamour. Her characters do not wear heavy or loud make-up. They are discreet. Yet, her biography is complete with details about her relationships with at least four men at different stages of her life, two actors, one singer, and a writer, two of whom she married: Coluche, Patrick Dewaere, Julien Clerc, and Jean Teulé, as well as details about her two daughters.

Very few academic studies are devoted to her; it is mostly through blogs, Facebook, or other fan pages, and popular press reviews that one can form any opinion of the actress, besides her films, and still one has to sift through the *people* like public biographical and personal data. French film history books do not cover her, but gloss over her, while discussing the films she has been in.

She rarely made the covers of film magazines or fashion magazines. *Studio* magazine – now defunct – featured her in profile, embraced by Gérard Depardieu, her acting partner in Claude Berri's 1993 heritage epic *Germinal* with the line: « Depardieu–Miou-Miou – *Des Valseuses* à *Germinal* – 20 ans déjà » ['Depardieu–Miou-Miou – From *Going Places* to *Germinal* – 20 Years Already'],[12] evoking the reunion between the two actors, twenty years later. Miou-Miou played with Depardieu at least three times, if not more. She made the cover once earlier, and alone, with her portrait in a short haircut « Miou-Miou – Les amours d'une blonde » ['Miou-Miou – The loves of a blonde'].[13]

Miou-Miou is a politically committed actress. She has embraced several important causes and feminism is one of them. Gisèle Halimi is a long-time friend of hers and together they fought in the 'trenches'. She is deeply committed to the cause of homeless people and the right to lodging; she has belonged to the D.A.L. association since the 1990s.[14]

In Michel Deville's successful *La Lectrice /The Reader* (1988), an adaptation of Raymond Jean's eponymous 1987 novel, Miou-Miou takes a more literary orientation, with a playful character – Marie-Constance G., a young woman who loves to read, and decides to make it her profession as a reader to people in a provincial town. She puts an ad in the newspapers. As she reads to others, she in turns becomes the character of the text. It is a charismatic role where the actress finds and uses her beautiful voice. The film for the first time agrees with her:

Jusque là, ma filmographie se résumait en un musée de personnages dans lesquels je m'efforçais d'entrer en m'abstrayant de tout et, en premier lieu, de ma vie même. J'étais aux ordres du scénario. Aujourd'hui, pour la première fois, j'ai l'impression que...le scénario m'obéit.

[Until then, my filmography was summed up as a gallery of characters, which I would try to enter, while making abstraction of all, and in the first place, of my life itself. I was under the orders of the script. Today, for the first time, I have the feeling that...the script obeys me.] [15]

The actress's 'comically dead-pan' performance was at her best although American reviewers did not seem to appreciate the wordiness of the script.[16] The problem was further complicated by the fact that they had to read subtitles and follow the text within the (film) text. Michael Hastings found that her 'delicate, nuanced performance is at the heart of veteran French director Michel Deville's entertaining confection. In other hands, the film's story-within-a-story of a professional reader and her indisposed clients could have been precious and saccharine, but Deville and Miou-Miou achieve a bittersweet, gently erotic tone.' [17]

Miou-Miou is actively playing in *auteur* films, more recently in *Quand je serai petit* (Jean-Paul Rouve, 2012); *Marcher*, a short film directed by her daughter Jeanne Herry, where she plays herself (2009), and *Bienvenue parmi nous /Welcome Aboard* (Jean

Becker, 2012). There was a four-year interruption from 2000-2004.[18]

Sylvie BLUM-REID
University of Florida, Gainesville

1. Patrick Schupp, « Miou-Miou ou la vulnérabilité souriante », *Séquences : La revue du cinéma* 138 (1989): 64-65.
2. Miou-Miou, www.ina.fr/arts-et-culture /cinema/video/TLC900201354.milou-en-mai-de-louis-malle.fr.html
3. Ibid.
4. Robert Stam, '*Jonah Who Will be 25 in the Year 2000*. The subversive charm of Alain Tanner,' *Jump Cut. A review of Contemporary Cinema* 15 (1977), http://www.ejumpcut.org/ archive/onlinessays/JC15folder/JonahStam.html.
5. Christiane Jouve, cited in Phil Powrie, *French Cinema in the 1980s. Nostalgia and the Crisis of Masculinity* (Oxford: Oxford UP, 1997), 64.
6. Isabelle Regnier, «Miou-Miou: le conte de fée d'une actrice malgré elle», *Le Monde*, July 7, 2004.
7. Powrie, *French Cinema in the 1980s*, 10.
8. Jill Forbes, *The Cinema in France after the New Wave* (London: BFI/MacMillan, 1992), 178.
9. Powrie, *French Cinema in the 1980s*, 173.
10. http://www.imdb.com/name/nm0591877/bio
11. Sabine Cayrol, « Miou-Miou : Amour, Gloire, et Beauté », *Paris Match*, April 28, 2010, accessed October 17, 2013, http://www. parismatch.com/People/Musique/miou-miou-julien-clerc-148100
12. *Studio* 78 (October 1993).
13. *Studio* 16 (1988).
14. «Miou-Miou, compagne de Julien Clerc», http://www.julien-clerc.net/biographie/famille/ miou_miou.html, accessed February 15, 2013.
15. Patrick Schupp, « Miou-Miou ou la vulnérabilité souriante ».
16. Vincent Canby, 'Miou-Miou as a Paid Reader in *La Lectrice*,' *New York Times*, April 21, 1989, accessed October 17, 2013, http:// www.nytimes.com/1989/04/21/movies/review-film-miou-miou-as-a-paid-reader-in-la-lectrice-by-deville.html; http://www.julien-clerc .net/biographie/famille/miou_miou.html
17. Michael Hastings, *Rovi*, http://www. answers.com/topic/la-lectrice.
18. 'Miou-Miou,' Unifrance films, http://www. unifrance.org/annuaires/personne/5644/miou-miou.

Eddy MITCHELL (1942–)
[Claude MOINE]

Black Socks,
Mint Eyes,
and
Timeless
Rock

C LAUDE MOINE was from early on fascinated by the American rock-n-roll scene. He began performing as a teenager with the group *Les Chaussettes noires* (The Black Socks), known as the first rock group in France, and took the stage name Eddy MITCHELL after the American expatriate actor Eddie Constantine. The band found success almost instantly, and before Mitchell was twenty years old he had sold over two million records. His voice has a unique blend of honeyed gruffness, his signature sound in such classics as *Couleur menthe à l'eau, L'Esprit grande prairie* with its nuances of the American West, and the iconic *Pas de boogie-woogie* (the tongue-in-cheek rock-n-roll confession of a priest troubled by the duty to tell his congregation to stop having sex). His last (2011) album *Ma dernière séance*, in which he sounds like a Continental Johnny Cash without the whiskey, features lyrics about his fifty-year career as a musician and vows « je ne vous ferai pas le coup du 'comeback' » ['I won't pull the "comeback" trick on you'] – much to the disappointment of fans spanning both generations and several bodies of water.

Mitchell left the Chaussettes and went solo in 1963, a move that cost him in court: his band members sued for breach of contract. Undeterred, Mitchell went on to record some of the best-selling rock singles of the 60s and 70s, including *Daniela, Sur la route de Memphis*, and the French adaptation *Danser le twist*. He also began an acting career that would span at least five decades and cover both television and movies. On the silver screen, he worked notably with director Bertrand Tavernier for 1981's *Coup de torchon /Clean Slate*, in a role that revealed his flair for comedy and earned him a César nomination. Mitchell has continued making mostly comedies, but has not shied away from other kinds of roles either. In 1991 he played in Wim Wenders's sci-fi road-movie *Until the End of the World*. In 1995, he played car-salesman Gérard in *Le Bonheur est dans le pré /Happiness is in the Field* (Étienne Chatiliez), and lent his voice to the character of Flappy in the 2005 *Pollux : Le Manège enchanté / Sprung! The Magic Roundabout* (dir. Dave Borthwick, Jean Duval, Frank Passingham).

Though Mitchell's film career has received less critical acclaim than his music career, he has nonetheless worked with some of the brightest stars of the French – and international – screen. He acted alongside fellow Americanophile *mélomane* Johnny Hallyday in *Les Parisiennes* (Marc Allégret, Claude Barma, Michel Boisrond, and Jacques Poitrenaud, 1962), *Cherchez l'idole /The Chase* (Michel Boisrond, 1964), and *Salaud on t'aime* (Claude Lelouch, 2014); with Michel Serrault in *Comment réussir en amour /How to Succeed in Love* (Michel Boisrond, 1962), *À mort l'arbitre /Kill the Referee* (Jean-Pierre

Mocky, 1984), *Ville à vendre /City for Sale* (Jean-Pierre Mocky, 1992), and *Le Bonheur est dans le pré* (1995); with Chantal Lauby in *La Cité de la peur /Fear City: A Family-Style Comedy* (Alain Berbérian, 1994), *Kitchendales* (Chantal Lauby, 2000), *Les Clefs de bagnole /The Car Keys* (Laurent Baffie, 2003), *Le Grand Départ* (Claude Meunier, 2008); and with Miou-Miou in *Attention une femme peut en cacher une autre ! /My Other Husband* (Georges Lautner, 1983), *La Totale ! / The Jackpot!* (Claude Zidi, 1991), and *Populaire* (Régis Roinsard, 2012).

And we cannot forget his work on television. Since 1969, Mitchell has been featured in at least nine telefilms and TV series, from 1969's *L'Homme qui venait du Cher* to *Au siècle de Maupassant : Contes et nouvelles du XIXe siècle* in 2009, to 2011's *Le Grand Restaurant II*. But his longest running, and most significant, television work was the six years he spent hosting *La Dernière Séance*, a show dedicated exclusively to American movies from the 1950s. (This show also inspired the title for his farewell album in 2011.)

As for what the future holds... Mitchell's farewell to the singing stage has left him ample time for cinematic work, and since 2011 he has appeared in six films, including one in post-production and another filming in early 2013. Longtime fans can rejoice in his continuing cinematic career; and those disappointed by his absence from the recording scene can take comfort in the 100-best playlist on YouTube. Mitchell may not make a comeback, but his legacy promises to remain among us.

Rosemary A. PETERS
Louisiana State University, Baton Rouge

Yves MONTAND (1921–1991) [Ivo LIVI]

The French Dream

THE LIFE and career of Yves MONTAND embody a real success story from the French melting pot. From the lower migrant class to the upper Hollywood glamour through a strong and constant leftist commitment, Montand's life and multiple talents followed the ups and downs of the last decades of the twentieth century's troubled history, to shape one of France's most popular artists of his time.

Born in 1921 under the name Ivo Livi, his parents soon moved from Italy to Marseilles, escaping the rise of fascism. Living within the large Italian migrant community in the South of France, he stood out very soon as a handsome young man in the late forties, and began early on a dual career both as an actor and as a singer. This feature, fairly common in Hollywood, if one should think for instance of Frank Sinatra and Dean Martin (both also from the Italian-American community), was and still is less ordinary in the French star system, despite the brilliant examples of actresses Brigitte Bardot, Anna Karina, or Jeanne Moreau in the sixties. Therefore, this was very often something that would be held against him by his detractors, under the pretence that as an actor-singer, he had never fully been one or the other, behaving either too much like a singing actor, or an acting singer.

Nevertheless, his ravishing good looks soon led him to begin his career with the help (and seduction) of powerful women, the most famous of which was the aging Édith Piaf. His good looks and realistic as-natural-as-breathing style, not too dissimilar from Humphrey Bogart's manners, were the result of a very modern approach to acting that had not been forged on the stage. First perceived to be a new Jean Gabin (whom he replaced under the direction of Marcel Carné in 1946's *Les Portes de la nuit /Gates of the Night*), this feature allowed Montand to make a strong breakthrough in the movie industry in 1953, with the successful filmmaker Henri-Georges Clouzot's thriller *Le Salaire de la peur /The Wages of Fear*, where Montand played a poor truck driver carrying dangerous explosives shipments on bumpy South American roads.

In 1965's *Compartiment tueurs / The Sleeping Car Murders*, the actor began what would become a lifelong collaboration with the politically committed French director from Greece, Constantin Costa-Gavras. It would result in the late sixties and seventies in a brilliant series of pictures, from 1969's *Z* (a violent denunciation of the Colonels' regime in Greece) to the gripping *L'Aveu /The Confession* (1970), adapted from Artur London's experience of being tortured and tried in Czechoslovakia during the Spring of 1968. He therefore met and worked from time to time with a galaxy of committed first-rate directors, such

as Joris Ivens, Chris Marker, or Alain Resnais. This often self-righteous, pro-communist stance, though much more critical after 1956, has always been one of Montand's trademarks, leading him later to accept similar parts, such as in Henri Verneuil's heavy-going but efficient political thriller *I...comme Icare /I as in Icarus* (1979), giving him perhaps the stature and credibility he lacked in his youth as the handsome and glamorous leading man.

It was indeed in that respect that in 1960 he got a contract in Hollywood: his part in George Cukor's *Let's Make Love* (also known as *The Millionaire*), where he played a much contrite French lover figure, mainly based on this natural sophistication of his as well as on the actor's singing abilities. This episode of his life remained notorious for the famous public affair he briefly developed with co-star Marilyn Monroe, endorsing Montand's reputation as a womanizer. Since 1951, he nevertheless shared his life and political struggles with his long-time partner off-screen, Simone Signoret, also one of the great actresses of the time, known for her dashing blonde bombshell beauty and strong-minded views. For instance, they had trouble getting visas when Montand was touring the US as a singer.

In the second part of his career, from the mid-seventies, Yves Montand now appeared in more popular pictures as the middle-aged ordinary fellow, instantly known by a very wide audience, in Claude Sautet's society oriented films *Vincent, François, Paul et les autres... /Vincent, François, Paul and the Others* (1974) or *César et Rosalie* (opposite Romy Schneider, in 1972). Montand now looked forward to extending his range to comedy, with *La Folie des grandeurs /Delusions of Grandeur* (Gérard Oury, 1971), an adaptation of Victor Hugo's *Ruy Blas* (co-starring the hilarious Louis de Funès), or as Isabelle Adjani's immature father in Jean-Paul Rappeneau's *Tout feu, tout flamme /All Fired Up* (1982). He also wanted to play more ambiguous parts in edgy thrillers, either with famous director Jean-Pierre Melville, or in Alain Corneau's dark *Police python 357* (1976). As an aging man, Montand achieved what will remain one of his most acclaimed performances, the part of the evil ancient César Soubeyran /'Papet' in the modern adaptation of Pagnol's novels, Claude Berri's *Jean de Florette* and its sequel *Manon des sources /Manon of the Spring* (both 1986). This character-driven role (the very humanitarian Montand was still noticeably younger than the character) marked a return to his native South of France. However, he died suddenly in 1991, just after finishing shooting his last film, Jean-Jacques Beineix's *IP5 : L'île aux pachydermes /IP5: The Island of Pachyderms*, leaving a young son behind. Unfortunately, the decade has seen the development of a real life courtroom drama, since the late Montand was involved in a paternity suit on the one hand, and allegedly accused of child molestation on the person of his adoptive daughter on the other – cases that have both kept tabloid readers yearning for new instalments.

Jean-Christophe BLUM
Lycée Blaise Pascal, Clermont-Ferrand

Jeanne MOREAU (1928–)

The Fatal Femme Fatale

ROMANTICISM had the *belle dame sans merci*. Hollywood films noirs had the 'femme fatale.' The Nouvelle Vague had Jeanne MOREAU.

Her look is more haggard and tired than Lauren Bacall's, and she has never been cast as a blonde ingénue. She was never a conventional beauty, and as such, was not deemed pretty enough to become a typical 'movie star.' But somehow, the young woman with the sullen eyes, who dreamt of becoming a great tragedian while watching *Phèdre* at the Comédie-Française, transcended the expectations of the film industry and made herself a great 'actress.' The greatest in the world, Orson Welles once said.

She has worked with some of the most influential directors in the history of 20th century cinema, such as Louis Malle (*Ascenseur pour l'échafaud /Elevator to the Gallows*, 1958; *Les Amants /The Lovers*, 1958); François Truffaut (*Jules et Jim*, 1962; *La Mariée était en noir /The Bride Wore Black*, 1968); Orson Welles (*Le Procès /The Trial*, 1962); Peter Brook (*Moderato cantabile /Seven Days…Seven Nights*, 1960); Luis Buñuel (*Le Journal d'une femme de chambre /Diary of a Chambermaid*, 1964) and Michelangelo Antonioni (*La notte /The Night*, 1961).

She is the housewife bored into sin by bourgeois conventions, she is Truffaut's Hitchcock-like revengeful temptress, she is the hallucinated gambler who falls in love with her good luck charm,[1] and the playfully tragic heart of a love triangle. She is the eternal feminine.[2]

She once said that, past 25, features can no longer hide the soul, and she is among the few actresses whose souls become them quite gracefully. Marguerite Duras could have been thinking about her when she wrote: 'I have come to tell you that for me, I find you more beautiful now than when you were younger. I did not like your face as a young woman so much as the one you have now, all ravaged and ruined.'[3]

Miles away from baby-faced glamour, she epitomises desire and intelligence – broody eyes and a carefree smile. Her atypical face can turn into Diana, goddess of the hunt; into a portrait by one of the black bride's victims, or a Greek statue bewitching Jules and Jim alike. But it is not afraid of distortion either, when playing the *village fool*'s game with Catherine's two lovers and her daughter. Even a smile can be laden with omen when it appears right before driving over a bridge to kill yourself and one of your lovers.

But an actress such as her cannot be summed up in a glance – she has to be heard. French theatrical tradition gave her an unusually poised and elegant diction, which mysteriously suits Célestine the chambermaid as well as the manipulative Merteuil,[4] scheming to Thelenious Monk's piano. Her raw whisper of a voice blends with Miles Davis's music as Florence wanders aimlessly down the illuminated streets of Paris, and it can turn into a possessed cry when the mask of the bored bourgeoisie falls down. It also lingers in the mind, long after the movie is over, singing what may well be the most faithful portrait ever made of her, to the tune of a juvenile guitar:

> … Et puis elle chantait avec une
> voix qui sitôt m'enjôla.
> Elle avait des yeux des yeux
> d'opale, qui m'fascinaient qui
> m'fascinaient,
> Y'avait l'ovale d'son visage pâle,
> de femme fatale qui m'fut
> fatal,
> De femme fatale qui m'fut fatal.[5]

Emilie L'Hôte
Université Paris VII

1. *La Baie des anges /Bay of Angels* (Jacques Demy, 1963)

2. Sandy Flitterman-Lewis, 'Fascination, Friendship, and "the Eternal Feminine," or the Discursive Production of (Cinematic) Desire,' *French Review* 66, 6 (May 1993).

3. « Je suis venu pour vous dire que pour moi je vous trouve plus belle maintenant que lorsque vous étiez jeune. J'aimais moins votre visage de jeune femme que celui que vous avez maintenant, dévasté » (*L'Amant*, Marguerite Duras)

4. *Les Liaisons dangereuses 1960 / Dangerous Liaisons* (Roger Vadim, 1959).

5. *Le Tourbillon de la vie*, in *Jules et Jim*:
   'She was the kind of singer that
      put me under a spell.
   She had eyes, eyes of opal that
      fascinated me,
   Her pale face was an oval,
   What a fatal femme fatale!'

Yolande Moreau (1953–)

The Left-of-Centre Feminine

An actress consistently drawn to the offbeat, Yolande Moreau has shied away from typically sexualised feminine roles, favouring the atypical, maladroit, and comical in her film choices. Indeed, her most revered performances have embraced a rather unconventional femininity, such as the self-deprecating thespian Irène in *Quand la mer monte /When the Sea Rises* (Yolande Moreau and Gilles Porte, 2004) and the naïve and deranged artist Séraphine de Senlis in *Séraphine* (Martin Provost, 2008).

Moreau was born on 27 February 1953 in Brussels, Belgium to a Walloon father and a Flemish mother. She trained at L'École Jacques Lecoq and cut her teeth performing in the children's theatre in Brussels, where she honed her comic skills. She tried her hand at playwriting early in her career, writing, directing, and starring in the 1981 one-woman show *Sale affaire, du sexe et du crime*, in which she portrayed a woman who has just murdered her lover. Moreau toured the play around Western Europe to immense success, and was noticed by the famed filmmaker Agnès Varda.

Following the hype of *Sale affaire*, Moreau made her film debut in Varda's 1984 short film *7 p., cuis., s. de b.,... à saisir,*[1] closely followed by a secondary role in the latter's gritty feature *Sans toit ni loi /Vagabond* (1985) the following year. She then became known for her comedic talent when she teamed up with comic duo Jérôme Deschamps and Macha Makeïeff for their iconic sketch show *Les Deschiens*, televised at prime time on Canal+ through the mid-90s. Moreau played the blunt and uncultivated housewife Mme Morel, perpetually clad in kitsch monochromes and speaking in a gruff Belgian accent, quickly becoming a staple on the show.

Despite her early career popularity, Moreau's first great cinematic success was with the 2004 road-trip film, *Quand la mer monte*, in which she self-reflexively interprets Irène, an actress who becomes involved with the costume-maker Dries (Wim Willaert), while performing *Sale affaire* on tour around France and Belgium. Moreau again evokes an untraditional femininity in her portrayal of Irène, who adopts an unsightly mask and masculine suit during her performances. Her off-stage moments with Dries, however, reveal a more sensual side to her character, marking a clear departure from the Mme Morel of *Les Deschiens* stereotype. *Sale affaire* functions as a *mise en abyme* in the film, the protagonists' love affair mimicking aspects of the play itself. As well as starring in *Quand la mer monte*, Moreau co-wrote and co-directed the film with Gilles Porte. It received the 2005 César for Best First Film and Moreau was awarded Best Actress prize at the same ceremony.[2]

However, *Quand la mer monte* did not furnish Moreau with her only Best Actress César. She became the first Belgian actress to earn the award twice when she won it in 2009 for Martin

Provost's *Séraphine*, in which she portrays the all-but-forgotten artist, Séraphine de Senlis (1864-1942: real name Séraphine Louis), famed for her chimerical and vibrant floral paintings. Moreau's de Senlis is artless and naïve, her ignorance of social norms and obsession with the intricacies of nature the first subtle signs of the mental illness which cast its shadow over much of her life. Moreau depicts de Senlis's descent into madness with delicacy, capturing her fervent spirituality as well as her gripping paranoia and avoiding sensationalizing the artist's mental deterioration. *Séraphine* is widely touted as Moreau's finest performance to date.

Throughout her career, Moreau has often tended towards eccentric, unhinged characters, finding a place for herself among the whimsical, carnivalesque oeuvres of filmmakers such as Jean-Pierre Jeunet and Joann Sfar. In Jeunet's *Le Fabuleux Destin d'Amélie Poulain /Amélie* (2001), Moreau plays the lonely, erratic concierge Mme Wallace and incarnates a similarly dotty, motherly figure for his 2009 *Micmacs à tire-larigot /Micmacs*. She also made a memorable cameo appearance in Sfar's cartoonish *Gainsbourg (vie héroïque) / Gainsbourg: A Heroic Life* in 2010, as an ageing, alcoholic, yet ever-charismatic Fréhel. In the same year, she also portrayed a vengeful factory worker, Louise Ferrand, who plots to have her deserter boss assassinated in the black comedy *Louise-Michel* (Gustave de Kervern and Benoît Delépine, 2008). Yet while she gravitates towards quirky comedic characters, even taking on the role of a girl-mime for Sylvain Chomet's Tour Eiffel vignette in the 2006 ensemble film *Paris, je t'aime*,[3] Moreau's film choices remain markedly diverse: she has tried her hand not only at comedy, but also drama, the biopic, romance and even horror, appearing as the leader of a troupe of torturous ghosts in the 2010 *La Meute /The Pack* (dir. Franck Richard).

Yolande Moreau has often appeared on the silver screen in modest feminine roles: the maid, the concierge, the housewife, the working-class woman. Yet she has likewise distinguished herself in her portrayal of more fantastical characters: the thespian, the musician, the ghost, the mime, the artist. Her characters are rough around the edges, her performances infused with an eccentric womanliness that sets her apart from more typically sexualized actresses. Moreau is not afraid to play upon her gender, as the masked and androgynous on-stage Irène, or to embrace the unpalatable, as the naïve Séraphine who unashamedly urinates in public. And as is clear in her work on *Les Deschiens*, she is not afraid to poke fun at herself, having said « j'ai compris qu'on n'est jamais aussi drôle que lorsqu'on joue de ses défauts. » ['I've come to understand that one is never quite as funny as when one plays on one's faults.']

Gemma KING
The University of Melbourne, and Université Sorbonne Nouvelle - Paris 3

1. « 7 pièces, cuisine, salle de bain... »
2. For further discussion of this film, see Zachariah Rush, '*Quand la mer monte*,' in *Directory of World Cinema: Belgium*, ed. Marcelline Block and Jeremi Szaniawski (Bristol, UK: Intellect, 2013), 195-196. —Ed.
3. For further discussion of this film, see Oana Chivoiu, 'Two Mimes Fall in Love,' in *World Film Locations: Paris*, ed. Marcelline Block (Intellect, 2011), 110-111. —Ed.

François MOREL (1959–)

L'Éternel « Monsieur Morel »

FRANÇOIS MOREL has enjoyed a multifaceted career in the world of arts and entertainment. He is an ENSATT-trained theatre actor who achieved success on the big and small screens – initially attaining popularity as cheese shop proprietor 'Monsieur Morel' on the televised sketch comedy series *Les Deschiens* – as well as onstage, whether performing his own works (such as his one man show, *Les Habits du dimanche*) or in classics by Molière and Georges Feydeau. Morel is an entertainer in every sense of the term, as he is a director, comedian, singer, screenwriter, author, and playwright, with more than 85 film and television credits to his name in a range of roles – from supporting to starring, as well as voiceover parts – in films by cinéastes including Christophe Barratier (*Faubourg 36 /Paris 36*, 2008; *La Nouvelle Guerre des boutons /War of the Buttons*, 2011); Étienne Chatiliez (*Le Bonheur est dans le pré /Happiness is in the Field*, 1995); Guy Jacques (*Violetta la reine de la moto /Violetta the Motorcycle Queen*, 1997); Jean-Pierre Mocky (*Alliance cherche doigt*, 1997); Edouard Molinaro (*Beaumarchais l'insolent /Beaumarchais the Scoundrel*, 1996); Jacques Otmezguine (*Une employée modèle /A Model Employee*, 2002); Joann Sfar (*Gainsbourg (vie héroïque) /Gainsbourg: A Heroic Life*, 2010; *Le Chat du rabbin /The Rabbi's Cat*, 2011), and Pascal Thomas (*Le Grand Appartement*, 2006; *L'Heure zéro /Towards Zero*, 2007).

As a songwriter, Morel has penned verses for Anne Baquet, Juliette Gréco, Norah Krief, Natalie Miravette, and Maurane, as well as the songs for his own 2006 show *Collection Particulière* (which he subsequently recorded as an album), setting his lyrics to the music of Reinhardt Wagner and others. Morel's 2010 concert tour, *Le Soir, des lions*, was also recorded as an album, which was released that year; on it, along with Morel's own songs (again with Wagner), he covers classics by Dalida and Georges Brassens. Starting in 2009, Morel took on another type of role in the public eye, that of commentator on the radio programme *Le 7/9*, with a segment called *Le billet de François Morel* airing on France Inter (French public radio) every Friday morning. France Inter was also the inspiration for Morel's 2011 play *Instants Critiques*, which he directed and co-wrote (with Olivier Broche), and whose dialogue is taken from the iconic clashes between the film critics Georges Charensol and Goncourt Prize winning novelist Jean-Louis Bory on the France Inter radio program *Le Masque et la Plume* in the 1960s and 70s.

Born on June 10, 1959 in Flers (Normandy), Morel studied at the *École nationale supérieure des arts et techniques du théâtre* (ENSATT). He appeared on the Parisian stage in 1986 in two plays directed by Jacques Rosny: *Les Dégourdis de la 11e* by André Mouëzy-Éon at the Théâtre des Variétés and Serge Lama's musical *Napoléon* at the

Théâtre Marigny. Morel's first big onscreen break – for the small screen – arrived in 1988, when he was cast as the bellhop Alfred, a regular cast member of the now cult French television comedy series *Palace /Ça, c'est palace*, directed by Jean-Michel Ribes and written by Ribes alongside Gébé, François Rollin, Roland Topor, Jean-Luc Trotignon, Georges Wolinski, and Morel himself. Set in the titular luxury hotel, the show aired for six episodes in 1988, with an ensemble cast performing the roles of guests and staff members, whose interactions and scenarios form the basis of the program. Series regulars included Jean Carmet, Darry Cowl, and Valérie Lemercier (also making her screen debut) while special guest stars such as Pierre Arditi, Michel Blanc, Alain Chabat, André Dussolier, Roger Hanin, Les Nuls, Tonie Marshall, Daniel Prévost, and Jean Yanne, among others, all appeared on the show.

Shortly thereafter, Morel joined Jérôme Deschamps and Macha Makeïeff's theatrical troupe *Les Deschiens*, spending a decade with them, appearing in numerous theatrical productions of theirs throughout the late 1980s and 1990s (including their original works, such as *Lapin chasseur* along with their interpretations of Molière and Jacques Offenbach), and in their now iconic sketch comedy series *Les Deschiens*, broadcast on French television from 1993-1996. On *Les Deschiens*, Morel memorably incarnated the role of 'Monsieur Morel,' proprietor of the 'Fromagerie Morel' ['Morel Cheese Shop'] – with Yolande Moreau in the role of Madame Morel – becoming a familiar face to a broad viewing public. In his own words about this character, « Monsieur Morel de la fromagerie Morel était paternaliste,

autoritaire, incohérent, contradictoire. Je me souvenais de modèles intimes observés pendant l'enfance à qui je n'essaie pas de ressembler dans la vraie vie mais qui m'offrait devant la caméra une source inépuisable d'inspiration » ['Mr. Morel of the Morel cheese-shop was paternalistic, authoritarian, incoherent, contradictory. I remembered some models, closely observed during my childhood, whom I try not to resemble in real life but who offered me, in front of the camera, a source of unending inspiration.'] [1] Morel also appeared in the Deschiens ensemble comedy film, *Le Voyage à Paris /The Journey to Paris* (Marc-Henri Dufresne, 1999), which he co-wrote (his first time as a screenwriter). In this film, Morel plays Jacques Dubosc, a cab driver living in Rosny (suburban Paris), whose thirty-something cousin Daniel (Olivier Broche), still living at home with his mother, is determined to visit the City of Light (and Jacques), which he has never seen. Other members of the Deschiens troupe in the *Le Voyage à Paris* cast include Yolande Moreau.

In 2000, Morel took his one-man show, *Les Habits du dimanche*, his childhood remembrances of life with his family, directed by Michel Cerda, on a tour throughout France for three years (*Les Habits du dimanche* is published by Le Rocher Archimbaud). That same year, Morel joined the all-star cast of Bertrand Blier's film *Les Acteurs /Actors*. In 2002, Morel co-starred in the comedy *Un couple épatant /An Amazing Couple*, the second instalment of Belgian auteur Lucas Belvaux's critically acclaimed experimental, *Rashomon*-esque film trilogy in which the characters and narratives overlap throughout the three films, although the protagonists shift between each film. In *Un couple épatant*, a comedy (while the first trilogy film is a thriller and the third a gritty drama), Morel stars as Alain, whose strange behaviour causes his wife Cécile (Ornella Muti) to suspect him of infidelity (when he is actually hiding his upcoming medical operation from her because of his neurosis). When she hires private detective Pascal (Gilbert Melki) to follow Alain, complications ensue. Yet the humorous tone of this second film gives way to drama in the third, *Après la vie /After Life*, in which Morel's character Alain again appears, but this time, as a supporting character while Pascal – the cop hired to watch Alain in *Un couple épatant* – dealing with the drug addiction of his wife Agnès (Dominique Blanc), is the protagonist. For his performance, Morel (and the entire cast) was honoured with the Chlotrudis Award for Best Cast. The film trilogy also won the Prix Louis Delluc, Best Film from the French Syndicate of Cinema Critics, and the Chlotrudis Award for Best Movie. In Guy Jacques' 2005 *Ze film*, the banlieue-set film-within-a-film, Morel incarnates the villain Legros, who attempts to prevent the young *cité* residents from fulfilling their dream of making their own film version of *Romeo and Juliet* (with stolen cameras and film). *Ze film* won the Roger for Best Feature at the Avignon-New York Film Festival. In 2007, Morel starred in Pascal Thomas's *L'Heure zéro /Towards Zero*, an adaptation of Agatha Christie's *Towards Zero*, as Commissaire Martin Bataille (Superintendent Battle in Christie's original texts), investigating the murder of wealthy elderly woman Camilla (played by iconic French film

star Danielle Darrieux, then in her 91st year), killed in her own estate on the coast of Brittany, where her relatives have assembled for a reunion, and who are all now suspects in her death. The cast includes Laura Smet and Chiara Mastroianni. From 2007-2009, at the Théâtre du Rond-Point and on national tour, Morel starred opposite Jacques Gamblin in Anne Bourgeois's production of *Les Diablogues*, Roland Dubillard's 1975 comic/absurd dialogues between two friends. In Christophe Barratier's Oscar-nominated and award winning film *Faubourg 36 / Paris 36* (2008), which pays homage to the Parisian musical hall culture of the 1930s prior to World War II and the Occupation of France when 'there was…a "Paris Spring" just before the Nazi invasion,'[2] Morel plays bistro proprietor Célestin, a small but essential role. He is a loyal supporter of the members of his neighbourhood (*faubourg*) theatre troupe attempting to save their theatre, the Chansonia, from bankruptcy and destruction, as well as the encroachment of fascism. In the film, Célestin's café, next to the theatre, serves as the troupe's second home, where he furthermore recuperates the film's political context by naming his *plats du jour* after current events and leaders, such as Léon Blum or Charles de Gaulle. As Célestin, Morel also sang one of the film's songs, *Y'aura jamais d'accordéon*. With minimum screen time, Morel achieved maximum effect, due to the nuances of his performance, revealing his character's deep sense of loyalty to his neighbours and friends, as well as his own moral compass (such as refusing to serve a close friend who began entertaining the fascists). Of Morel, Barratier stated that he 'brought the character of Célestin into a poetic and comic dimension which reached well beyond the script.'[3] In 2011, Morel joined the cast of the silent film *Ni à vendre ni à louer /Holidays by the Sea* (dir. Pascal Rabaté), which pays homage to Jacques Tati's *Les Vacances de M. Hulot /Monsieur Hulot's Holiday* (1953). Morel played Monsieur Jourdain in a grand production of Molière's *Le Bourgeois gentilhomme*, from November 2011 to January 2013, directed by Catherine Hiegel (formerly of the Comédie-Française). Replete with a baroque orchestra playing the music of Jean-Baptiste Lully as well as ballet dancers, this is an authentic recreation of the original 1670 Molière production held at the Château de Chambord.

Morel is also a well-known voice performer. In Yolande Moreau's César-winning directorial and screenwriting debut, *Quand la mer monte /When the Sea Rises* (2004),[4] Morel's voice can be heard as a TV presenter. He also starred, in 2006, as the voice of Rantanplan – the 'stupidest dog in the universe' – from the Belgian comic series *Lucky Luke*, in the short cartoon films that were shown on France 3 television. Morel reprised his role as Rantanplan in the animated film *Tous à l'ouest : Une aventure de Lucky Luke* (Olivier Jean Marie, 2007). He also lent his voice to the titular talking cat of Antoine Delesvaux and Joann Sfar's *Le Chat du rabbin / The Rabbi's Cat* (2011), which won the César for Best Animated Film. Morel previously appeared in Sfar's directorial debut, the 2010 Serge Gainsbourg biopic, *Gainsbourg (vie héroïque) / Gainsbourg: A Heroic Life*. In this film, Morel had the small but nonetheless pivotal role of the schoolmaster of the boys' boarding school in the French countryside, which, during the Occupation of France, sheltered the young Serge Gainsbourg (then known by his birth name of Lucien Ginsberg). The schoolmaster saves Lucien's life by telling him to flee the school and hide in the forest just before the Germans arrive to raid the premises for hidden Jewish students. *Gainsbourg: A Heroic Life* won the César for Best First Film, among other awards. In the recent *Astérix : Le domaine des dieux* (Alexandre Astier, 2014), Morel voices the role of the fishmonger Ordralfabétix.

A truly versatile figure who has made significant contributions to and impact upon French arts in numerous disciplines – stage, screen, song, and letters, such as writing the preface to the complete theatrical works of Jules Renard (Omnibus, 2010) – Morel was honoured as an Officier de l'Ordre des Arts et des Lettres, which he was awarded in June 2013 from the French Ministry of Culture. A May 2013 episode of *Vivement Dimanche* was devoted to Morel – in which he sang with Juliette Gréco and others – and included guest appearances by Richard Berry, Rachida Brakni, Gérard Jugnot, Valérie Mairesse, Yolande Moreau, Micheline Presle, Daniel Pennac (Morel starred in Pierre Boutron's 1997 film adaptation of Pennac's *Messieurs les enfants*), Olivier Saladin, and Kristin Scott Thomas, among others. *La Fin du monde est pour dimanche* is one of Morel's latest one-man plays (which he calls an 'existential show'), and continues with the 'Sunday' theme of his earlier one man show, *Les Habits du dimanche*. In *La Fin du monde est pour dimanche*, Morel incarnates numerous elderly characters who are in the 'Sunday' of their lives. Raising questions about aging, mortality, and the meaning and purpose of life, *La Fin du monde* ran from April to June 2013 at the La Pépinière-Théâtre in Paris and toured throughout France in 2013-2014. Morel is currently in the midst of several theatrical and film productions, such as *Hyancinthe et Rose*, his musical homage to his grandparents and their lengthy marriage (despite being opposites in almost every way and never agreeing about anything) – based on his illustrated book of the same title (Editions Thierry Magnier, 2010) – performed at La Pépinière during 2013-2014 as well as on tour. François Morel, who previously wrote and co-directed short films (including directing Kristin Scott Thomas in his 1995 *Plaisir d'offrir*),[5] has his feature-film directorial debut in the co-directed animated *Socks*, being released in 2014.

Marcelline BLOCK
Princeton University and SAG-AFTRA

1. Morel cited in Eric Fourreau, *François Morel : Farceur enchanteur* (Editions de l'attribut, 2008), 53.
2. Dan Akira Nishimura, 'Douce Sings to the Man who wrote the Song,' in Marcelline Block, ed., *World Film Locations: Prague* (Bristol: Intellect, 2013), 104-105.
3. *Faubourg 36 /Paris 36* press kit, http://medias.unifrance.org/medias/62/144/36926/presse/paris-36-2008-press-kit-english-2.pdf.
4. Editor's note: for further discussion of this film, see Zachariah Rush, *'When the Sea Rises /Quand la mer monte,'* in *Directory of World Cinema: Belgium*, ed. Marcelline Block and Jeremi Szaniawski (Bristol: Intellect, 2013), 195-196.
5. Morel wrote and, with Marc-Henri Dufresne, co-directed the prizewinning short films *Les Pieds sous la table* (1994) and *Plaisir d'offrir* (1995).

Michèle MORGAN (1920–)
[Simone ROUSSEL]

From Poetic Realism to the Tradition of Quality

MICHÈLE MORGAN (born Simone Roussel in 1920) was one of the true 'film goddesses' of classical French cinema and the key female star of poetic realist cinema, for many the cinematic high point of the aesthetically rich 1930s. She rose to fame in the 1930s after being discovered sunbathing on a beach in her hometown of Dieppe by Marc Alizon, a director famed for his capacity to discover future stars – he was also responsible for spotting Brigitte Bardot and Simone Simon. As a 'discovery' who entered the cinema directly, rather than starting her career on stage – as was common at the time – Morgan was an important example of the period's new and glamorous 'cinematic' stardom. Her entry into the cinema was based on her extremely photogenic appearance, which consisted of a smooth, classically proportioned face, blonde hair, tall slim body, and, most importantly, mysterious pale, blue eyes.

Her first lead roles came with *Gribouille* (Marc Allégret, 1937) and *Orage /Storm* (Marc Allégret, 1938), in which she co-starred with Charles Boyer, a big Hollywood star at the time. However, her big break came with her role in Marcel Carné's Poetic Realist *Le Quai des brumes /Port of Shadows* (1938), in which she plays Nelly, who, wearing a humble overcoat and beret (though designed by Chanel), is presented as being at once an ordinary girl from a dreary Le Havre and an idealised and otherworldly 'goddess', a tension central to Morgan's persona in the 1930s. It was also in *Le Quai des brumes* that Gabin uttered the famous line: « T'as d'beaux yeux tu sais » ['You have beautiful eyes you know'] – her eyes became a key part of her identity, often discussed in fan magazine articles and mentioned in the title of her autobiography, *With Those Eyes* (1978). These qualities made her ideal for Poetic Realism, which balances a concern for the quotidian with a poetic sensibility, suggesting the elevated and otherworldly. Her success in this film led to her appearance in *Remorques /Stormy Waters* (Jean Grémillon, 1941), in which she was again teamed with Gabin. The couple appeared in one other film together in the 1930s, *Le Récif de corail /Coral Reefs* (Maurice Gleize, 1939) and became a celebrated star couple – according to her autobiography they also had a real-life relationship in the late 1930s, which was cut short by the arrival of war.

Upon the advent of war, Morgan, like a number of other prominent members of the French filmmaking community, went to make films in Hollywood. While she did not manage to attain the same level of success as she had in France, she appeared in some notable films, including *Joan of Paris* (Robert Stevenson, 1942), co-starring Paul Henreid, and *Passage to Marseille* (Michael Curtiz, 1944) with

Humphrey Bogart. This film was a follow-up to *Casablanca* (Michael Curtiz, 1942), with Morgan in the role of the mysterious foreign beauty played by Ingrid Bergman in the earlier film (Morgan had, in fact, also been considered for the role of Ilsa in *Casablanca*). Upon returning to France her career entered another important stage, with her appearing in a number of films belonging to the period's 'tradition of quality', including *La Symphonie pastorale / Pastoral Symphony* (Jean Delannoy, 1946), *Les Orgueilleux* (Yves Allégret and Rafael E. Portas, 1953), *Napoléon* (Sacha Guitry, 1955), and *Les Grandes manoeuvres /The Grand Maneuver* (René Clair, 1955). Here her identity shifted from her youthful ingénue persona to her being an embodiment of French sophistication, elegance, and refinement. She also began to appear on stage and on television, and while her film career more or less ended in the 1960s, she worked in these other forms until the late 1990s. Her work in film has been recognised by the French film establishment and beyond, with her winning an honorary César Award in 1992 and a Career Golden Lion at the 1996 Venice Film Festival.

Jonathan DRISKELL
Monash University Malaysia

Philippe NOIRET (1930–2006)

*An
Everyman
for All
Seasons*

FOR MORE than 50 years, Philippe Noiret graced French film screens as the 'Everyman' figure – at once apparently ordinary yet truly unforgettable – starting with a non-credited role in Jacqueline Audry's 1949 *Gigi*, adapted from Colette's eponymous 1944 novella. Born in Lille, Noiret was raised in Paris. He originally trained as a theatre actor, and, after having been a stand up comedian, Noiret worked with some of the most acclaimed French film directors, including Bertrand Blier (*Les Côtelettes*, 2003); Georges Franju (*Thérèse Desqueyroux*, 1962); Louis Malle (*Zazie dans le métro*, 1960); Bertrand Tavernier, for whom he starred in several important films, as per below; André Téchiné (*J'embrasse pas /I Don't Kiss*, 1991), and Agnès Varda, consecrated as Grandmother of the French New Wave. Noiret had the leading male role in Varda's first film, *La Pointe Courte* (1955), which introduced her signature aesthetic blending documentary and fiction. Edited by Alain Resnais, this film was, for François Truffaut, an 'ambitious experimental work.'[1] It 'was very well received by the group [*Cahiers du Cinéma*], especially by [André] Bazin…[and] has been cited as one of

the most important precursors of the Nouvelle Vague.'[2] Outside of France, Noiret worked with George Cukor (*Justine*, 1969) and Alfred Hitchcock (*Topaz*, 1969).

With his unremarkable facial features as well as a bearish physique awarding him the moniker of 'Everyman', Noiret accepted a broadly diverse range of roles throughout his prolific career, from comic to villainous, and from romantic to dramatic and even introspective characters. Some of the roles he undertook were controversial, such as his turn in Marco Ferreri's *La Grande Bouffe /The Big Feast* (1973), a grotesque, satirical critique about the hollowness of modern bourgeois society (*la société de consommation*) that emphasizes overconsumption and excess. In this film, Noiret plays the judge, Philippe, who along with his three friends (Marcello Mastrioanni, Michel Piccoli, and Ugo Tognazzi), engages in sex with prostitutes and gorges himself to death on massive quantities of beautifully prepared food (including pâtés ironically prepared in the shape of the Dome of Saint Peter's Basilica). Some of Noiret's other important roles include a breakthrough, humoristic performance in the farcical *Zazie dans le métro* (Malle, 1960) as the cross-dressing Gabriel who babysits his spoiled, curious pre-teen niece Zazie during her adventurous visit to Paris, which is reeling from a subway strike. This film is adapted from Raymond Queneau's eponymous novel, whose unique and inventive use of language is exemplary of the *OuLiPo* group (of which Queneau was a founder). As Lucien Cordier, Noiret is the scheming, corrupt, and murderous police chief of a French West African colony on the eve of World War II in the Academy-Award-nominated *Coup de torchon /Clean Slate* (Bertrand Tavernier, 1981), adapted from Jim Thompson's 1964 American novel *Pop. 1280*, transposing its Deep South setting to Colonial French West Africa. In Claude Chabrol's 1987 thriller *Masques*, Noiret's smiling and kindhearted 'Everyman' physique and persona hides the evil nature and deeds of his character. In this film, Noiret stars as Christian Legagneur (literally 'the winner'), who, on the surface, appears to be the congenial host of a popular televised game show that pairs together elderly men and women, helping them find love and companionship with each other during their twilight years, sending the winning couples paired up by the show on lavish, all-expense paid trips. Yet, Legagneur's 'mask' is eventually removed, revealing his manipulative, deceitful, and violent behaviour toward those around him. The following year, Noiret took on the role of Alfredo, the movie theatre projectionist who instils in the young protagonist/filmmaker-to-be a lifetime love for cinema in the crowd-pleasing, Oscar winning Italian film *Cinema Paradiso* (Giuseppe Tornatore, 1988). For his performance, Noiret received the BAFTA for Best Film Actor. In the post-World War I drama/romance *La Vie et rien d'autre /Life and Nothing But* (Bertrand Tavernier, 1989), Noiret is Major Dellaplane, whose searches for missing French soldiers form a haunting meditation on loss, trauma, and memory. Noiret played the role of Chilean poet Pablo Neruda, who,

while exiled to a small Italian island, encountered a postal worker and his family in the beloved romance/melodrama *Il postino /Il Postino: The Postman* (Michael Radford, 1994).

Noiret's collaboration with Bertrand Tavernier (born 1941) was impactful; the actor starred in several of this director's films, including *Que la fête commence... /Let Joy Reign Supreme* (1975), *Le Juge et l'Assassin / The Judge and the Assassin* (1976), and *La Fille de d'Artagnan /Revenge of the Musketeers* (1994). Some of Noiret's most remarkable roles have been in Tavernier oeuvres including *L'Horloger de Saint-Paul /The Clockmaker of St Paul* (1974), adapted from detective novelist Georges Simenon (Noiret won the New York Film Critics' Circle Award for Best Actor for this performance). In the Best Foreign Language Oscar-nominated *Coup de torchon* (discussed above) Noiret won Best Foreign Actor from the Italian National Syndicate of Film Journalists. For *La Vie et rien d'autre*, Noiret received his second Best Actor César – his first was for the World War II revenge drama *Le Vieux Fusil /The Old Gun* (Robert Enrico, 1975) based on the Nazi massacre of nearly 700 French civilians (the majority of whom were women and children) in the French village of Oradour-sur-Glane on June 10, 1944.

In a tour de force performance as Major Dellaplane in *La Vie et rien d'autre*, Noiret plays a gruff military man attempting to navigate the post World War I French political and social landscape in his search for missing soldiers, so that their remains can be properly buried and their names can be memorialized in dignity for their war duty. *La Vie et rien d'autre* demonstrates the damage that the The Great War inflicted upon France's territory as well as collective unconscious, and the socio-political upheavals and cultural shift it inaugurated. Central to the film is the desperate need to find and properly commemorate the war dead, satisfying a public hunger for building memorials: in one instance a small town demands to redraw its borders so that it can have the minimum number of dead soldiers required for building a lavish public war memorial. Dellaplane's near obsessive but ultimately futile quest to uncover and catalogue the remains of missing soldiers is a coping mechanism that allows him to continue living in the past rather than confront the painful loneliness of his current condition. By the film's end, he has begun the difficult process of moving forward through pursuing a romantic relationship with a soldier's widow. The fields and former battlegrounds throughout the French countryside form the backdrop to this tale of love and loss, whose final, bittersweet message is that what remains, after the horrors of war, is life, this present life – and nothing else. Anchored by Noiret's masterful performance as a man searching for his place in the post-war political climate – at a crossroads between the trauma of the past and the uncertainty of the future – *La Vie et rien d'autre* is one of the most important and powerful cinematic treatments of World War I in France and it raises relevant conversations about the recuperation/preservation of historical memory and its functions.

At the end of his life, Philippe Noiret's extraordinary presence and his still-deep voice shone at the Théâtre de la Madeleine alongside Anouk Aimée in the reading of Albert Ramsdell Gurney's *Love Letters* (2005).

During his lifelong career in French cinema, Noiret received numerous accolades, such as the Cinema Nuova award for his early starring role opposite Emmanuelle Riva's Thérèse (as her husband Bernard) in Georges Franju's *Thérèse Desqueyroux* (1962), adapted from François Mauriac's eponymous novel. Along with his two Best Actor Césars, among other prizes and awards, Philippe Noiret was decorated with the French Légion d'Honneur in 2005, before he died of cancer on November 23, 2006.

Marcelline BLOCK
Princeton University and SAG-AFTRA

1. François Truffaut, *The Films in My Life*, trans. Leonard Mayhew (New York: Da Capo Press, 1994), ebook version.
2. Alison Smith, *Agnès Varda* (Manchester University Press, 1998), 7.

Vanessa PARADIS (1972–)

*Paradise
Lost?*

IN 1998, Johnny Depp was working in France on Roman Polanski's *The Ninth Gate*: 'I was in the lobby of this restaurant and I just saw this back across the room. Suddenly, the back turned and looked at me. And then the eyes that were attached to the back walked towards me and said, "Hi. Do you remember me?" I said yes, but I didn't remember because we had actually met a number of years before. But this time I was caught.' Since then, Vanessa PARADIS (the 'back' mentioned here by Depp) and Johnny Depp have had two children, a daughter Lily Rose Melody (1999) and a son John Christopher II (or 'Jack') (2002). In 1998, the name Vanessa Paradis may have been unknown to people outside France, but the mention of her as Johnny Depp's companion would now instantly ring a bell. However rumours of separation were very quickly dismissed in early 2012 and then confirmed by June of that year; the news made the headlines worldwide as 'the ideal couple breaking up.'

As a matter of fact, Vanessa Paradis has two very successful and interesting careers as a singer and as an actress. She was a singer before she became an actress; very, very young indeed, at 7 years old she was discovered on Jacque Martin's TV show *L'École des Fans* in 1980. In 1985, she recorded her first single *La Magie des surprises-parties* at the age of 12 – her first step towards celebrity. Two years later, at the age of 14, her song *Joe le taxi* made her internationally famous. It was number 1 in France for 11 weeks. Unusually for a song sung in French, it was released in the United Kingdom and reached number 3 in 1988. In 1990 she got the prize for 'Best Female Performer of the Year' (feminine interpretation) at the Victoires de la Musique with *Variations sur le même t'aime*, written for her by Serge Gainsbourg. The same year, she left France for the United States, now 19 years old, to work with rock musician Lenny Kravitz, who was her boyfriend for a while. Paradis worked on a new album entitled *Vanessa Paradis*, sung in English and written and produced by Kravitz. One of the singles from it was 'Be My Baby' which made number 5 in France and gave her another Top 10 UK hit (number 6). In 2001 she was nominated for the NRJ Music Awards for both 'Francophone Female Artist of the Year' and 'Francophone Album of the Year' for *Bliss*, an album in which she recorded a song with Depp. The album was actually dedicated to Depp and to their daughter Lily. In 2007 she recorded her fifth album, *Divinidylle*, which was nominated for 'French Album of the Year' at the NRJ Music Awards. Her acoustic album *Une nuit à Versailles* (2010) was recorded at L'Opéra of the Palace of Versailles. A set of DVDs titled *Anthologie* (2010) had been released in 2010 and collects her rare live performances and interviews from 1987–2007.

On a parallel track, since 1989, she

also built a cinematographic career. She has appeared in several films alongside Daniel Auteuil, Gérard Depardieu, Alain Delon, and Jeanne Moreau. She received a César for Most Promising Actress for Jean-Claude Brisseau's *Noce blanche /White Wedding* (1989) with Bruno Cremer. She rejected offers from Pedro Almodóvar and John Boorman because she wanted to build on her singing successes. However, she appeared in *Elisa* (Jean Becker, 1995); *La Fille sur le pont /The Girl on the Bridge* (Patrice Leconte, 1999), a black and white romance co-starring Daniel Auteuil, for which she was nominated for a César Award for Best Actress, and *Mon ange /My Angel* (Serge Frydman, 2004). In 2008, she was nominated for Trophy Women's Gold in the category 'Shows'. In 2011, she starred in the animated film *Un monstre à Paris /A Monster in Paris* (dir. Bibo Bergeron), and the well-received romantic comedy *L'Arnacœur /Heartbreaker* (Pascal Chaumeil, 2010), co-starring Romain Duris and Andrew Lincoln. Canadian film director Jean-Marc Vallée chose Paradis for the main role in *Café de Flore* (2011), for which she won a Genie Award for Best Actress in a Leading Role (2012).

From her height of 5'3", Paradis has also modelled for Chanel and promotes their fragrances and make-up such as the lipstick Rouge Coco (2010) as well as accessories. She was named Chevalier des Arts et des Lettres in 2007 and has her look-alike puppet in the French show *Les Guignols de l'info*. No link between the last two distinctions we presume.

Fabienne H. BAIDER
University of Cyprus

Gérard PHILIPE (1922–1959)
[Gérard PHILIP]

Gone Too Soon, but Never Forgotten

GÉRARD PHILIPE's short lifespan – about the length of those of Raphael and Mozart – is in inverse proportion to the immense successes he experienced during his lifetime and beyond, with the French public as well as internationally. According to Georges Sadoul, in his book about Philipe, « aucun comédien de France ne connut après-guerre une telle popularité » ['no other French actor knew, postwar, such popularity.'] [1]

Gérard Philipe was unanimously hailed as a most handsome *jeune premier*. His physical attractiveness, combined with an elegant composure, impeccable theatrical technique, and a charismatic cinematic presence ranks him among the most popular actors in France, in spite of his reduced time on this earth. Philipe was not even 37 years old at the time of his death – which occurred while he was at the height of his glory – from terminal liver cancer that had been hidden from him by his entourage and his physician (as was the days' custom).

Although Gérard Philipe was considered among the preferred French actors at the prime of his life, he had one quarter Czech heritage through a grandmother, and was very popular in Czechoslovakia, as were his films. For example, Philipe's posthumous image, in his iconic role as the titular *Fanfan la Tulipe /Fan-Fan the Tulip* (Christian-Jaque, 1952), appears in the short Czech New Wave film *Romance* (dir. Jaromil Jireš), a segment of the 1966 omnibus Czech New Wave 'manifesto' *Pearls of the Deep*, in which a young Czech man, observing the poster of *Fanfan* in the window of a Prague movie house, tells his girlfriend that he wishes he could be Fanfan, even if for only one day, since he is so handsome.

Yet Philipe nonetheless was « une parfaite incarnation de sa patrie...[il] aida son public à mieux comprendre, de 1946 à 1959, la France de notre temps, l'après-guerre » ('a perfect incarnation of his country...[he] helped his public better understand, from 1946-1959, the France of our time, of after the war.') [2]

Born in Cannes on December 4, 1922 – his birth name was actually Gérard Philip, but he added an 'e' to it – he studied drama, before moving to Paris to continue at the Conservatoire d'art dramatique. Among his first theatrical roles was the titular figure of Albert Camus's *Caligula*, performed at Paris' Théâtre Hébertot in 1945, directed by Paul Oettly: 'the initial success [of the play] was due at least in part to the "creation" of the role of Caligula by the brilliant but at that time unknown Gérard Philipe.' [3] Another famous masterpiece in which Philipe exercised his acting talent was Corneille's *Le Cid* at the Festival d'Avignon in 1951, under the direction of Jean Vilar. In *Le Cid*, Corneille's adaptation of the legend of 'El Cid' ['The Lord'] – the title given to the

medieval Castilian leader Rodrigo Díaz de Vivar, the national hero of Spain – Philipe portrays Rodrigue, torn between his love for Chimène and his duty towards his father whom he must avenge from the father of the very Chimène he had hoped to marry. This typically Cornelian conflict between love and duty is particularly gripping, as expressed through the acting and impassible yet moving facial expressions of Gérard Philipe's Rodrigue.

In his private life, Gérard Philipe was a loyal husband to Nicole Fourcade, also known as Anne Philipe (1917–1990), whom he married in 1951. They had two children, Anne-Marie (born 1954) and Olivier (born 1956). In spite of the adulation of female fans around the world that were often literally throwing themselves at him, Gérard Philipe remained faithful to Nicole. Nor did becoming a major film icon, mobbed by women everywhere he went, negatively affect his pleasant demeanor, strong work ethic, and good-natured attitude. According to Georges Sadoul:

Tout autre que lui aurait succombé aux séductions d'une telle idolâtrie, proche de la semi-déification ...obligé d'accepter des hommages excessifs, il n'en ressentait aucune vanité. Il était la modestie même, il passait sa vie à travailler pour se perfectionner dans son métier de comédien, au théâtre comme au cinéma. ...

Il accueillait généralement les foules avides de le voir et même de le toucher avec la profonde gentillesse qui fut toujours le fond de son caractère. Une grande sincérité, une parfaite dignité dominèrent sa vie et son oeuvre.

[Anyone else other than him would have succumbed to the seductions of such an idolatry, which came close to near-deification ... obliged to accept these excessive homages, he did not express any vanity. He was modesty itself; he spent his life working to perfect himself in his craft as an actor, in theatre as well as film. ...

He generally welcomed these crowds, that were eager to see and even to touch him, with the profound kindness that fundamentally characterized him. A great sincerity, a perfect dignity dominated his life and his oeuvre.] [4]

Nicole learned of his terminal liver disease, but she hid this bad news from him, so that he would enjoy life to the fullest until the end. Such a deception may seem shocking today, but it was commonplace at the time to hide terminal diagnoses from patients (Simone de Beauvoir's *Une mort très douce /A Very Easy Death*, her 1964 memoir of her mother's death describes this custom in detail.)

As an actor in over 30 films in a movie career that began in 1944 and lasted until his death in 1959, Philipe worked with some of the best known and most influential directors of his era (Yves Allégret, Luis Buñuel, René Clair, René Clément, Marcel Carné, Sacha Guitry, Max Ophüls) in many classic *oeuvres* including the titular character of iconic *Fanfan la Tulipe / Fan-Fan the Tulip* (Christian-Jaque, 1952). Philipe starred in two cinematic

adaptations of Stendhal novels: first, in Christian-Jaque's 1948 *La Chartreuse de Parme*, in which he incarnated Fabrice del Dongo, and then went on to play Julien Sorel in Claude Autant-Lara's *Le Rouge et le Noir / The Red and the Black* (1954). In *Les Amants de Montparnasse /The Lovers of Montparnasse* (Jacques Becker, 1958), Philipe plays the painter Amedeo Modigliani, a tragic figure, whose life, like Philipe's own, was cut short due to disease (in Modigliani's case, it was tuberculosis that killed him at age 35). Some of Philipe's other roles include that of Le Comte in Max Ophüls' *La Ronde* (1950) and D'Artagnan in Sacha Guitry's *Si Versailles m'était conté /Royal Affairs in Versailles* (1954).

Toward the end of his life, Gérard Philipe acted in Roger Vadim's 1959 *Les Liaisons dangereuses /Dangerous Liaisons*, a cinematic adaptation of Choderlos de Laclos's 18th century epistolary novel which narrates how the villainous Vicomte de Valmont seduces two women in order to please/appease his former love interest/accomplice, the evil, vendetta-bound Marquise de Merteuil. This, although not his final film, was the last to appear during his lifetime, since he died shortly after it premiered. Vadim transposed Laclos's 18th century novel of intrigue, lies, and deception into modern-day France, including the setting of an elegant ski resort and Thelonious Monk's soundtrack. Gérard Philipe's malleability and versatility allows him to perform, to perfection, the perfidious Valmont. Philipe's handsome features and seductive expression contrast with the *noirceur* and design of the character Valmont. Jeanne Moreau plays Juliette de Merteuil, the female counterpart to Philipe's Valmont, with Annette Vadim – Roger Vadim's second wife, after Brigitte Bardot – in the role of Marianne, whom Valmont seduces and then cruelly abandons despite actually falling in love with her. But it had been only a game for him.

Vadim's version differs from the later film adaptations of Laclos's *Les Liaisons dangereuses*. Both Stephen Frears's Academy-Award-winning *Dangerous Liaisons* (1988), with Glenn Close as Merteuil and John Malkovich as Valmont, and Milos Forman's *Valmont* (1989), starring Annette Bening and Colin Firth, are English-language costume dramas that remain faithful to the book's 18th century setting – as does the South Korean film adaptation, *Untold Scandal* (E J-yong, 2003), which is set during the Joseon Dynasty in 18th century Korea. However, Roger Kumble's 1999 *Cruel Intentions* is updated to the contemporary world of upper class New York City adolescents, with Sarah Michelle Gellar and Ryan Phillippe (who is of French descent, although whether or not he is related to Gérard Philipe is not known), in the Merteuil and Valmont roles. Likewise, the 2012 Chinese adaptation, Hur Jinho's *Dangerous Liaisons*, updates the setting of the original epistolary novel to 1930s Shanghai.

Although Roger Vadim's version of *Les Liaisons dangereuses* is often discarded as a minor cinematic undertaking, particularly when compared to the subsequent reinterpretations of the novel for the screen, without Gérard Philipe the film would not be what it is and might be relegated to a much lesser position. The range of Gérard Philipe's acting – from the stage performance of a mad Roman emperor or a tormented lover torn between his loyalty to his father Don Diegue and his duty to his love interest Chimène to the ultimate onscreen villain in Valmont – endeared Gérard Philipe to his fans, and to this day, he remains popular and is remembered with devotion.

Philipe's last movie performance was in Luis Buñuel's political narrative *La Fièvre monte à El Pao /Fever Mounts at El Pao* (1959), released posthumously with reshoots as Philipe died while the production was underway. [5] After his death, Anne Philipe published two books about her husband: *Gérard Philipe* (with Claude Roy, 1960; 2nd edition in 1978) and *Le Temps d'un soupir* (1963), about the last weeks of his life. French film historian Georges Sadoul's *Gérard Philipe* was published in 1967: [6] it would be his final book, as Sadoul died in October of that year.

Marcelline BLOCK
Princeton University and SAG-AFTRA

1. Georges Sadoul, *Gérard Philipe* (Paris: Filméditions, ed. Pierre Lherminier, 1984 ; 3rd ed.), 6. [All translations mine.]

2. Ibid., 5.

3. E. Freeman, *The Theatre of Albert Camus: A Critical Study* (London: Methuen, 1971), 35.

4. Sadoul, 6.

5. According to Vincent Canby of the *New York Times*, in his review of the film, 'This is not vintage Buñuel, but Mr Philipe is unexpectedly good as the muddled idealist.' *New York Times*, February 12, 1988, http://movies.nytimes.com/movie/review?res=940DEFD61139F931A25751C0A96E948260.

6. Sadoul's *Gérard Philipe* was subsequently reissued, with a third edition appearing in 1984.

Édith PIAF (1915–1963)
[Édith Giovanna Gassion]

'La Môme' Onscreen

THE YEAR 2013 marked the 50th anniversary of the death of the legendary performer Édith PIAF, who succumbed to liver cancer at age 47 on October 11, 1963 at her home in Placassier near Grasse in the South of France. Piaf, a universally recognized emblem of French culture and a symbol of Paris who is 'integral to international commodification of Frenchness'[1] as well as 'arguably the last "genuine" representative of the *chanson réaliste*'[2] was of French, Italian, and Moroccan heritage. She was born Édith Giovanna Gassion in the impoverished Belleville neighbourhood of Paris on December 19, 1915, supposedly in the rue de Belleville, under a street light, on the cape of a police officer who came to her mother's assistance, although this myth has been debunked: Ginette Vincendeau notes that Piaf was 'not [born] on the pavement as a blue plaque would have it.'[3] Piaf's mother, the Italian-born Annetta Giovanna Maillard – who abandoned Piaf as an infant – was a street singer known as 'Line Marsa.' Annetta's mother, Aïcha Saïd ben Mohamed, aka 'Emma', who cared for Édith as a child after Annetta abandoned her, managed a flea circus.

As a teenager, Édith performed throughout France with her father, the street acrobat Louis-Alphonse Gassion, and his travelling circus troupe. From these humble beginnings Piaf rose to prominence in the 1930s and 40s as a cabaret and then music hall star, also appearing in films, which 'use her in more or less transparent form,'[4] in other words, showcasing her as a singer (her songs are featured on over 100 film and television soundtracks, from 1936 to the present). Piaf was discovered and then promoted by Louis Leplée, owner of the Parisian nightclub Le Gerny, where she had her first successes as a performer; it was Leplée who gave her the nickname « la môme Piaf » ['the kid sparrow' (as 'piaf' is slang for 'sparrow')] due to her petite physique and febrile, bird-like mannerisms that contrasted with the raw emotional power of her deep voice. However, Leplée was murdered in 1936, shortly after engaging Piaf to sing for him. This was a dark time for Piaf, as she was accused of being complicit in Leplée's murder – and although she was cleared, her reputation remained tainted. The songwriter Raymond Asso, then working for singing star Marie Dubas, became involved with Piaf, as her lyricist, manager, and lover. Asso made her over completely: he engineered her renewed image by writing songs for her with music composed by Marguerite Monnot, re-baptizing her 'Edith Piaf,' and obtaining her a major contract at the Théâtre de l'ABC. Their relationship ended when Asso was drafted in 1939, after which Piaf was involved with actor Paul Meurisse, with whom she starred in Jean Cocteau's play *Le Bel Indifférent* (discussed below): it was 'well known that the leading men of her films and plays...were her lovers or intimate friends,'[5] including Raymond Asso, Charles Aznavour, Yves Montand, and Georges Moustaki, among others.

Piaf's short and troubled life was plagued by personal tragedies: as a little girl, she almost went blind, and later on, her only child, a daughter named Marcelle (born in 1933, when Piaf was 18, from her relationship with local errand/delivery boy Louis Dupont), died, as a toddler, from meningitis. Édith Piaf's Dickensian childhood and adulthood are reminiscent of several works of French literature: she could be a character out of Victor Hugo's *Les Misérables*. Like Cosette, she was left by her mother in the care of others, although Cosette was a martyred child servant at the house of Les Thénardiers, whereas Édith was the pet of the prostitutes in the brothel in Normandy managed by her paternal grandmother Léontine Louise Descamps. Édith's life was punctuated by scandal and she relied on alcohol and drugs (to which she became addicted) to get her through many difficulties and dramas, such as when the great love of her life, boxer Marcel Cerdan – a married father of three – whose visit she anxiously awaited, died in a 1949 plane crash en route to meet her in New York, where they had a rendezvous. Their story and relationship is the subject of Claude Lelouch's 1983 film, *Édith et Marcel*, in which Marcel Cerdan Jr. stars as his father, with Evelyne Bouix playing Piaf. Piaf was married twice: first to singer Jacques Pills from 1952 to 1956 (which ended in divorce) and then to Franco-Greek singer/ actor/hairdresser Theo Sarapo (born Théophanos Lamboukas), who was about 20 years younger than the 46 year old Piaf when they married in 1962, a year before she died.

Ill-fated personal and romantic relationships were primarily the subject matter of Piaf's love songs and ballads. She became a national icon hailed among the greatest French singers, achieving major recognition during her American tours with performances in New York City at Café Versailles (no longer in existence), Carnegie Hall, and the Waldorf Astoria Hotel in midtown Manhattan, as well as multiple appearances on *The Ed Sullivan Show*. However, it was at the Paris Olympia Concert Hall that Piaf gave her most unforgettable concerts. Her last performance was in Paris at Bobino in February 1963, shortly before her death in October of that year.

Piaf recorded approximately 430 songs, many of which are timeless examples of the tradition of the French *chanson réaliste*, evoking a Parisian landscape of low-lifes, culture, and love – the woman's passionate love for her man who often leaves her desperate and wanting. The great singer/performer Marie Dubas graciously lent Piaf her song *Mon légionnaire*, originally composed and written for Dubas in 1936 by the team of Marguerite Monnot and Raymond Asso, and which became one of Piaf's signature songs. Her other best recognized songs include *L'Accordéoniste* (Michel Emer, 1942), *Padam...Padam* (N. Glanzberg/Henri Contet, 1951), *Milord /Ombre de la rue* (Georges Moustaki/Marguerite Monnot, 1959), and *Non, je ne regrette rien* (Charles Dumont/Michel Vaucaire, 1956). In 1945, with music by Marguerite Monnot/Louis Gugliemi, she wrote the lyrics of *La Vie en rose* – which describe seeing life 'through rose-tinted glasses' when she is in her lover's arms – and which she first performed in 1946 after World War II and in Georges Friedland's 1948 film *Neuf garçons, un cœur* (discussed below). *La Vie en Rose*, the smash hit that brought her worldwide consecration, became the English title of the 2007 Piaf biopic directed by Olivier Dahan, whose title in French is *La Môme*. In this film, Piaf is masterfully interpreted by Marion Cotillard, who won the Academy Award for Best Actress for her performance, a historical victory, as it is the first time a French-language role was awarded such an honour.

Over the years, *La Vie en rose* has been covered by a wide range of singers including Josephine Baker, Jeff Buckley, Belinda Carlisle, José Carreras, Bing Crosby, Céline Dion, Dalida, Grace Jones, Julio Iglesias, Patricia Kaas, BB King, La Toya Jackson, Cyndi Lauper, Bette Midler, Liza Minnelli, Iggy Pop, and Donna Summer, as well as has been featured in over 30 films, for example, in Alfred Hitchcock's *Stage Fright* (1950) and Billy Wilder's *Sabrina* (1954), in which it is performed by Audrey Hepburn in the titular role (this song is also featured in the 1995 remake of *Sabrina*, directed by Sydney Pollack and starring Julia Ormond). *La Vie en Rose* is also the title of the 1998 television documentary about Piaf.

Édith Piaf achieved success and recognition in theatre and film, working with leading figures of the French entertainment industry as well as frequently performing on musical variety programs. She appeared in eight fictional films, and sang in all of them, starting with the controversial 1936 flapper story *La Garçonne /The Tomboy* (dir. Jean de Limur) starring Arletty, in which Piaf has a small role as a seductive singer, for which she is already listed in the credits as 'la môme Piaff.' She sang the film's theme song, *Quand même* (Louis Poterat/Jean Wiener). A few years later, with her then-romantic interest, Paul Meurisse (1912-1979) – who was to become best known for Henri-Georges Clouzot's *Les Diaboliques /Diabolique* (1955) – Piaf starred in Jean Cocteau's one-act play *Le Bel Indifférent* in the spring of 1940 at the Théâtre des Bouffes Parisiens. Meurisse, as the titular 'indifferent lover', was cast in a silent role while Piaf performed her monologue. Cocteau had written this play specifically for Piaf, based on her relationship with Meurisse: 'Cocteau thought Meurisse was a dull bourgeois unworthy of his beloved sparrow. So he wrote a play about their relationship with the aim of showing Paris that the passionate, man-hungry, booze-thirsty, life-devouring Piaf was shacked up with a cold fish, and also with a powerful desire to drive the pair apart. Then...he inveigled Paul and Édith to play themselves self-destructing on stage.' [6]

Cocteau was a lifelong friend and admirer of Piaf; when he learned of her death, he went into cardiac arrest, and as he was already ill and recuperating from an earlier heart attack, did not survive, passing away a few hours after she did, on the same day, October 11, 1963. That Cocteau's death occurred immediately followed hearing of Piaf's demise seems to confirm *post hoc ergo propter hoc* as expressed in the 1963 newspaper headline, 'Cocteau Dies on News of Piaf's Death':

> The death of Cocteau at one o'clock today seems to have been directly linked with that of Édith Piaf, the popular singer, who died at seven in the morning...A representative of the Paris State Radio, who was also a friend of Jean Cocteau, rang him up to ask him if he felt well enough to take part in the commemoration of Édith Piaf's death in some form on the air. M. Cocteau was convalescing after a severe heart attack earlier in the summer, but had resumed working and was, in fact, this morning engaged on drafting a new stage set for *Pelléas and Mélisande*. He had felt last night that his unease was due to the death of some near and dear friend. Now he knew this was Édith Piaf. He then added that he felt the same stifling sensation as when he had his original heart attack. A few minutes later he was dead.[7]

Yet, as Stuart Jeffries notes, this narrative, well-accepted in popular culture, must be taken with a grain of salt as it is but one more element of the 'legend' surrounding Piaf:

> Édith Piaf and Jean Cocteau died on the same day. Cocteau, chivalrous at the last, obeyed the rule of ladies first. 'Ah, la Piaf est

morte,' he said on the morning of October 11 1963. 'Je peux mourir aussi.' ['Ah, Piaf's dead. I can die too.'] And then he promptly died of a heart attack. Or so legend has it. But in these matters, legend is all-important...[8]

In the film *Montmartre-sur-Seine* (Georges Lacombe, 1941), Piaf starred as Lily alongside Jean-Louis Barrault. In this tale of 'a street singer who becomes a cabaret star,'[9] Piaf sang several songs for which she wrote the lyrics (*J'ai dansé avec l'amour*, *Un coin tout bleu*, *L'Homme des bars*, and *Tu es partout*) with music composed by her long time collaborator Marguerite Monnot (1903-1961). With first-time actor Yves Montand (1921-1991) – whom she discovered, and with whom she was also romantically involved – Piaf starred in the 1946 melodrama *Étoile sans lumière /Star Without Light* (directed by Marcel Blistène), a precursor to the American musical film *Singin' in the Rain* (Stanley Donen, 1952), starring Gene Kelly. Set in the 1920s, *Étoile's* narrative takes place at the end of the silent film era, when a declining film star appropriates the singing voice of her chambermaid Madeleine (Piaf), passing it off as her own onscreen. This film again features Piaf singing songs composed by Monnot, including *La Chanson des pirates*, yet 'the pessimism of *chanson réaliste* transfers to her [Piaf's] inability to "make it" on her own when the star dies.'[10] In the 1948 musical comedy *Neuf garçons, un cœur* (dir. Georges Friedland), Piaf performs with the group Les Compagnons de la Chanson, which she also launched into international stardom. For the film's finale, Piaf sings *La Vie en rose*. In Sacha

Guitry's historical epic, *Si Versailles m'était conté /Royal Affairs in Versailles* (1954), Piaf performs with many major film stars – including Brigitte Bardot, Jean-Louis Barrault, Bourvil, Claudette Colbert, Jean Marais, Gérard Philippe, Tino Rossi, and Orson Welles (as Benjamin Franklin). Here, she plays *une fille du peuple* ['a girl of the people'], singing the rousing French Revolution anti-aristocratic hymn, *Ça ira* ['It'll be Fine'], whose militant refrain declares, 'the aristocrats, we'll hang them'. That same year, Piaf played real-life Belle Epoque French cabaret singer Eugénie Buffet (1866-1934) in Jean Renoir's *French Cancan*. In the Mexican film *Música de siempre* (Tito Davison, 1958), Piaf sang *La Vie en rose* in Spanish. Piaf was reunited with director Marcel Blistène of *Étoile sans lumière* in the poetic realist love story *Les Amants de demain* (1959), as protagonist Simone, the unhappily married proprietress of a shabby hotel/restaurant, when a new male guest (Michel Auclair) arrives on Christmas Eve. Her songs in this film include the titular one as well as *Fais comme si* and *Les Neiges de Finlande* (composed by Monnot). Incidentally, Marcel Blistène's short directorial career (10 films in total) is bookended by two films starring Piaf: *Étoile sans lumière* (1946) and *Les Amants de demain* (1959). Piaf also joined the all-star casts of the musicals *Paris chante toujours ! /Paris Still Sings!* (Pierre Montazel, 1951) and *Boum sur Paris* (Maurice de Canonge, 1953), playing herself in both films, singing her own songs, including *Hymne à l'amour* in *Paris chante toujours !* and *Je t'ai dans la peau* as well as *Pour qu'elle soit jolie ma chanson* (with Jacques Pills, her then-husband) in *Boum sur Paris*.

Many theatrical commemorations throughout 2013 marked the 50th anniversary of Piaf's passing, including the last run of Leslie Fitzwater's one-woman show, *Piaf On Stage in the United States* in February 2013. Across the Atlantic, running from September 2012 through April 2013, the musical biography *Piaf : Une vie en rose et en noir* was revived (and updated) at the Daunou Theatre in Paris, produced by Alain Delon, written by Jacques Pessis and starring (and directed by) Nathalie Lhermitte. The musical *Les Amants d'un jour* – whose title is taken from Piaf's eponymous 1956 song – narrates the love between a couple of 20-year-olds in 1957 Montmartre through Piaf's iconic *chansons*, directed by Jean-Louis Grinda, head of the Monte Carlo Opera, was performed from September through December 2013 at Bobino, where Piaf gave her last performance in February 1963. Throughout 2012-2013, French singer Patricia Kaas (born in 1966) toured with her one-woman tribute to Piaf, *Kaas Chante Piaf*, in which she sings 21 classic Piaf songs in performances at Piaf's haunts such as the Olympia in Paris and Carnegie Hall in New York City, among other sites. The accompanying album *Kaas Chante Piaf* was released in November 2012. In New York City, the 50th anniversary of Piaf's death was commemorated with the 'Francofolies New York – A Tribute to Piaf' concert, held on September 19, 2013, at the legendary Beacon Theatre on Manhattan's Upper West Side (this concert moreover functioned as the US premiere of the *Francofolies* music festival, held annually in La Rochelle). Along with Kaas, a large group of international stars paid homage to Piaf by performing her songs for the

Francofolies event, including, among others, Harry Connick Jr, Beth Ditto, Julien Clerc, and Charles Dumont, to name a few. The show was subsequently broadcast on France 2 television.

Fifty years after her death, Édith Piaf's legacy for cinematic, theatrical, and French culture is her lasting musical repertoire immortalized through recorded soundtracks, by her own singing performances in her films, as well as by the generations of entertainers who pay homage to her with innumerable reinterpretations of *la môme Piaf*'s repertoire on stage and onscreen.

Marcelline BLOCK
Princeton University and SAG-AFTRA

1. Ginette Vincendeau, 'The *Mise-en-Scène* of Suffering: French *Chanteuses Réalistes*,' *New Formations* (no. 3, winter 1987): 125.

2. Ibid., 107.

3. Ibid., 115.

4. Ibid., 116.

5. Ibid., 115

6. Stuart Jeffries, 'The Love of a Poet', *Guardian*, November 7, 2003, accessed October 1, 2013, http://www.guardian.co.uk/music/2003/nov/08/popandrock.art.

7. Darsie Gillie, 'From the Archive, 12 October 1963: Cocteau Dies on News of Piaf's Death,' *Guardian*, October 11, 2011 (Originally Published in The Guardian on 12 October 1963), accessed October 1, 2013, http://www.guardian.co.uk/theguardian/2011/oct/12/archive-jean-cocteau-dies-edith-piaf.

8. Jeffries, 'The Love of a Poet.'

9. Vincendeau, 'The Mise-en-Scène of Suffering,' 116.

10. Ibid.

Jean PIAT (1924–)

The Venerable

FOR MOST French viewers old enough to remember it, Jean PIAT remains the most famous actor in *Les Rois maudits*, the phenomenally popular 1972 television adaptation of Maurice Druon's historical series of the same name. Combining an exuberant and cheeky masculinity with political shrewdness and self-serving acumen, Jean Piat embodied the complexities of Count Robert d'Artois in all their fine intricacies. His performance remains unforgettable.

But Jean Piat's career has not been limited to *Les Rois maudits*, nor even to the acting profession. Born in the small town of Lannoy in the North of France on 23rd September 1924, and kicked out of the Conservatoire national, Piat sat an audition at the grand house of French classical theatre, the Comédie-Française, which he integrated in 1947, becoming one of its members (*sociétaires*) six years later. Starting with servant parts, Piat made his true debut in 1958 with Beaumarchais's *The Barber of Seville*. Six years later, and for over three hundred nights, Piat played Cyrano de Bergerac. Legend has it that following the première, there were over fifty encores! As per the regulations of the Comédie-Français at the time, which imposed a twenty-year 'enrolment' period on its *sociétaires* and restricted their choices in terms of plays and parts, Piat remained with the Comédie-Française until 31st December 1972, becoming one of its honorary members the following day.

A versatile thespian, during his time at the Comédie-Française Piat was equally at ease in vaudeville as in tragedies, in classical plays as in contemporary theatre, a talent he also demonstrated in his work as a stage director of a wide range of works, from Molière's *Les Femmes savantes* to Marcel Achard's *Jean de la Lune*. He also adapted non-French theatre, such as Bill C. Davis's *Mass Appeal* (*L'Affrontement*), for which he received the Molière Award for Best Adaptation of a Foreign Play in 1997. In 2002, he presided over the Night of the Molière Awards.

Piat made his cinematographic debut in 1946 performing the eponymous role of the famous journalist/investigator Rouletabille in Christian Chamborant's film adaptation of Gaston Leroux's novel, *Rouletabille joue et gagne* (1947). Two years later, he reprised the role in *Rouletabille contre la dame de pique* (Christian Chamborant, 1948). Despite his participation in twenty-three movies, including the 1970 René Clément *Le Passager de la pluie /Rider on the Rain*, with Charles Bronson and Marlène Jobert, which won the Golden Globe Award for Best Foreign Language Film in 1971, it is primarily for his participation in two of France's most popular TV

mini-series that Piat is remembered today as a screen actor. Piat became a regular on French television first with the 1967 cloak and dagger series *Lagardère*, in which he played the title role. Handsome and romantic, Henri de Lagardère has sworn to avenge his companion Philippe de Nevers, murdered by the abominable Philippe de Gonzague, played with sadistic relish by Sacha Pitoëf, and to conquer the heart of the beautiful Aurore; one line summarises the series: 'If you don't come to Lagardère, Lagardère will come to you.' In 1972, Piat appeared again on the small screen, as the formidable Robert d'Artois in *Les Rois maudits*, thus cementing his place as one of France's most popular and talented figure of the small screen.

Classically trained in the art of impeccable diction and provided with a deep and warm voice, Piat (who once stated that 'to speak in tune is like singing in tune; it's a gift, albeit a less surprising one') has lent his voice to a number of animated films, notably as Scar and Frollo in the French versions of Disney productions *The Lion King* (Roger Allers and Rob Minkoff, 1994) and *The Hunchback of Notre-Dame* (Gary Trousdale and Kirk Wise, 1996) respectively. More recently, he has dubbed the characters of Gandalf the Grey in the popular *Lord of the Rings* trilogy (Peter Jackson, 2001-2003) and of Iorek Byrnison in *The Golden Compass* (Chris Weitz, 2007). He also worked as a voice actor in French animated productions such as *Le Château des singes /A Monkey's Tale* (Jean-François Laguionie, 1999) and *Kaena, la prophétie /Kaena:*

The Prophecy (Chris Delaporte and Pascal Pinon, 2003).

Jean Piat is also a celebrated author. He compiled an anthology of the greatest theatrical lines, composed an imaginary encounter with Beaumarchais as well as with his long-time friend Sacha Guitry who died in 1957, entitled respectively *Beaumarchais : Un intermittent du spectacle* (for which he received the Prix de l'Académie française, 2004), and *Je vous aime bien monsieur Guitry*. Jean Piat has written three novels: *La Vieille Dame dans la librairie*; *Veille de fête*, and *Le Dîner de Londres*.

Lesser known is Jean Piat's philanthropic work, particularly in Lebanon, a country he discovered during a tour in 1964. In the 1980s, the priest in charge of an orphanage in the massacred village of Damour appealed to Piat. The actor rallied to the call and recorded the priest's book, *L'Enfant du Liban*, ensuring that all profits would go the orphans' cause. Since then, Piat visits Lebanon yearly, stopping in Damour to renew his links with the priest and the orphans. During his 2010 visit, Piat took part in the filming of a documentary about his work in Lebanon, *Jean Piat : Une aventure Libanaise*.

His contributions to the acting profession, as a stage actor, a film and television actor, a voice actor, a director, and an adaptor has led to Piat receiving a number of awards. In addition to his 1997 Molière, Jean Piat was made *Grand officier de l'Ordre national du mérite* in 2006, with President Jacques Chirac acknowledging this 'very remarkable thespian, who excels in all registers,' and reminding audiences of Piat's interpretations as Figaro and Cyrano. In 2007-2008, under the title *Grand portrait*, an homage was given to Jean Piat at the Théâtre du Vieux-Colombier in Paris. In 2012, under the presidency of Nicolas Sarkozy, Jean Piat was made Grand Officier (Grand-Croix) of the Légion d'honneur. Piat is also an Officier in the Ordre des Arts et Lettres.

France GRENAUDIER-KLIJN
Massey University, New Zealand

Michel Piccoli (1925–)

In 1994, in celebration of the centennial of the birth of cinema, Michel Piccoli was chosen for the role of old Mr Simon Cinéma in Agnès Varda's *Les Cent et une nuits de Simon Cinéma /One Hundred and One Nights* (1994), and it only seemed too natural a choice, since the actor had gone through, give or take, a hundred and fifty characters throughout the then fifty-year-long career that had seen him a favourite of almost every major filmmaker. Indeed, hardly had there been on screen such a versatile actor, given the ability proven by Piccoli to play the average Joe. Nevertheless, he remains best known for a couple of skills that he relished, brisk anger fits on the one hand, and a more silent weaker figure on the other, both at their peak in perhaps his most famous and acclaimed performance, as screenwriter Paul Javal in Jean-Luc Godard's *Le Mépris /Contempt* (1963).

Like Yves Montand, Michel Piccoli was born into a family of Italian descent where both parents worked as musicians. After going to study in Paris, he discovered drama and joined the well-known Renaud-Barrault company. After a few cameos as an extra on movie sets, he started shooting in 1948, beginning quite

an amazingly long and diverse film career, undoubtedly helped by a very handsomely dark physique, though not overwhelmingly beautiful. He first worked mainly as a supporting actor in *films noirs*, where he impersonated mysterious, seductive (he was, after all, married to Saint-Germain des Prés muse and singer Juliette Gréco in the late sixties), troubling, and sometimes even scary characters, as in Costa-Gavras's first feature *Compartiment tueurs /The Sleeping Car Murders* (1965) or in Jean-Pierre Melville's much praised *Le Doulos* (1962). His career really took off in the mid-fifties when his path met with Jean Renoir's in *French Cancan* (1954) and Luis Buñuel's in *La Mort en ce jardin /Death in the Garden* (1956), arguably two of greatest filmmakers ever. He subsequently began a long term working relationship with the latter that lasted almost two decades, from *Le Journal d'une femme de chambre / Diary of a Chambermaid* (1964) to *Le Fantôme de la liberté /The Phantom of Liberty* (1974), through other masterpieces like *Le Charme discret de la bourgeoisie /The Discreet Charm of the Bourgeoisie* (1972) or *Belle de jour* (1967), co-starring young French superstar Catherine Deneuve. Piccoli even participated forty years later in the making of its sequel, *Belle toujours*, under the direction of Portuguese master Manoel de Oliveira and co-starring Bulle Ogier (in Catherine Deneuve's stead).

Besides his participation in genre films with older-generation artists Henri-Georges Clouzot, Melville, or Alfred Hitchcock (*Topaz*, 1969), Piccoli's talent really bloomed in auteur films, and found itself in perfect harmony with the spirit of the New Wave filmmakers and critics, from the predecessor Alexandre Astruc to Jacques Rozier (in *Adieu Philippine /Farewell, Philippine*, 1962, or in his short piece *Paparazzi*, shot on location in Capri, while Brigitte Bardot was filming *Contempt* there), or Claude Chabrol and Jacques Demy. He was also perfectly at ease with Alain Resnais, or Agnès Varda's more conceptual projects (for instance her 1963 still-framed picture *Salut les Cubains*). In the late sixties, Michel Piccoli's career took yet a new turn, with once again two filmmakers whose styles and projects could not be more distinct, Claude Sautet and Marco Ferreri. Claude Sautet leaned on a more mature manly character, presenting Piccoli as a lonely bourgeois figure (opposite friend and co-star Romy Schneider) in a depiction of contemporary French society, while the Italian filmmaker explored the edgy aspects of his characters. In a subversive series of protest films, Ferreri and Piccoli worked hard at undermining and finally destroying bourgeois values: the epitome of their adventure probably remains 1973's *La Grande Bouffe /The Big Feast*, where four friends choose to be secluded in a house in order to eat themselves to death. The film famously shocked the Cannes film festival, but was a huge box-office hit.

In the eighties, Piccoli engaged the last shift in his career, choosing to impersonate from now on either border-line characters or whimsical elderly ones, often working with younger uncompromising directors, such as Leos Carax (*Mauvais sang / The Night Is Young*, 1986; *Holy Motors*,

2012), Jacques Doillon, or even the late Raúl Ruiz. However, he cherished a special relationship with former New Wave directors like Jean-Luc Godard (becoming the angry factory manager of *Passion*, 1982), Louis Malle (in *Atlantic City* (1980) and the 1990 *Milou en mai /May Fools*, a period movie about a family spending a month at the countryside during the events of May 1968), and Jacques Rivette. The latter gave him one of his most touching roles in *La Belle Noiseuse* (1991), adapted from Balzac's novella *Le Chef-d'oeuvre inconnu /The Unknown Masterpiece* (1931), a radiant three-hour depiction of a melancholic painter doomed by an inspiration block, lost love, and bygone youth. Though he never stopped working, either as a stage actor or as an inspired new director in the years 2000, Piccoli's craft never ceased to improve, and could be compared with fine quality lace, using silence as well as a soft playful voice with great accuracy. In 2006, his deeply moving impersonation of King Lear at the Théâtre de l'Odéon showcased every skill he was gifted with, able to play emotions ranging from childlike madness to an old man's anger or despair, and reminded everyone that he used to be a convincing repertoire actor and a definitive Don Juan on television (directed by Marcel Bluwal, after Molière's play). Symbolically, one of Piccoli's most unforgettable characters was offered to him in 2000 by Oliveira in *Je rentre à la maison /I'm Going Home* (2001), where he played a famous actor confronted by the sudden death of his family and having to support his only remaining grandson. There he reached the very peak of his subtleness. His popularity reached new heights thanks to Nanni Moretti's *Habemus Papam /We Have a Pope* (2011), where Piccoli shows an equally unfathomable distress as a newly elected pope deeply upset by his fate. Both the film and the performance got rave reviews at the 2011 Cannes Film Festival, even winning the 2012 David di Donatello Award for best actor in Italy. Although his condition now only allows him to work as a supporting actor, the actor does not seem to be losing his passion for his craft, and he has kept shooting at a very sustained pace since the late 2000s: still very sought after by directors, he remains one of the last living legends of French cinema.

Jean-Christophe BLUM
Lycée Blaise Pascal, Clermont-Ferrand

Denis PODALYDÈS (1963–)

The Comedy of Innocence

BORN IN bourgeois Versailles, Denis PODALYDÈS had the audacity to leave the family nest, giving up his studies in philosophy and literature in order to take drama classes at the Cours Florent,[1] before entering the Conservatoire.[2] This early choice of stage-acting was confirmed in 1997 when he became a member of the Comédie-Française. Better known by the general public as a film actor, he is not really a star, but he is famous and successful with a certain audience.

From the start, cinema was, for him, a family business: his brother Bruno Podalydès directed him in two films on the city where they were born: *Versailles rive-gauche /A Night in Versailles* (1992) and *Dieu seul me voit /Only God Sees Me* (1998). In both, Denis Podalydès embodies a thirty-year-old single man, shy and awkward with girls, an eternal blunderer, an expert in putting himself into impossible and ridiculous predicaments. Not very tall, a little dishevelled, losing his hair because of stress, he is not very handsome, rather ordinary in appearance, but quite charming and touching. He believes his talent with women is his humour and tries to convince himself that: « C'est très bien les gens qui n'ont pas

peur du ridicule, c'est très touchant »
['It is a good thing not to be afraid
of looking ridiculous, it is a touching
feature in someone'].

Podalydès is perfect in the role of
the young adult a little out of touch
with reality, who does not really know
what to do with himself. Constantly
analysing situations and his own
reactions to them, we often find him
speaking to himself, trying to figure
out if he is making the right decisions.
We laugh at his embarrassment, his
awkwardness.

There is in him something a little
outdated. Both he in his acting and
his brother through the stories he
makes up, appear slightly out of step,
ill-suited to adult life, to modern life.
Both are fans of Tintin, in their films
and in real life, as if nostalgic for this
outmoded universe.

The two films on Versailles enabled
Denis Podalydès to assert his talent as
a comic actor and to forge his acting
personality. But in between the two,
he was also given chances to play in
more dramatic films, and to endorse
more substantial roles, not the leading
ones, but noticeable performances with
such directors as Arnaud Desplechin
(in *Comment je me suis disputé…(ma
vie sexuelle) /My Sex Life…or How I
Got into an Argument*, 1996), François
Dupeyron (*La Chambre des officiers /
The Officers' Ward*, 2001), and Bertrand
Tavernier (*Laissez-passer /Safe Conduct*,
2002).

In 2003, he had the leading role
of the detective Rouletabille in the
film adaptation of Gaston Leroux's
detective novel *Le Mystère de la chambre
jaune /The Mystery of the Yellow Room*
(2003) and its sequel *Le Parfum de la
dame en noir* (2004), both directed by

Bruno Podalydès. If his acting here
is more serious, more conventional,
and consensual, there is still this note
of amusing originality that always
characterises him. Here again the
parallel with Tintin is telling: Denis
Podalydès has the same innocence,
the same asexual appearance, the
determination, and playful airs of his
favourite hero.

But if he is perfect at playing
this comedy of innocence, he is also
capable of interpreting darker and
more complex roles (such as the
neurotic husband and father in the
ambiguous comedy *Liberté-Oléron*
(Bruno Podalydès, 2001), or of the
war veteran in *La Chambre des officiers*
(2001). Polite, kind, touching, and
amusing, this good boy from Versailles
has also proved that he could free
himself from these images and rise to
the level of melancholy and tragedy.

Podalydès is a workaholic. He
multiplies the roles in the theatre and
cinema, as well as stage readings. He
triumphs in Molière's *L'Avare* at the
Comédie-Française (2009). In the
film *La Conquête /The Conquest* (Xavier
Durringer, 2011), presented outside the
competition at the Cannes Festival,
he plays French President Nicolas
Sarkozy.

Céline VITARD
Lycée Camille Saint-Saëns, Rouen

1. A famous drama course in Paris.
2. The oldest and the most renowned
acting school in France.

Benoît POELVOORDE (1964–)

Tragically Funny

BENOÎT POELVOORDE is, without a doubt, one of the best known Belgian comedians. With a career spanning more than two decades and a repertoire of more than thirty movies, he has reached French stardom status. He went from being a 'nobody' to a 'star' during the 'Semaine de la critique' at the 1992 Cannes film festival where, with his school friends, Rémy Belvaux and André Bonzel, he was presenting their black and white film *C'est arrivé près de chez vous / Man Bites Dog*, 1992. Based on a Belgian TV show called *Strip-tease* and the adventures of *Torpedo*, a cult comic book from the 80s, the movie, filmed as a parody of a documentary, tells the story of a serial killer with a 'big heart.' The movie has no real pretensions or even political message. It is simply a film about freedom, the freedom to make films, away from the usual cliché about two people falling in love in a hotel in the 16th arrondissement, and of course, a film about the excesses of television. Belvaux, Poelvoorde, and Bonzel wanted to show that anybody would do anything to be on television and television would do anything to get something sensational; in other words, they wanted to show with a cringing, exaggerated humour the worst and most perverted aspects of television.[1]

An actor with an intricate personality, a crude but never vulgar sense of humour, a *sensibilité à fleur de peau*, Poelvoorde was not destined to become one of the most acclaimed, best paid, and one of the most loved actors of French cinema. Indeed, Benoît Poelvoorde comes from a poor family: his father, a lorry driver, died in a road accident when Benoît was a young teenager, and his mother, a shopkeeper, raised him alone with his brother and sister. He came to acting not through the mysterious ways of luck but simply because he wanted to meet a young woman who was participating in a class play. At the time, he was studying drawing – he wanted to draw comic books professionally and was very gifted at it – and had offered to do the poster for the play in the hope that he would be able to talk to the young woman. This is when fate struck. One of the main actors was not able to make the performance, so Benoît Poelvoorde was asked to replace him. It became immediately clear that Benoît Poelvoorde was a natural. He kept on acting, mostly as favours for the school projects of his best friend Rémy Belvaux. In 1992 they went on to make the movie *C'est arrivé près de chez vous* which became what the critics at the time called a cinematographic UFO and the movie cult of a generation. It received three awards at the Cannes festival of the same year, and Benoît Poelvoorde instantly became the talk of the Croisette.[2]

Critics viewed him as a cross between Raymond Goethals [3] and Robert De Niro. After this unbelievable experience, he told his mother that the advantage of him doing cinema was that from now on she would be called Miss Poelvoorde (even if most French people don't know how to pronounce her name) and people would hold the door for her.

Before acting in his second film, Benoît Poelvoorde went back to theatre and more importantly created for Canal+ a TV show called Les Carnets de Monsieur Manatane. Drawing on the caustic humour from C'est arrivé près de chez vous, he created a character who, through his own life experience takes an ironic and sarcastic view on contemporary and controversial subjects such as alternative sexuality, death, colonialism, and religion. During the three seasons of this show Benoît Poelvoorde attempted to make provocation a major art.

The real acting career only really began in 1997, when the director Philippe Harel asked him to star in his new movie Les Randonneurs / Hikers. This was Benoît Poelvoorde's first real experience with film making, sets, and relationships with other real actors and technicians. The movie went on to become an enormous success and some quotes, such as « À cinq on est partis, à cinq on arrivera, d'accord, we are together » immediately took their place in French lingo. He went on to make two other movies with Philippe Harel, the first one in 2001, a comedy, Le Vélo de Ghislain Lambert /Ghislain Lambert's Bicycle (2001), which tells the story of a professional cyclist born the same day as Eddy Merckx but who cannot reach the same glory, was also very well received. The second, in 2008, is the sequel of Les Randonneurs, Les Randonneurs à Saint-Tropez. As is often the case during his career, Benoît Poelvoorde chooses films he makes as a result of friendships with directors, and most of these films go on to be successful. Following Les Carnets de Monsieur Manatane, he acted in Christian Merret-Palmair's comedy Les Portes de la gloire /Days of Glory (2001). With Gilles Lelouche he made Narco in 2004, and for Benoît Delépine and Gustave de Kervern, played in Aaltra (2004), Louise-Michel (2008), and Le Grand Soir (2012).

Among all these films, one must absolutely remember the comedy, Podium, which propelled Benoît Poelvoorde to stardom in 2004. Yann Moix, the director, knew immediately that Benoît Poelvoorde was the ideal actor for that role. In fact he wrote it especially for Poelvoorde and in order to convince him to make the movie, Yann Moix wrote and published a novel about Bernard Frédéric whose profession is impersonating the famous pop French singer Claude François, whilst on the side working as a bank employee. With his friend Couscous, a Michel Polnareff lookalike, they embark on the preparation of the most important contest of their life, La Nuit des sosies. Upon reading the novel, Benoît Poelvoorde immediately understood that this role was perfectly tailored for him, and against the advice of his entourage, he went on to make the film with Yann Moix who had previously only directed one short movie. The movie was the success of 2004 and, that year, Poelvoorde was nominated for the César for best male actor.

In the meantime, Benoît Poelvoorde has not stopped making films with his Belgian compatriots. In 1996 he acted in Lucas Belvaux's *Pour rire !*, and he made two successful movies with Benoît Mariage, *Les Convoyeurs attendent / The Carriers are Waiting* (1999) and *Cowboy* (2007), and finally to reflect or give way to his personality, his sense of humour and subversiveness he played, in 2002 in Jan Bucquoy's controversial and rebellious film *La Vie politique des Belges*.

There are obviously many more comedies, some good, some bad, and some very bad which saw Benoît Poelvoorde considered as the new Bourvil. The enormous amount of filming finally took its toll however, and in the mid-noughties (2008), Benoît Poelvoorde suffered from depression and alcoholism to the point that he announced his retirement from cinema. Suddenly, he appeared to the public a man with a complex personality, great human fragility, and hopeless despair. He felt he had no legitimacy in the movie business and the fact he did not win the César in 2004 was the justification for this feeling.

Anne Fontaine is the director who saw the joyful melancholy, the human depth, and Shakespearean side of Benoît Poelvoorde, as it happened with Coluche when he acted as the lead actor in *Tchao Pantin /So Long, Stooge* (Claude Berri, 1983). He made three very powerful films with her: *Entre ses mains* (2005) where Poelvoorde played the complex role of Laurent Kessler – a seducer/serial killer who falls in love with Claire, a young insurance employee played by Isabelle Carré. Anne Fontaine then gave him the part of Etienne Balsan in *Coco avant Chanel /Coco Before Chanel* (2009), and finally she made him come back to his love of comedy by making him share the main role with Isabelle Huppert in the powerful, poignantly funny film *Mon pire cauchemar /My Worst Nightmare* (2011).

Benoît Poelvoorde came out of his period of existential and cinematographic crisis and has gone on to make other movies, maybe now trying to avoid roles which would once again corner him in the image of the sad clown, a label he forcefully rejects. This can certainly be seen in the quality and variety of his recent films such as Jean-Pierre Améris' *Les Émotifs anonymes /Romantics Anonymous* (2010), Gustave Kervern and Benoît Delépine's *Le Grand Soir* (2012), Hélène Fillières' *Une histoire d'amour /Tied* (2013), and with his friend Dany Boon the blockbuster *Rien à déclarer /Nothing to Declare* (2010).

Benoît Poelvoorde explained that out of his depression he learnt to be honest with himself, to question himself, and most importantly how to be sincerely nonchalant, and this is perhaps best seen in his role of a Belgian customs agent facing a rival French customs agent (Dany

Boon) in *Rien à déclarer /Nothing to Declare* (2010). This film epitomises the fact that he decided to embrace once again the joyful melancholy which constitutes his Belgitude. Benoît Poelvoorde intimately and profoundly feels Belgian. Indeed he is the embodiment of this kind of sad voluntarism, this ubiquitous grace one can find in the Belgian character and without which Benoît Poelvoorde, the actor, would have never been born.

Jean-Fréderic HENNUY
National University of Ireland, Maynooth

1. Editor's note: for further discussion, see Christophe Den Tandt, '*Strip Tease*: Documentary Realism as (Post)modernist Art' in *Directory of World Cinema: Belgium*, ed. Marcelline Block and Jeremi Szaniawski (Bristol: Intellect, 2013), 165-169. Other Benoît Poelvoorde films that are discussed in this article which are reviewed in *The Directory of World Cinema: Belgium* include *C'est arrivé près de chez vous* and *Les convoyeurs attendent*.
2. The boulevard/promenade de la Croisette, at Cannes. —Ed.
3. Raymond Goethals was a Belgian football trainer who notably led the Olympic of Marseille to win the European championship in 1993.

Jean POIRET (1926–1992)
[Jean Gustave POIRÉ]

A Waggish Kind of Gentleman

BORN INTO a modest family in Paris (under the name Jean Gustave Poiré), Jean POIRET grew up in the suburbs of Paris. He took drama classes during his youth and at the age of 25, after some years of working menial jobs, he got his first role on the radio. In 1951, he met Michel Serrault and together they put on a cabaret act. Their friendship was to last a lifetime, and their acting partnership set them both on the road to fame.

We get a glimpse of the duo in *Cette sacrée gamine /Naughty Girl* (Michel Boisrond, 1956), a comedy with Brigitte Bardot that did not age very well but shows how comfortable the two actors were together. Their few appearances still resemble cabaret acts and their short dialogues, mostly about food, have very little to do with the actual plot. This was just a beginning though, and a year later, *Naughty Girl*'s director Michel Boisrond again cast them together in a film, giving them a significant opportunity with *Assassins et Voleurs /Lovers and Thieves* (1957) in which Poiret plays a bored aristocrat who kills his lover's husband and lets a burglar (Michel Serrault) go to jail in his place. This time the duo actually makes the film. Poiret's delicate manners serve him again in *Le Mur de l'Atlantique /Atlantic Wall* (Marcel Camus, 1970), another comedy in which he appears as Armand, a well-born Gaullist caught between the Nazis, the hard-core bullying resistance, and the whining anti-hero played by Bourvil.

With his predilection for irony, Poiret proved to be at his best alongside foolish or hysterical counterparts. Fully at ease in roles of cynical characters or superior authorities, Poiret is generally shown as a middle or upper class protagonist, but Jean-Pierre Mocky challenged this image by casting him as a small time crook faking paralysis in the bawdy anti-clerical comedy *Le Miraculé* (1987).

Not all of Poiret's films are subtle and many have fallen into obscurity. However, a few have become French classics, such as François Truffaut's *Le Dernier Métro /The Last Metro* (1980), a World War II drama about a theatre trying to stay afloat during the Occupation of Paris. Poiret's role as a substitute stage director is discreet but allowed him to prove that he was worthy of the most prestigious directors. Claude Chabrol, another giant of the New Wave, cast him in the memorable role of Inspecteur Lavardin in *Poulet au vinaigre / Chicken with Vinegar* (Chabrol, 1985), *Inspecteur Lavardin* (Chabrol, 1986), and the TV series *Les Dossiers secrets de l'inspecteur Lavardin* (1988-1990). Poiret investigates, using smooth and unconventional methods, against the provincial bourgeois backdrop, becoming one of the most well-known detectives of the French cinema.

Jean Poiret's international fame was however not earned in films, but at the theatre, and more precisely as a playwright. His stroke of genius is *La Cage aux folles* (1973), whose characters had already been outlined in early sketches such as *Les Antiquaires* (1959), but reached their full potential in *La Cage aux folles*, a boulevard comedy about a gay male couple that runs a drag cabaret in St. Tropez. Poiret plays the owner of the drag club who, when asked by his beloved son to meet his fiancée's conservative parents, reluctantly agrees to pose as a traditional father. His partner, Michel Serrault, refuses to be ousted from the official introductions and makes a dramatic entrance as – the mother (in drag).

Jean Poiret handed over his part to Ugo Tognazzi for the 1978 screen adaptation directed by Edouard Molinaro, but one thing is sure: Poiret's pronounced taste for light-hearted comedy never expressed itself more naturally and graciously than in this play.

La Cage aux folles was a major hit in theatres and in cinemas all over the world, and spawned several sequels: Molinaro's 1980 *La Cage aux folles II* and Georges Lautner's 1985 *La Cage aux folles III – 'Elles' se marient /La Cage aux Folles 3: The Wedding* (with Serrault and Tognazzi reprising their roles in both remakes). It was especially well received in America (where it was also given the title *Birds of a Feather*): it was adapted for Broadway and first staged in 1983 (music and lyrics by Jerry Herman/book by Harvey Fierstein), garnering Tony Awards for Best Musical, Best Score, and Best Book, with two Broadway revivals: 2004 and 2010. It was remade onscreen by Mike Nichols as *The Birdcage* in 1996, starring Robin Williams and Nathan Lane, as well as featuring an up-and-coming Calista Flockhart (just before she became a household name as the titular character of the TV show *Ally McBeal*) as the son's fiancée.

As an actor, parody singer, producer, screenwriter, and playwright, Jean Poiret was a prominent figure of the French cultural scene for forty years. He tried his hand at directing with an adaptation of Alexandre Jardin's novel, *Le Zèbre* (1992). This burlesque drama is the portrait of a whimsical, middle-aged notary (Thierry Lhermitte) who annoys his wife (Caroline Cellier) with all manners of attempts to prolong their romance within the bonds of marriage. Poiret died of a heart attack on 14th March 1992, just two months before *Le Zèbre* was released. This film can be seen as his last contribution to French cinema, and maybe his most personal. Caroline Cellier was Poiret's spouse in real life, and the portrait retains something of Jean Poiret himself, for he too was a great promoter of self-derision, discarding all notions of respectability with a mocking smile and devoting his life to the amusement of others.

Sophie BOUVIER
University of Bristol

Albert Préjean (1894–1979)

The Odd Job Man of the Cinema

ALBERT Préjean was born in Pantin (Paris area) and died in Paris in 1979. As a child he dreamt of running away, which got him as far as boarding school where he quickly discovered his talent for comedy. He loved sport – running, wrestling, fencing, and especially boxing and cycling.[1] Nonetheless, Albert tried to follow his father's wish for him to become a businessman, but when he met the charming Mistinguett, the Queen of Music-Hall, his newfound passion for singing made it hard to focus on studying the stock market.[2] Just as he was exploring this exciting new world, the Great War broke out and Albert enlisted in the regiment. He was wounded, but would not let that keep him from serving. Upon his recovery, he joined the Air Force and went on to become a great pilot, decorated with the Croix de Guerre and the Légion d'honneur.[3]

Following the war, he met Augusta Favas, known as Lulu, a milliner and model, and they married in 1920.[4] Enrolling in a class called 'Be a Star in 30 lessons,' Albert took his first steps in *le milieu*.[5] By chance, Henri Diamant-Berger attended one of the sessions and noticed Albert. The director was looking for someone who could convincingly fight with a sword for his next project, the short film *Les Trois Mousquetaires* (1921). Préjean was on screen for only a few minutes in that film, but it was to be the beginning of his collaboration with Diamant-Berger; Préjean would act in several Diamant-Berger films from 1921 to 1927, including the sequel of the famous Mousquetaire story, *Vingt ans après* (1922).[6] Préjean's career was slow to take off, but in these early years, he laid the foundation for a lifetime in film. In 1922 on the set of Diamant-Berger's *Gonzague*, he met Maurice Chevalier, who would become a great friend.[7] In 1923, Diamant-Berger introduced Préjean to René Clair,[8] with whom he would make five films, including the director's first project, *Paris qui dort /At 3:25* (1925), and the musical *Sous les toits de Paris /Under the Roofs of Paris* (1930). Préjean's career finally took off in 1925 when he landed his first big role, starring in *Amour et carburateur* by Pierre Colombier. He also began working with Raymond Bernard, with whom he would collaborate on a few more films between 1923 and 1927.

While his career soared, things were not going well in his personal life, and he divorced Lulu in 1932. After *Voyage de noces /Honeymoon Trip* (Germain Fried, Joe May, Erich Schmidt, 1933), he played opposite Raimu in *Théodore et cie /Theodore and Company* (Pierre Colombier, 1932),[9] and then shared the screen with Danielle Darrieux in *Volga en flammes /Volga in Flames* (Viktor Tourjansky, 1933).[10] The pair would go on to star together in five

films during their careers. In 1935, he played opposite Josephine Baker in *Princesse Tam-Tam* (Edmond T. Gréville), and a year later met Marcel Carné and worked on *Jenny* (1936).[11] He continued to thrive, acting in rich and various collaborations with Pierre Chenal (*L'Alibi /The Alibi*, 1937),[12] Pierre Billon (*La Piste du sud*, 1938),[13] André Berthomieu (*L'Inconnue de Monte Carlo /Unknown of Monte Carlo*, 1939),[14] and Jacques Becker and Jean Stelli (*L'Or du Cristobal /Cristobal's Gold*, 1940).

During the war, Préjean portrays Maigret [15] after Harry Baur on three occasions, embodying the famous lieutenant in *Picpus* (1943) and *Les Caves du Majestic /Majestic Hotel Cellars* (1945) both by Richard Pottier, and *Cécile est morte /Cecile is Dead* by Maurice Tourneur in 1944. In his personal life, he reconnected with Lulu; they would remarry in 1937, only to divorce again at the end of World War II in 1945. The divorce was prompted by his meeting Jacqueline Le Haranger, aka Lysiane Rey, whom he married in 1946. Together, they had a son, Patrick, in 1944, who is known today for his roles in boulevard theatre and his work on dubbing.[16]

After the war, Préjean was still very active on screen, playing opposite the biggest stars, including Madeleine Robinson, Yves Montand, and Charles Vanel, and acting for the best directors, including Maurice Cloche, Henri Decoin, and Henri Verneuil. He ended his film career in 1962 with *Bonne chance Charlie / Good Luck Charlie* by Jean-Louis Richard, and turned his attention to the circus where he was not afraid to enter the lions' cage.[17] He married for the fourth and final time in 1977, wedding Jeanne Poché. Albert Préjean died of a heart attack on November 1st, 1979. He is buried in Auteuil.

The most famous roles of Préjean's career are:

1930 – *Sous les toits de Paris /Under the Roofs of Paris* (René Clair).

This is known as the first French filmed musical and the first speaking film by René Clair. Albert (Albert Préjean) is a street singer, living in a small room under the roofs of Paris. He meets the lovely Pola (Pola Illéry), already courted by his best friend Louis (Edmond T. Gréville) as well as Fred the crook (Gaston Modot). Pola falls in love with Albert, but he is framed for a crime and sent to prison. Once released, Albert has to meet again with his past, and his love.[18]

1931 – *L'Opéra de quat' sous /The Threepenny Opera* (G.W. Pabst).

A German musical created by Bertold Brecht and Kurt Weill in 1925, *L'Opéra de quat' sous* was soon after adapted for the screen, first in Germany and then in France. Set in London in 1900, it relates the story of Mackie (Albert Préjean), the king of the bandits. Polly (Florelle) marries Mackie against the will of her father, the king of the beggars. The outraged father, Peachum (Gaston Modot), manages to have Mackie arrested and sentenced to death, but he escapes and eventually joins with his father-in-law. Even if it diverges

from Brecht's version, the film is a poignant depiction of the economics of society and its dropouts, with an unconcealed allusion to the approach of the Second World War.

1935 – *Princesse Tam-Tam* (Edmond T. Gréville).

Max de Mirecourt (Albert Préjean), a famous French author, takes a trip to Tunisia to rediscover his inspiration for writing but instead meets the beautiful Alwina (Josephine Baker). Knowing that his wife Lucie (Germaine Aussey) is flirting with the Maharadjah de Datane (Jean Galland), Max has a plan. He brings Alwina back to France, making her the protagonist of his next novel and introducing her to Paris society as 'Princesse Tam-Tam' from India. The young girl needs to adapt to her new life, and the writer to win back his wife.

1936 – *Jenny* (Marcel Carné).

Jenny is Marcel Carné's first film and also the first of a fruituous collaboration with Jacques Prévert:

'His first sole film was the moody melodrama Jenny. This story of doomed love and star-crossed lovers marked the beginnings of Carné's romantic and fatalist mode of address that would endure up to *Les Portes de la nuit*.'[19]

Jenny (Françoise Rosay) and Benoît (Charles Vanel) run a so-called respectable nightclub, which is actually a place where rich men meet attractive young women. Jenny is also Jeanne, and has a daughter, Danielle (Lisette Bricart). Danielle soon meets

Lucien (Albert Préjean) and cannot help falling in love with him; but unfortunately he is already...Jenny's lover![20]

Candice NICOLAS
Loyola Marymount University,
Los Angeles

1. Patrick Préjean, *Albert Préjean* (Paris: Editions Candeau, 1979), 23-24.

2. Ibid., 29.

3. Ibid., 144-45.

4. Ibid., 38-40.

5. Ibid., 41.

6. Ibid., 48.

7. Ibid., 51.

8. Ibid., 62.

9. Ibid., 113-16.

10. Ibid., 121-28.

11. Ibid., 138-39.

12. Ibid., 130, and see pictures on 96-97.

13. Ibid., 133-35.

14. Ibid., 137.

15. Ibid.

16. Ibid., 42-47, and pictures.

17. See picture of 'Albert en tournée avec le cirque Jean Richard,' in Préjean, 144-45.

18. See pictures in Préjean, 48-49.

19. Ben McCann, 'Marcel Carné,' *Senses of Cinema* 59 (March 2011), http://sensesofcinema.com/2011/greatdirectors/marcel-carne/.

20. More on *Jenny* in Danièle Gasiglia-Laster, « Double jeu et 'je' double. La question de l'identité dans les scénarios de Jacques Prévert pour Marcel Carné », *Cinémaction* 98/1 (2001).

RAIMU (1883–1946)
[Jules Auguste César MURAIRE]

Genius of the People, Pure and Unrefined

THE CURTAIN was raised on Raimu's remarkable life not far from the military port of Toulon, where he came into the world as Jules Auguste César Muraire on 18 December 1883. After training as an upholsterer, he went on to forge a career as a travelling performer and actor, a long and arduous process in which he displayed great patience and fortitude.

His efforts were crowned with success when he took to the stage in the sumptuous silks of Molière's *Bourgeois Gentilhomme* and the pallid linen of his *Malade Imaginaire*, triumphs which won him the admiration not only of the fastidious audiences of the Comédie Française but also of luminaries such as Jean Cocteau.[1]

Raimu's affinity with Molière, whose works he played so brilliantly at the Théâtre Français in 1944 and 1945 (he had become a *sociétaire* of this bastion of national cultural resistance in 1943), stretched far beyond the confines of the stage: Molière himself had been born to a humble upholsterer. The inimitable voice of this apparently invincible hulk of a man, the *grande gueule* of the inter-war years, fell silent on 20 September 1946 in Neuilly at the age of just 62.

Preternaturally, even pathologically, demanding, and often the most difficult individual to work with on stage, in his forty-five-year career this great performer – artist and labourer rolled into one – attempted almost everything possible, in the theatre and then briefly on film, and succeeded at most of it.[2] The news of his demise prompted a shower of eulogies, including legendary tributes by Marcel Pagnol and Marcel Achard. To these can be added the verdict of Orson Welles, who during a stay in Paris shortly after the actor's death stated that Raimu was 'the greatest of us all.' Welles went to see *La Femme du boulanger /The Baker's Wife* (Marcel Pagnol, 1938), possibly Raimu's greatest film, no fewer than ten times. It was screened constantly in New York for nearly five years.[3]

In the course of his career Raimu appeared in just about every costume imaginable in theatre or film – from Clemenceau's frock coat to General Cambronne's uniform, from ecclesiastical regalia to the dinner jackets and tails of worldly sybarites, from the anonymous suit of a kind-hearted mobster to the black robes of a courtroom lawyer, the outfit of a school gym instructor or the tricolore sash of a town Mayor. His booming voice and forceful gestures, his titanic temper and mischievous tomfoolery assumed all these guises with consummate ease, but his truly unforgettable performances came when he was dressed in the humblest and poorest of clothes. In the first of these roles he donned the crumpled jacket of a lanky soldier, during his beginnings in the music hall and café concert; [4] then on three separate occasions he was to be found sporting a grimy apron behind the counter of the Bar de la Marine as César in Pagnol's trilogy (*Marius, Fanny, César*); [5] this was followed by the coarse, filthy woollen hat of a baker (*La Femme du boulanger*), the threadbare breeches of a well-digger (*La Fille du puisatier / The Well-Digger's Daughter*, dir. Marcel Pagnol, 1940) and, most squalid of all, the rotten greatcoat of a one-armed cavalryman who had survived the carnage of Eylau (*Le Colonel Chabert*, dir. René Le Hénaff, 1943).

From the late 1920s onwards, Raimu gradually metamorphosed from Provençal comedian into prominent figure of Parisian life, his face appearing on posters all over the capital, where he played in every theatre and soon became a member – and eventually a pillar – of the most flamboyantly fashionable circles, a veritable dandy.[6] He had begun as one of the *comiques à l'huile* (comprising the trio Raimu, Tramel, and Sardou) – indeed the foremost member of the group, once he had been recognised and appreciated as one of their number – who had graduated from the music halls of Marseilles to those of Paris. This eccentric bunch of *tourlourous* with their colourful southern French twang (the young Raimu imitated his great predecessor Polin) were following in the footsteps of their idol, Félix Mayol.[7] Other figures who had paved the way for this general gravitation north, which culminated in Raimu's repeated success in the light comedies of the prestigious Paris Boulevard theatres, included the scriptwriter and master of dialogue Yves Mirande, who was constantly at Raimu's side until 1946, and Rip (Georges-Gabriel Thenon), the skilled producer of shows featuring dancing girls with feathers, who was best known as a teacher of etiquette. Their ranks were then swollen with the names (and titles) of numerous patrons and associates, such as queen of the stage Réjane (Gabrielle Réju), father and son Lucien and Sacha Guitry, Marcel Pagnol and Roger Richebé, and later Marie Bell.[8]

Although he was not a great admirer of filmed stage productions, André Bazin considered Raimu, one of its central figures, as the Inheritor (with a capital I) of the French burlesque tradition.[9] Bazin anticipated Ginette Vincendeau in his suggestion that Raimu found the transition relatively straightforward from strongly regional theatre and film, with its emphatic enunciation and exaggerated gestures, to relatively neutral, i.e. Parisian, forms of acting (*Ces messieurs de la santé*, Pierre Colombier, 1934; *Un carnet de bal /Dance Program*, Julien Duvivier, 1937).[10] For all this, the Raimu myth, in film, is based on three great roles created for him by Marcel Pagnol, three men in their fifties, working-class men from the south: César Ollivier, Aimable Castanier, and Pascal Amoretti, each of them at once the hero, host, and arbiter of the drama in which they appeared.

It was not until *Marius*, directed by Alexander Korda for Paramount in 1931, that Raimu truly became a name in cinema, at the age of 48, and his on-screen success lasted only fifteen years.[11] Though a latecomer to the seventh art, he embraced film with great enthusiasm: from 1929, the year

Marius was staged at the Théâtre de Paris, until 1943 when he joined the Comédie-Française, Raimu made forty-odd films but only performed in the theatre on four occasions. His popularity, which rested largely on his powerful and often humorous portrayal of paternal and patriarchal values, grew to such an extent that the magazine *Cinémonde* devoted its 1 April 1939 issue to him, with the topical joke 'Raimu is in the Elysée, the country is saved.'[12] Two weeks later, the journal *Pour Vous*, an associate publication of *La Cinématographie Française*, published the result of a survey, in which cinema directors across France and its empire, as well as in Belgium and Switzerland, had voted for the most bankable French actors of the day: Raimu was riding high in fourth place, some way behind Jean Gabin (1904–1976), but almost on a par with Fernandel (1903–1971) and Louis Jouvet (1887–1951).[13] These four were far ahead of the rest of the field. Several screenplays brought members of this illustrious quartet together in front of the camera, in combinations of two (*La Fille du puisatier*; and *Les Rois du sport*, Pierre Colombier, 1937) or three (*Les Gaîtés de l'escadron /Fun in Barracks*, Maurice Tourneur, 1932; and *Un carnet de Bal*, 1937) – unsurprisingly, this guaranteed the film a devoted, often passionate, following.

Pierre LETHIER
University of Buckingham (BUCSIS)

1. Jean-Jacques Jelot-Blanc, *Pagnol et Raimu : l'histoire vraie* (Monaco: Editions Alphée-Jean Paul Bertrand, 2010), 257.

2. Paul Olivier, *Raimu ou l'épopée de*

César (Paris: Editions France-Empire, 1977), 70.

3. Raymond Castans and André Bernard, *Les Films de Marcel Pagnol* (Paris: Julliard, 1982), 100.

4. Yves Mirande, *Souvenirs d'Yves Mirande* (Paris: Librairie Arthème Fayard, 1952), 117.

5. Editor's note : for further discussion of Pagnol's Marseilles trilogy, see Rebecca Prime, 'Marcel Pagnol's Marseilles : *Marius, Fanny, César,*' in *World Film Locations: Marseilles,* ed. Marcelline Block (Bristol : Intellect, 2013), 8-9, as well as individual reviews of *Marius, Fanny,* and *César* in this volume, 16-17, 18-19, and 22-23).

6. Paulette Brun, *Raimu mon père* (Paris: Hachette Littérature, 1980), 12.

7. Pascal Djemaa, *Raimu, l'immortelle voix du cinéma français* (Gémenos: Editions Autres Temps, 2011), 34.

8. Daniel Lacotte, *Raimu, biographie* (Paris: Ramsay, 1998), 38, 217.

9. André Bazin, *Qu'est-ce que le cinéma ?* (Paris: Le Cerf, 1994), 100.

10. Ginette Vincendeau, 'Les Acteurs méridionaux dans le cinéma français des années 1930,' in *L'Acteur de cinéma : approches plurielles,* ed. Vincent Amiel, Jacqueline Nacache, Christian Viviani, and Geneviève Sellier (Paris: Presses Universitaires de France, 2007), 218.

11. Roger Richebé, *Au-delà de l'écran : 70 ans de la vie d'un cinéaste* (Monte Carlo: Editions Pastorelly, 1977), 78.

12. Claudette Peyrusse, *Le Cinéma méridional 1929–1944* (Toulouse: Eché, 1986), 128-9.

13. Claude Gauteur and Ginette Vincendeau, *Jean Gabin, anatomie d'un mythe* (Paris: Editions Nathan, 1993),

Serge Reggiani (1922–2004)

From Screen to Song

THERE ARE very few French singers that succeeded in establishing themselves as an actor after a singing career. Apart from the names of Maurice Chevalier, Charles Aznavour, and Yves Montand that come immediately to mind, one should without a doubt mention the career of Italian-French singer and actor Serge Reggiani, which has a place of its own in the pantheon of French cinema.

Originating from a very modest Italian family from Reggio Emilio (his father was a barber and his mother a worker), he moved to France at the age of 8 with his family to flee Mussolini's dictatorship. His father was a particularly active antifascist. While starting a career as a barber like his father, he developed an interest in boxing. However, his career took a completely different turn in 1937 when he was accepted in an acting school (Le Conservatoire des arts cinématographiques). After a promising theatre career during the war with *Le Loup-Garou* by Roger Vitrac and *Britannicus*, he was later discovered by Jean Cocteau who gave him a part in his production of *Les Parents terribles / The Storm Within* (1948). His acting career granted him several awards. During World War II, he left Paris to join the French Resistance.

He met his first wife, the actress Janine Darcey during the shooting of Léo Joannon's *Le Carrefour des enfants perdus /Children of Chaos* (1944). In Marcel Carné's *Les Portes de la nuit / Gates of the Night* (1946) a psychological urban drama, depicting postwar Paris, he acts alongside the singer/actor Yves Montand. He would then appear in more than 80 films, but one of his major parts was that of Georges Manda in Jacques Becker's *Casque d'or* (1952) with Simone Signoret. Now considered a masterpiece, it was a complete flop when it was first released. The waltz performed by Marie and Manda remains a moment of legend: not only did Reggiani break his fibula prior to shooting the scene, but also, Signoret could not dance. However, the way it was shot nobody could notice that he actually had to carry her throughout. Serge Reggiani would later compose the song *Un menuisier dansait*, as a tribute to the film and to Simone Signoret. In the 1952 version of *La Bergère et le ramoneur /The Curious Adventures of Mr Wonderbird* (dir. Paul Grimault), Serge Reggiani lent his voice to the chimney sweep.

Reggiani is particularly convincing as a rising talent in the part of Manon's brother in Henri-Georges Clouzot's eponymous film (1949), in Max Ophuls's delightful *La Ronde* (1950) as Franz the soldier suitor, and as Antoine Rougier, a printer in love with Danielle Darrieux, who plays the titular character of Duvivier's *Marie-Octobre* (1959). His performance in Jean-Paul Sartre's play *Les Séquestrés d'Altona* was particularly well-received. Following roles in *Le Doulos* (Jean-Pierre Melville, 1962) and *Il gattopardo /The Leopard* (Luchino Visconti, 1963), he started his singing career at the age of 43 with the help of Simone Signoret and Yves Montand. In 1965, his first album was a record suggested by Jacques Canetti, the discoverer of French music talents, based on texts by Boris Vian that would appeal especially to the *soixante-huitard* youth and to the singer Barbara. She would consequently ask him to do the first part of her singing tour.

In 1974, he acted in the emblematic Claude Sautet film *Vincent, François, Paul et les autres... /Vincent, François, Paul and the Others*, alongside very talented actors such as Gérard Depardieu, Yves Montand, and Michel Piccoli. Facing a mid-life crisis like his two other friends, Serge Reggiani is Paul, the writer with a serious case of writer's block. In 1975, he starred in Claude Lelouch's mystery film *Le Chat et la Souris /Cat and Mouse*. With age he became more and more an acclaimed interpreter of French songs and *chansons à textes* relying on the poetry of emblematic literary figures such as Rimbaud, Apollinaire, and Prévert.

In 1980, his son Stéphan committed suicide at the age of 33 and Reggiani, devastated, retreated from his singing career for a while and fell into depression and alcoholism. His performances became rarer, but his albums were as successful.

In 1986, he is the beekeeper in Théo Angelopoulos's *L'Apiculteur / The Beekeeper*, with fellow Italian actor Marcello Mastroianni. In the 1990s, he made a successful comeback to the concert stage, while devoting his time to his painting passion.

Serge Reggiani was not only one of the most acclaimed French singers of his time but a very gifted actor and painter who marked a whole generation.

Michaël Abecassis
The University of Oxford

Jean RENO (1948–)
[Juan MORENO Y HERRERA-JIMÉNEZ]

*Hollywood
Frenchman*

JUAN MORENO Y HERRERA JIMÉNEZ, better known as Jean RENO, was born in Casablanca, Morocco on July 30, 1948. His Spanish-Andalusian parents had fled to North Africa to escape Franco's dictatorship, and the family relocated again in 1965, this time to Paris, where Reno attended state-sponsored drama school. Stage work and cinema bit-parts followed, until *Le Dernier Combat /The Last Battle* (1983), Reno's debut for director Luc Besson, who would hone Reno's enduring screen persona – imposing tough guys, leavened by wry humour, wide-eyed innocence, or soft-centred sensitivity at anachronistic odds with his hulking 6'2" frame and hawk-like visage – over a series of subsequent collaborations.

The wordless *Le Dernier Combat*, Besson's first film, takes place in a blasted post-apocalypse world in which all survivors have been rendered mute. Reno's nameless 'Brute' is an antagonist to Pierre Jolivet's 'Man', repeatedly attempting ingress to a hospital with Wile E. Coyote-like ingenuity and tenacity.

His next role for Besson was the equally nameless and almost as wordless Drummer in *Subway*

(1985),[1] but Besson broke this trend with *The Big Blue* (1988), giving Reno one of the most verbose roles of his entire career as the flamboyant and egotistical free-diving champion Enzo Molinari. Reno was nominated for a César award for his performance, and the film, the most successful French production of the 1980s, won France's National Academy of Cinema's Academy Award in 1989.

Reno was silent again for Besson's *La Femme Nikita /Nikita* (1990) as Victor the 'cleaner': little more than a cameo appearance in the thriller starring Anne Parillaud. But Victor would prove to be the inspirational spark for *Léon /The Professional* (1994), arguably still Reno's most iconic role, a taciturn yet child-like hit man developing a peculiarly moving relationship with twelve-year-old Matilda (Natalie Portman). Besson has suggested that Victor and Léon are cousins, although Reno laughs this off as 'too much of an extrapolation.' To date, *Léon* marks the end of Reno and Besson's collaborations as actor and director, but Reno has continued to appear in films produced and/or written by the prolific Besson: *Wasabi* (Gérard Krawczyk, 2001); *Les Rivières pourpres 2 – Les Anges de l'apocalypse /Crimson Rivers 2: Angels of the Apocalypse* (Olivier Dahan, 2004); *L'Immortel /22 Bullets* (Richard Berry, 2010).[2]

Away from Besson, Reno's comedic performance in *Les Visiteurs* (Jean-Marie Poiré, 1993) constituted one of his greatest popular successes (another César nomination, and the highest French box office of the year) as the time-travelling medieval Comte Godefroy de Papincourt. The film engendered a sequel in *Les Couloirs du temps: Les visiteurs 2* (Poiré, 1998), and an American remake, also starring Reno, in *Just Visiting* (Poiré, 2001), although neither managed to match the original's success.

Comedy was also, at least, the intention, when Reno played Ponton, the hapless chaperone of Steve Martin's Inspector Clouseau in the *The Pink Panther* (Shawn Levy, 2006) and *The Pink Panther 2* (Harald Zwart, 2009). He struck more serious notes as a sentimental romantic lead in *Roseanna's Grave* (Paul Weiland, 1997); in a brief, uncredited role in Terry George's *Hotel Rwanda* (2004); for Roberto Benigni's *La tigre e la neve* (2005), as the exiled Iraqi poet Fuad; and in *La Rafle /The Round Up* (Roselyne Bosch, 2010) as a Jewish doctor embroiled in the infamous Vélodrome d'Hiver round-up of 1942.

However, his stock in trade has continued to be cops, gangsters and secret agents, in action thrillers and American blockbusters. He played Franz Krieger, member of Tom Cruise's team in *Mission: Impossible* (Brian de Palma, 1996); Agent Philippe Roaché in *Godzilla* (Roland Emmerich, 1998); co-starring with Robert De Niro as special-ops expert Vincent in *Ronin* (John Frankenheimer, 1998); Commissaire Principal Pierre Niemans in *Les Rivières pourpres /The Crimson Rivers* (Matthieu Kassovitz, 2000); and Captain Bezu Fache in the adaptation of Dan Brown's paperback juggernaut *The Da Vinci Code* (Ron Howard, 2006).

Reno endorsed Nicolas Sarkozy in the 2007 French presidential elections, and Sarkozy was best man at his third marriage, to Polish model and actress Zofia Borucka, in 2006. Nominated for a European Film Awards Audience Award for *Les Rivières pourpres*, along with his two previous César nods, he has yet to score an actual win for a performance. He did, however, take home a European Film Award for Outstanding European Achievement in World Cinema in 2000. Possible future projects at time of writing include *Fantômas* for Christophe Gans, a potentially mesmerising *Raspoutine* for Roselyne Bosch, and a sequel to *Les Visiteurs* for a 2015 release.

Owen WILLIAMS
Journalist, Southampton

1. For further discussion of this film, see Zachariah Rush, 'Héléna Offers Fred the Ransom for the Stolen Documents,' in *World Film Locations: Paris*, ed. Marcelline Block (Bristol : Intellect, 2011), 62-63. —Ed.

2. For further discussion of *22 Bullets /L'Immortel*, see Katherine A. Wagner, 'Interrogation in an Empty Seaport Warehouse,' in *World Film Locations: Marseilles*, ed. Marcelline Block (Bristol: Intellect, 2013), 120-121. —Ed.

Pierre RICHARD (1934–)
[Pierre DEFAYS]

Mister
Disaster

PIERRE DEFAYS, also known as Pierre RICHARD, was born in Paris in 1934. Though his wealthy parents wanted him to work in the family business, he decided to become an actor. His first teacher was Jean Vilar. He also worked for a while with the dancer Maurice Béjart. At first he acted in cabarets as a humorist, sometimes with Victor Lanoux. His first role was in Yves Robert's *Alexandre le bienheureux /Very Happy Alexander* (1968) with Philippe Noiret. Richard quickly decided to direct, and to act in, his own films: *Le Distrait / The Daydreamer* (1970), *Les Malheurs d'Alfred /The Troubles of Alfred* (1972), *Je ne sais rien mais je dirai tout /Don't Know Anything But I'll Tell All* (1973), *Je suis timide mais je me soigne /Too Shy to Try* (1978). Thanks to his physical agility and sensitivity, he managed to invent a burlesque and poetical character: the unlucky and clumsy young man. As an actor, Richard played naïve and fake heroes with Yves Robert in *Le Grand Blond avec une chaussure noire /The Tall Blond Man with One Black Shoe* (1972), Claude Zidi in *La Moutarde me monte au nez* (1974), and Gérard Oury in *La Carapate* (1978). He played a comical

duo with Gérard Depardieu in several of Francis Veber's movies which were big successes: *La Chèvre /The Goat* (1981), *Les Compères /ComDads* (1983), and *Les Fugitifs* (1986) – in this last film, his shyness contrasts with the smart and strong character played by Depardieu. He later played more melancholic parts (*La Partie d'échecs / The Chess Game*, dir. Yves Hanchar, 1994), sometimes in his own films (*On peut toujours rêver*, 1991), in television films (*Sans famille /Without Family* in 2000, *Robinson Crusoé* in 2003). His ageing figure increases the light, naïve, and comic fragility of his moving characters, as in *Et si on vivait tous ensemble ? /All Together* (2011).

Pierre Richard has created a type. Just to mention his name is to refer to this character, also known by other names: François Perrin, François Pignon. He is dogged by ill luck, but is also a public nuisance. On top of this, Pignon is a benevolent scatterbrain, a careless daydreamer, who is punished for being a naïve idealist. Pierre Richard is a lanky giant and his elastic, springy body fits his burlesque acting style. This gangly clown loves to perform acrobatics and spectacular movements. He thus created a character that is moving, innocent, and easy-going, even when he is in the deepest trouble. His gestures are too broad, his movements are too quick, and the soles of his shoes too slippery. This clown is sometimes aware of this curse: in *Les Malheurs d'Alfred*, as a tile falls from a roof, he tells his friends: 'Don't worry, folks! That is for me!' – just before the tile falls onto his head. Yet, most of the time, François Perrin is naïve and so blind that he feels he can dare to boast. With his excellent diction he pretends to be self-confident. He tries to act tough: sometimes he plays the spy, waddling along to gain self-assurance before stumbling over a carpet. In *La Chèvre*, he even tells Depardieu: 'I can confess it to you now: I haven't always been lucky in my life...' Half Rimbaud and half Jacques Tati, he looks like an angel with his wide and naïve blue eyes and his unruly blond hair. He creases his brow with astonishment and always has his head in the clouds. He was chosen by Yves Robert to play the *Grand Blond* with his stunned look and odd shoes. This angel oversteps the limits, however, being too tall and too thin. This restless acrobat has the skills of a dancer and an incredible sense of fancy. He is a talented improviser: in *Le Grand Blond*, he plays a violin virtuoso and, in an exhilarating sketch, he improvises a contemporary solo without any direction from Yves Robert. He is incredibly funny, but he is also moving. Because fragile characters are always fooled in this world, they are victims, scapegoats. There is no pity for the weak. Pierre Richard knows how to describe this silent distress, even through the funniest means. He did it as early as 1972 in *Les Malheurs d'Alfred*. In *On peut toujours rêver*, this rich businessman is no jester: he can no longer laugh, and is ready to accept everything just to have one friend and to have fun. Yet, this character becomes mighty. The stout Depardieu is touched by his fragility. The Grand Blond is clowning around and finally misleads those who tried to manipulate him.

Violaine HEYRAUD
Université Sorbonne Nouvelle – Paris 3

Emmanuelle RIVA (1927–)
[Paulette RIVA]

An Exceptionally Bookended Career

KNOWN FOR her artistic film choices, Emmanuelle RIVA's career has been punctuated by poignant performances in strong, often tragic female roles, from the anonymous 'Elle' in Alain Resnais' *Hiroshima mon amour* (1959) to her intimate portrayal of Anne in Michael Haneke's *Amour* (2012), 53 years later, for which she was nominated for an Academy Award for Best Actress. At the age of 85, she became the oldest Best Actress nominee in history, and the Oscar ceremony was held on February 24, 2013 – Riva's 86th birthday. Although Riva did not win the Oscar – which was ultimately awarded to the American actress Jennifer Lawrence for *The Hunger Games* (Gary Ross, 2012) – Lawrence memorably wished Riva a happy birthday from the stage during her acceptance speech. However, *Amour* did receive the Academy Award for Best Foreign Language film and for her riveting performance, Riva was universally lauded, recognized with the Best Actress César as well as Best Actress accolades from BAFTA, the National Society of Film Critics, the International Cinephile Society, the European Film Awards, and Lumières de la presse étrangère, among others.

Originally destined to become a seamstress, Emmanuelle Riva was not raised for a life of stardom. Born Paulette Riva in Chéniménil, Vosges, on February 24, 1927, it was only in 1952 that Riva left her provincial hometown, against her family's wishes, to study under the much-lauded Jean Meyer at L'École de la rue Blanche in Paris.

While she is best known for her cinematic roles, Riva's first passion lay in theatre. Launching her career with a part in George Bernard Shaw's *Le Héros et le Soldat* (1954), she received a steady stream of theatrical roles through the mid-to-late 1950s. Indeed, she would continue to hold a place on the French theatre scene throughout her career, concluding only in 2001 with the grandiose *Médée* at Paris's Théâtre Odéon. Despite her theatrical success, Riva moved on to cinema in 1958 with a minor role as a secretary in Denys de la Patellière's *Les Grandes Familles /The Possessors*. Yet it was only when Alain Resnais cast her in the lead role of his first feature film, *Hiroshima mon amour*, the following year, that Riva's career truly took off.

The film rapidly gained the reputation of a masterpiece and is now touted as a hallmark of the Nouvelle Vague era. Depicting the brief love affair between a French actress (Riva) and a Japanese businessman (Eiji Okada) in 1950s Hiroshima, the film explores the suffering of a couple at once divided by their disparate cultures and united by their shared trauma. With his confronting juxtaposition of brutal, real-life footage of wartime Hiroshima with the tragic narratives of each character's tale of personal loss, Resnais captured the grief and horror rife in French – and indeed global – society in the wake of the war. Based on the eponymous novel by Marguerite Duras, who also wrote the screenplay, *Hiroshima mon amour* delves into themes of memory, trauma and scarring, depicting each protagonist's suffering as representative of that of their respective nations. Riva brought a remarkable depth to the role, her resonant, haunting voice evoking a grief at once subtle and raw.

Hiroshima mon amour was awarded a Special Prize at Cannes Film Festival in 1959, but was excluded from mainstream competition due to its sensitive material. The film was however nominated for the Best Screenplay Oscar and Best Film BAFTA in 1961, where Riva also received a nomination for Best Actress. With the film's critical and popular success, Riva was thrust into the cinematic spotlight.

In the wake of *Hiroshima mon amour*, Riva's career continued to gather momentum and she appeared in a number of critically acclaimed films in the early 60s. In 1961 she starred in Jean-Pierre Melville's *Léon Morin, prêtre /Léon Morin, Priest*, set in a village in occupied France, where she played Barny, a communist militant who provokes a local Catholic priest (Jean-Paul Belmondo). A year later, she received the Volpi Cup for Best Actress at the Venice Film Festival, as well as the Silver Goddess Award from the Mexican Cinema Journalists panel, for her portrayal of the title character in Georges Franju's *Thérèse Desqueyroux* (1962), based on the eponymous 1927 novel by François Mauriac. Riva again incarnated a powerful female figure for this role, infusing Desqueyroux, who is imprisoned by her husband after she attempts to poison him, with a passion and darkness which she would continue to summon in several of her other performances.

While Riva occasionally dipped into popular genres, such as for Jean-Pierre Mocky's 1982 comedy *Y-a-t-il un français dans la salle ? /Is there a Frenchman in the House?*, she developed a reputation for her more artistic choices, working with an array of esteemed auteurs including Marco Bellocchio, Georges Franju, Michael Haneke, Krzysztof Kieslowski, Jean-Pierre Melville, and Alain Resnais. Riva has even remarked that her selectiveness could have hindered her career, or at least her public image, lamenting that she may have been considered snobbish: « j'aurais peut-être dû accepter davantage le cinéma commercial » ['I should perhaps have embraced commercial cinema more']. It is certain that Riva made a name for herself as a high-brow, rather serious actress. She certainly epitomised the passionate and anguished woman in many of her roles. Yet while she pursued a prolific career throughout the twentieth century, performing in over fifty films and nearly forty plays – indeed, her talents even stretched to poetry, of which she published three volumes, *Le Feu des miroirs* (1975), *Juste derrière le sifflet des trains* (1976), and *L'Otage du désir* (1982) – Riva never truly regained the heights of success she experienced with *Hiroshima mon amour*.

That is, not until 2012, when the Austrian director Michael Haneke's film *Amour* won the Palme d'Or at the Cannes Film Festival. Riva stars in the film alongside fellow octogenarian Jean-Louis Trintignant as the latter's beloved wife Anne, who is grappling with the effects of a paralysing stroke. The film deftly depicts the poignancy of a loving relationship in its final stages, and of the helplessness and distress of a family threatened by chronic illness. Riva's portrayal of the waning Anne is both delicate and moving, constituting somewhat of a return to her quintessential break-through performance.

To accompany Haneke in his win for *Amour*, Riva travelled to Cannes in 2012, rather poetically, for the first time since 1959. She was 85 years of age at the time. Indeed, it could be said that Riva's varied and illustrious career, spanning the realms of cinema, theatre, and poetry, has been bookended by two exceptional films, over fifty years apart.

Gemma KING
The University of Melbourne
and
Université Sorbonne Nouvelle – Paris 3

Jean ROCHEFORT (1930–)

« Le
Moustachu »

WITH HIS trademark moustache and with well over one hundred feature film appearances to his name, Jean ROCHEFORT is one of the most familiar and recognisable French actors. Thin and long-limbed, Rochefort's dandyish, slightly comic elegance has been put to good use in fashion industry satires *Qui êtes-vous, Polly Maggoo ? /Who Are You, Polly Magoo?* (William Klein, 1966) and *Prêt-à-porter /Ready to Wear* (Robert Altman, 1994). He is typically impeccably groomed in Guillaume Canet's *Ne le dis à personne /Tell No One* (2006), in which showjumping events provide a backdrop to virtually all of Rochefort's scenes. A horse breeder off-screen, Rochefort's expertise in this field allowed him to authoritatively commentate on equestrian events for French television during the 2004 Athens Olympics. As an elderly accomplished horseman with an appropriately sad countenance and natural comic timing, Terry Gilliam had identified Rochefort as the ideal candidate for the lead role in his adaptation of Cervantes's *Don Quixote* for which filming commenced in October 2000. Indispensable for the authenticity of the character, Rochefort's advancing

years introduced a further level of uncertainty to an already unwieldy production and, as recounted in Keith Fulton and Louis Pepe's fascinating documentary *Lost in La Mancha* (2002), the actor's inability to appear on horseback because of a double herniated disc played a decisive role in the project's ultimate collapse. Despite the curtailment of his horse riding, ageing has certainly not been a wholly negative experience for Rochefort the actor. Indeed, he has arguably become more familiar, at least to non-French audiences, in his later work (especially in Patrice Leconte's films) in which his characters' negotiations of the ageing process have been thematically foregrounded.

Jean Rochefort was born in Dinan (Brittany) in 1930 and, after training for the stage at the Paris Conservatoire, his first appearances on the silver screen came about in the late 1950s. Rochefort's emergence as a film actor thus coincided with the initial blossoming of the French New Wave but he did not appear in any of the key works of this vastly influential movement. Without the scruffiness of Jean-Paul Belmondo, the youth of Jean-Pierre Léaud, or the simmering anger of Gérard Blain, for New Wave *auteurs* like Jean-Luc Godard, François Truffaut, and Claude Chabrol, Rochefort was too classical and controlled in both his look and acting style to embody the kind of novelty and spontaneity that these directors were seeking to introduce. The New Wave was, of course, a reaction against the dominant currents in French cinema of the time, the literary adaptations and historical costume dramas that Truffaut had so scathingly identified as 'the Tradition of Quality' in his famous 1954 polemic 'A Certain Tendency of the French Cinema.' Despite the New Wave's initial successes at the box-office, 'the Tradition of Quality' did not fade away however and it was in this undoubtedly more traditional but also more consistently popular strand of French cinema that Rochefort initially found his natural home. Rochefort appeared alongside swashbuckling hero Jean Marais in *Le Capitaine Fracasse / Captain Fracasse* (Pierre Gaspard-Huit, 1961) and *Le Masque de fer /The Iron Mask* (Henri Decoin, 1962) and, as the lawyer Desgrez, he provides vital support and encouragement to Michèle Mercier's heroine in the first three films of Bernard Borderie's extremely popular *Angélique* series (1964-68). Like Borderie, Philippe de Broca repeatedly cast Rochefort in his films, helping to establish the actor's comic credentials with roles alongside Belmondo in *Cartouche /Swords of Blood* (1962) and *Les Tribulations d'un Chinois en Chine* (1965). In these early comedic roles, Rochefort typically plays the straight man, drawing attention to the more exuberant antics of fellow performers, such as with Yves Montand and Jean-Pierre Marielle in de Broca's *Le Diable par la queue /The Devil by the Tail* (1969).

Voted the seventh most popular actor in France in a poll conducted by Ifop [1] for *Le Figaro* in 2009, Rochefort has continued to appear in the mainstream genre films that made his name. From the mid-1970s onwards, however, his persona has also attracted the attention of directors operating on the more intellectual end of the French cinematic spectrum.

The breakthrough film in this regard was Bertrand Tavernier's *L'Horloger de Saint-Paul /The Clockmaker of St Paul* (1974) – based on a Georges Simenon novel – in which Rochefort's performance as Commissaire Guilboud communicated a jaded, tortured cynicism that evidenced an emotional range largely stifled in his previous roles. In Tavernier's next film, *Que la fête commence... /Let Joy Reign Supreme* (1975), Rochefort again played alongside his great friend Philippe Noiret and his efforts were recognised with the César for best supporting actor. After roles in films by Luis Buñuel (*Le Fantôme de la liberté /The Phantom of Liberty*, 1974), Bertrand Blier (*Calmos /Femmes Fatales*, 1976), and Claude Chabrol (*Les Magiciens / Death Rite*, 1976), Rochefort was back at the César podium in 1978, this time receiving the best actor award for his role as a naval captain with terminal cancer in Pierre Schoendoerffer's *Le Crabe-tambour /Drummer-Crab* (1977).

In 1980s French comedy films like the revealingly named *Le Moustachu /The Field Agent* (Dominique Chaussois, 1987), Rochefort regularly took top billing. It was in a comedy film, *Les Vécés étaient fermés de l'interieur* (1976) that the actor first worked with director Patrice Leconte and, after a substantial hiatus, the two embarked on a highly productive period of collaboration which has seen them making five films together since 1987. *Tandem* (1987), *The Hairdresser's Husband* (1990), and *L'Homme du train /Man on the Train* (2002) present intelligent and thought-provoking reflections on ageing, explored primarily through Rochefort's performances in leading roles. In

L'Homme du train, Rochefort's M. Manesquier, a retired French teacher, a man of imagination, suffocating under the weight of the heirlooms that surround him, is contrasted with a gangster, the drifter Milan, played by Johnny Hallyday. Neither character – man of imagination nor man of action – is content with the life he has lived. Envious of the experiences of the other, these figures are presented as two sides of the same coin as illustrated in the moving and comic sequence where Rochefort surreptitiously tries on Hallyday's leather jacket. Aged he may be, but with performances in the latest instalment of the *Astérix* franchise and in Fernando Trueba's 2012 *El artisto y la modelo /The Artist and the Model*, for which he is nominated for a 2013 Best Actor Award from the Spanish Cinema Writers Circle, it would seem that Jean Rochefort's elegance, versatility, and range remain at the height of fashion.

Jim MORRISSEY
Newcastle University

1. Ifop : *Institut français d'opinion publique* [French Institute of Public Opinion]. —Ed.

Viviane ROMANCE (1912–1991)
[Pauline Arlette ORTMANS]

Queen of the 1930s Femmes Fatales

As one of the great screen vamps of the 1930s and 1940s, it is fitting that Viviane ROMANCE began her career thanks to a series of scandals. Born in 1912 in the northern city of Roubaix, as a teenager, the young Pauline Ortmans left her modest beginnings behind for Paris, where she adopted her pseudonym for a stage career that began in her teens. After some formal training in dance, she became a can-can girl at the Tabarin nightclub, then danced at the Moulin Rouge until her career was interrupted by a highly publicized scuffle with Mistinguett, the *grande dame* of the Parisian music hall (according to legend, Romance yanked the star's hair). The flurry of publicity that followed this fated encounter pulled her from the ranks of dancing girls and started her winding path to movie stardom. Romance encountered another kind of scandal when, at age 18, she was elected 'Miss Paris' only to have her title withdrawn because it was discovered that she had given birth to a child.

The same year she won and lost Miss Paris – a title the popular cinephile press rarely refused her despite its official annulment –

Viviane Romance began to appear as a movie extra, occasionally landing small speaking roles as well. Over several years, she amassed a lengthy filmography that boasts a number of major figures in the industry: Jean Renoir's *La Chienne* (1931), Fritz Lang's *Liliom* (1934), and Edmond T. Gréville's *Princesse Tam-Tam* (1935), a vehicle for Josephine Baker, another (very different) music hall diva. After Romance made a brief appearance in Julien Duvivier's *La Bandera* (1935), the director offered her the role that would bring her bona fide stardom: the gold-digging ex-wife Gina in *La Belle Équipe /They Were Five* (1936). A touchstone of Popular Front cinema, *La Belle Équipe* featured the newly minted star Jean Gabin, longtime screen veteran Charles Vanel as Gina's ex-husband, and character actor Raymond Aimos as the pillars of a band of five working-class friends who win the lottery and remake their lives. When Gina enters the mix, her manipulations destroy their friendship. This role made Romance a headlining performer, but it also typed her as a vamp for the rest of her career.

Three years after *La Belle Équipe*, in 1939, *Pour Vous* named Romance the top female draw at the French box office, outdoing the second-ranked Danielle Darrieux by a comfortable margin. Sex sold tickets, and Romance's brand of seduction quickly trumped that of her competitors. As the quintessential *femme fatale*, Romance brought connotations of exoticism to a more familiar Frenchness, a core national identity she strengthened by ignoring calls from Hollywood. Her dark hair and sultry look added a touch of foreign flair to her persona, a clear advantage at a time when French cinema was catering to public taste for exotic star types. She played an Italian 'other woman' opposite Tino Rossi in *Naples au baiser de feu /The Kiss of Fire* (Augusto Genina, 1937); a Spanish spy opposite Erich von Stroheim in *Gibraltar* (Fyodor Otsep, 1938); a gypsy in *Cartacalha, reine des gitans* (Léon Mathot, 1942) – and, perhaps the most emblematic expression of her paradoxically exotic Frenchness, she played Carmen in Christian-Jaque's 1944 adaptation of Mérimée. Romance also incarnated the Frenchwoman abroad; her Safia in *La Maison du Maltais /Sirocco* (Pierre Chenal, 1938) was born in Marseilles but stuck in Tunisia until a French archaeologist persuaded her to abandon her true love and return with him to Paris. In *L'Esclave blanche* (Marc Sorkin, 1939), she played the French wife of an Ottoman pasha in fin-de-siècle Istanbul. A departure from the conventions that defined her more typical roles, Romance gives a particularly strong performance in *L'Esclave blanche*, whose plot gave her a firm platform to showcase both her sensuality and her feistiness.

After amassing more than a dozen film credits in three years, after the onset of World War II, Romance remained in France and continued to work. Abel Gance cast her as the lead in his infamous flop *Vénus aveugle / Blind Venus* (1942), a ponderous melodrama chronicling the onset of a woman's blindness – a strong allegory in an Occupation-era film. While *Vénus aveugle* failed to win over its audiences, it put Romance in a much more sympathetic position than her most famous prewar roles; no longer a predatory seductress, Romance pushes away her lover (played by her then-husband Georges Flamant) to spare him the burden of her disability. But this reprieve from typecasting expired with the war, and Romance revived her signature *femme fatale* once again for Duvivier in *Panique /Panic* (1946), in which she seduces an innocent man in order to frame him for murder.

Viviane Romance continued to make films into the 1950s, but at a much slower pace and with far less success than she had enjoyed at her peak. Among her last films was *Pitié pour les vamps /Pity for the Vamps* (1956), which she co-produced with her third husband Jean Josipovici, who also directed the film. The title alone makes evident Romance's frustration at her limited offerings, but her efforts to steer her career in new directions as she aged out of seductress roles made little headway. She retired from filmmaking, emerging occasionally for television work and for two small film roles that echoed her previous persona: as the wife of Jean Gabin's aging convict in Henri Verneuil's 1963 film *Mélodie en sous-sol /Any Number Can Win*, which also starred Alain Delon; and as a brothel madam in Claude Chabrol's *Nada /The Nada Gang* (1974), which was her final screen appearance before definitively withdrawing from the industry. She died in 1991.

Colleen KENNEDY-KARPAT
Bilkent University, Ankara, Turkey

Ludivine SAGNIER (1979–)

—*The Divine*

S HE IS blonde, she is voluptuous, she has a gorgeous, mischievous smile, a pair of twinkling blue eyes, as well as that freshness and energy that makes her acting so special. The young actress Ludivine SAGNIER is definitely what we call a *sacrée bout de femme* ['one hell of a woman'].

Born on July 3rd, 1979 in La Celle-Saint-Cloud (Yvelines department), Ludivine became an actress at an early age. She was only 10 years old when she made her debut in two films released in 1989: *Je veux rentrer à la maison /I Want to go Home* directed by Alain Resnais and *Les Maris, les femmes, les amants* directed by Pascal Thomas. The next year, she even appeared in Jean-Paul Rappeneau's screen version of *Cyrano de Bergerac*. She also starred in some films for television in 1990. However this was far from being enough for the ambitious Ludivine who was ready to work hard to achieve what she wanted. After eight years of acting classes in Sèvres, she went to the Versailles Academy of Dramatic Arts, where she finally took two first prizes. And as we shall see, these were certainly not the last awards she would receive.

In 1999, having finished her theatre studies, she was now ready to have a professional career and immediately was cast in numerous small parts in movies such as in Diane Kurys' *Les Enfants du siècle /Children of the Century*, in which she plays Hermine, Alfred de Musset's sister, and *Acide aminé*, a short film by Guillaume Bréaud.

But Ludivine Sagnier's life as an actress took a completely different turn when she met the French director François Ozon, already known for his movie *Sitcom* (1998). Ozon acted as a real Pygmalion for the young actress whose expressiveness and talent were really brought to light. In 2000 she starred in his movie *Gouttes d'eau sur pierres brûlantes /Water Drops on Burning Rocks*, a very sensuous and bold adaptation of R.W. Fassbinder's theatrical play, in which Ludivine plays the part of Vera, a young girl deeply in love with a boy himself obsessed by a fifty-year old man. The following year came the film *Ma femme est une actrice /My Wife is an Actress*, directed by Yvan Attal, in which Ludivine has a small but funny part, and above all Ozon's *8 femmes /8 Women* (2002), which really gave her national exposure. Indeed she received top billing, along with already very famous actresses like Fanny Ardant, Catherine Deneuve, and Emmanuelle Béart.

Far from being inferior to the others, Ludivine, who plays the part of a malicious child, reveals all her talent. For this role she was required to bandage her chest in order to portray this young girl. Her performance earned her the Romy Schneider Award and a nomination for the French César Award for Most Promising Actress. She also shared the

Silver Bear Award for Outstanding Artistic Achievement at the 2002 Berlin International Film Festival and the European Film Award for Best Actress along with the distinguished cast of *8 femmes*.

In 2003, her already promising career reached even higher heights when she re-teamed with François Ozon for his movie *Swimming Pool*, in which Ludivine starred with Charlotte Rampling. In contrast to her role in *8 femmes*, in *Swimming Pool*, Ludivine embodies a very voluptuous and provocative woman, a role for which she was recognized with her second César nomination – this time, for Best Supporting Actress – as well as numerous other prestigious nominations including the Boston Society of Film Critics Award for Best Supporting Actress, the Chlotrudis Award for Best Supporting Actress, and the European Film Audience Award for Best Actress. That same year she acted in Claude Miller's *La Petite Lili /Little Lili*, which was a great success abroad, bringing Ludivine much international attention and a Silver Hugo Award from the Chicago International Film Festival for Best Actress. Both films were indeed official 2003 Cannes Festival Selections. Moreover, Ludivine played the part of little Tinker Bell in P.J. Hogan's adaptation of *Peter Pan* the same year, for which she was nominated by the Visual Effects Society for the Award for Outstanding Performance by a Male or Female Actor in an Effects Film.

Ludivine has another hidden talent, namely, dubbing. You might hear her fragile and slightly rasping voice in *Gang de requins*, the French-language version of DreamWorks's animated film *Shark Tale* (Bibo Bergeron, Vicky Jenson, Rob Letterman, 2004), in which she voices the role of Angie (originally voiced in English by Renée Zellweger).

Her career now seems to flow steadily, as Ludivine is a mother. The father of her child is the young French actor Nicolas Duvauchelle. In 2006, Ludivine acted in *La Californie /French California* (dir. Jacques Fieschi), along with Nathalie Baye, and also appeared in the collaborative *Paris, je t'aime* in the segment 'Parc Monceau,' directed by Alfonso Cuarón. 2006 was another good year for the young actress as she was given top billing in the widely anticipated *Molière* (Laurent Tirard, 2007). For her turn in Claude Miller's *Un secret /A Secret* (2007), Ludivine received her third César nomination for Best Supporting Actress, for her role as Hannah, a young Parisian Jewish wife and mother whose life takes a tragic turn during the Nazi Occupation of France. She also starred in Christophe Honoré's ménage-à-trois musical film *Les Chansons d'amour /Love Songs* (2007).

As an ambiguous figure between child and woman, Ludivine enchants audiences. Ludivine herself, aware of the duplicity of her own appearance, ironically said during an interview: 'I am often given the part of a child or a young girl. This is not frustrating at all: people in my family look very young but die very old!' We hope to see a lot more of this promising French actress in the future.

Aurore GOUNAUD
École Normale Supérieure, Paris

Édith Scob (1937–)
[Édith Helena Vladimirovna Scobeltzine]

The Masked Actress

BORN THE 21st October 1937 in Paris, Édith Helena Vladimirovna Scobeltzine – stage name, Édith Scob – was the granddaughter of a general in the Russian Army and the daughter of an émigré architect and a strict Protestant. As a young girl, she suffered from anorexia and believed that success could mask her insecurity, having been influenced by the example of her older brother's exploits in cycling. She went to theatre classes whilst studying literature at university despite her family's mistrust for the performing arts. She was soon discovered by the French master of *fantastique-noir*, Georges Franju, with whom she has been forever associated. He was looking for an actress for a walk-on part for his feature film set in a mental hospital, *La Tête contre les murs /Head Against the Wall* (1959). Once he started shooting Édith Scob, whom he had chosen from a picture, it was clear to him she would be his muse: the mute extra became therefore a more significant character.

She was offered one of the leading parts in Franju's subsequent, controversial film, *Les Yeux sans visage /Eyes Without a Face* (1960) opposite Pierre Brasseur, with whom she had already performed in Henry de Montherlant's *Don Juan* (1958) at the Théâtre de l'Athénée, directed by Georges Vitaly. In *Les Yeux sans visage*, Brasseur played the part of a mad-scientist whose daughter Christiane, played by Scob, has been disfigured. Desperate to restore Christiane's beauty, he secludes her in order to perform heterograft surgeries at a horrifying price: kidnapping other girls to use their skin. Her face covered by a stiff mask for most of the film, Édith Scob's part was a key moment in the history of cinema and influenced generations of filmmakers. More than the part itself, Scob's face was unforgettable. Strangely, when the mask was removed for a few seconds, the audience could discover how immaculate her real face was, a mirror of the white mask itself. This unconventional role would associate her forever with a mask-like face with a virginal look. The same mask shows as well how she was objectified both by her fictional father and by Franju himself, known for his tendency to focus on women as objects of fantasy. 'The young masked girl' with 'fairy lightness', as Jean Cocteau described her, haunted Franju's imaginary world.

Her career was equally haunted by this film and four others later directed by Franju, notably *Thérèse Desqueyroux* (1962) and *Judex* (1963) in which she again played pure and passive characters faced alongside criminals. Even if she worked with other filmmakers, including the famous Julien Duvivier, she has always been known internationally thanks to Franju's dark poetical universe. She did not, despite her rapid rise to fame, leave the stage, and was associated with some of the greatest theatre directors, amongst others, Roland Piétri and Jean Anouilh.

During the seventies, she appeared mainly in television series. Her cinematic career was unsuccessful despite her part in Luis Buñuel's surrealist anti-Catholic film *La Voie lactée /The Milky Way* (1969) in which unsurprisingly she played an unconventional Virgin Mary. In the aftermath of the events of May 1968, Édith Scob devoted her time and energy to experimental theatre. With her husband, the composer Georges Aperghis, she founded the music and theatre company ATEM (*Atelier théâtre et musique*) in Bagnolet, with the aim of bringing the arts to a more disadvantaged audience. She took on challenging responsibilities, remaining faithful to her previous communist leanings, but nevertheless continued her career in the theatre. In total, she has participated in more than fifty plays since her first steps on stage, directing five of them between 1993 and 2003. In comparison, her work in cinema was much more irregular. In the eighties, she was offered mainly small and disappointing parts. Furthermore, these parts were often connected with Franju's films. For instance, in Jean Becker's popular success *L'Été meurtrier /One Deadly Summer* (1983), based on Sébastien Japrisot's novel, her character as a psychiatrist was inextricably linked to Franju's mad universe of oppressed women.

With the end of her experiment with ATEM, she did not have to wait long to embark on a new challenging work. Thanks to the Portuguese filmmaker Pedro Costa, she took on the rewarding part of Edite, a French émigré isolated in Cape Verde in *Casa de lava /Down to Earth* (1995). Shot with local people, acting their own parts in creole, this art-house film was the beginning of a new phase in Scob's career. With the producer Paulo Branco's help, she appeared in an adaptation of Marcel Proust's *Le Temps retrouvé /Time Regained*, directed by Raúl Ruiz (1999). In this film, Scob starred as Oriane de Guermantes, a part which allowed her to expand her acting skills, playing a more sadistic character rather than a victim. She successfully embodied the famous duchess's panache, dry wit, and theatrical elegance. From then on, her ability to play darker roles inspired numerous filmmakers such as Andrzej Żuławski (*La Fidélité / Fidelity*, 2000) and Christophe Gans (*Le Pacte des loups /Brotherhood of the Wolf*, 2001). Even if it was mainly in supporting roles, a new audience could see her in big productions and not only in art-house films: the television film *La Chambre des magiciennes /Of Woman and Magic* (Claude Miller, 2000); *L'Homme du train /Man on the Train* (Patrice Leconte, 2002), and *Bon voyage* (Jean-Paul Rappeneau, 2003). She was sought after by a new generation of female filmmakers, notably Viviane Candas (*Suzanne*, 2006); Sophie Laloy (*Je te mangerais /You Will be Mine*, 2009), and Karine Silla (*Un baiser papillon /A Butterfly Kiss*, 2011).

Radiant as ever, the passing years did not affect Édith Scob's aura and vitality. Nevertheless, she symbolises nowadays an earlier type of filmmaking, more artistic but financially unsustainable in the present era. It was for that reason Olivier Assayas offered her the part in *L'Heure d'été /Summer Hours* (2008) of a septuagenarian grand-mother who has tried to preserve the family art collection, but, once dead, leaves her children and grand-children with the difficult responsibility of deciding what to keep and what to discard. Furthermore, in Leos Carax's nostalgic homage to auteur cinema, *Holy Motors* (2012), she is Denis Lavant's driver on a journey to a new fragmented, masked postmodern world in which Lavant continuously changes his identity while she remains the same: Édith, who wears Franju's mask before leaving the screen.

Karine CHEVALIER
University of Roehampton, London

Jean SEBERG (1938–1979)

*A Life
from Iowa
to the
Champs-
Élysées*

THE FRENCH Film Director
François Truffaut once described
Jean SEBERG, the American actress of
the sixties and seventies as 'the best
actress in Europe', perhaps because
she epitomized the quintessential
American girl in Paris, the *gamine* who
symbolised the French Free Spirit.
Rising from Midwestern American
small town obscurity, Seberg became
a cinematic icon on both sides of the
Atlantic, but especially in France. She
belonged to the French *Nouvelle Vague*
or New Wave, a movement widely
regarded as one of the most important
ever to take place in cinema. This
movement produced groundbreaking
films that changed filmmaking forever.
Jean Seberg starred in 36 films, some
in English and some in French, but
it is her performance in Jean-Luc
Godard's *À bout de souffle /Breathless*
(1960) – ranked among the most
influential films of all time – that
catapulted her to super stardom.[1]

Jean Seberg was born in
Marshalltown, Iowa, on the 13th of
November 1938. Just before her 18th
birthday, the American director Otto
Preminger cast her in his film *Joan of
Arc*. It became the biggest commercial
and critical flop of Preminger's
career; virulent attacks soon followed

and focused on the inexperienced
newcomer whom Preminger had
'discovered'. In 1957, Preminger filmed
Bonjour Tristesse (based on Françoise
Sagan's novel), again casting Jean
Seberg in the main role of Cécile. It
was filmed in Cinemascope; many
scenes show Cécile remembering in
flashbacks the glory days of a past
summer spent on the French Riviera;
these scenes are juxtaposed with black
and white scenes filmed in dirty
monochrome and show Cécile in
grey Paris, where she has to live with
the aftermath of her actions on the
Riviera. *Bonjour Tristesse* (1958) was
criticized severely by both the public
and critics. However, today, fifty years
after its release, *Bonjour Tristesse* is
widely regarded as a prime example of
Hollywood's golden age and has been
newly restored in Blu-Ray format.

In 1960, Jean-Luc Godard brought
Seberg renewed international attention
when he cast her in *À bout de souffle*.
At that time, she was married to
François Moreuil whom she would
later divorce. Godard's film also
starred Jean-Paul Belmondo; it follows
the trials and tribulations of Michel
(Belmondo), a young petty criminal
who, after stealing a car in Marseilles,
kills the policeman who is pursuing
him. Now wanted by the authorities,
Michel arrives in Paris and seeks
the help of Patricia (Seberg) a chic,
young American woman studying at
the Sorbonne. He plans to leave Paris
with Patricia and hide in Italy, but
not before collecting a debt from an
underworld acquaintance. Unaware of
his troubles with the police, Patricia
agrees to hide him in her apartment.
Upon learning that Michel is on the
run, she betrays him to the authorities.

When he tries to escape, he is shot, and after a prolonged run in the streets of Paris, dies *à bout de souffle*. Michel's death scene is considered one of the most iconic scenes in the film, when, before dying, he utters these words: « C'est vraiment dégueulasse », to which she answers, « Qu'est ce que c'est 'dégueulasse' ? ». The entire film was shot on a hand-held camera, with next to no lighting; it attracted much attention for its bold visual style and innovative use of jump-cuts. Today, *Breathless* is ranked as the No. 15 best film of all time in the British Film Institute's 2002 *Sight and Sound Critics' Poll*, moving up to the No. 13 slot in the 2012 poll. Moreover, according to the *New York Times*, *Breathless* is both 'a pop artefact and a daring work of art...a bulletin from the future of movies.' [2]

By 1963, Seberg was living in Paris with her second husband, the famous French writer and diplomat Romain Gary. At that time, her influence in France and in other parts of Europe was phenomenal; she was known not only for her impeccable acting abilities, but also for being a fashion trendsetter. She was admired for her simple yet sophisticated look, and her modern pixie hairdo. In 1964 she moved temporarily to the US for the filming of Robert Rossen's *Lilith*, where she gave a memorable performance as a mysterious young schizophrenic woman being treated in an elite sanitarium in New England. The film also starred Warren Beatty as the novice counsellor, Vincent Bruce, who comes into contact with Lilith. Lilith manipulates all those who come into contact with her, and soon makes Vincent, as well as others, fall under

her erotic spell. Critics were especially impressed by the film's depiction of her lesbian association with another female patient, a relationship that Lilith flaunts in order to further disturb the defenceless Vincent.

In 1968, Seberg returned once again to Hollywood to film the western musical *Paint Your Wagon* directed by Joshua Logan, which also starred Lee Marvin and Clint Eastwood. The mid-sixties was a period of deep civil unrest, civil rights activism, and protests in the US. Seberg, like many other Hollywood stars of that time, became involved in anti-war politics; she associated herself openly with left-wing organizations like the Black Panthers and the National Association for the Advancement of Colored People (NAACP). After she finished filming *Paint Your Wagon*, she remained in the US in order to continue with her anti-war and anti-poverty activism. Her husband Gary, meanwhile, stayed in Paris. By 1970 Gary and Seberg had drifted more and more apart and were in the process of a divorce.

Sometime during the 1970's, she started a relationship with a revolutionary student named Carlos Navarra and became pregnant with his child. Her associations with the Black Panthers, however, had put her on the radar of FBI director J. Edgar Hoover, who considered her a genuine liability. The FBI made her the target of a horrendous smear campaign; they used Counterintelligence Program techniques to harass, intimidate, defame, and discredit her, as well as spread the rumour that the child that she was carrying was actually Raymond Hewitt's, one of the leaders of the

Black Panther movement. Seberg was so traumatized by this false allegation that she gave birth prematurely to a stillborn child. Soon after this sad incident, she left Hollywood for good and returned to live in Paris. In 1972, she married her third husband, the film director Dennis Berry, but the smear campaign contributed to her ever increasing depression, and ultimately wrecked her physical and emotional health. For some time, she seemed to have recovered from her depression, and even planned a return to filmmaking. In 1979, however, she was reported missing in Paris. On the 7th of September 1979, she was found dead in the back seat of her car in a Paris suburb. She had taken a massive overdose of barbiturates, and had been dead for about ten days.

In December 1980, Seberg's former husband Romain Gary also committed suicide; but in Gary's suicide note, he indicated that he had not killed himself over the loss of Seberg, but rather, for his own reasons which remain unexplained even to this day.

Vina Tirven-Gadum
Athabasca University, Alberta, Canada

1. Editor's note: for further discussion of this film, see Lance Lubelski, 'Michael and Patricia Reunite,' in *World Film Locations: Paris*, ed. Marcelline Block (Bristol: Intellect, 2011), 30-31.
2. A. O. Scott, 'A Fresh Look Back at Jean-Luc Godard's *Breathless*,' *New York Times*, May 21, 2010, accessed October 20, 2013, http://www.nytimes.com/2010/05/23/movies/23scott.html?pagewanted=all&_r=0.

Emmanuelle Seigner (1966–)

Unforgettable

For Emmanuelle Seigner, show business is second nature. Born in 1966 to a photographer father and journalist mother, granddaughter of Comédie Française veteran Louis Seigner, the ethereal blonde has spent much of her life in the public eye. After leaving her Catholic convent school for a career in fashion modelling at age fourteen, she made her film début in Christopher Frank's *L'Année des méduses* (1984) and rose to a young and fervent stardom, appearing in Jean-Luc Godard's film-noir homage *Détective* (1985), then opposite Harrison Ford in Roman Polański's *Frantic* (1988). She married Polański in 1989, thus stepping into the somewhat murky limelight the director (now in his 80s) has attracted through most of his own public career. Their marriage came just one year after Polański was sued by Samantha Geimer, the 13-year-old girl he was arrested for raping in 1977. This criminal case still haunts Polański, who had fled the United States in 1978, fearing deportation; it was reopened and Polański's extradition was sought by US authorities when he was arrested in Switzerland in 2006.

Seigner, however, has managed to

keep her cool, and her own reputation remains (mostly) unmuddied by Polański's moral waters. Her film career has showcased her as a versatile actress capable of taking on a wide variety of roles in different genres, from romantic dramas to thrillers to futuristic fantasy. She has played alongside French cinema greats Catherine Deneuve, Gérard Depardieu, and Charlotte Gainsbourg, as well as more recent revelations Marion Cotillard and Sylvie Testud. She has demonstrated her ability to cross language borders, joining colleagues Johnny Depp and Kristin Scott Thomas in bridging the Paris-Hollywood divide. Her role in Julian Schnabel's adaptation of Jean-Dominique Bauby's memoir *Le Scaphandre et le Papillon /The Diving Bell and the Butterfly* (2007) showed quiet, subtle strength, while Polański's 2013 'erotic dark comedy' *Venus in Fur* (an adaptation of David Ives's Broadway play, itself based on Wolfgang von Sacher-Masoch's 1870 novella of the same name) lets Seigner flex her muscles, perhaps literally: she portrays a dominating actress whose work with the unsuccessful director of a play-adaptation of Sacher-Masoch's novella puts the 'meta-' in 'masochist.'

Emmanuelle Seigner has more than one trick up her sleeve: after her roles as fashion model, film star, and mother, at age 40 she became the lead singer of the pop band Ultra Orange, which then changed its name to Ultra Orange & Emmanuelle. They recorded a self-titled album in 2007, and their sound has been compared to such electro-alternative bands as Mazzy Star and Sonic Youth. Seigner went on to record a solo album, 2009's *Dingue*, which includes duets with Iggy Pop and Roman Polański. In July 2012, her vocal work was featured in the B-movie-inspired interactive music video 'Forget Me Not', available for multi-layered viewing at http://forgetmenot.tv. It comes as no surprise to find well over 12,000 'likes' on the actor's Facebook page. Seigner is a versatile artist who spans generations, genres, and continents.

Rosemary A. PETERS
*Louisiana State University,
Baton Rouge*

Mathilde SEIGNER (1968–)

« *La Gourde
la plus
insupportable
du cinéma
français* » ?

H ER TWITTER feed (@M_Seigner)
includes affectionate repartee
with her 4,000 followers, alongside
congratulations and « gros poutouxxx »
for her latest film (from @
guccimimi56: « J'ai vu *Max* :-) au
TOP !! »), interspersed with a healthy
dose of opinion on, for example,
the outcomes of télé-réalité contests
like *Star Academy* and *À la Recherche
de la Nouvelle Star* (for the record,
@M_Seigner decries judging based on
« tout sauf la voix »).

The affection may be hard-won,
but not short-lived. Mathilde SEIGNER
raked in scathing derision from all
across the public spectrum for her ill-
placed commentary during the 2012
César ceremony (including the title
quote of this entry). While presenting
the coveted prize, the first César of
his career, to Michel Blanc, Seigner
stated that she would have preferred
to see the award go to Joey Starr,
a.k.a. Didier Morville, formerly of the
controversial French hip hop group
NTM and her co-star in Stéphanie
Murat's 2012 film *Max*. (You should
have seen her Twitter feed then!)

Seigner, star of the feel-good
comedy *Max*, is well-placed to
comment on cultural phenomena.
Born in 1968, Mathilde Seigner is

granddaughter of Louis Seigner
(whose 50-plus-year career included
roles in films from Jean Renoir's 1933
Chotard et cie /Chotard and Company to
Robert Hossein's 1982 *Les Misérables*);
sister to actor/chanteuse Emmanuelle
Seigner (thus sister-in-law to Roman
Polański); partner to cameraman
Mathieu Petit, with whom she has a
son; friend to Johnny Hallyday and
his wife Laeticia; and star in her own
right. Since her early appearances in
the TV series *Cas de divorce* (1991) and
3000 scénarios contre un virus (1994),
Seigner has acted in over 50 titles,
from mainstream movies to telefilms,
shorts, theatrical productions, and
guest appearances on television
series. And she has seen her share of
feedback – good and bad press alike.
After her interruption at the 2012
César awards ceremony, she made the
headlines well beyond her proverbially
allotted fifteen minutes. It took an
official apology issued through her
lawyer to clear the slate for public
opinion's next preoccupation.

Seigner's career has certainly
experienced several bumps in the
road, even self-inflicted ones like
the César gaffe that had cinephiles
critiquing her as a French Kanye
West. From her first film appearances
in 1994's odd duo of Christine
Carrière's quiet *Rosine* – which earned
her the Prix Michel-Simon – and
Claude Miller's titillating *Le Sourire /
The Smile*, Seigner has taken on roles
of a virtuosic diversity that would
make her grandfather proud. Between
1999 and 2001 alone, the *comédienne*
performed to acclaim in a steady
accumulation of hits: *Vénus beauté
(institut) /Venus Beauty Institute* (Tonie
Marshall, 1999); *Le Temps retrouvé /*

Time Regained (Raúl Ruiz, 1999); *Harry, un ami qui vous veut du bien / With a Friend Like Harry...* (Dominik Moll, 2000); *Betty Fisher et autres histoires /Alias Betty* (Claude Miller, 2000), *La Fille de Paris /The Girl from Paris* (Christian Carion, 2001), and *Inch'allah dimanche /Inch'Allah Sunday* (Yamina Benguigui, 2001), to name but a few.

She has not slowed the pace since then. Her performance in 2006's *Camping* (dir. Fabien Onteniente) earned her the Prix TéléPoche de la Meilleure Actrice de comédie de l'année; for the sequel, 2010's *Camping 2*, she won the *Gérard du désespoir féminin*. The Gérard may be a tongue-in-cheek award, but Seigner can take the joke: according to figures released by *Le Figaro*, the 2.1 million euros she earned for *Camping 2* make her the best-paid actress in France. Not to mention that she has received three César nominations of her own for Best Supporting Actress (for *Harry...*, *Vénus beauté*, and the 1997 hit *Nettoyage à sec /Dry Cleaning*, directed by Anne Fontaine). Besides, known for her 'franc-parler,' Seigner has successfully handled a bad opinion or two in her time. What's that they say about all publicity being good publicity?

Rosemary A. Peters
*Louisiana State University,
Baton Rouge*

Michel Serrault (1928–2007)

From Farce to Fear

MICHEL SERRAULT was born on January 24th, 1928. As a child, he long hesitated between becoming a clown or a priest. He attended secondary school at a Catholic seminary, preparing himself for religious life, but still fascinated by the Medrano Circus. Eventually, though, with the advice and guidance of a priest who would stay a close friend all his life, he decided to become a comedian and took drama courses at the new school of the Rue Blanche in Paris. Years later, Serrault acknowledged that his religious background could explain many of his cinematographic choices.

Following a short tour in Germany in 1946, Serrault began his artistic career in the cabaret in the early 1950s. He first met Jean Poiret at the Sarah Bernhardt Cabaret and the pair formed a long-lasting comic duet, Poiret playing a serious clown in front of an extravagant Serrault. In the mid-fifties, with Jean Carmet, Louis de Funès, Jacqueline Maillan, and others, Serrault was part of the famous, wild post-war comic troupe *Les Branquignols*, conducted by Robert Dhéry. *Ah ! Les Belles Bacchantes / Peek-a-boo* (Jean Loubignac, 1954), a movie starring Dhéry and the whole

Branquignols troupe, gave Michel Serrault the opportunity to act in a film comedy. In 1955, he played the supporting role of a teacher in the dark thriller *Les Diaboliques /Diabolique* (Henri-Georges Clouzot, 1955) starring Simone Signoret, immediately followed by other suspense movies. Serrault's career would, indeed, silently bridge the gap between farce and fear, absurdity and monstrosity. In 1957, with Jean Poiret, he played the role of a burglar in Sacha Guitry's last movie, *Assassins et Voleurs /Lovers and Thieves*, a cynical comedy about crime, suicide, and guilt.

Serrault was very prolific at the start of the decade, obtaining leading roles as in *La Belle Américaine* (Robert Dhéry, 1961) or supporting ones, as in the sketch movie *Les Vierges / The Virgins* by Jean-Pierre Mocky (1962), under the direction of Georges Lautner (*Des pissenlits par la racine / Salad by the Roots*, 1964), and Jack Pinoteau (*Les Durs à cuire ou comment supprimer son prochain sans perdre l'appétit /Hard Boiled Ones*, 1964). He also acted in comedies of manners such as *La Chasse à l'homme /Male Hunt* (Edouard Molinaro, 1964). Like many of his friends, he accepted roles in low level comedies like *Les Combinards* with Darry Cowl (Jean-Claude Roy, 1966). In 1966, *Le Roi de cœur /King of Hearts*, by Philippe de Broca, with Jean-Claude Brialy and Pierre Brasseur, made American universities roar with laughter. But hard times continued, with B movies such as *Le Fou du labo 4 /The Madman of Lab Four* (Jacques Besnard, 1967) with Bernard Blier, Pierre Brasseur, and Jean Lefebvre. During this time, Serrault showed a voracious desire to act both in the cinema and on stage, and through his collaboration with playwright Jean Poiret (*La Cage aux folles*), Serrault's notoriety in the theatre increased.

In 1972 with *Le Viager /The Annuity*, the screenwriter and film director Pierre Tchernia transformed Serrault into a foremost cinema actor. This sarcastic farce shows a family (Michel Galabru as the father) unsuccessfully waiting for an old man to die. The same year, Serrault played in two social satires directed by Jean Yanne (*Moi y'en a vouloir des sous /Me, I Want to Have Dough* and *Tout le monde il est beau, tout le monde il est gentil /Everybody He is Nice, Everybody He is Beautiful*). On stage, *La Cage aux Folles* was created in 1973 and would be a daily success until 1978. The play, written by Jean Poiret, showed Serrault as Albin, an outrageous drag queen arguing with Renato (Jean Poiret), the owner of a club on the Riviera. This great success gradually led Michel Serrault to diverge from the conventional universe of classical comedy, and play more flamboyant roles, a model of which is the very bizarre goggle-eyed serial killer Jérémie in *L'Ibis rouge /The Red Ibis* (Jean-Pierre Mocky, 1975). With his little moustache, Serrault also played stubborn characters caught in absurd situations. In *Préparez vos mouchoirs /Get Out Your Handkerchiefs* (Bertrand Blier, 1978), he is a stressed storekeeper woken up at night by his neighbours (Gérard Depardieu and Patrice Dewaere), forced to religiously listen to Mozart's clarinet concerto and drink a glass of Pastis.

The film adaptation of *La Cage aux folles* (Edouard Molinaro, 1978), filmed at Cinecittà and starring Ugo

Tognazzi instead of Poiret, received the Golden Globe and National Board of Review awards as best Foreign Film. It was adapted in 1983 as the first gay musical on Broadway and was a major hit in the gay community. Serrault, awarded a César for Best Actor for this film, gradually left pure comedy. He was hilarious as a gay Julius Caesar in the very popular comedy *Deux heures moins le quart avant Jésus-Christ /Quarter to Two Before Jesus Christ* (Jean Yanne, 1982). But most of his artistic successes came from cold-blooded roles: a despicable bank owner (*L'Argent des autres /Other People's Money*, Christian de Chalonge, 1978); a common man in a strange, criminal, and anonymous modern suburban area (*Buffet froid*, Bertrand Blier, 1979); a cynical notary caught in a breathtaking police examination (*Garde à vue /The Grilling* by Claude Miller, 1981, for which he obtained another Best Actor César, and which, in 2000, inspired the American *Under Suspicion*, directed by Stephen Hopkins); a *petit bourgeois* well-reputed serial killer from Quimper (*Les Fantômes du chapelier /The Hatter's Ghost*, Claude Chabrol, 1982, based on a Georges Simenon novel); a bloody police superintendent opposed to the straight Alain Delon (*Ne réveillez pas un flic qui dort /Let Sleeping Cops Lie*, José Pinheiro, 1988), and a monstrous doctor (*Docteur Petiot*, Christian de Chalonge, 1990). Serrault never completely left this atmosphere: in 1997's *Assassins*, Mathieu Kassovitz's fourth film, he plays an ageing hitman teaching his art to the younger generation; in 2007, his very last role is in the dark *Pars vite et reviens tard /Have Mercy on Us All*

by Régis Wargnier.

Since the nineties, however, Serrault also excelled in films which are closer to common life, focusing on his older age and wisdom, and deal with one's desire to change one's life. This series started with an intimate and elegant relationship between his character and that of the younger, urbane, and soft Emmanuelle Béart in *Nelly et Monsieur Arnaud /Nelly and Mr Arnaud* (Claude Sautet, 1995) – a role which won him his third César for best actor. In 1995, he formed a father/daughter-like and partner in crime team with Isabelle Huppert (*Rien ne va plus /The Swindle*, Claude Chabrol, 1997). He obtained the same year his greatest comic success since the eighties in *Le Bonheur est dans le pré /Happiness is in the Field* (Etienne Chatiliez, 1995). In 2001, finally, he plays an old farmer from the Vercors region sarcastically observing a young Parisian woman (Mathilde Seigner) starting her own farm in *Une hirondelle a fait le printemps /The Girl from Paris* (Christian Carion, 2001).

In the public's mind, Serrault was mostly a comic actor. In large part, this is due to his extravagant appearances in public, including at the Cannes Festival, where one could feel his great sense for the absurd and the freshness of his childish mind. A true actor, he ventured to express the richness of humanity by playing a great diversity of roles. He died on July 29th, 2007.

Nicolas RIGAUD
The University of Oxford

Delphine SEYRIG (1932–1990)

*A Camera
of One's
Own*

A FASCINATING stage and film actress as well as film director, Delphine SEYRIG represents the new generation of women artists who accompanied experimental movements both in literature and cinema after World War II.

The daughter of archaeologist Henri Seyrig and navigator Hermine de Saussure, her childhood was spent primarily between Lebanon, the United States, and France.

After her *baccalauréat*, she studied acting at the Comédie de Saint-Étienne, training under Jean Dasté, and at the Centre Dramatique de l'Est. She appeared briefly in small roles in the TV series *Sherlock Holmes*. In 1956 she returned to New York and studied at the renowned Actors' Studio.

The first film in which she appeared was the short *Pull My Daisy* (Robert Frank, Alfred Leslie, 1959), also starring American poet Allen Ginsberg. The film was an adaptation by Jack Kerouac from the third act of his play, *Beat Generation*, to which he offered his own improvised narration. In New York, she met Alain Resnais who asked her to star in his film *L'Année dernière à Marienbad /Last Year at Marienbad* (1961). Her performance brought her international recognition and she moved to Paris. Among her roles of this period is the older married woman in François Truffaut's *Baisers volés /Stolen Kisses*, 1968. Jean-Pierre Léaud, as Antoine Doinel, the young man in love with her in the film, says of her character Fabienne Tabard, 'She is not a woman, she is an apparition.' This was the sentiment of many of her admirers. And Michael Lonsdale, who plays her husband in *Baisers volés*, referring to the unusual and mesmerizing quality of the timbre of her voice, called her 'the actress with the cello voice.'

Working again with Resnais in *Muriel ou le temps d'un retour / Muriel, or the Time of Return*, in 1963, she received the *Prix d'interprétation féminine* at the Venice Film Festival. Always interested in alternative cinema, Seyrig also acted in William Klein's political farce, *Mr Freedom*, in 1969, and the same year she began working with Luis Buñuel, in *La Voie lactée /The Milky Way*. She would work again with Buñuel in *Le Charme discret de la bourgeoisie /The Discreet Charm of the Bourgeoisie* in 1972.

She gleefully varied her roles too: from a prostitute in *La Voie lactée*, she became a fairy the following year, in *Peau d'âne /Donkey Skin*, the 1970 musical film by Jacques Demy, and a lesbian vampire in *Le Rouge aux lèvres /Daughters of Darkness* – a 1971 Belgian horror film by Harry Kümel.[1]

Among the many film genres in which she starred one also finds political thrillers, like Fred

Zinnemann's classic *The Day of the Jackal* in 1973, and spy thrillers, such as *The Black Windmill* directed by Don Siegel and starring Michael Caine (1974). Between the two she had acted alongside Jane Fonda in an adaptation of Ibsen's play, *A Doll's House*, directed by Joseph Losey (1973). She had already worked with Losey in *Accident* (a 1967 film adaptation of a Nicholas Mosley novel – screenplay by Harold Pinter).

In 1975, she worked with Michael Londsdale once more in the most famous of Marguerite Duras's films, *India Song*. She had first worked with Duras in *La Musica* in 1967. She continued with *Son nom de Venise dans Calcutta désert* in 1976, and *Baxter, Vera Baxter* in 1977. Consistent with her feminist positions both in her political views and her profession, Seyrig chose to work with female directors from Liliane de Kermadec (in *Aloïse* in 1975) to Ulrike Ottinger (in *Freak Orlando* in 1981 and *Joan of Arc of Mongolia* in 1989) and, most notably, with Chantal Akerman (in *Jeanne Dielman, 23 Quai du Commerce, 1080 Bruxelles* – also in 1975).[2]

Throughout her career, Seyrig used her celebrity status to promote women's rights. Along with Stéphane Audran, Simone de Beauvoir, Catherine Deneuve, Marguerite Duras, Françoise Fabian, Gisèle Halimi, Bernadette Lafont, Ariane Mnouchkine, Jeanne Moreau, Marie-France Pisier, Micheline Presle, Romy Schneider, and Agnès Varda, she signed the *Manifesto of the 343* (in French *Le Manifeste des 343 Salopes*), published in April 1971 in the French left-wing weekly, *Le Nouvel Observateur*. It was a declaration signed by 343 women who admitted to having had an abortion at some stage in their lives, thereby exposing themselves to criminal prosecution, since abortion was then illegal in France. In November of the same year, she also took part in the famous 'Marche des Femmes', a large demonstration organised by the *Mouvement de libération des femmes* which took place in Paris: it demanded sexual liberation, free contraception, and the legalization of abortion.

Feminism naturally drove her own directorial work. With Carole Roussopoulos, a video pioneer, she directed two daringly militant films: *Maso et Miso vont en bateau* in 1975, and *SCUM Manifesto* a year later. From 1976 to 1981, Seyrig worked on the most important of the three films she directed, *Sois belle et tais-toi /Be Pretty and Shut up*, a documentary film based on a series of interviews (twenty or so) with various well-known actresses, including Juliet Berto, Ellen Burstyn, Marie Dubois, Jane Fonda, Shirley MacLaine, and Maria Schneider, sharing frankly their experiences of sexism in their professional careers within the film industry. In 1982, with Carole Roussopoulos and Ioana Wieder, Seyrig established the *Centre Audiovisuel Simone de Beauvoir* based in Paris (where her film *Sois belle et tais-toi* is available), which maintains a large archive of audiovisual documents concerning women's rights, struggles, and artistic creation. It produces as well as distributes works by and about women.

A year before she died, in 1989, Seyrig was given a festival tribute at the Créteil International Women's Film Festival, in France.

Seyrig married (and was later divorced from) American painter Jack Youngerman. Their son, Duncan Youngerman, is a renowned musician and composer.

Delphine Seyrig is buried in the Cimetière du Montparnasse, in Paris.

Brigitte LE JUEZ
Dublin City University

1. For further discussion of this film, see Michael Cramer, '*Daughters of Darkness*,' in *Directory of World Cinema: Belgium*, ed. Marcelline Block and Jeremi Szaniawski (Bristol: Intellect, 2013), 134-135. —Ed.

2. For further discussion of this film, see Marcelline Block, '*Jeanne Dielman, 23 Quai du Commerce, 1080 Bruxelles*,' in *Directory of World Cinema: Belgium*, ed. Block and Szaniawski, 81-84. —Ed.

Simone SIGNORET (1921–1985)
[Simone Henriette Charlotte KAMINKER]

Activist,
Author,
Academy
Award
Winner

AN ICONIC figure of French cinema for more than four decades as well as a writer and political activist, Simone SIGNORET (1921-1985) has the distinction of being the first woman to win an Oscar for a non-US film, receiving the Best Actress prize for her role in the British film *Room at the Top* (1959, Jack Clayton). Along with the Oscar for her powerful, sensual performance as the married, tragic figure Alice Aisgill – killed in a car crash after her younger lover Joe (Laurence Harvey) abandons her for a wealthy, well-connected woman his own age – Signoret was recognized with best actress awards from the Cannes Film Festival, the National Board of Review, and the British Academy of Film and Television (BAFTA). After Signoret's Oscar victory, two French actresses went on to win Oscars: Juliette Binoche received the Best Supporting award for *The English Patient* (1996, dir. Anthony Minghella) and Marion Cotillard as Édith Piaf in *La Môme /La Vie en Rose* (2007, dir. Olivier Dahan) was named Best Actress (for a French-speaking role). For the 1965 drama *Ship of Fools* (Stanley Kramer), Signoret was again nominated for a

Best Actress Oscar as well as a Golden Globe for her turn as a drug-addicted, prison-bound Spanish countess.

Signoret's birth name was Simone Henriette Charlotte Kaminker; she adopted her French Catholic mother's maiden name rather than using that of her Polish-Jewish French-born father, since she began acting during the Nazi Occupation of France in small, often uncredited roles in films including Marcel Carné's *Les Visiteurs du soir /The Devil's Envoys* (1942). However, less than ten years later, Signoret would star as the titular adulteress/murderess in Carné's Silver Lion winning film *Thérèse Raquin* (1953), adapted from Emile Zola's novel of the same name.

Although perhaps best known in the United States for her historic Oscar victory, Signoret's legacy is evidenced in other ways, too, in particular her political activism, with her husband Yves Montand, for left-wing causes such as the anti-war movement. Montand and Signoret starred in *Les Sorcières de Salem /The Crucible /The Witches of Salem* (1957, dir. Raymond Rouleau), a cinematic adaptation of Arthur Miller's *The Crucible* (1953), a play, which, although set during the Salem Witch Trials of the American colonial epoch, was actually an allegory for McCarthyism and made a strong anti-McCarthy statement. Jean-Paul Sartre wrote the screenplay for *Les Sorcières de Salem*, adapting Miller's theatrical work for the screen. For her leading performance as Elizabeth Proctor, wife of John Proctor (Montand) – both of whom were falsely accused of witchcraft – Signoret won the BAFTA award for Best Foreign Actress.

The actress and writer Catherine Allégret (born 1946) is Signoret's daughter from her first marriage, to French filmmaker Yves Allégret (1905-1987). Allégret directed Signoret in several of her early films, including *La Boîte aux rêves* (1945) – in which her appearance is uncredited – and her secondary role as Lily in the World War II drama *Les Démons de l'aube / Dawn Demons* (1946) about the Allied landings in Normandy. In Allégret's poetic realist *Dédée d'Anvers /Dédée / Woman of Antwerp* (1948), Signoret gave her breakthrough performance as the titular character, the prostitute Dédée, playing opposite '*l'immortel*' Marcel Dalio as her pimp and Bernard Blier as the bar owner. As in *Dédée*, throughout the 1950s, Signoret frequently incarnated femme fatales and prostitutes in noir and gangster films such as Allégret's *Manèges /The Cheat* (1950), in which she was reunited with Blier, this time, in the role of his conniving wife Dora. In Max Ophuls's period piece *La Ronde* (1950) set in turn of the century Vienna, Signoret again played a lady of the evening, Léocadie. That same year, Signoret starred as Denise Vernon, the former lover of a gangster, in Frank Tuttle's classic noir, *Gunman in the Streets*, set in the gritty Paris of the era.[1] Two years later, Signoret gave one of the performances of her lifetime as the eponymous protagonist of Jacques Becker's tragedy *Casque d'or /Golden Marie* (1952), set again in the criminal milieu of Paris, this time in the Belle Epoque. In this doomed love story, Signoret incarnated the role of Marie – called « Casque d'or » ['Golden Helmet'] because of her 'helmet'-like blonde updo – a gangster's girlfriend who falls for a carpenter, Georges Manda (Serge Reggiani), newly released from prison. Their love is not to be, as the film ends with Manda's execution for the murders of Marie's boyfriend and her boyfriend's gang's boss. Signoret received the BAFTA award for Best Foreign Actress for her performance. Moreover, *Casque d'or* is considered one of the most important movies in the history of French cinema, functioning as a key transitional work situated between the 'French tradition of quality' and the New Wave, which followed soon after *Casque d'or*'s release, and upon which it had profound influence. In 1955, Signoret starred in the critically acclaimed noir/psychological thriller, Henri-Georges Clouzot's sordid masterpiece *Les Diaboliques /Diabolique*, as Nicole, a teacher who is the mistress of the school's headmaster Michel (Paul Meurisse). Nicole plots – along with Michel's fragile, pious wife Christina (Véra Clouzot) – to murder him. *Diabolique* greatly impacted Alfred Hitchcock's 1960 *Psycho* – indeed, Hitchcock had wanted to direct *Diabolique* himself – and was remade in the US by Jeremiah Chechik as the poorly received *Diabolique* (1996), starring Sharon Stone (in Signoret's role), Isabelle Adjani as the headmaster's wife and Chazz Palminteri as the headmaster.

As the leading female character, Mathilde, in Jean-Pierre Melville's *L'Armée des ombres /Army of Shadows* (1969), a bleak and uncompromising portrayal of the French Resistance during World War II – adapted from Joseph Kessel's eponymous quasi-autobiographical 1943 novel as well as inspired by Melville's own Resistance activities – Signoret gave a powerfully understated performance as a woman who sacrifices herself for her family. Mathilde, at the helm of a Resistance *réseau*, is seemingly unstoppable when it comes to evading the enemy, due to her many disguises and false identities; her loyalty to her fellow *résistants* is fierce. Yet when her daughter is threatened by enemy forces, Mathilde must denounce her Resistance colleagues in order to save her child, for which she pays the ultimate price: death at the hands of her former comrades. *Army of Shadows*'s ending, with Mathilde's assassination by gunshot in a Paris street, overdetermines its harsh outlook on and depiction of the realities of Resistance and Collaboration in Occupied France, rather than upholding the idealistic Gaullist myths surrounding that dark and complex episode of French history, a terrain still not completely explored. Signoret returned to this subject in one of her final performances, when she narrated the controversial documentary *Des terroristes à la retraite /Terrorists in Retirement* (Mosco Boucault, 1985), which shed light upon a small group of former French Resistance fighters – primarily Eastern European immigrants to France – living in obscurity in Paris, having never received full recognition for their acts of valor as part of the FTP-MOI (*Francs-tireurs et partisans – main-d'œuvre immigrée* /'Immigrant Workforce Sharpshooters and Partisans') combat group during World War II.

Shortly after *Army of Shadows*, Signoret starred with Jean Gabin in *Le Chat /The Cat*, Pierre Granier-Deferre's 1971 cinematic adaptation of Georges Simenon: 'In *The Cat*, we find Gabin for the last time alone with Simone Signoret as they are sequestered behind the closed doors of a home scheduled for impending demolition.'[2] For their performances in this harrowing film as a long time married couple, no longer speaking, for whom the husband's beloved cat becomes the object of the wife's extreme jealousy, leading her to commit an act of violence against it, Signoret and Gabin were both awarded the Silver Bear Best Acting awards at the 1971 Berlin International Film Festival.

As she aged, Signoret continued appearing onscreen in some of her most prominent roles, not only without altering her looks but also openly accepting the process of aging: in a 1978 article, she is described as follows: 'it is clear that Signoret isn't what she used to be... The smouldering temptress of *Dédée d'Anvers* and *Les Diaboliques* is gone, replaced by a thick-set, worn woman of 57. Her face is lined, like a map of the Tour de France, without a trace of makeup to disguise the years; her wayward hair is flecked with white.'[3]

Signoret played the eponymous protagonist of *Madame Rosa* (1977, dir. Moshé Mizrahi), the adaptation of Romain Gary's Goncourt Prize-winning novel *La Vie devant soi* (1975, written under the pseudonym of Emile Ajar). As the formidable Madame Rosa – a former prostitute and Auschwitz survivor – who now ekes out a living by running an unlicensed daycare for the children of prostitutes in a small apartment in an unfashionable district of Paris, Signoret gave a tour de force performance. For her portrayal of the elderly, hard-as-nails victim of life haunted by the trauma of the Holocaust who forms a close, quasi-maternal bond with one of the children in her care, Mohammed /'Momo' (Samy Ben Youb), Signoret was awarded the Best Actress César, and the film received the Oscar for Best Foreign Language film.

Signoret studied English and Latin in Paris, and was considered the 'thinking man's sex symbol', a title reinforced by her literary endeavors, including her work as the translator of Lillian Hellmann's play *The Little Foxes* from English to French. She was also a published author with particular admiration for William Faulkner. Her memoir, *La Nostalgie n'est plus ce qu'elle était* was published in 1976 by Seuil (translated into English as *Nostalgia Isn't What It Used to Be* and published in 1978 by Harper and Row). Her historical novel *Adieu Volodia* (Fayard, 1985; translated into English as *Adieu, Volodya: A Novel*, published in 1986 by Random House), about Eastern European Jewish immigrants to France in the interwar years, was published shortly before her death.

Married to Yves Montand for over 30 years, from 1951 until her death in 1985, Signoret weathered Montand's highly publicized affair with Marilyn Monroe – then married to Arthur Miller – after starring together in *Let's Make Love* (1960, dir. George Cukor). A 2011 play, *Marilyn*, by Sue Glover, explored the complexities of the friendship between the two women in an imagined conversation they have while having their hair dyed by the hairdresser they shared while living in adjacent bungalows in the Beverly Hills Hotel during the summer of 1960 when Monroe and

Montand filmed *Let's Make Love.* Signoret discusses this period in her memoir: 'Every Saturday morning the hair colorist of the late Jean Harlow would board her plane in San Diego and arrive in Los Angeles, where Marilyn's car would be waiting for her at the airport and would bring her to our kitchenette…then the hair dyeing party would begin.'[4] Of Monroe, Signoret wrote, 'She never knew to what degree I never detested her, and how thoroughly I had understood the story that was no one's business but ours, the four of us [Miller, Monroe, Montand, Signoret]. Too many people were concerned with it during troubled times when many more important things were happening.'[5] Signoret died in 1985 (more than twenty years after Monroe's death in 1962) and was survived by Montand, who passed away six years after her in 1991.

Marcelline BLOCK
Princeton University and SAG-AFTRA

1. For further discussion of this film, see Dennis Hanlon, 'Eddy Roback Escapes the Police in a Department Store,' in *World Film Locations: Paris*, ed. Marcelline Block (Bristol: Intellect, 2011), 12-13.

2. Christian Janssens, 'Georges Simenon and Cinema,' translated by Marcelline Block, in *Directory of World Cinema: Belgium*, ed. Marcelline Block and Jeremi Szaniawski (Bristol: Intellect, 2013), 263.

3. Pamela Andriotakis, 'At 57, Simone Signoret Decides "It Is Useless to Hang Onto the Branches of Youth",' *People*, June 12, 1978, http://www.people.com/people/archive/article/0,,20071049,00.html.

4. Simone Signoret, *Nostalgia Isn't What It Used to Be* (New York: Penguin, 1979), 331-332.

5. Ibid., 349.

Michel SIMON (1895–1975)

The Beauty of the Beast

ALTHOUGH beauty and regular features are clearly not Michel SIMON's main assets, he did have something in common with the young Alain Delon in that they both escaped a dreary career as pork butchers within the family shop; they also both were drafted for army duty, but the comparison ends here. In 1914, while on leave, Simon encountered the stage and found his way through a decisive encounter with the famous theatre director and actor George Pitoëff, who subsequently became his mentor. With Pitoëff's troupe, Simon went to Paris where he then began to work regularly as a character actor, known for his unflattering face, and his brilliant and often whimsical performances on the stage. But it was only after he met Louis Jouvet (one of the most famous actors and stage directors of the thirties) that Michel Simon really found true recognition and reached stardom. Logically, he continued pursuing a career onscreen, in talking pictures, through which he would truly be remembered: indeed, only the sound cinema could showcase both Simon's odd physique and distinctive voice, combining a rather high pitch with a somewhat chewy diction. His lifestyle was equally uncommon: he often shocked society with very liberal sexual behaviour, from a distinct taste for very young women to an even more radical relationship, according to consistent gossip, with a female monkey. Though every story about him might not be true, the man never bothered too much to embellish his reputation or contradict the most scandalous rumours. Actually, it even fit quite well with his most famous onscreen characters, as his best compositions led him to vividly play two kinds of characters.

Before the Second World War, Michel Simon often favoured portraying hobos and beautiful losers, in such masterpieces as Jean Renoir's *La Chienne /The Bitch* in 1931 and *Boudu sauvé des eaux /Boudu Saved from Drowning* (1932),[1] and in Jean Vigo's cult classic *L'Atalante* (1934). In the latter two, he depicts lonely characters willingly standing at the margins of society, and transgressing its rules either by staying out of it in a utopian stance, or by being reintegrated within the bourgeois world. In Renoir's film, Boudu becomes the embodiment of every basic impulse that is usually repressed, regressing to a childlike state when blowing his nose in the curtains, or turning to a satyr upsetting the well-balanced sexual organisation of the family. Both in real life and on screen, Michel Simon felt close to a certain rebellious anarchism that never really left him. Being a perfect character actor, Simon demonstrates as easily his skills in comedy (in two hit plays adapted for the screen, *On purge bébé /Baby's Laxative*, Jean Renoir, 1931 and *Drôle de drame /Bizarre, Bizarre*, Marcel Carné, 1937), or in realistic

drama with *Quai des brumes /Port of Shadows* (Carné, 1938). At his best in comedies where his poor facial looks work wonders, he shows his great versatility by playing much older men or by seeking parts that require him to wear several disguises.

After World War II, though, Michel Simon started regularly putting his immense talent (some even say genius) toward the crafting of morally ambiguous, hard-to-grasp characters, with Julien Duvivier's *Panique /Panic* (1946), René Clair's *La Beauté du diable /Beauty and the Devil* (1950), or with Guitry's *La Poison / Poison* (1951). However, having become one of the most acclaimed actors of the century and a familiar figure to the French viewers, appearing in numerous pictures, he found one of his most touching parts in 1967 with Claude Berri's *Le Vieil Homme et l'Enfant /The Two of Us*. In this autobiographical drama that moved generations of spectators, Simon's character effortlessly shifted to that of a grumpy old peasant with a heart of gold, forced by circumstances to shelter a young Jewish boy trying to escape Nazi terror in occupied France. His amazing natural craft and the genuine originality of his looks and personality made Michel Simon one of the most recognizable and admired figures in the history of French cinema.

Jean-Christophe Blum
Lycée Blaise Pascal, Clermont-Ferrand

1. For further discussion of *Boudu sauvé des eaux*, see Adam Bingham, 'Boudu's Journey to the Centre of Paris,' in *World Film Locations: Paris* (Bristol: Intellect, 2011), 10-11. —Ed.

Simone SIMON (1910–2005)

*Dangerous
Innocence*

SIMONE SIMON committed herself to a series of roles that prevented us from thinking of her outside of purely sexual terms. Yet when we review her films, we are struck by the radiant purity of her features rather than by any illicit connotations implied by her roles. No one exploited this dichotomy to greater effect than Jean Renoir who, in one of his many masterstrokes of truly great casting, chose Simon for the role of Séverine in his classic adaptation of Émile Zola's *La Bête humaine* (1938). During Séverine's entrance, we are instantly struck by exactly how the danger behind Simone's erotic appeal functioned: when Roubaud (Fernand Ledoux) returns home to Séverine, he pauses at the open door of his apartment as a grin slowly illuminates his face. Breathtakingly, he utters his wife's name. And there she is, smiling sweetly and innocently, as lush and intelligent as the cat she fondly strokes. All because of her simple smile and relaxed familiarity, we are immediately aware that she is the heartbreaker, the troublemaker, the *femme fatale*.

Although we can ascribe a large part of her magnificent performance to Renoir's world-renowned capabilities as a director of actors, it remains nonetheless remarkable that Simon's image had so little impact on the French public despite acting in his films for five years. Simon entered the French film scene in 1931, initially working with minor directors such as Serge de Poligny and Carmine Gallone. Following completion of *Les Beaux Jours /Happy Days* (1935), her fourth collaboration with Marc Allégret, Simon opted for Hollywood.

Simon signed with 20th Century Fox but her unique aura of childishness tinged with eroticism bore little impact on the American screen. Some of her native French critics viewed her American work as utter nonsense,[1] which was a reflection of both the unchanging nature of her mediocre acting style and the contrived material assigned to Simon during her contract with Darryl F. Zanuck. *Girls' Dormitory* (1936, Irving Cummings) placed her opposite Ruth Chatterton, whose impeccably pronounced words only served to highlight Simon's intrusively thick French accent. Of them all, her casting in *Ladies in Love* (1936) reveals the otherness of her beauty within its American context and grants insight into the reasons for her surprising lack of enduring success during this phase of her career: compared with the tame eyes of Loretta Young and the classy coolness of Constance Bennett, Simon is nothing short of redundant and seems years ahead of her time. That Bennett's career, at its peak during the early 1930s, subsequently went into sharp decline and Simon's rose higher than ever before is indicative of the changing tastes in American society and the emerging demand for a new, smart, fatalistic beauty that would soon be crystallised by the *femme fatale*. Simon returned to France following an unnecessary remake of *Seventh Heaven* (1937, Frank Borzage) and the justly forgotten *Love and Hisses* (1937, Sidney Lanfield).

For some, her return to France was a relief and her revelatory performance in *La Bête humaine* was even viewed as casting advice to Hollywood.[2] It is quite likely that, had she retired at this point in her career, Renoir's film at least would have ensured her survival. In France, her performance was praised as an evolution within her own career. Even in one of the film's less favourable reviews, Renoir was praised for washing the face of a star that once 'displayed the amusing little sulky looks of a child-woman in two or three films in her debut' and 'imagined she could mumble through all of her roles.'[3] Renoir himself was evidently taken by her performance and later tried to engage her for the role of Christine in *La Règle du jeu / The Rules of the Game* (1939) but was discouraged by Simon's exorbitant financial demands.[4]

One can argue that Simon's unfeasible fee was a sign that money was now her most pressing concern and that she longed for the security of her steady studio pay-cheques. She departed once more, this time for the second, more critically, and deservedly appreciated phase of her American career. The first concrete realisation in American film of the mystique and intelligence that pervaded her features was captured by William Dieterle in his Faustian fantasy, *The Devil and Daniel Webster* (1941). Her luminous entrance is one of the most memorable of any film and, in every

one of her scenes, Simon attains a perfect balance of alluring beauty and the plotting, menacing voice of doom. She graduated from this supporting role the following year in the hands of Val Lewton who, clearly taken by her own feline features, cast her in his first horror film, *Cat People* (1943, Jacques Tourneur). Her evident discomfort with English only strengthened her uncanny aura and Lewton later used her once more in *Curse of the Cat People* (1944). Other minor roles followed including *Johnny Doesn't Live Here Any More* (1944, Joe May) and *Temptation Harbour* (1947, Lance Comfort), the latter also starring fellow émigré and Renoir alumnus Marcel Dalio.

Yet again, Simone Simon returned to France where, remarkably, she obtained two erotically-charged roles from Max Ophüls at an age when most women would have been losing them. Her chambermaid remains one of the most memorable sexual deviants of the star-loaded *La Ronde* (1950). Amidst the presence of Simone Signoret and Isa Miranda on the poetic carousel of love, Simon again proved that a smile and relaxed suggestiveness beneath her matronly garb could be more potent than any garter. Such a film made it difficult to believe that Simone Simon could have ever been slighted by her beau but, nonetheless, Ophüls subsequently moulded her into a great *tragédienne* in the third segment of *Le Plaisir* (1952). Simon exploited her ever-innocent visage in the role of Maupassant's emotionally-doomed model who cruelly compromises her youth to allow her unrequited love for her artist-lover to flourish under the pact of marriage. Her parts were few after this and following *The Extra Day* (1956, William Fairchild), she accepted no roles until 1973, when she appeared one last time, still lovely, in *La Femme en bleu /The Woman in Blue* (1973, Michel Deville).

Although Simon was surely as great an object of desire in life as in art, she never married, and died in Paris at the age of 94.

Barry NEVIN
National University of Ireland, Galway

1. Georges Sadoul, 'A Masterpiece of Cinema: *La Bête humaine*,' in *French Film Theory and Criticism* vol. 2, ed. Richard Abel (Princeton University Press, 1993), 261.

2. Ibid., 261.

3. François Vinneuil, 'Screen of the Week: *La Bête humaine*,' in *French Film Theory and Criticism*, vol. 2, ed. Richard Abel (Princeton University Press, 1993), 258.

4. Keith Reader, *La Règle du jeu*, French Film Guide (London: I. B. Tauris, 2010), 15.

Jacques TATI (1907–1982)
[Jacques TATISCHEFF]

The Very Essence of French Comedy

BELOVED French director and actor Jacques TATI, born Jacques Tatischeff in 1907,[1] was French with Russian, Dutch, and Italian origins. After a successful music hall and theatre career in the 1930s, Tati played minor parts after the war in two of Claude Autant-Lara's films, *Sylvie et le fantôme /Sylvia and the Ghost* (1946) and *Le Diable au corps / Devil in the Flesh* (1947). In 1947, Tati wrote, directed, and starred in a short entitled *L'École des facteurs /The School for Postmen*, which pays tribute to Charlie Chaplin and Buster Keaton, silent American actors of the 1920s. With the success of this short film, he wrote the all-time classic *Jour de fête* (1949), for which he shot two versions: one in black and white and another in colour. It proved to be a huge success. His second full-length feature film, *Les Vacances de M. Hulot /Monsieur Hulot's Holiday* (1953) gave Tati international fame. *Mon oncle* (1958), continuing Hulot's saga, was, according to François Truffaut, a masterpiece. Tati's *Playtime* (1967) portrays the robotic and dehumanized technology of modern society. Not only was this film the most expensive film ever made at the time – to the extent that it bankrupted Tati – but also, it was considered retrospectively by many to be his best film.

Tati's early career as a mime accounts for his penchant for silent comedy. In his films, there is hardly any dialogue and sound effects, though scarce, amplify and nurture the background of hardly audible dialogues. Gifted with an extraordinary sense of observation, and taking care of every single detail (nothing appears by accident in his films), Tati created a surreal and absurdist universe where slapstick deadpan pantomimes, as well as visual gags, were all choreographed with perfection.

Clumsy and gangly characters impersonated by Tati – whether François the postman in *Jour de fête*, or his alter ego the ordinary-looking and accident-prone M. Hulot with his inimitable umbrella and trench-coat – have delighted generations of spectators and inspired actors and directors alike. Isn't the character of Mr Bean, played by Rowan Atkinson, a modern version of Tati's Monsieur Hulot?

When Tati had the financial means, he would invest all his money in his next production. At the end of his life, he lost nearly everything following the *Playtime* extravaganza and would only travel second class. When arriving in stations where he was awaited by the press, he would exit the train from the first-class carriage in order to conceal his limited financial resources. His films *Trafic* (1971) and *Parade* (1974) were made on very low budgets, which drastically reduced the scope of his talent, preventing it from fully flourishing. The latter film was never released in cinemas.

In 2010, Sylvain Chomet released the animated film *L'Illusionniste /The Illusionist*, a semi-autobiographical script Tati had written in 1956, which was given to Chomet by his younger daughter. The unproduced script that gave birth to Chomet's *The Illusionist* was inspired by a letter Tati wrote to his elder daughter, in a remorseful attempt to reconcile with her (as he had abandoned her). Originally, the lost film was to be set in Prague, but Chomet relocated it to Edinburgh. It is as if Tati is resuscitated in this film. The tall and stooped magician character that is central to the film, billed as Tatischeff (Tati's original surname), is, with his magic sleights of hand and innumerable hat tricks, an extension of Tati's Monsieur Hulot. Inspired by *Playtime*, there are no close-ups and Chomet's 3D cartoon is virtually a silent movie in pure Tati style.

Tati has become iconic, not only in his own country, but also internationally. The style of his films, based on physical comedy, makes them accessible to all cultures, ages, and nationalities.

Michaël ABECASSIS
The University of Oxford

1. While Jacques Tati's birth year is variously published as 1907, 1908, and 1909, the editors are grateful to the *mairie* at Le Pecq for their confirmation that 'Jacques Tati est bien né au Pecq le 9 octobre 1907, dans le quartier dit de "l'Ermitage", dans la maison de son grand-père maternel qui exerçait la profession d'encadreur-doreur.'

Audrey TAUTOU (1976–)

The
Fabulous
Destiny
of —

B ORN ON 9 August 1976 [1] in the
tiny commune of Beaumont
(Auvergne), Audrey TAUTOU remains
closely associated with her widely
acclaimed heroine Amélie, and it is
difficult for spectators to dispel the
image of a young woman with a certain
air of innocence about her. Her big
brown eyes, gentle smile, and candid
beauty are so much part of her persona
that it is difficult to imagine how she
will be perceived in thirty years' time.

Tautou was in fact offered her
first major role precisely because
of the sensitivity and naivety she
radiates. Having missed her first
important audition after arriving
late, she burst into tears; the director,
Tonie Marshall, was touched by her
display of emotions and offered her
a second chance. Despite a disastrous
performance on that day, Tautou was
chosen by Marshall to play the part of
Marie in *Vénus beauté (institut) /Venus
Beauty Institute* (1999), a role for which
she won several awards, including the
César for Most Promising Actress,
Best Young Actress at the Cabourg
Romantic Film Festival, and the
Lumière Award for Most Promising
Young Actress.

Jean-Pierre Jeunet was the next
director to be captivated by her

charms and contacted her to audition
for the role of Amélie after seeing
a poster for *Vénus beauté (institut)*:
'Audrey looks like a little elf with
big eyes, like a deer.' Tautou's unusual
features coupled with her acting
talents made her the perfect actress
to embody the character of Amélie
Poulain. The film, *Le Fabuleux Destin
d'Amélie Poulain /Amélie* (2001),
was a phenomenal success and was
proclaimed a 'feel good movie' for
recreating an idealised Paris where the
smallest pleasures of life, too often
forgotten, are celebrated.[2] As the
character of Amélie is on a mission
to make the world a better place by
discreetly helping everyone around
her, the role undoubtedly reinforced
perceptions of Tautou as a benevolent
angelic figure. The identification
between the actress and the heroine
she personifies is such that Tautou
confessed in a TF1 news interview
that people often call her Amélie and
fail to remember her real name. The
success of *Le Fabuleux Destin d'Amélie
Poulain* was international and the film
quickly became a modern emblem
of Paris. Its worldwide success
undoubtedly boosted tourism in the
area of Montmartre with visitors
looking to retrace Amélie's footsteps
and attempting to recreate the beauty
of Paris they had seen on the film.

Shortly after this cinematic
triumph, Audrey Tautou agreed to
play the role of Angélique in *À la
folie...pas du tout /He Loves Me...He
Loves Me Not* (Laetitia Colombani,
2002). This was a strategic move on
her part that allowed her to play
with the image of *Amélie* without
completely departing from it. The first
part of the film shows the passionate

love of Angélique for a married doctor and the spectator feels sympathetic towards her, until it is revealed that Angélique is far from being as angelic as she may seem. Although it plays with the audience's expectations, the film still functions very much in reference to *Amélie* and there are recognisable similarities between the two characters: the innocent air and a preference for fantasy over the disappointments of reality.

Being acclaimed in the United States for her role as *Amélie* facilitated her entry in 2006 into the realm of Hollywood blockbusters, playing the part of Sophie Neveu for the cinematic interpretation of the immensely popular *The Da Vinci Code* (Ron Howard). Despite beating many other actresses for the part (including Julie Delpy, Virginie Ledoyen, and Sophie Marceau), Tautou's performance was not regarded as memorable, due to a perceived lack of chemistry between her and the film's lead actor, Tom Hanks. Although this represents her mainstream American breakthrough, the generally poor reviews that the film attracted make it hard to predict whether it will open doors to further Hollywood roles. In any case, Tautou has already proved that she can succeed in English-language roles, playing a Turkish immigrant worker in Stephen Frears's *Dirty Pretty Things* (2002).

Jeunet and Tautou returned to work together in 2004 on *Un long dimanche de fiançailles /A Very Long Engagement*, an adaptation of a novel by Sébastien Japrisot. As Mathilde, a young woman out to find her fiancé reported missing in action in the First World War, Tautou displays the same mixture of innocence and cunning which defined Amélie. However, the film lacked the sense of fantasy of their earlier collaboration and failed to repeat the incredible commercial and critical success of *Amélie*.

Among other film roles, Audrey Tautou played the part of French designer Coco Chanel in *Coco avant Chanel /Coco Before Chanel* (Anne Fontaine, 2009). This may be an attempt to produce the same mythologizing effect as in *Amélie* but this time with a character that existed and has achieved eternal recognition, leaving a permanent impression on the world of style and fashion. She was awarded the 'best actress' César for her performance in the film in 2010. That year, Tautou paired up again with Jean-Pierre Jeunet who directed the Chanel No. 5 *Train de nuit* commercial, shot on the famous Orient Express. 2010 marked her theatre debut in *A Doll's House* (Michel Fau, Théâtre de la Madeleine).

In 2011, the bubbly Tautou stars in David and Stéphane Foenkinos's light-hearted comedy *La Délicatesse / Delicacy*. There are numerous humorous moments in the film, as Audrey Tautou and the awkward character played by François Damiens establish levels of intimacy. Not only do Tautou's distinctive facial expressions and demeanour partake in the comedy, but her silences and moments of introspection reveal her depth as an actress. In 2012, Tautou starred in French director Claude Miller's *Thérèse Desqueyroux*, the closing-night film that year at Cannes as well as Miller's final film before his death. Her performance in *Thérèse Desqueyroux* is remarkable of finesse and gives a new dimension to François Mauriac's character which was played by Emmanuelle Riva in the previous version shot by iconic director Georges Franju in 1962. In Cédric Klapisch's latest film, the New-York-City-set romantic comedy *Casse-tête chinois /Chinese Puzzle* (2013) – the concluding episode of the *Auberge espagnole* trilogy – Tautou reprises her role as Martine, starring opposite Romain Duris as Xavier.

In Michel Gondry's adaptation of Boris Vian's 1947 novel *L'Écume des jours /Mood Indigo* (2013), Audrey Tautou once again blossoms onscreen alongside Romain Duris, with whom she had co-starred in Klapisch's trilogy. This romantic comedy, filmed in Gondry's signature exuberant and surreal style, is enticing, revolving around the now inseparable French cinema duo of Duris–Tautou. In Vian's imagination as revisited by Gondry, Chloé (Tautou), the love interest of wealthy bachelor Colin (Duris), is dying of a flower growing in her lungs. At the 2013 Cannes Film Festival, the now ubiquitous French actress hosted the opening and closing ceremonies. But despite such a prolific and successful career, will Audrey Tautou be able to carve another image of herself in the public consciousness beyond that of Amélie?

Lucie HINTON
The University of Oxford

1. Some sources suggest a 1978 birth year for Audrey Tautou, however the editors are grateful to Mᵐᵉ Tautou's agent, and to the Town Hall of Beaumont, for confirming 1976 as the correct year.

2. Re *Amélie*, see also: Arthur Lizie, 'Amélie and Nino in front of Sacré Cœur,' in *World Film Locations: Paris*, ed. Marcelline Block (Bristol: Intellect, 2013), 80-81. —Ed.

Sylvie TESTUD (1971–)

Pas typique

SYLVIE TESTUD complains that if others say she is not a 'typical'-looking actress, it is only because she is not obviously glamorous. However, the lithe actress's distinct – if average – appearance injects films with realism and originality. The French actress was first noticed in German films, starring at age 22 in the titular role of Niko von Glasow's *Maries Lied: Ich war, ich weiß nicht wo /Marie's Song: I Was I Know Not Where* (1994), and afterwards in Caroline Link's *Jenseits der Stille / Beyond Silence* (1996), in which she not only spoke German, but also sign language. Proving her dedication to the role, she additionally learned clarinet for the film, of which, like sign language, she had no previous knowledge. Despite Testud's relative success in Germany, the young actress continued to pursue star status in her homeland. At last Testud won renown in France with Chantal Akerman's *La Captive / The Captive* (2000),[1] an adaptation of *La Prisonière*, the fifth volume of Marcel Proust's *À la recherche du temps perdu*. Testud as Ariane (Proust's Albertine) psychologically dominates Simon (Proust's Marcel), played by Stanislas Merhar, and her cool, distanced, approach to the young man equally obsesses the audience. A lesbian scene of the seductress with her friend (Olivia Bonamy) began a trend in Testud's casting.

After the critical success of *La Captive*, Sylvie Testud gained widespread acclaim for *Les Blessures assassins /Murderous Maids* (Jean-Pierre Denis, 2000), in which she portrayed Christine Papin, who with her lover/sister Lea (Julie-Marie Parmentier) plans and kills the woman for whom they work as maids. Although the film and its director were both nominated for Césars, it was Testud's performance that garnered the award for the most promising actress. In fact the centre of *Les Blessures assassins* is Christine's delirium and the character's complicated attachment to her sister.

In 2003 after becoming known exclusively for dramatic roles, Testud starred in a comedy, *Filles uniques /Only Girls* (Pierre Jolivet, 2003), playing a newly released convict who befriends her judge. From this point forward, Testud has taken on both comedic and dramatic roles, producing a diverse acting oeuvre. In *Stupeur et Tremblements /Fear and Trembling* (Alain Corneau, 2003), Testud combines her naturalism with superior comedic timing as a low-level Belgian employee who fails at a Japanese corporation – this time, Testud mastered extensive Japanese dialogue for the role. Although the film, based on the Amélie Nothomb novel, portrays the Japanese office space and its staff in a stereotypical manner, the plot more subtly

alludes to the employee's lesbian desire for her immediate boss. The French public connected with the Francophone vision of Japan, and Testud won her second César, this time for best actress.

The genre-breaking comedy/ musical set in World War I, *La France* (Serge Bozon, 2007), demonstrates again Testud's ability to captivate the public in both light and dark subject matters. As Camille, Testud dresses as a male soldier to search for her boyfriend on the Western Front. Testud's slender form, clothed in military gear, confuses gender by enhancing the androgyny of the actress's frame. As her past roles hinged on androgyny and bisexuality, Testud was an obvious choice for *Sagan* (2008), Diane Kurys' biopic about Françoise Sagan, the bi-sexual author most famous for her first novel, *Bonjour Tristesse* (1954), published when she was eighteen years old. Testud researched radio and television interviews to achieve Sagan's precise diction and mannerisms, including the subtle changes of maturity in her voice. Although the film was not successful at the box office, Testud's mastery of Sagan surpasses a surface imitation and manages to depict the author's turbulent existence with emotional depth. Testud appears in another Kurys film, the semi-autobiographical family drama *Pour une femme /For a Woman* (2013), as Anne, a film director in the 1980s, who, upon the death of her mother, looks into her family history, particularly the experience of her parents in post World War II France.

Sylvie Testud was also the ideal

actress to play Françoise Sagan because of her own burgeoning literary career. Her first book *Il n'y a pas beaucoup d'étoiles* (2005) consists of droll journal entries concerning the life of an actress. However, Testud quickly pursued more serious writing forms, publishing two autobiographical novels, *Le Ciel t'aidera* (2007) and *Gamines* (2009), about her life pre-fame in an Italian immigrant family from Lyon. In 2009, invoking the circularity of Testud's relationship to literature and film, the actress starred as herself in a filmic adaptation of her novel *Gamines /Sisters* (2009) directed by Éléonore Faucher. Evidently the success of *Gamines* encouraged Testud to continue more boldly in the realm of fiction, and in 2012 she published a more abstract novel concerning a wife's obsession with cleanliness, with no overt autobiographical source. The title of the novel, *Chevalier de l'ordre du mérite*, is likely a wink at Testud's knighting to the national order of merit in 2009.

With her career as an actress and now as a novelist well established, Testud directed her first film, *La Vie d'une autre /Another Woman's Life* in 2012. The film is an adaption of a minor novel in which a woman wakes up to realize she has missed the last fifteen years of her life. Although the film's starring actors, Juliette Binoche and Mathieu Kassovitz, often take artistic chances, this clichéd plot under Testud's direction results in a banal romantic comedy. The film's heteronormativity is surprising when considering the bisexual, gender-blurring of Testud's most famous roles, but echoes the actress's increasingly mainstream trajectory, including her appearance on an episode of the French television documentary series *Rendez-vous en terre inconnue /Rendez-vous in an Unknown Region*, broadcast on the France 2 television channel in October 2012. Testud's current projects include the Paris segment of David Allain and Alexandra Billington's *Geography of the Heart* (2014) and *Mesyats v derevne /Two Women* (Vera Glagoleva, 2014), a Russian period drama adapted from Ivan Turgenev's play. In April 2012, Sylvie Testud was named Chevalier de la Légion d'honneur.

Nicole Beth WALLENBROCK
The City University of New York

1. For further discussion of *La Captive*, see David Sterritt, 'The Captive,' in *Directory of World Cinema: Belgium*, ed. Marcelline Block and Jeremi Szaniawski (Bristol: Intellect, 2013), 93-94. —Ed.

Jean-Louis TRINTIGNANT (1930–)

A Great Silence

BEFORE Jean-Louis TRINTIGNANT made his triumphant return at the Cannes Film Festival in May of 2012 with Michael Haneke's Palme d'Or winning film *Amour*, he had essentially retired from cinema to devote himself to working full-time in theatre. Indeed, he had not appeared in a major movie role since Patrice Chéreau's *Ceux qui m'aiment prendront le train /Those Who Love Me Can Take the Train* in 1998, in which he played a recently deceased artist, Jean-Baptiste Emmerich, whose death forces the other characters in the film to come to terms with themselves, with their previously difficult relationships with Emmerich, and with one another. Yet the Chéreau film – with an almost *Kane*-like narrative structure in which Trintignant's character is defined as much in relation or reaction to others as by his own personal attributes – would, in many ways, have been an excellent summation of Trintignant's cinema career. In a host of film performances noteworthy for their brooding intensity, his presence manifested itself most forcefully as an absence. Though they would never work together, he might have been the perfect *modèle* for a film by Robert Bresson; in his most famous roles

he served as the blank canvas upon which arthouse *auteur* and commercial filmmakers alike could project their own preoccupations.

The essential interiority of his performances introduced an unsettlingly universal note of moral ambivalence touching both the leading men, and the outright villains he portrayed. In his first high-profile roles, as the honourable but deluded Michel Tardieu, the man who agrees to marry feral sex kitten Brigitte Bardot in Roger Vadim's *Et Dieu... créa la femme /And God Created Woman* (1956), and, three years later, as Danceny to Jeanne Moreau's Juliette de Merteuil in Vadim's *Les Liaisons dangereuses 1960 /Dangerous Liaisons* (released 1959), he was too withdrawn and too secretive to be entirely convincing as the righteous champions of romantic morality for which the rather pedestrian scripts called. His guardedness could impart a certain moral weight, as in Sergio Corbucci's spaghetti western *The Great Silence* (1968), in which, as the mute gunslinger nicknamed Silence, he champions the citizens of a town terrorized by bounty hunters, or Costa-Gavras' taut thriller *Z* (1969), where he plays an incorruptible *juge d'instruction* investigating a politically motivated assassination. Yet, in David Thomson's estimation, from 'the mid-1960s, [Trintignant] found his diffidence leading him in to increasingly detached, voyeuristic characters.'[1] In fact, his emotional reticence on screen made him the perfect cypher for the prurient desires of cinema audiences themselves. This was never more obvious than in the *nouveau romancier* Alain Robbe-

Grillet's *Trans-Europ-Express* (1967), a film which explicitly conflates the gazes of Trintignant's character Elias, the camera, and the viewer, in protracted sequences that detail the sexual humiliation of Elias's possible lover Eva (Marie-France Pisier).

If his face betrayed little of the inner lives of his characters, the same could not be said of Trintignant's body, which could imbue the most mundane and mechanical of actions with an unexpectedly powerful eloquence. Nephew of the Formula One racers Louis and Maurice Trintignant, he had a natural aptitude for driving, and did so with a charismatic physicality fetishized by Claude Lelouch in the three films they made together – *Un homme et une femme /A Man and a Woman* (1966), *Le Voyou /The Crook* (1970), and *Un homme et une femme, 20 ans déjà /A Man and a Woman: 20 Years Later* (1986). There is, perhaps, more wit to Eric Rohmer's focus on Trintignant's sensuous handling of the stick shift in that most 'talky' of films, *Ma nuit chez Maud /My Night at Maud's* (1969); as the emotionally repressed Jean-Louis cruises the vertiginous streets of Clermont-Ferrand in search of Françoise (Marie-Christine Barrault), the supposedly pure Catholic girl that he has encountered at morning Mass, the grinding of the gear box is a supremely physical reminder of his sublimated passions and searing sexual frustration.

Yet Trintignant's gift for expressionless impassivity, and his strangely compelling physical presence, were never married to more stunning effect than in Bernardo Bertolucci's masterpiece *The Conformist* (1970).[2]

In the role of Fascist informant Clerici, who wavers in his resolve when asked to assassinate his old professor, a left-wing activist in exile from Italy, he seemed positively to embody the fundamental ambiguity of moral agency: the human capacity to make knowingly immoral choices. To David Thomson, in Trintignant's portrayal, Clerici chooses to mock his own sidling style, the walk of a captive creature – it's his way of being ironic, of pretending he has a greater intellectual liberty. But when most himself, he shrinks, occupying smaller spaces in hunched and tentative postures. He is in the dark or in a recess; he stands where the film lacks light. His pale, boy's face has to be coaxed into those alarming, tender and cruel close-ups. And then we hate what we see.

With the slightly curdled handsomeness of a 15th century Italian painting and the scuttle of an invertebrate insect, he is, as Thomson puts it, 'practising the anonymity of the Jew who prays not to be identified when the trains are filled.'[3]

It was possibly this impression of studied anonymity which helped Trintignant to step aside, 'as he grew older…to become a character actor, underplaying but commanding…'[4] He displayed an unexpected facility for comedy, both as the estate agent wrongly accused of his wife's murder in François Truffaut's last film, the romantic mystery *Vivement dimanche !* */Confidentially Yours* (1983), and as the voice of the talking brain, Irving, in Jean-Pierre Jeunet and Marc Caro's dystopian fantasy *La Cité des enfants perdus /The City of Lost Children* (1995). But it was as the lonely eavesdropper befriended by a young woman in the conclusion to Krzysztof Kieslowski's *Three Colours* trilogy, *Trois couleurs : Rouge /Three Colours: Red* (1994), that he offered his most significant late performance. It is to be hoped that Haneke's *Amour*, about the relationship between a man and his wife after she suffers a debilitating stroke, will signal the start of career renaissance for an actor who has for too long been absent from the screen.

Celia NICHOLLS
University of Warwick

1. David Thomson, *The New Biographical Dictionary of Film* (London: Little Brown, 2010), 977.

2. For further discussion of this film, see Giovanna Summerfield, '*La bella città* : Paris Through the Lens of Italian Directors,' in *World Film Locations: Paris*, ed. Marcelline Block (Bristol: Intellect, 2013), 86-87. —Ed.

3. David Thomson, 'The Killer Inside,' *Sight and Sound* 18:3 (March 2008): 28.

4. Thomson, *The New Biographical Dictionary of Film*, 978.

Charles VANEL (1892–1989)

Seven Decades of Cinema

A WORKING ACTOR for more than 70 years, Charles VANEL had what remains the longest French screen career of all time, appearing in film and on television well into his 90s. Born in Rennes in 1892 (even before the birth of cinema itself), Charles-Marie Vanel began acting for the stage while still in his teens. His first film role followed in 1912, and after he hit the big screen he definitively abandoned the theatre. In the late 1920s, Vanel tried his hand at directing, but gave it up after only two films, recognizing that his clearest strength was performing. By the time of his death in 1989, Vanel's filmography surpassed 160 titles, and while most of these roles did not grant him top billing, his cultural legacy far exceeds the sum of his work.

Vanel's longevity was matched only by his versatility; it would be practically impossible to encapsulate his career in a single role, or even a single character type. He had a penchant for playing the everyman, a talent that suited his perspective vis-à-vis his profession. In a 1938 issue of *Ciné-Miroir*, Vanel admitted his distaste for 'big, sensational roles…where vice and virtue are easily recognizable. I prefer roles that exist in real life, which is made up of suffering, of beauty and ugliness.' Throughout his career, Vanel followed this guideline almost religiously, playing characters that were neither deeply villainous nor mythically heroic. Instead, he opted for roles that aimed to convey a full spectrum of human experience.

The 1930s were Vanel's busiest working years, during which he played a wide variety of roles. Vanel occasionally incarnated the low-life – for instance, the suspicious mechanic Michaux in *Daïnah la métisse* (Jean Grémillon, 1932), the lecherous expatriate Clément in *Le Grand Jeu* (Jacques Feyder, 1934), and the businessman backing a brothel madam in *Jenny* (Marcel Carné, 1936) – but he was better known for characters that conveyed a more benign paternalism, such as policemen and military officers (some of his military roles helped him indirectly realize his childhood dream of becoming a sailor, a goal he was forced to abandon due to problems with his eyesight). Vanel also built a reputation for playing the cuckold, a casting pattern rooted in his ability to combine a uniquely vulnerable masculinity with an understated authority. Among the most famous of these roles was opposite Viviane Romance, who played his manipulative ex-wife in Julien Duvivier's Popular Front classic *La Belle Équipe /They Were Five* (1937), which also featured Jean Gabin as Vanel's friend and romantic rival. But this vulnerability did not always lead to victimhood; in Jean Grémillon's *Le Ciel est à vous /The Woman Who Dared* (1944), Vanel plays a husband who supports his wife (Madeleine Renaud) in her burgeoning passion for aviation despite the complications her hobby brings to their family. While adultery never enters the picture, the singular success of his wife and the equanimity with which he handles her rise to fame both point to a singular brand of manhood.

Never limiting his work to French productions, Vanel also made films in Italy and Germany. The 1950s marked the apex of Vanel's international appeal, with his best-known and most enduring films earning high praise at major festivals. Two of these films were directed by Henri-Georges Clouzot, a French filmmaker known for his tense, morally complicated thrillers. Clouzot's multilingual *Le Salaire de la peur /The Wages of Fear* (1953) brought Vanel particular acclaim in the role of Jo, a French expatriate in Central America who volunteers to deliver a truckload of nitroglycerine to the site of an oil field wildfire. His complex portrayal reveals Jo's charisma as well as his cowardice, both of which counterbalance the youthful bravado of his driving partner Mario (Yves Montand). *The Wages of Fear* earned Vanel a special mention at the Cannes film festival; the film also won the Grand Prix at Cannes, the Golden Bear at Berlin, and a BAFTA from Britain. Two years later, Vanel rejoined Clouzot for *Les Diaboliques /Diabolique* (1955), this time covering more familiar territory as a police commissioner investigating a scandalous murder. The same year, Vanel incarnated the wrong side of the law in Alfred Hitchcock's *To Catch a Thief* (1955), a film that today, thanks to Hitchcock's imprimatur, may be Vanel's most recognized work outside France.

In the 1960s, Vanel began to appear on the small screen as well, with TV movies, mini-series, and cameos alternating with continued work in feature films. Thanks in large part to television, his career showed little sign of slowing through the 70s and 80s. He continued to portray the firm but gentle patriarch, as illustrated by his portrayal of the eponymous Père Goriot in a 1972 TV adaptation of Balzac. In 1986, at the age of 93, Vanel declared that 'as long as one has the strength to do it, you can act,' a statement that appeared in his *New York Times* obituary three years later. Vanel's legacy to French cinema comes down to this persistent and omnivorous pursuit of his craft. Over more than seven decades, Charles Vanel crossed national borders as comfortably as he crossed into a new visual medium, and no matter how large or small his role, Vanel eschewed the extreme conventions of screen narrative in order to portray characters who lived life as though they might have been real.

Colleen Kennedy-Karpat
Bilkent University, Ankara, Turkey

Lino Ventura (1919–1987)

Whose Bark Was Worse Than His Bite

Lino (Angiolino) Giuseppe Pasquale Ventura was born in Parma in 1919. He emigrated to France with his family in 1927. Early on, he started to work as a professional wrestler and a fight organiser (sometimes using his mother's name Borrini). Jacques Becker gave him his first part in *Touchez pas au grisbi /Grisbi* in 1954, acting alongside the superstar Jean Gabin. With his stout figure and self-assurance, he always played policemen or gangsters. With Bernard Borderie's *Le Gorille vous salue bien /The Gorilla Greets You* (1958), Claude Sautet's *Classe tous risques /The Big Risk* (1960), and especially Denys de la Patellière's *Un taxi pour Tobrouk /Taxi for Tobruk* in 1961, he became a real star. As he specialised in playing the man of action, he was asked to act in parodies of gangster films, which, thanks to Michel Audiard's dialogues, soon became cult comedies: Georges Lautner's *Tontons flingueurs /Crooks in Clover* (1963), *Les Barbouzes /The Great Spy Chase* (1964), and *Ne nous fâchons pas /Let's Not Get Angry* (1966). He subsequently chose more pessimistic and disenchanted characters in Jean-Pierre Melville's *Le Deuxième Souffle /Second Breath* (1966) and *L'Armée des ombres /Army of Shadows* (1969),

Francesco Rosi's *Cadavres exquis / Illustrious Corpses* (1975), and Jacques Deray's *Un papillon sur l'épaule / Butterfly on the Shoulder* (1978). In 1981, he is the charismatic inspector Gallien for Claude Miller's melodrama *Garde à vue*, in which he forms a triangle with Michel Serrault and Romy Schneider. Lino Ventura was also famous for the charity he created for mentally handicapped children, 'Perce-Neige.' He died of a heart attack in St Cloud in 1987.

This instinctive actor, a superstar comparable to Jean Gabin, has the Italian type, but with the addition of cheeky Parisian humour. Lino Ventura has a powerful and calm style of acting, a quiet assurance together with an indisputable presence and an impressive stature. He is perfectly suited to playing enigmatic characters that make decisions without uttering a word and he can also be a hard hitter. This requires a very intense method of acting: Lino Ventura fills his silences with unexpressed doubts. At the end of Claude Lelouch's *La Bonne Année /Happy New Year* (1973), he stares at Françoise Fabian for one minute without moving or saying a thing; yet by a simple long look he expresses mute questions, deep disappointment, and then, the final acceptance of the woman who betrayed him. He can reveal the character's anxiety when he is cornered, just taking his head in his hands, although this man has the hands of a fighter. He agreed to deride this model of his own creation in the parodies of gangster films. A bit reluctant at first, he was the unique Uncle Fernand in *Crooks in Clover* with his shifty looks, his suspicious pout, his meditative bulldog face, his blunt and naïve fits of anger, his air of consternation, and his famous punches. These comedies underline his strange assurance and spontaneity. In *Crooks in Clover*, somebody asks: 'What do you think about this man? Is he a fake big chief, or is he a real wash-out?' Whatever the plot, he is always meant to be the boss. He is a silent and feared chief. In the comedies, he lends great sincerity and intensity to Michel Audiard's dialogues, which are known for their musicality and their misanthropic sentiments. As Ventura never took any lessons, he acts instinctively – hence his roles as impulsive men capable of the greatest violence despite their self-control. He was a generous man: on set, he was known for cooking delicious pasta dishes for the whole cast. He liked to have all his friends gathered for dinner; on these occasions they helped create some of the famous sayings that could later be found in Audiard's dialogues… This mighty figure was modest, too: very few directors managed to persuade him to kiss a woman on film. However, they did know how to take advantage of his contradictions in order to build characters. In his films, behind his rough looks, his taciturn face, and his husky voice, one can feel the sensitivity of a shy brute who throws punches to hide his deep anxiety.

Violaine HEYRAUD
Université Sorbonne Nouvelle – Paris 3

Boris VIAN (1920–1959)

'The Prince of Saint-Germain-des-Prés'

BORIS VIAN has always been a fascinating phenomenon and a multitalented, multifaceted figure in the French horizon of letters, performance, and music. Vian impacted numerous creative fields as an actor, novelist, playwright, poet, musician, prolific songwriter who 'wrote songs with Aznavourian profligacy: over 700 of them' [1] – quite a record for someone with such a short lifespan – critic, and translator of Raymond Chandler (among other authors) from English to French. Vian often signed his written pieces with pseudonyms such as Bison Ravi – a clever anagram of his own name, which means 'delighted bison' in English – and Vernon Sullivan. He was interested in existentialism, and participated in the Collège de 'Pataphysique (out of which the OuLiPo grew) alongside such renowned writers as Eugène Ionesco, François Le Lionnais, Raymond Queneau, and Roger Shattuck. Vian, who also received an engineering degree, is the exemplary *pantophile* à la Diderot.

Vian was born on March 10, 1920 in an upper middle class family in Ville d'Avray, a chic suburb of Paris. With his brothers, he had a golden childhood, although he was sickly, suffering from a heart problem. Boris' first name has nothing to do with Russia other than that his mother had attended the opera *Boris Godunov* by Mussorgsky (in an interesting twist, Vian's novel *L'Écume des jours* was made into an opera in 1981 by the Russian composer Edison Denisov). When the Vian family suffered financial difficulties during the Great Depression of the 1930s, they rented their villa 'Les Fauvettes' to Yehudi Menuhin and his family, a story related by Menuhin to artist Jenny Batlay, who at age 13 painted Menuhin's portrait (and who was at the time reading Vian's iconic novel *L'Écume des jours*, prompting Menuhin to mention his connection to Vian). Julian Barnes refers to a photograph of Vian, 'aged twelve, [standing] behind a chubby adolescent in long shorts and a criss-cross sweater who turns out to be the fourteen-year-old Yehudi Menuhin.' [2]

Vian was influential to the French cinematic landscape, as many of his stories and novels were adapted for the screen. His best known work is the above-mentioned bittersweet 1946 novel *L'Écume des jours /Froth on the Daydream* (or *Foam of the Daze*), in which Chloé, the protagonist's wife, dies of a bizarre condition: a water-lily growing in her lung. This novel was dubbed by Raymond Queneau as « le plus poignant des romans d'amour contemporains » ['the most poignant of the contemporary novels about love']. According to Jenny Batlay, « dans ce roman, bien que le pathétique soit privilégié, l'amour est traité d'une façon nouvelle. Malgré la tristesse qui le sous-tend, le récit est mené avec gaieté et humour…l'amour et l'humour s'y reflètent l'un dans l'autre au point de former un couplage de notions complémentaires, parfois même interchangeables » ['in this novel, even if the pathetic is privileged, love is treated in a new manner. Despite the sadness that underlies it, the narrative is conducted with gaiety and humour... love and humour are reflected in each other to the point of forming a coupling of complementary concepts, sometimes even interchangeable'].[3]

L'Écume des jours is also filled with Vian's signature puns, wordplay, and references to actual figures of the French cultural scene of Saint-Germain-des-Prés, in which Vian was a participant (and dubbed its 'Prince'): 'Vian's world, especially the world of his novels, is...rich in humour, acerbic wit, and fantastic imagery, all of which are grounded in his sophisticated manipulation and subversion of language through the invention of neologisms, puns, arcane references, and wordplay of the subtlest sort.'[4] For example, in *L'Écume des jours*, the character of the philosopher Jean-Sol Partre is modelled on Jean-Paul Sartre, who was, in reality, a friend and colleague of Vian's, as they frequented the same intellectual, literary, and artistic circles in Paris's Left Bank.

Vian's *L'Écume des jours* brings to the surface his iconic cinematic presence, unforgettable – and not forgotten – as it has been adapted for cinema on three occasions: first in 1968 as *L'Écume des jours /Spray of the Days* (dir. Charles Belmont), starring Jacques Perrin as Colin, Annie Buron as Chloé, Sami Frey as Colin's best friend Chick, Marie-France Pisier as Chick's love interest Alise, and Bernard Fresson in the role of Colin's cook, Nicolas; in

the 2001 Japanese film *Kuroe /[Chloe]* (dir. Gô Rijû) – named after the book's doomed female protagonist; and most recently in 2013 by Michel Gondry, whose *L'Écume des jours /Mood Indigo* has a cast of contemporary French stars: Romain Duris (Colin), Audrey Tautou (Chloé), Gad Elmaleh (Chick), Aïssa Maïga (Alise), and Omar Sy (Nicolas).

Vian also appeared in numerous films as an actor, including playing himself in 1946-50 for a documentary *Saint-Germain-des-Prés* by Jean Suyeux and Freddie Baume, alongside other habitués of the quartier (Alexandre Astruc, Dizzy Gillespie, Juliette Gréco, Raymond Queneau, and Roger Vadim...) and set in their local haunts Le Tabou and Le Caveau des Lorientais – the only copy of this film was confiscated because it reportedly showed a nude woman. In narrative fiction films, Vian performed roles such as the Cardinal in Jean Delannoy's adaptation of Victor Hugo's *Notre-Dame de Paris /The Hunchback of Notre Dame* (1956); the manager of the baths in Pierre Kast's *Un amour de poche / Girl in his Pocket* (also 1957), with a star-studded cast including Alexandre Astruc, Jean-Claude Brialy, Christian-Jaque, Jean Marais, and Jean-Pierre Melville, and as Prévan in Roger Vadim's *Les Liaisons dangereuses 1960*, a modern-day adaptation of Choderlos de Laclos' 18th century epistolary novel, starring Jeanne Moreau and Gérard Philipe. Vadim's *Les Liaisons '1960'* was released in 1959, the year that witnessed the deaths of both Vian and the popular French actor and heartthrob Philipe. Tragically, both Vian and Philipe died before reaching the age of 40: Philipe at 36 of liver cancer, and Vian at 39, on 23ʳᵈ June 1959, from cardiac arrest. (Vian suffered from poor health his whole life, causing him to be home-schooled as a child and later on, forcing him to stop playing the trumpet.) Vian's death was closely connected to cinema as well, as he went into cardiac arrest during a preview séance, at the Cinema Marbeuf, of the film adaptation of his (in)famous novel *J'irai cracher sur vos tombes /I Spit on Your Graves* (Michel Gast, 1959). Vian was upset with the filmic interpretation of his book. He thought the film was so bad that he wanted his name removed from the credits completely, and while sitting in his seat, he famously shouted, after only a few minutes of the film, 'These guys are supposed to be American? My ass!' He tried to get up to leave the theatre before having a massive heart attack, dying en route to the hospital.

Vian's novel *J'irai cracher sur vos tombes* blends elements of lurid pulp fiction with the Southern Gothic, dealing with racial and sexual tensions in the American South – centring upon the light-skinned African-American protagonist Lee Anderson seeking revenge for his brother's lynching – and was written under the pseudonym Vernon Sullivan (an inside joke combining the names of musician Paul Vernon and jazz pianist Joe Sullivan). With this novel, Vian perpetuated a literary hoax, claiming that he was actually its translator and that he had come across the manuscript by Sullivan, the book's actual author, an African-American writer (now living in Paris) whose text was censored in the US because of its explicit content. In reality, Vian had written the book in two weeks: 'in *J'irai cracher*,

Vian is playing with the readers, presenting them with a salacious thriller purportedly translated into French while at the same time telling them how low their tastes are.' [5] *J'irai cracher sur vos tombes* was a bestseller, yet Vian, in 1950, was taken to court and fined 100,000 francs because of it: the book was deemed 'objectionable literature' (it was the first French novel after Gustave Flaubert's 1856 *Madame Bovary* to be put on trial for obscenity). Moreover, a copy of *J'irai cracher sur vos tombes* was found in a hotel room – with highlighted excerpts of a scene in which a woman is strangled – adjacent to the corpse of a young woman who had been strangled by her lover (who then committed suicide). According to J.K.L. Scott, 'the novel led to Vian's prosecution, stigmatization, and, arguably, to his death…the work which had destroyed his literary status seems to have had an equally cataclysmic effect on his life.' [6]

J'irai cracher sur vos tombes went on to impact American film. The legacy of Vian's novel is evident in the title of the infamous 1978 American exploitation/rape-and-revenge film *I Spit on Your Grave* (dir. Meir Zarchi), which was inspired by Vian's book. Zarchi's graphic and upsetting film (originally named *Day of the Woman* but retitled in the 1980s) – banned and censored in many countries – has achieved cult status in the rape-and-revenge genre (recalling how, in Vian's original text, the 'two themes are sex and revenge' [7]). Zarchi's *I Spit on Your Grave* is infamous for having the longest rape scene in US film history, depicting extreme, explicit male violence against the female protagonist as well as her exacting murderous revenge against each of her four rapists. Described as 'a vile bag of garbage' by the late film critic Roger Ebert – who did not die upon seeing this film, but rather, 'walked out of the theatre quickly, feeling unclean, ashamed and depressed' [8] – *I Spit on Your Grave* has been recuperated by feminist film critics including Carol J. Clover. In her classic text *Men, Women and Chainsaws: Gender in the Modern Horror Film*, Clover writes, 'for all its disturbing qualities, at least it problematizes the issue of male (sexual) violence.' [9] *I Spit on Your Grave* was revived in the 21st century, with 2010 and 2013 remakes by Steven R. Monroe.

Throughout his short life, Vian was well known in musical (especially jazz), film, and literary circles. With his friends, he organized many parties and get-togethers, and introduced jazz onto the French scene, including the American musicians Hoagy Carmichael, Miles Davis, and Duke Ellington. Recently, in the biopic *Gainsbourg (vie héroïque) /Gainsbourg: A Heroic Life*, Joann Sfar's 2010 César-winning film about the life of Serge Gainsbourg, Boris Vian (played by French singer and actor Philippe Katerine) made an appearance. This character sings, with a soft, slightly high-pitched voice, « je bois pour oublier les amants de ma femme » ['I drink to forget my wife's lovers']. One is not convinced that Boris Vian, in the film, is upset about his wife's lovers (although, in reality, Vian's wife Michelle did have a liaison with Vian's good friend Jean-Paul Sartre, after which their marriage suffered until they divorced). Like Vian, Geroges Brassens, Jacques Brel, and Gainsbourg have all written melancholy and bittersweet songs from the point of view of the man being cuckolded by his wife or girlfriend – not from a vengeful, but rather, a philosophical, perspective, such as Jacques Brel in *Le Moribond*, saying goodbye to his friend: « C'est dur de mourir au printemps, tu sais / Mais j'pars aux fleurs la paix dans l'âme /Car vu que tu étais son amant /Je sais qu'tu prendras soin d´ma femme » ['It's difficult to die in the spring, you know /But I am leaving with peace in my soul /And because you were her lover /I know you will take good care of my wife'].

Brassens, Gainsbourg, and Vian also have in common political messages embedded in their original lyrics filled with humour, irony, and personal failures, as well as wordplay. The three of them seem to have no illusions about life, and see it 'as it is,' without sentimentality – they accept and reject it at once: 'Vian, wry and urbane, sang at the world with a cutting edge of sardonic disbelief.' [10]

Indeed, Boris Vian was a talented jazz musician (a trumpeter, which he had to forsake due to his ill health) and songwriter credited with the success of several Parisian jazz clubs such as Le Tabou. He founded the chorus called *La Petite Chorale de Saint-Germain-des-Pieds* – again demonstrating his penchant for irreverent wordplay – and also often wrote articles in jazz-related publications (such as *Jazz Hot*, to whose editorial board he belonged). Vian supported and helped launch Serge Gainsbourg's career. Vian had immediately recognized Gainsbourg's talent, and wrote a convincing article about him in *Le Canard enchaîné*, the satirical newspaper. Some of Vian's most famous songs include *C'est le be-bop*, sung by Henri Salvador (Salvador and Vian collaborated throughout the 1950s) as well as *Ah ! Si j'avais un franc cinquante* ['Oh, If I Only Had One Franc Fifty'], the anthem of the Le Tabou club. Vian's 1954 anti-war song *Le Déserteur* ['The Deserter'] – whose historical context was the battle of Dien Bien Phu – was banned until 1962 because of its strong anti-war message. It was initially interpreted by French singer Marcel Mouloudji and later, French singer/actor Serge Reggiani when he embarked upon his singing career, as well as many other anti-war protest singers throughout the world, such as the American folk trio Peter, Paul and Mary and singer Joan Baez. Yet, 'despite *Le Déserteur*, [Vian] didn't write "protest songs" so much as songs of satirical provocation, anarchic moralities…sly and worldly songs.' [11]

After his death, Boris Vian was canonized by young people in the 1960s and 1970s who idolized him; he was truly the guru of the young, and during the May 1968 revolution in France, his name became even more famous, particularly his song *Le Déserteur*, in which he addresses the president of France to tell him he would go to jail rather than go to war.

Vian was the 'Prince of Saint-Germain-des-Prés' [12] (indeed, he wrote a touristic guide entitled *Le Manuel de Saint-Germain-des-Prés*) at the time that Saint-Germain was Paris's intellectual district, where the likes of the unforgettable Barbara, Juliette Gréco, and Cora Vaucaire congregated, and where one could glance at Jean-Paul Sartre – whom Vian immortalizes as Jean-Sol Partre in *L'Écume des jour* – and Simone de Beauvoir, all of whom created their unforgettable masterpieces

in those days. In his *Manuel de Saint-Germain-des-Prés*, Vian, 'through a series of literary sketches…captures the essence of the beauties, philosophers, and the scenesters that shaped the Left Bank's boulevards and clubs…reading *Saint-Germain-des-Prés* feels like racing through its streets and nightclubs with Vian.' [13] Boris Vian also sang at Les Trois Baudets, a cabaret frequented by intellectuals, among others; this is where Serge Gainsbourg met Vian. Boris Vian will always be part of this pre-1968 Parisian scene of intellectuals, poets, singers, artists, and writers – and the post-1968 youth culture and rebellion against *les vieux poncifs*.

Vian was commemorated at the Colloque de Cerisy, with a colloquium dedicated to him that took place in July–August 1976, headed by Noël Arnaud and Henri Baudin, and attended by leading international Vian scholars and aficionados including Jenny Batlay, Gérard Durozoi, Michel Fauré, Guy Laforêt, Gilbert Pestureau, Michel Rybalka, and Jean-Pierre Vidal. The Cerisy proceedings were published in 1977 (previously, Arnaud edited a 1976 issue of *Obliques* dedicated to Vian). Although Cerisy sometimes holds colloques devoted to authors who are still alive, such as Roland Barthes, Régis Debray, and Francis Ponge, Vian was not there as he had passed away in 1959. Yet his presence was felt throughout the conference, as *maître de conférences* Arnaud – a living Vian encyclopedia who died in 2003 – carried Vian's torch very high: *canulars*, puns and plays on words, as well as an excursion to an *équarisseur de chevaux* [14] (in homage to *L'Équarissage pour tous*, Vian's farcical 1947 play set during the Allied liberation of France in 1944), were part of the Cerisy Vian colloquium. The published proceedings of the Vian Cerisy conference starts with Arnaud's essay « Boris Vian sauvé des veaux » [15] which is a play not only on Vian's famous castigation of the critical establishment when he declared, « Critiques, vous êtes des veaux ! » ['critics, you are cattle!'], but also on the title of Renoir's 1932 film, *Boudu sauvé des eaux /Boudu Saved from Drowning* (based on René Fauchois' play), itself referring to the biblical story of *Moïse sauvé des eaux*. This mise-en-abyme of the rescue of Moses, Boudu, and Vian raises the readers' awareness to the near-mythical yet farcical quality which is emblematic of Vian's œuvre: Vian treated the most serious and complex subject matter with this kind of *désinvolture* that is the true style of Saint-Germain-des-Prés where intellectual and artistic royalty mingled with students and American jazz musicians as well as the many other unique, unusual, and memorable characters who frequented this celebrated neighbourhood and its cafés, nightclubs, and theatres.

Although he was rejected by the critical establishment during his brief lifetime, after his death, Vian's lasting legacy has greatly impacted youth, film, musical, and literary culture in France and the United States. Vian was recently consecrated with one of the establishment's highest honours and tributes, a Pléaide edition of his complete works (two volumes, published in 2010), while a major exhibition devoted to him was held at the Bibliothèque Nationale de France (François-Mitterrand) in Paris in 2011–2012. Films treating Vian's relationship with cinema include the documentary

Le Cinéma de Boris Vian (Yacine Badday and Alexandre Hilaire, 2010) and the made-for-television biopic *V comme Vian /Vian was his Name* (Philippe Le Guay, 2011), starring Laurent Lucas.

Marcelline BLOCK
Princeton University and SAG-AFTRA

1. Julian Barnes, *Something to Declare: Essays on France and French Culture* (Vintage, 2003), Kindle file.

2. Ibid.

3. Jenny Batlay, 'Une chanson d'Hamour de Boris Vian: La valse dingue' in *Boris Vian de A à Z*, ed. Noël Arnaud, special edition of *Obliques* (no. 8-9, 1976): 319. Translation mine.

4. Paul Knobloch, Translator's note, Boris Vian, *The Manual of Saint-Germain-des-Prés* (Rizzoli, 2005), iv.

5. JKL Scott, '*J'irai cracher sur vos tombes*: A Two-Faced Translation,' in *On Translating French Literature and Film*, ed. Geoffrey Harris (Amsterdam: Rodopi, 1996), 215.

6. Ibid., 209.

7. Ibid., 215.

8. Roger Ebert, '*I Spit on Your Grave* (1980),' http://www.rogerebert.com/reviews/i-spit-on-your-grave-1980.

9. Carol J. Clover, *Men, Women and Chainsaws: Gender in the Modern Horror Film* (Princeton University Press, 1993), 115.

10. Julian Barnes, *Something to Declare*.

11. Ibid.

12. Tosh Berman, introduction, Boris Vian, *The Manual of Saint-Germain-des-Prés*, translated by Paul Knobloch (Rizzoli, 2005), iii.

13. Ibid, ii.

14. The place where horse carcasses are transformed into glue and other products, whose odour caused the august Cerisy congregants to hold their noses during the entire visit to the *équarisseur*.

15. Noël Arnaud, 'Boris Vian sauvé des veaux,' in Noël Arnaud and Henri Baudin, eds., *Centre Culturel International de Cerisy-la-Salle: Boris Vian I* (Paris: Union Générale d'Éditions, 1977), 9-21.

Jacques VILLERET (1951–2005)
[Mohammed BOUFROURA]

Unfinished
Sympathy

JACQUES VILLERET, born Mohammed Boufroura on February 6th 1951 in Tours, was a beloved supporting actor whose popularity never stopped growing from the early 1980s up until his death on January 28th 2005. His mother took her 9-year-old son nicknamed Jacky with her when she left his Algerian father and the child took the name of his stepfather, Raymond Villeret. His physical appearance as a podgy little chap, combined with a kind of naïve sincerity, was much appreciated and led him to act mostly in comic movies such as Jean Girault's *La Soupe aux choux /Cabbage Soup* (1981), Thomas Gilou's *Black mic mac* (1986), and Francis Veber's *Le Dîner de cons /The Dinner Game* in 1998. However he also agreed to act in a few dramatic films such as the recent *Vipère au poing /Viper in the Fist* (Philippe de Broca, 2004), and *Les Âmes grises / Grey Souls* (Yves Angelo, 2005). The latter offered him an unusual role as a gloomy judge. But in other dramatic films his comic features (general appearance, simplicity, artless look) stuck to the characters: for instance, in *Vipère au poing*, his natural kindness and sympathetic aspect were quite

convincing in the role of Monsieur Rézeau, the placid and powerless husband of a tyrannical mother played by Catherine Frot (nicknamed 'Folcoche' by her children). The 1987 movie *L'Été en pente douce* (dir. Gérard Krawczyk) offered him a role of an autistic character, a naturally naïve person whose condition was sad, but whose kindness and sincerity were refreshing and engendered a few comic situations within a rather dramatic movie: the character was mocked, but his simple and naïve reactions could sometimes de-dramatize his condition.

One of the most relevant roles as a naïve character was given to him in the comic film – directly adapted from the play in which he had appeared five years before its cinematic adaptation – *Le Dîner de cons*, in which he was supposed to be the dummy (le Con). In this film, a pair of arrogant, upper-middle class friends like to mock ordinary, naïve people by inviting them to a dinner during which they make a fool of them. Jacques Villeret was one such victim, but the audience understands that what appears to be his naïveté is in fact kindness, generosity, and sincerity, and that the dinner-game principle was, actually, the dumbest of all.

One of the roles that made him popular was *La Soupe aux choux* with Louis de Funès in which he played an extra-terrestrial landing on a farm; once again, he used his naïve aspect to enrich the character with a convincing lack of knowledge of terrestrial civilisation; but the more he learns, the more he understands, and even evolves hierarchically on his planet. In *Un crime au paradis /A Crime in Paradise* (Jean Becker, 2001), a remake of Sacha Guitry's *La Poison /Poison* (1951), Villeret plays the role of the husband (Michel Simon in the original version) looking for a cunning plan to kill his wife – who appears to be truly poisonous – by the least illegal means possible: paradoxically, in this film, the murderer seems less cruel than the victim. The audience is moved by the sensitivity of the husband and understands that his life is closer to Hell than to Heaven (« un crime au paradis »): the spectator is automatically on the side of the murderer who is a kind person. The naïve aspect of Villeret helps make us believe he was not a natural-born killer: not having a killer's instinct, he went to see an attorney claiming he had killed his wife, and with cunning questions, he managed to learn from the man of the law how to kill his wife and receive the lowest possible penalty.

His skills as an actor were recognized shortly after the start of his career, with a César Award in 1979 for Best Supporting Actor for his role in *Robert et Robert* (Claude Lelouch, 1978). He was always referred to as a comic actor, even though in real life he was rather shy. In a satirical movie about the French resistance, *Papy fait de la résistance /Gramps is in the Resistance* (Jean-Marie Poiré, 1983) the contrast of his image (naïve and sensitive) and of the role he incarnates (that of a German officer) created a comic effect. In *Effroyables jardins / Strange Gardens* (Jean Becker, 2003), he happened to be on the other side, that is to say, on the side of the Résistance which was threatened by the Nazis. Once again his characteristics brought a realistic and contrasting aspect to

his role: as a *résistant*, he did not really fit with the stereotype of a brave and fearless hero. He embodied rather a normal person with fears and ordinary cowardliness, the 'heroic' side of the character being simply his lack of collaboration (with the Nazis). In spite of being well-liked in the 1980s, it was more towards the end of his life that he came into demand by many filmmakers – between 1990 and 2000 he appeared in three plays, the first being Patrick Suskind's *La Contrebasse* (1981), a play characterised by a long monologue given by the single actor on stage. For this play he was nominated for the Molière Award. Sadly, among the mass of new films in which he acted, some of them were of low quality (*Iznogoud*, Patrick Braoudé, 2005; *L'Antidote*, Vincent de Brus, 2005), but as he appeared in these posthumously, they were relatively successful: indeed, people wanted to see him one last time. This post-mortem success showed definitively the real and unconditional popularity he could have enjoyed.

Igor BRATUSEK
Université Paris-Sorbonne

Jacques WEBER (1949–)

*Cyrano
on Stage
but Not
on Screen*

WITH HIS sturdy, stocky build and a charismatic personality, Jacques WEBER is a leading figure in theatre, born in 1949 in Paris. The character of Cyrano would stick to him his whole life on stage, a bit like Pierre Brasseur with the role of Frédérick from *Les Enfants du paradis /Children of Paradise* (Marcel Carné, 1945), the legend with whom he would begin his career on stage in the 1970s and who would become his mentor. Weber was destined to play *Cyrano* on the cinema screen. Fate alone had other plans.

Studying under François Florent, well-known for the courses of the same name which would open in 1967, he won first place at the *Conservatoire National d'art dramatique*. Along with the theatre, he made noteworthy appearances on screen partly due to his large size and physical beauty in his roles as seducer. In particular, we see him in *Raphaël ou le débauché* (Michel Deville, 1971); Costa-Gavras' *État de Siège /State of Siege* in 1972 alongside Yves Montand, *Le Malin Plaisir / Evil Pleasure* (Bernard Toublanc-Michel, 1975), and *Bel ami* in 1983 in an adaptation by Pierre Cardinal.

He burst onto the stage in 1983 when playing Edmond Rostand's *Cyrano de Bergerac* over a hundred times, directed by Jérôme Savary. At the last performance of *Cyrano* he threw his fake nose to the audience, only for fate to have it fall in the lap of Gérard Depardieu. The role of *Cyrano* for cinema was in fact first offered to Jacques Weber, but the day he celebrated getting the role, producer Gérard Lebovici was assassinated. From then on the project was abandoned and in the end it was Gérard Depardieu who would play *Cyrano* on screen.

It was in 1991 that Weber achieved recognition, winning the César for best supporting male for his interpretation of the Comte de Guiche, for lack of playing Cyrano, in Jean-Paul Rappeneau's screen adaptation of *Cyrano de Bergerac* in 1990.

In 2008, Jacques Weber directed Isabelle Adjani and his son Stanley in the telefilm *Figaro* where he played Count Almaviva.

Following in the footsteps of Dullin, Jouvet, and Pierre Brasseur, whom he fervently admires, Jacques Weber, during his lifetime, belongs in the hall of fame of classical theatre. He has a stage presence that fills the theatre with his aura, and is one of those theatrical voices, deep and distinct, that is unforgettable.

Michaël ABECASSIS
The University of Oxford

Lambert WILSON (1958–)

*Face
to
Faiths*

Dubbed the 'sexiest actor alive', Lambert WILSON has also expressed, through the distinctive warm timbre of his voice, the many facets of his talent and commitment, including repeated forays into ecological, social, political, and spiritual causes. Actor, director, singer, model, but also activist, Lambert Wilson is an *Officier des Arts et Lettres* and holds the highest French honour, the Légion d'Honneur. This multilingual and proteiform chameleon has now made this established versatility his trademark.

Born in 1958, Lambert Wilson is the son of Georges Wilson, a prominent actor who directed the Théâtre National Populaire. Hardworking and eager to prove his own theatrical abilities, Lambert Wilson graduated from the prolific Drama Centre in London in 1977 and soon played a leading role in Fred Zinneman's *Five Days One Summer* (1982), appeared in Peter Greenaway's *The Belly of an Architect* (1987), and a number of French television drama and feature films, among which his father's successful *La Vouivre* (1989). His sensitive portrayal of l'Abbé Pierre, a prominent French figure of generosity, and his work with famous

directors such as Claude Chabrol (*Le Sang des autres /The Blood of Others*, 1984), Andrzej Wajda (*Les Possédés / The Possessed*, 1988), and Carlos Saura (*El Dorado*, 1988), brought him international fame. The many facets of the characters he plays, Wilson claims, correspond to 7 to 9 characters he bears within himself which allow him to impersonate a pompous dandy just as well as a Trappist monk or Céline Dion.

Throughout the 1990s, Wilson also became well-known for his memorable and high-profile theatrical acting alongside confirmed stars such as Judi Dench (*A Little Night Music*), and his father (*Eurydice*). A director himself, Lambert Wilson successfully directed Alfred de Musset's *Les Caprices de Marianne*, Marivaux's *La Fausse Suivante* and Racine's *Bérénice*. But aside from this high-brow profile, Lambert Wilson does not deny himself the pleasure of popular culture. Indeed, his more intellectual experiences seem to feed off his crowd-pleasing roles and vice-versa – and that is precisely where his English and French experiences fully blend. While giving 'commercial works' the lightness of his talent, he also elegantly fills them with the serious work he puts in everything he touches: songs, comedies (Alain Resnais's *On connaît la chanson /Same Old Song*, 1997; Fabien Onteniente's *Jet Set*, 2000; Valérie Lemercier's *Palais royal !*, 2005; Victor Levin's 2014 romantic comedy *5 to 7*); sci-fi (Merovingian in the Wachowskis's *The Matrix* films; the 2014 short film *The Nostalgist* by Giacomo Cimini); cartoons (*Ernest et Célestine*, Stéphane Aubier, Vincent Patar, Benjamin

Renner, 2012), ads and even TV games subtly allow him to defend the causes he believes in. Half-way between Jean Anouilh's depictions of a grotesque society and Paul Claudel's cosmic mysticism, Lambert Wilson acts for and on the public whom he seduces by never fully revealing himself and always looking for *other* roles.

All at once studious, funny, and self-deprecating, Lambert Wilson is also a man of faiths. He actually calls himself a believer, but not in religion. Determined to surpass himself, he actively supports several causes such as the environment – he professes a passion for trees – and joined Greenpeace and Europe Écologie in 2009 in order to better fight against nuclear and oil policies. This commitment led him to chain himself to gates of the Prime Minister's official residence in 2002. Politically, he supported socialist women presidential candidates Ségolène Royal and Eva Joly, whom he praised for the intelligence of her visionary analyses. His fight for social fairness addressed issues such as same-sex parenting (*Comme les autres*, Vincent Garenq, 2008) or temporary show-business workers' rights (he read a letter to the Minister of Culture at the César ceremony in 2005). His concern for this material survival echoes his spiritual, although not religious, leanings. Indeed, he asked Abbé Pierre to baptize him and said he was changed after *Des hommes et des dieux /Of Gods and Men* (Xavier Beauvois, 2010) – if not religiously, then at least spiritually: 'I am a temporary faith-business worker.'

What he has the most faith in however is tireless work, attested by his flawless English (his first months in London were a total linguistic blur), and his meticulous voice training (a baritone, Lambert Wilson has sung Bernstein, Gershwin, Cole Porter, and Kurt Weil). He has directed actress Fanny Ardant in *Music Hall*, learned how to chant for *Of Gods and Men*, and lent his voice to the role of Ernest in *Ernest et Célestine* (which won the 2013 César for Best Animated Film and was nominated for the Oscar for Best Animated Film). He has demonstrated musical comedy skills, and overall leadership as a theatre and music-hall director, and as president of the Champs-Elysées Film Festival. There is now a wax statue of him at the Grévin museum.

His only lack of faith: himself ('I can't stand the fact that I can't stand myself, my constant self-flagellation'), but the underlying anxiety of this narcissistic, discreet, and humorous romantic has also been his best engine.

Marked by a Claudelian name (he was named after Lambert de Besme, a passionate noble and aching father figure), Lambert Wilson seems to rehearse, through his eclectic artistic trajectory an elusive, 'You ain't seen nothing yet' – which is, incidentally, the title of his latest Resnais film, *Vous n'avez encore rien vu /You Ain't Seen Nothin' Yet* (2012). We, spectators, have certainly already seen a lot, with more in his five appearances in films released in 2014. Keep the faiths, brother !

Noëlle ROUXEL-CUBBERLY
Bennington College, Vermont

Elsa ZYLBERSTEIN (1968–)

*The Shy
Seductress,
the
Chameleon
Actress*

WITH A prolific career of more than fifty films, Elsa ZYLBERSTEIN (born October 16, 1969 in Paris) inscribes herself within a line of contemporary, talented French actresses equally at ease in any role. She stands out for her graceful and expressive performances that always add rich complexity to her characters. Femininity, sensitivity, elegance, child-like innocence, and powerful acting are only a few words that describe Zylberstein.

Cultivating her early artistic inclination, Zylberstein studied classical dance and dramatic art and enjoyed her first cinema success when director Maurice Pialat cast her as the prostitute Cathy in *Van Gogh* (1991) earning her the Michel Simon prize and her first nomination for the César for Most Promising Actress. She incarnated the role of the muse several times. As a shy seductress and a beauty from another era, Zylberstein embodied the painter Suzanne Valadon, Toulouse-Lautrec's lover and inspiration in *Lautrec* (Roger Planchon, 1998). In 2004, the American filmmaker Mick Davis offered her the role of Jeanne Hébuterne in his critically contested and highly fictional biography,

Modigliani. Here, Zylberstein personified a powerful character, a young Catholic student who inspired the great painter (Andy Garcia) and who was castigated by her parents because of her relationship with the bohemian Jewish artist.

As an actress, Zylberstein reached the realm of international recognition once she began her collaboration with American and British directors. Having studied English, and then acting in New York, the actress was eager to perform in English-language films. In interviews, she has often shown her enthusiasm for working with Hollywood stars. Before filming *Modigliani*, she brought to life, with humour and intelligence, the character of Madame de Lafayette in James Ivory's *Jefferson in Paris* (1995). Later, in the literary adaptation and British drama *Metroland* (1997) by Philip Saville, she interpreted Annick, Chris' former French girlfriend. While Chris (Christian Bale) who has been married to Marion (Emily Watson) for ten years nostalgically recalls his love story with Annick, the atmosphere of the 1970s in Paris is recreated through flashbacks and music such as the Françoise Hardy song *Tous les garçons et les filles*. Probably in none of her other films has Zylberstein incarnated so perfectly the irresistibly chic French girl as in *Metroland*.

Far from forgetting her cultural origins, Zylberstein has inspired directors who create films that represent various aspects of Jewish culture. Her substantial collaboration with filmmaker Martine Dugowson resulted in the two vehicles in which Zylberstein delivers her most memorable performances: *Mina Tannenbaum* (1994) and *Les Fantômes de Louba* (2001). Both cinematic creations artistically convey an awareness of perpetually problematic Jewishness as a background for themes such as female friendship, identity crises, and a repressed past. In the first film, Zylberstein plays Ethel, a pretty young woman who becomes the jealous and unscrupulous friend of Mina (Romane Bohringer). Zylberstein's interpretation of the dually natured, good and evil Ethel, demonstrates once again her impeccable capacity to skilfully personify diverse characters. In the second film, the actress embodies Louba, a young Jewish woman whose parents disappeared during the Nazi occupation and who is haunted by memories of a traumatic childhood. With a high calibre performance, Zylberstein succeeds in expressing the complexity of a character struggling with understanding and accepting her past and who finally overcomes her own fears. Zylberstein appears in another film that references her Jewish cultural heritage, *Little Jerusalem* (2005) by Karin Albou. It tells the story of Laura (Fanny Valette) and Mathilde (Elsa Zylberstein), two Orthodox Tunisian sisters living in France with their Jewish migrant family, refugees fleeing the consequences of the Arab-Israeli war of 1967 in North Africa. Zylberstein's elegant interpretation of the elder sister who lives by strict religious rules marks the star's advancement to more mature roles.

One of Zylberstein's most complex performances has been her portrayal of Léa in *Il y a longtemps que je t'aime /I've Loved You so Long* (2008), Philippe Claudel's film drama that explores Léa's efforts to rebuild her relationship with her sister Juliette (Kristin Scott Thomas) after Juliette returns from prison. The film's focus on its characters and its mixture of a gloomy and sentimental atmosphere add depth to Zylberstein's role for which she received the César for Best Actress in a Supporting Role. Critics praised her for her acting in this film, which confirmed yet again her theatrical skills. The actress's numerous appearances on stage have inspired and completed her screen persona. She has had a presence on the theatre scene in numerous dramatic representations such as Luigi Pirandelli's *Six Characters in Search of an Author* (1997); Marcelle Sauvageot's *Commentaire* (2005), and Antoine Rault's *Le Démon de Hannah* (2009).

If comedy is one of the most difficult genres to film and play, Elsa Zylberstein, with her grace and capacity to express the tragicomic, to be funny even when she cries, is the perfect artist for it. In Jean-Jacques Zilbermann's *L'Homme est une femme comme les autres /Man Is a Woman* (1998), she incarnated Rosalie, an Orthodox Jewish woman married to Simon, a gay Klezmer musician, who marries her due to religious and family obligations. Zylberstein reprised her collaboration with Zilbermann ten years later in the sequel, *La Folle Histoire d'amour de Simon Eskenazy /He is my Girl* (2009).

As she declared in an interview for *Cahiers du cinéma* (no. 477, p. 101):

« fondamentalement, chacun a tout à l'intérieur, on possède toutes les émotions possibles et on est tout, potentiellement. On a mille facettes et il suffit d'en ouvrir quelques-unes plus spécifiquement en fonction des rôles »

['fundamentally, everyone already has everything on the inside, we possess all the necessary emotions and we are everything, potentially. We have a thousand facets and it suffices to just open a few of them more specifically depending on the role'].

The actress Elsa Zylberstein has demonstrated her infinite potential to interpret the most diverse roles while remaining an original, alluring screen presence.

Adela Lechintan-Siefer
The Ohio State University, Columbus

INDEX OF FILM TITLES

TITLES WITH INITIAL DIGITS

2 Days in New York   155
2 Days in Paris   155
3 amis   75
5 Fingers   145
5 to 7   397
7 p., cuis., s. de b.,... à saisir   301
*8×8, A Chess Sonata in 8
Movements*   125
*8 femmes
/8 Women*   v, 8, 44, 145, 261, 353
8½   257
*9 mois ferme
/Nine Month Stretch*   184, 245
15 août   218
*17 fois Cécile Cassard
/17 Times Cécile Cassard*   186
18 ans après /18 Years Later   74
*20 ans déjà /A Man
and a Woman: 20 Years Later*   58
*36 Quai des Orfèvres
/36 /36th Precinct*   21
*37°2 le matin
/Betty Blue*   139, 142, 271
99 francs   182
*100% cachemire
/The Ultimate Accessory*   143, 263
1492: Conquest of Paradise   165
1900   162
1986   326

A

Aaltra   330
*À bout de souffle
/Breathless*   48, 244, 357
*Absolument fabuleux
/Absolutely Fabulous*   43
*Abus de confiance
/Abused Confidence*   144

Accident   366
Acide aminé   353
À cœur ouvert /An Open Heart   60
*Adieu Berthe – l'enterrement de mémé
/Granny's Funeral*   10, 263
Adieu Gary /Goodbye Gary   28
*Adieu Philippine
/Farewell, Philippine*   326
*Adieu, poulet
/The French Detective*   172
A Doll's House   366
À double tour /Leda   247
Adrenalin: Fear the Rush   252
Agathe Cléry   263
A Good Year   133
*Ah ! Les Belles Bacchantes
/Peek-a-boo*   362
*Ah ! Si j'étais riche
/If I Were a Rich Man*   58, 135, 182
*Aimer, boire et chanter
/Life of Riley*   23
Akoibon   31
À l'abri des regards indiscrets   181
*À la folie...pas du tout /He Loves
Me...He Loves Me Not*   377
*À la petite semaine
/Nickel and Dime*   130
*À la place du cœur
/Where the Heart Is*   18
*À la vie, à la mort !
/Til Death Do Us Part*   17
*Alceste à bicyclette
/Bicycling with Molière*   276
*Alexandre le bienheureux
/Very Happy Alexander*   102, 344
Algiers   82
Ali Baba et les quarante voleurs   46
Alice et Martin   59
*Alice ou la dernière fugue /Alice or the
Last Escapade*   103, 187, 259
À l'intérieur /Inside   140
A Little Night Music   397
Allez France   102
Alliance cherche doigt   303
All This, And Heaven Too   83

Aloïse   366
À l'origine /In the Beginning   170
Alphaville   244
Alyse et Chloé /Alyse and Chloe   9
À ma soeur ! /Fat Girl   285
Amateur   237
Amélie   377, 378
À mort l'arbitre /Kill the Referee   296
Amour   237, 345, 347, 382
Amour et carburateur   335
An American Werewolf in Paris   155
And Then There Were None   24
Angèle   192
Angélique series   349
Anna   244
Anna Karenina   282
À nos amours /To our Loves   70
À nous deux /Us Two   22
Anthony Zimmer   283
Antichrist   214
Antoine Rives, juge du terrorisme   36
À perdre la raison /Our Children   12
Après la vie /After Life   208, 305
Après vous   22, 245
Ararat   25
Archimède, le clochard
        /The Magnificent Tramp   100, 101
Arch of Triumph   83
Arlette   21
Army of Shadows   369
Around the World in 80 Days   149
Arrête ton char...bidasse !   136
Arsène Lupin   225
Arsène Lupin contre Arsène Lupin
        /Arsène Lupin vs. Arsène Lupin   97
Arsène Lupin, Detective   55
À s' baraque /At One's House   73
Ascenseur pour l'échafaud
        /Elevator to the Gallows   97, 299
Assassins   364
Assassins et Voleurs /Lovers and
        Thieves   134, 332, 363
Associés contre le crime /Partners in
        Crime   188, 209
Astérix   164

Astérix et Obélix : Au service de sa
        majesté /Astérix and Obélix: God
        Save Britannia   31, 72, 242, 263
Astérix et Obélix aux jeux olympiques
        /Asterix at the Olympic Games   130
Astérix et Obélix : Mission Cléopâtre
        /Asterix and Obelix Meet
        Cleopatra   29, 113, 142, 147
Astérix : Le domaine des dieux
        3D   306
A Thousand Times Good Night   60
Atlantic City   326
Atomik circus, le retour de James
        Bataille
        /The Return of James Batalle   284
Attention aux yeux !
        /Let's Make a Dirty Movie   22
Attention une femme peut en cacher une
        autre ! /My Other Husband   297
Attila Marcel   250
Auberge espagnole trilogy   379
Au bout du conte
        /Under the Rainbow   28, 239
Au fil des ondes   178
Augustin roi du kung-fu
        /Augustin   135
Au Long de la rivière Fango   172
Au plus près du paradis
        /Nearest to Heaven   158
Au revoir les enfants   4, 50
Au siècle de Maupassant : Contes et
        nouvelles du XIXe siècle   297
Autour de minuit
        /'Round Midnight   121
À vendre /For Sale   16, 246

B

Babette s'en va-t-en guerre
        /Babette Goes to War   37, 63
Babylon A.D.   162
Baisers volés
        /Stolen Kisses   94, 254, 274, 365
Bancs publics (Versailles rive droite)
        /Public Benches   10

Bande à part
    /*Band of Outsiders*   88, 244
Banzaï   129
Barbe-Bleue   92
Barcarolle   195
Barnie et ses petites contrariétés   220,
    276
Barocco   163
Baxter, Vera Baxter   162, 366
Beaumarchais l'insolent
    /*Beaumarchais the Scoundrel*   36,
    223, 276, 303
Beau Père   172
Before Midnight   155
Before Sunrise   155
Before Sunset   155
Bel ami   396
Bellamy   162
Belle de jour   63, 158, 325
Belle toujours   325
Belphégor – le fantôme du Louvre
    /*Belphegor, Phantom of the
    Louvre*   36, 282
Benvenuti al sud
    /*Welcome to the South*   72
Beowulf   252
Bérénice   397
Bernadette Lafont, exactement   249
Bernie   184
Bête mais discipliné
    /*Dumb but Disciplined*   22
Bethsabée   287
Betty Blue   142
Betty Fisher   218
Betty Fisher et autres histoires
    /*Alias Betty*   245, 362
Bien agités !   36
Bienvenue à bord   263
Bienvenue chez les Ch'tis
    /*Welcome to the Sticks*   72
Bienvenue parmi nous
    /*Welcome Aboard*   295
Big Fish   133
Bimboland   223
Birds of a Feather   333

Birthday Girl   110
Black mic mac   394
Black Swan   110
Blah Blah Blah   155
Blanc comme neige /*White Snow*   122
Blanche et Marie
    /*Blanche and Marie*   293
Blank Generation   76
Blood Ties   99, 133
Bon anniversaire Juliette   86
Bonheur en location   102
Bonheur, impair et passe   35
Bonjour la chance   102
Bonjour Tristesse   357
Bonne chance Charlie
    /*Good Luck Charlie*   335
Bon voyage   261, 356
Borsalino   153
Borsalino and Co.
    /*Blood on the Streets*   153
Boudu   209
Boudu sauvé des eaux /*Boudu Saved
    from Drowning*   209, 372
Boum sur Paris   321
Branquignol /*Crazy Show*   102
Braveheart   282
Breathless   358, 359
Brève rencontre à Paris
    /*Two People*   42
Brice de Nice
    /*The Brice Man*   130, 181, 182
Brodeuses /*A Common Thread*   18
Buffet froid
    /*Cold Cuts*   65, 76, 77, 162, 364
*Butch Cassidy and the Sundance
    Kid*   79

C

Ca$h   130
Caché /*Hidden*   22, 59, 222
Cadavres exquis
    /*Illustrious Corpses*   387
Café de Flore   313
Café de Paris   55

Ça ira mieux demain
  /Tomorrow's Another Day   146
Callas Forever   8
Calmos /Femmes Fatales   284, 349
Camille Claudel   1, 50, 166
Camille Claudel 1915   60
Camping   362
Camping 2   362
Can-Can   118
Cap Canaille   141
Capitaine Conan   50
Carnages /Carnage   130
Carrefour /Crossroads   55
Cartacalha, reine des gitans   351
Cartouche /Swords of Blood   48, 349
Casablanca   137, 256, 257, 308
Casa de lava /Down to Earth   356
Casino Royale   225
Casque bleu /Blue Helmet   242, 263
Casque d'or
  /Golden Marie   341, 368, 369
Casse-tête chinois
  /Chinese Puzzle   149, 186, 379
Catch-22   138
Catch Me if You Can   43
Cat People   374
Cause toujours !   146
Cavale /On the Run   208
Cécile est morte
  /Cecile is Dead   335
Celles qu'on n'a pas eues   145
Celui qui doit mourir
  /He Who Must Die   258
César   206, 338
César et Rosalie
  /César and Rosalie   235, 298
Ces messieurs de la gâchette   136
Ces messieurs de la santé   339
C'est arrivé près de chez vous
  /Man Bites Dog   329, 330
C'est beau une ville la nuit /A City is
  Beautiful at Night   67, 69
C'est la vie   71
C'est le bouquet !
  /Special Delivery   146

Cet obscur objet du désir /That Obscure
  Object of Desire   75
Cette femme-là /Hanging Offense   33
Cette sacrée gamine /Naughty Girl   332
Ceux qui m'aiment prendront le train
  /Those Who Love Me Can Take the
  Train   382
Chacun sa chance
  /Everyman for Himself   211
Chanel solitaire   197
Changement d'adresse
  /Change of Address   19
Chaos   208, 272
Charade   25, 244
Charlotte Gray   204
Chateaubriand   36
Cherchez Hortense
  /Looking for Hortense   28
Cherchez l'idole /The Chase   296
Cheval de guerre /War Horse   12
Chicken Run   263
Chinese Puzzle   150
Chloe   165
Chocolat   59
Choisir d'aimer   46
Chotard et cie
  /Chotard and Company   361
Chouchou   190, 191
Christine   153
Ciao, les mecs /Ciao, You Guys   251
Cinema Paradiso   310
Circulez y'a rien à voir! /Move Along,
  There is Nothing to See   61
Clara et les chics types   269
Classe tous risques /The Big Risk   386
Cléo de 5 à 7 /Cleo from 5 to 7   244
Cliente   33, 34
Clouds of Sils Maria   60
Clubbed to Death (Lola)   140
Club de femmes   144
Cluny Brown   83
Cocktail Molotov   121
Coco   190, 191
Coco avant Chanel
  /Coco Before Chanel   331, 378

Code inconnu /Code Unknown 59

Cœur de lilas /Lilac 204

Cœurs /Private Fears in Public
Places 9, 23, 187

Combien tu m'aimes ?
/How Much do You Love Me? 162

Comme les autres 398

Comment j'ai tué mon père
/How I Killed my Father 78

Comment je me suis disputé…(ma vie
sexuelle)
/My Sex Life…or How I Got into
an Argument 4, 132, 170, 328

Comment réussir en amour
/How to Succeed in Love 296

Comment réussir quand on est con et
pleurnichard
/How to Make Good When One Is a
Jerk and a Crybaby 103, 174

Comme une image /Look At Me 239

Compartiment tueurs /The Sleeping Car
Murders 86, 249, 298, 325

Complices /Accomplices 170

Contagion 133

Contempt 37, 38, 326

Contre-enquête
/Counter Investigation 182

Copie conforme
/Certified Copy (2010) 60

Copie conforme
/Confessions of a Rogue (1947) 102

Coquecigrole 144

Correo 268

Cosmopolis 60

Coup d'éclat /Fabienne 210

Coup de foudre à Rhode Island
/Dan in Real Life 60

Coup de foudre /Entre Nous
/At First Sight 292, 293

Coup de tête /Hothead 145, 173

Coup de torchon
/Clean Slate 20, 296, 310

Cours privé 245

Cowboy 331

Cracks 226

Crésus /Croesus 192

Crooks in Clover 387

Cruel Intentions 316

Cuisine et Dépendances /Kitchen with
Apartment 28, 146, 238

Curse of the Cat People 374

Cyrano de Bergerac 163, 166, 245, 352

D

Daïnah la métisse 385

Dancer in the Dark 157

Dangerous Liaisons (1988) 316

Dangerous Liaisons (2012) 316

Daniel 54

Dans la maison /In the House 36, 276

Dans Paris /In Paris 186

Danton 166

Dark Shadows 226

David Golder 40, 41

Débats 1974-1981 36

De battre mon cœur s'est arrêté
/The Beat That My Heart
Skipped 12, 186

Décalage horaire /Jet Lag 60

Dédée d'Anvers /Dédée
/Woman of Antwerp 90, 368, 370

De Jeanne d'Arc à Philippe Pétain 125

De l'autre côté du lit
/Changing Sides 72

Delicatessen 175, 176

Demain les mômes
/Tomorrow's Children 44

Dernier été /Last Summer 17, 289,
290

De rouille et d'os /Rust and Bone 133

Derrière la façade 55

Descente aux enfers /Descent into
Hell 88, 282

Désengagement /Disengagement 60

Des hommes et des dieux
/Of Gods and Men 274, 398

Désordre 125

Des pissenlits par la racine
/Salad by the Roots 63, 363

Des poupées et des anges /Dolls and Angels 46

Des terroristes à la retraite /Terrorists in Retirement 369

Détective 42, 154, 230, 255, 359

Deux grandes filles dans un pyjama 216

Deux heures moins le quart avant Jésus-Christ /Quarter to Two Before Jesus Christ 364

Deux jours, une nuit /Two Days, One Night 133

Deux sous de violettes /Two Pennies Worth of Violets 79

Deux vies...plus une /Two Lives Plus One 143

Diabolique (see *Les Diaboliques*) 369

Diary of a Chambermaid 105

Didier 112

Diên Biên Phu 36

Dieu a besoin des hommes /God Needs Men 102

Dieu seul me voit /Only God Sees Me 327

Dieu vomit les tièdes 17, 290

Dinner for Schmucks 95, 209

Dirty Pretty Things 378

Diva 66, 142, 179

Divine 266

Divorce et fiançailles /Divorce and Engagement 18

Dobermann 111

Docteur Françoise Gailland 222

Docteur Petiot 364

Domicile conjugal /Bed and Board 94, 254

Don Camillo /The Little World of Don Camillo 193

Don Juan 75

Donnie Darko 253

Donovan's Reef /La Taverne de l'Irlandais 138

Double zéro /French Spies 29

Drôle de drame /Bizarre, Bizarre 39, 241, 372

Drôle de Félix /The Adventures of Felix 17

Du bleu jusqu'en Amérique /Blue Away to America 132

Du vent dans mes mollets /The Dandelions 239

E

Eastern Promises 110

Édith et Marcel 318

Edy 51

Effroyables jardins /Strange Gardens 278, 395

Églantine 98

El artisto y la modelo /The Artist and the Model 350

El Dorado 397

Elena et les hommes /Elena and Her Men 97, 280

Elisa 313

Elizabeth 110

Elle boit pas, elle fume pas, elle drague pas, mais... elle cause ! /She Does Not Drink, Smoke or Flirt, But... She Talks 103, 221

Elle cause plus... elle flingue /She No Longer Talks, She Shoots 103

Elle court, elle court la banlieue /The Suburbs Are Everywhere 291

Elle et moi /She and Me 102

Elle s'appelle Sabine /Her Name Is Sabine 71

Embrassez qui vous voudrez /Summer Things 61

En attendant Godot 35

En avoir (ou pas) /To Have (or Not) 245, 246

Encore /Once More 183

Enfants de salaud /Bastard Brood 122

Enfermés dehors /Locked Out 184

Ensemble c'est tout /Hunting and Gathering 99

Ensemble, c'est trop /Together Is Too Much 43

Ensemble nous allons vivre une très,
    très grande histoire d'amour 234
Entrée des artistes
    /The Curtain Rises 64, 241
Entre ses mains 331
Equinoxe 36
Ernest et Célestine 397, 398
Escale au soleil 193
Escale /Thirteen Days of Love 178
Escalier C 208
Espionne et tais-toi 35
Est-ce bien raisonnable ? 145
État de Siège
    /State of Siege 396
Et Dieu...créa la femme
    /And God Created Woman 37, 382
Et là-bas quelle heure est-il ?
    /What Time is it Over There? 255
Étoile sans lumière
    /Star Without Light 320, 321
Et si on vivait tous ensemble ?
    /All Together 344
Et ta soeur 97
Eugénie Grandet 103
Europa Europa 155
Eurydice 397
Exiles 186

F

Faisons un rêve
    /Let's Make a Dream 227
Fait-divers 14
Fanfan la Tulipe
    /Fan-Fan the Tulip 314, 315
Fanfare d'amour
    /Fanfare of Love 100
Fanny 116, 206, 338
Fantômas 151, 280, 343
Fatale /Damage 59
Fat Girl 285, 286
Father's Day 164
Faubourg 36
    /Paris 36 131, 303, 305, 307
Faustine et le bel été 235

Fauteuils d'orchestre /Avenue
    Montaigne 150, 184, 263
F comme Fairbanks 172
Feu ! 195
Feux rouges /Red Lights 147
Figaro 1, 396
Filles uniques
    /Only Girls 246, 380
Fils unique 99
Fin août, début septembre
    /Late August, Early September 260
First a Girl 100
Fitzcarraldo 174
Five Days One Summer 397
Flic ou Voyou /Cop or Hood 35, 48
Folies bourgeoises /The Twist 25
Folle embellie 293
Force majeure
    /Uncontrollable Circumstances 121
Fortress 252
Fortress 2 252
Fort Saganne 281
For Your Eyes Only 75
France boutique 223
François premier
    /Francis the First 193
François Villon 102
Franklyn 225
Frantic 359
Franz 95
Freak Orlando 366
Fred 51, 272
Frédérica 62
French Cancan 203, 212, 321
French Kiss 121
Freud, The Secret Passion 259
Fugueuses /Runaways 50

G

Gadjo Dilo
    /The Crazy Stranger 186
Gainsbourg (vie héroïque)
    /Gainsbourg: A Heroic Life 202,
    229, 302, 303, 306, 391

Gamines /Sisters   381
Gang de requins   353
Garde à vue /The Grilling   364, 387
Garden of Allah   83
Gaslight   82
Gaspard et Robinson
   /Gaspard and Robinson   142
Gazon maudit /French Twist   33, 113
Gendarme de Saint-Tropez   151
Généalogies d'un crime
   /Genealogies of a Crime   249
Génial, mes parents divorcent !   253
Gentlemen Prefer Blondes   138
Geography of the Heart   381
George et Fanchette   18
Georges et Georgette   100
Germinal   162, 164, 294
Ghost Rider: Spirit of Vengeance   253
Gibraltar   351
Gigi   116, 118, 309
Gil Blas de Santillane   35
Girl, La Fille de 15 ans
   /The 15 Year Old   223
Girls' Dormitory   373
Gloria   211
Godzilla   60, 343
Golden Eighties
   /Window Shopping   35
Golgotha /Behold the Man   195, 267
Gonzague   335
Goupi mains rouges
   /It Happened at the Inn   259, 268
Gouttes d'eau sur pierres brûlantes
   /Water Drops on Burning Rocks   353
Green Card   163, 167, 168, 169
Greystoke: The Legend of Tarzan, Lord
   of the Apes   251
Gribouille   307
Grosse fatigue /Dead Tired   61, 213
Grossesse nerveuse /False Pregnancy   17
Guernica   107
Gueule d'amour /Lady Killer   211
Gunman in the Streets   368
Gunmen   252

H

Habemus Papam
   /We Have a Pope   327
Hamlet   162
Happy Feet   131
Harry, un ami qui vous veut du bien
   /With a Friend Like Harry...   362
Hasards ou coïncidences
   /Chance or Coincidence   10
Haute tension
   /High Tension   149
Heaven's Gate   237
Hélas pour moi
   /Oh, Woe is Me   162
Hellphone   182
Henri IV, le bien aimé   36
Hereafter   150
Heureux anniversaire
   /Happy Anniversary   104
Heureux qui comme Ulysse...
   /Happy He Who Like Ulysses   193
Hieronymus Bosch   109
Highlander   252
Highlander II: The Quickening   252
Highlander III   252
Highlander: Endgame   252
Hiroshima mon amour   105, 345, 346,
   347
Histoire de Piera   237
Histoire(s) du cinéma   108
Holy Motors   326, 356
Hommes, femmes, mode d'emploi
   /Men, Women, A User's Manual   10
Hors de prix
   /Priceless   190
Hors-la-loi
   /Outlaws   130
Hôtel des Amériques
   /Hotel America   173
Hôtel du Nord   13, 64, 241
Hotel Rwanda   343
Humour noir
   /Black Humour   92

I

I...comme Icare /I as in Icarus   298

Icon   99

*Identificazione di una donna
    /Identification d'une femme
    /Identification of a Woman*   86

Il buon soldato   35

Il gattopardo /The Leopard   153, 341

Il postino /Il Postino: The Postman   310

Il reste du jambon ?   46

*Ils se marièrent et eurent beaucoup
    d'enfants /...And They Lived
    Happily Ever After*   213

*Il y a des jours...et des lunes
    /There Were Days...and Moons*   141

*Il y a longtemps que je t'aime
    /I've Loved You so Long*   400

Images   86

Impardonnables /Unforgivable   76, 188

*Impasse des deux anges
    /Dilemma of Two Angels*   288

Inception   133

*Inch'allah dimanche
    /Inch'Allah Sunday*   362

India Song   366

Indigènes /Days of Glory   148

Indochine   158

Innocents   224

*Inspecteur la Bavure
    /Inspector Blunder*   129

Inspecteur Lavardin   333

Intouchables /The Intouchables   123

*IP5 : L'île aux pachydermes
    /IP5: The Island of Pachyderms*   299

Irène   149

Irma Vep   255

Irréversible   III, 184

I Spit on Your Grave   390, 391

Itinéraire bis   46

*Itinéraire d'un enfant gâté /Itinerary of
    a Spoiled Child*   6, 48, 49

I Want to Go Home   162

Iznogoud   395

J

Jack and Jill   191

*J'ai épousé une ombre
    /I Married a Dead Man*   42

J'ai pas sommeil /I Can't Sleep   208

*J'ai toujours rêvé d'être un gangster /I
    Always Wanted to be a Gangster*   30

Jaloux comme un tigre   135

*Jane B. par Agnès V.
    /Jane B. for Agnès V.*   213

Jane Eyre   213

Jappeloup   99, 235

*J'aurais voulu être un danseur
    /Gone for a Dance*   150

Jean de Florette   22, 162, 164, 299

*Jeanne Dielman, 23 Quai du
    Commerce, 1080 Bruxelles*   366

*Jeanne et le garçon formidable
    /Jeanne and the Perfect Guy*   260

Jeanne la Pucelle   70, 71

Jean-Philippe   275

Jefferson in Paris   399

J'embrasse pas /I Don't Kiss   44, 309

*Je ne sais rien mais je dirai tout
    /Don't Know Anything But I'll Tell
    All*   344

Jenny   335, 336, 385

*J'enrage de son absence
    /Maddened by his Absence*   71

Jenseits der Stille /Beyond Silence   379

Je préfère qu'on reste amis   222

*Je rentre à la maison
    /I'm Going Home*   326

*Je suis timide mais je me soigne
    /Too Shy to Try*   344

*J'étais une aventurière
    /I was an Adventuress*   195

Je te mangerais /You Will be Mine   356

Jet Set   397

*Jeux d'enfants
    /Love Me If You Dare*   99, 133

Jeux interdits /Forbidden Games   197

*Je veux rentrer à la maison
    /I Want to go Home*   352

Je vous aime /I Love You All   162
Je vous salue, Marie /Hail Mary   59
*Je vous trouve très beau
    /You Are So Beautiful*   61
*J'irai cracher sur vos tombes
    /I Spit on Your Graves*   390
Joan of Arc   357
Joan of Arc of Mongolia   366
Joan of Paris   308
*Johnny Doesn't Live Here Any
    More*   374
*Jonah qui aura 25 ans en l'an 2000
    /Jonah Who Will Be 25 in the Year
    2000*   292
Jo /The Gazebo   216
Jour de fête   375, 376
Joyeuses Pâques   282
Joyeux Noël /Merry Christmas   72, 99
Judex   355
Jules et Jim   165, 250, 299, 300
Julie pot de colle /Julie Gluepot   98
Jurassic Park   59
*Juste avant la nuit
    /Just Before Nightfall*   20, 79, 103
Justine   3, 309
Just Visiting   343

K

*Kaena, la prophétie
    /Kaena: The Prophecy*   323
Kamikaze   68
Karnaval   130
Katia   144
Killing Zoe   155
Ki lo sa ?   17, 146
Kingdom of Heaven   225
King of Kung-Fu   135
Kitchendales   297
Knock   102, 241
*Knock, ou le triomphe de la
    médecine*   241
Kung Fu Panda   10
Kuroe /[Chloe]   389

L

*La Baie des anges
    /Bay of Angels*   300
La Balance /The Nark   42, 50, 58
*La Bande à Bonnot
    /Bonnot's Gang*   94
*La Bande des quatre
    /The Gang of Four*   183
*La Bandera
    /Escape from Yesterday*   211, 267, 351
La Banquière /The Lady Banker   269
La Baraka   141
La Bataille silencieuse   206
La Baule-les-Pins /C'est la vie   43
*La Beauté du diable
    /Beauty and the Devil*   372
La Belle Américaine   102, 363
*La Belle Équipe
    /They Were Five*   211, 351, 385
*La Belle et la Bête
    /Beauty and the Beast*   124, 279
*La Belle Histoire
    /The Beautiful Story*   141, 142, 272
La Belle Marinière   211
La Belle Noiseuse   44, 326
La Belle verte   272
*La Bergère et le ramoneur /The Curious
    Adventures of Mr Wonderbird*   341
La Bête humaine   101, 211, 258, 259,
    373, 374, 375
La Bigorne, caporal de France   102
La Boîte aux rêves   368
La Boîte noire /The Black Box   58
*La Bonne Année
    /Happy New Year*   387
La Bostella   31
La Boum /The Party   70, 66, 88, 219,
    281, 282
La Boum 2   70, 197, 281
La Bourse et la Vie   102
La Brigade /The Brigade   197
La Bûche /Season's Beatings   146, 213
La Cage aux folles   89, 333, 363
La Cage aux folles II   86, 333

La Cage aux folles III – 'Elles' se
    marient /La Cage aux Folles 3: The
    Wedding   333
La Californie /French California   354
La Captive
    /The Captive   379, 380, 381
La Carapate   344
L'Accompagnatrice
    /The Accompanist   68
La Cérémonie   71, 236, 260
La Chambre des magiciennes
    /Of Woman and Magic   356
La Chambre des officiers
    /The Officers' Ward   188, 328
La Chambre verte
    /The Green Room   42
La Chartreuse de Parme /The
    Charterhouse of Parma   108, 315
La Chasse à l'homme /Male Hunt   363
La Chèvre /The Goat   162, 344, 345
La Chienne   351
La Chienne /The Bitch   372
La Chinoise   254
La ciociara /Two Women   132
La Cité de la peur
    /Fear City: A Family-Style
    Comedy   112, 143, 263, 297
La Cité des enfants perdus
    /The City of Lost Children   175, 383
La Clef /The Key   270
La Communion solennelle
    /Solemn Communion   16
La Comtesse /The Countess   155
La Conquête /The Conquest   328
La Coquille et Le Clergyman
    /The Seashell and the Clergyman   14
La Course de lièvre à travers les champs
    /And Hope to Die   44
La Crise   272
La Cuisine au beurre /My Wife's
    Husband   80, 193
La Dame aux camélias
    /Camille   53, 206
L'Addition   66
La Délicatesse /Delicacy   378

La Demoiselle d'honneur
    /The Bridesmaid   278
La Dentellière
    /The Lacemaker   23, 236
La Dernière Femme
    /The Last Woman   162
La Dérobade
    /Memoirs of a French Whore   11
La Désenchantée
    /The Disenchanted   223
Ladies in Love   373
La Différence, c'est que c'est pas
    pareil   51
La Dilettante   208
La Discrète /The Discreet   276
La Disparue de Deauville
    /Trivial   282
La dolce vita   3
L'Adolescente /The Adolescent   35
La Doublure
    /The Valet   72, 95, 190, 261
La Duchesse de Langeais
    /Wicked Duchess   195
L'Adversaire /The Adversary   121, 218
Lady Chatterley   233, 235
Lady Jane   18, 290
La Fausse Suivante   245, 397
La Faute d'orthographe   257
La Femme d'à côté /The Woman Next
    Door   7, 8, 163, 165
La Femme de chambre du Titanic /The
    Chambermaid on the Titanic   69
La Femme de mon pote /My Best
    Friend's Girl   269
La Femme du boulanger
    /The Baker's Wife   338
La Femme d'une nuit   15
La Femme en bleu
    /The Woman in Blue   375
La Femme flic /The Woman Cop   11
La Femme infidèle
    /The Unfaithful Wife   79
La Femme Nikita /Nikita   342
La Femme qui pleure au chapeau
    rouge   18

La Ferme du pendu
/Hangman's Farm 80
L'Affaire des poisons
/The Case of Poisons 287
L'Affaire est dans le sac
/It's in the Bag 101
L'Affaire farewell /Farewell 11
L'Affaire Marcorelle
/The Marcorelle Affair 255
L'Affaire Sacha Guitry 36
La Fiancée du pirate
/A Very Curious Girl 249
La Fidélité /Fidelity 233, 282, 356
La Fièvre monte à El Pao
/Fever Mounts at El Pao 316
La Fille coupée en deux
/The Girl Cut in Two 51, 278
La Fille de d'Artagnan /Revenge of the
Musketeers 281, 310
La Fille de l'eau 90
La Fille de Monaco
/The Girl from Monaco 21
La Fille de Paris
/The Girl from Paris 362
La Fille d'un soldat ne pleure jamais
/A Soldier's Daughter Never
Cries 260
La Fille du puisatier /The Well-Digger's
Daughter 22, 192, 338, 339
La Fille du RER
/The Girl on the Train 158
La Fille seule /A Single Girl 260, 278
La Fille sur le pont
/The Girl on the Bridge 22, 313
La Fine Combine 194
La Fleur du mal
/The Flower of Evil 43, 278
La Folie des grandeurs /Delusions of
Grandeur 151, 152, 299
La Folle Histoire d'amour de Simon
Eskenazy /He is my Girl 400
La France 380
L'Africain /The African 35
La Garçonne /The Tomboy 319
La Gifle /The Slap 57

La Grande Bouffe
/The Big Feast 63, 309, 326
La Grande Illusion /Grand Illusion
90, 100, 137, 204, 205, 206, 211
La Grande Lessive /The Big Wash 63
La Grande Peur de Monsieur
Clément 94
La Grande Vadrouille
/Don't Look Now...We're Being Shot
At! 80, 81, 151, 152
L'Agression /Act of Aggression 22
La Guerre des boutons
/War of the Buttons 215
La Guerre des gosses 24
La Guerre des polices /The Police
War 88, 89
La Haine /Hate 109, 110, 111, 278
La Honte de la famille 216
L'Aile ou la Cuisse /The Wing or the
Thigh 129, 151, 152
L'Air de Paris /Air of Paris 13
Laissez-passer /Safe Conduct 328
Laissons Lucie faire ! 220
La Journée de la jupe /Skirt Day 1
La Jument verte /The Green Mare 63,
81, 101
La Lectrice /The Reader 108, 294
L'Alibi /The Alibi 335
La Lune dans le caniveau
/The Moon in the Gutter 162
La Lune et le téton
/La teta y la luna 143
La Madelon 102
La Main du diable
/Carnival of Sinners 207
La Maison de Nina 239
La Maison du bonheur 72
La Maison du Maltais
/Sirocco 137, 351
La Maison sous la mer 2
La Maladie de Sachs
/Sachs' Disease 184
La Malibran 125
La Maman et la Putain /The Mother
and the Whore 204, 248, 255

*La Marche de l'Empereur
/The March of the Penguins* 69

*La Mariée était en noir /The Bride
Wore Black* 79, 161, 250, 299

La Marseillaise 101

*La Meilleure Façon de marcher
/The Best Way to Walk* 172

La Meilleure Part /The Best Part 86

La Menace 35

L'Américain /The American 86

La Meute /The Pack 302

*L'Ami de la famille
/A Friend of the Family* 97

L'Ami Giono: Jofroi de la Maussan 17

La Môme /La Vie en Rose 131, 132,
163, 166, 180, 203, 319, 367

La Mort dans l'île 198

*La Mort en ce jardin
/Death in the Garden* 325

*L'Amour à mort
/Love Unto Death* 8, 9, 23, 187

L'Amour à vingt ans /Love at 20 254

L'Amour braque 282

*L'Amour dure trois ans
/Love Lasts Three Years* 263

*L'Amour en douce
/Love on the Quiet* 44

*L'Amour en fuite
/Love on the Run* 94, 254

*L'Amour par terre
/Love on the Ground* 187

L'Amour violé /Rape of Love 9

La Moustache 272

La Moutarde me monte au nez 344

La Musica 366

L'An 01 /The Year 01 119

Landru /Bluebeard 160, 161

*L'Anglaise et le Duc
/The Lady and the Duke* 175

*L'Année dernière à Marienbad
/Last Year at Marienbad* 105, 365

L'Année des méduses 359

*L'Année prochaine si tout va bien /Next
Year if it All Goes Well* 269

L'Année sainte /Holy Year 97

L'Année suivante 18

La noche oscura 154

La Note bleue 282

La notte /The Night 299

La Nouvelle Eve /The New Eve 208

*La Nouvelle Guerre des boutons
/War of the Buttons* (2011) 303

L'Antidote 395

*La Nuit américaine
/Day for Night* 42, 254, 255

*La Nuit de Varennes
/That Night in Varennes* 39, 98

*La Partie d'échecs
/The Chess Game* 344

La Passion Béatrice /Beatrice 154

La Patronne /The Patron 102

*La Petite Apocalypse
/The Little Apocalypse* 188

*La Petite Lili
/Little Lili* 168, 218, 353

La Petite Voleuse /The Little Thief 213

*La Pianiste
/The Piano Teacher* 222, 237

L'Apiculteur /The Beekeeper 341

*La piel que habito
/The Skin I Live In* 92

La Piste du sud 335

*La Plus Belle Soirée de ma vie
/The Most Wonderful Evening of My
Life* 91

La Pointe Courte 309

La Poison /Poison 372, 395

*La Possibilité d'une île
/Possibility of an Island* 278

*L'Appartement
/The Apartment* (1996) 69, 110

L'Appât /Fresh Bait 50, 58

L'Apprentissage de la ville 17

*La Princesse de Clèves
/Princess of Cleves* 280

La Question 217

*La Question humaine
/Heartbeat Detector* 5

La Rafle /The Round Up 191, 343

L'Arbalète /The Syringe 22

L'Arbre de Nöel
    /The Christmas Tree   81
La Règle du jeu /The Rules of the
    Game   90, 101, 137, 138, 374, 375
La Reine Margot
    /Queen Margot   1, 98
La Religieuse /The Nun   244
La Révolution française   35
L'Argent   15, 55
L'Argent des autres
    /Other People's Money   364
L'Argent fait le bonheur
    /Money Makes Happiness   17
La Ritournelle /Paris Follies   237
L'Armée des ombres
    /Army of Shadows   288, 369, 386
L'Armoire volante
    /The Cupboard was Bare   193
L'Arnacœur /Heartbreaker   186, 313
La Ronde /Circle of Love   145, 244,
    315, 341, 368
La Route de Corinth
    /Who's Got the Black Box   79
La Route joyeuse   197
L'Art d'aimer
    /The Art of Love   19, 223
L'Art (délicat) de la séduction   58, 149
La Rupture /The Breach   79, 103
L'As des as /Ace of Aces   48
La Sirène du Mississippi
    /Mississippi Mermaid   158
La Sonate à Kreutzer   97
La Soupe aux choux /Cabbage
    Soup   151, 152, 394
La Source des femmes /The Source   47
L'Assassinat du Père Noël
    /Who Killed Santa Claus?   41, 267
L'Assassin habite...au 21 /The Murderer
    Lives at Number 21   207
La strada   203
Last Tango in Paris   255
La Symphonie fantastique
    /The Fantastic Symphony   39
La Symphonie pastorale
    /Pastoral Symphony   308

L'Atalante   372
La Tête contre les murs
    /Head Against the Wall   24, 92, 354
La Tête d'un homme
    /A Man's Neck   40
La tigre e la neve   343
L'Atlantide
    /Missing Husbands
    or Lost Atlantis   257
La Totale ! /The Jackpot!   270, 297
La Tour de Nesle
    /The Tower of Lust   79
La Tourneuse de pages
    /The Page Turner   208
La Tour, prends garde !
    /King on Horseback   254
La Traversée de Paris
    /Four Bags Full   81, 151
La Truite /The Trout   237
L'Auberge espagnole /The Spanish
    Apartment   149, 186, 223
L'Auberge rouge
    /The Red Inn   101, 193
Laurence Anyways   43
Lautrec   399
L'Auvergnat et l'autobus   102
La Vache et le Prisonnier
    /The Cow and I   193
La Valise /Man in the Trunk   284
L'Avare /The Miser   151, 216
La Vengeance d'une femme
    /A Woman's Revenge   236
L'Aventure, c'est l'aventure /Money,
    Money, Money   95, 160, 230
La Vérité ou presque
    /True Enough   122
La Vérité si je mens
    /Would I Lie to You?   6, 67
La Vérité si je mens ! 2
    /Would I Lie to You? 2   6, 190
La Vérité si je mens ! 3   6
La Vérité /The Truth   37, 259
L'Aveu /The Confession   298
La Veuve de Saint-Pierre
    /The Widow of Saint-Pierre   59

La Victoire en chantant (noirs et blancs en couleurs)
  /*Black and White in Color*   103
La Vie à l'envers
  /*Life Upside Down*   160
La Vie de château
  /*A Matter of Resistance*   92
La Vie de famille /Family Life   59
La Vie d'une autre
  /*Another Woman's Life*   60, 381
La Vie en Rose   203, 319
La Vie est un long fleuve tranquille
  /*Life is a Long Quiet River*   278
La Vie est un roman
  /*Life is a Bed of Roses*   9, 23, 187
La Vie et rien d'autre
  /*Life and Nothing But*   310, 311
La Vie, l'amour, la mort
  /*Life Love Death*   86
La Vie politique des Belges   331
La Vie séparée   35
La Ville est tranquille
  /*The Town is Quiet*   18, 290
L'Avion   272
La Voie lactée
  /*The Milky Way*   105, 355, 365
La Vouivre   397
La Voyante /The Clairvoyant   54

LE–

Le affinità elettive /Les Affinités électives /Elective Affinities   237
L'Eau à la bouche
  /*A Game for Six Lovers*   247
L'Eau froide /Cold Water   260
Le Bal   144
Le Bar de la fourche /The Bar at the Crossing   95, 141, 235
Le Baron fantôme
  /*The Phantom Baron*   125
Le Beatnik et le Minet   162
Le Beau Mariage
  /*A Good Marriage*   187
Le Beau Serge
  /*Handsome Serge*   97, 247

Le Bonheur est dans le pré
  /*Happiness is in the Field*   23, 296, 297, 303, 364
Le Bossu (1959)   81, 265
Le Bossu /On Guard (1997)   21, 220
Le Boucher /The Butcher   20
Le Camion /The Lorry   162
Le Candidat /The Candidate   12
Le Capitaine Fracasse
  /*Captain Fracasse*   279, 349
Le Capital   191
Le Caporal épinglé
  /*The Elusive Corporal*   89, 102
Le Carrefour des enfants perdus
  /*Children of Chaos*   341
Le Cavaleur   218
Le Cercle rouge /The Red Circle   153
Le Cerveau /The Brain   81
Le Chandelier   35
L'Échange /The Exchange   39
Le Charme discret de la bourgeoisie
  /*The Discreet Charm of the Bourgeoisie*   325, 365
Le Chat du rabbin
  /*The Rabbi's Cat*   303, 306
Le Château des singes
  /*A Monkey's Tale*   323
Le Chat et la Souris
  /*Cat and Mouse*   341
Le Chat /The Cat   369
Le Choc /Contract in Blood   157
Le Ciel est à vous
  /*The Woman Who Dared*   385
Le Ciel, les oiseaux...et ta mère !
  /*Boys on the Beach*   147
Le Cinéma de Boris Vian   393
Le Clan des siciliens
  /*The Sicilian Clan*   153, 212
L'Éclipse /The Eclipse   153
Le Code a changé
  /*Change of Plans*   72, 234
L'École de la chair
  /*The School of Flesh*   50, 271, 285
L'École des facteurs
  /*The School for Postmen*   375

Le Colonel Chabert /Colonel
    Chabert 276, 338
Le Comte de Monte-Cristo /The Count
    of Monte-Cristo 279
Le Concierge 136, 216
Le Convoyeur /Cash Truck 182, 184
Le Corbeau /The Raven 205, 207
Le Corniaud
    /The Sucker 80, 81, 151, 152
Le Cou de la girafe
    /The Giraffe's Neck 70
Le Coup du Berger 97
Le Courage d'aimer 10
Le Cousin 114
Le Créateur /The Creator 184
Le Cri du cormoran le soir au-dessus des
    jonques /Cry of the Cormoran 103
Le Crime de Monsieur Lange /The
    Crime of Monsieur Lange 40, 55
Le Crime est notre affaire /Crime Is
    Our Business 188, 208, 209
L'Écume des jours /Mood Indigo
    (2013) 187, 191, 379, 389
L'Écume des jours /Spray of the Days
    (1968) 389
Le Déménagement 72
Le Dernier Combat
    /The Last Battle 342
Le Dernier Métro
    /The Last Metro 158, 163, 333
Le Dernier Vol /The Last Flight 133
Le Derrière /From Behind 263
Le Deuxième Souffle
    /Second Breath 86, 288, 386
Le Diable au corps
    /Devil in the Flesh 375
Le Diable et les dix commandements
    /The Devil and the Ten
    Commandments 24
Le Diable par la queue
    /The Devil by the Tail 283, 349
Le Diner 220
Le Diner de cons /The Dinner
    Game 95, 208, 209, 270, 394
Le Distrait /The Daydreamer 344

Le Divorce 270
Le Doulos 325, 341
Le Drapeau noir flotte sur la marmite
    /The Black Flag Waves Over the
    Scow 103
Le Duel 206
Le Duel d'Hamlet 53
Le Fabuleux Destin d'Amélie Poulain
    /Amélie v, 188, 204, 302, 377
Le Fantôme de la liberté
    /The Phantom of Liberty 325, 349
Le Farceur /The Joker 2
Le Far-West /Far West 95
Le Faux-cul /The Phoney 141
Le Festin de Babette
    /Babette's Feast 20
L'Effrontée
    /An Impudent Girl 213, 249
Le Fils de l'autre
    /The Other Son 170
Le Fou du labo 4
    /The Madman of Lab Four 363
Le Futur est femme
    /The Future is Woman 11
Le Gai Savoir /Joy of Learning 254
Le Gamin au vélo
    /The Kid with a Bike 150
Le Garçu 162
Le Gendarme à New York
    /The Troops in New York 216
Le Gendarme de Saint-Tropez
    /The Troops of St. Tropez 215
Le Gendarme en balade
    /The Troops on Vacation 216
Le Gendarme et les Extra-terrestres
    /The Troops & Aliens 216
Le Gendarme et les Gendarmettes
    /The Troops & Troop-ettes 151, 216
Le Gendarme se marie
    /The Troops Get Married 216
Le Genou de Claire
    /Claire's Knee 98, 276
Le Gigolo /The Gigolo 98
Le Gitan /The Gypsy 86
Légitime violence 89

Le Gorille vous salue bien
  /The Gorilla Greets You   386
Le Goût des autres   239
Le Goût des autres
  /The Taste of Others   28, 239
Le Grand Appartement   303
Le Grand Blond avec une chaussure
  noire /The Tall Blond Man with One
  Black Shoe   65, 103, 344
Le Grand Carnaval   58
Le Grand Chemin
  /The Grand Highway   66
Le Grand Jeu   385
Le Grand Meaulnes
  /The Wanderer   197
Le Grand Pardon   27, 58, 142
Le Grand Pardon 2   58, 142
Le Grand Restaurant
  /What's Cooking in Paris   152
Le Grand Restaurant II   297
Le Grand Soir   330, 331
Le Guignolo   49
Le Havre   147
Le Hérisson /The Hedgehog   18, 33
Le Hussard sur le toit /The Horseman
  on the Roof   10, 59, 121
Le Joli Mai   244
Le Jouet /The Toy   79
Le Joueur de violon
  /The Violin Player   58
Le Jour et l'heure
  /The Day and the Hour   86
Le Journal d'une femme de chambre
  /Diary of a Chambermaid   105,
  299, 325
Le Jour se lève
  /Daybreak   13, 56, 64, 211
Le Juge et l'Assassin
  /The Judge and the Assassin   98,
  216, 236, 242
Le Juge Fayard, dit le Shérif /Judge
  Fayard Called the Sheriff   173
Le Juif errant   14
L'Élégance du hérisson /The Elegance of
  the Hedgehog   18, 33

Le Lieu du crime
  /Scene of the Crime   145
Le Lièvre de Vatanen
  /Vatanen's Hare   253
Le Lit à colonnes   258
Le Magnifique
  /The Man from Acapulco   49
Le Magot de Josefa /Josefa's Loot   92
Le Maître d'école   129
Le Malin Plaisir /Evil Pleasure   396
Le Mardi à Monoprix   176
Le Mariage de Figaro   35
Le Mas des alouettes
  /The Lark Farm   188
Le Masque de fer
  /The Iron Mask   280, 349
Le Meilleur de la vie
  /A Better Life   70
Le Mépris /Contempt   37, 325
Le Mille-pattes fait des claquettes   216
Le Miracle des loups
  /Blood on his Sword   39
Le Miraculé   333
Le Miroir à deux faces   81
Le Misanthrope   36
L'Emmerdeur
  /A Pain in the Ass   58, 95, 261
Le Moustachu
  /The Field Agent   349
Le Mouton enragé
  /Love at the Top   35
Le Mur de l'Atlantique
  /Atlantic Wall   333
Le Mystère de la chambre jaune
  /The Mystery of the Yellow
  Room   10, 328
L'Enfer /Hell   44, 121, 220
L'Ennemi intime
  /Intimate Enemies   278
L'Ennemi public n°1
  /Mesrine: Public Enemy #1   5, 111
Le Nombril du monde   75
Le Nouveau Protocole
  /The New Protocol   130
Léon /The Professional   342

Léon Morin, prêtre
    /Léon Morin, Priest   48, 346
Le Pacha /Pasha   212
Le Pacte des loups
    /Brotherhood of the Wolf   110, 356
Le Parfum de la dame en noir
    /The Perfume of the Lady in
    Black   10, 328
Le Passager de la pluie
    /Rider on the Rain   323
Le Passe-muraille
    /Mister Peek a Boo   81
Le Pavillon brûle   102
Le Pays d'où je viens
    /The Country I Come From   86
Le Père Noël a les yeux bleus
    /Santa Claus has Blue Eyes   254
Le Père Noël est une ordure /Santa
    Claus is a Stinker   32, 242, 269
Le Péril jeune   185, 186
Le Péril jeune /Good Old Daze   185
Le Petit Criminal
    /The Little Gangster   6
Le Petit Lieutenant
    /The Young Lieutenant   43
Le Petit Nicolas   245
Le Petit Poucet /Tom Thumb   69
Le Petit Soldat /The Little Soldier   244
Le Petit Théâtre de Jean Renoir   102
Le Pistonné
    /The Man with Connections   129
Le Placard   270
Le Placard
    /The Closet   21, 95, 162, 165, 270
Le Plaisir   145, 212
Le Pornographe
    /The Pornographer   69, 255
Le Poulpe /The Octopus   146
Le Pressentiment   147
Le Procès /The Trial   299
Le Promeneur du Champ de Mars
    /The Last Mitterrand   17, 78
Le Quai des brumes /Port of
    Shadows   91, 308
Le Quart d'heure américain   35

Le Récif de corail /Coral Reefs   308
Le Retour de Casanova /Casanova's
    Return   153, 276
Le Retour de Martin Guerre /The
    Return of Martin Guerre   42, 165
Le Retour du grand blond
    /The Return of the Tall Blond Man
    with One Black Shoe   103
Le Révélateur   249
Le Roi danse
    /The King is Dancing   278
Le Roi de cœur
    /King of Hearts   98, 363
Le Roi de la Chine   35
Le Roi se meurt   78
Le Roman d'un jeune homme
    pauvre   188
Le Roman d'un tricheur
    /The Story of a Cheat   204, 227
Le Rosier de Madame Husson
    /He   192
Le Rouge aux lèvres
    /Daughters of Darkness   365
Le Rouge est mis
    /Speaking of Murder   221
Le Rouge et le Noir /The Red and the
    Black   145, 223, 315

LES–
Les Acteurs /Actors   10, 49, 188, 284
Les Adieux à la reine
    /Farewell, My Queen   261
Les Affinités électives
    /Elective Affinities   220
Le Salaire de la peur
    /The Wages of Fear   298, 385
Les Amants de demain   321
Les Amants de Montparnasse
    /The Lovers of Montparnasse   315
Les Amants du Pont-Neuf
    /The Lovers on the Bridge   59
Les Amants /The Lovers   97, 299
Les Âmes grises /Grey Souls   233
Le Samouraï
    /The Samurai   153, 230

Les Amours de la reine Élisabeth
/*Queen Elizabeth* 53

Le Sang des autres
/*The Blood of Others* 20, 35

Le Sang d'un poète
/*The Blood of a Poet* 124

Les Apprentis
/*The Apprentices* 122, 166

Les Assassins de l'ordre
/*Law Breakers* 95

Les Aventures de Rabbi Jacob
/*The Mad Adventures of Rabbi
Jacob* 138, 142, 151, 152, 291

Les Aventures des pieds-nickelés 265

*Les Aventures de Tintin : Le Secret de
la Licorne /The Adventures of Tintin:
The Secret of the Unicorn* 191

*Les Aventures du roi Pausole /The
Adventures of King Pausole* 195

Les Barbouzes
/*The Great Spy Chase* 63, 65, 386

Les Bas-fonds
/*The Lower Depths* 211, 267

Les Beaux Jours
/*Happy Days* 8, 373

Les Biches /The Does 20

Les Bien-aimés /Beloved 157

Les Blessures assassins
/*Murderous Maids* 380

Les Bonnes Causes
/*Don't Tempt the Devil* 92

Les Bonnes Femmes
/*The Good-Time Girls* 20, 247

Les Bons et les Méchants
/*The Good Guys and the Bad* 197

Les Bricoleurs
/*Who Stole the Body?* 63

Les Brigades du Tigre
/*The Tiger Brigades* 30

*Les Bronzés /French Fried
Vacation* 32, 119, 242, 269

Les Bronzés font du ski 32, 119, 242,
269

Les Bronzés 3 : Amis pour la vie
/*Friends Forever* 32, 62, 119, 271

Le Scandale
/*The Champagne Murders* 20

Le Scaphandre et le Papillon
/*The Diving Bell and the
Butterfly* 5, 11, 234, 360

Les Caprices de Marianne 397

*Les Carnets de Monsieur
Manatane* 330

Les Caves du Majestic
/*Majestic Hotel Cellars* 335

Les Cent et une nuits de Simon Cinéma
/*One Hundred and One
Nights* 163, 325

Les Chansons d'amour
/*Love Songs* 354

Les Chevaliers du ciel
/*Sky Fighters* 278

Les Choristes /The Chorus 51, 242

Le Schpountz 192

Les Cinq Gentlemen maudits
/*Moon Over Morocco* 267

L'Esclave blanche 351

Les Clefs de bagnole
/*The Car Keys* 182, 297

Les Clés du paradis
/*The Keys to Paradise* 109

Les Collégiennes 157

Les Combinards 363

Les Compagnons de la Marguerite
/*Order of the Daisy* 63

Les Compères
/*ComDads* 95, 162, 164, 344

Les Convoyeurs attendent
/*The Carriers are Waiting* 331

Les Corps impatients
/*Eager Bodies* 231

Les Côtelettes 309

*Les Couloirs du temps:
Les visiteurs 2* 343

Les Cousins
/*The Cousins* 19, 97

Les Dames du Bois de Boulogne
/*Ladies of the Park* 108, 124

*Les Demoiselles de Rochefort /The Young
Ladies of Rochefort* 145, 157

Les Démons de l'aube
/*Dawn Demons* 102, 368

Les Derniers jours du monde
/*Happy End* 23

Les Deux Anglaises et le continent
/*Two English Girls* 254

Les Deux mémoires 109

Les Diaboliques /*Diabolique* 230, 288,
319, 363, 369, 370, 385

*Les Durs à cuire ou comment supprimer
son prochain sans perdre l'appétit*
/*Hard Boiled Ones* 363

Les Émotifs anonymes
/*Romantics Anonymous* 331

Les Enfants du paradis
/*Children of Paradise* 13, 38, 39,
56, 91, 102, 108, 268, 396

Les Enfants du placard
/*Closet Children* 197

Les Enfants du siècle
/*Children of the Century* 59, 60,
278, 353

Les Enfants /*The Children* 188

Le Septième Ciel /*Seventh Heaven* 50,
245, 246, 272, 287

Le Serpent a mangé la grenouille 17

Les Espions /*The Spies* 171

Les Fantômes de Louba 400

Les Fantômes du chapelier
/*The Hatter's Ghost* 25, 364

Les Femmes de l'ombre
/*Female Agents* 169, 220, 282

Les Femmes du 6e étage
/*The Women on the 6th Floor* 245

Les Fleurs du miel
/*The Honey Flowers* 197

Les Fugitifs /*Fugitives* 103, 162, 344

Les Gaîtés de l'escadron
/*Fun in Barracks* 339

Les Gardiens de l'ordre
/*Off Limits* 150

Les Godelureaux /*Wise Guys* 247

Les Gorilles 216

Les Grandes Familles /*The
Possessors* 91, 92, 346

Les Grandes manoeuvres
/*The Grand Maneuver* 308

Les Grands Ducs 86, 284

Les Gueux au paradis
/*Hoboes in Paradise* 192

Les Herbes folles /*Wild Grass* 187

Les Hommes de l'ombre
/*The Men in the Shadows* 43

Les Hommes préfèrent les grosses
/*Men Prefer Fat Girls* 32, 50

Le Signe du lion /*The Sign of Leo* 19

Les Inconnus dans la maison
/*Strangers in the House* 206

Les Infidèles /*The Players* 183

Les Innocents /*The Innocents* 98

Les Intrus /*The Intruders* 25

Les Invasions barbares
/*The Barbarian Invasions* 233

Les Jolies choses /*Pretty Things* 132

Les Joyeux Lurons 216

Les Juifs contre la France
/*The Jews against France* 267

Les Keufs /*Lady Cops* 33

Les Kidnappeurs 243

Le Skylab /*Skylab* 155, 249

Les Liaisons dangereuses
/*Dangerous Liaisons* (1988) 316

Les Liaisons dangereuses 1960
/*Dangerous Liaisons* (1959) 300,
315, 382, 389

Les Liens du sang /*Rivals* 123

Les Lions sont lâchés
/*The Lions are Loose* 98

Les Livreurs 63

Les Magiciens /*Death Rite* 349

Les Malheurs d'Alfred
/*The Troubles of Alfred* 344

Les Malheurs de Sophie 98

Les Mariés de l'an deux
/*The Scoundrel* 92, 172

Les Maris, les femmes, les amants 352

Les Marmottes
/*The Groundhogs* 260

Les Mauvais Jours 18

Les Mendiants /*The Beggars* 223

Les Misérables   40, 48, 80, 81, 103, 222, 259

Les Mistons /The Mischief Makers   247, 250

Les Mots pour le dire   217

Les Mystères de Paris /The Mysteries of Paris   102, 280

Les Naufragés de l'île de la Tortue /The Castaways of Turtle Island   35

Les Neiges du Kilimandjaro /The Snows of Kilimanjaro   18, 147

Les Nuits de la pleine lune /Full Moon in Paris   276

Les Nuits fauves /Savage Nights   68

Les Orgueilleux   308

Le Soulier de satin /The Satin Slipper   38

Le Souper /The Supper   88, 89

Le Soupirant /The Suitor   105

Le Sourire /The Smile   361

Les Paradis de Laura   285

Les Parapluies de Cherbourg /The Umbrellas of Cherbourg   157, 250

Les Parents terribles /The Storm Within   279, 340

Les Parisiennes   296

Les Patriotes /The Patriots   245

Les Perles de la couronne /Pearls of the Crown   39

Les Petits Mouchoirs /Little White Lies   99, 123, 133

Les Pieds sous la table   307

Les Poneys sauvages   35

Les Portes de la gloire /Days of Glory   330

Les Portes de la nuit /Gates of the Night   91, 298, 341

Les Possédés /The Possessed   237, 397

Les Poupées russes /Russian Dolls   149, 186

Les Prédateurs /The Hunger   158

Les Princes   141

Les Quatre Cents Coups /The 400 Blows   97, 125, 253, 254, 255

Les Randonneurs /Hikers   330

Les Randonneurs à Saint-Tropez   330

Les Rencontres de Mérimée   109

Les Ripoux /My New Partner   270

Les Risques du métier /Risky Business   94

Les Rivières pourpres /The Crimson Rivers   109, 110, 343

Les Rivières pourpres 2 – Les Anges de l'apocalypse /Crimson Rivers 2: Angels of the Apocalypse   230, 278, 342

Les Rois du sport   193, 339

Les Routes du sud /Roads to the South   293

Les Saisons du plaisir   136, 223

Les Saveurs du Palais /Haute Cuisine   208, 210

Les Seigneurs   191, 285

Les Seins de glace /Someone is Bleeding   88, 89

Les Sorcières de Salem /The Crucible /The Witches of Salem   368

Les Sous-doués /The Under-Gifted   22

Les Sous-doués en vacances   70

Le Stade de Wimbledon /Wimbledon Stage   4

Les Témoins /The Witnesses   169

Les Temps qui changent /Changing Times   163

Les Tontons flingueurs /Crooks in Clover or *Monsieur Gangster*   63, 65

Les Tribulations d'un Chinois en Chine /Up to His Ears   49, 349

Les Tricheurs   46

Les Trois Mousquetaires (1921)   335

Les Trois Mousquetaires /The Three Musketeers (1953)   81

Les Trois Mousquetaires : Première époque – les ferrets de la reine   102

Les Trois Valses /Three Waltzes   206

Le Sucre   103

Les Vacances de M. Hulot /Monsieur Hulot's Holiday   104, 306, 375

Les Vacances du petit Nicolas   250

Les Vacanciers   216

Les Valseuses /*Going Places*   162, 164,
    172, 197, 235, 291, 292, 293, 294
Les Vécés étaient fermés de
    l'interieur   349
Les Veinards /*People in Luck*   63
Les Vierges /*The Virgins*   63, 363
Les Visiteurs /*The Visitors*   119, 120
    262, 342, 343
Les Visiteurs 2 : Les Couloirs du
    temps   120
Les Visiteurs 3 : La Terreur   120
Les Visiteurs du soir /*The Devil's*
    Envoys   v, 55, 102, 258, 368
Les Volets clos /*Closed Shutters*   98
Les Voleurs /*Thieves*   278
Les Yeux sans visage
    /*Eyes Without a Face*   92, 354, 355
Le Talisman Balzac-Beethoven   36
L'Étalon /*The Stud*   63
Le Tartuffe   163
L'État de grâce /*State of Grace*   10
L'Été en pente douce   394
L'Été meurtrier
    /*One Deadly Summer*   1, 121, 355
Le Temps de l'aventure
    /*Just a Sigh*   171
Le Temps des cerises   12
Le Temps des vertiges   80
Le Temps du loup
    /*Time of the Wolf*   140
Le Temps retrouvé
    /*Time Regained*   36, 157, 356, 361
L'Été prochain /*Next Summer*   223
L'Éternel retour /*Love Eternal*   279
Le Testament d'Orphée /*The Testament*
    of Orpheus   108, 124, 279
Le Théâtre et son double
    /*Theatre and Its Double*   14
Le Théâtre national populaire   107
Le Thé d'Ania   18
Le Tigre se parfume à la dynamite
    /*Our Agent Tiger*   79
Le Transfuge   35
Le Triporteur
    /*The Tricyclist*   134, 135, 235

Let's Make Love   298, 370, 371
L'Étudiante   271, 281
Le Vélo de Ghislain Lambert
    /*Ghislain Lambert's Bicycle*   330
Le Viager /*The Annuity*   363
Le Vicomte de Bragelonne
    /*The Last Musketeer*   102
Le Vieil Homme et l'Enfant
    /*The Two of Us*   372
Le Vieux Fusil /*The Old Gun*   310
Le Vilain /*The Villain*   184
Le Voleur d'enfants
    /*The Children Thief*   260
Le Voleur et la Menteuse   143
Le Voleur /*The Thief of Paris*   249
Le Voyage à Paris
    /*The Journey to Paris*   304
Le Voyage du père /*Father's Trip*   193
Le Voyage en Arménie /*Armenia*   18
Le Voyageur sans bagages   207
Le Voyou /*The Crook*   383
Lévy et Goliath
    /*Levy and Goliath*   6, 75
Ley del mar   268
Le Zèbre   334

L'H–
L'Heure d'été /*Summer Hours*   60, 356
L'Heure zéro
    /*Towards Zero*   303, 305
L'Histoire d'Adèle H.
    /*The Story of Adele H.*   1
L'Histoire de Jen /*Story of Jen*   234
L'Homme à femmes /*Ladies Man*   145
L'Homme aux clefs d'or /*The Man with*
    the Golden Keys   222
L'Homme de Rio
    /*That Man from Rio*   48
L'Homme du large
    /*Man of the Sea*   82
L'Homme du train /*Man on the*
    Train   231, 349, 350, 356
L'Homme est une femme comme les
    autres /*Man Is a Woman*   190, 400
L'Homme-orchestre /*The Band*   152

L'Homme qui aimait les femmes /The Man Who Loved Women   161, 197

L'Homme qui rit /The Man Who Laughs   164

L'Homme qui venait du Cher   297

L'Homme qui vendit son âme   268

L'Homme qui voulait vivre sa vie /The Big Picture   12

L'Homme qu'on aimait trop /In the Name of My Daughter   99

L'Honorable Catherine   195

L'Horloger de Saint-Paul /The Clockmaker of St Paul   310, 349

L'Horoscope   216

L'Humeur vagabonde /Vagabond Humour   141

Liberté-Oléron   328

Liberty Belle   59

L'Ibis rouge /The Red Ibis   266, 363

Life of Pi   162

Life Without Zoe   76

Liliom   351

Lilith   358

L'Illusionniste /The Illusionist   376

Lily, aime-moi   172

L'Immortel /22 Bullets   58, 342

L'Inconnu dans la maison /Stranger in the House   48

L'Inconnue de Monte Carlo /Unknown of Monte Carlo   335

L'Incorrigible /The Incorrigible   49

L'Increvable /The Indestructible   135

L'Insoutenable légèreté de l'être /The Unbearable Lightness of Being   59

L'Inspecteur Lavardin   247

L'Instinct de mort /Mesrine: Killer Instinct   5, 46

L'Intrépide   216

L'Intrus /The Intruder   140

L'Invitation   12

L'Irrésolu /The Indecisive Guy   246

L'Italien des roses /The Italian of the Roses   66

Little Jerusalem   400

L'Ivresse du pouvoir /The Comedy of Power   36, 51, 236

L'Oeil de Vichy /The Eye of Vichy   79

L'Oiseau rare /A Rare Bird   98

Lola   3

LOL (Laughing Out Loud)   281

Looking for Jimmy   155

L'Opéra de quat' sous /The Threepenny Opera   336

L'Opération corned-beef /Operation Corned-beef   119, 262

Lord of the Rings   323

L'Or du Cristobal /Cristobal's Gold   335

L'Orpheline avec en plus un bras en moins   175

Lost in La Mancha   348

Louder than Bombs   237

Louise-Michel   302, 330

Loulou   162, 164

Love Affair   83, 84

Love and Hisses   374

Love in the Afternoon   118

Love Me   246

Love Me Tonight   116

Luca il contrabbandiere /Luca le contrebandier /Contraband   86

Lucie Aubrac   76

Lucky Luke   36

Lumière d'été   91

L'Un reste, l'autre part /One Stays, the Other Leaves   213

M

Ma Bonne Étoile /My Lucky Star   253

Macadam   288

Macbeth   134

Madame Bovary   36, 236, 267

Madame de... /The Earrings of Madame de...   83, 145

Madame Rosa   370

Made in U.S.A.   106, 244

Madeline   21

Mademoiselle Chambon   245, 246, 272

Mademoiselle et son gang 102
Ma femme est une actrice
  /My Wife is an Actress 213, 353
Ma femme, ma vache et moi 215
Ma femme…s'appelle Maurice
  /My Wife Maurice 21
Mahjong 260
Main dans la main
  /Hand in Hand 263
Mains armées /Armed Hands 47
Mais qu'est-ce que j'ai fait au bon Dieu
  pour avoir une femme qui boit dans
  les cafés avec les hommes ? /What
  Did I Ever Do to the Good Lord to
  Deserve a Wife Who Drinks in Cafes
  with Men? 74
Maléfique 130
Malpertuis
  /Legend of Doom House 79, 230
Ma mère /My Mother 237
Manèges /The Cheat 368
Mange ta soupe 4
Manon 79
Manon des sources
  /Manon of the Spring 22, 44, 299
Man on the Train 231
Ma nuit chez Maud
  /My Night at Maud's 383
Ma petite enterprise
  /My Little Business 51, 272
Marche à l'ombre 50, 61
Marcher 295
Mariage mixte 143
Mariages ! 182
Marie 219
Marie baie des anges
  /Marie from the Bay of Angels 285
Marie-Jo et ses deux amours /Marie-Jo
  and Her Two Lovers 18, 290
Marie-Octobre 287, 341
Maries Lied: Ich war, ich weiß nicht wo
  /Marie's Song: I Was I Know Not
  Where 379
Marius 205, 206, 338, 339
Marius et Jeannette 17, 289, 146

Marius-Fanny-César trilogy 22
Marquise 282
Marseille contrat
  /The Destructors 86
Marseilles Trilogy 17, 19, 116, 206
Marthe Richard, au service de la France
  /Marthe Richard 195
Martin et Léa 50
Ma saison préférée
  /My Favorite Season 22, 158
Masculin féminin 254
Maso et Miso vont en bateau 366
Masques 248, 310
Master Class 8
Mauvaise foi /Bad Faith 46, 150
Mauvaise Passe /The Escort 61
Mauvais garçon 36
Mauvais sang
  /The Night Is Young 154, 326
Ma vie en l'air
  /Love Is in the Air 133
Ma vraie vie à Rouen
  /My Life on Ice 17
Max 361
Mayerling 83, 144
M comme Mathieu 197
Mean Guns 252
Meeting Venus 11
Méfiez-vous, mesdames ! 287
Melancholia 214
Mélo 8, 9, 23, 188
Mélodie en sous-sol /Any Number Can
  Win 102, 153, 352
Memento 231
Mensonges et trahisons et plus si
  affinités /The Story of My Life 130
Merci la vie
  /Thank You, Life 61, 103, 162, 213
Merci pour le chocolat 236
Mères et Filles /Hidden Diary 234
Mères françaises
  /Mothers of France 54
Mes amis, mes amours
  /London mon amour 261
Mes héros 131, 242

Mes meilleurs copains
/*My Best Pals* 28, 119, 146
Mes nuits sont plus belles que vos jours
/*My Nights are More Beautiful than
Your Days* 282
Mesrine : l'instinct de mort /*Mesrine:
Killer Instinct* 111, 150
Messieurs les enfants 306
Mesyats v derevne /*Two Women* 381
Metroland 399
Mia et le Migou
/*Mia and the Magoo* 72
Micmacs à tire-larigot
/*Micmacs* 72, 188
Midnight in Paris 133, 191
Mille milliards de dollars
/*A Thousand Billion Dollars* 173
Milou en mai
/*May Fools* 50, 262, 291, 326
Mima 260
Mina Tannenbaum 69, 400
Mission: Impossible 45, 343
Mississippi Mermaid 79
Miss Mona 103
Miss Montigny 18
Miss O'Gynie et les hommes fleurs /*Miss
O'Gynie and the Flower Man* 11
Moche et Méchant
/*Despicable Me* 191
Model Shop 2
Moderato cantabile
/*Seven Days...Seven Nights* 299
Modigliani 399
Moi César, 10 ans ½, 1m39
/*I, Cesar* 58
Moi y'en a vouloir des sous /*Me, I want
to Have Dough* 363
Molière 186, 276, 354
Mon ange /*My Angel* 313
Mon colonel /*The Colonel* 150
Mon idole /*Whatever You Say* 99
Mon meilleur ami
/*My Best Friend* 72
Monocle series 287
Mon oncle 375

Mon oncle Benjamin /*My Uncle
Benjamin* 94, 95
Mon oncle d'Amérique /*My American
Uncle* 9, 162, 208, 217
Mon père avait raison
/*My Father Was Right* 227
Mon père ce héros /*My Father the
Hero* 219
Mon petit doigt m'a dit... /*By the
Pricking of My Thumbs* 188, 209
Mon pire cauchemar /*My Worst
Nightmare* 188, 331
Mon pote 30
Mon premier amour 58
Monseigneur /*Monsignor* 259
Monsieur Batignole 242
Monsieur Fabre 171
Monsieur Hire 61, 70, 71
*Monsieur le président-directeur
général* 216
Monsieur Naphtali 243
Monsieur Vincent 79, 102, 207
Monster 131
Mont-Dragon 95
Montmartre-sur-Seine 287, 320
Moonraker 274
Mortal Kombat 252
Mort d'un président
/*Death of a President* 36
Mouche 260
Mourir d'aimer /*To Die of Love* 221
MR73 /*The Last Deadly Mission* 21
Mr Freedom 365
Munich 274
Muriel ou le temps d'un retour
/*Muriel, or the Time of Return* 365
Música de siempre 321
My Fair Lady 203

N

Nada /*The Nada Gang* 352
Nadia et les hippopotames
/*Nadia and the Hippos* 17
Nag la bombe 17

Naïs 192

Naples au baiser de feu
  /The Kiss of Fire 351

Napoléon 15, 212, 308

Narco /The Secret Adventures of
  Gustave Klopp 263, 330

Nathalie... 165

Nathalie Granger 162

Ne le dis à personne
  /Tell No One 99, 123, 188, 234

Nelly et Monsieur Arnaud
  /Nelly and Mr Arnaud 44, 364

Ne nous fâchons pas
  /Let's Not Get Angry 386

Ne réveillez pas un flic qui dort
  /Let Sleeping Cops Lie 364

Nettoyage à sec /Dry Cleaning 293, 362

Neuf garçons, un cœur 319, 320

New York Stories 76

Ni à vendre ni à louer
  /Holidays by the Sea 306

Nid de guêpes /The Nest 278

Night on Earth 140

Ni pour ni contre (bien au contraire)
  /Not For, or Against (Quite the
  Contrary) 220

Nobody Wants the Night 60

Noce blanche /White Wedding 313

Noroît 249

Nos enfants chéris
  /Our Precious Children 69

Nosferatu 15

Notre-Dame de Paris /The Hunchback
  of Notre Dame 389

Notre histoire /Our Story 145, 174

Nous deux /Us Two 141

Nous irons à Deauville 102

Nous York 47

Nouvelle vague /New Wave 153

Novecento 36

Nuit d'ivresse 269

Nuit et Brouillard /Night and Fog 79

Nuovo Cinema Paradiso
  /Cinema Paradiso 197

Nymphomaniac 214

O

Occupe-toi d'Amélie..!
  /Keep an Eye on Amelia 101

Ocean's Twelve 110, 111

Odette Toulemonde 184, 208, 209

Of Gods and Men 398

Olé 190

On aura tout vu /The Bottom Line 23

On connaît la chanson
  /Same Old Song 9, 23, 146, 188

One Hour with You 116

On l'appelle catastrophe 216

On ne choisit pas sa famille
  /You Don't Choose Your Family 120

On ne meurt que deux fois
  /He Died with His Eyes Open 145

Onorato 17

On peut toujours rêver 344, 345

On purge bébé /Baby's Laxative 372

On s'en fout... nous on s'aime 216

Orage /Storm 307

Orphée /Orpheus 108, 124, 279

Orpheus 280

OSS 117 movies 181

OSS 117 : Le Caire, nid d'espions /
  OSS 117: Cairo, Nest of Spies 182

OSS 117 : Rio ne répond plus
  /OSS 117: Lost in Rio 182

Où est la main de l'homme sans tête
  /Hand of the Headless Man 150

Out 1, noli me tangere 248

Out 1 : Spectre 248

P

Paint Your Wagon 358

Palais royal ! 263, 397

Panique /Panic 352, 372

Papa 114

Paparazzi 272, 326

Papy fait de la résistance /Gramps is in
  the Resistance 61, 119, 269, 395

Parade 376

Paradis pour tous 173

Par-delà les nuages
   /Beyond the Clouds 282
Par effraction
   /Breaking and Entering 60
Parfum de famille 36
Par ici la monnaie 216
Paris 60, 186
Paris-béguin /The Darling of Paris 211
Paris brûle-t-il ?
   /Is Paris Burning? 171
Paris chante toujours !
   /Paris Still Sings! 321
Paris, je t'aime 45, 60, 302, 354
Paris nous appartient
   /Paris Belongs to Us 97
Paris qui dort /At 3:25 335
Paris s'éveille /Paris Awakens 223
Parlez-moi d'amour
   /Speak to me of Love 11, 282
Parlez-moi de la pluie
   /Let It Rain 28, 239
Paroles et musique /Love Songs 252
Pars vite et reviens tard
   /Have Mercy on Us All 364
Partage de Midi
   /The Break of Noon 39
Pas de problème ! /No Problem! 172
Pas de scandale
   /Keep it Quiet 237, 271
Passage to Marseille 308
Passion 326
Passionnément 213
Pas sur la bouche
   /Not on the Lips 9, 23, 135, 187
Pater 272
Pattes blanches /White Paws 259
Paulette 249
Pearls of the Deep 314
Peau d'âne
   /Donkey Skin 259, 280, 365
Pédale douce 8
Pépé le Moko 82, 137, 199, 200, 203,
   204, 211
Perceval le Gallois /Perceval 187, 276
Père et fils /Father and Sons 75

Perfect Sense 226
Péril en la demeure 218
Persepolis 145
Peter Pan 353
Petites coupures /Small Cuts 22
Petit jour 94
Peur sur la ville /The Night Caller 35
Peut-être 186
Picpus 335
Pierrot le fou 48, 244
Pile ou face /Heads or Tails 9
Pillow Talk 138
Pinocchio v
Pinot simple flic 242
Pitié pour les vamps
   /Pity for the Vamps 352
Place Vendôme 50, 158
Plaisir d'offrir 307
Playboy of Paris 116
Playtime 375, 376
Pleins feux sur l'assassin
   /Spotlight on a Murderer 92
Plein soleil /Purple Noon 153
Podium 330
Poil de carotte /The Red Head 40
Polar 35
Police 70, 162, 165, 282
Police python 357 299
Pollux : Le Manège enchanté /Sprung!
   The Magic Roundabout 72, 296
Populaire 186, 297
Possession 1
Potiche /Trophy Wife 159, 162, 223
Pouic-Pouic 151
Poulet au vinaigre
   /Chicken with Vinegar 79, 247, 333
Poulet aux prunes /Chicken with
   Plums 30, 31
Pour 100 briques t'as plus rien /For 200
   Grand, You Get Nothing Now 22
Pour l'amour de Dieu 45
Pourquoi (pas) le Brésil
   /Why (Not) Brazil? 10
Pour rire ! 331
Pour Sacha /For Sasha 142

Pour une femme
  /For a Woman 279, 380
Premier rendez-vous
  /Her First Affair 258
Premiers désirs /First Desires 44
Préparez vos mouchoirs /Get Out Your
  Handkerchiefs 162, 172, 363
Président 184
Prêt-à-porter /Ready to Wear 121, 348
Prête-moi ta main /I Do: How to Get
  Married and Stay Single 248
Pretty Baby 203
Princesse Tam-Tam 335, 336, 351
Prison à domicile /House Arrest 243
P.R.O.F.S. 276
Psy 145
Psycho 369
Public Enemies 133
Pull My Daisy 365
Pulp Fiction 220

Q

Quadrille 188, 245, 263
Quai des brumes
  /Port of Shadows 211, 372
Quai des Orfèvres 241
Quai d'Orsay
  /The French Minister 12, 270
Quais de Seine 46
Quand je serai petit 295
Quand j'étais chanteur 149
Quand la mer monte
  /When the Sea Rises 301, 306
Quantum of Solace 5
Quatre étoiles 121
Que la fête commence... /Let Joy Reign
  Supreme 284, 310, 349
Quelle drôle de gosse ! 144
Quelque chose d'organique
  /Something Organic 69
Quelques jours avec moi
  /A Few Days with Me 22, 70, 71
Quelques jours en septembre
  /A Few Days in September 60

Qu'est-ce qu'on a fait au Bon
  Dieu ? 120
Qui êtes-vous, Polly Maggoo ?
  /Who Are You, Polly Magoo? 348
Qui plume la lune ? 147

R

Radiostars 131
Raging Bull 131
Raphaël ou le débauché /Raphaël or the
  Debauched One 197, 396
Rashomon 304
Raspoutine 343
Ratatouille 284
Razzia sur la chnouf /Razzia 212
Remorques
  /Stormy Waters 211, 258 308
Rendez-vous 59
Renoir 80
Repulsion 158
Requiem pour une tueuse
  /Requiem for a Killer 130
Resurrection 253
Retiens la nuit 17
Retour à la bien-aimée
  /Return to the Beloved 236
Retour à Marseille
  /Return to Marseilles 16
Rê\ve de singe /Bye Bye Monkey 162
Ridicule 223
Rien à déclarer
  /Nothing to Declare 72, 331, 332
Rien de grave 181
Rien ne va plus
  /Out of Whack (1979) 35
Rien ne va plus /The Swindle
  (1997) 36, 121, 236, 364
Riens du tout
  /Little Nothings 146, 276
Rien sur Robert 276
Ripoux contre ripoux
  /My New Partner II 270
Ripoux 3 270
Rive droite, rive gauche 76, 77

Roadflower   252

Robert et Robert   395

Robinson Crusoé   344

Rocco e i suoi fratelli
   /Rocco et ses frères
   /Rocco and His Brothers   153, 221

Rois et Reine
   /Kings and Queen   4, 170

Romance   314

Ronin   343

Room at the Top   132, 367

Roseanna's Grave   343

Rosebud   237

Rosine   361

Rouge midi   17

Rouletabille contre la dame de
   pique   323

Rouletabille joue et gagne   323

RRRrrr !!!   113, 263

Rue du départ /The Way Out   121, 142

Rupture   104

S

Sabrina (1954)   138, 261, 319

Sabrina (1995)   263, 319

Sac de noeuds /All Mixed Up   33

Sagan   380

Saint-Cyr
   /The King's Daughters   36, 237

Salaud on t'aime
   /We Love You, You Bastard   230

Salut cousin ! /Hey Cousin!   190

Salut les Cubains   326

Sans famille /Without Family   344

Sans regrets   234

Sans toit ni loi /Vagabond   70, 71, 301

Sarah's Key   11

Sarati   41

Sauve qui peut (la vie)
   /Every Man for Himself   42

SCUM Manifesto   366

Secret défense /Secret Defense   71

See How They Dance   234

Selon Charlie /Charlie Says   218

Selon Matthieu /To Matthieu   278

S'en fout la mort /No Fear, No Die   98

Séraphine   301, 302

Serial Lover   184

Série noire   173

Seventh Heaven   374

Sexes faibles ! /The Weaker Sexes!   262

Sexes très opposés
   /Very Opposite Sexes   286

Sex is Comedy   286

Sex-shop /Le Sex Shop   284

Shark Tale   354

She Hate Me   148

Sheitan   286

Ship of Fools   367

Signé Furax   266

Si jeunesse savait   55

Singin' in the Rain   320

Si Paris nous était conté
   /If Paris Were Told To Us   228

Sitcom   353

Si Versailles m'était conté /Royal Affairs
   in Versailles   228, 315, 321

Smoking /No Smoking   9, 23, 238

Snobs !   63, 274

Socks   307

Sœur Sourire /Sister Smile   150

Sois belle et tais-toi
   /Be Pretty and Shut up   366

Soldat Duroc, ça va être ta fête !
   /The Dangerous Mission   216

Some Like it Hot   100

Someone Else's America   109

Sommersby   165

Son nom de Venise dans Calcutta
   désert   366

Souls, Les Âmes grises /Grey   394

Sous le soleil de Satan /Under the Sun
   of Satan   70, 162, 164

Sous les toits de Paris
   /Under the Roofs of Paris   335, 336

Sous le vent des Îles Baléares   39

Southland Tales   253

Souvenirs perdus /Lost Souvenirs   92

Sport de filles   235

Stage Fright   319
Stavisky...   11, 48, 162
Stealing Beauty   280
Strictement personnel   10
*Stupeur et Tremblements
/Fear and Trembling*   380
Subway   27, 252, 342
Superman   10
Superstar   150
Surcouf /Adventure   14
*Sur le bout des doigts
/At My Fingertips*   233
*Sur mes lèvres
/Read My Lips*   110, 170
Suzanne   356
Sweeney Todd   175
Swimming Pool   353
*Sylvie et le fantôme /Sylvia and the
Ghost*   101, 375
*Symphonie eines Lebens
/Symphonie d'une vie*   41

T

T4xi   132
Tais-toi /Ruby and Quentin   162
Tandem   175, 349
Tango   76, 223
Tanguy   23, 188
Tartarin de Tarascon   63
Tarzan   263
Taxi   132
Taxi 2   132
Taxi 3   132
Taxi Driver   109
*Tchao Pantin
/So Long, Stooge*   6, 129
T'empêches tout le monde de dormir   22
Temptation Harbour   374
Tenue de soirée /Ménage   61, 162, 293
Teorema /Theorem   243
Tête d'or   39, 140
The 33 /Los 33   60
The Artist   123, 181, 182
The Beach   99, 261

The Belly of an Architect   397
The Big Blue   342
The Big Pond   116
The Big Red One   20
The Birdcage   334
The Black Windmill   366
The Cat   370
The Conformist   383
The Constant Nymph   83
The Dark Knight Rises   133
The Da Vinci Code   284, 343, 378
The Day of the Jackal   274, 366
The Devil and Daniel Webster   374
*The Discreet Charm of the
Bourgeoisie*   20
The Dreamers   224, 225, 255
The English Patient   59, 367
The Extra Day   375
The French Connection   85, 86
The Godfather   121
The Golden Compass   225, 323
The Graduate   172
The Great Silence   382
The Hairdresser's Husband   349
The Happy Road   171, 197
The Hunchback of Notre-Dame   323
The Hunger Games   345
The Illusionist   376
The Immigrant   133
The Lion King   323
The Longest Day   13, 82, 259
The Love Parade   116
The Magus   244
The Man in the Iron Mask   223
The Man Who Knew Too Much   206
The Matrix   397
The Merry Widow   116
*The Messenger: the Story of Joan of
Arc*   110
The Milky Way   105
The Millionaire   298
Themroc   129, 172
The Name of the Rose   274
The Night of the Hunter   40
The Ninth Gate   312

The Nostalgist 397
Théodore et cie
   /Theodore and Company 335
The Passion of Joan of Arc 15
The Pink Panther 343
The Pink Panther 2 230, 343
The Point Men 252
The Rage of Paris 144
Thérèse Desqueyroux 309, 311, 346,
   355, 378
Thérèse Raquin 368
The Screen Illusion 5
The Short Night 158
The Sicilian 252
The Smiling Lieutenant 116
The Stranger 244
The Testament 125, 126
The Three Musketeers 155
The Tin Drum 25
The Trial 259
The Truth About Charlie 25, 244
The Voyager 155
The Wages of Fear 385
The Wolf of Wall Street 183
The World is not Enough 282
Three Men and a Baby 74, 188
Three Men and a Little Lady 74
Tir à vue /Fire on Sight 70
Tirez sur le pianiste /Shoot the Piano
   Player 24, 25, 26
Titanic 81, 151
To Catch a Thief 385
Together Again 83
To Have and Have Not 138
Toi, moi, les autres /Leila 47
Tontons flingueurs
   /Crooks in Clover 386
Topaz 309, 325
Topaze 192, 195
Total Eclipse 69
Toto le Héros /Toto the Hero 79
Touche pas à la femme blanche
   /Don't Touch the White Woman! 135
Touchez pas au grisbi /Grisbi 212, 386
Tournée /On Tour 4

Tous à l'ouest : Une aventure de Lucky
   Luke 306
Tous les garçons et les filles de leur
   âge 260
Tous les matins du monde /All the
   Mornings of the World 166, 284
Tout ça ne vaut pas l'amour 211
Tout ça...pour ça ! /All That...for
   This?! 141, 272, 276
Tout ce qui brille
   /All That Glitters 46
Toutes les filles pleurent 223
Toutes les filles sont folles
   /All Girls are Crazy 182
Toutes nos envies
   /All Our Desires 220
Tout feu, tout flamme
   /All Fired Up 299
Tout le monde il est beau, tout le monde
   il est gentil /Everybody He is Nice,
   Everybody He is Beautiful 363
Tout peut arriver /Don't Be Blue 276
Trafic 376
Train de vie /Train of Life 190
Trans-Europ-Express 383
Trésor 114
Trois couleurs : Blanc
   /Three Colours: White 59, 155
Trois couleurs : Bleu 59
Trois couleurs : Rouge
   /Three Colours: Red 59, 384
Trois hommes et un couffin
   /Three Men and a Cradle 74, 188
Trop belle pour toi /Too Beautiful for
   You 33, 34, 76, 77, 121, 162
Trouble Every Day 139
True Lies 270
Twist again à Moscou
   /Twist Again in Moscow 119

U

Un air de famille
   /Family Resemblances 28, 146, 208,
   209, 238

Un amour de poche
  /Girl in his Pocket 389
Un amour de Swann
  /Swann in Love 35
Una stagione all'inferno
  /A Season in Hell 98
Un baiser papillon
  /A Butterfly Kiss 356
Un balcon sur la mer
  /A View of Love 182
Un bonheur n'arrive jamais seul
  */Happiness Never Comes
  Alone* 283, 191
Un bon petit diable 98
Un carnet de bal
  /Dance Program 40, 339
Un cœur en hiver
  /A Heart in Winter 22, 44, 188
Un cœur simple /A Simple Heart 70
Un conte de Noël
  /A Christmas Tale 4, 157
Un couple /A Couple 63
*Un couple épatant /An Amazing
  Couple* 208, 304, 305
Un crime au paradis
  /A Crime in Paradise 394
Under Suspicion 364
Un dimanche à la campagne
  /A Sunday in the Country 23
Un divan à New-York
  /A Couch in New York 59
Un drôle de colonel
  /A Strange Kind of Colonel 216
Un drôle de Paroissien /Heaven Sent 63
Une affaire de femmes
  /Story of Women 236
Une affaire privée
  /A Private Affair 270
Une belle fille comme moi
  /Such a Gorgeous Kid Like Me 161,
  187, 248
Une employée modèle
  /A Model Employee 303
Une époque formidable...
  /Wonderful Times 67

Une étrange affaire
  /Strange Affair 35, 42
*Une exécution ordinaire /An Ordinary
  Execution* 30, 31, 234
Une femme est une femme
  /A Woman is a Woman 98, 244
Une femme française
  /A French Woman 44
Une hirondelle a fait le printemps
  /The Girl from Paris 364
Une histoire d'amour /Tied 331
Une histoire simple
  /A Simple Story 88
Un éléphant ça trompe énormément
  /Pardon Mon Affaire 88, 89
Une liaison pornographique
  /An Affair of Love 43
Une nouvelle amie
  /The New Girlfriend 187
Une nouvelle vie /A New Life 223
Une nuit au Moulin Rouge 178
Une page d'amour 35
Une pour toutes /One 4 All 50
Une ravissante idiote 37
Un été d'orages /Stormy Summer 223
Un étrange voyage 50
Une veuve en or 103
Une vie de chat /A Cat in Paris 248
Une vieille maîtresse
  /The Last Mistress 286
Une vie meilleure /A Better Life 47
Un flic /A Cop 157
Un héros très discret
  /A Self-Made Hero 50, 184
Un homme et son chien
  /A Man and His Dog 49
*Un homme et une femme /A Man and
  a Woman* 3, 58, 222, 383
Un homme et une femme, 20 ans déjà
  */A Man and a Woman: 20 Years
  Later* 383
Un homme marche dans la ville
  /A Man Walks in the City 254
Un homme qui me plaît
  /Love is a Funny Thing 86

Un idiot à Paris   102

Un indien dans la ville
    /Little Indian, Big City   270

Un long dimanche de fiançailles
    /A Very Long Engagement   130,
    169, 175, 184, 188

Un mauvais fils /A Bad Son   173, 197

Un mauvais garçon   144

Un monde à nous   30

Un monstre à Paris
    /A Monster in Paris   313

Un papillon sur l'épaule
    /Butterfly on the Shoulder   387

Un pont entre deux rives
    /The Bridge   77

Un printemps à Paris
    /A Winter in Paris   36

Un prophète /A Prophet   12, 46, 47

Un secret /A Secret   150, 168, 354

Un singe en hiver
    /A Monkey in Winter   48

Un taxi pour Tobrouk
    /Taxi for Tobruk   386

Untel père et fils
    /The Heart of a Nation   258

Until September   270

Until the End of the World   296

Untold Scandal   316

Up   25

Up, Down, Fragile   244

Upgrade   242

Uranus   61, 162, 164, 276

Urgence   35

Utrillo   178

V

Valmont   316

Van Gogh   399

Varsovie, quand même...   107

Vatel   164

V comme Vian
    /Vian was his Name   393

Vendredi soir /Friday Night   263, 272

Vengeance   230

Vent d'est   36

Vénus aveugle /Blind Venus   351

Vénus beauté (institut) /Venus Beauty
    Institute   43, 361, 377

Venus in Fur   360

Vercingétorix /The Gaul   252

Verdun, visions d'histoire   16

Versailles rive-gauche
    /A Night in Versailles   327

Victoria   244

Vidocq   99

Vie privée /A Very Private Affair   37

Vigo, histoire d'une passion   69

Viktor und Viktoria   100

Ville à vendre /City for Sale   297

Vincent, François, Paul et les autres...
    /Vincent, François, Paul and the
    Others   162, 298, 341

Vingt ans après   335

Violetta la reine de la moto /Violetta the
    Motorcycle Queen   303

Violette Nozière   20, 103, 236, 247

Vipère au poing   394

Vipère au poing
    /Viper in the Fist   210, 394

Viva Maria !   38

Vive Henri IV...vive l'amour !
    /Long Live Henri IV...Long Live
    Love   92

Vive la sociale !   17, 121

Vivement dimanche !
    /Confidentially Yours   8, 383

Vivre ensemble   244

Vivre pour vivre /Live for Life   222

Vivre sa vie /My Life to Live   244

Volga en flammes
    /Volga in Flames   335

Volpone   41

Vous n'aurez pas l'Alsace et la
    Lorraine /You Won't Have Alsace-
    Lorraine   128

Vous n'avez encore rien vu /You Ain't
    Seen Nothin' Yet   9, 23, 398

Voyage au bout de la nuit   36

Voyage de noces /Honeymoon Trip   335

W

Waiting for the Moon   249
Wasabi   342
Week-end /Weekend   106
Welcome   272, 273
Welcome to New York   167, 168
Welcome to the Sticks   72, 73
When Tomorrow Comes   83
White Material   253
White Nights   280
Womb   226
Words and Pictures   60

X

XXL   190

Y

Y-a-t-il un français dans la salle ?
   /Is there a Frenchman in the
   House?   347

Z

Z   86, 298
Zazie dans le métro   309
Ze film   305
Zonzon   148

Drawings index

by Jenny Batlay
on pages:

1, 2, 14, 16, 19, 23, 24, 32, 34, 37, 42,
44, 52, 68, 70, 74, 75, 78, 82, 85, 93,
115, 119, 144, 154, 156, 167, 170, 174,
177, 194, 199, 208, 213, 219, 221, 223,
224, 233, 238, 244, 245, 247, 256,
257, 262, 266, 291, 299, 303, 307,
309, 312, 317, 340, 350, 354, 357, 361,
365, 367, 379, 388, 396, & 399.

by Igor Bratusek
on pages:

4, 6, 7, 9, 11, 13, 21, 27, 29, 38, 40,
45, 48, 50, 55, 57, 59, 61, 62, 64, 65,
72, 80, 87, 90, 97, 99, 100, 102, 104,
106, 109, 112, 121, 124, 127, 130, 131,
134, 136, 139, 141, 145, 147, 149, 151,
152, 159, 162, 171, 181, 183, 185, 187,
189, 192, 197, 205, 210, 215, 217, 227,
228, 235, 240, 242, 243, 251, 253,
260, 264, 269, 271, 273, 275, 278,
279, 281, 283, 285, 286, 289, 296,
297, 301, 313, 322, 325, 327, 329, 332,
334, 337, 342, 344, 345, 348, 352, 359,
362, 371, 373, 375, 377, 382, 384, 386,
394, & 397.

EDITORS AND ARTISTS

Editors

Dr Michaël Abecassis (DEA Grenoble, DLang St Andrews) is a Senior Instructor in French and a college lecturer at the University of Oxford. He has published widely on French linguistics and cinema. His publications include *The Representation of Parisian Speech in the Cinema of the 1930s* (Peter Lang, 2005); *Le français parlé au XXIème siècle* in two volumes (L'Harmattan, 2008), with Laure Ayosso and Élodie Vialleton; *Les Voix des Français* in two volumes (Peter Lang, 2010) and *Écarts et apports des médias*  *francophones: Lexique et grammaire* (Peter Lang, 2013), both with Gudrun Ledegen.

 Marcelline Block (BA Harvard, MA Princeton, PhD cand. Princeton) has edited several volumes on literature and cinema. Her publications include *The Directory of World Cinema: Belgium* (Intellect, 2014), *World Film Locations: Boston* (Intellect, 2014), *World Film Locations: Prague* (Intellect, 2013), *World Film Locations: Marseilles* (Intellect, 2013), *World Film Locations: Las Vegas* (Intellect, 2012), *World Film Locations: Paris* (Intellect, 2011), and *Situating the Feminist Gaze and Spectatorship in Postwar Cinema* (Cambridge Scholars, 2008, 2nd ed. 2010).

Artists

Jenny Batlay (PhD Columbia University) had her first painting exhibition at age 12 in Montpellier, France, and her second at age 14 in Paris at the Galérie Marcel Bernheim. A portrait painter, she has painted violinists David Oistrakh and Yehudi Menuhin (in the collection of the late Queen Elisabeth of the Belgians), Pablo Casals, Henri Mondor, and many actors in Hollywood and France. She now lives in New York. Her article  'L'art du portrait dans Gil Blas: Effet d'esthétique à travers le mouvement' in *Studies on Voltaire* (1974) is in the *Bibliographie des Études sur Gil Blas et Lesage*, Journées d'agrégation (Paris: 2002).

 Igor Bratusek was born in France and graduated at Paris Sorbonne, where he is now employed. His passion for cinema, drawing, and photography has motivated him to illustrate this book on French actors. He particularly likes to draw portrait caricatures and drawings with an emphasis on word plays.

CONTRIBUTORS

Michaël ABECASSIS, *The University of Oxford*, (Editor, and:
Audran, Baye, Richard Berry, Blanche, Boujenah, Canet [with
Marcelline Block], Le Poulain, Reggiani, Tati, Weber)
Benjamin ANDRÉO, *Monash University, Melbourne* (Artaud, Casarès, Cocteau)
Fabienne H. BAIDER, *University of Cyprus* (Adjani, Bonnaire, Fossey, Paradis)
Jenny BATLAY, *PhD Columbia University* (Drawings [as listed in Index] and:
Aznavour, Chevalier, Julie Depardieu, Dubas)
Nicoleta BAZGAN, *University of Maryland Baltimore County* (Ledoyen, Marceau)
Sophie BELOT, *The University of Sheffield* (Ardant)
Marcelline BLOCK, *Princeton University and SAG-AFTRA*, (Editor, and:
Carole Bouquet, Michel Bouquet, Bozzuffi, Brel, Canet [with Michaël
Abecassis], Darmon, Deneuve, Gérard Depardieu, Dreyfus, Fréhel, Frot,
Hallyday, Lafont, Lebeau, Morel, Noiret, Philipe, Piaf, Signoret, Vian)
Jean-Christophe BLUM, *Lycée Blaise Pascal, Clermont-Ferrand* (Blier, Duris,
Gabin, Guitry, Jouvet, Montand, Piccoli, Michel Simon)
Sylvie BLUM-REID, *University of Florida, Gainesville* (Miou-Miou)
Sophie BOUVIER, *University of Bristol* (Poiret)
Cristian BRATU, *Baylor University, Texas* (Balmer, Carmet, Coluche, Dujardin, Galabru)
Igor BRATUSEK, *Université Paris – Sorbonne* (Drawings [as listed in Index] and:
Bourvil, Cowl, Fernandel, Villeret)
William BROWN, *University of Roehampton, London* (Green, Hands)
Céline CANDIARD, *Université Lumière Lyon 2* (Barrault, De Funès)
Karine CHEVALIER, *University of Roehampton, London* (Delpy, Scob)
Marion COSTE, *École Normale Supérieure de Lyon* (Baer, Chabat, Cluzet)
Marina DAVIES, *NYU Paris [New York University, Paris Campus]* (Bacri, Jaoui)
Kath DOOLEY, *Flinders University of South Australia* (Bernhardt)
Jonathan DRISKELL, *Monash University Malaysia* (Darrieux, Morgan)
Emilie FRENKIEL, *Université Paris 8* (Delon)
Michael GOTT, *University of Cincinnati, Ohio* (Boon)
Aurore GOUNAUD, *École Normale Supérieure, Paris* (Sagnier)
France GRENAUDIER-KLIJN, *Massey University, New Zealand* (Marielle, Piat)
Jean-Frédéric HENNUY, *National University of Ireland, Maynooth* (Gillain, Poelvoorde)
Violaine HEYRAUD, *Université Sorbonne Nouvelle – Paris 3* (Belmondo, Richard,
Ventura)
Lucie HINTON, *The University of Oxford* (Tautou)
Thomas HINTON, *The University of Durham* (Balasko, Cassel)
Christa JONES, *Utah State University, Logan* (Bekhti, Elmaleh)
Sonali JOSHI, *Film Curator, London* (Léaud)
Colleen KENNEDY-KARPAT, *Bilkent University, Ankara, Turkey* (Romance, Vanel)
Gemma KING, *The University of Melbourne and Université Sorbonne Nouvelle –
Paris 3:* (Arestrup, Yolande Moreau, Riva)

Olga Kourelou, *King's College, London* (Aimée, Dalle)
Adela Lechintan-Siefer, *The Ohio State University, Columbus* (Denner, Zylberstein)
Aurélie Ledoux, *École Normale Supérieure, Paris* (Arletty, Azéma)
Brigitte Le Juez, *Dublin City University* (Dussollier, Seyrig)
Pierre Lethier, *University of Buckingham (BUCSIS)* (Lonsdale, Meurisse, Raimu)
Emilie L'Hôte, *Université Paris Diderot – Paris 7* (Marais, Jeanne Moreau)
François Massonnat, *Villanova University, Pennsylvania* (Berléand)
Joseph Mai, *Clemson University, South Carolina* (Boyer, Claude Brasseur, Meylan)
Ben McCann, *University of Adelaide* (Jules Berry, Ledoux)
Christophe Miqueu, *Université Montesquieu – Bordeaux IV* (Dupontel, Luchini)
Jim Morrissey, *Newcastle University* (Cotillard, Rochefort)
Elisabeth-Christine Muelsch, *Angelo State University, Texas* (Carette, Le Vigan)
Katharina Müller *Universität Wien /University of Vienna* (with Daniel Winkler:
    Arditi, Ascaride, De France)
Stéphane Narcis, *Bath Spa University* (Blanc, Clavier)
Barry Nevin, *The National University of Ireland, Galway* (Fresnay, Simone Simon)
Mame-Fatou Niang, *Carnegie Mellon University, Pittsburgh, Pennsylvania*
    (Richard Bohringer, Romane Bohringer)
Celia Nicholls, *University of Alberta, Edmonton, Canada* (Dalio, Trintignant)
Candice Nicolas, *Loyola Marymount University, Los Angeles* (Pierre Brasseur, Préjean)
Julie Parson, *The Ohio State University, Columbus* (Feuillère)
Arina Patrikova, *The University of Oxford* (Auteuil, Béart, Magimel, Mesquida)
Rosemary A. Peters, *Louisiana State University, Baton Rouge* (Cornillac,
    Kiberlain, Mitchell, Emmanuelle Seigner, Mathilde Seigner)
Gaëlle Planchenault, *Simon Fraser University, British Columbia, Canada*
    (Devos, Garcia)
Keith Reader, *University of London Institute in Paris* (Baur)
Nicolas Rigaud, *The University of Oxford* (Brialy, Darroussin, Dewaere,
    Huppert, Serrault)
Jonathan Robbins, *Columbia University, New York* (Amalric, Jugnot, Karina)
Caroline Rossi, *Université Stendhal – Grenoble 3* (Bardot, Debbouze)
Noëlle Rouxel-Cubberly, *Bennington College, Vermont* (Lemercier, Wilson)
Nathalie Ségeral, *Virginia Polytechnic Institute and State University [/Virginia
    Tech]* (Binoche, Gainsbourg, Godrèche)
Jamie Steele, *University of Exeter* (Carrière)
Vina Tirven-Gadum, *Athabasca University, Alberta, Canada* (Seberg)
Isabelle Vanderschelden, *Manchester Metropolitan University* (Lhermitte,
    Lindon)
Céline Vitard, *Lycée Camille Saint-Saëns, Rouen* (Podalydès)
Nicole Beth Wallenbrock, *The City University of New York* (Girardot, Testud)
Robert Watson, *Stetson University, Florida* (Anconina, Kakou)
Owen Williams, *Journalist, Southampton* (Lambert, Reno)
Daniel Winkler *Universität Wien /University of Vienna* (with Katharina Müller:
    Arditi, Ascaride, De France)

BRIGHTER FRENCH
—Colloquial & Idiomatic, for Bright Young People (who already know some) *by* Harry Thompson RUSSELL
illustrated by Eric FRASER

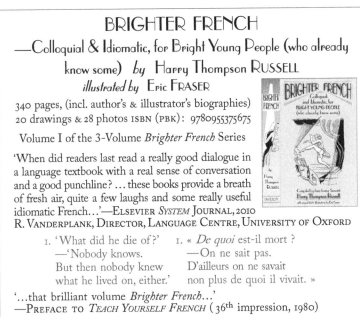

340 pages, (incl. author's & illustrator's biographies)
20 drawings & 28 photos ISBN (PBK): 9780955375675

Volume I of the 3-Volume *Brighter French* Series

'When did readers last read a really good dialogue in a language textbook with a real sense of conversation and a good punchline? ... these books provide a breath of fresh air, quite a few laughs and some really useful idiomatic French...'—ELSEVIER *SYSTEM* JOURNAL, 2010
R. VANDERPLANK, DIRECTOR, LANGUAGE CENTRE, UNIVERSITY OF OXFORD

    1. 'What did he die of?'   1. « *De quoi* est-il mort ?
     —'Nobody knows.   —On ne sait pas.
     But then nobody knew   D'ailleurs on ne savait
     what he lived on, either.'   non plus de quoi il vivait. »

'...that brilliant volume *Brighter French*...'
—PREFACE TO *TEACH YOURSELF FRENCH* (36th impression, 1980)

'Great Fun.' —*BOOKS IRELAND*, 2010

'Regarded as one of the best French language learning guides ever written.' —*WILTSHIRE TIMES*, 2010

PHAETON PUBLISHING LTD. DUBLIN IRELAND

EXTREMELY ENTERTAINING SHORT STORIES
—Classic Works of a Master
by Stacy AUMONIER

576 pages: biography, 29 stories, 1 essay
ISBNS (PBK): 9780955375637 (HBK): 9780955375651

Stories of World War I & the 1920s
in England and in France

'Stacy Aumonier is one of the best short story writers of all time. His humour is sly and dry and frequent... And can't he write!' —JOHN GALSWORTHY (winner of the Nobel Prize for Literature).

'...a very elegant volume...short stories that invite comparison with those of Saki, O. Henry and even Guy de Maupassant.'—*BOOKS IRELAND*

BROADCAST ON BBC RADIO 4 *Afternoon Readings* in 2011.

'... in England, my first trip there in 25 years ... I bought the new Phaeton collection of *Extremely Entertaining Short Stories* by Stacy Aumonier ... greatly appreciated in his time for his wit and neatly contrived plots. Back now in New York, it's a heavy volume to cart back and forth as subway reading, but it's well worth the weight!' —*LIBRARY JOURNAL*, NEW YORK, 2009

'...a great holiday read.' —BRENTANO'S, PARIS

Lightning Source UK Ltd.
Milton Keynes UK
UKOW06f2146260515

252337UK00003B/63/P

9 781908 420114